Digital Marketing and Consumer Engagement:

Concepts, Methodologies, Tools, and Applications

Information Resources Management Association
USA

Volume I

Published in the United States of America by
    IGI Global
    Business Science Reference (an imprint of IGI Global)
    701 E. Chocolate Avenue
    Hershey PA, USA 17033
    Tel: 717-533-8845
    Fax: 717-533-8661
    E-mail: cust@igi-global.com
    Web site: http://www.igi-global.com

Library of Congress Cataloging-in-Publication Data

Names: Information Resources Management Association. editor.
Title: Digital marketing and consumer engagement : concepts, methodologies,
  tools, and applications / Information Resources Management Association,
  editors.
Description: Hershey : Business Science Reference, [2018]
Identifiers: LCCN 2017037831| ISBN 9781522551874 (hardcover) | ISBN
  9781522551881 (ebook)
Subjects: LCSH: Electronic commerce.
Classification: LCC HF5548.32 .D5384 2018 | DDC 658.8/72--dc23 LC record available at https://lccn.loc.gov/2017037831

British Cataloguing in Publication Data
A Cataloguing in Publication record for this book is available from the British Library.

All work contributed to this book is new, previously-unpublished material. The views expressed in this book are those of the authors, but not necessarily of the publisher.

For electronic access to this publication, please contact: eresources@igi-global.com.

List of Contributors

Table of Contents

Section 2
Development and Design Methodologies

Volume III

Section 5
Organizational and Social Implications

Section 6
Critical Issues and Challenges

Preface

The constantly changing landscape of Digital Marketing and Consumer Engagement makes it challenging for experts and practitioners to stay informed of the field's most up-to-date research. That is why Business Science Reference is pleased to offer this three-volume reference collection that will empower students, researchers, and academicians with a strong understanding of critical issues within Digital Marketing and Consumer Engagement by providing both broad and detailed perspectives on cutting-edge theories and developments. This reference is designed to act as a single reference source on conceptual, methodological, technical, and managerial issues, as well as to provide insight into emerging trends and future opportunities within the discipline.

Digital Marketing and Consumer Engagement: Concepts, Methodologies, Tools, and Applications is organized into six distinct sections that provide comprehensive coverage of important topics. The sections are:

1. Fundamental Concepts and Theories;
2. Development and Design Methodologies;
3. Tools and Technologies;
4. Utilization and Applications;
5. Organizational and Social Implications; and
6. Critical Issues and Challenges.

The following paragraphs provide a summary of what to expect from this invaluable reference tool.

Section 1, "Fundamental Concepts and Theories," serves as a foundation for this extensive reference tool by addressing crucial theories essential to the understanding of Digital Marketing and Consumer Engagement. Introducing the book is "A Literature Survey on the Usage of Fuzzy MCDM Methods for Digital Marketing" by Cengiz Kahrama, İbrahim Yazıcı, and Ali Karaşan: a great foundation laying the groundwork for the basic concepts and theories that will be discussed throughout the rest of the book. Section 1 concludes and leads into the following portion of the book with a nice segue chapter, "Investigating the Mechanics of Affiliate Marketing Through Digital Content Marketing: A Key for Driving Traffic and Customer Activity" by Parag Shukla, Parimal Hariom Vyas, and Hiral Shastri.

Section 2, "Development and Design Methodologies," presents in-depth coverage of the conceptual design and architecture of Digital Marketing and Consumer Engagement. Opening the section is "Digital Marketing Strategy for Affinity Marketing" by Aster Mekonnen. Through case studies, this section lays excellent groundwork for later sections that will get into present and future applications for Digital Marketing and Consumer Engagement. The section concludes with an excellent work by Nursel Bolat, "The Functions of the Narrator in Digital Advertising."

Section 3, "Tools and Technologies," presents extensive coverage of the various tools and technologies used in the implementation of Digital Marketing and Consumer Engagement. The first chapter, "Augmented Reality as an Emerging Application in Tourism Marketing Education" by Azizul Hassan and Timothy Jung, lays a framework for the types of works that can be found in this section. The section concludes with "Web 2.0 Technologies and Marketing" by Dora Simões. Where Section 3 described specific tools and technologies at the disposal of practitioners, Section 4 describes the use and applications of the tools and frameworks discussed in previous sections.

Section 4, "Utilization and Applications," describes how the broad range of Digital Marketing and Consumer Engagement efforts has been utilized and offers insight on and important lessons for their applications and impact. The first chapter in the section is "Digital Marketing in Online Education Services" written by Surabhi Singh. This section includes the widest range of topics because it describes case studies, research, methodologies, frameworks, architectures, theory, analysis, and guides for implementation. The breadth of topics covered in the section is also reflected in the diversity of its authors, from countries all over the globe. The section concludes with "Building China's Global Brands" by Donald E. Sexton, a great transition chapter into the next section.

Section 5, "Organizational and Social Implications," includes chapters discussing the organizational and social impact of Digital Marketing and Consumer Engagement. The section opens with "Engaging Consumers via Twitter: Three Successful Communicative Strategies" by Veronica Ravaglia, Eleonora Brivio, and Guendalina Graffigna. This section focuses exclusively on how these technologies affect human lives, either through the way they interact with each other or through how they affect behavioral/workplace situations. The section concludes with "Evaluating the Relevance of Contextual Hyper-Advertising on Social Media: An Empirical Study" by Dhote Tripti and Zahoor Danish.

Section 6, "Critical Issues and Challenges," presents coverage of academic and research perspectives on Digital Marketing and Consumer Engagement tools and applications. The section begins with "What Social Media Marketing Content Is Best to Engage Consumers? A Content Analysis of Facebook Brand Pages" by Chedia Dhaoui. Chapters in this section will look into theoretical approaches and offer alternatives to crucial questions on the subject of Digital Marketing and Consumer Engagement. The final chapter of the book looks at an emerging field within Digital Marketing and Consumer Engagement, in the excellent contribution, "The Organization of the Future and the Marketing Function: Marketers' Competencies in the Era of Information Technology" by Mario Gonzalez-Fuentes.

Although the primary organization of the contents in this multi-volume work is based on its six sections, offering a progression of coverage of the important concepts, methodologies, technologies, applications, social issues, and emerging trends, the reader can also identify specific contents by utilizing the extensive indexing system listed at the end of each volume. As a comprehensive collection of research on the latest findings related to using technology to providing various services, *Digital Marketing and Consumer Engagement: Concepts, Methodologies, Tools, and Applications* provides researchers, administrators, and all audiences with a complete understanding of the development of applications and concepts in Digital Marketing and Consumer Engagement. Given the vast number of issues concerning usage, failure, success, policies, strategies, and applications of Digital Marketing and Consumer Engagement in countries around the world, *Digital Marketing and Consumer Engagement: Concepts, Methodologies, Tools, and Applications* addresses the demand for a resource that encompasses the most pertinent research in technologies being employed to globally bolster the knowledge and applications of Digital Marketing and Consumer Engagement.

Section 1
Fundamental Concepts and Theories

Chapter 1
A Literature Survey on the Usage of Fuzzy MCDM Methods for Digital Marketing

Cengiz Kahraman
Istanbul Technical University, Turkey

İbrahim Yazıcı
Istanbul Technical University, Turkey

Ali Karaşan
Istanbul Technical University, Turkey

ABSTRACT

Digital marketing is the integrated processes of building and maintaining customer relationships using online channels to establish the exchange and flow of products, and services in the market. It is the marketing that bridges electronic technology with psychology in the marketplace. Fuzzy sets can handle the uncertainty and human-manner linguistic evaluations in digital marketing. The objective of this chapter is to summarize and classify the literature on digital marketing, which uses the fuzzy multicriteria decision making methods (MCDM), and predict the future directions for digital marketing. Our chapter will include the main definitions and principles of digital marketing with its challenges. We also give a brief definition of the fuzzy MCDM used methods in the literature. We use graphical illustrations techniques for summarizing the survey results.

1. INTRODUCTION

Digital marketing is the marketing which aims to promote brands and reach customers by using all advertisement segments in electronic medium. It makes use of electronic devices such as personal computers, cell phones, game consoles etc. The Digital Marketing Institution's (DMI) definition for digital marketing is "The use of digital technologies to create an integrated, targeted and measurable communication which helps to acquire and retain customers while building deeper relationships with them". Simply

DOI: 10.4018/978-1-5225-5187-4.ch001

Digital Marketing's definition for digital marketing is "Digital Marketing is a sub branch of traditional Marketing and uses modern digital channels for the placement of products e.g. downloadable music, and primarily for communicating with stakeholders e.g. customers and investors about brand, products and business progress" (Royle & Laing, 2014).

Digital marketing differs from traditional marketing in that enabling an organization to analyze marketing campaigns and follow the actions such as which item is being viewed, how often the item is being viewed, sales event analyze, what content is not efficient, in real time. Digital marketing sometimes is called as online marketing especially in the U.S due to the fact that its proliferation area is mainly internet. Websites, blogs, e-mails, apps and social media are the platforms of digital marketing. Social media is the leading and most growing area for digital marketing.

In the U.S., online consumer spending exceeded USD 100 billion, and there is a growing rate of on-line demands for information goods. For example, online demands for information goods such as books, magazines and software are between 25% and 50%. Another remarkable example is Amazon. Amazon is used as a transaction channel in digital marketing. On the peak day of sellings in Amazon, November 26, 2012, 26.5 million items are ordered worldwide in all product categories. It is a record-breaking selling 306 items per second.

Digital marketing consists of five levers (Royle & Laing, 2014): Attract, Engage, Retain, Learn, and Relate. Attract part is related to acquiring and directing customers to website or webpage that selling are done. Mnemonic branding, listing in search engines, adequate bandwidth, promotions, piggyback advertising, affiliate program, banner ads are the most used tools in this part of digital marketing. Engage part is related to customers' interest and participations engagement to achieve an interaction or transaction. Informative and useful content, transaction capabilities, unique content, creative programming, lucky draws/contests, creating virtual communities, multilingual website, forums/discussion groups are the most used tools in this part of digital marketing. Retain part is related to making current customers loyal to company or brand. Dynamic content, security features, rapid information loading time, privacy statements, hyperlinks to related sites, loyalty programs, providing online order tracking, creating switching costs via communities, interactive functions are the most used tools in this part of digital marketing. Learn part is related to knowing and determining customers' behaviors to reach targets. Information capture, feedback via online surveys, webpage tracking devices, feedback via open-ended survey forms, gathering information about new potential customers, cookies, holding virtual focus groups, supporting chat groups are the most used tools in this part of digital marketing. Relate part is related to applying the learnings from previous phase to constitute value chain. Personalized communications about product/service, customized product/service, e-mails to update about new products, customized webpages, linkages to core business, real time interactions are the most used tools in this part of digital marketing (Teo, 2005; Royle & Laing, 2014; Albert & Sanders, 2002).

In digital marketing, marketing channels are important as in traditional marketing because digital marketing strategies are organized considering these channels. Mostly used digital marketing channels are e-mail, social media, content, events and Search Engine Optimization (SEO). Mostly budget allocated areas in digital marketing are data and analytics, marketing automation, e-mail marketing, social media marketing and content management.

Digital marketing's scope spans to many areas with specific goals and criteria. Tiago and Verissimo (2014) adopt the perspective of the firm to facilitate an understanding of digital marketing and social media usage as well as its benefits and inhibitors. The second generation of Internet-based applications enhances marketing efforts by allowing firms to implement innovative forms of communication and co-create content with their customers. Based on a survey of marketing managers, they show that firms face internal and external pressures to adopt a digital presence in social media platforms. Firms' digital marketing engagement can be categorized according to perceived benefits and digital marketing usage. To improve digital marketing engagement, marketers must focus on relationship-based interactions with their customers. They demonstrate how some firms are already accomplishing just that. Gao et al. (2012) show that unconscious thought moderates the relationship between information quality and consumer satisfaction towards their decision making when shopping experience products online, and is thus worthy of special attention in the design of e-commerce websites. The study contributes to both unconscious thought theory and information processing theory by exploring the interaction effect of the quantity and quality of information with thought mode in affecting the quality of purchasing decisions. Li et al. (2011) present a Web-based hybrid knowledge automation system, called WebDigital, for formulating digital marketing strategies. Within this system, various digital marketing strategy models are computerized, adapted and extended. On-line Monte Carlo simulation is employed to capture the stochastic behavior of relevant factors or variables influencing digital marketing decision making. Web-based fuzzy logic is applied to model the uncertainty surrounding the input and strategic options.

Digital marketing problems are fuzzy MCDM problems since they include many qualitative criteria evaluated by using linguistic terms and some quantitative criteria with incomplete or vague data. The fuzzy set theory can capture this vagueness and handle the linguistic evaluations within numerical calculations. Fuzzy MCDM methods have extensively been developed and applied to a large variety of multi criteria problems. The existing outranking methods ELECTRE, PROMETHEE, and ORESTE have been extended to their fuzzy versions (Xu & Chen, 2014; Chen, 2014; Wu & Chen, 2011; Kaya & Kahraman, 2011b; Lin et al., 2007; Wei-xiang & Bang-yi, 2010; Chen et al., 2011; Ishizaka & Nemery, 2011; Chen & Xu, 2015, Chou et al., 2007). Pairwise comparisons based methods AHP and ANP have also been extended to their fuzzy versions by several researchers with different approaches (Rezaei et al., 2014; Song et al., 2014; Chou et al., 2013; Ishizaka & Nguyen, 2013; Wu et al., 2012; Ayağ & Özdemir, 2013; Zaim et al., 2014). Negative and positive ideal solutions based methods TOPSIS and VIKOR have been developed under fuzziness and applied to many multicriteria decision making problems (Ye & Li, 2014; Mandic et al., 2014; Wang, 2014; Chang, 2014; Kim & Chung, 2013).Other classical multicriteria methods such as DEMATEL, MACBETH, COPRAS and MAUT have been extended under fuzzy environment and used for the solution of multicriteria problems (Tavana et al., 2013; Patil & Kant, 2014; Mokhtarian, 2011; Dhouib, 2014; Jiménez et al., 2013).

This chapter surveys the fuzzy multicriteria decision making methods used in the evaluation of digital marketing problem. We search the Scopus database for digital marketing and e-commerce, and give the obtained review results in tabular and graphical forms.

The rest of this chapter is organized as follows. Section 2 presents a literature review for evaluation criteria of digital marketing. Section 3 also gives a literature review with tabular and graphical illustrations for fuzziness in digital marketing. Section 4 presents fuzzy MCDM applications in digital marketing and e-commerce. Section 5 includes an illustrative application of fuzzy MCDM for evaluating digital marketing performance. Section 6 concludes the chapter.

2. EVALUATION CRITERIA FOR DIGITAL MARKETING: LITERATURE REVIEW

For measuring the success of digital marketing, the most used common criteria in the literature are measuring ROI, lack of budget, content management system, generating leads and conversion, speed and innovation, social CRM capability:

- Measuring ROI is important for budget allocation to which channel, which channel delivers the best leads and which channel generates the most profit or revenue. Each digital marketing channel require different scales and measurement for ROI.
- Lack of budget is problematic for digital marketers. Under budget constraints, some allocations on marketing channels could not be done.
- Content management system is a competition indicator in digital marketing. Strategies of producing and integrating content across all channels will contribute significantly to competitiveness.
- Engagement and conversion of customers is related to analyzing your visitors' behavior through the social media activity. The activities including analyzing visitors' behavior as potential customers, then influencing and making them your customers are the meaning of generating leads and converting. The activities will require a lot of efforts to gain new customers. Engagement rate, ROI and conversion rate are indicators of success in digital marketing.
- In digital channels, once marketing is started, users will immediately react. This immediate reaction will require speed in digital marketer data compiling, writing performance reports and optimizing activities in real time. Customers' reaction estimation and pre-plan actions with quick reactions under some scenarios will enable digital marketers to innovate the marketing. Speed and innovation capability will contribute significantly to competitiveness in rapid changing digital medium.
- Customer Relationship Management (CRM) is valuable communication tool for companies both in digital and traditional marketing. CRM used in digital marketing is social CRM. Social CRM aims to provide special profiles and making personalization for customers by using marketing, sales, collaboration, innovation, service and support, customer experience insights. Efficient social CRM will construct long term relationship with customers besides loyalty of them for companies or brands.

In the literature, many researchers evaluated the digital marketing performances of firms by using different evaluation criteria since they had different viewpoints to the problem. In the following sections, we summarize the used criteria in the recently published papers.

Huang et al. (2009) develop a performance assessment model for e-commerce; it included indicators, indicator weights, and evaluation methods. The model has seven methods of assessing e-commerce performance and uses four criteria to compare and select the appropriate one for a particular situation. This model is tested in the retail sector of China. According to the data collected from 70 Chinese retailers, 16 indicators of e-commerce performance consist of four constructs: marketing and sales, customer service, supply chain efficiency, and financial performance. The indicators for those constructs provide a comprehensive measurement of performance. Then weights are assigned for each indicator using a majority aggregation method. Comparison of the results from seven evaluation methods shows that discordance analysis and simple additive weighting were the best evaluation methods for the enterprises they had sampled.

Sun et al. (2012) examine Customer Decision Making (CDM) in web services with a novel P6 model, which consists of the 6 Ps: privacy, perception, propensity, preference, personalization and promised experience. This model integrates the existing 6P elements of marketing mix as the system environment of CDM in web services. The new integrated P6 model deals with the inner world of the customer and incorporates what the customer thinks during the DM process.

Aydin & Kahraman (2012) evaluate the websites by considering the following criteria given in Figure 1: ease of use (1) is main criterion, and sub-criteria are completing a transaction quickly (1a), ease of navigation (1b), easy to find needs (1c), ease of online transaction (1d), easy to get different pages in website (1e). Product (2) is the second main criterion, and sub-criteria are product detail (2a), product price detail (2b), product quality (2c), comment on products by customer (2d), competitive product price (2e). Security (3) is the third main criterion, and sub-criteria are online purchase security (3a), protection personnel information (3b), and privacy statement (3c). And the fourth main criterion is customer relationship (4), and its sub-criteria are; quick response to customer demands (4a), direction of registration (4b), and online customer service support and help (4c), online order status tracking (4d). And final main criterion is fulfillment (5), and sub-criteria are on-time delivery (5a), accurate delivery of products (5b), accurate billing (5c).

Royle & Laing (2014) aim to specify any digital marketing skills gaps encountered by professionals working in communication industries. In-depth interviews are undertaken with 20 communication industry professionals. A focus group followed, testing the rigour of the data. They find that a lack of specific technical skills; a need for best practice guidance on evaluation metrics, and a lack of intelligent future proofing for dynamic technological change and development are skills gaps currently challenging the communication industry. However, the challenge of integrating digital marketing approaches with established marketing practice emerges as the key skills gap. Emerging from the key findings, a Digital Marketer Model is developed, highlighting the key competencies and skills needed by an excel-

Figure 1. Hierarchy for e-commerce website selection

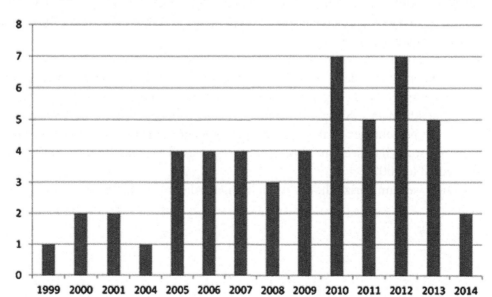

lent digital marketer. The research concludes that guidance on best practice, focusing upon evaluation metrics, future-proofing and strategic integration, needs to be developed for the communication industry.

Chen et al. (2014) propose an analytic decision-making framework for multi-channel evaluation. They first develop an analytic network, based on the inputs of managers and literature, to depict the interrelationships between decision criteria. Multi-Criteria Decision Making methods are then adapted to determine the weight of each evaluation criterion and to rank the practicality of alternative marketing channels. The model is tested with Cisco China. Sensitivity analysis is conducted in order to understand the impact of criteria uncertainties on channel rankings and the robustness of the proposed model. The management at Cisco found the model to be transparent, logical, practical, and it provided a valid and reliable guide for evaluating channel alternatives.

For a successful digital marketing management, the literature says the following main criteria: focusing the plan around customers; learning from competitors; having a clear vision for the year; identifying content resources; making fact-based plans; and creating an actionable scorecard.

3. FUZZINESS IN DIGITAL MARKETING: A LITERATURE REVIEW WITH TABULAR AND GRAPHICAL ILLUSTRATIONS

The concepts "digital marketing" and "e-commerce" are often misused interchangeably. The synonyms to digital marketing are e-marketing, online marketing, or web-marketing and it is related to e-commerce in that manner digital marketing is the tool supporting e-commerce process with supplementary ways such as email marketing, search engine marketing, and social media marketing.

A search in the SCOPUS database for the concept "digital marketing" gives only 73 papers while the search for "e-commerce" gives 2,334 papers, using these concepts in their titles. There are few works on fuzzy multicriteria digital marketing in the literature. Hence we give the literature review results for fuzzy e-commerce in the following. These results present the distribution of the papers with respect to their publication years, distribution of published papers with respect to their journals, and percentages of the published e-commerce papers with respect to their subject area.

The distribution of fuzzy e-commerce papers is as in Figure 2. Table 1 illustrates the journals most publishing fuzzy e-commerce papers.

Figure 3 shows the journals which published the most of the fuzzy e-commerce papers.

With respect to subject areas, the distribution is in that way: 39 of the papers are related to computer science (39 papers); engineering (22 papers); business, management and accounting (8 papers); decision sciences (8 papers); mathematics (8 papers); social sciences (2 papers); other areas (5 papers).

Figure 4 shows the percentages of the published e-commerce papers with respect to their subject areas. Since there are some intersections between subject areas of papers, the total of the percentages in Figure 4 is not equal to 100%.

In the next section we summarize the fuzzy multicriteria digital marketing and e-commerce works in a tabular form.

Figure 2. Fuzzy e-commerce publications with respect to years

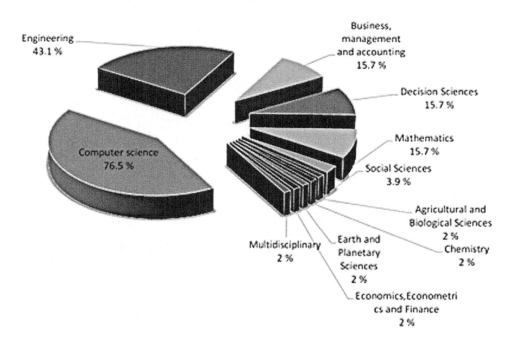

Table 1. The journals most publishing fuzzy e-commerce papers

Expert Systems with Applications	ESWA
Electronic Commerce Research and Applications	ECRA
Dongbei Daxue Xuebao Journal of Northeastern University	DDXJNU
Journal of Software	JS
Annual Conference of the North American Fuzzy Information Processing Society NAFIPS	ACNAFIPS
Applied Soft Computing Journal	ASCJ
Computers and Industrial Engineering	CIE
ACM Transactions on Internet Technology	ACMTIT
Dalian Haishi Daxue Xuebao Journal of Dalian Maritime University	DHDXJDMU
Decision Support Systems	DSS
Electronic Commerce Research	ECR
Computers in Industry	CI

4. FUZZY MCDM APPLICATIONS IN DIGITAL MARKETING AND E-COMMERCE

We give a broader literature review in tabular form together with the advantages and disadvantages of the proposed solution methods under fuzziness. Table 2 presents the researchers, problem definitions, analysis methods, considered criteria, advantages and disadvantages of the proposed methods.

Figure 3. Distribution of published papers with respect to their journals

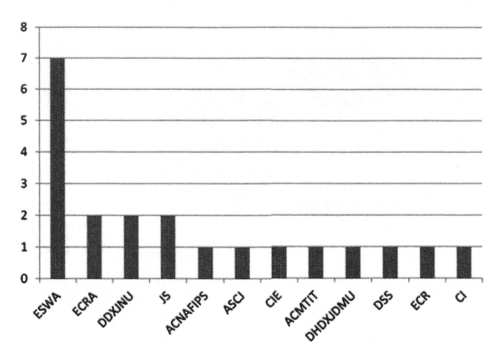

Figure 4. Percentages of the published e-commerce papers with respect to their subject areas

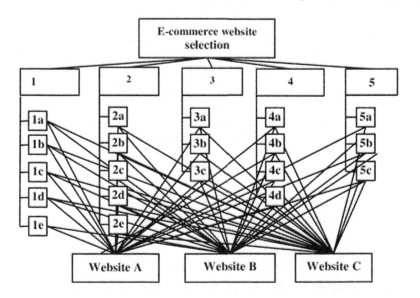

Table 2. The researchers, problem definitions, analysis methods, considered criteria, advantages and disadvantages of the proposed methods

Researchers	Problem Definition	Analysis Method	Considered Criteria	Disadvanteges of the Proposed Method	Advantages of the Proposed Method
Liu et al. (2008)	Customer satisfaction	Fuzzy e-commerce customer satisfaction index (ECSI)	Customers' cognition Customers' expectation, Customers' loyalty behavior Customers' grumble behavior	Integrated additional cultural factors are not considered.	A five levels quantity based fuzzy index is used.
Yu et al. (2011)	Ranking B2C e-commerce websites in e-alliance	AHP and fuzzy TOPSIS	Price Abundance Appearance Ease use Security Intelligence Confidence Trust Speed	Subjective or vague data must be considered during the process.	Ranking e-alliance alternatives has significant impacts to the success and efficiency of e-alliance.
Ngai & Wat (2005)	Risk Analysis	Fuzzy Risk Analyzer	Ease of interaction, Capabilities Efficiency Speed Reliability Produces useful results	The validity of the system is difficult. studies. The prototype only considers the classified risk items in the framework Membership functions are evenly distributed by triangular fuzzy numbers.	Evaluators can simply use the risk evaluation checklist and use the linguistic terms to evaluate the e-commerce development risk level. Prioritization of risks is considered. Therefore, the most serious risk item will be addressed first.
Mohanty & Passi (2010)	React To Buyers' Feedbacks	Fuzzy Linear Programming	Re-sale value Comfort Maintenance cost Popularity	The problem becomes large and complex, if the agent will suggest a big number of products initially. A huge number of market transaction data is required to accurately estimate the weights.	An agent based e-commerce system is introduced which takes the buyers' feedbacks as input and recommends the products in an ordered sequence of preference. The method derives the degree of customer focus on the final recommended products.
Akhter et al. (2005)	Reliability in e-commerce	Fuzzy logic	Security Familiarity Design layout, Competitiveness Trust	Existence of a feature is only relevant to the user if it can be acknowledged, otherwise the vendor must seriously reconsider inclusion of this aspect on the website.	An added advantage would be to feed these data to the FIS for Trust and B2C and the user could compare his/her buying decision with that of others based on the outcome of the fuzzy expert system.
Wang & Lin (2009)	Predicting the success of B2B	Multi-criteria decision-making; Consistent fuzzy preference relation	Management support Firm size IT integration Organizational culture Government policies Industry characteristics	Application of the proposed approach is clearly faster and more efficient than the conventional analytic hierarchy methodologies.	Method considers only (n-1) judgments whereas the traditional analytic hierarchy approach (that is AHP or FAHP) uses $\frac{n*(n-1)}{2}$ judgments in a preference matrix with n attribute or alternatives.
Lee & Ahn (2009)	Designing of controls in B2C e-commerce web-based systems	Fuzzy cognitive map Structural equation modeling	IS infrastructure Organizational requirement for security Controls for system continuity Access controls Communication controls Informal controls Implementation Performance	LISREL offers several advantages over other multivariate techniques but the same relationships cannot be tested by other multivariate techniques.	ECFCM can provide an answer to "what-if" questions by entering an input case offering an ordered list of consequences and diagnoses. ECWS will provide a consistent approach in processing relevant cases, interpreting and applying them to problem solving in control design. Structural equation modeling is used to derive the causal relations among factors in ECWS controls.
Ajayi et al. (2010)	Improving response time	Fuzzy logic-based information retrieval model	Processor speed Memory size Resolution Availability of anti-virus	A comparative analysis between Mamdani and Sugeno type fuzzy inference systems is needed.	The proposed model reduces the response time, which is experienced by users, especially when they are performing a search operation on e-commerce servers.

continued on following page

Table 2. Continued

Researchers	Problem Definition	Analysis Method	Considered Criteria	Disadvanteges of the Proposed Method	Advantages of the Proposed Method
Ramkumar et al. (2010)	Scoring products	Fuzzy logic	duplicate of any review written before semantically similar to any review written before. Helpfulness Number of lines that speak about the brands Number of lines that speak about the model Number of lines that do not speak of product features Position of the review in the sorted order by date of the reviews Total number of reviews written for the product Average rating of the product and the deviation of the review rating from the average rating Price and sales rank of the product	The usage of the sales rank of the product in prediction of future sales rank needs to be considered and the application of genetic algorithms on the prediction should be studied. The efficiency of the review analysis step by looking on the effects of contextual valence shifters on the calculation of the product ratings should be improved.	System not only generates user profiles but also calculates the reputation of each user based on the application of fuzzy logic to the data collected for each user.
Chan et al. (2007)	Bargaining strategy formulation	Fuzzy inference system	Total product categories clicked for the current visit Total product items clicked for the current visit Total product items sent to shopping cart for the current visit Total number of products purchased A5 Total monetary amount of products purchased Total number of visits The time between the customer's first visit and now	Due to the limited information content of weblog data, the used index may not provide an accurate estimate of a customer's potentiality and hence limit the use of the proposed approach The proposed approach does not take the customer's preferences into account in the bargaining process.	Bargaining agent reaches the final agreed price faster than the other three agents. Bargaining agent creates greater customer satisfaction and customer loyalty to the shopping mall.
Huang & Liang (2010)	Negotiation process for B2C e-com Merce	Fuzzy multi-attribute selection using axiomatic design and the AHP	Price Spec. Dividend Giveback	The proposed model is not applicable to the real world with its current status. The approach to enhancing the negotiaiton model needs to be explored in future.	The model presents a multiple attributes negotiation model to B2C e-commerce, which deploys intelligent agents to facilitate autonomous and automatic on-line buying and includes a 4-phase model, information collection, search, negotiation, and evaluation.
Nassiri-Mofakham et al. (2009)	Multi-issue bargaining model	Fuzzy Inference Engines	Openness Conscientiousness Extraversion Agreeableness Negative emotions	Any logical possibility of personality descriptions (resulted from the simulation) in n-dimensional facet space may be unlikely to co-occur within a given individual.	Approach calculates the best offer near to the opponent's offer without prior knowledge about the criteria weights in the opponent's viewpoint and is based only on his previous offer. The approach presented in this study can be adapted to any other descriptive personality model, so that, needed facets or traits are filtered to compute appropriate Risk and Cooperation factors.
Vahidov & Ji (2005)	Infrequent purchase decision support	Fuzzy weighted-sum model and cluster analysis	Price Brand name Producer Supplier Cpu Memory Hard drive Screen sizes	The major limitation of the study is the preliminary nature of the experiments. This topic requires a thorough treatment and will be the subject of future research. In this regard the effectiveness of the method needs to be tested through statistical hypotheses.	Their design bases on imprecise searching and divergent browsing could have a positive impact on customer's trust level.
Buyukozkan & Cifci (2012)	Strategic analysis of electronic service quality	Combined of fuzzy AHP and fuzzy TOPSIS	Tangibles Responsiveness Reliability Information quality Assurance Empathy	The research might be the application of a hybrid method that combines ANP and TOPSIS methods to the service quality performance problem and the comparison of the results.	Humans are often uncertain in assigning the evaluation scores. Therefore AHP and TOPSIS methods are performed in fuzzy environment to capture this difficulty.

continued on following page

Table 2. Continued

Researchers	Problem Definition	Analysis Method	Considered Criteria	Disadvanteges of the Proposed Method	Advantages of the Proposed Method
Lee & Li (2006)	Forming an e-marketplace	Fuzzy Delphi Fuzzy Multiple Criteria Decision Making Kano analysis	Accuracy of order processing Trading credit investigation Order processing correctness Trading credit investigation Quality check Production project	The model use only Kano analysis to realize the supplier's attitude towards all the preferred operation modes. A comparative analysis is required.	Their study shows that the e-commerce mechanism of the e-marketplace can improve trading efficiency and lower the cost of collecting information as well as the purchase price.
Zandi & Tavana (2011)	Assessment in agile manufacturing	Four-phase fuzzy QFD model	Strategic Agility Criteria Operational Agility Criteria Functional Agility Criteria	Managerial judgment is an integral component of e-CRM framework evaluation and selection decisions; therefore, the effectiveness of the model relies heavily on the decision maker's cognitive capabilities.	Their approach helps the decision makers to think systematically about complex multi-attribute decision making problems and improves the quality of the decisions.
Chiu et al. (2012)	Mining framework into e-commerce environment	Cluster-based fuzzy rules	Clustering Association Rule Semantic Web Web Page Content Mining Search Result Mining Text Mining Image Mining	Authors use virtual-time databases. Therefore, it is unrealistic that the most approximate fuzzy sets can always be provided in advance.	They take the transaction data and web usage data to mine multiple-level association knowledge for analyzing the customer's behavior and to aid the enterprises for determining the suitable marketing and business strategies.
Pan et al. (2014)	Provider selection in data communication services	Fuzzy multi-objective model	Cost Reliability Delay Reliability Bandwidth	The model is used under simplfying assumptions.	They transform the fuzzy multi-objective provider selection problem into a weighted max–min deterministic-crisp non-linear programming model. This transformation simplifies the solution process, giving less computational complexity, and makes the application of fuzzy methodology more understandable.
Castro-Schez et al. (2013)	Taking advantage of acquired knowledge	Hierarchical Decision Support System based on the Fuzzy Repertory Table (HDSS-FRT) method	The relevant attributes or criteria used to assess each one of the alternatives Almost complete absence of experts' advices in the process of knowledge acquisition Descriptive, linguistic, ordinal variables Support explanation facilities	It is a prototype intended to serve as a vehicle for exploring and testing the ideas proposed here. It is not a commercial application, therefore little attention is paid to usability issues of the portal website.	The suggested system models the behaviour of a consumer when it is searched in a database (a catalogue) for a product that matches according to the requirements, needs, tastes, preferences and so on.
Miao et al. (2007)	Agent-based personalized recommendation	Fuzzy cognitive agents	Make Model Age Mileage Price	Fuzzy decision trees combine symbolic decision trees with approximate reasoning offered by fuzzy representation. But the trees grows very fast if many factors are taken into account. Yet they are difficult to represent causal relationships between factors. Users often make decisions based on the impact factors and the causal relationships between them.	The case study shows that fuzzy cognitive agents can be applied into various e-commerce/business/service applications.
Lucas et al. (2013)	recommendation approach for a tourism system	Fuzzy Cost-Benefit Analysis	Religion Landmarks Shopping Sport Eating Leisure Cultural Exhibitions City tours Festivities Performing Arts	The number of users and items are constantly increasing in web systems due to their popularization and, therefore, future adaptation and extensions would be needed in the proposed technique.	The model includes the discretization process and the definition of the degrees of membership to the generated intervals and, hence, it brings more significance and value to data.
Liu & Chen (2009)	Prioritization of digital capital measures	Fuzzy AHP	Public relationships School relationships Image creation Word of mouse Public trust Timely response Security Career planning Stability	This study is still exploratory in nature, as it is the first attempt to investigate digital capital of recruiting websites of national armed forces, and further work needs to be done. For example, as the expert sample used is quite small, the next step need to be done is to enlarge the sample size to achieve more objective.	The main contribution of this study is to develop the dimensions/subdimensions of recruiting websites of national armed force and to identify their priorities that help the national armed force by providing a guideline for conducting recruiting programme through websites successfully.

5. AN ILLUSTRATIVE APPLICATION: FUZZY MCDM FOR EVALUATING DIGITAL MARKETING PERFORMANCE

Fuzzy TOPSIS is one of the most used multicriteria decision making methods in the literature. The steps of fuzzy TOPSIS method can be found in (Kaya & Kahraman, 2011a). Because of the space constraints, we will not give these steps in this chapter.

As an illustrative example, we make a digital marketing performance evaluation with respect to five criteria under fuzziness. Let A_1, A_2, and A_3 be three competitors in digital marketing. Five criteria for measuring the performance of the alternatives are ROI capability (ROIC), social customer relationship management capability (SCRMC), budget allocation (BA), content management system (CMS), and usability of web-page (UW). We use the linguistic assessment scale in Table 3 to evaluate the alternatives with respect to the criteria.

Table 4 is used for weighting the criteria.

After experts' evaluations based on Tables 3 and 4, the compromised decision matrix in Table 5 has been obtained.

The three experts have assessed the criteria as in Table 6. The mean values of the assessments in Table 6 are obtained as (0.83, 0.97, 1) for ROIC; (0.07, 0.23, 0.43) for SCRMC; (0.63, 0.83, 0.97) for BA; (0.5, 0.7, 0.87) for CMS; and (0.23, 0.43, 0.63) for UW.

Table 7 presents the transformation to their numerical assessments from the linguistic assessments in Table 6. w denotes the weight of the considered criterion.

Table 8 gives the normalized decision matrix obtained from Table 7.

Table 9 gives the weighted normalized decision matrix. This matrix is obtained by fuzzy multiplication of weights and alternative values in Table 8.

Calculating the distances to positive and negative ideal solutions of each alternative, Table 10 is obtained.

Table 11 presents the closeness coefficients (CC) to ideal solutions of each alternative.

According to Table 11, the best alternative is Alternative 3 since it has the largest CC value. Alternative 2 takes the second rank and Alternative 1 takes the last rank.

Table 3. Fuzzy evalutaion scores for the alternatives

Linguistic Terms	Fuzzy Score
Very Poor (VP)	(0,0,1)
Poor (P)	(0,1,3)
Medium Poor (MP)	(1,3,5)
Fair (F)	(3,5,7)
Medium Good (MG)	(5,7,9)
Good (G)	(7,9,10)
Very Good (VG)	(9,10,10)

Table 4. Fuzzy evalutaion scores for the criteria

Linguistic Terms	Fuzzy Score
Absolutely Low Importance (ALI)	(0,0,0.1)
Very Low Importance (VLI)	(0,0.1,0.3)
Low Importance (LI)	(0.1,0.3,0.5)
Equal Importance (EI)	(0.3,0.5,0.7)
High Importance (HI)	(0.5,0.7,0.9)
Very High Importance (VHI)	(0.7,0.9,1)
Absolutely High Importance (AHI)	(0.9, 1, 1)

Table 5. Decision matrix

Alternatives	ROIC	SCRMC	BA	CMS	UW
A_1	VG	MG	F	G	MG
A_2	G	G	G	F	F
A_3	MG	G	MG	VG	VG

Table 6. Criteria assessments by the experts

Experts	ROIC	SCRMC	BA	CMS	UW
Expert-1	AHI	VLI	VHI	EI	LI
Expert-2	VHI	LI	HI	HI	EI
Expert-3	AHI	LI	VHI	VHI	EI

Table 7. Transformation to numerical assessments from linguistic assessments

	W_{ROIC}			W_{SCMRC}			W_{BA}			W_{CMS}			W_{UW}		
Alternative	0.83	0.97	1	0.07	0.23	0.43	0.63	0.83	0.97	0.5	0.7	0.87	0.23	0.43	0.63
A1	9	10	10	5	7	9	3	5	7	7	9	10	5	7	9
A2	7	9	10	7	9	10	7	9	10	3	5	7	3	5	7
A3	5	7	9	7	9	10	5	7	9	9	10	10	9	10	10

Table 8. Fuzzy normalized decision matrix

	ROIC			SCMRC			BA			CMS			UW		
	W_{ROIC}			W_{SCMRC}			W_{BA}			W_{CMS}			W_{UW}		
Alternatives	0.83	0.97	1	0.07	0.23	0.43	0.63	0.83	0.97	0.5	0.7	0.87	0.23	0.43	0.63
A1	0.9	1	1	0.5	0.7	0.9	0.3	0.5	0.7	0.7	0.9	1	0.5	0.7	0.9
A2	0.7	0.9	1	0.7	0.9	1	0.7	0.9	1	0.3	0.5	0.7	0.3	0.5	0.7
A3	0.5	0.7	0.9	0.7	0.9	1	0.5	0.7	0.9	0.9	1	1	0.9	1	1

Table 9. Weighted fuzzy normalized decision matrix

	ROIC			SCMRC			BA			CMS			UW		
A1	0.747	0.97	1	0.035	0.161	0.387	0.189	0.415	0.679	0.35	0.63	0.87	0.115	0.301	0.567
A2	0.581	0.873	1	0.049	0.207	0.43	0.441	0.747	0.97	0.15	0.35	0.609	0.069	0.215	0.441
A3	0.415	0.679	0.9	0.049	0.207	0.43	0.315	0.581	0.873	0.45	0.7	0.87	0.207	0.43	0.63

6. CONCLUSION

In this chapter we have made a literature survey on the usage of fuzzy MCDM methods for digital marketing. The SCOPUS database has been searched for the keywords *digital marketing* and *fuzzy sets*. It has been seen that there are few works on fuzzy digital marketing. However, when another term, e-commerce, being under the main term digital marketing, is searched, we have obtained more than 50 papers published in international scientific journals. These papers have been analyzed with respect to their subject areas, journals and years they have been published. A detailed table on fuzzy digital marketing has been prepared by considering analysis methods, performance criteria, advantages and disadvantages of the used methods. An illustrative numerical application has also been given to show

Table 10. Sum of the distances

D_1^*	2.706555
D_2^*	2.824417
D_3^*	2.79592
D_1^-	2.655186
D_2^-	2.564328
D_3^-	2.986745

Table 11. Closeness coefficients to ideal solutions

CC_1	0.49521
CC_2	0.47587
CC_3	0.51650

how the digital marketing performances of three competitive firms can be compared by using a fuzzy multicriteria decision making method. We have used fuzzy TOPSIS method in our application because it is one of the most used MCDM methods in performance measurement and comparisons.

As a conclusion, we have detected that digital marketing is not a research area frequently researched by using fuzzy sets as many as it is with other fuzzy research areas such as fuzzy energy, fuzzy supplier selection, fuzzy mathematics, etc. Its reasons might be the term digital marketing has many equivalent terms and sub-terms, such as e-commerce, e-marketing, online-marketing, web-marketing, which are generally preferred to research under fuzziness. However, the fuzzy set theory has been rarely used with digital marketing and its sub-terms till now.

The direction of digital marketing in the future may be in that way the convergence of marketing, public relations and advertising will accelerate in the next years. Content creation, search optimization and social media will find a wider application area across the organization. Fuzzy multicriteria decision making methods should be introduced to the firms using digital marketing media since they can evaluate the systems by capturing the uncertainty of vague and imprecise information.

For further research, we recommend that the other publications rather than journal papers, such as conference papers, scientific books, and book chapters to be also reviewed for digital marketing.

REFERENCES

Ajayi, A. O., Aderounmu, G. A., & Soriyan, H. A. (2010). An adaptive fuzzy information retrieval model to improve response time perceived by e-commerce clients. *Expert Systems with Applications, 37*(1), 82–91. doi:10.1016/j.eswa.2009.05.071

Akhter, F., Hobbs, D., & Maamar, Z. (2002). A fuzzy logic-based system for assessing the level of business-to-consumer (B2C) trust in electronic commerce. *Expert Systems with Applications, 28*(4), 623–628. doi:10.1016/j.eswa.2004.12.039

Albert, T. C., & Sanders, W. B. (2002). *E-Business Marketing*. Prentice Hall.

Ayağ, Z., & Özdemir, R. G. (2012). Evaluating machine tool alternatives through modified TOPSIS and alpha-cut based fuzzy ANP. *International Journal of Production Economics, 140*(2), 630–636. doi:10.1016/j.ijpe.2012.02.009

Aydin, S., & Kahraman, C. (2012). Evaluation of E-commerce Website Quality Using Fuzzy Multi-criteria Decision Making Approach. *IAENG International Journal of Computer Science, 39*(1), 64–70.

Buyukozkan, G., & Cifci, G. (2012). A combined fuzzy AHP and fuzzy TOPSIS based strategic analysis of electronic service quality in healthcare industry. *Expert Systems with Applications, 39*(3), 2341–2354. doi:10.1016/j.eswa.2011.08.061

Castro-Schez, J. J., Miguel, R., Herrera, V., & Albusac, J. A. (2013). Supporting multi-criteria decisions based on a hierarchical structure by taking advantage of acquired knowledge. *Applied Soft Computing, 13*(1), 509–526. doi:10.1016/j.asoc.2012.08.001

Chan, H. C.-C., Cheng, C.-B., & Hsu, C.-H. (2007). Bargaining strategy formulation with CRM for an e-commerce agent. *Electronic Commerce Research and Applications, 6*(4), 490–498. doi:10.1016/j.elerap.2007.02.011

Chang, T.-H. (2014). Fuzzy VIKOR method: A case study of the hospital service evaluation in Taiwan. *Information Sciences, 271*, 196–212. doi:10.1016/j.ins.2014.02.118

Chen, K., Kou, G., & Shang, J. (2013). An analytic decision making framework to evaluate multiple marketing channels. *Industrial Marketing Management, 48*(3), 1420–1434.

Chen, N., & Xu, Z. (2015). Hesitant fuzzy ELECTRE II approach: A new way to handle multi-criteria decision making problems. *Information Sciences, 292*, 175–197. doi:10.1016/j.ins.2014.08.054

Chen, T.-Y. (2014). An ELECTRE-based outranking method for multiple criteria group decision making using interval type-2 fuzzy sets. *Information Sciences, 263*, 1–21. doi:10.1016/j.ins.2013.12.012

Chen, Y.-H., Wang, T.-C., & Wu, C.-Y. (2011). Strategic decisions using the fuzzy PROMETHEE for IS outsourcing. *Expert Systems with Applications, 38*(10), 13216–13222. doi:10.1016/j.eswa.2011.04.137

Chiu, H.-P., Tang, Y.-T., & Hsieh, K.-L. (2012). Applying cluster-based fuzzy association rules mining framework into EC environment. *Applied Soft Computing, 12*(8), 2114–2122. doi:10.1016/j.asoc.2011.08.010

Chou, J.-S., Pham, A.-D., & Wang, H. (2013). Bidding strategy to support decision-making by integrating fuzzy AHP and regression-based simulation. *Automation in Construction*, *35*, 517–527. doi:10.1016/j. autcon.2013.06.007

Chou, W.-C., Lin, W.-T., & Lin, C.-Y. (2007). Application of fuzzy theory and PROMETHEE technique to evaluate suitable ecotechnology method: A case study in Shihmen Reservoir Watershed, Taiwan. *Ecological Engineering*, *31*(4), 269–280. doi:10.1016/j.ecoleng.2007.08.004

Dhouib, D. (2014). An extension of MACBETH method for a fuzzy environment to analyze alternatives in reverse logistics for automobile tire wastes. *Omega*, *42*(1), 25–32. doi:10.1016/j.omega.2013.02.003

Gao, J., Zhang, C., Wang, K., & Ba, S. (2012). Understanding online purchase decision making: The effects of unconscious thought, information quality, and information quantity. *Decision Support Systems*, *53*(4), 772–781. doi:10.1016/j.dss.2012.05.011

Huang, C.-C., Liang, W.-Y., Lai, Y.-H., & Lin, Y.-C. (2010). The agent-based negotiation process for B2C e-commerce. *Expert Systems with Applications*, *37*(1), 348–359. doi:10.1016/j.eswa.2009.05.065

Huang, J., Jiang, X., & Tang, Q. (2009). An e-commerce performance assessment model: Its development and an initial test on e-commerce applications in the retail sector of China. *Information & Management*, *46*(2), 100–108. doi:10.1016/j.im.2008.12.003

Ishizaka, A., & Nemery, P. (2011). Selecting the best statistical distribution with PROMETHEE and GAIA. *Computers & Industrial Engineering*, *61*(4), 958–969. doi:10.1016/j.cie.2011.06.008

Ishizaka, A., & Nguyen, N. H. (2013). Calibrated fuzzy AHP for current bank account selection. *Expert Systems with Applications*, *40*(9), 3775–3783. doi:10.1016/j.eswa.2012.12.089

Jiménez, A., Mateos, A., & Sabio, P. (2013). Dominance intensity measure within fuzzy weight oriented MAUT: An application. *Omega*, *41*(2), 397–405. doi:10.1016/j.omega.2012.03.004

Kaya, T., & Kahraman, C. (2011a). Multicriteria decision making in energy planning using a modified fuzzy TOPSIS methodology. *Expert Systems with Applications*, *38*(6), 6577–6585. doi:10.1016/j. eswa.2010.11.081

Kaya, T., & Kahraman, C. (2011b). An integrated fuzzy AHP–ELECTRE methodology for environmental impact assessment. *Expert Systems with Applications*, *38*(7), 8553–8562. doi:10.1016/j.eswa.2011.01.057

Kim, Y., & Chung, E.-S. (2013). Fuzzy VIKOR approach for assessing the vulnerability of the water supply to climate change and variability in South Korea. *Applied Mathematical Modelling*, *37*(22), 9419–9430. doi:10.1016/j.apm.2013.04.040

Lee, S., & Ahn, H. (2009). Fuzzy cognitive map based on structural equation modeling for the design of controls in business-to-consumer e-commerce web-based systems. *Expert Systems with Applications*, *36*(7), 10447–10460. doi:10.1016/j.eswa.2009.01.070

Lee, T.-R., & Li, J.-M. (2006). Key factors in forming an e-marketplace: An empirical analysis. *Electronic Commerce Research and Applications*, *5*(2), 105–116. doi:10.1016/j.elerap.2005.10.004

Li, S., Li, J. Z., He, H., Ward, P., & Davies, B. J. (2011). WebDigital: A Web-based hybrid intelligent knowledge automation system for developing digital marketing strategies. *Expert Systems with Applications, 38*(8), 10606–10613. doi:10.1016/j.eswa.2011.02.128

Liu, C.-C., & Chen, S.-Y. (2009). Prioritization of digital capital measures in recruiting website for the national armed forces. *Expert Systems with Applications, 36*(5), 9415–9421. doi:10.1016/j.eswa.2008.12.051

Liu, X., Zeng, X., Xu, Y., & Koehl, L. (2008). A fuzzy model of customer satisfaction index in e-commerce. *Mathematics and Computers in Simulation, 77*(5-6), 512–521. doi:10.1016/j.matcom.2007.11.017

Lucas, J. P., Luz, N., Moreno, M. N., Anacleto, R., Figueiredo, A. A., & Martins, C. (2013). A hybrid recommendation approach for a tourism system. *Expert Systems with Applications, 40*(9), 3532–3550. doi:10.1016/j.eswa.2012.12.061

Mandic, K., Delibasic, B., Knezevic, S., & Benkovic, S. (2014). Analysis of the financial parameters of Serbian banks through the application of the fuzzy AHP and TOPSIS methods. *Economic Modelling, 43*, 30–37. doi:10.1016/j.econmod.2014.07.036

Miao, C., Yang, Q., Fang, H., & Goh, A. (2007). A cognitive approach for agent-based personalized recommendation. *Knowledge-Based Systems, 20*(4), 397–405. doi:10.1016/j.knosys.2006.06.006

Mohanty, B. K., & Passi, K. (2010). Agent based e-commerce systems that react to buyers' feedbacks – A fuzzy approach. *International Journal of Approximate Reasoning, 51*(8), 948–963. doi:10.1016/j.ijar.2010.07.002

Mokhtarian, M. N. (2011). A note on "Developing global manager's competencies using the fuzzy DEMATEL method". *Expert Systems with Applications, 38*(7), 9050–9051. doi:10.1016/j.eswa.2011.01.080

Nassiri-Mofakham, F., Nematbakhsh, M. A., Ghasem-Aghaee, N., & Baraani-Dastjerdi, A. (2009). Ghasem-Aghaee, N., Baraani-Dastjerdi, A., A heuristic personality-based bilateral multi-issue bargaining model in electronic commerce. *International Journal of Human-Computer Studies, 67*(1), 1–35. doi:10.1016/j.ijhcs.2008.08.001

Ngai, E. W. T., & Wat, F. K. T. (2005). Fuzzy decision support system for risk analysis in e-commerce development. *Decision Support Systems, 40*(2), 235–255. doi:10.1016/j.dss.2003.12.002

Pan, W., Yu, L., Wang, S., & Wang, X. (2014). A fuzzy multi-objective model for provider selection in data communication services with different QoS levels. *International Journal of Production Economics, 147*, 689–696. doi:10.1016/j.ijpe.2013.04.030

Patil, S. K., & Kant, R. (2014). A hybrid approach based on fuzzy DEMATEL and FMCDM to predict success of knowledge management adoption in supply chain. *Applied Soft Computing, 18*, 126–135. doi:10.1016/j.asoc.2014.01.027

Ramkumar, V., Rajasekar, S., & Swamynathan, S. (2010). Scoring products from reviews through application of fuzzy techniques. *Expert Systems with Applications, 37*(10), 6862–6867. doi:10.1016/j.eswa.2010.03.036

Rezaei, J., Fahim, P. B. M., & Tavasszy, L. (2014). Supplier selection in the airline retail industry using a funnel methodology: Conjunctive screening method and fuzzy AHP. *Expert Systems with Applications*, *41*(18), 8165–8179. doi:10.1016/j.eswa.2014.07.005

Royle, J., & Laing, A. (2014). The digital marketing skills gap: Developing a Digital Marketer Model for the communication industries. *International Journal of Information Management*, *34*(2), 65–73. doi:10.1016/j.ijinfomgt.2013.11.008

Song, Z., Zhu, H., Jia, G., & He, C. (2014). Comprehensive evaluation on self-ignition risks of coal stockpiles using fuzzy AHP approaches. *Journal of Loss Prevention in the Process Industries*, *32*, 78–94. doi:10.1016/j.jlp.2014.08.002

Sun, Z., Sun, J., & Meredith, G. (2012). Customer decision making in web services with an integrated P6 model. *Physics Procedia*, *24*, 1553–1559. doi:10.1016/j.phpro.2012.02.229

Tavana, M., Momeni, E., Rezaeiniya, N., Mirhedayatian, S. M., & Rezaeiniya, H. (2013). A novel hybrid social media platform selection model using fuzzy ANP and COPRAS-G. *Expert Systems with Applications*, *40*(14), 5694–5702. doi:10.1016/j.eswa.2013.05.015

Teo, T. S. H. (2005). Usage and effectiveness of online marketing tools among Business-to-Consumer (B2C) firms in Singapore. *International Journal of Information Management*, *25*(3), 203–213. doi:10.1016/j.ijinfomgt.2004.12.007

Tiago, M. T. P. M. B., & Verissimo, J. M. C. (2014). Digital marketing and social media: Why bother? *Business Horizons*, *57*(6), 703–708. doi:10.1016/j.bushor.2014.07.002

Vahidov, R., & Ji, F. (2005). A diversity-based method for infrequent purchase decision support in e-commerce. *Electronic Commerce Research and Applications*, *4*(2), 143–158. doi:10.1016/j.elerap.2004.09.001

Wang, T.-C., & Lin, Y.-L. (2009). Accurately predicting the success of B2B e-commerce in small and medium enterprises. *Expert Systems with Applications*, *36*(2), 2750–2758. doi:10.1016/j.eswa.2008.01.033

Wang, Y.-J. (2014). The evaluation of financial performance for Taiwan containershipping companies by fuzzy TOPSIS. *Applied Soft Computing*, *22*, 28–35. doi:10.1016/j.asoc.2014.03.021

Wei-xiang, L., & Bang-yi, L. (2010). An extension of the Promethee II method based on generalized fuzzy numbers. *Expert Systems with Applications*, *37*(7), 5314–5319. doi:10.1016/j.eswa.2010.01.004

Wu, J., Huang, H.-B., & Cao, Q.-W. (2013). Research on AHP with interval-valued intuitionistic fuzzy sets and its application in multi-criteria decision making problems. *Applied Mathematical Modelling*, *37*(24), 9898–9906. doi:10.1016/j.apm.2013.05.035

Wu, M.-C., & Chen, T.-Y. (2011). The ELECTRE multicriteria analysis approach based on Atanassov's intuitionistic fuzzy sets. *Expert Systems with Applications*, *38*(10), 12318–12327. doi:10.1016/j.eswa.2011.04.010

Ye, F., & Li, Y. (2014). An extended TOPSIS model based on the Possibility theory under fuzzy environment. *Knowledge-Based Systems*, *67*, 263–269. doi:10.1016/j.knosys.2014.04.046

Yu, X., Guo, S., Guo, J., & Huang, X. (2011). Rank B2C e-commerce websites in e-alliance based on AHP and fuzzy TOPSIS. *Expert Systems with Applications*, *38*(4), 3550–3557. doi:10.1016/j.eswa.2010.08.143

Zaim, S., Sevkli, M., Camgoz-Akdağ, H., Demirel, Ö. F., Yayla, A. Y., & Delen, D. (2014). Use of ANP weighted crisp and fuzzy QFD for product development. *Expert Systems with Applications*, *41*(9), 4464–4474. doi:10.1016/j.eswa.2014.01.008

Zandi, F., & Tavana, M. (2011). A fuzzy group quality function deployment model for e-CRM framework assessment in agile manufacturing. *Computers & Industrial Engineering*, *61*(1), 1–19. doi:10.1016/j.cie.2011.02.004

This research was previously published in Fuzzy Optimization and Multi-Criteria Decision Making in Digital Marketing edited by Anil Kumar and Manoj Kumar Dash, pages 1-19, copyright year 2016 by Business Science Reference (an imprint of IGI Global).

Chapter 2
Halal Branding:
A New Trend in Islamic Marketing

Ali Shahnazari
Payame Noor University, Iran

ABSTRACT

Muslim and Islamic marketing is very important on the global level. This chapter investigates Muslim's food market. In the first section, the foundations of Halal food are explained, and the roots of the concept of Halal and the challenges facing it are described. The second section includes Islamic branding and the foundations of Islamic branding. The Islamic foundation of Halal is a subject that comes together with the description of Halal food in the Holy Quran and is the subject of the third section. In the fourth section, Halal branding is explored, and in the fifth section, the legal and practical issues of Halal branding are analyzed. The final section includes models of Halal food and brand in which six models are put forward. The most recent of these models includes all the essential concepts of the previous models.

INTRODUCTION

While many people believe that Muslims live mainly in the Middle East, in fact it is wrong. Based on the report made by Pew Forum in 2011 regarding people's religion and general life, around 1.56 billion people are Muslim. This number is 23% of the whole population of the world. It has been estimated that 60% of the Muslims live in Asia, 20% in North Africa and Middle East, and the remaining 20% live in other places across the world. Although the population of Muslims in the Middle East is considerable, great populations also live in Indonesia, Malaysia, India, Pakistan, Turkey, Nigeria, and other countries. Muslim customers have expanded over the Middle East countries. The Muslim population in Europe has grown 140% within a decade and that growth is more than the growth of non-Muslims. Around 30 million Muslims live in the Russian Federation. The Muslim population across North and South Americas is expanding, too. In the U.S. there are around 2.6 million child and adult Muslim which comprises 0.8% of the population of the U.S. It has been predicted that up to 2030, this number will reach 6.2 million which equals 1.7% of the whole population of the U.S. (Rarick, 2011).The Musmims' market includes 20.01% of the whole population of the world. Muslims include the population of more than 50

DOI: 10.4018/978-1-5225-5187-4.ch002

countries in Asia, Africa, and Europe and Islam has had the fastest rate of growth among all religions of the world. The biggest Islamic organization (Islamic Conference Organization) consists of 57 countries among which 50 countries are completely Muslim. Although in the other countries Muslims are not the major population, they have big populations. These 57 countries altogether have an $8 trillion GDP which equals that of the U.S. (before the oil boom in 2008). Halal market comprises a significant share in the economy of these countries.

Also, the countries which are not members of the Organization of Islamic Cooperation but have access to smaller populations of Muslims have shares in the global Halal market to the extent that recently it has been estimated around $760 billion. The growth rate of this market has been estimated as 15% and this makes it the fastest-growing market in the world (Al-Serhan, 2010: 105).

FUNDAMENTALS OF HALAL FOOD

Origins of Halal

Halal is an Arab`ic term which is connected to the Islamic tradition. Generally, Halal can be defined as "allowed" or "permitted". The acceptance and understanding of what means Halal is at the center of Muslims' beliefs. The opposite of Halal in Arabic is the term "haram" or unlawful. Islamic tradition considers everything as Halal unless the opposite has been proven. So, a Muslim must distinguish between Halal and unlawful foods. On the other hand, it seems that "haram" causes much strong feelings in people. That is because the voluntary consumption or involvement in unlawful activities will lead to spiritual or physical punishments. So, Muslims prefer to avoid such activities when they are doubtful. For Muslims, Halal is not just a brand but a part of their belief system and ethical program in their everyday lives. The literature review in the current study points to the exact and uniform definitions of Halal. Generally, such definitions fall into the field of marketing. However, experts claim that "Halal" as a concept contains some characteristics that give it the features of a phenomenon and spirituality. Anything which is presumed as Halal is driven by the spiritual world and as a result cannot be confined to the physical dimensions of branding (Wilson, 2010:115).

The Origins of the Concept of Halal

If the nature of Halal exists for the theories of brand and product, a questions arises as whether Halal can be defined successfully as forming a commercial product, a brand, or a combination of both? Experts believe that Halal is a concept that cannot be placed completely within the framework of these concepts. More than being a philosophy for brand marketing and product development, the concept of Halal is involved with such principles as the organizational behavior, cultural anthropology, and sociology. The origins of Halal date back to the times before the formation of branding and marketing activities. So, attempts to place it within these concepts are a cumbersome task. In fact, branding and marketing thought should attempt to adjust themselves to what really is Halal and not vice versa. If Halal be considered as a brand, the chances are not so high for the name "Halal" to be accepted completely. So, usually it is proposed that Halal be determined as a synthetic brand or a synthetic word in which case the role of a co-brand will be assumed for that. A global organization by the use of a "co-brand" can start a section which can use the term "Halal". However, this may cause more intense scrutiny over the activities of the organization. For example, the activities of the companies in the field of food service must be in accordance with the characteristics of Halal and observe such Islamic traditions as Ramadan and prayers (Wilson, 2010: 114).

Challenges Facing Halal

For Muslim consumers, those products that have Halal logo have a deeper concept and more importance than the ones having ISEO or similar certificates. Halal not only presupposes the standard cleanse but the products and production machines must be clean inward and outward. Muslim consumers should ask producers, importers, or business people to put Halal logo on their goods to give their costumers more confidence. Halal certificate not only does not have any negative impacts on business, but also is compatible with scientific and technological developments; so putting Halal certificate on products will not leave any doubt for people (Shahidan, 2004: 5).

ISLAMIC BRANDING

The big size of the Islamic market, the increasing trend of multi-national companies in this market, and the fact that powerful companies in this market are targeting non-Islamic markets has led to an increase in Islamic branding. A review of the insufficient literature of the subject shows that the meanings for this concept are quite vast. In fact, different people use this concept in a different way by assuming that they are making correct usage of the descriptive term "Islamic" (Alserhan, 2010: 101).

Up to now, there has not been a clear understanding of the term "Islamic Branding" and this has led to the incorrect usage of the word "Islamic". For more clarity, this term can be used to describe brands as "Islamic" for the following reasons:

1. These brands correspond with the Islamic Law (Islamic brands based on religion)
2. Their origins are Muslim nations (Islamic brands based on the origin country)
3. They target Muslims (Islamic brands based on targets)

Foundations for Islamic Branding

For a Muslim, brand cannot be separated from a religion that necessitates all actions to be divine and says that likes and dislikes of a person are not because of the human desires but of those emotions that are being guided by God. What differentiates Islamic branding from others is that the producers do not produce goods but honesty, they do not sell products but invite people to a life filled with beneficence, and buyers do not buy their needs and comforts but are being involved in worshipping. Such an understanding of Islamic branding gives it a higher impetus and in making relations with customers, makes it stronger in comparison with traditional branding. Islamic branding deals with the mixing of religion with materials and spirituals with physicals. Islamic branding talks about the religious mixing of brand with religious people who live assured of the divine rewards. In Islam, all actions are judged by their true motive or goal. So, all actions of a Muslim are considered good if the motive behind them was pure, no matter how the final results were. By having good intentions, simple acts like breathing, eating, and washing, among other things, are considered good actions which make God happy and guarantee his satisfaction. So, when a Muslim rejects anunlawful product or consumes a Halal one, this is considered as a good act. While non-Muslim consumers can be persuaded by the superficial advantages that can be identified in the short run, Muslim consumers are being affected by a much stronger factor and that is doing a good act. Brands that have been permitted by the Religion turn into good act and this is the thing that all of the brands targeting Muslims must try to achieve. Anything that God has created and has taught human beings about them is Halal and in the opposite direction, anything that Humans do in an arbitrary and irresponsible way is unlawful. For example, grapes have been called as heavenly fruit in the Holy Quran but turning them into inebriant drinks has been called unlawful. The Internet is Halal but making use of that in order to spread chastity pictures is considered unlawful. Cutting a tree to make a shelter for one's family is Halal but doing that to make a summer house is called squander. Remembering the small list of unlawful entities in Islam is not such a difficult task. In fact saying that Islam has forbidden wine is not difficult but it is difficult to understand the power of Muslims' emotions with regard to wine. What is of interest here is that brands correlate significantly with emotions and their success depends on the life styles or people's emotions. In addition to the insufficient knowledge of the experts of Islamic branding with regard to the Islamic lifestyle, they also need a high level of motivation, sincerity, and truthfulness in discussing with merely academic methods. Drinking alcoholic beverages and the consumption of pig meat and discussing about the Islamic brands is clearly non-Islamic and this is probably the reason that the Western experts have failed in their prediction of the leading brands despite their leading attempts related to the Islamic branding. They have failed in keeping these brands alive since their fundamental motive in their attempts is merely commercial and ignore the describing "good deeds" of a brand. What many experts see is just an opportunity to make money what is not being considered is an opportunity to add a moral dimension to created brand. Muslims naturally and actively reject those brands that they view as inconsistent with some Islamic teachings. The term "actively" means that they encourage others to reject those products, too (Alserhan, 2010: 104).

Halal Food in the Holy Quran

After an analysis and study on the verses of the Holy Quran, six key words including eating, Halal, unlawful, clean things, made clean, and livelihood and later we found that there are 41 verses in the Holy Quran that are related to Halal foods and drinks (Abdolnaqi, 1994). Next, we referred to two authoritative sources and extracted those points related to the discussion of Halal food in those verses. The extracted points are as follows:

1. Verse no. 168 Chapter 2. Al-Baqarah:people, eat of what is lawful and good on the earth and do not walk in Satan's footsteps, because he is for you a clear Enemy.

    Messages:

1. The essential thing in the consumption is two things: Being Halal and being clean and desirable.
2. Making use of unlawful and unclean things is following Satan (Qera'ati, 2006).
3. Chapter 2. Al-Baqarah, Verse 172: O ye who believe! Eat of the good things wherewith we have provided you, and render thanks to Allah if it is (indeed) he whom ye worship.

Messages:

1. In Islam, materials are a prerequisite to the spirituals.
2. Islam pays attention to hygiene in nutrition (Qera'ati, 2006).
3. Chapter 2, Verse 173: he hath forbidden you only carrion, and blood, and swine flesh, and that which hath been immolated to (the name of) any other than Allah. But he who is driven by necessity, neither craving nor transgressing, it is no sin for him. Lo! Allah is forgiving, merciful.

Imam Sadeq (peace be upon him) says: Carrion causes asthenia, sterilization, and sudden death and the consumption of blood leads to inclemency and barbarity. God's prohibitions are not just for medical and hygienic (like carrion and blood) but sometimes the reason for prohibition is doctrinal, intellectual, and behavioral issues. For example, the reason for the prohibition of an animal's meat that has been dedicated to other than Allah is to oppose paganism. Sometimes we do not eat a person's food as a result of his poor hygiene, and sometimes we do not eat to show our protest and objection (Qera'ati, 2006:261).

4. Chapter 3, Verse 93: All food was lawful to the children of Israel (Jacob) except what Israel (Jacob) forbade himself before the Torah had been sent down.

Messages: 1: In all religions, the food as being Halal is a fixed concept; 2: Without canonical reasons, do not consider Halas as unlawful (Qera'ati, 2006).

5. Chapter 5, Verse 3: you are forbidden (to consume) the dead, blood and the flesh of swine; also flesh dedicated to any other than Allah, the flesh of strangled (animals) and of those beaten, that which is killed by falling, gored to death, mangled by beasts of prey, unless you find it (still alive) and slaughter it; also of animals sacrificed on stones (to idols). (You are forbidden) to seek division by the arrows, that is debauchery.

HALAL BRANDING

Halal Certificate

Halal certificates can be seen on packages and mainly on the ads of Halal restaurants. Since there is no single legislative figure in Islam, some differences can be observed in the interpretations of Islamic principles. This leads to the situation that there are various Halal certificates being used within a country or between countries. This situation has been reported to exist in countries like Malaysia. The importance degree of Halal certificates depends on the agency issuing that and its popularity. Certificates' fame and fee differ greatly from each other. In the United States, the agency responsible to issue such certificates is the Islamic Food and Nutrition Council of America. In order to get Halal certificates in their target country, marketers must receive that from that country's official agencies.

Treats and Opportunities of Halal

In England, companies have faced problems since the time Muslim clergymen asked their followers not to dine in restaurants because it is unlawful. Food suppliers in these companies anesthetize chickens before butchering them and also use mechanical equipment in the process of butchering. While the Islamic Council that is the highest authority in Muslims' issues has declared the use of anesthetics in the process of butchering animals as Halal, local clergymen have their own opinions and based on these opinions guide their on followers. When there is conflict between the opinions of local clergymen, marketing becomes difficult. Lack of certainty and conflict makes the customers to buy these products. In France, fast food restaurants have some conflicts with politicians because they had decided to delete pork from their menu and just to offer Halal food in selected markets. In France there lives a significant population (around 5 millions) of Muslims. This country has experienced some political pressure in some cultural activities. The mayor of one of the cities in France decided to sue the owners of this restaurant because of prejudice against non-Muslims. Also, Germany that contains a considerable number of Muslims has moved very slowly toward conquering the Muslims' market. Some German retailers are worried about offering Islamic products since this will cause their non-Muslim customers to be disappointed. Such worries and perceptions has led the German market to be underdeveloped in religious and moral fields. Countries like the Philippines hope to conquer the Muslims' expanding market by introducing a national standard to authorize companies issuing Halal certificates. The Philippines expects to assure Muslim customers of their products being Halal by standardizing the process of issuing Halal certificate and in so doing attract them to its products. Although many American companies have made some reforms in their foreign products and services, the companies that have adjusted themselves to the requirements of Halal are not many in the U.S. Jalel Aossey, the CEO of a chain food company, says: "you must consider the requirements of the countries that you are going to target them "This is like you are the guest house of a person". His point of view can be very popular. In the global Halal market, so many western and active business people can be found that are marching together with the experts and exchange views on the future of this expanding and lucrative market (Rarick, 2011).

Brand and the Challenges of Halal

After reviewing the definitions of Alserhan (2010) and OgilvyNoor (2010) it cannot be concluded that all the Islamic brands are necessarily Halal, or at least completely halal. In the following, this point is described using 4 examples:

1. Cobra Zero Beer is "Halal" which is consumed by Muslims, but in the classical sense it is not Islamic and it has no trace in the Islamic tradition.
2. Mecca Bingo and Mecca USA contain commercial names that are clearly connected to Islam and Muslims' holiest places. Apart from this, they want to inspire their consumers by the association of meanings. Although, none of these commercial brands can claim to be Islamic. In addition, such weak bonds have the potential to face these brands with problems.
3. Virgin Megastore in Jeddah, Saudi Arabia.

Together with Virgin Cafe, it provides a Halal atmosphere for consumers. These stores and products are being considered as Islamic. However, some traditional regions might consider them as insulting because of some music CDs that contain a special sort of material. Also, Virgin adopts its logo from Arabic and Arabic is a major language in Islamic countries. Arabic script has a high amount of respect. Not only because of this, but also because it is used as the Islamic output for artistic and creative works. Emirates Airlines uses Islamic and Arabic calligraphy. They offer services to their Muslim customers by providing them with Halal services and flying mainly to Muslim countries. Although, they have tried to attract customers with various tastes and values by offering alcoholic beverages and a uniform for the female flight attendants that covers just a part of their hair. Wilson and Liu (2010) say that "the current literature shows that the exact and same definitions of Halal mainly exist within the field of product marketing". However, authors claim that Halal, as a concept, contain some characteristics that make it both phenomenal and spiritual. In addition, "Halal as a concept cannot be bound merely and completely within these structures". Also, the theory of Brand brings up the case that a brand can be split from the product or service in terms of: name, personality, identity, relations, and so on. Within the Halal industry, it is Islam or more particularly Halal that bears this conceptual position instead of any other brand or company name. So, it is Halal that turns into a pattern instead of branding. Although it can be argued that branding in the field of Halal is expanding with a superficial logic and act, Halal cannot completely allow for that based on its classic definition. What is considered Halal is, at its most, very pure, praiseworthy, and useful. So, these characteristics should be assumed and rendered in all products. The argument that can be brought up only for "Halal" products is that the intention of those involved in the process of production is important. They guide the consumers towards a lifestyle which is Islam. So, a brand is supported or rejected by an Islamic standard. While this is developing and facing various interpretations, it remains stable at its core principles (Wilson, 2011).

Halal Branding

Multi-national companies need to develop brand with local qualities in order to maximize their success in the Islamic markets. As long as branding is considered important, multinational companies, by having a key advantage in marketing and general management qualifications compared to their local Muslims competitors, start to work. These companies have branding and marketing skills that are much more complicated and developed than their local rivals. Multi-national companies should try to increase their cultural understanding in time of entering to the Islamic markets. Only relying on branding skills without taking into account or understanding the importance of cultural knowledge or sensitivities can turn these efforts as inconclusive. Entering in a hurried way to the Islamic markets without having a comprehensive understanding of cultural and religious motives and also the underlying reasons for a Muslim consumer's behavior would be unsuccessful for a brand. There are many examples of multi-national companies that have caused disastrous consequences for themselves in the global level by committing simple mistakes. The lesson that companies should learn from these examples is that their precision will not be exact while working in a different cultural situation or targeting customers with different cultures. In an Islamic setting, global knowledge would not be enough because the Islamic market is thoroughly different in terms of motivational factors, structure, and behavior. Religion plays a central role in Muslims decision making process and attempts to counteract its influences on customers' decisions will lead to a backfire. Finally, those multi-national companies that want to enter the Islamic market should carefully evaluate the diverse and accessible methods of entering a brand to the Islamic market like developing new brands, making use of the available brands, making use of pilot brands, and a mixture of all. This choice should be related to the overall strategy of the company and simultaneously be done based on a thorough understanding of a Muslim customer, the Islamic law, and the influences of the concept of Halal on the aspects of marketing. Companies should recognize that the Halal qualification must be obtained from the whole chain of offer. The implementation of Halal in some stages and not doing that in others can turn the brand into a non-Islamic one (Alserhan, 2010).

The Customers of a Halal Product

Halal is an Arabic term and its counterpart in English would be "lawful" and "healthy". Halal is a vast concept that encourages Muslims to consume products that promote goodness on all respects of life, are healthy, and have been produced in a healthy and clean condition. It has been predicted that the significant growth in Halal market would continue. Halal products are moving toward the mainstream and it will have attraction for those look for moral and high-quality products. Some companies have revealed that not all of their customers are Muslims. One-fourth of the customers of Marhaba, that produces chocolates and candy, are non-Muslims. Grocery stores that learn the guiding principles of Muslims will be successful in circle of faithful customers. Nowadays, supermarkets are offering many types of Middle Eastern dishes in way that more American customers have inclined towards them. This can be a process that is the result of more profitable and higher sells of those supermarkets that offer service to the Islamic market. As an example, a recent survey done by JWT on Muslim customers in the United States puts a significant emphasis on the Muslims' market as a special one. Food plays an important in Islam. Muslims are inclined to have big families, so their food expenses are high. Also, they buy big cars and spend more money on their house decoration and entertainment Estimates all around the world reveal that 70% of Muslims follow Halal principles. But before food suppliers try to provide Muslims with their nutritional requirements, they should understand the nutritional limitations that influence their purchases. Although there are clear instructions for a Muslim's diet, there is no global authority supervising the Halal standards. Now, there are more than 15 Halal logos in this market (Alserhan, 2010).

The Levels of Halal

The Halal industry is expanding both in size and maturity. This industry is not limited to meat, but include various products such as cosmetics, vaccines, and savings accounts. Generally, Halal market can be divided into three interdependent levels including food, lifestyle, and services. The first level, food, is now under the control of the non-Muslim, multi-national companies. However, there are some Muslim companies in this level such as Al-Islami brand in the UAE, Al-Marai in Saudi Arabia, and also thousands of small, local companies that are developing very fast. The reason for the lack of Islamic Halal brands in the market is that the concept of Halal food has never been discussed in Islamic countries because of the assumption that all the foods sold in these markets are guaranteed as Halal. Recognizing the products as Halal was an issue until the doors of Muslims' market were opened to the global market and products from non-Muslim countries flew into them. The second level, lifestyle, is under the control of non-Muslim multi-national companies, too. The producers of Halal cosmetics, containing no alcohol or animal fats, introduced their products in a slow way to Muslims. The slow development of this level in comparison with the first level has two reasons. The first is that these products are not as essential as food and the second reason is that both Muslims and multi-national companies have paid attention very late to the fact that Halal can be spread to fields other than food. In this way, usual and routine activities also can be Islamic and be classified as Islamic. By establishing such an understanding, Islamic products specially lifestyle started to develop in order to satisfy the needs of these markets. The third level, services, includes such areas as financial services, hospitality and provision, and transportation. Of all these services, Halal financial services have spread the most through the Islamic banks. These banks which operate according to Islami law have had a good performance during the economic depression because they were inclined more toward conservatism. In the areas of hospitality, hotels have had a good development (Alserhan, 2010).

Halal Creativity

Halal companies have understood that in their expansion they cannot merely rely on religion as a stimulus for supporting their marketing activities. Finally, people do not buy Halal products just because they are Halal. They attempt to buy high-quality products. This is possible for the rival companies to duplicate the ideological aspects of a product in order to gain profits. So, it is essential for them to have creativity all the time. Halal products and services include both food and non-food items. These items originate from the Middle East, Europe, and South-East Asia. Nestle is a leading company in this field. This company has started a Halal committee and also distinct facilities for its Halal products since 1980s. As a result, this company has gained $3.6 billion from in Halal products and 75 out of 456 factories in this companies are fitted to produce Halal products. In non-food items, companies such as LG from South Korea and Nokia from Finland have targeted Muslim customers. LG offers an application that helps users to connect live with Mecca. Also, Nokia provides Muslim customers with downloadable versions of the Holy Quran and maps for finding the location of the major mosques in the Middle East.

Such products and services increase loyalty to brands. In fact, famous and popular brands can be attractive to Muslims without making changes in their main products.

Halal Brands and Morality

The point here is that there would be problems in the supply chain optimization if only administrative issues be taken into account about the value of a brand. This is the result of the fact that those Halal cannot be achieved just by introducing high-quality products, delivering them faster, or by starting a more powerful brand. In order to make it more clear, in the following there is a verse from the Holy Quran and a Hadith about the foundations for judgment in Islam:

By the time of the afternoon! Surely, the human is in a (state of) loss, except those who believe and do good works and charge one another with the truth and charge one another with patience.

All actions are judged by their intentions.

This shows that the motivational factors for a Muslims are being guided by right thoughts and intentions. Following the suggestions by Maklan and Knox (1997, 2010), the experts in the field of business claim that morality can play an effective and fundamental role, too. As an instance, Prophet Muhammad (peace be upon Him) has deprived 10 types of people from his mercy in relation to alcoholic drinks: the person who makes alcoholic drinks, the person who orders others to make alcoholic drinks, the person who drinks that, the person who carries that, the person for whom it is taken, the person who prepares that, the person who sells that, the person who gates profit from the money paid for them, the person who buys that, and the person from whom it is bought. While drinking alcoholic drinks for fun has been prohibited in Islam, this hadith shows that being involved in encouragement and consumption of that has also been banned. So, one point is considering the concepts of Halal as a set of processes. This topic leads the efforts toward such points of view as fair trade, corporate altruism, sustainability and green marketing. Products that claim to have such levels of morality are inclined to introduce themselves as the carriers of reward. On the other hand, many Halal products at present are pricing less than their equivalent products. This is because of encouraging people to consume them, or for commercial reasons, or both (Wilson, 2010).

Strategic Halal Branding

Keller (1993, 1998, 2001, and 2003) introduces the consumer-based brand (CBBE) model as a method to investigate the value of a brand. There, a brand shows its value within the customers' minds and are processed and known as unique, desirable, and powerful collections. In addition, it seems that it seems that the concept of Halal, apart from being a brand, can gain a similar status among Muslims by creating a real situation. Anyway, the question that comes to mind is whether these products can attain such a stable status by acquiring a Halal title as a form of manifest branding. Brands which misuse the term "Halal" in fact weaken their power and statues among customers through losing their reputation. Neumeier (2009) says that an empirical concept can be achieved through an ideology in the field of creativity design; where all the sides involved are connected in some way to the brand. Within the framework put forward by Neumeier (2009) culture, both socially and organizationally, helps in the formation of a conception. It is evident that understanding culture, specifically Halal culture, is one of the essential components in every stage. So, branding should lead to the influence of cultural concepts centering Halal so that stable and strategic competitive advantages be gained (Wilson, 2010).

Offensive or Defensive Strategy

There is a growing trend in the influx of products other than food to the Halal market. For example, Halal soap, perfume, chocolate, etc. this phenomenon can be seen from two perspectives: from an optimistic perspective, they revive the need for such products and as a result the economic capacity of the market in a positive way. However, such an expansion can increase worries in Islamic societies. Muslims might feel that their needs have not been met sufficiently. There might be a pessimism towards bigger companies or some feeling that Islamic standards are not being controlled completely. There has been cases that some products contained alcohol or unclean animal parts, though they had Halal brand. This indicates that there are some worries left among Muslims. Another perspective, without considering any optimism or pessimism, is that forms of presence for Halal products are among companies' offensive or defensive strategies. The purification of a person's wealth and actions leads to a level of spirituality. Such feelings provide praiseworthy states and are a great potential for marketers and brands. As a result of these feelings, they see their customers as companions of products and services that get Halal certificates (Wilson, 2010).

LEGAL AND PRACTICAL ISSUES IN HALAL BRANDING

After explaining the Islamic foundations of Halal, it seems necessary, for the use of concepts in a practical way, to survey and study the legal and practical foundations of Halal and provide the grounds of its practical use both objectively and subjectively.

The Standards and Procedures of Halal

In definitions offered for Halal, cleanness and quality control has been mentioned together with spiritual issues. Raw materials, mediatory goods, and all the equipment used in the process of production of Halal products must be in accordance with Islamic law. Also, the process of food production must be observed and supervise by Muslim experts. Such processes that conform to the Halal standards and procedures attain the required credibility for a Halal food. So, Halal authentication can be a useful tool in observing and supervising over the process of producing Halal food. It includes food storage and transportation (Issa, 2009).

Halal Certificate

Companies use Halal certificate as a way to establish awareness and certainty among Muslim costumers towards the fact that they are making use of products that are in accordance with the Islamic Sharia. In other words, Halal certificate confirms that the products are lawful according to the Islamic law. In order for a product to get Halal certificate, it must get through an inspection phase which is performed by an Islamic agency that issues certificates. However receiving a Halal certificate causes some alterations in the process of production, which is a worthwhile act since nowadays Muslims comprise the largest amount of customers all over the world (Alserhan, 2010). Halal certificate is one of the ways of telling the customer that the product is not only Halal and in accordance with the Islamic Sharia, but also clean and healthy. The label which is put on the product must have enough transparency and content lest the customer be confused. The main concern of customers is the Halal logo and some of the Muslim customers have more confidence in Halal logo than any other logos such is ISEO ones. Nevertheless, some customers do not have confidence in Halal logos' credibility and this originates from governments' weakness in describing the benefits of certified Halal logos. So, it seems necessary to study and analyze food companies' experiences and impressions on Halal processes and procedures (Issa, 2009).

Halal Guarantee System

This is a system that is established by the producer individual or company to guarantee that the products are Halal. It is based on three concepts:

1. **Limitation:** No unlawful raw material has been used in the process of production.
2. **Disinfection:** No unlawful product has been produced.
3. **Threats:** No destructive threats are being accepted by the producer.

Any producer wishing to produce Halal food must operationalize the above mentioned system. The system has five elements: Halal management system and Halal system, the accounting system standard, the unlawful analysis control point, Halal solution, and Halal database. The general solutions of all these elements should be documented in the form of a Halal system. Of course, this system includes the policies of producers and objectives of the system. The producers' commitment to produce Halal food is regularly checked and evaluated through this system. The investment in the effective system for guaranteeing halal can create a competitive advantage for companies via development of values throughout the supply chain (Maheran, 2009).

Halal Logo

This is natural that as much as Muslims become more aware about their religion, they want to pay more attention to products and services that they use. In addition, once the customers become more careful about their meals and issues related to health, the appearance of informative labels and the need for information becomes more urgent. Halal logo contains signs that informs Muslims of what types of food they are allowed to consume. As a result, a logo can be profitable for the producers in this way that it informs the target customer that their product is in accordance with Islamic standards. This creates a competitive advantage against those companies that do not have Halal certificate. It has been many years that Halal logo is use for food products; as the term "Halal" is used among Muslims and non-Muslims to refer to a type of food which is permitted to use. Such a logo is not applied to other products. The common terms used in the service sector such as banking or insurance are "according to Islam" or "according to Sharia" (Shahidan, 2004).

Halal Provisions

Many countries all over the world are investing considerable amounts in order to become regional hubs for Halal products. These centers offer special production sites and also Halal provision systems to maintain the product in a Halal state throughout shipping or storage stages. Halal market's supply chains are attempting to change the process of production not only in Islamic countries but also in non-Muslim countries. For example, Brazilian meat providers have made modern facilities for slaughtering chickens exported to the Islamic countries. New Zealand, the largest producer of Halal lamb, has chosen native agencies in Muslim countries. Also, the Netherlands has built warehouses to keep Halal products apart from unlawful ones such as pork or alcohol. Food products that Muslim experts have classified into Halal and unlawful are being coded with small, green labels to notify customers of being Halal or unlawful. Unlawful products such as products that contain alcohol, pork, or narcotics are being kept in a glass room in the back of the store. In addition, those unlawful products are wrapped into pink, air resistant plastic covers and are being packed after purchase by workers that wear special, blue-colored gloves. In this way, the main store will not be contaminated. Halal industry is not being stopped for a long while in the stage of production. Storage and transportation companies from Dubai to Rotterdam have stabilized their position as providers of Halal provisional activities and has become very modern and equipped. For example, the National Shipping Company of Malaysia provides weekly and express Halal services and has a shipping line of importing Halal beef from New Zealand and Australia to the Far East and further. This company has built a hub for Halal provisions in the west of Kuala Lampur having such facilities as refrigerated warehouses, sterilization units, and also a laboratory for making sure that the products are Halal (Alserhan, 2010).

MODELS OF HALAL BRAND AND FOODS

The Model of Halal Food Choice

In Figure 1, attitude has a direct impact on the choice of Halal products. Also, subjective norms can be an important factor that may influence customers' attitude towards Halal products. Subjective norm can

Figure 1. Halal food choice

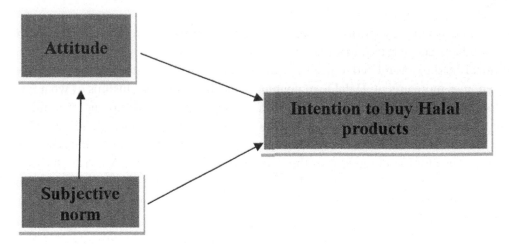

also influence the intention of choosing Halal products in a direct ay. Subjective norm refers to those expectations that exist toward customers (Lada, 2009).

The Model of Influential Factors on the Perception of Halal Food

One of the important points mentioned in this model is the special emphasis and focus on religious issues and more exactly, the religious approach in Figure 2 that makes it distinct from other models (Salman, 2011).

The Model of Intention to Buy Halal Food

Figure 3 has a behavioral approach toward the purchase of Halal food and it can be said that it is more detailed and more specific than other models, while the rest are more general and macro *(Alam, 2011)*.

Figure 2. Influential factors on the perception of Halal food

Figure 3. Intention to buy Halal food

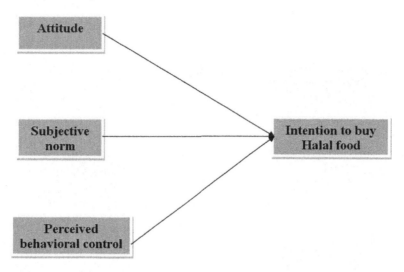

The Programmed Behavior Theory Model for the Consumption of Halal Meat

Figure 4 has two approaches toward the behavior of customers and brand and Halal food: a behavioral perspective and a religious one. Of course, it should not be forgotten that this model has been designed for a specific type of product, namely Halal meat, so it might have so much generality (Bonne, 2007).

The Fish Bone Model of Halal Purchase Intention

Figure 5 has more generality compared to the previous models in a way that it contains both marketing concepts and religious beliefs and indicators form behavioral discussions.

At the end, the ten models have been illustrated in a brief way with some considerations. The objective of doing this is to present a general image and perspective of the models and their indicators and concepts put forward by experts and designers in order to design and present new ideas and models (Shaari, 2010).

The Model of Promoting the Halal Brand in the Global Markets

Figure 6 includes four main dimensions and 28 peripheral variables. It seems that this is the most comprehensive model in the field of Halal branding which was designed in 2013 by the researcher during a comprehensive field study and was operationalized by the use of Delphi technique and forming a panel of experts in the Islamic Republic of Iran. What is important abut this model is that only the balanced enhancement of 28 peripheral variables would leave to the enhancement of the status of Halal brand in the global markets (Shahnazari, 2013).

Figure 4. The programmed behavior for the consumption of Halal meat

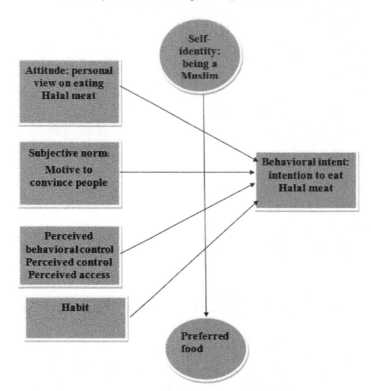

Figure 5. Halal purchase intention

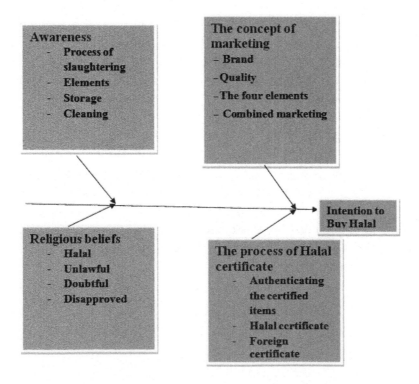

Figure 6. Promoting the Halal brand in the global markets

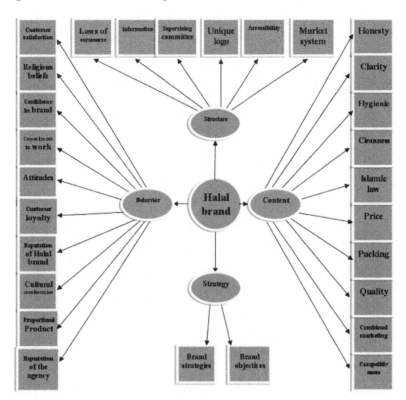

CONCLUSION AND SUGGESTIONS

At the end, the researcher presents the following suggestions as ways to improve Halal branding:

1. Formation of a trade union for Muslims centering the Organization of Islamic Cooperation for the purposes of facilitating commercial exchanges and unity among Muslim to establish Islamic laws.
2. Take advantage of the yearly Hajj ceremony to enhance trade and business grounds, regarding the fact that a considerable population of Muslims gather around each year.
3. Practical and intellectual battle against Wahhabism and Baha'ism that nowadays try to spread superficiality and Satanism. This will be operationalized when Muslims understand the concept of cleanness deeply and implement that in their life. Such an analysis and understanding can be confirmed by looking deeply into the verses of the Holy Quran.

Any attempt and action in the course of planning, design, production, and presentation of a Halal product are inseparable elements of a Halal brand. In other words, Halal brand is not limited just to quantity and exteriors but is quire vast. It can be argued that a notable definition of brand and Halal brand has been presented here. Concerning the increasing trend among Muslims and non-Muslims to Halal products and services, it should be said that Muslims all over the world, in a united way, should consider the shared concepts among Islamic branches and implement concepts taken from the Holy Quran and Islamic Jurisprudence in business environment.

REFERENCES

Alam, S. (2011). Applying the theory of planned behavior in halal food purchasing. *International Journal of Commerce and Management, 21*, 23–29. doi:10.1108/10569211111111676

Alserhan, B. A. (2010). On Islamic branding: Brands as good deeds. *Journal of Islamic Marketing, 1*, 45–53. doi:10.1108/17590831011055842

Alserhan, S. A. (2010). Islamic branding: A conceptualization of related terms. *Journal of Brand Management, 18*, 30–41. doi:10.1057/bm.2010.18

Karin, B. (2007). Determinants of halal meat consumption in France. *British Food Journal, 109*, 1–39.

Lada, S. (2009). Predicting intention to choose halal products using theory of reasoned action. *International Journal of Islamic and Middle Eastern Finance and Management, 2*, 45–58. doi:10.1108/17538390910946276

Maheran, N. (2009). Positioning Malaysia as halal –hub: Integration role of supply chain strategy and halal assurance system. *Asian Social Science, 5*, 21–29.

Mat, I. (2009). Practices of food producers in producing halal food products in Malaysia. *Interdisciplinary Journal of Contemporary Research in Business, 1*, 23–29.

Qeraati, M. (2007). *Tafsir noor* (Vol. 1). Tehran, Iran: Cultural Center of Quran's Lessons.

Rarick, C. (2011). *Is it kosher? No it is halal: A new frontier in niche marketing*. London: International Academy for Case Studies.

Salman, F. (2011). An exploratory study for measuring consumer awareness and perceptions towards halal food in Pakistan. *Interdisciplinary Journal of Contemporary Research in Business, 3*, 52–64.

Shaari, J. N. (2010). Dimension of halal purchase intention: A preliminary study. *International Review of Business Research, 6*, 90–102.

Shahidan, S. (2004). *Halal certification: An international marketing issues and challenges*. Malaysia: Malaysian International Marketing and Service.

Wilson, J. (2011). The challenges of Islamic branding: navigating emotions and halal. *Journal of Islamic Marketing, 2*, 76–84. doi:10.1108/17590831111115222

KEY TERMS AND DEFINITIONS

Halal Certificate: Halal certificates can be seen on packages and mainly on the ads of Halal restaurants. Since there is no single legislative figure in Islam, some differences can be observed in the interpretations of Islamic principles. In order to get Halal certificates in their target country, marketers must receive that from that country's official agencies.

Halal Food: Halal is an Arabic term which is connected to the Islamic tradition. Generally, Halal can be defined as "allowed" or "permitted". The acceptance and understanding of what means Halal is at the center of Muslims' beliefs. The opposite of Halal in Arabic is the term "Haram" or unlawful. Islamic tradition considers every food as Halal unless the opposite has been proven. So, Muslims distinguish between Halal and unlawful foods.

Islamic Branding: The term "Islamic" can be used to describe brands that correspond with the Islamic Law, their origins are Muslim nations, and they target Muslims.

This research was previously published in Marketing in the Cyber Era edited by Ali Ghorbani, pages 160-176, copyright year 2014 by Business Science Reference (an imprint of IGI Global).

Chapter 3
Defining Place Image

Candi Clouse
Cleveland State University, USA

Ashutosh Dixit
Cleveland State University, USA

ABSTRACT

The image of a place is important as it has implications for investments made in cities, workforce locations, and tourism. Place image incorporates concepts including brand, visual image, reputation, the sense of place, and the identity of the place - all of which create an overall image of a place and can lead to investment or abandonment. Place image has ramifications for decisions made about the place, including where businesses locate, where workers live, and where tourists visit (Smith, 2006). Place image has serious ramifications for decisions made about the place as people choose to stay, work, visit, and invest. This research outlines the inconsistencies in the literature, clarifies the terminology, and begins to set research standards for how place image is described through a conceptual model.

INTRODUCTION

The image of a place is important as it has implications for investments made in cities, workforce locations, and tourism which can include upwards of 600 significant new expansions or relocations in a state in a given year with each creating jobs and value to the economy (Conway, 2015). Place image incorporates concepts including brand, visual image, reputation, the sense of place, and the identity of the people - all of which create an overall image of a place and can lead to either investment or abandonment. Place image has ramifications for decisions made about the place, including where businesses locate, where workers live, and where tourists visit (Smith, 2006; Zenker, Eggers, & Farsky, 2013). Place image has serious ramifications for decisions made about the place as people choose to stay, work, visit, and invest. This research outlines the inconsistencies in the literature, clarifies the terminology, and begins to set research standards for how place image is described through a conceptual model.

Promoting places requires the "sale" of the image of particular place "so as to make it attractive to economic enterprises, to tourists, and even to inhabitants of that place" (Philo & Kearns, 1993). The goal of promoting cities is to encourage interest and investment to a specific place. Promoting places is

DOI: 10.4018/978-1-5225-5187-4.ch003

one way to boost regional growth through self-promotion and to "manufacture an environment that will secure the acceptance and even the affection of peoples who might otherwise rebel against it" (Philo & Kearns, 1993). Selling places makes one location stand out from the competition (Trejo, 2008; Avraham & Ketter, 2008). The marketing of places is crucial because practitioners argue that 71% of location decisions are based on image and these decisions are made based on emotions and rationalized with data (personal communication).

Place brands are now disseminated through a variety of tools including advertising, direct marketing, sales promotion, public relations and personal selling (Kotler, et al, 1993). Close attention should be paid to how valuable marketing dollars are spent and where the best impact for the money will be seen. Experts have said that an audience is perhaps five times more likely to be influenced by editorial copy than by advertising (Kotler, et al, 1993). As Andy Levine, President of Development Counsellors International noted, "If Money magazine says you're a great place to live that means more than if you say it. If a corporation says you're a great place to do business, that's more credible than your ad" (as quoted in Baker, 2007). Oftentimes, the media has a great influence on prospective place buyers by highlighting current events, sports highlights and publicized rankings ranging from most walkable to most miserable places.

There has been a major global shift toward increasing activity at the urban level to attract attention, capital, residents, and tourists, and one of those activities is place branding (Jensen, 2007). Anholt (2010) argues that given the effects of globalization, every country and every region must compete with every other for its share of the commercial, political, social, and cultural transactions. The brand is the shortcut for the "informed buying decision" about a region (Anholt, 2010). The brand, however, may not be known in- depth by the people who are potential residents or tourists. For example, a person may make a decision to visit Orlando because of Disney World, not knowing anything else about the region or its image.

CONCEPTS OF PLACE IMAGE

"The Image of the City" written by Kevin Lynch (1960), is a well-cited resource on city image. He calls for future research on how images develop and how this process can be influenced. The concepts and terminology surrounding place image are inconsistent in both the academic literature and among practitioners to this day. What one source calls image, another calls identity, and a third will term brand (Stock, 2009). This confusion is one of the major challenges for those researching this topic. The literature offers few empirical studies of this topic and instead relies mostly on case studies and anecdotal practitioner information (Dinnie, 2004; Uhlir, 2005; Herstein & Jaffee, 2008; Fan, 2010; & personal communications). Due to the inconsistencies in the literature, there is a great need to clarify the terminology and begin to set research standards for how place image is examined.

This lack of cohesiveness on definitions for all concepts of image includes concepts such as brand, image, reputation, stereotypes, sense of place, quality of place, identity, and quality of life. Gertner (2011) brings out this subject in a meta-analysis of the place marketing and place branding literature between 1990 and 2009. He found that most articles were not concerning business, management, marketing, or branding, but instead in the fields of public diplomacy, urban planning, geography, and political science, perhaps due to the lack of collaboration between disciplines. He also notes that most articles were essays or editorials with "doubtful scientific value" and 200 of 212 were subjective and anecdotal. He reported that several articles talked about brand and image as interchangeable concepts; he stated that out of the

212-article sample, 144 were based on personal opinions and secondary sources and 187 did not refer to any theoretical framework. In fact, only 16 articles reported statistics leading to his argument that little progress had been made in building theoretical knowledge in the field (Gertner, 2011). This thorough analysis demonstrates the need for research that explains the terminology surrounding place image.

Based upon a review of the literature and interviews with place marketing and attraction practitioners, a framework of five concepts of place image is presented: brand, visual image, reputation, sense of place, and identity. These concepts together herein will be referred to as place image. It is important to examine all five of these concepts as they all interact in the system of how a place is seen by various actors working on place promotion as well as those that may live in, visit, or invest in a place. After each component of place image is presented, a model outlining the concepts of place image will be offered.

The body of this chapter will further delve into the literature on place image and it will outline the definitions of the five aspects of place image. This includes the brand: the intended message of the place, the visual image: the symbolic knowledge of a place, the reputation: specific knowledge about a place, the sense of place: subjective experience in a place, and identity: the extents to which people are willing to associate themselves with a place. These five aspects are proposed here as a framework for understanding the complexity of place image.

BRAND

Promoting a city is usually means adopting a new tagline and a logo, for example *The Best location in the Nation* or *Cleveland's a Plum* or even *Believe in Cleveland*. Taglines offer no information about a place and have a very short shelf-life. A real brand is more than these taglines.

Branding is the intended message of the place. Branding is often presented as half science, and half art (Franzen & Moriarty, 2009). It is a complex bundle of images, meanings, associations, and experiences in the minds of people (Fan, 2010). A brand is the personality of a product and that personality is how people associate with it (Aaker, 1997). The brand enables the place to differentiate itself from the competition, plan its future economic, human, social and cultural developments, retain and create new human capital, develop and capitalize on its cultural heritage, sports teams and attributes, attract major investment, and define or redefine what it does well and upon which it is capable of building (Allan, 2004). The brand is a complex bundle of what the place offers.

Branding is story-telling about a place which compels people to see it in a certain way by articulating it as such (Jensen, 2007). Branding can be defined as a combination of imaginative marketing, supported by investment in key services and facilities which is required to deliver the experience (Hankinson, 2004). It is argued that branding is truly not a sales pitch or slogan; it is about creating a place (Hankinson, 2004; On Three Communication Design Inc., 2008). Branding can be demonstrated through various means including both functional, symbolic, legal, strategic, differentiating, and ownership devices (Medway & Warnaby, 2008). Branding generates a set of expectations and images and positioning those shows off what a community has to offer (Runyan & Huddleston, 2006). Also, branding should bridge the gap between what a place is, how people perceive it, and how it wishes to be seen (Alonso & Bea, 2013). The brand must be factual and offer insight on the realities of the place.

A brand is the promise of the value that the place offers (Van Gelder, 2008). Branding, according to Allan (2006), is about creating value for all that have a stake in the brand, its reputation, products and services, as well as for the customers who purchase those items. A brand is also an organizing tool and can be seen as the way in which products and services are created and brought to market (Allan, 2006). The brand can be reinforced by positive associations with companies located within a place's boundary as is the case with Cleveland being on the healthcare radar due in large part to the presence of the world-renowned Cleveland Clinic. The brand of a place organizes the stakeholders around a common value.

Branding requires resident recognition and adoption. Branding a place is different from branding a product because you cannot control or change the product easily when dealing with an entire city (Hankinson, 2004). It is important to see how the public sees a place in order to improve it (Nasar, 1990). As Jensen (2005) points out, "You don't have to ask the beans in the can how they feel about the label." Taking stock of the people is of the utmost importance as residents are necessary for the success of the campaign.

Branding is the aspect of place image in which the heaviest investment is often made. The brand of a place is often what is found leading the brochures, advertisement, and communications to the world about a place. To conclude, a brand is the intended message of the place.

VISUAL IMAGE

Visual image represents what people know and visualize about a place. For example, when Toledo, Ohio began working through a branding campaign, they found that it was not that they had a bad image to outsiders, it was that they did not have one at all (Baker, 2007). People may picture the Empire State Building, the Sydney Opera House, or the Eiffel Tower. People distinguish that Orlando is a family tourist destination and that Las Vegas is a city of vice. As Downs and Stea (1973) note, "We rely on these images for understanding and explaining the event because 'you would expect that sort of thing to happen there.'" Images of the social system, attitudes of the people, culture, and food are envisioned about places (Downs & Stea, 1973). The visual image is what people see when they think of a place and represent a simplification of all of the information one has of each place. They are the product of each person trying to essentialize huge amounts of information about a place (Kotler et al., 1993). Lynch (1960) argues that image is a "purposive simplification…made by reducing, eliminating, or even adding elements to reality." He further argues that people are always trying to organize their surroundings to understand them and that people create their own meanings and connections (Lynch, 1960). These connections become their visual image of a place.

A prevalent definition of place image is that it represents the sum of beliefs, ideas, and impressions that people have of a place (Kotler et al., 1993). Image also includes evaluations of these items (Burgess, 1982 as cited in Ashworth & Voogd, 1990). Images are the "mental conceptions" that pull together everything that an individual knows, evaluates, and prefers about places (Walmsley, 1988 as cited in Ashworth & Voogd, 1990). Thus, images are preferences which have been filtered through each individual's own personality construct (Ashworth & Voogd, 1990). Visual images are individually held.

Image is formed through different mechanisms. Luque-Martinez et al. (2007) modeled how city image is formed in Granada, Spain through a detailed survey of residents. The authors identified twelve dimensions of city image, which lead to a level of satisfaction living in the city (Luque-Martinez et al., 2007). Authors argue that all of the factor dimensions (physical, social, cultural, and economic) which they included have an impact on how the residents see the city. The nine factors in their model suggested that image had a high positive influence on how satisfied people felt living the city (Luque-Martinez et al., 2007). Image can affect how people feel about places.

Some authors argue that positive image is crucial to places. Visual image has become an active part of the economic success or failure of a region (Ashworth & Voogd, 1990). A place with a positive visual image has an easier time exporting goods and attracting talent (Anholt, 2010b). Ergo, visual image is important in the way a place is represented. A visual image of a place involves more than a tagline or brand; it is the personal embodiment of how an individual symbolically thinks about a place. To summarize this section, a visual image is the symbolic knowledge of a place.

REPUTATION

A reputation is how a city is colloquially known. Reputation represents feedback from the outsiders about claims made from those endogenous to the city (Fan, 2010). Reputation is based on certain firm clichés and prejudices (Anholt, 2007). It represents a widely held belief that is simplistic and carries a certain attitude about a place that is either positive or negative (Kotler et al., 1993). Reputations include that Paris is romantic and Baghdad is dangerous. Public opinion is usually in agreement on the reputation of places (Nasar, 1990). Reputations exist outside of the physical place and can be held by people that have never even visited it (Anholt, 2010a). The reputation is specific knowledge about a place that is a pre-conceived notion about the place.

Often the reputation of a city is a reflection of a real-life problem or condition (Avraham, 2004); the reputation can be both positive and negative, however, cities must work to solve the real problems to curb some of the negative attention placed on them (Avraham, 2004). The real-life situation is more important than any media strategy invoked to counter a negative reputation (Avraham, 2004). Barber (2008) states that the relationship between a place and its reputation is a "chicken-and-egg scenario." A place could have reflected their reputation first or it could be that a place grew to accept and become a likeness of said reputation.

Place representation is built through various mechanisms. The media plays a role in the creation and dissemination of reputation (Pocock & Hudson, 1978). Part of this is the popularity of negative stories (Avraham & Ketter, 2008). According to Allan (2006) the role of the media is even more important now as they assist in making the place recognizable. With their reach in print, television, and the internet, the representation that the media creates and distributes play a role in defining places by shaping opinions of them (Allan, 2006). The media can, because of the proliferation of negative stories, reinforce adverse stereotypes of places (Baker, 2007). In addition, the media can send outdated messages further impacting a city (Baker, 2007). Avraham and Ketter, (2008) note that the media is the very mechanism through which the way we see places is constructed. They argue the idea that if crime is the main topic of news stories that are told about a place, any positive stories will be lost (Avraham & Ketter, 2008). Anholt and Hildreth (2004) argued that good stories just do not have the same power as bad ones and they further argue that the public is not likely to "trade down" from a juicy story to a boring one. The media works not just as an adversary, but it can also act as an ally as many cities promote themselves through this medium. Reputations are convenient and fit within what Anholt and Hildreth (2004) called the "spirit of the times." This zeitgeist is largely influenced by the media.

As with visual image, reputation is defined by public perceptions (Barber, 2008). Reputation is distributed through a wide network for the public to accept or reject (Barber, 2008). However, by the very nature of the media distribution network, the portrayed reputations of places are the work an elite group that possesses the power to command these forums (Barber, 2008). Often the reputation of a city is cemented into place, even if positive change occurs in the area. Places or regions with poor reputations like the rust belt may have a harder time attracting people and investment due to the way the region is seen.

Many cities believe that a poor reputation is an obstacle for economic growth (Avraham, 2004). Residents often lack pride in their city when it has a bad reputation. This can lead to a lack of investment in the city and even to its abandonment (Avraham, 2004). Thomas Waltermire, {now former} Chief Executive Officer of TeamNEO, the business attraction organization for Greater Cleveland, states "It's not often easy to be a realistic optimist in Northeast Ohio because the culture is so much more attune to badmouthing, that if you aren't doing that, you are an outcast" (personal communication). When a city is suffering from major economic issues, it is often hard to change how the residents see the city which can lead to decline. To conclude, a reputation is defined as specific knowledge about a place.

SENSE OF PLACE

Unlike branding, visual image, and reputation, the sense of place must be experienced on the ground. Every neighborhood or city has a distinct sense of place stemming from its physical infrastructure and sociological make-up (Billig, 2005). Sense of place is the experience of being involved in the human aspect of place (Birch, 2001). Jorgensen and Stedman (2006) argue that it is a multidimensional construct made up of beliefs, emotions, and behavioral commitments about a specific geography. The sense of place is an attachment held by people to specific places which is deeply personal. It represents the idea of "topophilia" – from the Latin word meaning "to love" (Barber, 2008; Holcomb, 1993). This may be an experience held by a vacationer, a person doing business, or residents. People remember the unique atmosphere of places as it relates to them and their interests (Billig, 2005). Shamai (1991) states that places are not just objects, but instead the experiences in places. A sense of place is the feelings, attitudes, and the behavior toward a place: an essence that exists in the beholder's senses and mind (Shamai, 1991). The character of a place is defined by the people in it imposing upon it their views, attitudes, beliefs, symbols, and myths (Shamai, 1991). The former marketing director of Positively Cleveland notes,

We need to address an attitude…thinking about Cleveland as a tourist destination. I'm imagining that if you talk to most people walking down the street and asked if they think Cleveland is a tourist destination, the answer would be no. We need to change that thinking. We need to be welcoming. We need to stop asking visitors why they are here and really roll out the red carpet because if you have a great experience, you're going to post it on Facebook, you're going to tweet about it, all of your friends are going to hear about it and they are going to want to come visit. We need to make sure that people are running into very happy, very positive ambassadors for this region. (personal communication).

Sense of place is a feeling within a place that can be held by anyone there.

The sense of place is often inspired by the natural environment or skyline (Barber, 2008). The sense of place is made up of the scenic nature of a place which is often used to make inferences about the local people (Nasar, 1990). The sense of place includes the density of the area, variety of offerings, urban qualities, and positive "street culture" (Jensen, 2007). It is how one feels when inside a place and what one remembers about it. Here again, Lynch (1960) notes that the "vividness and coherence" of a place was crucial for enjoyment and use. He further notes "By appearing as a remarkable and well-knit place, the city could provide a ground for the clustering and organization of these meanings and associations.

Such a sense of place in itself enhances every human activity that occurs there, and encourages the deposit of a memory trace." Hay (1998) argues that a sense of place can "provide feelings of security, belonging and stability, similar to the feelings that arise from a fully developed pair bond." Sense of place is the memory and the associations made about a place.

Chamlee-Wright and Storr (2009) found in their research on the former residents of New Orleans's ninth ward after Hurricane Katrina that residents that returned to The Big Easy desired the unique characteristics that cannot be found elsewhere. The sense of place was found to be a strong determinant for those that returned quickly (Chamlee-Wright & Storr, 2009). The sense of place for these displaced people was raised up to a level of consciousness with which most people are not in touch. This sense of happiness, well-being, and even their sense of self was tied to the city. The sense of place for those that returned was so high that they even expected other people to hold it as well (Chamlee-Wright & Storr, 2009). The sense of place itself was brought back to New Orleans.

German sociologist Gerhard Schulze argued that we are living in "erlebnisgeschellschaft" or "experience society" (Jensen, 2005, 2007). The primary concern has shifted away from mere sustenance toward seeking ever more stimulating experiences (Jensen, 2007). The way a place is represented has profound implications on the level of *erlebnisgeschellschaft* offered. Orleans (1973) argues that any knowledge of a place comes from how it is experienced. Evans (2003) argues that city location alone is not enough to generate interest but the package of entertainment can capture those looking for an urban consumption experience. Boddy (1992) states that people may even prefer stimulation to reality. Take the case of Disneyland as presented by Sorkin (1992); often a popular vacation spot – it is by its very nature created space. Sorkin (1992) argues, "Disneyland is just like the world, only better." Travelers to Disney are putting a preference on stimulation over reality – urbanism without the city. The promotion of places should focus not as much on the place, but on what can be done and experienced in the place.

The sense of place, or way a place is experienced, has an impact on decisions that are made whether or not to stay or invest. The sense of place concept requires that one experience the place first-hand. If this experience is positive, it may encourage further exploration or investment. The importance of this is shown by regional marketing and attraction agencies that invite site selection experts to visit their cities to see what it is really like. Dave Shute, the Senior Strategic Adviser at the Global Center for Health Innovation in Cleveland, noted that getting people to the city and the site was key in his ability to attract businesses and because of the low expectations held by some visitors, they are overwhelmed by the city (personal communication). To summarize, the sense of place is the subjective experience in a place.

IDENTITY

The concept of places and people in them having a unique identity is not new. Back to agrarian societies, people have felt connected to the land and identified themselves by where they are from. This is easily demonstrated through the many surnames that were used which identified location, such as the "Tweedie" clan of Scotland and their roots on the River Tweed. Clans, tribes, and city-dwellers throughout history have identified themselves by location. Finding out where people are from is often one of the first questions asked when meeting a new person. Based on his analysis of mining towns in Mexico, Harner (2001) argues that identity is "a cultural value shared by the community, a collective understanding about social identity intertwined with place meaning. Place is a process, and it is human experience and struggle that give meaning to place" (Harner, 2001). The identity is an attitude held by the residents.

The identity of a place is the personal connection that residents have to it. It is how one is a "Cleve-lander" or a "New Yorker"; a self-image (Twigger-Ross & Uzzell, 1996). The identity exists within the people within a place (Anholt, 2010a). Proshansky (1978) defines a "place-identity" in terms of the self as all pieces of the person as they relate to their environment. People organize their place identity as it suits them. It should also be noted that places do not have single identities but like all characterizations of place representation instead have different meanings to different people (Goodwin, 1993). Those that live in an affluent section of town will identify with a city very differently than those that reside in low-income housing. Former employees identify with an abandoned factory town in a very different way than a politician or a developer (Goodwin, 1993). Identity is tied to how one interacts with their environment.

People want to be proud of their city and where they come from. Lalli (1992) contends that self-esteem has been positively correlated with living in a prestigious place. This is found through the attributes of a place and through positive feedback given to people in a place (Twigger-Ross & Uzzell, 1996). Positive place identity, simply pride in where they live and work, is notably not a characteristic held by people in the industrial Midwest given deindustrialization and the weak economy. Anholt (2010a) argues that "loyalty builds success, and success builds loyalty, and no place on earth – city, town, country, village or region – can hope to make others respect and admire it unless it first respects and admires itself." The identity, formed through unique culture, history, land, traditions, genius, and imagination, are a strong force in creating identity (Anholt, 2010a). Anholt (2010b) argues that "… people want their nation to *count*. They want to feel proud of where they come from" (Anholt, 2010b). Identifying with a place is essential to residents and the stronger the identification is, the more likely they will remain.

Changing the way people feel about their home is not easy but it can be enriched through improvements. Lowe (1993) argues that any physical improvement, although important to the place image, may be even more important to the confidence of the residents which arguably will lead to further regional regeneration in the long run. Improving a place not only has implications for how it is seen outside, but it also has a large impact on how people within the place interact and identify with it. If people have a strong identity due to being from a certain place, they are likely more apt to stay in that place. As the company Monolith was looking for a new location, they wanted to be in a place "where people share their values, who are very hardworking, and who they can trust" (Bartles, 2015). To conclude, identity is the extent to which people are willing to associate themselves with a place.

MODEL OF PLACE IMAGE

Many case studies regarding how the way places are represented can be found in extant academic and practitioner literature (Barber, 2008; Birch 2001; Boyer, 1992; Herstein, & Jaffe, 2008; Laurier, 1993; Ong & Horbunluekit, 1997). Figure 1 proposes how the five concepts of place image may fit together, using the definitions outlined previously.

The model ties the five concepts of place image together. There are two groups: the attraction focus (brand, visual image, reputation) and the retention focus (sense of place, identity). The brand, visual image, and reputation of the place are all place characteristics utilized by marketing professionals to attract businesses to a specific place. These characteristics can develop away from the place and live outside of it. These three concepts are propagated by organizations and governments as well as by the media and individuals, both inside and outside the place. These concepts are conveyed through pictures and text and do not require people to physically experience a place; they are the broad characteristics of

Figure 1. Conceptual model of place image

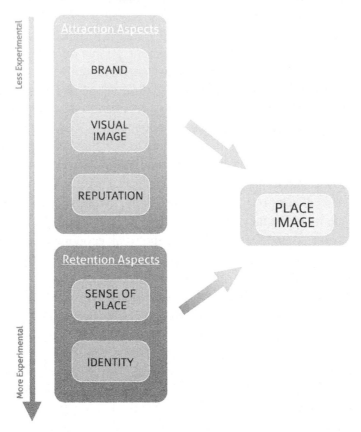

a place. However, the concepts of sense of place and identity are concrete place characteristics that can be used by marketing and site selection professionals to primarily retain businesses. To experience sense of place, one needs to be present in the place, one needs to identify with the place, and one must live there. These concepts play a role in the retention of businesses – instead of the solely attraction focus above. An interesting sense of place and a positive place identity will retain residents and businesses in addition to aiding in attraction efforts.

Additionally, the model shows a hierarchy from brand to identity, showing an increasing experiential relationship to the physical space (leftmost arrow). The brand can live completely outside the space and be completely unrelated to it. For example, the brand for the city of Pittsburgh is "Mighty. Beautiful" and shows a logo of a bridge over water (Visit Pittsburgh, 2014). The visual image that a person has of a place can also live outside the place but requires some knowledge of the place, like visualizing Niagara Falls outside of Buffalo. The reputation of a place requires more specific knowledge, like the burning Cuyahoga River for which Cleveland is often remembered. All three can persist in the absence of any direct experience with a place. However, the sense of place can be experienced by any visitor as in Detroit's North End neighborhood filled with art and agriculture creating an interesting sense of place (Huffington Post, 2013). Identity is the concept that is most closely tied with an individual. One must be a current or a former resident of a place to identify with it, as those from the Canton, Ohio region identify strongly with their football-centric home town. The concepts of sense of place and identity require experience with the place.

The five concepts of place image presented here are intended to guide the further research into how place image factors into the location decision process and economic health of places. As Hill, et al, (1995) argued, "If the region has a poor image, risk perceptions will increase, business start-ups with locational choices will take place elsewhere, and plants and other operations will have strong incentives to do their expanding in other places." This model will help guide further research surrounding place image as it clarifies the common terms and presents a framework for future research. Figures 2-6 show how each of the aspects of place image currently fits in the context of Cleveland.

The Five Aspects of Place Image: Cleveland

Brand: The Intended Message of the Place

"Grit meets sophistication in a town where you can browse modern art inside a turn-of-the-century transformer station, hear the orchestra perform live inside the local hot dog joint and chow down on pierogi stuffed with beef cheek. We've got world-class experiences without the world-class ego. And for that, you're welcome."

Over time, the city has also been "The Best Location in the Nation," and even "Cleveland is the Plum."

Visual Image: The Symbolic Knowledge of a Place

The most recognizable image of the city – the Rock & Roll Hall of Fame and Museum. Other notable images include the skyline of the city sitting on Lake Erie including the historic Terminal Tower, Severance Hall (home to the world-renowned Cleveland Orchestra), the West Side Market (the oldest market in the city), and the East 4th Street entertainment district.

Reputation: The Specific Knowledge About a Place

The reputation of Cleveland has formed through many events, most notably:

Figure 2. Brand
www.thisiscleveland.com

Figure 3. Visual image
www.rockhall.com

Figure 4. Reputation
http://clevelandhistorical.org/items/show/63#.VmdfJLgrK70

1964: The last time a professional Cleveland sports team won a championship.
1966: Race riots occurred in the Hough neighborhood.
1969: The industrial Cuyahoga River caught fire.
1978: The city became the first major American city to default on debts since the Great Depression.

   Additional items that cross time include the Cleveland Orchestra, the Cleveland Clinic, the Rock & Roll Hall of Fame and Museum, the sports teams, and specifically, LeBron James and the 2016 NBA Champion Cleveland Cavaliers. The reputation of Cleveland has been mainly negative due to some of the aforementioned events, which led to the adoption of the "Mistake on the Lake" moniker which was propagated largely by late night television host Johnny Carson as he continually poked fun at the city.

Sense of Place: The Subjective Experience in a Place

The sense of place in Cleveland varies greatly depending on what parts of the city are visited. There is the bustling downtown which houses shopping, restaurants, and a casino, with three sports stadiums within walking distance. The theater district, the largest in the country outside of New York City's Lincoln Center, is home to five major theaters as well as smaller performance spaces. Additionally, the city sits on the banks of where the Cuyahoga River and Lake Erie meet and recreation and entertainment options are located along the shores.

Identity: The Extent to Which People Are Willing to Associate Themselves With a Place

While traditionally, Clevelanders themselves have tended to badmouth the city, most residents are die-hard fans that were born and stayed in the city. Also, a new generation of people is being welcomed that was not party to the issues that created any bad visual image or reputation of the city. These new arrivals are quickly making the city their own which in turn has helped improve the identity of many long-time residents.

INVESTING IN CITIES

Cities continue to invest in themselves and their image. Kotler et al. (1993) argue, for example, that economic weakness throughout the Midwest is often measured by population loss, decreasing incomes,

Figure 5. Sense of place
www.east4thstreet.com

Figure 6. Identity
www.livecleveland.org

and investment. Places need to find ways to sustain themselves and grow, but also prevent unmanaged growth or further decay from destroying them. Not everything that happens to a place is within its control: there are natural disasters, business location changes, or what Joseph Schumpeter called "creative destruction" (Kotler et al., 1993). Business, industry, and population once had a large concentration in the Midwest, and specifically in the central cities in this region. In the current market, however, businesses have many more options for their location decisions. As Hill, et al (2012) notes, "Central cities that at one time dominated their regional markets for business locations are now just one potential location among many in much less dense and much larger metropolitan areas." Job losses and the decline in the manufacturing industry has been a huge factor in their economies.

At a summit of 2,000 citizens in the Ohio capital city of Columbus, 19% of them stated that self-image was a factor standing in the way of the greatness of the city (Smyth, 2008). The common name of the city and the lack of professional sports teams were cited as a major impetus in their image creation (Smyth, 2008). These same citizens recommended capitalizing on the downtown riverfront, adding a downtown trolley and becoming a center for green construction to improve the city (Smyth, 2008). These residents note their city lacks an image (and arguably also a brand).

A successful place must be able to look honestly at its situation. By examining the attributes of a place from a regional standpoint, it is easier to see how the place functions in the national and international marketplace (Kotler, et al, 1993). Any effort to improve the image of a place must begin with a strategic market planning process (Kotler, et al, 1993). This process must be a collaborative effort of all of the relevant players within the place including city leaders, government, institutional, nonprofit, business representatives (both large and small), and representatives from the citizenry and daytime employment population. When the city of Dallas, Texas worked on its plan, the city council sent questionnaires to citizens asking what they would like their city to look like in ten years and this information helped guide the direction of their process (Kotler, et al, 1993). Working in a partnership, the interests of the entire community can be represented. Sometimes, the image of a place change just by a change in the way the leadership and government treats the citizenry through education, housing, training, social security, culture, and the environment (Allan, 2006). Strong, engaged leadership is key to a positive place image.

All cities have challenges from their history and infrastructure which leads to issues with planning and development (Morrison & Dewar, 2012). This is where public investment can make a difference. Changing the way a city is perceived may require public investment and government intervention both in infrastructure as well as in the way these cities are seen. Public investments may contribute to forging positive images that eventually affect could location decisions. Government outlays signal willingness to invest in the future. Lynch (1960) noted that merely investing in a place can improve its image regardless of how the investment turns out in the end. The idea that merely showing investment can improve the way a place is seen is one reason places invest in themselves. It is imperative that those investing in cities and their marketing focus on each of the aspects of place image to improve the overall conditions.

During the 1990s, in the midst of a boom in development in the urban core including new skyscrapers and sports stadiums valued at approximately $1.2 billion (in 2015 dollars), Cleveland billed itself as a "Renaissance City." This level of major investment and development may lead people to perceive it as progress and to assume that the city is improving. Currently, projects valued at an estimated $8.7 billion in construction are set to be completed in Cleveland, including the Global Center for Health Innovation (formerly called the Medical Mart), the Horseshoe Casino, and skyline-altering new office and residential buildings (personal communication). Since investment is perceived as progress, Cleveland may be positioning itself to change the perception of being known as the "mistake on the lake."

Growth of a city is important to its success. Pocock and Hudson (1978) examined reasons areas grow and decline with regard to public investment. They note one frequent strategy for solving regional problems is to encourage growth by changing the area and its industrial structure through business retention and attraction. To accomplish this, many changes have to take place in both the people and the place. They argue that "Places regarded as having growth potential have had public sector investment channeled to them; places perceived as lacking growth potential have been denied these resources" (Pocock & Hudson, 1978). Whichever came first, the investment or the success of the city, the two items are intertwined.

In his seminal work on city image, Lynch (1960) begins by noting that "the city is a construction in space," meaning that what people know of a city is constructed by a variety of actors. The way places are represented can be influenced by marketing and a place can be sold just like any other product (Allen, 2007). Stakeholders in each place need to meticulously define, design, and market to the outside world the assets of their place (Kotler et al., 1993). In the absence of attention to marketing, places run the risk of (further) decline and failure (Kotler et al., 1993). Places and their images are constructed for the purpose of encouraging growth.

The act of selling a place is popular to economic development professionals because it offers a chance to improve prospects for "trade, aid, economic development, political influence and general respect" (Anholt, 2010a). The increasing importance of place image may be due several factors including the media and declining cost of travel. Any way that professionals within a place can work to improve the five aspects of place image will advance the overall environment and will therefore lead to increased interest and investment.

Roles certain cities and regions played historically have adjusted, adapted, or disappeared (Sadler, 1993). At the height of the industrial Midwest, Pittsburgh was known as the location for steel production and Akron, Ohio dominated rubber manufacturing. Competition has increased with globalization and the relevance of place is becoming less important for business (Sadler, 1993). Each place must compete with every other for its share of commercial, political, social, and cultural transactions (Anholt, 2010a; Short et al., 1993). This competition forces places to work on their image in order to improve their attraction efforts.

Spreading the word that Cleveland has a strong bioscience industry or that Pittsburgh is a city with a concentration of technology companies can contribute to the economic success of these cities. Regions throughout the Midwest are trying to turn around negative images. The word "industrial" itself may be associated with negative images of a deteriorating economic base, pollution, and obsolescence (Short et al., 1993). Even the recent renaming of the region to "Legacy Cities" invokes a sense of obsolescence. Regions going through deindustrialization or having become post-industrial face "a deep sense of insecurity that grows out of the collapse all around them of the traditional economic base of their community" (Bluestone & Harrison, 1982). Cities in the Midwest have not only their individual place image issues to content with, but additionally those from a broader, regional scale.

Major improvements and investments may lead people to take a closer look at a place, whether at the city or national level. An executive with Visit Buffalo Niagara, stated that their work to improve the waterfront, art, and architecture are leading people to take a closer look at Buffalo. He noted "The story that I would have to tell would just be empty spin if all of this very concrete investment weren't taking place…there is real substance behind the story we are trying to tell" (personal communication). A former executive of the Allegheny Conference in Pittsburgh notes "A lot of Pittsburgh's transformation was very place-based and focused – improving the appearance and the land use" (personal communication). New positive promotion, which showcases new assets, may lead people to look at a place differently and piques their interest about places to which they may have been indifferent previously or about which they had a negative opinion. Changes in the way a place is seen do not happen suddenly; however, as shown when Pittsburgh's previously dominant steel industry all but died by 1983 and its official transformation did not begin until 2005 (personal communication). Improvements to a place are important to place image, but they alone cannot change it completely.

Public and private investment can shift beliefs about a city. According to an article in the Chicago Sun Times (as quoted by Uhlir, 2005), "You can't put a monetary value on public works that enhance the image and quality of life of a city." Chicago created the Millennium Park, one of the largest public works projects the city has ever undertaken. The park is built on land that previously housed outdated rail yards which is now an immense outdoor recreation and arts area. The city now boasts an iconic park which is not only enjoyable and useful, but also beautiful and its likeness is used in many regional promotion pieces. The park has even been showcased in national advertising focused on archetypal places throughout the country and shows that a major investment can affect the image of the place.

Whether or not there is a problem with the image of certain cities or if this has any impact on the location decisions, actors in these cities feel that there are problems and therefore invest in image. In Greater Cleveland for example, the promotion of individual cities is handled internally by each locality with their own budgets. However, two organizations represent a regional collaboration that works to target business and people. TeamNEO is a collaboration of the largest metro chambers of commerce in Northeast Ohio. The organization is tasked with attracting businesses from around the world to the 18-county region. In 2011, they had $3.3 million in revenue generated from local communities and spent $2.9 million on business attraction and marketing (Guidestar: Team NEO, 2013). Positively Cleveland, the Convention and Visitors Bureau of greater Cleveland, is tasked with marketing, sales, and promotion of the region for tourism, conventions, and trade shows. They raised a 2011 budget of $8.9 million from membership fees of businesses and the hotel bed tax and they spent $8.8 million on their mission that year (Guidestar: Positively Cleveland, 2013). So in Greater Cleveland alone, with just the work of these two organizations, $11.7 million was spent on place promotion, without verification that these efforts yield results.

ECONOMIC CHALLENGES IMPACTING THE CONCEPT OF PLACE

While the image of a place may not be on the first list of considerations when a business selects a new site, it is however important when final considerations are being made. The research shows that factors important to the business location decision include demographics, education, environment, financing, government, industry, infrastructure, transportation, workforce, necessities of life, and quality of life. The concepts of image are not a common topic in the literature. After the initial set of criteria is met, the importance of image comes into play. Anecdotal evidence shows that when companies are left with the final two to three options, the image of the place becomes the deciding factor (personal communication). Image was an important factor when Facebook established a presence in Austin (personal communication). Also, for headquarter locations, image is very important as the company looks to match their specific brand and culture. Office Max moved to Chicago because it offered something their previous location could not (Miller, 2005).

Image is also shaped by the workforce. The people, or the identity of the residents, are a huge factor when a business is looking to make a location decision. Businesses want to be in a place where their employees and executives want to live which can offer them a certain set of amenities. When a site is being considered, if the feel of the location does not meet the expectations and desires of the company, the city will be snubbed. For example, Sierra Nevada was looking for a certain image so as to recruit a talented workforce and they chose Ashville – notably a city for the outdoors, food, and craft brewing. The company wanted employees who identified with that culture (personal communication). A site selection consultant that owns his own consulting firm notes, "25 years ago, it was all about cost: utility, labor, transportation, taxes. Today, these aren't the drivers as it's more about maintaining competitive edge in their businesses: labor, skilled workforce, and local communities' ability to generate quality workers (pipeline of future workers is awesome – that's the image part)" (personal communication).

Additionally, when faced with the decision of potentially relocating or taking a vacation, individuals examine different aspects of place image. Each individual, like businesses, are looking for a certain set of criteria. When a job offer is made for with options in Seoul or Cairo, the image of Egyptian politics alone will likely steer the job-seeker to Korea. Again, investments made in the different aspects of place image can improve the prospects for attracting people to places.

The International Image

When competing in the international market, the place image of cities is second to that of the nation itself. In fact, countries spend immense amounts of money developing brands that convey certain images in the hopes of increasing tourism, investments, and exports (Pipoli de Azambuja, 2010).

The country brand is important when decisions are made based on the good name of the country of origin (Anholt & Hildreth, 2004; Samiee, 2009). Often, buyers develop stereotypical images of countries (macro) and products (micro) which include the total of all descriptive, inferential, and informational beliefs about a particular country (Pappu, Quester, & Cooksey, 2004; Martin & Eroglu, 1993). These images are based on politics, economics, technology, and social desirability. Arguably, there are three aspects of country-related image: cognitive (the beliefs about the country), affective (emotional reaction to the country), and conative (the behavioral intentions about the country) (Brijs, Bloemer, & Kasper, 2011); which all factor into decisions made about the country.

CONCLUSION

It can be argued that image is everything and that this above all can predict destiny or that it has no bearing on the market whatsoever. Merely discounting this concept can be challenged on the basis that images change over time and flow with the economy of cities (Pocock & Hudson, 1978). While Detroit was once known as a world center for the automotive industry as well as research and development, the city center is now seen as a place abandoned and struggling to hold what employment base remains from its legacy. On the flip side, ask anyone 25 years ago how they felt about Silicon Valley and their answer would have been nil. Birch (2001) argues that image develops in an incremental fashion - when one image dominates, it is already it in the state of change as was the case in his study on the Bronx moving from the "shame of the nation" to the "all-American city." Because of the transient nature of images, they cannot predict success or failure, but remain an important concept regarding city life and investment. Image can be a very strong determinant when the business site selection decision is considering their top options and therefore cities should strive to improve and maintain strong images in the market.

REFERENCES

Allan, M. (2006, January). *Place Branding. Proceedings of the Seventh International Conference on Urban Planning and Environment.*

Allen, G. (2007). Place Branding: New Tools for Economic Development. *Design Management Review*, Spring.

Anholt, S. (2010). Editorial. Definitions of place branding - Working towards a resolution. *Place Branding and Public Diplomacy*, *1*(6), 1–10. doi:10.1057/pb.2010.3

Anholt, S. (2010a). *Places: identity, image and reputation*. New York: Palgrave Macmillan.

Anholt, S., & Hildreth, J. (2004). *Brand America: the mother of all brands*. London: Cyan Communications Limited.

Avraham, E., & Ketter, E. (2008). *Media Strategies for Marketing Places in Crisis*. Oxford: Elsevier Linacer House.

Baker, B. (2007). *Destination Branding for Small Cities: The Essentials for Successful Place Branding*. Portland: Creative Leap Books.

Baloglu, S., & McCleary, K. W. (1999). A Model of Destination Image Formation. *Annals of Tourism Research*, *26*(4), 868–897. doi:10.1016/S0160-7383(99)00030-4

Barber, A. (2008). *Reno's Big Gamble: Image and Reputation in the Biggest Little City*. Lawrence, KS: University Press of Kansas.

Bartels, J. (Ed.). (2015). *Nebraska Economic Development Overview (Summer 2015)*. Columbus, Nebraska: Nebraska Public Power District.

Birch, E. L. (2001). From Flames to Flowers: The role of planning in re-imaging the South Bronx. In L. J. Vale & S. B. Warner (Eds.), *Imaging the City: Continuous struggles and new directions* (pp. 33–55). New Brunswick, NJ: Center for Urban Policy Research.

Bluestone, B., & Harrison, B. (1982). *The deindustrialization of America*. New York: Basic Books.

Boyer, M. C. (1992). Cities for Sale: Merchandising History at South Street Seaport. In M. Sorkin (Ed.), Variations on a Theme Park. New York: The Noonday Press.

Brijs, K., Bloemer, J., & Kasper, H. (2011). Country-image discourse model: Unraveling meaning, structure, and function of country images. *Journal of Business Research*, *64*(12), 1259–1269. doi:10.1016/j.jbusres.2011.01.017

Chamlee-Wright, E., & Storr, V. H. (2009). "There's no place like New Orleans": Sense of place and community recovery in the ninth ward after Hurricane Katrina. *Journal of Urban Affairs*, *31*(5), 615–634. doi:10.1111/j.1467-9906.2009.00479.x

Conway. (2015). New Plant Database. Retrieved from http://siteselection.com/newplant/

Dinnie, K. (2004). Editorial. Place branding: Overview of an emerging literature. *Place Branding*, *1*(1), 106–110. doi:10.1057/palgrave.pb.5990010

Fan, Y. (2010). Branding the nation: Towards a better understanding. *Place Branding and Public Diplomacy*, *6*(2), 97–103. doi:10.1057/pb.2010.16

Gertner, D. (2011). Unfolding and configuring two decades of research and publications on place marketing and place branding. *Place Branding and Public Diplomacy*, *7*(2), 91–106. doi:10.1057/pb.2011.7

Goodwin, M. (1993). The City as Commodity: The Contested Spaces of Urban Development. In G. Kearns & C. Philo (Eds.), *Selling places: the city as cultural capital, past, and present* (pp. 145–162). Oxford, England: Pergamon Press.

Guidestar: Positively Cleveland. (2013). Positively Cleveland 2011 IRS Form 990. Retrieved from http://www.guidestar.org/organizations/34-0149652/positively-cleveland.aspx

Guidestar: Team NEO. (2013). TeamNEO 2011 IRS Form 990. Retrieved from http://www.guidestar.org/organizations/34-1885408/team-neo.aspx

Harner, J. (2001). Place Identity and Copper Mining in Sonora, Mexico. *Annals of the Association of American Geographers, 91*(4), 660–680. doi:10.1111/0004-5608.00264

Hay, R. (1998). Sense of Place in Developmental Context. *Journal of Environmental Psychology, 18*(1), 5–29. doi:10.1006/jevp.1997.0060

Herstein, R., & Jaffe, E. D. (2008). The children's city – The transition for a negative to a positive city image. *Place Branding and Public Diplomacy, 4*(1), 76–84. doi:10.1057/palgrave.pb.6000082

Hill, E., Wolman, H., & Ford, C. C. (1995). Can Suburbs Survive without their Central Cities?: Examining the Suburban Dependence Hypothesis. *Urban Affairs Review, 31*(2), 147–174. doi:10.1177/107808749503100201

Hill, E., Wolman, H., Kowalczyk, K., & St. Clair, T. (2012). Forces Affecting City Population Growth or Decline: The Effects of Interregional and Inter-municipal competition. In A. Mallach (Ed.) Rebuilding America's Legacy Cities: New Directions for the Industrial Heartland (pp. 31-79). New York: The American Assembly.

Hosany, S., Ekinci, Y., & Ulsal, M. (2006). Destination image and destination personality: An application of branding theories to tourism places. *Journal of Business Research, 59*(5), 638–642. doi:10.1016/j.jbusres.2006.01.001

Jensen, O. B. (2007). Culture Stories: Understanding Cultural Urban Branding. *Planning Theory, 6*(3), 211–236. doi:10.1177/1473095207082032

Kotler, P., Haider, D., & Rein, I. (1993). *Marketing Places: attracting investment, industry, and tourism to cities, states and nations*. New York: The Free Press.

Laurier, E. (1993). 'Tackintosh': Glasgow's Supplementary Gloss. In G. Kearns & C. Philo (Eds.), *Selling places: the city as cultural capital, past, and present* (pp. 267–290). Oxford, England: Pergamon Press.

Lynch, K. (1960). *The Image of the City*. Cambridge: MIT Press.

Martin, I., & Eroglu, S. (1993). Measuring a Multi-Dimensional Construct: Country Image. *Journal of Business Research, 28*(3), 191–210. doi:10.1016/0148-2963(93)90047-S

Miller, J. (2005). OfficeMax picks suburban Chicago. Crain's Cleveland Business. Retrieved from http://www.crainscleveland.com/article/20050815/FREE/50815002/officemax-picks-suburban-chicago

Morrison, H., & Dewar, M. (2012). Planning in America's Legacy Cities: Toward Better, Smaller Communities after Decline. In A. Mallach (Ed.), Rebuilding America's Legacy Cities: New Directions for the Industrial Heartland (pp. 31-79). New York: The American Assembly.

Nasar, J. L. (1990). The Evaluative Image of the City. *Journal of the American Planning Association, 56*(1), 41–54. doi:10.1080/01944369008975742

Ong, B. S., & Horbunluekit, S. (1997). The Image of a Thai Cultural Show on Thailand's Destination Image. *American Business Review, 15*(2), 97–103.

Pappu, R., Quester, P. G., & Cooksey, R. W. (2007). Country image and consumer-based brand equity: Relationships and implications for international marketing. *Journal of International Business Studies*, *28*(5), 726–745. doi:10.1057/palgrave.jibs.8400293

Philo, C., & Kearns, G. (1993). Culture, History, Capital: A Critical Introduction to the Selling of Places. In G. Kearns & C. Philo (Eds.), *Selling places: the city as cultural capital, past, and present* (pp. 1–32). Oxford, England: Pergamon Press.

Pipoli de Azambuja, G. (2010). The Importance of Using Slogans in Country Brand Strategies when Building Country Image. *Review of Management Innovation & Creativity*, *3*(8), 1–12.

Pocock, D., & Hudson, R. (1978). *Images of the Urban Environment*. New York: Columbia University Press.

Sadler, D. (1993). Place-marketing, Competitive Places and the Construction of Hegemony in Britain in the 1980s. In G. Kearns & C. Philo (Eds.), *Selling places: the city as cultural capital, past, and present* (pp. 175–192). Oxford, England: Pergamon Press.

Samiee, S. (2010). Advancing the country image construct — A commentary essay. *Journal of Business Research*, *63*(4), 442–445. doi:10.1016/j.jbusres.2008.12.012

Short, J. R., Benton, L. M., Luce, W. B., & Walton, J. (1993). Reconstructing the Image of an Industrial City. *Annals of the Association of American Geographers*, *2*(83), 207–224. doi:10.1111/j.1467-8306.1993.tb01932.x

Smith, A. (2006). Assessing the Contribution of Flagship Projects to City Image Change: A Quasi-Experimental Technique. *International Journal of Tourism Research*, *8*(6), 391–404. doi:10.1002/jtr.586

Smyth, J. C. (2008). Ohio capital strives for big-city image. *USA Today*. Retrieved from www.usatoday.com

Stock, F. (2009). Identity, image and brand: A conceptual framework. *Place Branding and Public Diplomacy*, *5*(2), 118–125. doi:10.1057/pb.2009.2

Trejo, F. (2008). City "Branding" Essential Ingredient for Attracting Tourism Dollars; Cities Spend Thousands for Logo Development and Research. *Hotel Online*. Retrieved from www.hotel-online.com/news

Uhlir, E.K. (2005). The Millennium Park Effect. *Economic Development Journal*, Spring, 7-11.

Zenker, S., Eggers, F., & Farsky, M. (2013). Putting a price tag on cities: Insights into the competitive environment of places. *Cities (London, England)*, *30*, 133–139. doi:10.1016/j.cities.2012.02.002

KEY TERMS AND DEFINITIONS

Brand: The intended message of the place.

Identity: The extent to which people are willing to associate themselves with a place.

Place Image: Represents the sum of beliefs, ideas, and impressions that people have of a place (Kotler, et al, 1993).

Reputation: The specific knowledge about a place.

Sense of Place: The subjective experience in a place.

Visual Image: The symbolic knowledge of a place.

This research was previously published in Strategic Place Branding Methodologies and Theory for Tourist Attraction edited by Ahmet Bayraktar and Can Uslay, pages 1-20, copyright year 2017 by Business Science Reference (an imprint of IGI Global).

Chapter 4
Mobile Customer Relationship Management:
An Overview

Tolga Dursun
Abant İzzet Baysal Üniversity, Turkey

Süleyman Çelik
Abant İzzet Baysal Üniversity, Turkey

ABSTRACT

Electronic platforms provide many advantages both customers and companies due to development of communication technology. Today almost every people have smartphones and tablets. Thus mobile customer relationship management became an significant concept for generating long-term relationships and increasing customer satisfaction, retention and loyalty. In addition companies use mobile CRM to facilitate salespeople for better performance in marketing activities. M-CRM offers interactive relationships between firms and companies. In this study, we define what is customer relationship management and origins of CRM. After that we stated electronic customer relationship management concept and finally we mentioned about mobile CRM especially benefits and characteristics of it.

INTRODUCTION

Today, companies have to develop long-term relationships with their current and potential customers to survive and maintain their lifes in intensive competitive environment. In this context, customer relationship management is considered as an important tool to achieve lasting relationships. Especially advances in internet and technology shifted these relationships to the electronic environenment. Furthermore, developments in mobile broadband connections (3G,4G) and with the advent of smartphones, world is seeing a huge migration to the mobile technologies and mobile CRM which is a type of e-CRM is emerged. Consequently, mobile CRM has become vital to determine customers' needs and requirements properly and boots satisfaction of customer.

DOI: 10.4018/978-1-5225-5187-4.ch004

EVOLUTION OF CUSTOMER RELATIONSHIP MANAGEMENT

The roots of CRM can be traced back to the term of relationship marketing (RM) (Zablah et al, 2004). Since the competition has changed and structural changes in operations have led to the emergence of the relationship concept for generating long-term relationships among customers and suppliers. Due to the globalisation of business, internationalisation, information technology progression, shorter product life cycles, and the evolving recognition of the relationship between customer retention and profitability (Morgan and Hunt, 1994; Zineldin and Jonsson, 2000; Chandra and Kumar, 2000; Sahay, 2003; Stefanou et al., 2003; cited in Osarenkhoe and Bennani, 2007).

According to Parvatiyar and Sheth (1995), "developing customer relationships has historical antecedents going back into the pre-industrial era. Much of it was due to direct interaction between producers of agricultural products and their consumers. Similarly, artisans often developed customized products for each customer. Such direct interaction led to relational bonding between the producer and the consumer. It was only after the advent of mass production in the industrial era and the advent of middlemen that interaction between producers and consumers became less frequent leading to transaction oriented marketing" (Parvatiyar and Sheth, 2001).

After industrialization and mass production, companies have lost their control over their customers and it became very hard to manage and remember informations about on a large number of consumers. But parallelly advances in information technology, computer technology and wireless communication led to start new possibilities to companies for customer relations.

Recently, several elements have contributed to thedevelopment and evolution of customer relationship management rapidly. These elements are the changes in intermediation process in many industries due to the progression of advanced computer and telecommunication technologies that allow producers to directly communicate with customers. For instance, in many industries such as the airline, banking, insurance, computer software, or household appliances industries and even consumables, the de-intermediation process is fast changing the nature of marketing and consequently making relationship marketing more popular. Databases and direct marketing instrumentsprovide these industries the means topersonalize their marketing endeavours. (Parvatiyar and Sheth, 2001).

As a result since many companies compete in industries, customers have many options to buy product or services and customers became the center of competition. So in addition to advances in technology led to development of CRM, changes in customers' behaviours play an active role in the emergence of CRM.

Definition of Customer Relationship Management

In the marketing literature there are many definitions of customer relationship management from different perspectives. Vavra (1992) defines customer relationship management only as providing customer retention through implementing several after marketing tactics that lead to customer bonding or staying in touch with the customer after a sale is made.Another perspective of CRM database marketing underlying the promotional aspects of marketing linked to database efforts (Bickert, 1992).

According to Hamilton (2001) CRM is the process of storing and analyzing the vast amount of data produced by sales calls, customer service centers, actual purchased, supposedly yielding greater insight into customer behavior. As a result CRM can be defined as an interactive process achieving the excellent balance between corporate investments and the satisfaction of customer needs to generate the maximum profit. It involves (Gebert, et al, 2002):

Figure 1. The CRM continuum
(Payne, A. and Frow, P., 2005)

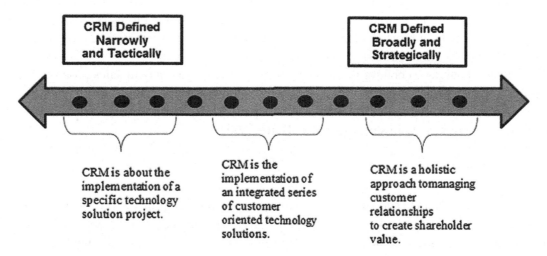

- Measuring both inputs across all functions including marketing sales and service costs and outputs in terms of customer revenue, profit and value.
- Acquiring and continuously updating knowledge about customer needs, motivations and behavior over the lifetime of the relationship.
- Applying customer knowledge to continuously improve performance through a process of learning from successes and failures.
- Integrating the activities of marketing, sales and service to achieve a common goal.
- Implementing appropriate systems to support customer knowledge acquisition, sharing and measuring CRM effectiveness.
- Constantly flexing the balance between marketing, sales and service inputs against changing customer needs to increase profit.

THREE LEVELS OF CUSTOMER RELATIONSHIP MANAGEMENT

As we see, there is no absolute definition of CRM. Some of the complexity comes out since the term is used in a number of different ways. CRM can be seen at three levels: strategic, operational, analytical (Buttle, 2004).

Strategic CRM

Strategic CRM is focused on the development of a customer-centric business culture. This culture is dedicated to winning and keeping customers by creating and delivering value better than competitors (Buttle, 2004).There has been not only customer centric but also it could be found three others orientations such as production, product, sales (Kotler, 2003).

Product-oriented businesses believe that customers always choose best quality products with best design or features. These businesses are often highly innovative and entrepreneurial. Many new business start-ups are product-oriented. In these firms the customer's voice generally to be missing when important marketing decisions are made. There is a little or no customer research is carryed out. Management makes assumptions about what customers want. The outcome is that products are overspecified or overengineered for the requirements of the market, and therefore too costly for the majority of customers (Rogers, 1962; cited in Buttle, 2004).

Sales-oriented businesses believe that if they focus on investing money in sales promotions, advertising, public relations, customers will be keen on buying products of companies.Very often, a sales orientation follows a production orientation. The company produces low-cost products and then they have to promote them heavily to shift inventory (Buttle, 2004).

Operational CRM

Operational CRM contributes and automates customer supporting programs in the business process by using software for marketing, service and selling functions to be integrated. Operational CRM are divided into three forms: Marketing automation, Sales force automation, Service automation (Buttle, 2004).

Marketing automation (MA) uses technology to carry out marketing efforts. A variety of compentences are offered by MA software: customer segmentation, campaign management and event-based marketing. Software enables users to determine their customer data for the purpose of developing targeted communications and offers. In addition MA enables companies to develop budget and execute communication campaigns. MA can also audit and analyse campaign performance, and direct leads from advertising campaigns to the most appropriate sales channel. Sales-force automation (SFA) was the original form of CRM. It applies technology to the management of a company's selling activities. Sales-force automation software enables companies automatically to record leads and track opportunities as they progress through the sales pipeline towards closure. (Buttle, 2004).Service automation facilitate activities of businesses to retain customers by offering best quality of service and building strong relationship. It includes issue management to fix customers' problems, customer call management to handle incoming/outgoing calls, service label management to trace quality of service based on key performance indicators (www.techonestop.com).

Analytical CRM

This is concerned with customer related data such as obtaining, storing, interpreting, integrating, reporting and distributing data to improve not only customer loyalty but also firm's value too. Those data could be internal such as sales data, marketing data, financial data and service data and also external data such as geodemographic data by measuring customer's propensity, response, and value (Greenberg, 2002).

From the customer's point of view, analytical CRM can offers better and more timely, further personally customized solutions to the customer's problems, thereby providing customer satisfaction. From the company's point of view, analytical CRM offers the prospect of more powerful crossselling and up-selling programmes, and more effective customer retention and customer acquisition programmes (Buttle, 2004).

Electronic Customer Relationship Management

Developments ininternet-based technology led to change the way of customers behavior and customers become online consumers. In parallel with companies also changed the way of managing relationships with customers. Thus electronic customer relationship management was emerged. Since traditional CRM become incapable of meeting requirements of online customers. Companies sustain exercises online platforms for retention and acquisition of customers to survive in competitive environment and to gain financial benefits. Because electronic CRM presents faster and more effective way to interact with customers.

With the rapid advancement in technology especially information and communication technology has helped the scale and scope of customer relationship management. Thus it leads to the increasing use of E-CRM. By integrating and simplifying the customer-related processes through the internet, E-CRM helps to improve customer development, customer acquisition and customer retention (Chang, Liao & Hsiao, 2005).

Although electronic CRM is a new form, there are many different definitions. E-CRM also has no universal specific definition like CRM concept. According to Dyche (2001) E-CRM refers to electronic customer relationship management or, more simply, CRM that is web-based. Dyche (2001) also suggested that there are two main types of e-CRM. These are operational e-CRM and analytical e-CRM. Operational e-CRM is dealt with customer touch points, that is, all methods of customer contact, including Web-based, in person, e-mail, telephone, direct sales, and fax. Analytical e-CRM focuses on technology to process vast amounts of customer data. The purpose is to build new business opportunities via analysing informations such as customer demographics, purchasing patterns, and other factors.

E–CRM is a part of E-business, which describes the use of electronic platforms to conduct a company's business. Electronic business has been heavily influenced by the Internet, which enables firms to serve the customers faster, more accurately, over a wide range of time and space, at a reduced cost, and with the ability to customize and personalize customer offerings (Kotler, 2003).

According to Gilbert, and Mannicom (2003) E-CRM refers to the marketing activities, tools and techniques delivered over the Internet with a specific aim to locate, build and improve long-term customer relationships to enhance their individual potential (Harrigan et al, 2011).

Benefits of E-CRM

E-CRM provides a wide variety of benefits to companies such as improving customer retention, gaining potential customers, determining customers' needs, ensuring satisfied customers and increasing companies' profits etc. All benefits can be achieved by implementing successful E-CRM applications Adebanjo (2003) determined fundamental benefits of E-CRM as below:

- Reducing the cost of contacting customers by making customer details readily available, customer contact personnel have better opportunities to resolve customer enquiries in less time, thereby freeing them for other productive work.
- Transferring some responsibility to the customer (e.g. product configuration, order tracking, online customer details collection) reduces administrative and operational costs for the organization and therefore, increases the value that an ECRM solution will deliver to the organization.
- Integration of E-CRM applications with back-office systems such as finance supply chains and production can enhance work flow and consequently, the efficiency of the organization, thereby delivering cost savings. For example, field salespeople could use hand-held devices to initiate orders, check stock, track orders, check production status, request invoices and with minimum cost and effort.

- E-CRM applications also can improve sales by customer profiling, automated campaign management, e-mail marketing, etc., thereby improving the bottom line for the organization.
- Improving the overall interaction with customers would lead to better service and improve customer satisfaction, loyalty and ultimately customer life-time value.

In addition Chen and Chen (2004) considered E-CRM benefits with two dimensions as tangible and intangible:

INTRODUCTION OF MOBILE CUSTOMER RELATIONSHIP MANAGEMENT (M-CRM)

The mass migration of internet users from desktop PCs to mobile devices is global and universal. The proportion of internet traffic coming from mobile devices grew from 1% in 2009 to 13% in 2013, and it's still growing (http://www.salesforce.com/uk/crm/mobile-crm/). Mobile is at the forefont of the new digital age. Mobile is driving the development of new services in areas such as social networking, digital content and electronic commerce. Mobile is delivering a new and vibrant ecosystem which is based on mobile broadband networks, advanced tablets and smartphones and a growing range of other connected technological devices and objects (GSMA, 2015).

According to GSMA Global Mobile Economy Report (2015) The world is seeing a rapid technology migration to both higher speed mobile broadband networks and the increased adoption of smartphones and other connected devices. Mobile broadband connections will account for almost 70% of the global base by 2020, up from just under 40% at the end of 2014. Smartphone adoption is already reaching critical mass in developed markets, with the devices now accounting for 60% of connections. It is the developing world—driven by the increased affordability of devices—that will produce most of the future growth, adding a further 2.9 billion smartphone connections by 2020.

The mobile industry contiunes to scale rapidly, with a total of 3.6 billion unique mobile subscribers at the end of 2014. Half of the word's population now has mobile subscription. An additional one billion subscirbers are predicted by 2020 taking the global penetration rate to approximately %60. There were 7.1 billion global sim connections at the end of 2014. In addition, At the end of 2014, the number

Table 1. Tangible and intangible benefits of E-CRM

Tangible Benefits of E-CRM	Intangible Benefits of E-CRM
Decrease internal cost	Improve customer service
Increase revenues and profitability	Streamlined business process
Higher employee productivity	Increased dept and effectiveness of customer Segmentation
Higher customer retention rates	Acute targeting and portfolio of customers
Preserved marketing investments	Increase customer satisfaction
Decrease marketing cost	Better understanding of customer requirements
Maximized returns	Closer contact management

(Chen and Chen, 2004)

of people using the mobile internet reached 2.4 billion. This is expected to rise to 3.8 billion by 2020 (GSMA, 2015).

There is an accelerating technology shift to mobile broadband networks across the world. Mobile broadband connections (i.e. 3G and 4G technologies) accounted for just under 40% of total connections at the end of 2014, but by 2020 will increase to almost 70% of the total. This migration is being driven by greater availability and affordability of smartphones, more extensive and deeper network coverage, and in some cases by operator. The increasing proportion higher speed connections largely reflects the accelerating rate of smartphone adoption. Adoption rates have already reached 60% of the connection base in the developed word. Over the next four years, smartphone adoption in the developed word is expected to reach the 70-80% ceiling, the level at which growth tends to slow (GSMA, 2015). 2012, about a quarter of all mobile users were smartphone users. By 2018, this number is expected to double, reaching 50 percent. The number of smartphone users worldwide is expected to grow by one billion in a time span of five years, which means the number of smartphone users in the world is expected to reach 2.6 billion by 2019 (http://www.statista.com/statistics/274774/forecast-of-mobile-phone-users-worldwide/).

All these statistics show that the most people use smartphones every hour of the day all over the world to fulfill their daily transactions thanks to technological development in mobile industry. Since mobile devices mostly are used nowadays, Mobile CRM is the critical factor for companies to develop personalized long-term relationships with their potential and current customers. What companies have to do is to set up proper mobile CRM systems to survive in the competitive environment.

Mobile CRM

Mobile CRM can be defined as the communication, either one way or mutual, that is related to marketing, sales and customer service activities through mobile technologies in attemp to build and maintain relationships between the costumer and the company (Kim et al, 2015). Mobile CRM allows companies' employees use mobile devices such as smartphones and tablets to access, update and interact with customer data wherever and whenever they are (http://www.tendigits.com/about-mobile-crm.html).

According to Nguyen and Waring (2013) m-CRM can be defined from two perspectives. From the perspective of technology, m-CRM is seen as a technological tool applied to marketing for the purpose of reducing costs and increasing the efficiency of the processing information between buyer and seller. On the other side, from strategic perspective, m-CRM is seen as a long-term management approach that companies fulfill through mobile channels in order to get benefits (San- Martin et al, 2015).

Recently, Software Advice (2014) carried out a survey including severeal questions and 1,940 responses are acquired from sales professionals in the U.S. who currently access their company's CRM system through a mobile device. Their aim was to find out how it benefits their companies, which features they commonly use and what requirements they feel are most important for a mobile CRM system to meet.

Accordingly their research nearly half of 1,940 sales professionals who are CRM users Access their system via smartphones (48 percent) and/or tables (45 percent). Furthermore, a significant majority (81 percent) say they access their system on multiple types of devices and 20 percent use the combination of three of the above listed devices and 29 percent of participants use four devices to Access CRM system (Software Advice, 2014).

Another important output of research shows that most common used mobile crm applications and features are consecutively sales content management, review/input customer data, sales reporting and analytics, business card scanning and geolocation (Software Advice, 2014).

Figure 2. Devices used to access CRM system
(Software Advice, 2014)

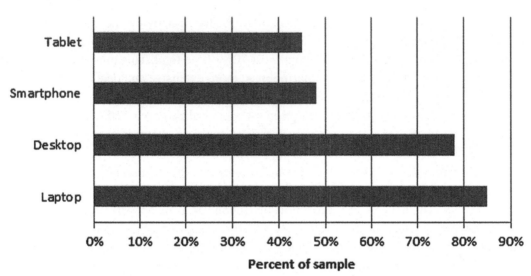

37 percent reported regularly using their mobile CRM system to manage sales content, such as slide presentations and reports. This reflects the increasing importance of tablets, in particular, as a vector for delivering sales content during presentations. In addition 31 percent said that they regularly use mobile CRM to arrange customer informations. 26 percent routinely used business-card scanning—a relatively niche mobile feature—as used such core functionality as reporting or database access (Software Advice, 2014).

Figure 3. Most used mobile CRM applications and features
(Software Advice, 2014)

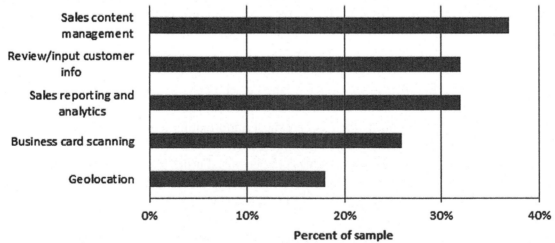

Chracteristics and Benefits of Mobile CRM

According to Deans (2004), the convergence of mobile internet and wireless communication technology has promised users the concept "anytime anywhere", which implies access to information for work and personal communication. The mobile medium and wireless technology enable companies' four reasons to build relationships with its customers, which are:

- Personalize content and services.
- Track customers or users across media and over time.
- Contribute content and service at the point of need.
- Contribute content with highly engaging characteristics.

According to Durlacher Research (1999) m-CRM overcomes existing traditional CRM limitations such as obtaining customer information through face-to-face interactions and wired networks by enabling the ability to easily obtain customer information anytime, anywhere. In addition, employees can benefit from rapid and continuous information updates and engage in real-time marketing (Kim et al., 2015).

Verma and Verma (2013) mentioned that m-CRM provides personalized and two- way communication with customers, thereby improving customers' intelligence by making employees easier to gather data on each customer. This allows employees to figure out customer needs better and develop suitable responses as well as to improve interactions with customers by retaining a record of their inquiries, transactions, complaints, and problems solved (Kim et al., 2015).

Turban et al. (2004) proposed mobility and accessibility as the most important characteristics of mobile computing and business and suggested that mobility enables employees to access systems through wireless networks and devices to execute real-time business as well as to search for and process information (Kim et all., 2015).

According to Li and Mao (2012) m-CRM can provide optimal information and services by synthetically considering information on customers, including their location, personal identification, personal background, individual preference, and purchase history as well as other types of information extracted from the CRM database (Kim et al., 2015).

According to the authors Sinisalo et. al. (2006), consider mobile medium of being a powerful opportunity to reach customers, by offering different ways for companies to plan and implement more advanced ways to communicate with their customers. One particular way is SMS, which is seen to be immediate, automated, reliable, personal, and customized channel, which allows an effective way to reach customer directly. Other benefits of mCRM are that mobile medium allows high speed message delivery, relatively low cost and high retention rates. Mobile CRM also provides interactive communication in real-time between companies and their customers (Belachew et al., 2007).

According to Software Advice Research (2014), There are important benefits using mobile CRM such as increased efficiency, better decision making, better follow ups, higher end user adoption. Research results revealed that participants who use smartphones and tablets get higher benefits than only one device users. Important outputs of research as follows:

50 percent of the respondents say that mobile CRM increased their efficiency, and 42 percent say it facilitated "faster, more informed decision-making." In both cases this was over twice the number of single-device users who said the same and furthermore 23 percent of multiple-device users and 15 percent of single-device users said mobile CRM access resulted in higher end-user adoption.

Figure 4. Top benefits realized through mobile CRM
(Software Advice, 2014)

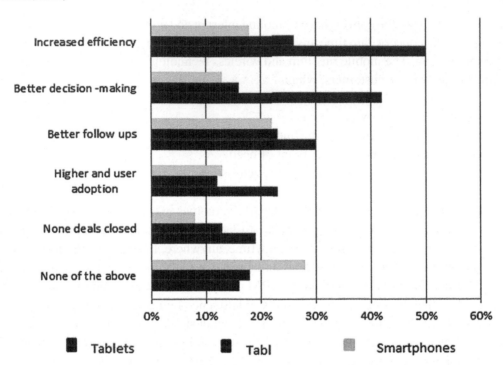

A research made by Nucleus (2012) found that mobile access to CRM increases productivity of sales people by 14.6 percent. This significant increase in productivity is driven by the development of custom, device-specific applications that take advantage of the form factors of individual device. Vendors and consultants are increasingly delivering task-specific, role- and vertical-based views of mobile CRM data that make it easier for salespeople to go beyond updating their pipeline through their smartphones.

Furthermore, research by Innoppl Technologies showed that 65% of sales representatives that adopted mobile CRM achieved their sales quotas while only 22% of representatives using non-mobile CRM reached the same targets (www.hso.com).

Kim et al. (2015) mentioned that characteristics of mobile CRM are information quality, system quality and service quality. They examined the role of characteristics of m-CRM on employees' personal performance through the full mediating effects of user satisfaction and system use. They found that m-CRM is crucial not only for firms' growth but also for the significant improvement of employees' performance.

San-Martin et al. (2015) examined the perception of companies on the benefits of implementing a m-CRM strategy from relationship marketing and TOE model and found that companies perceived better technologial compentence is more willingness to innovative, the more employee support and the better management of customer information which results in improving customer loyalty and increasing firm's global profits.

Mobile CRM activities also provides trustworthiness which leads to customer loyalty. Sohn et al. (2011) analysed the effect of mobile CRM activities on trust-based commitment and found that trust plays the role of mediator between commitment and mobile CRM activities. Customers who experience mobile CRM activities trust the company and finally commit to the company.

Figure 5. Effect of having mobile CRM on sales quotas
(www.hso.com)

■ Achieved sales quotas   ▨ Non-achieved sales quotas

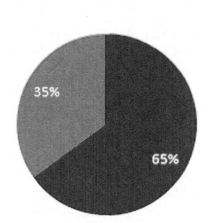

Figure 6. Effect of not having mobile CRM on sales quotas
(www.hso.com)

■ Achieved sales quotas   ▨ Non-achieved sales quotas

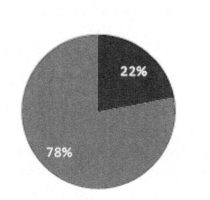

CONCLUSION

Developments in mobile technologies led to smartphones is essential tool for people in the world. Thus mobilizing customer relationship management is necessity for companies to improve and to maintain its relationships with customers. Mobile CRM provides interactive communication with customers on the contrary traditional CRM. Therefore m-CRM enables companies to increase sales people performance, to improve customer service and to facilitate other marketing activities. Thanks to mobile CRM, sales people can use it anywhere and anytime which impacts performance of users positively. If companies want to be successful, they have to improve relationships with their customers. In this context, mobile CRM is a neccessity for companies to have satisfied and loyal customers.

REFERENCES

Adebanjo, D. (2003). Classifying and Selecting E-CRM Applications: An Analysis Based Proposal. *Management Decision, 41*(6), 570–577. doi:10.1108/00251740310491517

Belachew, Y., Hoang, A., & Kourieh, J. (2007). *Mobile Customer Relationship Management: A Study of mCRM adoption in the Swedish Market* (Unpublished Master's Thesis). Jönköpıng University, Sweden.

Bickert, J. (1992). *The Database Revolution*. Target Marketing.

Buttle, F. (2004). *Customer relationship management: concepts and tools*. Oxford, UK: Elsevier Butterworth-Heinemann.

Chang, T., Liao, L., & Hsiao, W. (2005). An Empirical Study on the e-CRM Performance Influence Model of Service Sectors in Taiwan. *Proceedings of the 2005 IEEE International Conference on e-Technology, e-Commerce and e-Service (EEE'05) on e-Technology, e-Commerce and e-Service*, 240-245. doi:10.1109/EEE.2005.33

Changsu, K., In-Seok, L., Tao, W., & Mirsobit, M. (2015). Evaluating effects of mobile CRM on employees performance. *Industrial Management & Data Systems, 115*(4), 740–764. doi:10.1108/IMDS-08-2014-0245

Chen, Q., & Chen, H. M. (2004). Exploring the Success Factors of E-CRM Strategies in Practice. *Journal of Database Marketing & Customer Strategy Marketing, 11*(4), 333–343. doi:10.1057/palgrave.dbm.3240232

Deans, P. C. (2004). *E-commerce and M-commerce technologies*. IRM Press. doi:10.4018/978-1-59140-566-5

Dyche, J. (2001). *The CRM handbook: A business guide to customer relationship management*. Boston: Addison-Wesley.

Gebert, H., Geib, M., Kolbe, L., & Riempp, G. (2002). Towards Customer Knowledge Management. *Proceedings of the 2nd International Conference on Electronic Business (ICEB 2002)*.

Greenberg, P. (2002). *CRM at the speed of light: capturing and keeping customers in ınternet real time*. Berkeley, CA: McGraw-Hill.

Hamilton, D. P. (2001, May 21). Making Sense of It All. *The Asia Wall Street Journal*, p. T4.

Harrigan, P., Ramsey, E., & Ibbotson, P. (2011). Critical factors underpinning the e-CRM activities of SMEs. *Journal of Marketing Management, 27*(5-6), 503–529. doi:10.1080/0267257X.2010.495284

Kotler, P. (2003). *Marketing management* (11th ed.). Prentice Hall.

Nucleus Research. (2012). *Market focus report: The value of mobile and social CRM* (Report No. M13). Author.

Osarenkhoe, A., & Bennani, A. E. (2007). An exploratory study of implementation of customer relationship management strategy. *Business Process Management Journal, 13*(1), 139–164. doi:10.1108/14637150710721177

Parvatiyar, A., & Sheth, J. N. (2001). Customer relationship management: Emerging practice, process and discipline. *Journal of Economic & Social Research, 3*(2), 1–34.

Payne, A., & Frow, P. (2005, October). A Strategic Framework for Customer Relationship Management. *Journal of Marketing, 69*(4), 167–176. doi:10.1509/jmkg.2005.69.4.167

San-Martín, S. Jimenez N.H. Lopez-Catalan, B. (2015). The firms benefits of mobile CRM from the relationship marketing approach and the TOE model. *Spanish Journal of Marketing – ESIC, 26,* 18-29.

Sohn, C., Lee, D. I., & Lee, H. (2011). The effects of mobile CRM activities on trust-based commitment. *International Journal of Electronic Customer Relationship Management., 5*(2), 130–152. doi:10.1504/IJECRM.2011.041262

Vavra, T. G. (1992). *After marketing: how to keep customer life through relationship marketing*. Homewood, IL: Business One – Irwin.

Verma, D., & Verma, D. S. (2013). Managing customer relationships through mobile CRM In organized retail outlets. *International Journal of Engineering Trends and Technology, 4*(5), 1696–1701.

Zablah, A. R., Bellenger, D. N., & Johnston, W. J. (2004). An evaluation of divergent perspectives on customer relationship management: Towards a common understanding of an emerging phenomenon. *Industrial Marketing Management, 33*(6), 475–489. doi:10.1016/j.indmarman.2004.01.006

ADDITIONAL READING

GSMA. (2016) GSMA mobile economy 2016. *GSMA*. Retrieved from: http://www.gsmamobileeconomy.com/GSMA_Global_Mobile_Economy_Report_2015.pdf

HSO. (n.d.) The rise of CRM and how it's transforming business interactions. *HSO*. Retrieved from: https://www.hso.com/fileadmin/user_upload/CRM_manufacturing_Whitepaper.pdf

Sales Force. (n.d.) Mobile CRM – Responding to a connected world. *Sales Force*. Retrieved from: http://www.salesforce.com/uk/crm/mobile-crm/

Software Advice. (2014) Mobile CRM Software UserView. *Software Advice*. Retrieved from: http://www.softwareadvice.com/crm/userview/mobile-report-2014/

Statista (n.d.) Number of mobile phone users worldwide from 2013-2019. *Statista*. Retrieved from: http://www.statista.com/statistics/274774/forecast-of-mobile-phone-users-worldwide/

Taylor, M. (2016) 18 CRM Statistics You need to Know for 2017. *Super Office.* Retrieved from: http://www.superoffice.com/blog/crm-software-statistics/

TechOneStop. (n.d.) Types of CRM- operational, analytical, collaborative. *TechOneStop.* Retrieved from: http://techonestop.com/types-of-crm-operational-analytical-collaborative

Ten Digits. (n.d.) About Mobile CRM. *Ten Digits.* Retrieved from; http://www.tendigits.com/about-mobile-crm.html

This research was previously published in Mobile Platforms, Design, and Apps for Social Commerce edited by Jean-Éric Pelet, pages 309-321, copyright year 2017 by Business Science Reference (an imprint of IGI Global).

Chapter 5

Investigating the Mechanics of Affiliate Marketing Through Digital Content Marketing:
A Key for Driving Traffic and Customer Activity

Parag Shukla
The Maharaja Sayajirao University of Baroda, India

Parimal Hariom Vyas
The Maharaja Sayajirao University of Baroda, India

Hiral Shastri
Independent Researcher, India

ABSTRACT

The domain of online marketing and internet advertising is going through radical changes. In context to Indian online market, according to Internet and Mobile Association of India (IAMAI), the digital commerce market has seen a growth by 33% reaching to a figure of 62,967 Crore in the year 2015 which is predicted to touch $50 to $70 Billion by the year 2020 owing to the increasing popularity of online shopping and increase in internet penetration. Affiliate marketing is referred as performance marketing and associate marketing (IAMAI Research Report, 2014). Affiliate marketing is a type of online marketing technique where an affiliate/promotes a business through an advertisement on their web site and in return that business rewards the affiliate with commission each time a visitor, customer generates sales. The objective is to analyze by conceptualizing the mechanics of affiliate marketing through judicious and optimum use of digital content marketing by e-tailers so as to engage customers and create boundless business opportunities for growth, expansion and profitability.

DOI: 10.4018/978-1-5225-5187-4.ch005

INTRODUCTION

The domain of online marketing and internet advertising is going through radical changes. Rapid technological advancements and breakthroughs have led to the digitalization of the media, which in turn has resulted in ferocious marketing strategies aimed at promotion of brands by businesses. Internet advertising has gained prominence with the high growth rate of online media penetration at global level because it offers richer possibilities to directly make targeted communications to global consumers and segmenting them. In context to Indian online market, according to Internet and Mobile Association of India [IAMAI], the digital commerce market has seen a growth by 33 per cent reaching to a figure of 62,967 Crore in the year 2015 which is predicted to touch a mammoth figure of $50 to $70 Billion by the year 2020 owing to the increasing popularity of online shopping and increase in internet penetration (IAMAI Research Report, 2014). Online retailers like Flipkart, Amazon, and Yatra.com have already started affiliate marketing in India and it is gaining popularity in digital market. Affiliate marketing has emerged as one of the choicest promotional tools for lead generation the digital promotion through seamless integration of variety of programmes. In an online affiliate program advertising website offers their affiliates revenues based on provided website traffic and associated leads and sales. If a website decides to join another websites affiliate program, it has to host a coded link on its website that directs a visitor to the parent website. If the customer makes a purchase from the parent website through this affiliate link, the host website will get a percentage of that sale. To summarise, Affiliate marketing is a type of online marketing technique where an affiliate/publisher promotes a business through an advertisement on their web site and in return that business rewards the affiliate with commission each time a visitor, customer generates sales. Affiliate marketing is also referred as performance marketing and associate marketing (ibid).

The objective of this research paper is to analyze by conceptualising the mechanics of affiliate marketing through judicious and optimum use of digital content marketing by e-tailers so as to engage customers and create boundless business opportunities for growth, expansion and profitability. E-retailers intend to take advantage on it in spite of impediment and escalated competition of e-tailers. Tomorrow's high-performing businesses will use technology to strengthen their relationships with customers, leverage their data, optimize and secure their critical systems, and enable their workforces with leading tools.

Technology is also enabling customers to take more control of their shopping experiences, and new approaches to shopping and fulfilment are opening the doors to competition that would not have been viable just a few years ago and it's all changing at warp speed. Retailers are increasingly leveraging their presence across channels of catalogue, web, stores and kiosks, to increase their share of the customer's wallet and expand across consumer segments. The retailers should be able to actively engage with customers on various social media platforms and essentially working towards making a truly integrated multichannel experience, that is the future of e-retailing.

In the last few years, brands have become very good at targeting people of a specific demographic or geographical location. However, to create really compelling content for a customer, they must be targeted according to what they do, not just what they look like, or where they live. Today, brands can access data about each individual customer's buying behaviour, and use it to craft uniquely relevant content, that provides utility and real value to a customer. This can also help the company in converting a loyal customer or visitor into a close affiliate. This strategy is far more effective in getting customers to take up the real revenue generating actions through affiliate marketing, rather than simply being customers. Information technology [IT] drives innovation and innovation is the path to business success. It's hard to imagine any business that has not benefited from the digital revolution. Innovation results in smarter apps, improved data storage, faster processing, and wider information distribution. Innovation makes businesses run more efficiently. And innovation increases value, enhances quality, and boosts productivity. The affiliate Marketing is a good example of this (Ventuso LLC, 2010).

Thus the modern day retailers need to synergistically join in the value co-creation process to meet the restless hyper-connected shopper. The technology changes of the last five years have changed customers and their expectations. Looking ahead, these changes will continue to influence the relationship between the customer and the set of retailers they choose to interact with. This poses a set of opportunities for retailers to view technology as an enabler to providing richer experiences that appeal to discerning customers and that differentiate the business enough to stand out among a sea of online and offline competitors.

BACKGROUND OF THE STUDY

The future may seem uncertain at times, but we do know that every retailer must be a digital retailer to outpace competitors and appeal to the unique wants and needs of today's customer. The task may seem insurmountable, but new tools and technologies can ease the journey.

The authors in this research work attempt to conceptually study and posit the tools and technologies along with the nitty-gritty associated with affiliate marketing through digital content marketing and offer a succinct view into the aspects concurrent with it.

In this research study an attempt has also been made to understand the consumer attitude towards affiliate marketing through proper content management by organisations which has a direct influence on customer engagement, enhanced visibility of the company as a brand and eventually resulting into enhanced store/website traffic. It also attempts to outline the benefits of affiliate marketing from the organisational perspective that gives e-tailers a competitive edge over others through cost optimisation, capabilities of market expansion by going global, agility in tracking results and reports which culminates into robust business strategy and enhanced competitiveness in the digital world.

In business world the success depends upon the partnering organizations and their ability to generate and support business process. Even in digital world success of e-commerce business depends upon partnering organizations like affiliates who help the firm in bringing customers. Affiliate marketing is one of the online marketing tactic in which online firms partner with online content providers who bring traffic to the firm's website. The firm in turn pays commission to the content providers over the converted sales from given customers. Online firms in western countries have been adopting the tactic. Businesses through affiliate marketing in the USA are expected to rise from $1.6 Billion in 2007 to $4.1 Billion in 2015 (Birkner, 2012).

An attempt has been made to understand the basic working model of Affiliate Marketing to understand the concept of Affiliate Marketing. (Please refer to Figure 1.)

As depicted in the above figure the affiliate marketing or associate marketing is an arrangement by which advertiser pay commission to affiliate for generating sales or traffic on its website. Affiliate website may posts ads, banners, and links of products or services from merchant's website. Affiliate marketing is relationship between three parties' i.e. Advertiser or Merchant, the Affiliate himself and the customer.

The word "digital" is an all-encompassing term for all digital channels, in practice, most companies take channel specific approach to customer engagement. The social, web store, mobile and e-commerce teams all operate on their own terms, with their own creative content, budgets and strategies (Altimeter

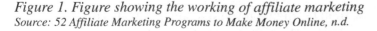

Figure 1. Figure showing the working of affiliate marketing
Source: 52 Affiliate Marketing Programs to Make Money Online, n.d.

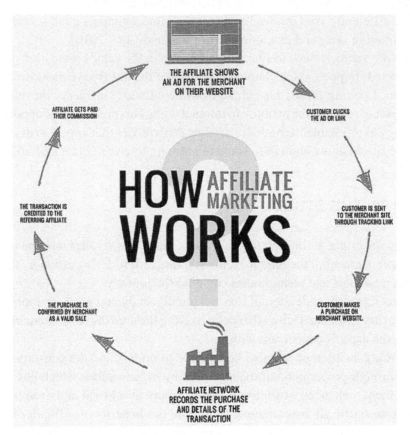

Research Study, 2015). By reviewing this study it can be deduced that customers and shoppers' want to be recognized as unique individuals across all touch points with a brand, and the only way to fulfill this demand is to coordinate the efforts of all channel offerings with a single, unified strategy which can be done by proper content marketing. While brands have been crafting messages with the goal of driving people into stores, they often lack a clear strategy for doing it effectively, especially when it comes to synchronizing all the channels of communication to enhance effectiveness. This is the focal theme of this research study.

In this chapter the study the fundamental element that in which way the retail businesses in India should leverage their organisational competencies to get the benefits of affiliate marketing which is still at the nascent stage specifically for e-tailers in India.

A BRIEF REVIEW OF LITERATURE

In this section an attempt has been made to review the literature in brief on Affiliate Marketing.

Internet users' population is young, mobile and well educated. They are driven by aspirations and they strive to achieve their goals. Previous researchers have argued that attitude towards internet advertising consists of both cognitive and affective antecedents (Ducoffe, 1996; Shimp 1981). Pollay and Mittals model (1993) presented seven belief factors underlying consumers' beliefs and classified those factors into two categories. The first category labeled as personal use consists of factors including product information, social role and image and entertainment. The second category labeled as social effect, includes value corruption, falsity, good for economy and materialism. In today's competitive advertising environment, it is increasingly impossible to stand out of the crowd. In addition, consumers easily ignore advertising and consider it to have little value (Wang et al, 2002).

Also, the media costs are too high forcing the advertisers to search for the factors that contribute to effective advertising. Ultimately, the goal of advertising is to influence consumer behavior (Petty & Cacioopo, 1983).

The growth of affiliate marketing has been rapid in recent years. The major online seller Amazon, as a pioneer of affiliate marketing, has attracted over 1,000,000 content providers that have been cooperating with the company since their affiliate program was introduced in 1996. Rowley claims that quarter of Amazon's revenue is generated by affiliates (Rowley, 2004).

Nowadays, more and more companies have started their affiliate programs in order to efficiently acquire new customers. Affiliate networks have emerged and position themselves as intermediaries between content providers and merchants providing technical solutions to manage affiliate programs. Such networks are for example Commission Junction, Zanox or TradeDoubler. Affiliate marketing provides even further ways of targeting. According to Hoffman and Novak, whereas in traditional online advertising it is the merchant, who decides how to target the advertising, by employing affiliate marketing, content providers themselves asses which merchants and products best suit their audience (Hoffman & Novak, 2000). Nevertheless, merchants can still decide, which content providers they want to cooperate with (ibid).

As Papatla and Bhatnagar proved, content providers benefit most from the participation in the affiliate program, if there is close connection between the website and products or services offered through the program. The connection does not only apply to product types, which should match website orientation, but also to brand perceptions, consumer loyalty etc. (Papatla & Bhatnagar, 2002). Moreover, some content providers can participate in affiliate marketing programs, because they perceive it as a good service for their visitors such as providing sale coupons, updated information about new products etc. (Duffy, 2004).

Several studies (such as Hoffman & Novak, 2000; Papatla & Bhatnagar, 2002) had been conducted focusing on the companies offering affiliate marketing programs, however none of the studies was concerned with the perspective of content providers.

As demonstrated above, content providers can nowadays choose out of thousands of affiliate programs and marketing these programs towards content providers is crucial.

If the merchants do not attract enough content providers into their affiliate programs, their links and banners will be exposed to fewer customers than their competitors', resulting in losing positions in the sales, brand management and product awareness (Hoffman & Novak, 2000). The digital content marketing is the key for the retailers to succeed in order to better engage the customers' and to increase foot-falls and traffic in the retail stores.

As Hoffman and Novak demonstrated, affiliate marketing enables better targeting of online advertising which improve their effectiveness. Retailers have to choose affiliate programs very carefully, because of the opportunity cost connected with not employing competing programs. Therefore, they target the advertising even more precisely than merchants themselves, as otherwise they would not get optimal income. (Hoffman & Novak, 2000).

Recommendation of a product or service on a partner website can create halo effect and thus encourage the customers to purchase (Gallaugher et al., 2001). Apart from increasing the sales, employing the content providers for online promotion is also beneficial for enhancing the reach and creating broader exposure (Chatterjee, 2002). Moreover, through content providers, companies can gain customers that are usually very difficult to reach and save on online campaigns planning (Hoffman & Novak, 2000).

Gallaugher et al. add that using affiliate marketing is more cost-effective to the merchants than other forms of online advertising, because it diminishes the administrative costs connected with buying advertising. If the program is managed well, it can enable advertising on such a great amount of websites that would be otherwise impossible to acquire (Gallaugher et al., 2001).

Driving customers into stores has long been the end-goal of nearly all types of advertising. However, traditional campaigns are limited in their ability to continue doing this, as consumers require more than just brand awareness to make a purchasing decision. Fortunately, there is a great opportunity in harnessing the power of digital content and media to reach customers, and influence their decision not just to come into a store, but to take action once they're there. Brands can now communicate with customers in the way they demand, which is to be recognized as unique individuals, with unique histories, preferences and buying behavior. By embracing the one-to-one advertising model instead of one-to-many, brands stand not only to gain foot-traffic into their stores; they are able to gain the all important patronage of the digital shopper.

Despite the rise of the internet, e-commerce and Amazon, in-store purchases still account for 90 per cent of customer transactions. No matter how digitally savvy the customer, walking into a physical store to purchase has been, and will continue to be not just a significant part of the shopping experience, but by far the most important touch point (A.T. Kearney, Incorporation. (2014). On Solid Ground: Brick-and-Mortar Is the Foundation of Omnichannel Retailing. India. Michael, Mike, & Andres Mendoza-Pena).

By reviewing the relevant literature it can be deduced that although it would be hard to find a brand that doesn't make use of digital channels today, most of them believe digital marketing is best deployed as a brand-building tool. That's why the social media presence of retailers is limited to being entertaining, and announcing upcoming promotions. While online display ads are usually no different than what a customer might see in a magazine or a billboard, containing much of the same taglines and visual content. By focusing only on awareness, brands end up not taking the entirety of the offline/online customer journey into account when planning advertising experiences. Today's digitally empowered shopper doesn't just need a brand message, or generic item and price; they need/expect/demand more robust and relevant information to make decisions.

Digital channels such as social media, mobile and online display are well suited for delivering a consistent brand message to a lot of eyeballs at once, but they also present opportunities for reaching individual customers with unique messages that are relevant only to them. This allows digital channels to act not just as brand building vehicles, but as a place where customers can be convinced to take action that translates into actual revenue.

Although "digital" is an all-encompassing term for all digital channels, in practice, most companies take a siloed, channel-specific approach to customer engagement. The social, web, mobile and e-commerce teams all operate on their own terms, with their own creative content, budgets and strategies. However, customers want to be recognized as unique individuals across all touch points with a brand, and the only way to fulfill that demand is to coordinate the efforts of all channel silos with a single, unified strategy.

OBJECTIVES OF THE RESEARCH STUDY

The Chief Objective of the research study is to conceptualize the mechanics of affiliate marketing which is done through sensible and optimum use of digital content marketing by retailers so as to connect customers at different touch points and create illimitable business opportunities for growth, expansion and profitability.

For this the researchers intend to make use of content analysis for drawing inferences and conclusions about the subject matter of affiliate marketing.

This study also attempts to understand the consumer attitude towards affiliate marketing which has a direct influence on customer engagement, enhanced visibility of the company as a brand and eventually resulting into enhanced store/website traffic. It also attempts to chart out the benefits of affiliate marketing from the organisational viewpoint that enables organizations to gain a competitive advantage over others through cost optimisation, capabilities of market expansion by going global, agility in tracking results and reports which finally culminates into robust business strategy and enhanced competitiveness in the digital world.

The other *peripheral objectives* of this research study are as follows:

1. To investigate the mechanism of affiliate marketing for retailers and business in India.
2. To study the role of Affiliate marketing in India this is likely to become the principal mainstream marketing strategy for e-commerce businesses in the future.
3. To identify the critical success factors in affiliate marketing in India.
4. To outline a roadmap for organisations and retailers to get started by creating targeted content, unifying messages across multiple digital channels, and building long-lasting relationships with their customers.
5. To demystify the various aspects and issues related with the role of information technology in affiliate marketing.
6. To study the emerging affiliate marketing models used by contemporary organisations.

A CONCEPTUAL MODEL OF AFFILIATE MARKETING

The apprehension that Affiliate marketing can be an effective tool for only e-retailers is a wrong notion. In fact, the physicality of the retail store will always be preferred by the shoppers' who seek entertainment value from shopping activities. For the brick and mortar stores the Affiliate marketing can be used by creating a customized content marketing strategy by judicious use of digital content which can be used to drive customer traffic and engagement across all touch points in not only the digitally relevant environment but also drawing the shoppers'' to the retail stores. The Mechanics of Affiliate Marketing is shown in below figure. (Please refer to Figure 2.)

ROLE OF INFORMATION TECHNOLOGY FOR AFFILIATE MARKETING

Information technology drives innovation and innovation is the path to business success. It's hard to imagine any business that has not benefited from the digital revolution.

Figure 2. Figure showing mechanics of affiliate marketing
Source: Model Conceptualized by the Authors

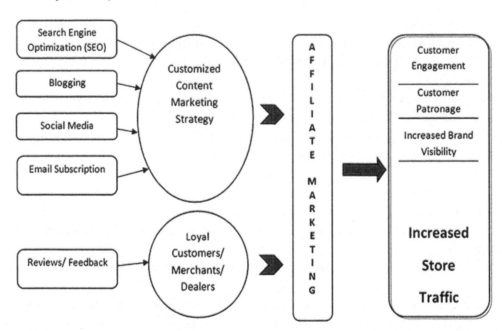

The affiliate marketing constitutes of four main players; the affiliate network, the affiliate program, the publisher and the user. The Affiliate Network is the platform, software, tracking and asset tools that will connect advertisers with publishers. It's the entity which connects advertisers and publishers, it's who manages the technical interactions between the advertiser and publisher, oversees the payments and provides the neutral party of trust between the entity paying the commissions and the entity receiving the commissions.

The advertiser is an entity with a web presence who sells things online, generates mobile app downloads, compiles lead gen forms, captures email sign ups and much more. Basically, an advertiser or often referred to as merchant, is any entity who is able to process an action, captured on their site and can monetize that conversion. The publisher, or often called the affiliate, is the entity within this ecosystem which has access to traffic.

They don't sell an end service or product, but drive website traffic and want to partner with businesses who are able to monetize that traffic and share with them a piece of the pie (ibid). Publishers are often times content specialists, masters of their niche and provide valuable information to people seeking out solutions.

In providing this information, the publisher is able to make recommendations, reviews, savings and more, all while promoting their partner advertisers. By providing a link from their site to an advertiser's site, their web traffic can easily take the next step in the conversion process by investigating the advertiser's site. The user is simply the internet user seeking out information online. They have some form of a relationship with a publisher, either through an email list, memberships, loyalty, trust or something else. They seek out information and recommendations to help provide a solution to their problem. The publisher of course, is able to solve that problem with detailed information about the solution. The solution being, the product or service offered by their affiliate partnership with their advertisers.

The affiliate marketing programs comes with bundle of attributes to be configured as per the needs of an organization. The major components of an affiliate program may include; the log in page, terms and condition agreements, the interface, tracking capabilities, messaging tools, managing log in credentials and accounts, account IDs, reporting system, payment integrations, image hosting and tracking, fraud monitoring and much more. A few examples of affiliate tools could be webinars for your affiliates to learn more about your products and services - in use, it could also be whitepapers you provide your publishers to educate them on what they're recommending. Some affiliates love coupon codes and drive lots of traffic through providing exclusive savings to their members. Other affiliates like to have state-of-the-art widgets which their users can interact with on their site and be seamlessly integrated with the advertiser's site with one click. It is necessary to understand the basic characteristics required by Affiliate marketing. The below given table compares the technology levels and what they can offer for Affiliate Marketing. (Please refer to Table 1.)

This suggests that the mobile devices are going to be the next era changing technology for affiliate marketing; it is now with retailer, affiliates and technology people to how to provide the seamless integration with web and provide ultimate user experience to unfold the potential of latent affiliate marketing.

KEY DISCUSSIONS

Retailers and brands have an opportunity to connect with their customers on a far more meaningful level than simply advertising at them. Through targeting, they can create solutions for a customer that solves problems that are specific to those individuals and their lifestyles. Knowing a customer's likes and dislikes, what time of the month they are most likely to buy, or what type of promotion they are most likely to take advantage of is crucial information, for personalizing content. Until a customer walked into a store and bought an item, it was difficult to know who they were, not just in terms of demographics, but in terms of their interests, habits and responsiveness to content. All of that can now be measured by reaching customers at all the digital locations they visit before coming to the store.

Table 1. Emerging digitalized media's adoption of affiliate marketing

Necessary Characteristic	ITV/Radio	Websites	Mobile Devices 3g & 4G/Other Tablets Devices
Commercial	These are highly accepted and used as commercial medias.	The websites have gained strong position and loyal customer base.	Until now, mobile or other devices have only to a very limited degree functioned as a marketing medium.
Interactivity	These media have high degree of challenge to conceptualize the tracking.	Provides variety of solutions and ways for interaction, tracking, reporting.	Provides variety of solutions and ways for interaction, tracking, reporting.
Decentralization	As the history suggest these media are far too away from adopting any decentralized structure.	Best suitable ways and decentralization can be adopted and implemented easily.	As mobile devices are also highly controlled by few players, limitations are highly to emerge.
User-friendly Interface	New technology advancements enabled better user experience.	It is the market of vibrant changes and user-friendly innovative tools.	Mobile devices have emerged as the highly convenient devices changing the online market.

Source: Compiled by Authors' from Review of Literature

This includes the company website, search results, mobile, social media and email. Instead of building the store and waiting for them to come, marketers can engage customers where they already are.

Mobile is an especially potent addition to this mix, since it is a gateway to the customer at all times. There is a delicate balance to be implemented, which avoids bombarding a customer with constant messaging, and instead sending them a meaningful message at the moment when they are most likely to take action. The channels might change but the customer remains the same. It only makes sense then to have a marketing strategy that is not specific to the channel, but specific to the customer. To truly have a chance of engaging a customer where they are most likely to respond, a brand must adopt a mindset where it can create equally engaging touch points across mobile, social, the web, email or a point-of-sale. The end goal must not be an engagement metric for that specific channel; it must be to get the customer into the store.

In an Omni-channel digital approach, content plays a key role in influencing the actions of a customer. To be truly effective, the content needs to solve a problem, or provoke some sort of interest in the audience, rather than having a purely commerce aspect to it. This is why it's important to have a content strategy that is centered on the customer, and not the brand's efforts to sell to them.

The content created must be modular enough to be used and re-used across multiple channels and media, while at the same time having enough elements of personalization to make each customer feel unique. Thus the key is to create a shopper centric digital content by seamless integration.

Once a unified, sustainable strategy is put in place that extends through all departments of the organization, it must be executed with the help of the right technology platform. These platforms should enable cross-departmental teams to have a single, up-to-date view of the customer that allows for real-time engagement on whatever channel they are present on. The capabilities of these platforms must go beyond boilerplate Customer Relationship Management [CRM] systems, and allow for plenty of integrations that enable data influx from varied sources, and predictive intelligence and marketing automation.

In addition to a data platform, content management is key, and a dedicated digital asset management platform can enable brands to create an infinite number of personalized versions of ads, using the same basic creative elements. To truly deploy dynamic content, or versioning at scale, a high-functioning Digital Asset Management platform that connects to a personalization engine or website optimization solution is a must-have. While the tools are important, they cannot be solely relied upon, especially when brands get into local targeting. In these instances, agencies and other service providers can be valuable partners. Plans and technologies are only as good as the people putting them to use, and in when it comes to digital marketing, the right personnel can make all the difference. In addition to cross-departmental leaders to supervise the strategy through all the different channels, a brand needs data scientists to make sense of all the information, content experts that can create vast amounts of creative that can be customized automatically, and finally it needs leadership that has the belief (and the budget) to see it all way through. However, this doesn't mean that every organizational aspect of these efforts needs to be put in place before a company starts executing on the plan. This is more of a continuous journey of innovation, with plenty of the data already at hand for an organization to start connecting the dots. All it needs is a few motivated individuals.

MANAGERIAL IMPLICATIONS AND CONCLUDING REMARKS

Incentivize visits to retail locations, with features such as order online, pick-up in store, store returns. These can be used in addition to sales, coupons and other promotional activity designed to attract foot traffic.

The physical retail stores needs to be mobile first, or at least primary, when it comes to formulating a content engagement strategy. When it comes to reach, and opportunities for right-time and location targeting, few channels are better than mobile. The retailers operating with the physical retail stores should leverage the mix of paid, earned and owned media to maximize value from your budget, and engage customers outside the usual realms. They should plan for online cross channel content with similar teams and processes that are in place for delivering offline content. This enables a coordinated strategy across paid, earned and owned channels, without having to start completely from scratch. The special focus should be to reconsider budget allocation to devote more towards digital spending, as well as identify the digital marketing tactics that give the most return on investment.

When it comes to digital advertising by retail stores, the most commonly used metric for success is number of impressions. While this may serve as a good indicator of how much reach a brand has on any given channel, it's not necessarily a measure of engagement, and its link to sales is tenuous at best. Focusing on impressions usually means the goals at the top of the funnel and the bottom of the funnel aren't aligned. It's only when digital advertisements are coupled with targeting and action-driven messaging that they start truly contributing value. This is to be taken care by retailers. The term "local" immediately brings to mind "location," and indeed there is great value in being able to target customers based on their geo-location. However, "local" can mean so much more than a zip code. There is a tangible value in expanding "local" to include Who, What and When in addition to Where. While proximity to a store can make a customer walk into it, messages that target customers based on who they are, and the previous actions they have taken are far more effective in getting them to spend money once they enter.

Thus the physical retail stores need to embrace the new digital technology and to do this retailers' must understand evolving customer behaviour and heed the shoppers of all ages and their level of technology adoption. Retail organizations often fail to realize their full return on investment for digital projects. That is because they are implemented in a piecemeal fashion rather than addressed from the top down as a business transformation effort. Physical stores are not going to disappear. Customers will always have different motivations to shop and hence will be looking for different purchase environments. Retailers need to understand how to address these shopping motivations online and offline.

REFERENCES

Altimeter Research Report. (2015). *A though Leadership Study by Rebecca Leib "From Web Traffic to Foot Traffic: How Brands and Retailers Can Leverage Digital Content to Power In-Store Sales"*. Author.

Birkner, C. (2012). *The ABCs of affiliate marketing*. Marketing News.

Brown, M., Mendoza-Pena, A., & Moriarty, M. (2014). *On Solid Ground: Brick-and-Mortar Is the Foundation of Omni channel Retailing*. Retrieved on May 12, 2016 from http://www.atkearney.com/documents/10192/4683364/On+Solid+Ground.pdf/f96d82ce-e40c-450d-97bb-884b017f4cd7

Chatterjee, P. (2002). Interfirm alliances in online retailing. *Journal of Business Research, 57,* 714723.

Ducoffe, R. H. (1996). Advertising value and advertising on the web. *Journal of Advertising Research, 36*(5), 21–35.

Duffy, D. L. (2005). Affiliate marketing and its impact on e-commerce. *Journal of Consumer Marketing, 22*(3), 161–163. doi:10.1108/07363760510595986

Gallaugher, J. M., Auger, P., & Barnir, A. (2001, August). Revenue Streams and Digital Content Providers: An Empirical Investigation. *Information & Management, 38*(7), 473–485. doi:10.1016/S0378-7206(00)00083-5

Hoffman, D. L., & Novak, T. P. (2000, May - June). How to Acquire Customers on the Web. *Harvard Business Review, 78*(3), 179–183. PMID:11183979

Internet and Mobile Association of India (IAMAI). (2014). *Final_IAMAI_Annual Report 2014-15 copy-AnnualReport2014-15.pdf.* Retrieved May 8, 2016 from http://www.iamai.in/sites/default/files/annual_report/AnnualReport2014-15.pdf

Papatla, P., & Bhatnagar, A. (2002). Choosing the Right Mix of On-line Affiliates: How Do You Select the Best? *Journal of Advertising, 31*(3), 69-81.

Petty, R. E., Cacioppo, J. T., & Schumann, D. (1983). Central and peripheral routes to advertising effectiveness: The moderating role of involvement. *The Journal of Consumer Research, 10*(2), 135–146. doi:10.1086/208954

Pollay, R. W., & Mittal, B. (1993). Heres the beef: Factors, determinants and segments in consumer criticism of advertising. *Journal of Marketing, 57*(3), 99–114. doi:10.2307/1251857

Rowley, J. (2004). Just another channel? Marketing communications in e-business. *Marketing Intelligence & Planning, 22*(1), 24–41. doi:10.1108/02634500410516896

Shimp, T. (1981). Attitude towards the ad as a mediator of consumer brand choice. *Journal of Advertising Research, 10*(2), 9–15. doi:10.1080/00913367.1981.10672756

Wang, C. N., Zhang, P., Choi, R. S., & D'Eredita, M. (2002). *Understanding consumer attitudes toward advertising.* Retrieved July 10, 2011 from http://sigs.aisnet.org/sighci/amcis02/RIP/Wang.pdf

KEY TERMS AND DEFINITIONS

Affiliate Marketing: Affiliate marketing is a type of performance-based marketing in which a business rewards one or more affiliates for each visitor or customer brought by the affiliate's own marketing efforts (https://en.wikipedia.org/wiki/Affiliate_marketing).

Content Marketing: Content marketing is the marketing and business process for creating and distributing relevant and valuable content to attract, acquire, and engage a clearly defined and understood target audience – with the objective of driving profitable customer action (contentmarketinginstitute. com/2012/06/content-marketing-definition).

Digital: Digital describes electronic technology that generates, stores, and processes data that creates value for organisations. Digital is a new way of engaging with customers. And for others still, it represents an entirely new way of doing business (www.mckinsey.com/industries/high-tech/our-insights/what-digital-really-means).

Web Traffic: Web traffic is the amount of data sent and received by visitors to a web site. This is determined by the number of visitors and the number of pages they visit (https://en.wikipedia.org/wiki/Web_traffic).

This research was previously published in Driving Traffic and Customer Activity Through Affiliate Marketing edited by Surabhi Singh, pages 113-128, copyright year 2018 by Business Science Reference (an imprint of IGI Global).

Section 2
Development and Design Methodologies

Chapter 6

Digital Marketing Strategy for Affinity Marketing:
Utilising the New Marketing Arena

Aster Mekonnen
GSM London, UK

ABSTRACT

Integration of digital marketing into overall business strategy is no longer an option, it is imperative for success. Yet, not all have tapped into this. Another opportunity that could leverage an organisation in today's competitive environment is affinity marketing. Successful implementation of affinity marketing has the potential to enhance participation, raise revenue, increase retention and provide a mutually beneficial arrangement for the partners involved. Yet, despite its appeal and the popularity it achieved in the late 1980s and early 1990s, uptake of the scheme has slowed down. Whilst some affinity partners have embraced digital marketing to an extent, most are not using it effectively to drive and sustain their affinity marketing scheme. Cognisant that affinity marketing is still a lucrative area, this chapter sets forth a digital marketing strategy for affinity marketing, e-affinity marketing, as this is where the added value for the 21st century customer is envisioned.

INTRODUCTION

Businesses in the 21st century are hugely reliant on the internet to support the growth of their organisations. Whether one should integrate internet technology as part of their business plan is no longer questionable, but rather a matter of how it may be most effectively deployed (Michael Porter, 2001). The growth of and investment in digital marketing is astounding. For instance, an industry survey conducted by Pricewater house and Cooper (PwC) and sponsored by the Interactive Advertising Bureau (IAB) has shown that in US alone the revenue generated for half-year 2014 totalled $23.billion, 15% higher than the previous year (IAB, 2014). Coupled with the digital era, affinity marketing presents a unique opportunity for organisations to strengthen their competitiveness as well as build on their customer's loyalty. The internet presents the ultimate interactive and integrative communications system (Schultz, 1996).

DOI: 10.4018/978-1-5225-5187-4.ch006

Given that affinity marketing (i.e. the triadic relationship between the affinity group, the customer and the service provider) is said to be built on the affinity that customers already have with their affinity group, integrating and implementing digital marketing effectively has the potential to further enhance the customer-affinity group as well as the customer-service provider relationship.

Given the minimal integration of digital marketing in driving affinity marketing, the challenge is to determine the extent to which marketers are using it and to propose ways of enhancing usage. As noted above, unlike most media the internet is interactive and provides marketers with a wide variety of potential uses that range from marketing research to advertising and selling. One of the most significant contributions of the internet is that of value-added marketing – adding value to visitors' experience by allowing marketers to give them additional information as well as services. "The concept of value-added marketing creates loyalty to one or more homepage sites and consequently to the homepage sponsor. Such loyalty is the corner-stone of building lasting relationships with customers" (Husted & Whitehouse, Jr., 2002, p.4).

In the face of today's rapidly changing environment, with the advent of a technology revolution and associated trends such as social media, customers' needs and demands (and even decision making processes) are changing. Recent studies have elicited that companies which master the process of digital integration are 2.5 times more likely to convert their customers (Bughin, 2013). Unfortunately, affinity marketers have not risen to the challenge. The investigation by the author has shown that most affinity marketing schemes are not adequately visible on the internet, therefore failing to capitalise on the opportunity that the digital platform presents.

This chapter intends to provide a strategy that enables affinity partners to integrate their business plan with digital marketing as a key component to drive success. The rest of the chapter is organised under three main areas: the new marketing arena; affinity marketing and digital marketing; and strategic integration. The new marketing arena gives an overview of the 'technology behind digital marketing', looking at the impact of technology and the internet. It also introduces such concepts as e-business, e-commerce and e-marketing with a view to clarifying terminologies, as well as to help put digital marketing into context. The first section will also outline some of the popular 'digital marketing strategies' adopted by marketers to date. Part two on affinity marketing and digital marketing reviews the origins and core values of affinity marketing under the section 'affinity marketing – the big opportunity', highlighting some of the challenges faced by affinity marketers. It then explores how this could be utilised to formulate objectives for e-affinity marketing. Part three – 'strategic integration' – begins with an investigation into 'affinity marketing on the web', a key step in planning the process for e-affinity marketing strategy. This is followed by a discussion on 'knowing the customers', as understanding visitors' needs is an important step in determining what they are offered. Then the 'strategy to activity' proposes steps to help set appropriate strategy and related activities based on knowledge of the target group. The last step in the process – 'performance analysis' – is designed to review the effectiveness of the new initiatives.

1. THE NEW MARKETING ARENA

Aghaei et al. (2012) describes the four generations of the web as follows: Web 1.0 as a web of information connections, Web 2.0 as a web of people connections, Web 3.0 as a web of knowledge connections and Web 4.0 as a web of intelligence connections (the future). The internet has grown from strength to strength since its innovation phase 1964 - 1974 (creation of the fundamental building blocks), through the institutionalisation phase 1975 - 1995 (when large intuitions were provided funding and legitimisation), up to today's commercialisation phase 1995 – present (private corporations take over, expand the backbone of the internet and local services) (Laudon & Travis, 2013). By the end of 2014, the number of internet users in the world is predicted to reach almost 3 billion, with two-thirds of them coming from the developing world (ICT Publication, 2014). Today, the web provides a tremendous opportunity to reach customers directly. A recent survey of digital marketing spending indicated that up to 2.5% of a company's revenue is used in this area (Gartner, 2013). This report suggests that the three top digital activities key to marketing success are the operation of a corporate website, social marketing and digital advertising. Social media is undoubtedly gaining in prominence, with over 72% of internet users now active on social media. The likes of Facebook and Google+ now have over 1 billion users and the potential to attract more (Laudon & Travis, 2013).

Advances in technology and the evolution of marketing are inseparable. The printing press, radio, television and now the internet are all examples of major breakthroughs in technology that also advanced the field of marketing. Technology has the ability to open up new markets and to radically change existing ones. The rapidness of changes in technology makes it necessary to continuously study consumer behaviour. As soon as one thinks that they may have a grasp on what their archetypal consumer wants, those wants will have changed. In the developed world, the digital revolution is changing the way we choose and buy our products and services. People are now going online on a daily basis to fulfil needs such as banking, shopping, recreation and communication.

Some marketing principles never change. Companies must meet the needs of their customers, the need now is digital integration, which is further fuelled by digitally enabled social networking (more commonly known as social media).

The Technology Behind Digital Marketing

The terms internet marketing, e-marketing and digital marketing are often used interchangeably. However, e-marketing is sometimes considered to have a broader scope than internet marketing since it refers to digital media such as web, e-mail and wireless media, but also includes management of digital customer data and electronic customer relationship management systems (E-CRM systems). The term 'digital marketing' was first used in the 1990s and was then described as 'the marketing of products or services using digital channels to reach consumers (Dorie 2012). The key objective is to promote brands through various forms of digital media. To help clarify these alternative terminologies and definitions, in collaboration with the Institute of Digital Marketing, Chaffey (2005) proposed an all-encompassing explanation of digital marketing, describing it as an activity that involves the application of technologies which form online channels to market; that's web, e-mail, databases, plus mobile/wireless and digital TV.

The internet began in the late 1950s in the military and was gradually advanced by computer scientists. The digital revolution, also called the third industrial revolution, is the change from analogue, mechanical, and electronic technology to digital technology (Ryan & Jones, 2012). The digital age as we know it now began with the internet and the Web 1.0 platforms of the early 1990s. This was a rather static world in which users could get the information they desired but it could not be shared on the web. There was no such thing as interaction, as the only activity was reading of content. In 1993, we saw the entrance of the first clickable banner ad and by the next year online magazine Hotwired had begun to purchase huge numbers of banner ads. This was the first step towards shifting the market into a new digital age.

Web 1.0 then slowly progressed into Web 2.0. This is not a new version of Web 1.0; it is about enhancing how people use technology. People were no longer passively taking in information, but instead the internet became a sort of super-highway where users could directly interact with both other users and businesses, the collaborative potential enabling users to share, interact and communicate via rich media content such as Facebook, Instagram, YouTube, FaceTime, Skype and many more. In the early 2000s, supported by the capabilities of broadband and fibre optics, numerous networks and social platforms were developed. This finally enabled Web 2.0 to become truly social. Social media has now become a thriving entity.

In the 2000s and the 2010s, as digital marketing continued to get more sophisticated, it became recognised as an effective technology to enable and foster a relationship with more concisely targeted consumers. With this came the need to formulate a strategy specifically tailored to meet the demands of the internet audience. Digital marketing has changed drastically since its conception in the early 1990s and will continue to change.

Which Digital Marketing Strategy?

Although the term 'strategy' has been used in many different contexts, they are all synonymous in being described as the means to achieve a goal. One simple definition is that it is "a plan of action designed to achieve a long-term or overall aim" (Strauss & Frost, 2014, p. 72). In comparison to traditional strategy, e-business strategy is described as "the deployment of enterprise resources to capitalise on technologies for reaching specified objectives that ultimately improve performance and create sustainable competitive advantage" (Strauss & Frost, 2014). This is inclusive of information technology components such as the internet, digital data, databases, etc.

There are several tools that have been developed or adapted by marketers in their effort to integrate digital marketing strategy into their overall business strategy. Chaffey and Chadwick's generic digital marketing strategy development process (2006, 2012); Chaffey and Smith's 'SOSTAC© Planning Framework for e-Marketing' (2012); and Strauss and Frost's 'E-Marketing Plan' (2014) being amongst such theories. The foundation of these strategies is traditional marketing with common elements, such as; assessing the marketplace; defining objectives; selecting a strategic approach; implementing actions or activities; measuring results or performance (being comparable).

When considering the formulation of a strategic plan suitable for e-affinity marketing, first and foremost one has to examine the unique features inherent to affinity marketing. The review of generic and specific digital marketing strategies, as well as current best practice, can also aid the building of an e-affinity marketing strategy as it will undoubtedly unveil some of the most essential elements required in order to develop a robust digital marketing strategy. Therefore, highlights from some of the notable literature mentioned in the subject area are discussed below.

In a comprehensive study on internet marketing, Chaffey and Chadwick (2006) suggest that the internet marketing strategy should follow a similar form to the traditional strategic marketing planning process and should include: goal setting, situation review, strategy formulation and resource allocation and monitoring. The authors highlight that this plan should also take into consideration external and internal factors that could affect the organisation. In their discussion of digital marketing, the authors further outline three key steps that need to be followed: defining the online opportunity, selecting the strategic approach and delivering results online.

A similar concept was proposed in in the late 1990s by PR Smith, who developed a marketing planning system represented by SOSTAC©, which stands for situation, objectives, strategy, tactics, actions and control. This model was voted as the third most popular marketing model by the Chartered Institute of Marketing (CIM). This could be attributed to its simple, all-encompassing features. At a later date, in 2008, Chaffey and Smith proposed an overall strategy process model for strategic internet marketing - the SOSTAC© planning framework for digital marketing strategy development, which incorporated unique features and capabilities of the internet.

The environment, strategy and performance (ESP) model created by Strauss and Frost (2014) is an alternative approach to e-marketing strategy, which builds on the idea that businesses need a well formulated process on which to determine the success of their strategy. ESP is supported by key marketing tools such as the SWOT (strength, weakness, opportunity and threat), and e-marketing mix to create a comprehensive strategy.

Deviating from the process or plan orientated approaches described above, Ryan and Jones (2012) identified five key components that generally form the foundation of a digital marketing strategy as follows; knowing your business; knowing your competition; knowing the customer; knowing what you want to achieve and knowing how you are going to do it. The authors argue that this process "forces you to sit down and analyse the market in which you are operating in with a critical eye, and to really think about the different components of your business and how digital marketing can help you to achieve your business goal" (Ryan & Jones, 2012, p.23).

Another recent work with an alternative focus is Scott's (2013) investigation of the use of social media, in which he discusses the importance of setting a clear goal when building a digital marketing and PR plan. Here, the author places emphasis on a buyer orientated focus in the context of the organisational goals. Scott suggests that organisations should learn as much as they can about their buyers and segment them into groups identified by 'buyers' persona'. This, he notes, should be the first and single most important step that an organisation needs to take in creating a digital marketing plan. Scott also explained other components that need to be included in the overall planning, such as tactics for the implementation and measurement of the marketing effort and success.

What is clear from the review is that the digital marketing strategy must support and be integrated with the overall business and marketing plans. The review has also shown that there is no single common approach to building a digital marketing strategy, nor should there be one. But, there are essential elements that every marketing strategy must have. This should include (but not be exclusive to); setting digital goals or objectives; analysing the situation; knowing one's customer; setting the strategy and tactics by which to execute it and having a control mechanism for evaluating performance. To the same effect, one must design a strategy or plan that is well structured and comprehensive in the context of the specified sector. With an informative overview of the key components required to build a digital marketing strategy, let us now turn to the context in which we want to develop it for – affinity marketing.

2. AFFINITY MARKETING AND DIGITAL MARKETING

Affinity marketing is widely recognised as a scheme that:

Involves customers who already have sympathy to one brand (be it commercial, not-for-profit or another membership organisation) being sold another service, by another organisation, with the endorsement of the affinity organisation and using its channels of communication. (Mintel, 2000)

Considering how affinity marketing fits within the broader field of services marketing, while most of the studies to date placed it within the context of relationship marketing, associations of the topic have also been made with cause-related marketing. The first time affinity marketing appeared in association with cause-related marketing was in Varadarajan and Menon's (1988) work on the concepts of cause-related marketing. In this work, the authors described affinity marketing as an extreme type of highly targeted cause-related marketing. Varadarajan and Menon (1988) defined cause-related marketing as:

The process of formulating and implementing marketing activities that are characterised by an offer from the firm to contribute a specified amount to a designated cause when customers engage in revenue-providing exchanges that satisfy organisational and individual objectives. (Varadarajan & Menon, 1988, p. 123)

Similarly, Macchiette and Roy (1992) suggested in their study of affinity marketing that the revenue generated by affinity could be seen as cause-related marketing. Soon after, in Schlegelmilch and Woodruffe's (1995) comparative analysis of the affinity card markets (the most popular affinity marketing scheme in the USA and the UK) it was suggested that affinity credit cards fit with cause-related marketing because a firm (the card issuing service provider) uses an association with a designated cause (for example a charity) to market its product or service. Another view that follows the same line of discussion is Worthington and Horne's (1992) proposal that affinity marketing is a sub-set of cause-related marketing, representing a step-change in the nature and intensity of the triadic relationship between the commercial and non-profit partners and consumers. Both cause-related marketing and affinity marketing are premised on the idea that linking specific products to a credible and respected cause or non-profit organisation (in return for a contribution to that cause or organisation) will make the product offering more attractive to consumers (Ross et al, 1992).

Currently, there is growing interest in the use of cause-related marketing as a corporate communication strategy in encouraging sales and as a tool for competitive differentiation (Bigné et al., 2012). Therefore, due to their similarity, equal interest could be expected for affinity marketing. Moreover, one should also note that the role of information communication technology in philanthropy is growing. There is a new culture of generosity, for instance in the UK, between 2007 and 2008 online donations almost doubled, rising from 4% to 7% of UK wide giving (Honoré, 2011). In light of the role of technology and the 'big opportunity' presented through affinity marketing, this section starts with an in-depth review of affinity marketing, highlighting the key principles underpinning its foundation. It then explores how this could be utilised to formulate 'objectives for e-affinity marketing'.

Affinity Marketing: The 'BIG' Opportunity

The first significant academic perspective of affinity marketing was offered by Macchiette and Roy (1992), who described it as a blending of affinity and existing marketing concepts. Affinity, they suggest, is "an individual level of cohesiveness, social bonding, identification and conformity to the norms and standards of a particular reference group" (p.48), while the marketing concept focuses on the "expectation of benefit for the individual, satisfying consumer wants and needs" (p.48). Therefore, the main component in affinity marketing is the customer/affinity group relationship, upon which the affinity marketing scheme is leveraged. Affinity marketing is therefore based upon a strategic partnership between complementary brands, in which a mutually beneficial triadic relationship is formed between the group, the members of the group and the service provider of the product being used for marketing purposes.

There were several organisations linked to affinity marketing schemes. For example, work related organisations, charities, educational institutes and leisure clubs could all be linked to such a scheme. It is worth noting that different types of affinity groups are likely to exhibit differing types of relationships (Worthington, 2001; Laing et al., 2004). This is suggestive that each type of group is influenced by different sets of values that could potentially affect an individual's decision making process with regards to an affinity product. Popular industries that utilise affinity schemes include financial services (often related to the issuance of credit cards), insurance, communications, travel and tourism.

In examining affinity relationships and related schemes, one also needs to be aware that strength of these relationships may vary. Consequently the strength may influence customers' decision making processes and levels of engagement with the affinity group and associated partners, be it offline or online. In addition, the nature of the customer - service provider relationship needs to be taken in to consideration in order to get a full picture of the triadic relationship. This will enable us to gauge why and how the relationship developed, the extent to which the affinity group affects the relationship and how this could aid in the development of a digital strategy.

As previously noted, the affinity marketing partnership (described as a triadic relationship) is based on Macchiette and Roy's (1992) 'affinity interaction model'. The model depicts the triadic relationship formed between the consumer, the affinity group and the commercial organisation. Varied adaptations of the triadic relationship have since been proposed (Mekonnen, 2012, Worthington. 1997). In a triadic relationship it is assumed that a long-term ongoing relationship is formed. Moreover, it is believed that value is created to all partners involved in the triad, provided the relationships are managed well (Worthington, 2001). The triadic relationship provides tangible and non-tangible benefits to all the partners involved (i.e. the customer, the affinity group and the service provider). A summary of these benefits are illustrated in Figure 1.

Utilising the concept of affinity marketing, affinity credit cards provided the main focal point for affinity schemes, especially in the early days of the development and growth of affinity marketing. Consequently, most of the literature on the subject is based on affinity credit cards. Affinity cards were also the earliest adopted and have been perhaps one of the most successful affinity products. Therefore some of the examples in this chapter may draw on affinity credit cards to demonstrate key concepts in relation to digital marketing

Affinity credit cards are like conventional credit cards for the most part, except that they are affiliated to particular affinity groups and it is therefore presumed that they are taken out by people with common interests. Usually, an affinity credit card will display the logo of the particular affinity group, along with the name of the service provider and the card scheme mark (Visa or MasterCard). The key difference between the affinity credit card and the generic bank card is that when a member or supporter of the affinity group signs up for the card, a payment is made by the affinity credit card service provider to the affinity group. Most affinity credit card agreements include both an initial donation from the service provider to the affinity partner (ranging from £5 to £10 per card issued) and an ongoing turnover related payment (usually around 20p to 25p per £100 spent on the card). The USA is the leader of affinity marketing and can often serve as a useful indicator for the UK market. A recent report on credit cards conducted by the USA's Government of Accountability Office (GAO, 2014) indicated that the University

Figure 1. Triadic relationship and associated benefits: The case of affinity credit cards
Key: T- Tangible benefit NT- Non-tangible benefit

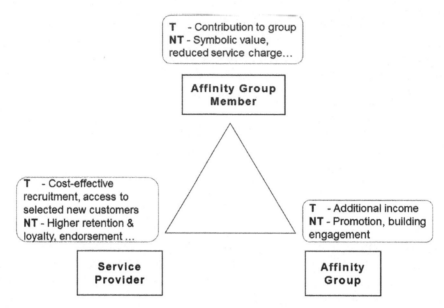

of California received about $1.5 million through its agreement with FIA card services, the largest payment to an institute of higher education in 2012. The University of Cambridge, whose alumni affinity credit card launched in 1993, had 10,000 card holders by 1999 and had generated over £250,000 for the university by that date (Mintel, 2000). Thus, there is undoubtedly a 'big opportunity' to raise funds and promote the standing of an organisation or a cause through affinity marketing.

Affinity Marketing Challenges

Looking at the affinity card industry in particular, despite sounding like the ideal partnership, the decline in the number of charity credit cards available is a sure sign that these partnerships have encountered some problems. Horne et al. (2000) have shown that there was a gap in how the affinity partners understood the benefits each gained (i.e. there was a knowledge gap between the customer, the affinity group and the service provider). Such a gap in knowledge could potentially lead to mismanagement of the scheme, particularly mismanagement of the customers and possibly even lead to the dissolution of the customer-service provider relationship (Mekonnen, 2012). Such problems could hamper the growth of the affinity marketing industry.

Mintel (2004) has reported that the number of affinity credit cards in issue, as a proportion of all credit cards, has fallen from a peak of 8.6% in 1998 to 3.4% in 2003. More recently, a market research report on affinity credit cards has indicated that payment card affinity schemes fell in number by over 25% between 2008 and 2010 (Finaccord, 2010). This report also notes that many credit card schemes have been discontinued either through lack of demand or lack of profitability. Supporting this, in a study relating to all types of credit cards in the UK, Euromonitor (2011) reported that the total number of personal credit cards that use affinity has fallen from 69,927.4 million in 2005 to 55,894.3 million in 2010. However, the reason behind the fall was not explored. Furthermore, due to the difficulty in obtaining access to customers holding affinity products, there is a gap in understanding customers' attitudes towards this product and the nature of the relationship customers have with their affinity groups. More often than not, affinity partnerships end due to one member of the party failing to receive comparable benefits to the other (Bumell, 2013). A recent example of this can be seen in the demise of the Lloyds Banking Group's partnerships with charities such as Cancer Research UK, the NSPCC and the Scottish SPCA. In the case of Cancer Research UK, Lloyds ceased offering their charity credit card in 2012 after a 23-year partnership which raised a total of £14.5 million for the charity (Howard, 2012).

There is no known study to date that explains why the growth of affinity marketing schemes has stagnated, or any that have considered why there is limited integration of affinity marketing in the digital landscape. Yet the coupling of these two areas has huge potential in capturing a unique market. Having reviewed alternative digital strategies for business and the core concepts of affinity marketing, let's now turn to the setting of a plan for e-affinity marketing in the 21st Century.

3. STRATEGIC INTEGRATION

This strategic integration identifies the key steps required for planning a digital marketing strategy for affinity marketing. The 'E-Affinity Marketing Planning Process' presented in Figure 2 illustrates the step-by-step process for creating an e-affinity marketing plan. Each step is not necessarily conducted in isolation and there is likely to be an iterative process of back and forth to fine-tune essential elements that need to be reviewed within each step.

Setting E-Affinity Marketing Objective

One main area highlighted in relation to planning a digital marketing strategy is the need to clearly identify the goal or objective desired from the digital channel. It is important that organisations build on

Figure 2. E-Affinity Marketing Planning Process

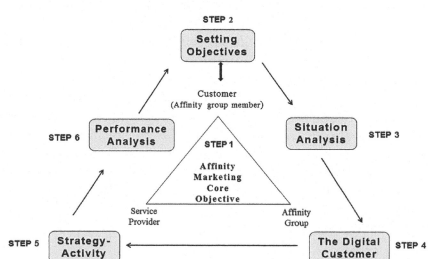

their overarching objectives in the advent of digital integration. Likewise, affinity marketing schemes should follow the same ethos, as it is an extension of the channel or means by which the organisation reaches customers. Therefore, to help create objectives for e-affinity marketing, the recommendation is to initially evaluate the core values related to the scheme and then consider how this can be enhanced or achieved via digital channels. Informed by knowledge of the core objective, the next step in the process is setting e-affinity marketing objectives (Step 2).

A review of digital marketing strategies to date indicates that most of the e-marketing planning tools proposed begin with an evaluation of the environment before commencing with the designated steps. However, given the nature of affinity relationships and the overarching aims and principles underpinning affinity marketing, this paper opted to diverge from this approach as it was felt necessary that the digital objectives for e-affinity marketing should be defined from the outset.

In the SOSTAC© model for digital planning, the objective is denoted by the statement "Where do we want to be?" It is further noted that the model can be used to identify what a business wants to achieve through online channels, as well as to question what the benefits might be (Chaffey & Smith, 2008). This model is encompassed by five broad benefits of, reasons for or objectives of e-marketing: 1) to grow sales 2) to add value 3) to get closer to customers 4) to save costs and 5) to extend the brand online. What is striking about these objectives is that most of it is already aligned with the principles and aims underpinning affinity marketing.

In digital marketing, there are a number of different objectives that can be set; for example, lead generation, acquisition, engagement or retention. In previous studies it has been proposed that an *explorer* could be converted to a *supporter* – thereby strengthening the customer-affinity group relationship as well as the customer-service provider relationship (Mekonnen, 2012). Therefore, if one was to consider a charity group seeking to raise more donations through long-term commitment, one objective could be to convert x% of its episodic donors or members on the newsletter mailing list to the affinity credit card scheme by July 2016. As shown by Mintel's 2000 report, customer acquisition through affinity-based direct mail communication to a 'warm' audience may yield a 6% to 7% response, whereas direct mail into the mass 'cold' market may only yield at best a 1% response. Therefore, it could be said that such a strategy has a high potential of succeeding, given that the target audience are already said to have sympathy for the affinity group. Ultimately, the objectives should relate to what an affinity group and partner aspires to achieve in their overall business objective. Once the objectives for e-affinity marketing have been clearly defined, the next step is to analyse the digital marketspace in the context of affinity marketing.

The remainder of the discussion in this section logically follows the rest of the e-affinity marketing process demonstrated in Figure 2 and is organised accordingly from Step 3 through to Step 6. Step 3 reviews the current practice of 'Affinity marketing on the web' (situation analysis on Figure 2). The next logical step would be to ensure the needs of affinity marketing customers are understood, in both an online and offline sense (Step 4, the digital customer on Figure 2). This is a fundamental requirement for any business striving to succeed in today's competitive environment. *'Knowing the customer'* is crucial for affinity marketing given the unique affinity relationship that the scheme is leveraged upon. Based on the analysis of the situation and the customers' persona, strategies for e-affinity marketing need to be identified (Step 5, strategic-activity on Figure 2). The last step in the process is to formulate a control mechanism with key performance indicators (KPIs) to measure and analyse performance (Step 6, performance analysis on Figure 2).

Affinity Marketing on the Web

The situation analysis (Step 3 of the process in Figure 2) should provide an overview of your organisation (who you are, what you do and how you interact and trade online) by addressing internal and external factors impacting on the business. For e-marketing, it is suggested that this analysis should include growth in users, changes in the market place as well as examples of good and bad e-marketing practices (Chaffey & Smith, 2013 and Strauss & Frost, 2014). Extending this, in the context of e-affinity marketing analysis an assessment of members or supporters' engagement with the group via the web should also be included.

It is important to have an honest and realistic baseline of your current capabilities and activities in order to define a meaningful digital marketing plan for the future. In order to analyse the situation in the first instance, affinity partners (in particular the affinity groups) should consider encompassing the following areas and answering related questions:

1. **Identification of the Digital Customer:** The affinity group needs to know who the digital customers are (with a demographics breakdown), how they interact with the brand, and what platform(s) they use.
2. **SWOT Analysis:** What are the strengths, weaknesses, opportunities and threats of digital integration in relation to the affinity scheme to the organisation as a whole. This should be inclusive of the affinity groups internal capabilities, skills and knowledge with respect to digital marketing.
3. **Competitor Analysis:** The affinity group should identify its competitors and assess how they compete. In terms of added value, to what extent have competitors incorporated an affinity scheme? Competitors overall product offering (i.e. inclusive of price, customer service, and their key differentiators). Furthermore, affinity groups should take this opportunity to assess their competitive position with respect to digital marketing in the industry they operate in and in relation to their close competitors.
4. **Digital Channels Analysis:** The affinity group should list the various digital channels used and success of each in different areas of the organisation. In other words, the affinity groups should be able to assess the scope, depth and effectiveness of their current digital marketing activities across the range of digital channels.

Currently it is apparent that the main presence of affinity marketing on the web is on the affinity groups website. This could be attributed to the complicated nature of the triadic relationship and due to the fact that the initial contact with the affinity group members or supporters is often made via the affinity group. However, once the customer sign up to the affinity scheme, the affinity product provider is primarily in charge of the relationship, and subsequently the one that has regular contact with the member with regards to the scheme.

Taking the above into consideration, following on the affinity credit card theme, the author investigated the presence of the affinity marketing scheme on the websites of affinity groups. Past studies have shown charity, sports, and university affinity groups to be amongst the most popular ones from the array of affinity groups at present (Mintel, 2000 and Mekonnen et al., 2008). Therefore, the websites of 10-15 affinity groups within each of the above category were investigated to evaluate the current situation. Visibility and activity of each group in relation to the prominence of the scheme in the homepage as well as related sub-pages were examined.

An e-commerce presence map is one way of identifying presence in the context of the website, email, social media and offline media, with presence identified on different platforms including the traditional desktop, tablet, and mobile (Laudon & Traver, 2013). Activities one should look for when evaluating presence should include search, display, newsletter, conversation, engagement and sharing. Ideally an extensive investigation of all of the above would be recommended, but in this case the author had already uncovered that current digital integration of affinity marketing to be minimal. Therefore, the information the researcher was able to unearth was limited.

The key findings from the investigation into affinity scheme presence on the web include the following:

1. In extreme cases there were affinity groups with a robust website dedicated to the main function, but they did not have a page on their website for the affinity schemes which they are participating in offline. Therefore, in these cases no further investigation could be conducted.
2. With the affinity groups who had their affinity scheme represented on the website, at the time the investigation was conducted, with the exception of a few the affinity schemes were not visible at all on the homepage. In a few of the cases where it appeared on the homepage, it was only visible as a side banner ad.
3. Where the affinity groups had incorporated the affinity scheme in their website, it was noted that there was no link associated to the scheme on the homepage. This suggests that affinity schemes may not be ranked highly in terms of the organisation's priority for digital integration.
4. In most cases it is evident that unless a potential digital customer actively searches for the affinity scheme, with existing knowledge the scheme, there was not much chance of the customer finding out about the scheme whilst navigating through the homepage. For the most part, there does not appear to be any consistency as to how the affinity groups are leading potential customers to the site dedicated to the affinity scheme. Out of the three categories investigated, universities appear to have adopted a relatively similar step for customers to reach the site dedicated to the affinity scheme. They all appear to lead their members or supporter to the page hosting the affinity scheme via the alumni page, for which the link is often visible on the homepage.
5. Once customers reach the page related to the affinity scheme, if they wish to proceed with signing up for the scheme, they will then be directed to the partner's (affinity product provider) website to complete the registration.

On the whole, all the affinity groups investigated appear to have the technological capability to fully integrate the affinity scheme as part of their digital activities, as can be evidenced by the depth of the activities they have integrated for some of the functions relating to the organisation's main offerings. For example, the University of Cambridge's magazine page gives visitors several opportunities to interact, e.g. play crosswords, download the magazine, link to the CAM reader app, etc. In comparison, the page related to the affinity scheme only has general information and a link to the service provider. Generally speaking, there is no indication to show that the same level of effort is exerted for affinity schemes. For many of the affinity groups, although the affinity scheme may not be their main priority in relation to their overarching business objective, if harnessed it has the potential to add value to the customers experience and consequently build a long-term relationship for all parties involved.

Knowing Your Customer

Once the overarching e-affinity marketing objective has been derived from the core values underpinning affinity marketing (Step 1 and 2) and the situation analysed (Step 3), the affinity groups needs to focus on their customer (Step 4) and work towards an appropriate digital strategy that meets customer's demands.

Identification of digital customers in situation analysis looked at a more generic set of information exploring their demographic breakdown, how they interact with the brand, and what platform(s) they use However, here the emphasis is to extend this knowledge and get a deeper understanding of customers' value in relation to their affinity relationship and the affinity scheme, with a view towards building a persona for the digital customer. A better understanding of how affinity group members or supporters perceive their group's unique qualities, social status and size may provide a way of assessing the strength of their 'affinity', therefore analysing their receptivity to affinity marketing. When an organisation considers the design of their site, they need to understand the differing mind sets of the visitors in order to reach them by building an effective content strategy (Scott, 2013). Scott demonstrates this point by explaining how a college website could have multiple goals such as: 1) Keeping alumni happy so that they donate money to their Alma matter (differentiating between the young and the older alumni), 2) Recruiting students (with sites that need to be tailored for both high school students who may be considering the college as well as the parents reviewing the college, with different information needs), 3) keeping current students happy. In total, five groups are identified here. By understanding the persona of these five groups, the college can create appropriate content to cater for each set of visitors. Similarly, when considering creating of an effective e-affinity marketing site, affinity groups needs to first understand the behaviour of each group of customers that are likely to visit the site.

With e-affinity marketing the affinity group can start by segmenting potential customers based on existing knowledge of the characteristics exhibited by members of the affinity group. For instance, three types of affinity marketing customers - *communicators, supporters* and *explorers* were identified in a recent study related to understanding their relationship with affinity marketing (Mekonnen, 2012). Explorers were primarily driven by opportunities in the marketplace (benefit sought: individual-functional). For communicators, conveying their profession as part of their identity was a strong influencing factor when considering an affinity scheme such as an affinity credit card. For supporters, the functional benefits (donations) were the main reason for acquiring the affinity product. With this knowledge in mind, for example, a professional group's website could place emphasis on the symbolic value of the affinity product on the page dedicated to the affinity scheme. Furthermore, the group could also promote the symbolic value of the scheme on its homepage as one of its online value propositions.

It is also important to recognise that the strength of relationships varies and customers with different strength of relationships (for instance high, medium or low) will require different levels of engagement. Once the organisation has a clear picture of its potential e-affinity marketing customers, it then needs to plan its digital strategy with these groups in mind. Subsequently, the marketing channels used, message, content, layout and structure, as well as wording and language intended to describe what the affinity group provides, should be guided by the defined persona (Scott, 2013).

Strategy to Activity

Having recognised the 'big opportunity', defined digital objectives in line with the organisation's core values and objectives (Step 1 and 2), conducted a situation analysis to assess the affinity scheme's presence on the web (Step 3) and defined the digital audience in relation to the affinity scheme (Step 4), the next step in the process is to set out a strategy and set of related activities (Step 5). This should be formulated to enable the affinity marketing partners to fulfil the objectives set.

Affinity partners should consider the following three steps in setting and implementing the strategy:

1. Initially, affinity partners need to clearly specify what they want to achieve. Strategy is the long-term vision and should be set for a defined period. There should also be an approved budget allocation. For example (continuing on the theme of the affinity credit card), if we revisit the example used in Step 2, if the objective is 'to convert x% of the members on the mailing list for newsletter to the affinity credit card scheme by July 2016', the strategy could be to send periodic communication to the target audience, from the mailing list. In this strategy the affinity group should strive to understand the existing customer database and learn how it interacts with the website. In addition the strategy should also question how the affinity group is currently communicating with its existing customer database?

2. The next step is the tactic. Tactics are the detailed plans to implement the strategy and tend to be short-term and flexible (Chaffey & Smith, 2012 and Strauss & Frost, 2013). Continuing on the theme of the affinity card example from Point 1 above, at this stage the affinity group can determine the exact online activities or communication channels suitable for each target identified. Furthermore, decision regarding the content and frequency of the communication can also be taken.

3. In the final stage the partners need to specify how each activity will be managed. Given the complexity of the scheme, partners may have different objectives and levels of responsibility at different stages in the relationship. This includes everything from the promotion, to the sales and on to the maintenance of the scheme. This is evident if we look at the nature of the triadic relationship demonstrated by the infographic diagram (Figure 1), which indicates the variety of benefits to be gained by each partner. The process of building the affinity scheme also demonstrates different levels of responsibility. For instance, whilst the introductory and initiation of customers often falls upon the affinity group, the signing up of customers is the affinity product provider's responsibility.

Earlier studies have already indicated that there has been a gap in how the affinity partners understood the benefits each gained by each (Horne et al., 2000). Mintel (2004) has also reported how the complex nature of triadic relationship might lead to a problem in relation to how the customers are managed. Technically, the affinity groups might feel that they should have a say in the relationship, since it is assumed that the customer will be a member or supporter of their organisation. Besides, it is assumed that the affinity group would obviously have been the host group that provided the service provider with details of the customers' names and addresses in the first instance. However, in reality it generally tends to be the service provider that takes control of the customer relationship in affinity marketing schemes. For example, with affinity credit cards, the service providers know who the card holders are, they speak or communicate with them regularly via email and the monthly statement; ultimately, they provide the customer service to their card holders. Moreover, due to data protection requirements, the affinity groups were not even always told which of their members have actually arranged a financial product via the scheme (Mintel, 2004). Therefore, when devising and implementing the e-affinity marketing strategy it is critical that both partners are involved in the design, management and maintenance of each tactical e-tool, as both will benefit if the site is fully optimised.

Performance and Analysis

The final step in the process of strategic integration is 'performance and analysis' (Step 6, Figure 2). This is designed to measure and analyse the performance of the website in order to determine the success of the strategies and the plans. As the result is intended help future developments of the site, this is indicated as an iterative process with the final arrow pointing back to e-affinity marketing objectives.

Performance analysis is primarily led by the objectives set at the outset, with the help of web analytics. Web analytics is the measurement, collection, analysis and reporting of the internet data for purposes of understanding and optimising web usage (Web Analytics Association WWW, 2008, p.3). Analytics is not just a tool for measuring web traffic, but can be used as a tool for business and market research, and to assess and improve the effectiveness of a website. The partners involved in the triadic relationship should be able to measure, monitor and review their e-affinity marketing campaign, updating and modifying elements as required.

Often the objectives set at the beginning should guide the identification of KPI at the start of the process. Other areas that need to be considered are the frequency of reporting and the analysis of performance, questioning why it is happening. Furthermore given the complex nature of the triadic relationship partners should also determine who measures what and reports to whom and finally who takes appropriate actions arising (what should be done about it). As with the previous step (strategies – activities) this is another area where the responsibilities and terms performance and analysis need to be clearly defined and agreed between the affinity scheme partners.

CONCLUSION

This paper was inspired by the dearth of literature and lack of practical guide on optimising affinity marketing schemes through digital integration. There is no known study to data that explains why the growth of affinity marketing scheme has stagnated or one that looks at why there is limited integration of the scheme in the digital landscape. Yet the coupling of these two areas has huge potential in capturing a unique market. The Internet is an ideal platform to target and engage customers, consequently encouraging a long term relationship. Moreover it has been shown that the role of information communication technology in philanthropy is growing, with donation via the internet nearly doubling between 2007 and 2008 (Honoré, 2011).

This paper proposes a strategic integration plan which identifies six key steps required for planning a digital marketing strategy for affinity marketing, 'E-Affinity Marketing Planning Process'. Initially, the core values related to the scheme needs to be evaluated (Step 1) as this will enable clear and concise e-affinity marketing objectives to be set (Step 2). Then the current situation or current practice of affinity marketing on the web needs to be reviewed (Step 3). The next step is to understand affinity marketing customers' persona (Step 4). Knowing the customer is fundamental for any business striving to succeed in today's competitive environment. Following this based on the situation analysis and the customers' persona, strategies and activities for e-affinity marketing need to be identified (Step 5). Finally the last step in the process is to formulate a control mechanism with KPIs to measure and analyse the performance of the scheme (Step 6).

On the whole all the affinity groups investigated appear to have the technology capability to successfully integrate affinity scheme as part of their digital activities, as evident by the depth of the activities they have integrated for some of the functions relating to the organisations main offerings. But the activities supporting the affinity scheme appears to be limited. Thus it is apparent that affinity groups are not exerting the same level of effort on their affinity schemes digitally as they are doing so in other areas of their website. There may be a number of factors contributing to the lack of the schemes presence on the web. For instance lack of digital collaboration between the affinity partners and not having a clearly defined responsibility with regards to the management of the scheme online could be possible reasons worth exploring.

Knowledge and understanding of customer is an asset for any organisation for better segmenting and management. As Scott (2013) has suggested, if organisations can segment their customers into distinct groups then it makes it easier to create content targeted to each group identified. As it stands the affinity scheme sites investigated did not exhibit segmentation or targeting. Yet there are some known characteristics associated with affinity marketing customers (Laing et al., 2004, Mekonnen, 2012; Worhington, 2001). For instance the typologies identified as 'explorer', 'communicator' and 'supporter' can give good insight as to what affinity marketing customers associated with a professional or a charity group would expect from an affinity scheme such as an affinity credit card. Such knowledge could be used as a starting point when formulating personas for e-affinity marketing customers in different sectors.

It is undeniable that all partners involved in the triadic relationship could benefit given that the digital integration is implemented and managed correctly. Specifying clear strategies guided by the digital objectives aligned with the core values underpinning affinity marketing is crucial to the success of the scheme. The strategy then needs to be implemented and executed properly with tactics formulated that takes into consideration partners responsibility. In the past affinity marketing schemes had faced some challenges with regards to customer ownership and responsibility. This needs to be clarified as failure to do so could impair successful digital integration. Whilst the initial engagement of the customers may primarily fall under the affinity group, management of the scheme is often undertaken by the affinity scheme service provider. With regards to converging and conflicting interests relating to customer ownership the affinity group and the affinity service provider should have an agreement in place as to how to manage the customers in the event where the terms of the partnership have to be altered or if the partnership has to end. This is strongly tied with good communication, sharing information, and collaborative working without compromising customers' confidentiality. Affinity partners' efforts in promoting the scheme to customers need to be aligned. Without breaching confidentiality, a possible plan of action for the service provider could be to collaborate with the affinity group in providing periodic updates to the customers. From the customers' perspective, lack of informative continuous communication could lead to relationship weakening (Mekonnen, 2012). This relates to communication during the periods when the customer-service provider relationship was stable as well as during the process of dissolution (Mekonnen, 2012). To avoid such pitfall the digital integration of affinity scheme, needs to ensure that there is a schedule or plan in place to harness communication online. Furthermore affinity partners need to understand the nature of communication desired by different segments.

Through performance analysis continuous improvement and sustainable growth could be achieved. Web analytics will bring this to life. The right KPI need to be set for this to be effective. Affinity marketing on the web has been explored to a degree but for the most part an untapped area.

REFERENCES

Aghaei, S., Nematbakhsh, A. N., & Farsani, H. K. (2012). Evolution of the World Wide Web: From Web 1.0 to Web 4.0. *International Journal of Web & Semantic Technology*, *3*(1), 1–10. doi:10.5121/ ijwest.2012.3101

Bigné-Alcañiz, E., Currás-Pérez, R., Ruiz-Mafé, C., & Sanz-Blas, S. (2012). Cause-related marketing influence on consumer responses: The Moderating effect of Cause-brand fit. *Journal of Marketing Communications*, *18*(4), 265–283. doi:10.1080/13527266.2010.521358

Bughin, J. (2013). Brand success in the era of digital Darwinism. *Journal of Brand Strategy*, *2*(4), 355–365.

Bumell, P. (2013). What happened to charity credit cards? *News archive*. Retrieved from http://www. affinitymarketing.co.uk

Chaffey, D., Ellis-Chadwick, F., Johnson, K., & Mayer, R. (2006). *Internet Marketing Strategy, Implementation and Practice* (3rd ed.). Harlow, UK: Prentice Hall FT.

Chaffey, D., Ellis-Chadwick, F., Johnson, K., & Mayer, R. (2012). *Internet Marketing Strategy, Implementation and Practice* (5th ed.). Harlow, UK: Prentice Hall FT.

Chaffey, D., & Smith, P. R. (2008). *EMarketing Excellence Planning and optimizing your digital marketing* (3rd ed.). London, UK: Elsevier.

Chaffey, D., & Smith, P. R. (2013). *EMarketing Excellence Planning and optimizing your digital marketing* (4th ed.). New York, NY: Routledge.

Dorie, C. (2012). The End of the Expert: Why no one in marketing knows what they are doing. *Forbes News archive*. Retrieved from http://www.forbes.com

Euromonitor International. (2011, March). Global Market Information Database GMID - Country Sector Briefing – credit cards London, UK.

Finaccord. (2010). *Affinity and Partnership Marketing in UK Payment Cards and Consumer Finance*. London: UK. April 2010

Gartner. (2013). *Gartner Survey Shows U.S. Digital Marketing Budgets Average 2.5 Percent of Company Revenue*, Stamford, CT, USA. Retrieved from http://www.gartner.com/newsroom/archive/

Honoré E. (2011). *The role of Information Communication Technology in Philanthropy*, Centre of charitable giving and philanthropy NCVO/CAF.

Horne, S., Naudé, P., & Worthington, S. (2000). Knowledge Gaps between Participants in a Triadic Relationship. *International Journal of Bank Marketing*, *18*(6), 287–293. doi:10.1108/02652320010358706

Howard, B. (2012, January 28). Cancer charity loses out as bank ends credit card deal. BBC News – Business. London, UK.

Husted, S. W., & Whitehouse, F. R. Jr. (2002). Cause-Related Marketing via the World Wide Web: A Relationship Marketing Strategy. *Journal of Nonprofit & Public Sector Marketing*, *10*(1), 3–22. doi:10.1300/J054v10n01_02

International Advertising Bureau IBA. (2014). Advertising Revenue Report HY 2014 DOC.

Laing, A., Harris, F., & Mekonnen, A. (2004). Deconstructing affinity relationships: Consumers and affinity marketing. *Journal of Customer Behaviour, 3*(2), 215–228. doi:10.1362/1475392041829500

Laudon, K., & Travis, C. (2013). *E-Commerce 2013: Global Edition* (9th ed.). Harlow, UK: Pearson Education.

Macchiette, B., & Roy, A. (1992). Affinity Marketing: What is it and How does it Work? *Journal of Services Marketing, 6*(3), 47–67. doi:10.1108/08876049210035935

Mekonnen, A. (2012). *Customer-service provider relationship dissolution: the case of affinity marketing*. Thesis ((Doctoral dissertation). Open University, UK. Available from ProQuest Dissertations and Theses database. (U581639)

Mekonnen, A., Harris, F., & Laing, A. (2008). Linking products to a cause or affinity group: Does this really make them more attractive to consumers? *European Journal of Marketing, 42*(1/2), 135–153. doi:10.1108/03090560810840943

Mintel. (2000). *Affinity and Store Cards October 2000*. London, UK Mintel.

Mintel. (2004). *Affinity Marketing UK 2004*. London, UK: Mintel.

Porter, M. E. (2001). Strategy and the Internet. *Harvard Business Review, 79*(3), 62–78. PMID:11246925

Ross, J. K., Patterson, L., & Stutts, M. A. (1992). Consumer Perceptions of Organisations that Use Cause-Related Marketing. *Journal of the Academy of Marketing Science, 20*(1), 93–97. doi:10.1007/BF02723480

Ryan, D., & Jones, C. (2012). *Understanding Digital Marketing* (2nd ed.). London, UK: Kogan Page.

Sanou, B. (2014). *ICT Facts and Figures, International Telecommunication Union (ICT)*. Publication.

Schlegelmilch, B. B., & Woodruffe, H. (1995). A comparative analysis of the affinity card market in the USA and the UK. *International Journal of Bank Marketing, 13*(5), 12–23. doi:10.1108/02652329510092176

Schultz, D.E., (1996, December 18). Integration and the Internet. *Marketing News*, No. 12.

Scott, D. M. (2011). *The New Rules of Marketing & PR*. Hoboken, NJ: Wiley.

Storbacka, K., Strandvik, T., & Grönroos, C. (1994). Managing Customer Relationships for Profit: The Dynamics of Relationship Quality. *International Journal of Service Industry Management, 5*(5), 21–38. doi:10.1108/09564239410074358

Strauss, J., & Frost, R. (2014). *E-marketing* (6th ed.). New Jersey: Pearson Education Limited.

United States Government Accountability Office. (2014). CREDIT CARDS: Marketing to College Students Appears to Have Declined (GAO-14-225).

Varadarajan, P., & Menon, A. (1988). Cause-Related Marketing: A Coalignment of Marketing Strategy and Corporate Philanthropy. *Journal of Marketing, 52*(3), 58–74. doi:10.2307/1251450

Vela-McConnell, J. A. (1999). *Who is my neighbour?: Social affinity in a modern world*. Albany, NY: New York Press.

Web Analytics Association (2008), *Web Analytics Definitions*. Draft for Public Comment, September 22ⁿᵈ 2008.

Worthington, S. (1997). Affinity Credit Card Issuers and their Relationship with their Alumni Affinity Group Partners. *International Journal of Bank Marketing*, *15*(2), 39–47. doi:10.1108/02652329710160448

Worthington, S. (2001). Affinity credit cards: A critical review. *International Journal of Retail & Distribution Management*, *29*(11), 485–512. doi:10.1108/EUM0000000006174

Worthington, S., & Horne, S. (1992). Affinity Credit Cards in the United Kingdom – Card Issuer Strategies and Affinity Group Aspirations. *International Journal of Bank Marketing*, *10*(7), 3–10. doi:10.1108/02652329210021113

KEY TERMS AND DEFINITIONS

Affinity Relationship: A relationship built on the notion of cohesiveness, bonding, liking, identification and related concepts.

Affinity Scheme: A way of adding value through differentiation by designing a product that is of interest to members, employees and supporters of the said affinity group.

Cause-Related Marketing: A marketing activity where by a product is linked to a cause or non-profit organisation in return for a contribution to that cause or organisation and to make the product offering more attractive to consumers.

Digital Integration: In the context of marketing, this refers to integrating online efforts and aligning it with overall business objective.

E-Affinity Marketing: Refers to the promotion and sales of products endorsed by affinity groups through the internet.

This research was previously published in Competitive Social Media Marketing Strategies edited by Wilson Ozuem and Gordon Bowen, pages 1-19, copyright year 2016 by Business Science Reference (an imprint of IGI Global).

Chapter 7
A Case–Based Identification of Internal and External Issues for Branding Strategies

Abu Sayeed Mondal
Swami Vivekananda Institute of Science and Technology, India

Dilip Roy
University of Burdwan, India

ABSTRACT

In this chapter, the authors offer a strategic platform to pinpoint the variables for developing branding strategies. The case elicits the internal and external aspects of a brand. These two aspects are considered to be the starting point of the strategic roadmap to reach success. A detailed discussion on the brand's internal and external aspects has been made with the help of a successful case. However, the authors go beyond the identification of internal and external aspects of brands and suggest a scheme for arriving at branding strategies. Basically, these two aspects of brands have been matched and a four-cell strategic guideline has been developed. The authors call this four-cell strategic guideline C_4 strategy matrix, wherein four types of branding strategies (Continuity, Caution, Change, and Correction) are available.

INTRODUCTION

It will be more important to own markets than to own factories. The only way to own markets is to own market dominant brands. - Larry Light (1991)

Branding is all about endowing product and services with the power of a brand. It is about creating differences in the market place. The process of branding involves educating consumers "who" the product is–assigning it a name and other brand elements to help consumers recognize it–as well as "what" the product does and "why" the consumers should care (Kotler & Keller, 2006). The organizations have conducted their marketing activities with the varying degree of weights to process, product and people (internal and external) across various industrial eras. These resulted in evolution of different marketing

DOI: 10.4018/978-1-5225-5187-4.ch007

concepts: production concept, product concept, selling concept, marketing concept and holistic marketing concept. Similarly, marketers have shifted orientations in branding domain to hit the jackpot of marketing success.

The process of branding has been existent for centuries as a means to differentiate the goods of one producer from those of another (Kotler & Keller, 2006). This very concept of differentiation is later on capitalized by the modern day marketers in the competitive market place. The focus shifted from producer to product and from product to consumers. The smart marketers go beyond the products' functional attributes for brand creations. They realize the fact that brand needs to be created in the psyche of the consumers. It is the consumers' minds where brands reside and branding is all about creating a mental structure reflecting the perceptions, even the idiosyncratic ideals, of the consumers (Kotler & Keller, 2006).

BRAND: DEFINITIONS AND ITS ROLES

There exists a plenty of definitions of brand in congruence with other areas (e.g. brand loyalty) of research in marketing (Chernatony & Riley, 1998). American Marketing Association defines (1960) brand as "A name, term, design, symbol, or a combination of them, intended to identify the goods or services of one seller or group of sellers and to differentiate them from those of competitors." According to Kapferer (1992), "A brand is both, tangible and intangible, practical and symbolic, visible and invisible under conditions that are economically viable for the company".

The traditional definition of brand offered by Kotler (2000) was: "the name, associated with one or more items in the product line, which is used to identify the source of character of the item(s)."A brand is a set of dimensions added to a product or service in order to differentiate it from other products and services developed to cater to the same need. The differentiating dimensions can be functional, rational, or tangible (related to the performance of the brand's product). The differences may be in terms of symbolic, emotional or intangible represented by the brand (Kotler and Keller, 2006). Although many researchers (Watkins, 1986; Aaker, 1991; Dibb et al, 1994; Kotler et al, 1996) follow the above definition, this was criticized by other researchers for being too product oriented (Crainer, 1995) and too mechanical (Arnold, 1995). According to Dibb et al. (1997) brand can be any other feature and is not limited to name, term, design, symbol, or a combination of them. American Marketing Association (2007) redefined brand as "a name, term, design, symbol, or any other feature that identifies the seller's good or services as distinct from those of other sellers'".

According to Brown (1992) "a brand name is nothing more or less than the sum of all the mental connections people have around it." In line with Brown (1992), brand is regarded as "shorthand device of emotional and functional characteristics" by Chernatony et al (1998).

Ambler's (1992) definition of brand is: "the promise of the bundles of attributes that someone buys and provide satisfaction . . . The attributes that make up a brand may be real or illusory, rational or emotional, tangible or invisible."

The researchers like Crainer (1995) and Cooper (1987) view brand as a legal instrument. Their concepts of brand are at par with the definition offered in the Oxford English Dictionary- "A particular sort or class of goods, as indicated by the trade marks on them". Webster's New Unabridged Dictionary defines brand as: "Kind, grade or make, as indicated by a stamp, trade mark or the like."

Kapferer (1992) is highly critical of perspectives of brand as a legal entity and as a logo (McWilliam, 1993). Kapferer (1992) attempts to define brand in holistic terms:

A brand is not a product, it is the product's essence, its meaning and its direction and it defines its identity in time and space…Too often brands are examined through component parts: the brand name, its logo, design, or packaging, advertising or sponsorship, or image or name recognition or very recently, in terms of financial brand valuation. Real brand management, however, begins much earlier, with a strategy and a consistent, integrated vision. Its central concept is brand identity, not brand image.

To define brand, the researchers (e.g. Martineau, 1959; Pitcher's, 1985; Joyce, 1963; Arnold, 1992; Keller, 1993) have adopted consumer oriented perspectives. They throw light on the fact that brand is a set of associations in consumer's mind. Martineau (1959) defines brand as "as images in consumers' mind of functional and psychological attributes. Pitcher (1985) holds that brand is a consumer's idea of a product. According to Keeble (1991), "a brand becomes a brand as soon as it comes in contact with the consumers." Gardner and Levy's (1955) definition, which provides a synthesis between identity and image, is:

A brand name is more than the label employed to differentiate among the manufacturers of a product. It is a complex symbol that represents a variety of ideas and attributes. It tells the consumers many things, not only by the way it sounds (its literal meaning if it has one), but, more important via the body of associations it has built up and acquired as public object over a period of time.

The definition of brand should incorporate the concept of added value which strikes a difference between brand and product (Jones, 1986). Jones (1986) defines brand as a "product that provides functional benefits plus added values that some consumers value enough to buy." The concept of added value finds an important place in the definition provided by de Chernatony and McDonald (1994):

Brands are an identifiable product, service, person or place augmented in such a way that the buyer or user perceives relevant unique added values which match their needs more closely.

A brand is not a name, logo, sign, symbol, advertisement, or spokesperson. A brand is not everything that an organization wants people, especially its target markets, to feel and believe about its products and services (Van deen Heever, 2000). A brand is a mixture of tangible and intangible attributes, symbolized in a trademark, which if properly managed, creates influence and generates value (Duncan, 2005).

Keller (2003) offers an account of the various roles played by brands. The roles played by the brand from consumer's point of view are summarized in the following points:

- Identification of source of product,
- Assignment of responsibility to product maker,
- Risk reducer,
- Search cost reducer,
- Establishes bond with the maker of a product,
- Serves as symbolic devise, and
- Signal of quality. (Source: Keller, 2003).

According to Davis (2002), the role of strong brands from company perspectives are considered in the following points:

- Generation of repeat business due to brand loyalty.
- Brand-based price premiums offer higher margins for the company.
- Strong brands endow credibility to the new products introduced in the market.
- Makes company less vulnerable to competitive actions because of strong brand's valued and sustainable point of differentiation.
- Brand strength enables company attract the best employees and keeping its satisfied employees.
- Strong brand facilitates greater shareholder and stakeholder returns.

BRANDING: A HISTORICAL OVERVIEW

The practice of branding is as old as human civilization. In ancient market place people used branding using symbols, signs, posters, pictorial symbols and trademarks. It was started ever since people owned cattle or created goods to be engaged in exchange. At the core of all branding activities there was human desire to be of someone consequence, to create a personal or social identity, to represent ownership, to stand out and to possess a good reputation. Branding was started as a sign to mean what an object is and then gradually took the form of naming it (Bastos & Levy, 2012). To ensure the ownership of cattle and sheep, they were branded with paint or pine tar and even with hot irons. Craftsmen used imprinted trademarks on the goods to denote the creator or the origin. Humans were branded too. Slaves were marked for assigning their ownership. For denouncing the criminals with disgrace, they were branded.

In primitive times the river side civilizations (Babylon, Egypt, and Greece) largely formed the major markets for trading and selling of goods. The goods were arrived at the riverside markets on ship. There were barkers who persuaded customers to buy with their barked out sales pitches describing spices, rugs, wines and other items. In Egypt information related to goods were written on papyrus papers which were posted on the walls and trees. Wall writings to advertise the goods were also in vogue. Writing on the walls in ancient city of Pompeii bore witness to this fact. To reach the illiterate mass pictorial signs were hung by the merchants and the store fronts were painted with colors. The same practices were prevalent in ancient Greece and Rome. In china at that time trade fairs were held. In the trade fairs the hawkers pitched displayed items. Branding was transformed from denotation to connotations implying something more than a name (Bastos & Levy, 2012). Negative connotations attached with branding started losing ground with the positive and commercial aspects taking upper hand.

At the outset of the Middle Ages commerce fell significantly with the collapse of the Roman Empire. Craftsmen took the back seat. Common mass were mostly illiterate except the clergy and a few rare people. At that time town criers played the major role of spreading information about goods and services. In the thirteenth century, the Magna Carta, the end of feudalism and trade between east and west brought betterment to the lives of people living in town. It was followed by the revival of crafts and emergence of the middle class. There was formation of craft guilds to control trade. The guild made the proprietary marks compulsory. Hand written handbills were distributed to advertise and woe customers. The merchants hung signs to help customers identify them and their type of business.

In China different forms of early branding and advertising were used with printed wrappers, banners, painted lanterns, painted pictures, and signboards, as well as printed advertisements. The Chinese did much progress in printing technology which, along with their great interests in painting, enabled them to devise these early methods of branding.

Invention of printing press by Johannes Gutenberg in 1448 in Germany ushered in a new era in branding and advertisement. The usage of this invention rapidly spread across Europe. From then it became very easy to reach public with printed information about the products and services and the popularity of advertising rose. By the late fifteen tenth century, the first English handbill announcing the availability of a book came into existence. The streets of London found its walls posted with huge numbers of printed advertisements promoting hawking goods. The first advertisement in the newspaper appeared in 1625 in England. The first known newspaper advertisement in America appeared in Boston Newsletter in 1704. The advertisements were restricted to the one section of the newspapers. These advertisements were mere the simple announcements about products and services and many newspapers repeated a single line copy of the advertisements several times to grab the attention of the customers. All these marked the advent of modern branding practices.

DEVELOPMENT OF BRANDING CONCEPTS VIS-À-VIS INDUSTRIAL DEVELOPMENT

Although the initiation of modern business practices dates back to 1820-30, the period from 1820-1900 was a land mark era in the history of management. This period was noted for unprecedented creative turbulence. Breakthroughs in the field of science and technology and economic unification due to construction of roads, rails and canals led towards a rapid industrial movement. The result was the evolution of modern business firms. This period was known as era of initiation or Industrial Revolution. Development of production technology and organization technology were the pre-occupations of the entrepreneurs. Not much time was spent for looking into the detailed operational aspect of the enterprises. Not much thought was devoted to branding. However, branding started evolving as a part of business activity. The product offering under brand names was introduced. The consumers started liking packaged branded goods. The practice of buying commodities out of barrels was fast losing ground. People wanted to buy readymade clothing, shoes and sealed goods for improved freshness. Branding involved helping consumers identify the products of their choices. For this purpose the manufactures sought to create visual identities. Manufacturers introduced labels, boxes and wrappers. Branding was aided by early form of advertising which aimed at disseminating information about goods to consumers. This period may well be called identification oriented branding era.

From 1900 onwards business houses started the consolidation effort to capitalize on the momentum of growth achieved in the previous era. In the previous era the business firms relied on the external technological environment and became successful. During this period, focus shifted to internal organizational environment to improve upon the production technology. The idea was to gain in proficiency in production by progressively reducing the average cost of production. Availability of cheap labor further provided the impetus to this effort. The market size was huge due to less number of competitors and demand was massive. The goods produced in bulk to meet this huge demand enabled the manufactures to enjoy the advantage of economies of scale. As result, the product was offered at the lowest possible price to the consumers who were primarily price-oriented. This phenomenon further pulled the demand in the market place. Thus, high volume and low price became the magic mantra of management. This continued till 1930's and the period is known as era of mass production. In mass production era basic products were offered to the consumers. Branding embraced the task of endorsing the basic commodity like products. Marketing became just an extension of production activity. Low priced branded products dominated the consumer economy created as a result of industrial growth. Through branding attempt was made to create identification systems for the manufacturers. Branding helped corporations achieve a visual image in the wake of minimum environmental challenges and little political interferences in business. However, branding did not restrict itself into the designing of logo or trade mark. Advertising agencies were evolved with the discovery new media types like radio and television. The manufacturers started sponsoring the radio programs to promote their brands. "Overblown" copy writing styles and melodramatic taglines were in vogue. This period of branding may be called generic branding era.

From 1930's another significant change was felt in the external business environment. Unlike the previous era, consumers started moving away from the low priced standard items. They were no longer satisfied with basic performance of these products. They demanded something more than that. Increasing number of affluent class of consumers pushed this trend. They were gradually getting interested in the high quality products without paying heed to the price of the same. Competition sneaked in the market. So, the concept of product differentiation was introduced to address this issue. It made the business firms adopt marketing orientation. The managers started paying more attention to the external environmental challenges. .Thus, a shift towards an extroverted perspective took place. New problem-solving approaches were developed. New types of organizational structures were devised. The managers formed a different attitude to arrest the uncertainty of business dynamics. This period is known as mass marketing era which continued till the last of 19350's. In this era, branding started attracting serious thoughts. It happened especially due to focus of business shifted from production to product. There was pressing need to make the consumers aware of the differentiated quality of the product. This task was achieved through creating images of brands' promised benefits to consumers. Initially images of brand's functional benefits (to satisfy the "utilitarian" needs of the consumers) were depicted; later on symbolic benefits (to satisfy the psychological and social needs of the consumers) were stressed upon. Thus, creating brand image became be all and end all of branding. The literature on branding started emerging rapidly and increased focus to brand image signaled the departure from viewing brands as merely from identifiers to viewing them in terms of images (Gardner & Levy 1955; Oxenfeldt & Swann 1964; White 1959). These images were the perceptions about the brands created by the firms (Park et al. 1986) to secure competitive advantages and their standing in the market place (Welcker, 1949). Communicating brand image became necessary for the firms to help consumers to both differentiate a brand from its competitors (DiMingo, 1988; Reynolds and Gutman, 1984) and identify the needs that a brand promised to satisfy (Roth, 1995).

During the late 1950's academic research on branding threw light on the fact that it became difficult for the consumers to differentiate brands at the time of purchase considering functional benefits that a brand promised to offer. Gardener and Levy (1955) pointed out that the consumers could not discern the differences among brands as, more or less, all the brands in the product category made similar claims of superiority. The researchers argued that the firms must satisfy the symbolic needs created as a result of the consumers' desire for self-enhancement, social position, group membership, ego-identification (Park et. al, 1986). Advertising professionals and marketing practitioners went beyond this and they started embedding human characteristics to the bands to create symbolic brand image. In 1958 Martineau used the word 'brand personality' to denote non-material dimensions that contributed to a store's special image. To advertising agencies the popular copy strategies were creation of brand image through projection of brand personality. This was how image-oriented branding era prevailed in the mass marketing era. The branding concepts that ruled the image-oriented branding era were- brand image and brand personality.

During the mid 1960's organizations were found establishing style and speed of progress. A new industrial era- the Age of Discontinuity- began. This period was marked by unforeseen environmental turbulence coupled with changes in business dynamics and business boundaries. Technological and political changes also contributed to create an environment of "discrete changes" (Roy, 2006). Organizations became information dependent to deal with the extreme uncertainty in the business environment. Shortening of product life cycle proved to be the new success mantra. Product line extension emerged as the strategic options for the many firms. Branding turned into a complex job due to brand proliferation. Noise level in the market place rose in an unprecedented way. Chaos reigned supreme as a result of marketers' attempt to reach consumers' minds with the messages of large portfolio of products and brands. Advertising failed to do the job as compared to the previous eras (Trout and Ries, 1972). In Trout & Ries' (1972) own words the state-of-affairs were brought to light:

Today's marketplace is no longer responsive to strategies that worked in the past. There are just too many products, too many companies and too much marketing noise. We have become an over communicated society.

Al Ries and Jack Trout advocated a new approach to branding what they called brand positioning. This concept evolved as an epoch making discovery in the field of branding. Positioning involved the act of making the brands secure a distinctive place in the minds of the target market through creation of value proposition for the consumers and clarification of brand's essence. According to Al Ries and Jack Trout (1982):

Positioning starts with a product. A piece of merchandise, a service, a company, an institution or even a person... But Positioning is not what you do to a product. Positioning is what you do to the mind of the prospect. That is, you position the product in the mind of the prospect.

The idea behind the positioning concept was not to change the mind of the prospect, as traditional advertising used to do through creation of brand image; rather the mission was to be in the mind itself. Thus, positioning stood out as the key concept in the communication- oriented branding era which lasted till the late 1990's.

During the mid of 1980's, researcher like Kapferer (1986) added a new perspective to communication-oriented branding. He argued that effective communication of brand should ensure sending out messages and their receiving at the consumers' end. He propounded the brand identity concept based on the communication model involving receiver and sender. According to him, brand must convey its identity in order to thrive and survive in the midst of "hurly-burly" created in the marketplace due to increased number media and high volume of advertising. He offered brand identity prism with six aspects of a brand- physique, personality, culture, relationship, consumer's reflection and self-image. Brand identity concept proved useful in case of managing multi-product brands. This issue could not get resolved through positioning concept. Unlike brand identity, brand positioning failed to reveal the brand's richness of meaning and uncover all its capabilities. Brand identity also enabled brand overcome the lacuna of brand image which focused too much on the brand appearance rather than brand essence (Kapferer, 2000). This how, brand identity emerged as a necessary concept in *communication-oriented* branding era (lasted till last half of 1990's) leaving behind the concepts of brand image, brand personality and brand positioning.

The current era, which started in the late 1990's, is the era of Reversing Industrial Revolutions as advocated by Hammer (1997). In the era of Industrial Revolution effective management practice involved fragmented and simple individual tasks. The present era calls for coordination and integration amongst these fragmented tasks and complex organizational processes. These complex organizational processes lead to high quality low cost performances on the part of the individuals who are now required to do the large components of the work. To ensure integration amongst different functional activities become the focal point of the business strategy. The firms are aiming to create value for its stakeholders to out-perform the rivals in a customer-centric environment (Roy, 2006). Superior customer value so created is brought to the customers through brands. Researchers (Aaker, 1991; Keller, 1993) argue that brand is one of the most important assets to the company. They support their arguments with the finding of the fact that a brand provides value to the firm as it possesses consumer awareness, customer loyalty and perceived quality. Brand has other proprietary assets in terms of access to critical distribution channels or to patents and brand associations; such as personality associations (Batra, Myers and Aaker, 2006). This new perspective to branding is known as the concept of brand equity which is enshrined in the branding literature as a path-breaking discovery. The brand equity concept, which aims to pinpoint the innate value of the brand, makes the practitioners realize that brands must be managed at a much higher level in the organization. Branding becomes the responsibility of the CEOs rather than being mere a communication issue (Kapferer, 2006). Business strategy should be the prime driver of brand strategy and the organization need to be adjusted to brand building with development of structures, cultures, people and systems supportive of brand building (Aaker, 2006). Thus, a new era–innate value oriented branding era–sets in.

BRANDING: A REVIEW OF LITERATURE

Branding discipline has attracted tremendous attention from the side of scholars and academicians in the 1990s. The researchers have dealt with a lot of issues in branding- replacement cost (Aaker, 1992), Price premiums (Aaker, 1992), Stock price analysis (Simon & Sullivian, 1990), and brand loyalty analysis (Fieldwick, 1996). Branding and marketing approach of Jenester & Smith (2005) and Schultz & Hatch (2003) is primarily based on organizational culture & core values which, according to them, are the building blocks of a brand. Cobb-Walgreen (1995) explores brand perception based on consumer preferences, where as Buzzel and Gale (1987) bring in economic perspectives centered on objective, financial and market based criteria. Ohnemus et al (2009) introduces resource based and economic views on branding which seek to address the questions - "are companies spending adequate resources on establishing and maintaining the optimal value of their brands, and can it be measured on their financial results?" Kerin and Sethuraman (1998) suggest a link between firm's enhanced branding efforts and higher market value, but they do not confirm that brand value growth at firm level necessarily ensures a proportionate growth in shareholder value. Olins (1989) proposes three types of branding strategies – "monolithic" (usage of one name and visual style throughout by the corporation. E.g. – Kellog), "endorsed" (usage of corporate identity along with name of subsidiaries having diverse visual styles. e.g. ICI), "branded" (having products under exclusively different brand names .E.g. - Procter & Gambles). Aaker (1991) argues that Olins' branding systems do not touch upon "some of the complexes of brand structures" due to "predominance of nested branding."On the other hand, some researchers report the benefits a firm can get by adopting Olins' approach. Monolithic branding strategy offers brand consistency, advantage out of deployment of corporate reputation in a number of products, economies of scale in advertising (Alessandari & Alessandari 2004, Olins 1990). Levy (1999) argues that emphasis on brand intangibles proves to be the important and unique aspect of branding. These intangibles elements help marketers differentiate their brands with consumers (Park, Jaworski and MacInnis 1986). Actual or aspirational user imagery, purchase and consumption imagery, history, heritage and experiences are the brand associations that form the intangible elements of brands (Keller 2001). Aaker (1999) explores different dimensions of brand personality and finds that these dimensions affect different types of people in different consumption settings. But, the conceptual validity of Aaker's brand personality scale has been challenged by Azoulay and Kapferer (2003). As brands are recognized as intangible assets, focus has been shifted to building, measuring and managing brand equity (Kapferer 2005; Keller 1993, 2003). Brand extension has come out as one of the critical areas of branding research (Czellar 2003). The studies of Aaker and Keller (1990), Klink and Smith (2001) show that successful extension is dependent on consumers' perception of fit between a new extension and parent brand. Consumers' evaluation of brand extension is largely affected by the positively evaluated symbolic brand associations (Reddy, Holak, and Bhat 1994; Park, Milberg and Lawson 1991). Consumer knowledge of the parent and extension categories also influences extension success (Moreau et al, 2001). Roy and Banerjee (2007) proposes CARE (credibility building, alteration, relationship building and expansion) –in strategies for integration of brand identity and brand image to cement a lasting bond of the brand with its consumers. The studies of Choi and Winterich (2013) investigate how moral identity of brand affects out-group brand attitudes of the consumers.

GENERATING FRESH INSIGHTS TO BRANDING STRATEGIES

In Search of a Starting Point

Branding brings benefits for the organization enabling the marketers to strategically address its products and markets. As a result, in most of the product categories marketing programs have largely become brand based. The major task that preoccupies the marketers is to develop branding strategies to triumph in the market place. Strategic thinking in terms of brand extension, brand revitalization, brand positioning and brand repositioning has surely empowered the brand managers. On the other hand, the concept of brand identity proves to be the password to unlock the mystery of branding. Although we talk of importance of branding strategies to be the key to success, conceiving strategies is not always easy on the part of the marketers. What could be the starting point of formulating branding strategies is also a baffling question.

C_4 Strategy Matrix: A Road Map to Branding Strategies

In various strategic approaches available in the literature, strategies have been developed through a matching process of the organization's internal factors and the factors external to it. Here, drawing an analogy with the strategic approach we would propose an approach involving a matching process of the brand's internal and external elements- internal effort and external realization. Internal effort signifies branding efforts to ensure brand's specific mode of communication, its adjustments to the external environment and its physical appearance. External realization is the brand's external effect realized by the consumers. The two dimensions – internal effort and external realization- vary from low to high and their interplay gives rise to four branding strategies- continuity, caution, change and correction.

Figure 1. C₄ strategy matrix

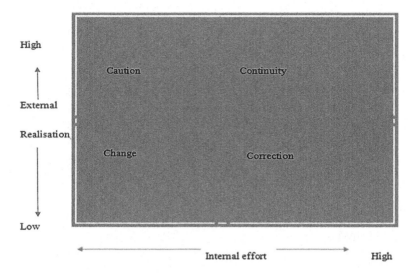

Details of the Branding Strategies

Continuity

When high degree of internal effort of branding has high external realization, continuity is the most suitable strategic choice. In this situation what brand is and how brand communicates are properly understood and perceived by the consumers in a highly favorable way. Here, brand requires investment in communication to maintain its strong strategic position. Since brand's embedded personality traits and physical qualities generate favorable external realization, brand should keep up the communication with these aspects as the main theme of communication. If the choice of brand name alludes to the brand's specific physicality and personality type and has significant contribution to creative strategy, highlighting of the same brand name should be considered. Personality and appearance of brand's creator may also play significant role in the brand theme. Communication should be maintained supporting this creator brand relationship. Sometimes type of product that brand endorses exhibits what the brand actually is or wants to be. If this is operating, communication should continue supporting that product or those product features should be made visible. No alteration in logo and visual symbol is desirable

Caution

Need for caution strategy arises when external realization of brand is high, even if internal effort for brand building has not been exerted. In this situation brand enjoys a favorable competitive position. Complacency on the part of the brand managers should be avoided. Here high external image is achieved due to functional performance of brand or due to attractive price- quality relationship or because of pioneer advantage of the brand in the product category. Under caution strategy possible areas of attack from the side of the competitor brands are to be ascertained. Means of protecting the brand need to be explored. Scope of further brand building is to be investigated through consumer research. High external realization of brand must be included in the content of advertising. If the users of the brand possess specific personality types and physical stature, these are to be embedded in the brand. Further investment in advertising is also a feasible proposition and it could serve as defense shield of the brand.

Change

This situation represents weakest strategic position of the brand. Here internal effort for brand building is not properly made. In view of the low internal effort and low external situation, this position poses a real problem to the brand managers. Failure in implementation of the caution strategy may lead to this situation also. Change strategy means discrete alteration in branding activities. There are two alternatives to the brand mangers. Management can drop the idea of brand building under the same creative strategy, because low external realization nullifies further allocation of resources. Otherwise, brand can be revived through change of brand name, total change in visual symbols or logos or packaging. Total change in either physique or personality or in both can be done. Selective promotion can be undertaken to make the brand turn around.

Correction

High internal effort and low external realization calls for correction strategy. When consumers do not perceive the brand building effort in a favorable way, this situation arises. The consequence of failure of development strategy can be this situation. It is also notable that if continuity strategy fails to retain the strong position of the brand, brand enters in this position. Under this strategy bottle necks in theme of the brand is to be eliminated. If there exists an abstract concept in communication aspect and physicality of the brand, that is to be simplified. Clarity of the content of advertising needs to be improved. Media plan of the brand is to be reengineered.

THE CASE OF SHAHNAZ HERBALS

Shahnaz Herbals was founded in 1970 by Shahnaz Hussain in her house in Delhi, India. The company was initially formed to offer beauty treatments to Indian women and later started offering its own beauty products. At the time of inception of Shahnaz Herbals Indian beauty and beauty service industry services were unorganized and fragmented. Basic beauty products like cold cream, shampoo, hair oil and toilet soap were available in the market for the consumers. People used to associate cosmetics with makeup items largely. All these products were chemical based. Shahnaz offered alternative methods of beauty services and alternative products- herbal method and herbal cosmetics- before the big companies in India could capture the markets with their existing cosmetics based products on which a good number of consumers were getting dependent to look good. Within three decades Shahnaz Herbals, with an estimated global worth of $ 500 million, had more than 350 products and 400 franchise salons operating in 138 countries across the world. The company, according to an FMCG analyst, registered annual turnover of Rs 650 crore. Shahnaz Herbals compete in India with the formidable skincare players like L'Oreal, Clarin's and BodyShop in Rs 5000 crore Indian beauty Industry which is expected, as per ASSOCHAM, to be Rs 10000 crore by 2014. The mid-to-upper market positioned aurvedic brand received tremendous popularity in Indian and international markets. Shahnaz herbals were the first Asian beauty products company to sell its products through reputed global stores like Bloomingdale's (New York), Galleries Lafayette (Paris), Seibu (Japan), Harrods, Selfridges (London) and La Rinaeccente(Milan).

The success of the company owes much to the Shanaz Hussain's branding which seems like an enigma to branding gurus and practitioners. "You (Husain) violate every norm that we teach of setting aside a part of your budget for advertising and publicity. It is not only her franchise-based enterprise but also her marketing strategies that are truly unique" said Dr Samuel Hayes, finance guru and Harvard Business School professor, about Shahnaz's branding. The 3 Cs – creator, creation and communication – particularly shape the realm of it. 'Creator' stands for Shahnaz Husain, creation denotes the brands and 'communication' is the iconoclastic approaches of the 'creator' making the 'creation' interact with the consumers.

Unlike the top international cosmetic brands which invest whopping amount in advertising, Shahnaz Husain did not advertise till the year 2008. Her brand's promise to offer customized and an alternative solution to the consumers were communicated through word-of-mouth publicity. "Advertising is a paid form of publicity; I have never relied on it" said Shahnaz.

Shahnaz Hussain brands are by far the best representatives of Shahnaz Hussain herself. She has put in all her experience, expertise, and rigorous training of ten years in chemistry and cosmetology in the various leading beauty schools of the west including L'Oréal and Schwarzkopf in her brands. Shahnaz becomes a prolific writer of beauty columns in reputed newspapers and magazines vouching for the benefits of the herbal cosmetics and cautioning against the use of chemical based products. She arranges seminars and conferences for this purpose on a regular basis. It has become a regular practice for her to reply personally to letters seeking beauty solutions. Mostly her brands carry her names and photographs to make consumers choose the brands counting on her expertise and experience. In Shahnaz's own words, "If it bears my name, it catches on". Shahnaz is also seen inaugurating her salons in various cities across the world wearing embroidered, self -designed clothes and with Louis Vuitton bag in her hands. In a word, Shahnaz Hussain is the real figurehead shaping the mode of communication of what the brand actually is.

For Shahnaz Hussain selling her beauty products and treatments is selling 5000 year old Indian civilization in a jar. In the startup years, she used to sell her own formulations in bottles bought from the local markets and she labeled them herself. One of her early creation is Shagrin which she formulated with the recipe of rice, rose petals, herbs and sandalwood oil. She has taken much care in packaging of her brands. She herself has visited khurja (a place in India known for pottery design going back centuries) for examining the pottery design and choosing jars for packaging for her products. The product ranges are based on specific extracts and accordingly they have been named like flower power, neem, oxygen, pearl concepts, 24 carat gold, and diamond collection etc. The physical appearances of the brands signify the natural ingredients of these products.

In 1980 Shahnaz Herbals went international with the participation of the festival of India in London. The huge customer acceptance of Shahnaz Hussain brands in Selfridges, London broke the stores cosmetic sales record for the sales of worth £2700 in two hours. The company broke another record in 2010 at Selfridges, London by selling the products of worth £4334 in a single transaction to an individual customer. In Galeries Lafayette (in Paris), the world's most prestigious cosmetic store, all the consignments were sold out during the India festival.

Shahnaz adopted franchise-based marketing strategies which enabled the brand Shahnaz Hussain to become the household names in India .The first Shahnaz Herbal franchise clinic was started in Kolkata in 1979. Shahnaz Hussain products are primarily sold through the franchise saloons. When a new salon is launched, it is done first in the international markets. In these salons clients are recommended products after diagnosis and clinical analysis of the skin and scalp condition.

The branding addressed the trend of rapid growth of male grooming products in the market. The company became one of the earliest players in the male hair and skin care market. Shahnaz Hussain brand was extended to the male segment with the launch of Shahnaz Herbal Salon for men in 1993.

The company plans to expand its operations in the markets across the globe through international branding, cementing the global franchise distribution channel and ensuring distribution of the brands in the unrepresented new markets by appointing distributors. It aims to improve its presence in major countries like USA, Canada, Kazakhstan and Kuwait, Bahrain, Oman, Australia, Singapore, Malaysia, South East Asia, New Zealand and other CIS countries including Russia, Belarus and Latvia by 2015.

CASE ANALYSIS

The close look at the above case enables us to identify two basic aspects of brand- one is the internal aspect and the other one is the internal aspect. From the above case it is evident how Shahnaz Hussain has played a pivotal role in making the brand effectively communicate with the consumers and making the consumers understand what the brand actually is. She truly defines the credo of the brand; she devises the momentum to reach success. Accordingly the brand is physically built. These two aspects can be considered under the internal aspect of a brand and this internal aspect is achieved through organization's internal brand building efforts.

One of the key external aspects of Shahnaz Hussain brands is consumers' projected image. Consumer's projected image is how the consumers want to be seen themselves after using the brand. This aspect unfolds the consumers' desire to move from being to becoming. In this case, consumers' projected image can be well understood by the brands' evoked image of the persons for whom beauty is an achievable reality, thanks to the Shahnaz Hussain brands. This aspect also gets integrated with the internal expects of the brands and contribute to brands' external effects. The brands' innovative products, which are the results of prolonged research and development activities, appeal to the consumers. Shahnaz Hussain's introduction of clinical system with client card- diagnosis and clinical analysis of the skin and scalp condition before recommending the products and individual consultations and treatments, is favorably perceived by the consumers. Shahnaz Hussain brands become the choice of women and men of India and foreign countries.

Her inauguration of salons, giving free consultation and pioneering of herbal products attracted media coverage and did publicity for her brands. Large pool of satisfied customer base and positive word of mouth has provided an impetus to Shahnaz Hussain brands. Uncompromising quality and alternative herbal based products behind the brands to potentially harmful chemical based ones win the minds of the many consumers. They are made more skin conscious, when they are aware of Shahnaz Hussain brands or interact with it. They also develop uncompromising attitude towards themselves at the time of making purchase decisions. The consumers' skin consciousness and uncompromising attitude toward themselves form the consumer's self-portrayal. Consumer's projected image and consumer's self portrayal, as mentioned above, are purely the consumer centric issues. These two issues form the external realization of the brand. Thus, the above case helps us derive two basic issues – internal effort and external realization- on which the branding strategies can be developed.

CONCLUSION

In this above case we have examined that there is high degree of internal effort for brand building both from communication and physicality perspectives. At the same time the high internal effort is accordingly realized by the consumers of the Shanaz Hussain brands. As per the C_4 strategy matrix when internal effort is high and external realization is also high, the recommended strategy is continuity strategy. The courses of action to be taken under continuity strategy are that investment in communication to maintain the strong position of the brand and advertising campaign is to be undertaken in selected media incorporating contribution of Shahnaz Hussain as brand's creator. Under the same creative strategy physical attributes of the brand are to be highlighted without any alteration in logo or visual symbols.

REFERENCES

Aaker, D. (1991). *Managing brand equity: Capitalizing on the value of a brand name*. New York: The Free Press.

Aaker, D. A. (1991). *Managing brand equity*. New York: Free Press.

Aaker, D. A. (1992). Managing the most important asset: Brand equity. *Strategy and Leadership*, *20*(5), 56–59. doi:10.1108/eb054384

Aaker, D. A., & Keller, K. L. (1990). Consumer evaluations of brand extensions. *Journal of Marketing*, *54*(1), 27–41. doi:10.2307/1252171

Aaker, J. L. (1999). The malleable self: The role of self-expression in persuasion. *JMR, Journal of Marketing Research*, *36*(2), 45–57. doi:10.2307/3151914

Alessandri, S. W., & Alessandri, T. (2004). Promoting and protecting corporate identity: The importance of organizational and industry context. *Corporate Reputation Review*, *7*(3), 252–268. doi:10.1057/palgrave.crr.1540224

Ambler, T. (1992). *Need-to-know-marketing*. London: Century Business.

American Marketing Association. (1960). *Marketing definitions: A glossary of marketing terms*. Chicago: IL AMA.

Ries, A., & Trout, J. (1982). *Positioning: The battle for your mind*. New York: Warner Books.

Arnold, D. (1992). *The handbook of brand management*. The Economist Books.

Aaker, D. A. (1991). Foreword. In *Managing brand equity* (p. ix). New York: The Free Press.

Azoulay, A., & Kapferer, J.-N. (2003). Do brand personality scales really measure brand personality? *Journal of Brand Management*, *11*(2), 143–155. doi:10.1057/palgrave.bm.2540162

Bastos, W., & Levy, S. J. (2012). A history of the concept of branding: Practice and theory. *Journal of Historical Research in Marketing*, *4*(3), 347–368. doi:10.1108/17557501211252934

Batra, R., Mayers, J. G., & Aaker, D. A. (2006). *Advertising management*. Delhi: Pearson Education.

Brown, G. (1992). *People, brands and advertising*. Warwick, UK: Millward Brown International.

Buzzell, R. D., & Gale, B. T. (1987). *The PIMS principle- Linking strategy to performance*. New York: Free Press.

Chernatony, L. D., & Riley, F. D. (1998). Defining a "brand": Beyond the literature with the experts' interpretations. *Journal of Marketing Management, 14*(5), 417–443. doi:10.1362/026725798784867798

Choi, W. J., & Winterich, K. P. (2013). Can brands move in from outside? How moral identity enhances out-group brand attitudes. *Journal of Marketing, 77*(2), 96–111. doi:10.1509/jm.11.0544

Cobb-Walgren, C. J., Ruble, C. A., & Donthu, N. (1995). Brand equity, brand preference, and purchase intent. *Journal of Advertising, 24*(3), 25–40. doi:10.1080/00913367.1995.10673481

Crainer, S. (1995). *The real power of brands: Making brands work for competitive advantage*. London: Pitman Publishing.

Czellar, S. (2003). Consumer attitude toward brand extensions: An integrative model and research propositions. *International Journal of Research in Marketing, 20*(1), 97–115.

Daniels, C. (2013). *Shahnaz Husain: The free spirit of an entrepreneur*. Retrieved February 17, 2014 http://news.in.msn.com/her_courage/shahnaz-husain-the-free-spirit-of-an-entrepreneur

Davis, S. (2002). Brand asset management: How businesses can profit from the power of brand. *Journal of Consumer Marketing, 19*(4), 351–358. doi:10.1108/07363760210433654

de Chernatony, L., & McDonald, M. (1994). *Creating powerful brands*. Oxford, UK: Butterworth-Heinemann.

Dibb, S., Simkin, L., Pride, W. M., & Ferrell, O. C. (1994). *Marketing: Concepts and strategies* (2nd ed.). Boston: Houghton Mifflin.

Dibb, S., Simkin, L., Pride, W. M., & Ferrell, O. C. (1997). *Marketing: Concepts and strategies* (3rd ed.). Boston: Houghton Mifflin.

DiMingo, E. (1988). The fine art of positioning. *The Journal of Business Strategy, 9*(2), 34–38. doi:10.1108/eb039211 PMID:10303386

Duncan, T. (2005). *Advertising & IMC*. New York: McGraw-Hill.

Fieldwick, P. (1996). What is brand equity anyway, and how do you measure it? *Journal of the Market Research Society, 38*(2), 85–104.

Flock, E. (2009). *If it bears my name: It catches on*. Retrieved February 19, 2014 http://forbesindia.com/printcontent/4702

Gardner, B. B., & Levy, S. J. (1955). The product and the brand. *Harvard Business Review, 33*, 33–39.

Hammer, M. (1997). Beyond the end of management. In *Rethinking the future*. London: Nicholas Barely Publishing.

Jenster, P. V., Hayes, H. M., & Smith, D. E. (2005). *Managing business marketing and sales- An international perspective.* Copenhagen Business School Press.

Jones, J. P. (1986). *What's in a name?* Aldershot, UK: Gower.

Joyce, T. (1963). Techniques of brand image measurement. In *New developments in research* (pp. 45–63). London: Market Research Society.

Kapferer, J.-N. (1986), "Beyond positioning, retailer's identity", paper presented at Esomar Seminar, 4-6 June, Brussels.

Kapferer, J.-N. (1992). *Strategic brand management.* London: Kogan Page.

Kapferer, J.-N. (2000). *Strategic brand management.* New Delhi: Kogan Page India.

Kapferer, J.-N. (2005). *Strategic brand management.* London, UK: Kogan Page.

Keeble, G. (1991). Creativity and the brand. In *Understanding brands by 10 people who do* (pp. 167–182). London: Kogan Page.

Keller, K. L. (1993). Conceptualizing, measuring, and managing customer-based brand equity. *Journal of Marketing, 57*(1), 1–22. doi:10.2307/1252054

Keller, K. L. (1993). Conceptualizing, measuring and managing customer- based brand equity. *Journal of Marketing, 57*(1), 1–22. doi:10.2307/1252054

Keller, K. L. (2001). *Building customer based brand equity: A blue print for creating strong brands.* Cambridge, MA: Marketing Science Institute.

Keller, K. L. (2003). *Strategic brand management: Building, measuring, and managing brand equity* (2nd ed.). Upper Saddle River, NJ: Prentice Hall.

Kerin, R., & Sethuraman, R. (1998). Exploring the brand value shareholder value nexus for consumer goods companies. *Journal of the Academy of Marketing Science, 26*(4), 260–274. doi:10.1177/0092070398264001

Klink, R. R., & Smith, D. C. (2001). Threats to external validity of brand extension research. *JMR, Journal of Marketing Research, 38*(3), 326–335. doi:10.1509/jmkr.38.3.326.18864

Kotler, P. (2000). *Marketing management.* Upper Saddle River, NJ: Prentice Hall.

Kotler, P., Armstrong, G., Saunders, J., & Wong, V. (1996). *Principles of marketing.* Hemel Hempstead, UK: Prentice Hall Europe.

Kotler, P., & Keller, K. L. (2006). *Marketing management.* New Delhi: Prentice Hall of India Private Limited.

Levy, S. J. (1999). *Brands, consumers, symbols and research: Sydney J. Levy on marketing.* Thousand Oaks, CA: Sage publications.

Martineau, P. (1958). The personality of a retail store. *Harvard Business Review, 36,* 47–55.

Martineau, P. (1959). Sharper focus for the corporate image. *Harvard Business Review, 36*(1), 49–58.

McWilliam, G. (1993). A tale of two gurus: Aaker and Kapferer on brands. *International Journal of Research in Marketing, 10,* 105–111.

Moreau, P., Lehmann, D. R., & Markman, A. B. (2001). Entrenched knowledge structures and consumer response to new products. *JMR, Journal of Marketing Research, 38*(1), 14–29. doi:10.1509/jmkr.38.1.14.18836

Ohnemus, L., & Jenster, P. V. (2009). Corporate brand thrust and financial performance. *International Studies of Management & Organization, 7*(4), 84–107.

Olins, W. (1989). *Corporate identity: Making business strategy visible through design.* London: Thames and Hudson.

Olins, W. (1990). *The Wolff Olins guide to corporate identity.* Ashgate Publishing.

Oxenfeldt, A. R., & Swann, C. (1964). *Management of the advertising function.* Belmont, CA: Wadsworth.

Park, C. W., Jaworski, B. J., & MacInnis, D. J. (1986). Strategic brand concept-image management. *Journal of Marketing, 50*(4), 135–145. doi:10.2307/1251291

Park, C. W., Milberg, S., & Lawson, R. (1991). Evaluation of brand extensions: The role of product feature similarity and brand concept consistency. *The Journal of Consumer Research, 18*(2), 185–193. doi:10.1086/209251

Pitcher, A. E. (1985). The role of branding in International advertising. *International Journal of Advertising, 4,* 241–246.

Raturi, P. (2013). *An interview with Shahnaz Husain: You can be what you will yourself to be.* Academic Press.

Reddy, S. K., Holak, S. L., & Bhat, S. (1994). To extend or not to extend: Success determinants of line extensions. *JMR, Journal of Marketing Research, 31*(2), 243–262. doi:10.2307/3152197

Reynolds, T. J., & Gutman, J. (1984). Advertising as image management. *Journal of Advertising Research, 24,* 27–38.

Roth, M. S. (1995). The effects of culture and socioeconomics on the performance of global brand image strategies. *JMR, Journal of Marketing Research, 32*(2), 163–175. doi:10.2307/3152045

Roy, D. (2006). *Discourses on strategic management.* New Delhi: Asian Books Private Ltd.

Roy, D., & Banerjee, S. (2007). CARE-ing strategy for integration of brand identity with brand image. *International Journal of Commerce and Management, 17*(1), 140–148.

Schultz, M., & Hatch, M. J. (2003). The cycles of corporate branding: The case of the LEGO company. *California Management Review, 46*(1), 6–26. doi:10.2307/41166229

Simon, C. J., & Sullivan, M. W. (1993). The measurement and determinants of brand equity: A financial approach. *Marketing Science, 12*(1), 28–52. doi:10.1287/mksc.12.1.28

Trout, J., & Ries, A. (n.d.). Positioning cuts through chaos in marketplace. *Advertising Age.*

Van den Heever, J. (2000). *Brands and branding in South Africa.* Johannesburg, South Africa: Affinity.

Watkins, T. (1986). *The economics of the brand.* McGraw Hill Book Company.

Welcker, J. W. (1949). The community relations problem of industrial companies. *Harvard Business Review*, *49*(6), 771–780.

White, I. S. (1959). The functions of advertising in our culture. *Journal of Marketing*, *23*(1), 8–14. doi:10.2307/1249358

KEY TERMS AND DEFINITIONS

Brand: A name, term, design, symbol, or any other feature that identifies the seller's good or services as distinct from those of other sellers.

Brand Identity: The way a brand attempts to identify itself or its product.

Brand Positioning: The act of making the brands secure a distinctive place in the minds of the target market through creation of value proposition for the consumers and clarification of brand's essence.

Branding: The process of endowing product and services with the power of a brand.

C_4 Strategy Matrix: A four-cell decision matrix involving the interplay of internal effort and external realization of a brand to conceive four types of branding strategies -continuity, caution, change and correction.

External Realization: The way the target audience perceives the internal effort of a brand.

Internal Effort: A set of practices to ensure brand's specific mode of communication and the way it adjusts to its external environment with a particular physical appearance.

This research was previously published in Cases on Branding Strategies and Product Development edited by Sarmistha Sarma and Sukhvinder Singh, pages 1-23, copyright year 2015 by Business Science Reference (an imprint of IGI Global).

Chapter 8
Using Social Strategy to Retain Customers:
Cases and Tips

Wafaa A. Al-Rabayah
Independent Researcher, Jordan

ABSTRACT

Customer retention is the process of keeping your current customers' set satisfied and loyal to your product, successful customer retention is not only related to the applied product or services, but strongly related to how the organization provide the services and the reputation it creates within and across the marketplace. This chapter mentions four different cases of using social media to achieve customer retention. Cases will be named based on services provided by the firm, theme park, personal care business, food business, and suppling athlete tools. Also set of tips and guidelines about planning social strategy presented, finally suggested tools support different platforms were mentioned.

INTRODUCTION

Organizations' structure is shifting toward customer-based structure rather than product-based structure, customer-based structure aims to consider the set of customers as the source of revenue, not the products or services, customer-base is a group of customers who purchase and get benefits of organization's products and services repeatedly, behaviors and actions of customers can be defined and predicted based on market researches and previous experiences (Ryals & Knox, 2001). This strategy is followed by large companies mainly, there are many factors driving this shift, like introducing Customer Relationship Management (CRM), convergence of Information Systems (IS), and developing supporting software. Organizations concern in building strong enough strategies to insure achieving their goals. Business strategy is the process of identifying major goals, objectives, policies, plans and initiatives of that business and implementing specific techniques and tools to achieve these objectives (Teece, 2010), based on consideration of resources and an assessment of the internal and external factors represented in strength/weakness points, and threat/opportunities might face the business (Porter, 1979) Various models and

DOI: 10.4018/978-1-5225-5187-4.ch008

frameworks were introduced to assist in strategic planning process in a competitive dynamics environment, like SWOT analysis, experience curve, and industry structure and portfolio. Figure 1 is the graphic representation of SWOT analysis (Jackson, Joshi, & Erhardt, 2003).

Strategies in general aims to achieve a specific goal, i.e. increase profits, niche products, expand market. One of most important goals is managing customers' relations, either current customers or potential customers (Teece, 2010). It is important to keep your current set of customers satisfied and loyal, at the same time to look forward to maximizing this set by attracting new customers. This chapter discusses the retention of current customers, it will contain three sections, the first section will go over the general concept of customer retention by discussing the concept definition, importance, and challenges. Three cases of real life companies applied social media strategies to ensure customer retention were mentioned in the second section, third section discuss social networks managing tools. And finally a set of guidelines and tips were mentioned to achieve customer retentions in the last section.

CUSTOMER RETENTION

The simplest definition of customer retention is the set of steps planned and implemented to reduce customer defections or churn rate. Keeping customers is more about keeping their lifetime value either in term of their expenses or their influence power on other potential customers, where retaining existing customers is profitable in about five times more than attracting new customers (Han & Hyun, 2015; Eid, 2011), there are four main reasons why retained customers are more profitable (Ryals & Knox, 2001; Meldrum & McDonald, 1995):

1. Acquisition of new customers could be high in cost, therefore to have profitable customers, organization should keep the relationship with the same set of customers for more than one season or year.

Figure 1. SWOT analysis matrix

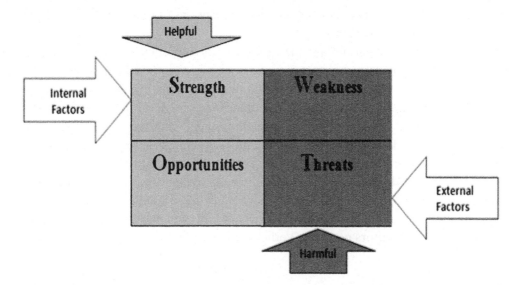

2. Profit stream of current customers will grow continuously after acquisition costs are covered, where customers tend to increase their purchases from places they already tried and go to it.

3. Customer retention is strongly connected to a satisfied customer, satisfied customers are more likely to become positive referrals and encourage other potential customers and enhance organization's image in market in a cost-effective way.

4. In backward looking, customers also get benefits of customers' retention, where they will spend less time in comparing prices against competitors so that they tend to become less price-sensitive.

The core of customers' retention is about defining needs and desired products/services and addressing them before losing the customer to another competitor, researchers define set of factors to ensure customer retentions such as: product and service quality, satisfaction, and commitment, (Dimitriades, 2006; Han & Hyun, 2015), senior management commitment, customer focused cultures, a clearly targeted marketing campaign and the identification of switching barriers (Ennew & Binks, 1996), these factors contribute to affect retention and loyalty of customers. The explosion of communication platforms and technologies in recent years reshape strategies and technique adopted in managing customers' relations and processes of retaining customers, using web 2.0 technologies provide the opportunities to instant interaction and capturing customer's feedback adequately about provided products/services (Sashi, 2012).

Problems may face organizations regarding keeping current customers which may be raised from issues like poor employee training, lack of dedicated resources, security and privacy issues in e-commerce environment, or unaddressed customer needs regarding needed products or services (Eid, 2011). Adding value to a product will overcome a huge problem in keeping customers, there are many components for adding value to a product such as: customers' service, quality, image, price, awareness, truth, and trust (Martisiute, Vilutyte, & Grundey, 2010).

Organizations and researchers face serious challenges when analyzing and planning techniques to retain current customers, such challenges include: appropriate differentiation of customers, where each customer demand a different set of serviced and customized products. Another challenge is gaining a satisfied employee. Where the more satisfied employees are the better the quality of the job delivered and that leads to better customers' management and retention. Self-reinforcing relationship strongly developed using internal marketing, an effective internal marketing strategy helps to strengthen customers' oriented service culture through enhancing employees' perceptions of their role and importance within the organization (Ennew & Binks, 1996).

After understanding the concept of customer retention, its importance, and challenges facing it, it is important to know the main strategies to achieve customer retention. Strategies have different goals, many strategies are developed to expand sales through market dominating, market penetrating, finding new market, and expanding the product range. Where other strategies developed to focus on employees to achieve commitment and satisfaction so that the job quality enhance and keep a pool of qualified employees, lastly strategies may be developed to concentrate on customers' relations (Meldrum & McDonald, 1995). Customer retention strategies include building effectively committed customers using a loyalty program, sending direct mailings, provide service calls, employing sales visits, that provide economic incentives; another important points is to compete other competitors variables such as competitive loyalty programs. Organizations should adopt regular research activities to analyze their customers' needs and study market status and competitors position (Verhoef, 2003).

Social Networks

Web has evolved from one way communication into more dynamic attractive environment. Social Networks (SNs) creates the opportunity to open communication channels between customers to share their experience and opinions regarding specific products, service, or brand in general (Mangold & Faulds, 2009). SNs create a new phenomenon of administrating business; it contributes in enhancing and creating new strategies to bond relations with allies, competitors, and customers, where it is essential for firms to keep following online presence presented in social network to avoid lagging behind a very dynamic competitive environment, online presence should deliver a tangible value in return for customers' time, attention, endorsement and data, so that customers will engage strongly with businesses' social pages (Heller & Parasnis, 2011). Firms can gain benefits of SNs by designing content with value to foster more intimate relationships with current and potential customers (Nezamabad, 2011). In fact, SNs is a double edged sword, it creates *social capital* for firms, by opening customers' relations, personal views, opinions, and attitudes to firms; so that analyst can follow the customers' status, updates, followings, and interests to create more related and successful plan; where the increase in customer retention by just 5 percent, can lead to increase in the firms' profits by 25 percent to 95 percent (Stillwagon, 2014), however at the same time SNs have increased challenges by opening the world and empower bargaining of customers, almost all information available online through SNs, so that firms should be aware of what to publish and how to communicate through SNs. This chapter will view a set of SNs implemented strategies cases from various domains and how do these cases help in changing and improving firm's position. Keeping customer's retention goes beyond giving the customer what they expect; it's more about exceeding their expectations to create a loyal customers advocate for your brand.

Social networks varies in its purposes and features, for example Facebook is a social network used to connect with friends and community by sharing posts, photos, and videos; organizations use it as a marketing platform, where LinkedIn is a more professional social network used to follow professionals, job opportunities and marketing qualifications of users. Whatsapp is smartphone based messenger which use the Internet to share texts, photos, videos, locations, and audio messages between contacts. Instagram is photo and video sharing stage supported by smart phones, both WhatsApp and Instagram applications started as a standalone platforms, but later on Instagram was acquired by Facebook for approximately 1 billion US$, and WhatsApp was also acquired by Facebook for approximately 19.3 billion US$. The following table presents a set of most important social networks and some of their features, important numbers related to each platform are mentioned.

METHODOLOGY

In this section, we will go over four different cases, of real businesses who integrate social network into their marketing strategy to insure customer retention objectives. Cases will be named based on services/products provided by the business, which are: theme park, personal care business, food business, and athlete tools supplies. In each case we discuss which social network platform is used and how.

Table 1. Popular social platforms

Social Platform	Features	Statistics
Facebook	• News Feed • Comments • Friends and followers • Wall and Timeline • Like, Love, HaHa, WoW, Sad, and Angry emotions • Messages and inbox • Notifications • Networks and groups • Private/Public options	• 12,691 employees. • 1.4 billion daily active user. • 934 million mobile daily active users. • 70+ supported language.
Twitter	• Write and read tweets (tweets and retweets) • Messaging (only 140 character) • Adding and following content • Send and receive updates via website, SMS, RSS, emails or a third party application. • Private/Public options • Third party application to send messages like Tweetie, Twitterrific, and Feedalizr.	• 3,900 employees. • 305 million monthly active user. • 80% active users on mobile. • 35+ languages supported.
WhatsApp	• Messaging application with sharing photo, video, location, contact and documents options. • Sound messages. • Rich and unique set of emotion options. • Pinch-to-Zoom videos for iOS users only. • Save link history. • Group of 256 members.	• 1 billion user. • 55 employees. • 32 languages supported.
YouTube	• Create personal channel and upload videos • view, pause, stop, rate, share and comment on videos, track • Auto-start track/ Series playlists • Monetization • Longer videos • Custom thumbnails • Paid subscriptions • Unlisted videos • Private videos • Live events • Channel customization	• Over a billion users. • 50% of users are active on mobile. • Launched local versions in more than 70 countries in total of 76 different languages.
LinkedIn	• Marketing personal qualifications • Connecting groups: used to amplifying messages through groups and nurture network. • Posting multimedia content including PDF files • Endorsements lists • Profile views report	• 9200 employee. • 414 million active user. • 24 languages supported.
Blog	• Create posts including multimedia and location. • Publish RSS feeds. • Host your blog. • Find support: either personalized assistance or answer questions.	• 275.9 million users. • 155 million monthly active users.
Instagram	• Part of Facebook, Inc. • Photographic filters. • Exploring tab. • Adding lux effect to pictures. • Uploading videos • Instagram direct: including private photo and video sharing, instant messaging, and sharing post and profiles from feeds directly to the user.	• 13 employees. • 300 million users. • 25 languages supported.

Case 1: Theme Park

This business is considered one of the largest eldest international entertainment businesses, it has more than 650 million guests since its opening. In March 2005, reports revealed that 65,700 jobs are supported by the resort, including about 20,000 direct employees and 3,800 third parties. They used SNs for different purposes, each platform supports different goals. For example, they use YouTube to create more entertainment value videos rather than to sell their products, their videos were rich in recognizable and popular characters, thus will make their audience talk about their products. Another platform is the Facebook were they create 267 pages across different countries they are constantly posting and talking to consumers; including individual pages for their consumer products. These pages are in a never-ending selling cycle, and need to advertise and endorse products around the year.

Managers create an engagement plan based on SNs features; they focused on two key principals:

- Reaching families and enthusiasts, encouraging them to share personal related content, SNs provide a sharing stage for voice, photos, and videos stories, this communication form of sharing fans' experience and endearing itself to customers in the process does three things: promotes firm's core values, celebrates its brand advocates and invites participation, which encourage brand loyalty
- Getting guests talking about the content and sharing it beyond their own profile, it is crucial for any business to have a strong expanded social media presence, it improve the opportunity to grow and ensure that consumers will be talking and passing on business related information to friends, family and peers.

Social Network's Activities

Using YouTube creates a challenge of providing entertaining, satisfying teases the paid for content at the same time to avoid seeming like you're providing nothing of value, provokes engagement and ultimately attract subscribers, the firm provides various channels for film trailers, music videos, and documentaries on the parks. The key for success in social media interaction is having good content, so keep your eyes open and be aware of what you post. Another important tip to consider the online presence is valuable for both customers and the firm, is the exclusivity of the content, where the firm provides an attractive content that users won't find anywhere else.

This firm runs an excellent Pinterest page, fully with a variety of boards, which makes the page visually interesting and improve brand reach. Pinterest content offer a rich valuable mixture content such as visual splendor, informative how-to-guides, behind-the-scenes photos, vintage treats from the past, sneak peeks of the future, which separates firm's brand identity from its competitor. The holiday board is updatable with pins relevant to the time of the year such as Christmas time, each pin contain a how-to guide on making a decoration or gift for the season. Another incredible success board is the recipes. Another used platform is the Instagram, where the firm provides a set of exclusive new content such as odd cheeky but necessary merchandise snap, and cute moments captured from around the park.

Unfortunately, frim's successful strategies failed in Facebook, Twitter, and Google+. Despite these platforms are more direct one-to-one channels, and provide great and regular content, but each one is used identically to the other, therefore a redundant content is available on these channels, audience will receive the same broadcasting three times, thus decrease the engagement with the large communities.

Based on this experience, what to do? Be careful of your content, and be aware of your broadcast. You don't need to be available on all SNs, you should have to focus on the right form that support your field, managers realize that multimedia "video mainly" will add a value to its present, so focus on YouTube to create a strategic plan to reach and strength relations with customers, while using Facebook, Twitter, and Google + add more burden on the firm to provide the same broadcast or information in three locations, but it should appear as new unique at each platform.

Case 2: Personal Care Business

This 32 years old "earth friendly" firm makes products for personal care, health, beauty, and personal hygiene. The total manufactured products in 2007 was over 197 products for facial and body skin care, lip care, hair care, baby care, men's grooming, and outdoor remedies, they disturbed their products in nearly 30,000 retail outlets across the United States, United Kingdom, Ireland, Canada, Hong Kong, and Taiwan.

Social Network's Activities

In celebrating its 30th birthday, customers were encouraged to submit their happy birthday wishes into Facebook, Blog, and Twitter; these wishes were then shared and read aloud on the firm's location. As a result of collaborating and inviting communities to celebrate this milestone the firm received wishes from people around the globe, the support and passion from customers strengthened the relation with existent community and enlarged it, managers arc cager to offer interactive and compelling content to keep relation with customers sustainable and productive.

Managers employ classic products into their brand's personality, they produced a series of six-second stop motion novellas, this campaign help the firm to earn an entirely new online audience generating more than 2,000 likes, 580 Revines, and close to 1,000 new followers.

As cosmetic business, the firm introduced a new service of online tutorials into its social strategy, you can see a 20-to-30-second social media lessons which gives the customers another reason to interact with the brand without products being the main focus, also set of product viral videos about the products' best using way, and advices of taking care in faces and hair improve relation among firm and its' customers.

The company goes beyond traditional social platforms, and added promotional messages and reminders to people's Yahoo, Google, Apple, or Microsoft calendars. Customers are invited to click on a link that automatically added a series of eight weekly calendar items, like "Workshop of best ways of personal hygiene", this teach us not to be afraid to experiment with new social tools or reach new audiences.

The last point is using hashtags strategically; the brand doesn't limit itself to using only campaign-related hashtags in its tweets and Facebook posts. It aims to reach a broader stage of audience; therefore it incorporates popular, existing hashtags. Take into consideration that limiting you to a specific or limited hashtag(s) set harm than good. Use keywords that your customers may use to find your brand or products and turn them into hashtags on social media

Case 3: Food Business/ Snacks

This case talks about large snack producer; the product was introduced before 100 years. Snacks market has very wide products categories; it is a challenge to keep in forefront of the market. Nevertheless this product has successfully proved its quality and dominated a wide portion of snacks market. Over the last three years it has followed an agile marketing strategies to insure its position. In total, this product has signed up to the creative direction and now has a catalogue of important online discussion topics, typically using Twitter as its vehicle.

Social Network's Activities

Achieving success is a target, but sustaining this success is a strategy. To achieve success this brand act in agile to stay ahead of the curve by adopting flexible visions and acting in responsive and adaptive way; the targeted platforms were Twitter, Instagram, and Pinterest. The following is a set of main points they focused on and working to achieve best results:

- **Twitter:** They used Twitter as a quick response stage, where customers' inquiries and communications were responded to in seconds. The product was collaborate with the huge electronic game producer, Sony, to create customized PS4 controller where they integrate the product's design into control hand, which leads to another modification of Xbox product to be introduced to support this specific brand. Thus a user watches brands and interacts with these brands in different times, therefore the personal engagement among various products at the same time increases product's followers and brand loyalty.
- **Instagram:** Was another support channel for the product; it knows exactly what makes its channel attractive for a user to follow. Lists of interesting images full of delicious looking food. This product was used over 100 years in same look, but the successful marketing secret lies on using the product itself as a blank canvas. A highly adaptable, moldable food stuff that the brand aren't afraid to mess with. Combination of multi strategies including sharing regular recipes' ideas, bizarre recipe ideas, and old school adverts, this product introduce a great entertainment. Lately, Instagram's video functionality was adopted to create added value communication channel.
- **Pinterest:** This platform used as main stage that contains all published materials on social channels, which creates a chance to acknowledge the brand's loyal followers by showcasing their pictures and creativity. Being visual, different, and resourceful create the opportunity to encourage interaction, brand loyalty, and spread awareness.

Case 4: Athlete Tools Supplies

This case discuss a multinational corporation, specialized in designing, developing, manufacturing and worldwide marketing and sales of footwear, apparel, equipment, accessories and services. It was launched in 1964 as distributer for foreign products, now after more than fifty years, it is known as one of the most popular supplier of athlete shoes and apparel. Facebook page of this corporation has more than 23 million likes, Twitter page of main account has more than 5.85 million followers, and more than 38 million followers on Instagram. Managers design corporation's strategy to achieve sustainable, long-term growth across its global portfolio of brands and businesses.

Social Network's Activities

- **Instagram:** This brand has the optimal exploitation of Instagram Features, from captivating, carefully shot photographs, to arty videos. Online material is always really high quality and befitting with brand image, that encourages high energy activity and adventure. They have developed a set of brand's hashtags, including trademark hashtag. They launch feminine support campaign to empower women in sport and create hashtag for this campaign. These hashtags are frequently adopted by other Instagram users; which help in forming brand's community to share their own fitness journeys. This encourages customers to frequently visit Instagram page to view latest updates and community events.

- **Twitter:** This brand start with one product, with time the corporation had grown and branched out into a number of departments. To support vision and goals of each department, separated Twitter accounts have been created, the summation of followers on these accounts is more than 8 million followers. They keep their tweets brief and tend to use sentence-long motivational statements, also tweets are enriched with photos; despite the simplicity of their tweets, they generally receive a couple of thousand retweets and favorites. They encourage their customers to engage with them on Twitter by asking questions about what their favorite products are and encouraging them to send in pictures of their own brand gear.

- **Facebook:** Facebook page not only works as a normal fan page, it also has customized tabs that link followers directly to their Instagram account and support page. In addition to this there is also a 'Shop Now' button that redirects users to their online store. Like on Twitter, they have multiple accounts on Facebook key account, and smaller specialized pages. Page's contents tend to receive a high level of engagement and a community of keen runners has been formed, who use the page as a forum for discussing their hobby, sharing tips and finding out about new products and events. Responding rate on Facebook is high, they make the effort to reply to nearly every comment or post on the page, whether it is in response to a purchase enquiry or just a general remark about a post.

SOCIAL NETWORK MANAGING TOOLS

Social network is one of the most effective means for businesses and organizations to adopt in marketing and managing their activities, it creates an open atmosphere between organization and the customers, allows infinite ways to communicate and deliver benefits for both sides. The complexity of creating appropriate social network strategy rises from the availability of various platforms of social networks with wide range of features and properties, where it is impossible to create fix standard strategy to follow in all social platforms, therefore it is better to plan and implement set of strategies instead of adopting one strategy. Any organization planned to measure success degree of its strategy, but it is difficult to measure exact earnings achieved based on social strategies. This section will introduce set of tools used to manage social network activities, help in implementing planned strategy, provide feedback of these strategies, and help in measuring success degree. Some of these tools available online for free, while other tools you have to pay for its services.

- **CrowdBooster:** Offers analytics with suggestions and tools to help improving online presence on Twitter and Facebook, it create the opportunity to schedule social media posts and offers important and relevant measurements in simplified charts (CrowdBooster, 2010), the most pros of this tool are:
  - Targeted recommendations: helps in understanding whom to engage with on Twitter and Facebook.
  - Clean and very intuitive user interface.
  - Fast and easy to get started.
  - Provide insightful and real time social media analytics
  - Empower its analytical results with graphs and percentage reports
- **HootSuite**: This tool allows managing up to 100 social profiles, scheduling up to 350 messages at a time, collaborating with others, and getting valuable, in-depth data with enhanced analytics. HootSuite provides 159 applications to facilitate managing of different social platforms, 84 free apps and 75 premium applications (HootSuite, 2008). Some of these applications are listed below
  - **Geopiq for Twitter:** This application used to monitor posts on Twitter by location, keywords, language or username. You can use combination of search terms for powerful targeting. It allows you to monitor and engage with users that are posting in your area, or an area you choose to follow, also you can monitor events to see what is being posted, by who, and to engage with them. It costs 4.99 US$ monthly
  - **Tailwind for Pinterest:** This free application used to manage Pinterest platform, it used to create new Pins, schedule drafts for later, or Pin to multiple boards at once.
  - **Crowd Analyzer:** This free application used as monitoring and analytics platform. It enables you to precisely listen and engage with your customers on social media. Crowd Analyzer monitors major social channels like Facebook, Twitter and Instagram.
- **TweetDeck***:* Is multi-platform desktop and web dashboard application, it is an effective tool for real-time tracking, organizing, and engagement Twitter accounts (TweetDeck, 2010), TweetDeck helps to:
  - Use one friendly interface to monitor multiple timelines.
  - Create schedule for future tweets posting.
  - Keep up with emerging information through turn on alerts.
  - Filter searches based on criteria like engagement, users and content type.
  - Build and export custom timelines to put on your website.
  - Use intuitive keyboard shortcuts for efficient navigation.
  - Mute users or terms to eliminate unwanted noise.
  - TweetDeck timelines stream in real-time, therefore there is no need to refreshing the page.
  - Work in group to manage a Twitter account.
- **Audiense (Formerly SocialBro):** Is a Twitter community analysis tool (Audiense, 2016), most important features of SocialBro are:
  - Define famous followers: the accounts of celebrities that have been verified by Twitter.
  - Define and validate new followers.
  - Knowing inactive friends – sort your friends by the date of their last tweet.
  - Search all Twitter when building list: lists will automatically sync up with Twitter, and it will saving transfer time.

- ◦ Follower bio tag cloud: through checking out the top keywords that appear most in the bios of followers.
  - ◦ Advanced search among friends or followers: search for connections from specific locations, mentioning specific keywords, or naming themselves in a specific manner.
  - ◦ Analyzing your lists: analyze your own lists as well as public lists created by other users
- **Tagboard:** Hashtag managing tool, support Facebook, Twitter, Instagram, Google+, and Vine. Managers can use Tagboard to search hashtags activities, which overlap and which match social marketing plan. This tool fit when a multi-platform strategy planned, it helps mangers to find out influencers to connect with and hot topics organization can cover (Tagboard, 2016).

Following table represent a summary of used managing tools, some of these tools provide free services, while other set provide free trial almost for one month, then the user should pay for full services version, which provide an entrepreneurs and professional view of managing tools.

ONLINE CUSTOMER RETENTION TIPS

Based on readings and researches, a set of important guidelines can be introduced to create solid strategy which aims to insure customer retentions, following are set of 8 main points to take into consideration:

- Be easy to find: keep consistent in user name and browsing image in all social networks, so that users will find you easily when they need you. Namech_K, Knowem, and Usernamecheck are example of tools used to check username availability across hundreds of online networks.
- Know your loyal customer: it is very important to know you customer, through online profiles activities, even better to communicate with them based on their preferences, interests and hobbies. Proactively engage with them about their favorite sports, music, foods, and media shows.
- Follow you brand on social network: use listening tools like Google Alerts, and Hootsuite, which provide immediate notifications to brand mentions and key phrases, that allow organizations to know their reputation and customer's opinion directly, this create the opportunity to avoid any potential problems and capture available but hidden opportunities.
- Keep your strategy dynamic by combining both consistent posting items and at the same time scheduling some posts to be productive, tools like Hootsuite, Buffer, and TweetDeck are examples of scheduling tools for future posts. Figure 2 represents Hootsuite options for scheduling post into tow social platforms which are Twitter and Facebook.
- Make each platform content unique, you can post shared information on all social platforms, but don't make you presence on various social platforms look like multiple versions of the same copy, give your customers reason to follow you on all social platforms. As you reach your customers on various different platforms, they will be more likely to build a long-term relationship with your business.
- Be close to your customers, businesses are available intensively in social platforms, you should be available all times for your customer, try to provide a real time engagement with customers, answer support questions on social platforms., where any asked question will be answered in fast time. Use a qualified employee/team "based on your business size" to follow and manage your social media presence.

Table 2. Social media management tools

Cost	Managing Tool	Objective	Supported Platform
Free	Hyperalerts	Create monitoring system	Facebook
	TweetDeck	Create a monitoring system	Twitter
	WhosTalkin	Monitor and Search social network content	Multi-platform Twitter, Facebook, LinkedIn, Google+,... etc
	Mentionmapp	View Twitters' connection in tree graphical representation, contains people connections, mentioned hashtags in recent tweets.	Twitter
Paid	Sprout Social	Monitoring and managing multiple social networks	Multi-platform Twitter, Facebook, LinkedIn, Google+,... etc
	Visually Google Analytics Report	Analysis tool	Google
Free trial for 30 days Paid for premium features	ShortStack	Add functionality	Facebook
	Tagboard	Find trending hashtags	Multi-platform Facebook, twitter, Instagram, Google+, and Vine
	Hootsuite	Managing multi account	Multi-platform Twitter, Facebook, LinkedIn, Google+,... etc
	Crowdbooster	Analysis tool	Facebook and Twitter.
	Agorapulse	Monitoring and managing multiple social networks	Multi-platform Twitter, Facebook, LinkedIn, Google+,... etc
	KnowEm	Search Social Network to find if brand's, trademark, or names mentioned	Multi-platform Twitter, Facebook, LinkedIn, Google+,... etc

Figure 2. Scheduling option in Hootsuite tool

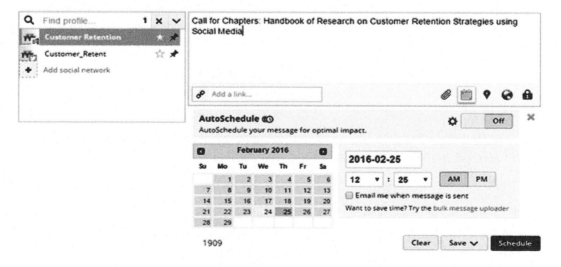

- Be careful of your personality and tone: customers are opening to other businesses on social networks, pay attention to how your audience engages on each specific platform.
- Be aware of outside potential customers: don't let your concerns focused only on your current customers, create a list up to 20 of people who are strangers to you and your business, use social platforms to communicate with them daily, but avoid spam unsolicited communications, contribute to their discussions and interesting's field, until they recognize you and your business.

CONCLUSION

Social network is now real trend in business world, business strategies built based on features of social networks to achieve various goals, such as improve customer retention opportunities. Cases discussed in this chapter showed how the firms planned its strategy based on social networks features to achieve required goals and to retain their customers', cases cover various ranges of businesses. Applying social network strategy is important and crucial step, yet managers can't be very sure about success degree or worthiness of effort applied on this strategy; list of tools is suggested, classified based on its cost, each tool can manage one social platform or various platforms. And each tool is specified to achieve specific goal.

REFERENCES

Audiense. (2016). *Audiense*. Retrieved 2016, from Twitter: https://www.audiense.com/

CrowdBooster. (2010). *CrowdBooster*. Retrieved 2016, from CrowdBooster web site: http://crowdbooster.com/about/

Dimitriades, Z. S. (2006). Customer satisfaction, loyalty and commitment in service organizations: Some evidence from Greece. *Management Research News, 29*(12), 782–800. doi:10.1108/01409170610717817

Eid, M. (2011). Determinants of e-commerce customer satisfaction, trust, and loyalty in Saudi Arabia. *Journal of electronic commerce research, 12*(1), 78-93.

Ennew, C. T., & Binks, M. R. (1996). The Impact of Service Quality and Service Characteristics on CustomerRetention: Small Businesses and their Banks in the UK. *British Journal of Management, 7*(3), 219–230. doi:10.1111/j.1467-8551.1996.tb00116.x

Han, H., & Hyun, S. S. (2015). Customer retention in the medical tourism industry: Impact of quality, satisfaction, trust, and price reasonableness. *Tourism Management, 46*, 20–29. doi:10.1016/j.tourman.2014.06.003

Heller, C. B., & Parasnis, G. (2011). From social media to social customer relationship management. *Strategy and Leadership, 39*(5), 30–37. doi:10.1108/10878571111161507

HootSuite. (2008). *HootSuite Corporation*. Retrieved 2016, from HootSuite web site: https://hootsuite.com/

Jackson, S. E., Joshi, A., & Erhardt, N. L. (2003). Recent Research on Team and Organizational Diversity: SWOT Analysis and Implications. *Journal of Management, 29*(6), 801–830. doi:10.1016/S0149-2063(03)00080-1

Mangold, G. W., & Faulds, D. J. (2009). Social media: The new hybrid element of the promotion mix. *Business Horizons*, *52*(4), 357–365. doi:10.1016/j.bushor.2009.03.002

Martisiute, S., Vilutyte, G., & Grundey, D. (2010). Product or Brand? How Interrelationship between Customer Satisfaction and Customer Loyalty Work. *European Journal of Interdisciplinary Studies*, *2*(1), 5-15.

Meldrum, M., & McDonald, M. (1995). Customer Retention Strategies. In Key Marketing Concepts (pp. 199-204). doi:10.1007/978-1-349-13877-7_38

Nezamabad, M. (2011). The Impact and Benefits of Internet on Marketing Mix. *Australian Journal of Basic and Applied Sciences*, *5*(9), 1784–1789.

Ryals, L., & Knox, S. (2001). Cross-Functional Issues in the Implementation of Relationship Marketing Through Customer Relationship Management. *European Management Journal*, *19*(5), 534–542. doi:10.1016/S0263-2373(01)00067-6

Sashi, C. (2012). Customer engagement, buyer-seller relationships, and social media. *Management Decision*, *50*(2), 253–272. doi:10.1108/00251741211203551

Stillwagon, A. (2014, Sep 11). *Did You Know: A 5% Increase in Retention Increases Profits by Up to 95%*. Retrieved April 20, 2016, from Small Buisness Trends: http://smallbiztrends.com/2014/09/increase-in-customer-retention-increases-profits.html

Tagboard. (2016). *Tagboard*. Retrieved from Tagboard Web site: https://tagboard.com/

Teece, D. J. (2010). Business Models, Business Strategy and Innovation. *Long Range Planning*, *43*(2-3), 172–194. doi:10.1016/j.lrp.2009.07.003

TweetDeck. (2010). *TweetDeck*. Retrieved 2016, from Twitter web site: https://tweetdeck.twitter.com/

Verhoef, P. C. (2003). Understanding the Effect of Customer Relationship Management Efforts on Customer Retention and Customer Share Development. *Journal of Marketing*, *67*(4), 30–45. doi:10.1509/jmkg.67.4.30.18685

This research was previously published in Strategic Uses of Social Media for Improved Customer Retention edited by Wafaa Al-Rabayah, Rawan Khasawneh, Rasha Abu-shamaa, and Izzat Alsmadi, pages 246-263, copyright year 2017 by Business Science Reference (an imprint of IGI Global).

Chapter 9
Branding Impetus for Start-Ups:
Relevance and Rhetoric

Umashankar Venkatesh
Great Lakes Institute of Management, India

ABSTRACT

Startups face multiple challenges in the initial stages of their existence, characterized by resource constraints, they encounter – financial, legal and reputational risks. Gaining traction in the market, and scaling-up is the main thrust of any such business. Most start-ups come into existence on the basis of an innovative idea for a service or product, presented in the form of a business proposition. The consequence of this is - how do they establish this 'new' idea/concept or product in the chosen market. A bigger question to answer is also the reputational non-existence of the start-ups when they are relatively unknown to most stakeholders and publics - relevant for growth and success. This chapter explores the relevance and importance of branding for startups based on literature and industry cases. The chapter concludes with outlining directions for brand building in the context of both B2C and B2B startups.

If you are not embarrassed by the first version of your product, you've launched too late. -Reid Hoffman (Founder of LinkedIn)

INTRODUCTION

The challenges that a startup organization encounters are myriad as they emanate both internally as well as externally to the organization. This is especially true for bootstrapped startups world-over wherein internally such organizations struggle with a skeletal manpower base in the form of the founders and a handful of multi-tasking people thereby facing a talent/expertise deficit in specific and crucial areas of business management (including marketing); coupled with capital constraints. On the other hand externally, it is endeavoring to establish awareness and trust in its chosen markets and among other stakeholders, while striving to scale-up in the shortest span of time. Thus the focus of the founders and managers in a startup is usually more on operations and all efforts are to streamline the same while grappling with quality issues and resource shortages.

DOI: 10.4018/978-1-5225-5187-4.ch009

At this stage, the articulation and enactment of any tactic or strategy that can help startups in establishing a quick foothold in their target markets and bridge the resource and trust gaps mentioned above, can prove to be a life-saver for such firms and may be the difference between a successful and a failed startup. Amongst other things, one of the possible theses that startup founders/managers may want to engage with is to explore the relevance and ramification of building a brand for the benefit of external stakeholders especially as well as internal ones too.

This chapter is focused at exploring the positive impact if any, of brand building in such startups. The chapter unfolds by investigating the nature of startups and their travails while trying to establish themselves in their chosen markets. Then based upon extant literature we identify and explore some of the branding models – both in the business-to-business (B2B) as well as business-to-consumer (B2C) space. Finally, with the help of some cases drawn from the Indian startup space encompassing B2B and B2C companies the chapter comes to a conclusion vis-à-vis the rationale and directions for enabling building of successful brands for such startup firms.

BACKGROUND

Branding as a concept as well as a tool and brand building activities thereon are considered important pillars of modern marketing. Traditionally, brands and branding activities have been associated more intently with marketing effort targeted at end customers in the B2C markets. However, there is a growing awareness of the virtues of brand building in the B2B arena as well. Brands are supposed to serve B2B markets for precisely the same generic purposes as it meant to achieve in B2C or consumer markets. This namely encompasses – facilitation of product identification by buyers of products, services and businesses as well as creation of differentiation against competitors (Anderson & Narus, 2004).

Commenting upon the importance of brands for corporations Steenkamp (2014), posits brands as the 'lifeblood' of companies as they are instrumental in – generating market share, increasing customer loyalty, amplifying channel power, enabling larger profit margins, and helping to guard against competitive attacks.

The importance and challenge of establishing a successful brand has led authors to say that - as far as marketing as a profession is concerned "perhaps the most distinctive skill of professional marketers is their ability to create, maintain, enhance, and protect brands" (Kotler & Keller, 2007, p. 157).

Expanding the ambit of this discussion further, within this framework, there is also a need to look at the special category of organizations that may benefit from branding and brand building effort, namely the startups. Startups are unique in the way that they usually come into fruition with an individual or a very small group of people getting convinced about an idea whose time they think has arrived and which has a market which is worth pursuing as a business model. Another category is when an existing company or entrepreneurial venture, which is relatively well established, plans to enter into a new business/category and to realize this plan creates a new company.

This chapter is focused upon the former category of startups wherein the founders are not part of an existing company and are endeavoring to create something from scratch.

To clarify and regulate the startup ecosystem, the Ministry of Commerce and Industry, Government of India, released a notification on April 17, 2015, classifying 'startups'. According to this notification, to qualify as a startup, an entity will be characterized by the following three features – (i) no more than five years from the date of incorporation; (ii) turnover does not exceed Rs. 25 crores ($3.75 million at current exchange rate) in the last five financial years; and (iii) it is working towards innovation, development, deployment, and commercialization of new products, processes, or services driven by technology or intellectual property. If one is planning to structure a part of an existing business into a separate entity, it won't be called a startup as it already forms a part of a registered entity (Dwivedi, 2016).

The Startup Eco-System

New businesses or startups are relatively uncertain about a variety of things during their inception stage. These uncertainties include – will they find acceptance in their chosen market segments; will their business model succeed as planned and scale-up in their planned time-frame; more fundamentally, have they zeroed-in upon the right bundle of values in their product/service design vis-à-vis the targeted customers; will they be able to withstand competitive pressures from existing players especially; and would they be able to create a differentiation for themselves in the chosen market and be able to realize the targeted price points etc.

Resource constraints are the order of the day, as most startups are relatively unknown and find it difficult to garner the immediate support of suppliers; channel partners; financial partners and other service providers, along with credibility, confidence and recognition in the eyes of the customers as well as existing and potential team members. This gets further accentuated by internal structures that are either ad hoc and not defined (Rode & Vallaster, 2005) and capital constraints (Abimbola, 2001).

Another characteristic of startups is that they are mostly working under extreme time pressure as they are racing against time to scale-up before their limited window of opportunity closes down (Timmons, 1999). This forces them to prioritize their activities and resources in a manner in which operational processes and deliveries gets focused upon and emphasized, whereas communication, especially meant for external stakeholders, is relegated to a lower order denomination, only to be seen as a chore rather than being of strategic importance. This limited window of opportunity is what is being emphasized in the opening comment of this chapter, attributed to Reid Hoffman, the Founder of LinkedIn. This brings out clearly the inherent nature of startups and their existential challenge as they setup as a relatively unknown entity. Also, the founders may be from technical (engineering) background and may not look at marketing as requiring professional capabilities or even effort.

Startups are also characterized by strong individual (founders') influences; a limited business network and reach; and an unstructured communication infrastructure (Drumm, 2002; Lechner, 2002). This often leads to a somewhat serendipitous outlook towards marketing; and communication and branding - as in the inception stages, startups are trying to engage with external stakeholders in a limited fashion with a clear outlook to create (only) those relationships that they feel are essential for the survival of their business.

Box 1. Opening vignette

Two new age Indian companies – Paytm (payment services and e-commerce firm); and Zomato (online restaurant discovery platform) have made it to the global list of emerging brands in the list of brands featured in the *Interbrand Breakthrough Brands,* published in July 2016. The study was compiled collaboratively between Interbrand, the New York Stock Exchange and the digital agency - Ready Set Rocket, New York. These two Indian companies/brands were among the top 60 brands chosen from 200 nominations. This study was restricted to brands that were less than 10 years old and the final 60 names were finalized on the bases of their growth potential; capacity to grab consumers' attention; and the strength of their business model.
Paytm figures in the 'Growing Global' brands, classified as a brand that has created a unique, differentiated approach, which is global. This list signifies brands that are "breaking ground fast and too big to ignore" (Mitra & Verma, 2016, p. 7).

A separate of line of thought will be to look at the antecedents of startup reputation and how that may be another challenge as far as building startup recognition as brands for superior market results is concerned. Research indicates that past performance is one of the clear and defining antecedents of a startup's reputation and awareness for it, among its stakeholders (Fombrun & Shanley, 1990). The other determinant of startup recognition is rooted in the substantiality of the brand building and advertising (marketing communication) investments made by the startup in its initial stages of inception (Milgrom & Roberts, 1986). The relative impossibility of both of these being present in a startups initial life is brought out succinctly by Petkova, Rindova, and Gupta, (2008, p. 320)

… this expectation to have performance track record and substantial resources available for reputation-building investments make reputation an almost impossible target for new ventures.

Most entrepreneurial intentions are usually focused at creating superior value which in turn creates superior returns for the firm (Schumpeter, 1936), variously based upon – an innovative product/service or a 'new-to-the-world' product; a parity product/service at much lower cost; or a superior product at the same cost.

Many entrepreneurs clearly think that – it's all about building the best ever product and when that happens, it will 'sell' itself. This clearly is the classic product-orientation that marketing theory talks about, one which ignores the dynamic marketing environment and the changing customer perceptions and wants. Whether they realize it or not, many companies don't have an accurate sense of how they are presenting themselves to the public. To help make the message clear, sometimes an outside perspective is in order. Andruss (2012), quotes Copywriter Laura Scholes, who while working for some entrepreneurs realized how these startups offered valuable products, but had no brand identity to support them –

They (founders of startups) came to me and said, 'I need help writing my website,' and I thought, 'No, you need help building your brand,'" she says, "They were so concerned with talking about what they did and how well they did it that they weren't connecting with their audience, which is crucial... (An-druss, 2012, p.59)

Therefore this lop sided focus on product again would render marketing as myopic and hence brand building as a low priority function or activity in startups.

THE CONTEXT FOR BRANDING

Is it important for new ventures to be concerned about and take steps in branding their enterprise or products for the reasons enumerated in the discussion above? One can try and answer this by revisiting the generic advantages of branding for any company - however it would be of greater relevance if we can specifically focus upon the relevance of branding for startups. The discussion here focuses a little more on the B2B context for startups and hence branding, as branding's relevance in B2C is largely established. However vignettes included would encompass both B2B and B2C categories of startups.

Traditionally B2B products such as components, spare parts, business services, consumables etc. are seen as being supposedly selected (for purchase) by organizational buyers through an objective decision-making process, solely based upon technical specifications and functionalities associated with the alternatives being considered along with specific benefits, price, service, and quality (Aaker & Joachimsthaler, 2000). Research on branding and brand management has conventionally focused on B2C branding (Homburg, Klarmann, & Schmitt, 2010; Sethuraman, Tellis, & Briesch, 2011), whereas as per Interbrand (2015), three out of the top ten global brands are – Microsoft, IBM and GE – which are largely B2B brands. Apart from these there are numerous global brands which are recognized and respected across markets and nations such as Oracle; FedEx; Sumitomo; Siemens; United Technologies; Boeing; Thyssen-Krupp; Tetra Pak, Tata Steel, Tata Consultancy Services (TCS), Infosys etc. are all B2B brands. These brands command respect, trust and preference over others, as well as many times a premium.

Finally, another perspective for brand building could be branding decisions and activities pertaining to the corporation/organization *per se* as a brand on one hand, and specific product(s)/category of the company being branded, on the other.

Logically, most companies evolve to a stage wherein they may have a portfolio of products/categories or services, if not a portfolio of multiple businesses. As per Aaker (2004), a corporate brand is a brand that defines the organization that will deliver and stand behind the offering. And that the corporate brand is defined primarily by organizational associations. Having said this, in the long run, it is better to develop separate product brands or category brands at least, within a given corporate brand house as the corporate brand is not always well suited for being a product master brand, especially in the following situations (Aaker, 2004) –

- The corporate brand's role becomes limited if it becomes too confining because of its product category associations. In a diversified company, the corporate name initially thought of in the context of a specific initial business may be rendered inappropriate at a later stage.
- If and when the corporate brand lacks a relevant value proposition then too creating a strong sub-brand or new brand would be a better proposition.
- When the corporate brand may have negative associations. For instance, the "Imperial Tobacco Company" in India was concatenated to ITC Limited for obvious reasons.

Therefore what this means is that a corporate entity may usually end up having multiple brands within the same company or across multiple companies, necessarily being different from the umbrella corporate brand.

For startups, this dichotomy may not be of immediate interest, especially during their inception phase. However, prudent startups, who have thought this through well, may decide to have a clear separation between the corporate brand and the product branding. (See: Exhibit 1).

Exhibit 1.

A good example of how this deliberate separation is worthwhile, could be from the Indian company, namely Intermesh Systems, which was set-up in 1996 in Delhi as a provider of wide range of web-based services via IndiaMART.com. The company has four other industry specific websites viz. – Indiantravelportal.com; Handicrafts.indiamart.com; and Finance.indiamart.com. Today, IndiaMART.com is considered as India's largest online marketplace, connecting buyers with suppliers.

After many years of successful operation of their marketplace business model, IndiaMART.com has added a new business by the name of Tolexo.com, which is a B2B e-commerce portal wherein companies and institutions may find and buy all kinds of business supplies that they may be looking for, directly from vendors. Each of the portals (especially IndiaMART and Tolexo) is being built as an individual brand, which embodies and manifests a specific promise targeted at specific buyer segments. This has given the company ample room and freedom to develop new products/services as per chosen growth strategies, ranging from intensive to integrative and finally to diversification based expansion plans.

The Value of Branding for Startups

Based upon the above case example, we may now deduce and specify the underlying value that brand building can add to startup businesses, whether operating in the B2C or B2B domain.

Fundamentally speaking, brands "survive and thrive on their ability to deliver on a compelling brand promise – to provide superior delivery of desired benefits in ways that can't be matched by another other brand or firm" (Keller, 2015).

Lynch and de Chernatony (2004), posit – trust inherent in the brand name; peace of mind; and security, as the emotional brand values that appears to be as the most appropriate advantage accruing out of B2B branding. Keller (2008), identifies the basic purpose of a brand as constituting a threefold impact that it aims to create – (i) simplifying decision making amongst buyers; (ii) reducing the perception of risk while making the purchase decision; and (iii) setting the right expectations reducing the perception of risk while making the purchase decision. All the three are legitimate purposes, whether we see them through the B2C or B2B prism. The fourth perspective is what brands and their underlying meanings can do for the organizational culture and values and what message does it deliver to the internal stakeholders. Finally, branding of startups has connotations for how it is perceived within special interest stakeholders such as financial institutions, venture capital firms, banks etc.

Branding Facilitates Complex Buying Behavior

In a B2B context, the buying decision is more complex as compared to the B2C segment, as accountabilities and goals are professionally specified with limited tolerances and there is not much room for leverage. There are usually a larger number of stakeholders in such buying processes and functions with relatively rigid standard operating procedures for each stage of buying, which many times creates contradictory pressures for professional buyers trying to balance the divergent objectives of different stakeholders or departments. This forces B2B buyers to setup a set of criteria or policies that govern the identification, communication and selection of vendors that may be deemed eligible to supply. At this stage the brand is more pertinent as a measure of corporate reputation as well as a promise based upon the buyers' own experience of dealing with the brand or the way the brand (value and functionality promise) is perceived within the buyers' industry or trade. Within the buyer system, stakeholders maybe more amenable to certain brands whereas their awareness and knowledge for certain other brands may not be sufficient to garner a sense of acceptance, anticipation and comfort associated with a known brand.

Similarly in B2C selling, especially for high involvement purchases, the end-use customers' in the B2C markets also exhibit a complex buying behavior (Kotler, 2010). Research indicates that evaluation difficulty pertaining to a product or service due to (say) poor or inadequate awareness among consumers increases the perceived risk in the product category perspective. Additionally, higher involvement generates a stronger relationship between evaluation difficulty and perceived risk for the product category perspective (Laroche, Nepomuceno, & Richard, 2010). This means that creating a brand and following it up with creating awareness of the brand will certainly help startups too in making breakthroughs in their chosen markets, especially if they are trying to market innovative products/services which are new-to-the-market or new-to-the-world offerings.

In the context of B2C e-commerce businesses, Ward and Lee (2000), have found that recent adopters of the Internet are less proficient at searching for product information and hence rely more on brands. But as they become more experienced in online purchasing, their search proficiency may rise, leading to a decrease in their brand reliance. This suggests that branding can facilitate consumers' acceptance of electronic commerce.

Brands Reduce Perception of Risk

Most startups are faced with what Stinchcombe (1968), termed as the 'liability of newness', which creates an aura of generic uncertainty around the existence and relevance of these entities. Being new, they suffer from a distinct lack of legitimacy, which is considered being absolutely paramount for firm performance and survival (Certo, 2003).

From this flows the perspective of the brand's purpose being one of a risk reduction proposition. It is clear that one of the 'non-tangible nonfinancial benefits' that Narayandas (2005), posits as one of the benefits accruing from brands in the B2B context, is also referring to the 'emotional' value of brands that Lynch and de Chernatony (2004), are referring to. The impact of this benefit has been identified to be of more critical for businesses in retaining buyers rather than during the customer acquisition process (Narayandas, 2005). Lennartz, Fischer, Krafft, and Peters (2015), have found that B2B customers not only value desirable product performance, but also reward emotional attributes.

For instance, the 'Intel Inside' badge on a computer evokes a sense of buying a benchmark product if not one of a superior than competition product among B2B as well as B2C buyers. For startups too, an appreciation from channel partners and buyers that the product/service brand of the startup encapsulates innovation or the best design/quality, will be of seminal importance in scaling up and expanding market share.

Brands Facilitate the Setting of Right Expectations

In the context of a New Task or New Buy situation, 'setting the right expectations' can be of extreme importance especially for a startup. Sweeney (2002), reported brands as being crucial determinants at the following four stages of the B2B buying process – deciding on the tender list; shortlisting for negotiation; signing of purchase agreement; and deciding on supply and support services. Another study by Blombäck and Axelsson (2007), reveals that corporate brand image maybe of special importance when business buyers need to identify new subcontractors. However, this process is only partly formalized, and coupled with limited resources and perceived risk, buyers need to rationalize the selection process. The brand's primary role in such a situation therefore is to attract interest and provide trust with regard to capacity, on-time delivery and competence.

In the case of a startup, if is going to market with a me-too product or service especially, any branding effort aimed at creating a differentiation amongst the channel partners first and then building engagement and conviction with the customers' customers could ease the market acceptance of the startup and its products and services. For instance, the market sits up and takes note if the startup releases a press note saying that it has secured funding from a well-known venture capital firm or personality. This is because any such funding reflects more upon the strength of the idea (or founders' background and capabilities; or product/service etc.) and has a salutary effect on -- channel partners, the customers' customers and all other stakeholders (See: Exhibit 2).

Exhibit 2.

In India, Caratlane.com, an online retailer of jewelry, became newsworthy the day Ratan Tata (Chairman emeritus of Tata Sons, the holding company of the $100 billion steel-to-software Indian conglomerate) invested in it in his personal capacity in 2014. The news reported this event as – "… he (Ratan Tata) joins a list of pedigree angel investors and venture capital firms backing the Bangalore-based company founded by IIT graduates …. and seed-funded by the serial entrepreneur duo Meena Ganesh and K Ganesh …" (Kurian & Sharma, 2014). The iconic status of Tata Sons as a company and Mr. Ratan Tata as a personality; the bellwether engineering institution of India - namely the Indian Institute of Technology (IIT) – all adds up and helps shape the brand image which then may suitably impress – customers; other potential investors and financial institutions as well as endow the startup with a sense of respect all around. One of the founders of Caratlane.com went on say that "… an investment by Ratan Tata who has been at the helm of India's most successful and respected conglomerate is a validation of our approach in building an innovative brand that is disrupting the jewelry market …". (Kurian & Sharma, 2014).

In 2016, Titan Industries Limited, a Tata Group Joint Venture company has acquired a majority stake in Caratlane.com. This was commented upon in the news as – "… the collaboration is sure to bring more credibility to CaratLane as Tata is among the most trusted brands in India …" (Nair, 2016). As a startup in the ecommerce space, the journey of the Caratlane.com has thus grown from strength to strength, this success can be safely said to be equally founded on the brand impact created by associating with and piggybacking upon some of the most iconic personalities and institutions in the country.

Brand Building and Corporate Values and Culture

Finally, another value of building a brand is what it does to the organizational climate and culture and its role in attracting the right talent. For startups the credibility issue is translated into skepticism among professionals who could be valuable for the organization, but they often baulk at the prospect of committing and joining a new entrepreneurial venture. There is tacit acceptance in the industry that for attracting the right talent, what the corporation needs to do is to build what is called an "employer brand". The term indicates specifically to an organization's reputation as an employer, as against its more generic corporate brand reputational image in the general public (Mosley, 2015). The fact that the corporation as an employer brand (as against a brand for consumers and/or other stakeholders) is pertinent to the corporation's ability to successfully attract top talent was validated in an 18 country survey of 'employer branding' as a phenomenon, by interviewing CEOs and HR Heads. One of the main findings of this study was that in the eyes of business leaders the primary responsibility of creating an 'employer brand' vests with the CEO or marketing as opposed to with recruiters and HR (Mosley, 2015).

The corporate brand in a startup's context can imbue a sense of focus and belief in the team and help articulate the organizational culture. Brands have been widely recognized as important sources of organizational value. Brand orientation basically describes the extent to which the organization is orientated around the brand and around maximizing the brand potential (Gyrd-Jones, Helm, & Munk, 2013). Brands, whether product or corporate, can serve therefore as a rallying point to instill the right (or desired) values across the organization. In the context of service organizations, Berry (2000), posits how brand meaning rallies internal stakeholders together around the brand to deliver superior services.

Thus, seen through the prism of the service dominant logic of marketing (See: Vargo & Lusch, 2004, 2008), in the context of brand building within a startup - whether in manufacturing or service businesses – the conclusion of Berry (2000), on the relationship between brands and corporate values and culture, assumes seminal importance.

Startup Branding in the Context of Garnering Support and Allegiance From Financial Publics

Researchers have concluded about the role of marketing for startups by inferring that – "while new ventures strongly emphasize their product and team when pitching in front of investors, they might also proactively communicate marketing capabilities and the value they assign to marketing to increase their chances of getting funding" (Homburg, Hahn, Bornemann, & Sandner, 2014, p. 640).

Compared to new businesses initiated by existing corporations, startups usually have – less capital resources; inadequate numbers of qualified manpower; less legitimacy or brand presence; lack strategic partners who can fill the resource and know-how gaps; informal and evolving organizational structures; and ill-defined or even non-existent business processes. Thus at an abstract level, young startups suffer due to the dual liabilities of being new and being small (Cyert & March, 1992; Hannan & Freeman, 1989).

Therefore, a well-conceived set of brand values and consequently communication of the same may very well mitigate this deficit among startups with respect to legitimacy and confidence, especially in the eyes of the financial publics.

Thus, as seen from multiple perspectives above - whether B2B or B2C - the generic rationale for brand building seemingly works for startups as well. What remains to be seen hereafter is what kind of models can be used for brand building as far as startups are concerned.

BRAND BUILDING FRAMEWORKS

Brand building approaches are numerous and it has received intense attention of various authors and researchers from a variety of perspectives. Simply stated, brands are mechanisms or constructs that help create an identity for an organization or its offerings that differentiates them in the eyes of their customers and other stakeholders.

The value that a brand represents or commands is defined in terms of the concept of brand equity. Brand equity is conceptualized –

… from the consumer perspective as a utility, loyalty, or a clear, differentiated image not explained by product attributes and from a firm perspective as the incremental cash flow resulting from the product with the brand name compared with that which would result without the brand name. (Ailawadi, Lehmann, & Neslin, 2003, p. 1)

There is almost always an element of subjectivity inherent in most brand building processes and the outcomes thereof, although there is a constant endeavor from practitioners and researchers to quantify the assumptions on which brands are built. This is especially so in B2C brands as most of the times the brand values that are manifest on part of marketers - targeted at consumers in particular and other stakeholders in general - are trying to establish an emotional and situational connect with their audiences. These connections therefore are given a relatively personalized context and engagement from the point of view of potential and existing customers. Further, if this theme/message positively reinforces the values sought by the customers, it is supposed to create a 'resonance' (see: Keller, 2001), with them, amplifying the relevance and fit of the brand in that chosen or desired consumer context and narrative.

At this stage, it is pertinent to look at the two possible scenarios of branding for startups in the B2C and B2B domains respectively. The eventual outcome of branding in both the domains may be similar but the 'emotionalism' inherent in the construct of brands is considered to be more pronounced in B2C brands targeted at end-customers, whereas B2B brands are supposed to be built upon more 'rational' foundations and logics. This is so, as the B2B buyer is usually perceived to be a 'professional' buyer who looks more intently at the functional benefits or capacities of the brands in consideration before choosing among them while making a purchase decision. The B2B buyers are also supposed to be more price-conscious and may not have the same price-quality associations as in B2C buying. B2B buying is thus driven by concerns about organizational productivity and profitability (McQuiston, 1989), whereas B2C buying is driven more by psychological and social needs and wants.

B2C Branding Models

In the B2C context, the following two models provide a well-established and proven model for conceptualizing and building brands – Aaker's (1991), Brand Equity Model and Keller's (2001), Customer Based Brand Equity Model.

Aaker (1996, p. 7), defines brand equity as the

… set of brand assets and liabilities linked to a brand, its name or symbol that add or subtract from the value provided by a product or service to a firm and/or to that firm's consumers.

The Brand Equity Model, (Aaker, 1991) posits brand equity as composed of the following five dimensions, namely - brand loyalty; brand awareness; perceived quality; brand associations; and other proprietary assets. The benefits of brand equity for customers are – it helps them process and interpret information about the company/product with certainty; helps reduce risk perceptions in buying; and builds use satisfaction. The benefits to the firm includes – increased efficiency and effectiveness of marketing programs; company/brand loyalty; pricing power and better margins; brand extensions; trade leverage; and hence competitive advantage.

The Customer Based Brand Equity (CBBE) Model enunciated by Keller (2001), proposes a four step process of building strong brands, namely – (i) establishing a proper brand identity, i.e. the breadth and depth of brand awareness (answering the question – 'Who' are you?); (ii) creating an appropriate brand meaning through strong, favorable and possibly unique associations (answering the question – 'What are you?); eliciting positive and accessible brand responses (answering the question – 'What about you; What do I think and feel about you?); and (iv) forging brand relationship with customers, characterized by intense and active loyalty (answering the question – 'What about you and me; What kind of association and how much of a connection would I like to have with you?).

The above process in the CBBE Model is conceptualized as being composed of six building blocks constituting a pyramid structure with 'brand resonance' as the final outcome of a successful brand building campaign (Figure 1).

For every startup, it is of extreme importance to decide upon and define the 'who are we' question very carefully. This is a long term existential question (for the organization as well as a product brand) and has bearing upon how they would want the external and internal stakeholder look at them and what meaning they want them to derive from it.

Figure 1. The Customer Based Brand Equity Pyramid (Keller, 2001)
Source: Keller. K.L. (2001) Building Customer Based Brand Equity: A Blue Print for Creating Strong Brands. Working Paper No. 01-107. Cambridge, MA: Marketing Science Institute. (Reprinted with permission from author)

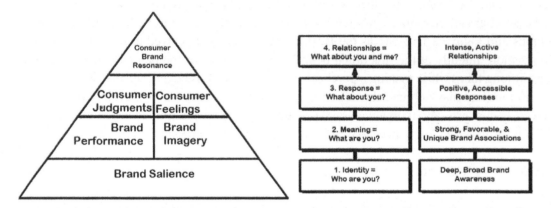

Thus the CBBE model can be used to conceptualize and flesh-out a startup B2C brand, with the clear message that the basic building blocks of brand salience and brand performance need to be passionately researched and assiduously defended against alienating elements that may creep in and destroy the purity of the brand and in effect degenerate the brand to another 'me-too' brand.

The key therefore in successful branding of a B2C startup product or brand, is in being 'honest' in crafting the value proposition in every way of conception and presentation. The salience has to be true and pure for it to be believable and resonate with the target customers.

B2B Branding Models

Branding in the B2B context is often mistakenly seen as a small subset of marketing management, which therefore puts brand building in a silo with its responsibility restricted to one of the teams within marketing. However, since a brand is reflected in everything the company does, a holistic branding approach requires a strategic perspective (Kotler & Pfoertsch, 2007).

It is also to be noted that for branding efforts to be successful in the B2B context, it is not enough to assign a brand manager with a typically short-term job horizon within the company as the sole driver of branding activities (Aaker & Joachimsthaler, 2000). Building, championing, supporting and protecting strong brands in B2B domain is posited to be everyone's job in the company, starting with the chief executive officer (Bedbury, 2002).

A McKinsey (n.d.) study proposes a Business Branding Stakeholder Matrix, classifying the relative importance of various stakeholders in the short-run as well as in the long run. The study concludes that in the short-term (*i.e.* in the inception period) of startups -- customers followed by employees are the two most important stakeholders for B2B startups. The study identifies other stakeholders such as – regulator; investors; suppliers and talent – as being of medium to low importance in the short-run. Thus for B2B startups, any brand building process should take into cognizance these two as crucial building blocks of their brand building foundation.

As far as brand building model for B2B brands, there are a range of models that are available for consideration. Some of these models are discussed after the ensuing case study. (See Exhibit 4).

Exhibit 3. Bunkaari India

The author successfully incubated a startup with a student of his in the retail domain. The business proposition was to showcase a part of the traditional and hand-woven textile weaving traditions of India.

The idea was to look at this as a social enterprise, to focus equally on the welfare of the traditional weaver families located in the vast hinterland of India, unknown and unsung as far as their master craftsmanship is concerned, ridden with resource constraints and poor or non-existent go-to-market strategies or plans. As a result they have traditionally been at the mercy of channel partners who exploit their fragmented existence and marketing resource and market knowledge limitations. The remuneration that the weavers of these traditional categories of hand-woven *Sarees¹* receive are usually far less from the final retail price, as the channel partners (wholesalers and retailers) control the market and the unorganized weavers have very little say in the margins they receive.

The business model was to open exclusive branded stores in different cities of India (including Tier-1, Tier-2 and Tier-3 cities) which would be stocked only with *Sarees*. The brand salience was built around the hand-weaving traditions and ethnic patterns and designs and colors prevalent in different regions of India.

The store brand was named '*Bunkaari*' (which literally means hand-weaving) with material sourced directly from weavers from 11 different regions of India to start with. Through word-of-mouth alone and having strategically located the stores in one city to start with; with no advertising budget and minimal presence in social media; conservative price points (as compared to other similarly themed retail store brands) – the business broke even in its first year of existence itself. People loved it for genuineness of the wares and the moderate pricing and the brand story pictorially depicted in the stores through still pictures and videos.

In the context of Keller's CBBE model, the brand salience was clearly and successfully established in constructing the brand persona of *Bunkaari* by keeping it true to the sub-culturally embedded values of – tradition; purity; honesty and timelessness. In the author's conviction the validation of the previous assertion being true was emphatically established when on day-one of opening of the second *Bunkaari* store in a Tier-2 city located in a Mall, a slow trickle of curious customers walked-in into the store. There was no preceding marketing communication and these were footfalls attracted naturally due to the Mall. There was a clear word-of-mouth effect visible as we witnessed young girls entering the store and browsing and then calling their mothers/sisters to come quickly; taking pictures on their mobile phones and sending it to family members/friends for approval. There was even a case of a family driving down forty kilometers from a nearby industrial city after being called by one of their acquaintances. It helped that the opening day coincided with a national holiday (15 August – Indian Independence Day).

There was a clear realization among the shoppers as witnessed by many of them verbalizing their recognition of certain styles of design/fabric as something they associated with certain regions of India and how authentic the wares were and there was also obvious reference to the 'amazing' (honest) price points (through overheard conversations). We had to entertain so many questions on the videos of weavers in their natural (rural) eco-systems – in various stages of their craft.

A major point of curiosity and interest was the specially designed labels that we had commissioned. These were large sized labels printed on hand-made paper with a concise description of the particular piece of *saree* in question; its history and symbolism (for instance – how the saree in question is relevant/allowed for certain rituals in the Hindu culture); and the region of India of which the particular object was a manifestation of.

We had deliberately avoided the store interior design to be bereft of the 'chrome and glass' look and industrial white lighting. The décor was natural wood paneled walls and shelves with yellow-lighting all around. We created a small central island for people to bring their *sarees* of choice from the racks; a life-size mirror to see the draping; and a small sofa and coffee table at one end of the store for the men/children accompanying the lady buyers to relax and have a cup of tea perhaps. The store was being managed by a mature lady manager who was highly knowledgeable and passionate about the world of *sarees*.

Today we have four stores in four different cities in India. We have not been successful in our original plan of growing through franchised stores. This was because we could not find the right people with the right mindset and passion to continue with the purity with which we had conceived the brand persona.

For this store brand, we depended upon the definition of brand salience to really be of value to the potential buyers. The brand performance was founded upon purity and honesty which helped us create the right 'brand imagery' – as one which was not a dishonest rip-off in the name of Indian tradition and culture as well as not being elitist or touristy.

The 'consumer judgment' was created by the authentic interactions in the store with the store personnel; the communication through pictures and videos; the ambience; and the 'story' narrated by the product *per se* and the other collaterals like labels etc. The 'consumer feeling' was readily witnessed by the excited word-of-mouth generated in the stores and the advocacy that was evident on behalf of real customers exhorting their friends and family members to come and 'experience' the brand.

The 'brand resonance' is manifest by repeat buyers enthusiastically committing themselves to the brand on one hand and their happiness in engaging with the brand across touchpoints and advocating the brand on the other going beyond positive word-of-mouth.

The '*Bunkaari*' brand was thus established without mass media communication. Social media (mainly Facebook) was the only digital marketing effort. More effort and energy was put on conceptualizing the brand salience and how we would portray that in the product/store design and assortment. Being initiated as an offline retail brand, choice of store location obviously has been a very important part of the branding strategy.

Exhibit 4. Happay (Va Tech Ventures Private Limited)

We look at another case study from India, wherein in the B2B space a startup – Va Tech Ventures was established in 2012, wherein they launched a new service product in the expense management space, namely – Happay. The brand Happay met with great success in its chosen market and in 2015 the company was rated as one of the 'Top 10 Hottest Startups' by the apex industry association of the Indian information technology and IT enabled industry – NASSCOM (Srivastava, 2015).

Happay is an online expense management system for businesses that lets them issue cards to employees and track the spending real time, define spending policies and set spending limits among other things. It is a Web- and mobile-based solution wherein all the transactions done using the Happay Card (accepted at all Visa points of sale online, offline and ATMs) are automatically recorded in the Happay mobile app. Employees using the card can click a picture of the receipt and tag it to the respective expense, select expenses based on trips and submit them for approval. Launched as a peer-to-peer (P2P) product, they moved from their P2P product to B2B (business-to-business) product. After they built the first version, they went back to these businesses and were in pilot mode for around four months before they came out in public (Srivastava, 2015).

Subscribing to McKinsey's - Business Branding Stakeholder Matrix, Happay most prominently lists its major customers (arguably, currently they have a customer base of 800 to 900 companies and firms) on the home page itself of their website, as a clear statement of its brand salience for any new and potential client (See: http://www.happay.in). Potential customers are also encouraged to look at some of the case studies published on their website to convince internal stakeholders (in the customer companies) to call Happay for a demo. They also proactively collect and circulate customer endorsements among existing and potential customers as 'brand performance' leading to positive 'customer judgment'.

They project the quality and credibility of their partners to lend credence to their solution in the eyes of discriminating business customers. They proudly proclaim the globally known brand of VISA as their main partner along with RBL Bank from India.

Secondly, the credibility and background of the founders and key employees is the second very important brand building block for B2B brands. This is validated in the case of Happay, as the young co-founders and their impeccable background is established in the eyes of Indian businesses and executives as both of them belong to one of the premier most engineering schools of India. By 2015, the company had acquired 500 business customers and was growing rapidly. But in their early days there were times when the founders felt as if they would fail. At times the founders desperately felt like getting back to the cushy corporate jobs that they had left behind. Anshul Rai and Varun Rathi the co-founders, had joined Tata Power and Microsoft, respectively, after graduating from the very prestigious Indian Institute of Technology (IIT) in 2010. Two years down, they quit their jobs to found Happay (Venkataraman, 2015).

The brand names of the IIT along with Tata and Microsoft indicates a pedigree that is immensely aspirational in a country like India. The IIT's are one of the toughest engineering colleges in the world to get in with about 1.2 million applicants in 2016 registering for the preliminary entrance test for admission to the IIT's (Rao, 2016), vying for about 10,500 total available seats across all the IITs in the country (Nanda, 2016).

Similarly, brand Tata is the most valuable Indian brand among all Indian companies. Valued at Rs. 669 billion ($9.96 billion), brand Tata stands heads and shoulders ahead of the next brand on this list – Reliance, which is valued at Rs. 340 billion ($5.06 billion) (Interbrand-ET, 2015). The brand Tata is itself synonymous with 'trust' as its core value and is much revered and respected brand name in India as a 'branded-house'. As a global company Microsoft was ranked fourth in the Interbrand Global Brand Ranking 2015 and was valued at $67.67 billion (Interbrand, 2015).

Thus, based upon the discussion above, Happay's brand building strategy especially in its initial 3 years as a startup has reaped great results by being intensely focused on –

1. Communicating and leveraging the reputation and number of existing customers
2. Communicating the endorsement from happy customers
3. Piggy-backing on the strength of strategic (channel) partners
4. Leveraging the pedigree and charisma of their co-founders

This Happay case is closely aligned to the Stakeholder Model for Brand Equity (Jones, 2008), which posits that brand value is co-created through interaction with multiple strategic stakeholders, including customers; channel partners; employees etc.

There are also manifest elements from the Network Actor Participation Model (Mäläskä, Saraniemi, & Tähtinen, 2011) in this case. The network actor participation model extends branding theory towards a network approach by defining and describing the direct and indirect activities performed by network actors which are relevant for branding.

The stakeholder model for brand equity (Jones, 2008), identifies the following stakeholders along with their key expectations from brands:

1. **Consumers:** Where Product quality leads to high reputation and high benefits.
2. **Public Opinion:** Rests on socially responsible behavior, Good environmental track record.
3. **Governments:** Look out for legality of operations and job creation.
4. **NGOs:** Expect socially responsible behavior and good environmental track record.
5. **Competitors:** Brand strength, reputation, market strength.
6. **Media:** Is happy with social, ethical, environmental and financially responsible behavior.
7. **Employees:** Seek job security and reputation.
8. **Distribution Partners:** Look for brand strength and reputation.
9. **Suppliers:** Value brand strength, reputation, market strength.
10. **Managers:** Look for market position and reputation of the brand.

On another dimension, based upon Keller's (2001), CBBE model focused on the building of B2C brands - Kuhn, Alpert, and Pope (2008), adapted the CBBE model to propose a revised brand equity model specifically applicable for building B2B brands. With reference to organizational buyers they have found a much greater emphasis on the selling organization, including its corporate brand, credibility and staff, than on individual brands and their associated dimensions. They propose the following changes in the B2C, CBBE pyramid model – (i) Instead of 'Resonance' as the final outcome, the revised model talks of achieving - "Partnership Solutions"; (ii) Consumer judgment is retained as – "Judgments" (of the business customer); however 'Consumer Feeling' is replaced with – "Sales force relationships" referring to the much closer and deeper relationship that business customers seek from vendors vis-à-vis retail customers; (iii) in the CBBE model Brand performance is supposed to result in the creation of 'brand imagery' whereas in the revised model 'Performance' is supposed to build 'reputation' of the brand; and (iv) finally, 'Salience' here refers to salience of the manufacturers' brand.

The Happay case can be seen through the prism of the brand building model adapted by Kuhn *et al.*, (2008), as well. Partnership solutions that they have built with clients are propagated from their website as well as case studies that they publish. Also, the communication of manifest customer endorsements, have also seemingly worked for them well.

In summation, the Stakeholder Model for Brand Equity proposed by Jones (2008), seems to be more comprehensive B2B brand building model, however in the context of a startup, all the stakeholders may not be at the cross-hairs of the company simultaneously, as in the initial stages their attention is more on customers, employees and partners, in that order.

FUTURE RESEARCH DIRECTIONS

The discussion in this chapter has been to establish the relevance of brands for startups, as they strive for establishing their presence in their chosen markets. Extant literature does help to provide foundational underpinnings to why startup managers should look at branding and brand building as an integral part of their go-to-market strategy. The cases presented in the chapter provide real-life examples of how startups in the business-to-business as well as business-to-consumer arenas have successfully incorporated tenets of brand building in their path to business success.

Future research may now focus on specific methodologies relevant to effective branding across different categories of startups in different parts of the world. Specific tools that can help startup brands as different from conventional brand building tools and media as well as the differential importance and hence emphasis needed to utilize these need also to be explored and validated.

CONCLUSION

To conclude, if we look at the concept of value chain as enunciated by Porter (1985), it implicitly identifies the internal competencies that underpin a firm's competitive advantage. This includes 'primary' activities such as – inbound/outbound logistics; operations; service; and marketing and sales. These primary activities are posited to be founded upon and facilitated by 'supportive' activities consisting of – technology, human resource management, procurement, along with firm infrastructure. Competitive advantage is thus construed to possibly emanate – from a superior execution of these activities; through a more synergistic coordination of these activities; and/or a superior management of the interface between the startup firm and the other stakeholders within its value network (Morris, Schindehutte, & Allen, 2005). In the context of managing this interface between the startup and its strategic stakeholders, marketing as a core activity and within that - branding as a tool - does constitute an integral part of any business model chosen by the startup.

The thesis of this chapter was to establish through extant literature and case studies, the relevance of branding for startups, both in the B2C as well as B2B domains. There is enough evidence available both in research literature as well as market events and real company cases to indicate that branding and brand building, seen in a holistic perspective, can serve startups in both B2C and B2B categories. It may be true that the startups have specific challenges in their initial life cycle stages which render them unique as far as brand building processes for an existing and long-standing company is concerned. However, the benefits of focused and creative brand building effort (notwithstanding the lack of resources of all kinds at the startup phase), companies can actually scale-up their businesses faster and have quicker market penetration and expansion outcomes.

The case studies juxtaposed with select brand building models provides rationale and directions for brand building in startups and also identify the foundational building blocks to be considered on priority in both B2C and B2B startups.

REFERENCES

Aaker, D. A. (1991). *Managing Brand Equity: Capitalizing on the Value of the Brand Name*. New York, NY: The Free Press.

Aaker, D. A. (1996). *Building Strong Brands*. New York, NY: The Free Press.

Aaker, D. A. (2004). Leveraging the corporate brand. *California Management Review*, *46*(3), 6–18. doi:10.2307/41166218

Aaker, D. A., & Joachimsthaler, E. (2000). *Brand Leadership*. New York, NY: The Free Press.

Abimbola, T. (2001). Branding as competitive strategy for demand management in SMEs. *Journal of Research in Marketing and Entrepreneurship, 3*(2), 97–106. doi:10.1108/14715200180001480

Ailawadi, K. L., Lehmann, D. R., & Neslin, S. A. (2003). Revenue premium as an outcome measure of brand equity. *Journal of Marketing, 67*(4), 1–17. doi:10.1509/jmkg.67.4.1.18688

Anderson, J. C., & Narus, J. A. (2004). *Business Market Management: Understanding, Creating, and Delivering Value*. Englewood Cliffs, NJ: Pearson Prentice-Hall.

Andruss, P. (2012). Branding Inc. *Entrepreneur, 40*(4), 59–60.

Bedbury, S. (2002). *A New Brand World*. New York, NY: Viking Penguin.

Berry, L. L, (2000). Cultivating service brand equity. *Journal of the Academy of Marketing Science, 28*(1), 128–137. doi:10.1177/0092070300281012

Blombäck, A., & Axelsson, B. (2007). The role of corporate brand image in the selection of new subcontractors. *Journal of Business and Industrial Marketing, 22*(6), 418–430. doi:10.1108/08858620710780181

Certo, S. T. (2003). Influencing initial public offering investors with prestige: Signaling with board structures. *Academy of Management Review, 28*(3), 432–446.

Cyert, R. M., & March, J. G. (1992). *A Behavioral Theory of the Firm*. Malden, MA: Blackwell Publishers Inc.

Drumm, H. J. (2002). *Organisation für Gründer*. Berlin: Springer-Verlag. doi:10.1007/978-3-662-00466-1_13

Dwivedi, A. B. (2016). *The government has finally defined the word 'startup'*. Retrieved July 28, 2016, from https://yourstory.com/2016/02/government-definition-startup/

Fombrun, C. J., & Shanley, M. (1990). Whats in a name? Reputation - building and corporate strategy. *Academy of Management Journal, 33*(2), 233–258. doi:10.2307/256324

Gyrd-Jones, R. I., Helm, C., & Munk, J. (2013). Exploring the impact of silos in achieving brand orientation. *Journal of Marketing Management, 29*(9/10), 1056–1078. doi:10.1080/0267257X.2013.811283

Hannan, M. T., & Freeman, J. (1989). *Organizational Ecology*. Cambridge, MA: Harvard University Press.

Homburg, C., Hahn, A., Bornemann, T., & Sandner, P. (2014). The role of chief marketing officers for venture capital funding: Endowing new ventures with marketing legitimacy. *JMR, Journal of Marketing Research, 51*(5), 625–644. doi:10.1509/jmr.11.0350

Homburg, C., Klarmann, M., & Schmitt, J. (2010). Brand awareness in business markets: When is it related to firm performance? *International Journal of Research in Marketing, 27*(3), 201–212. doi:10.1016/j.ijresmar.2010.03.004

Interbrand. (2015). *Best 100 Brands*. Retrieved July 4, 2016, from http://interbrand.com/best-brands/best-global-brands/2015/ranking/

Interbrand – ET. (2015). *Best Indian Brands 2015 - Poised to Rise*. Retrieved June 3, 2016, from http://interbrand.com/wp-content/uploads/2015/12/Interbrand-Best-Indian-Brands-2015.pdf

Jones, R. (2008). Finding sources of brand value: Developing a stakeholder model of brand equity. *International Retail and Marketing Review, 4*(2), 43–63.

Keller, K. L. (2001). *Building Customer Based Brand Equity: A Blue Print for Creating Strong Brands.* Working Paper, No. 01-107. Cambridge, MA: Marketing Science Institute.

Keller, K. L. (2008). *Strategic Brand Management* (3rd ed.). Upper Saddle River, NJ: Pearson Prentice-Hall.

Keller, K. L. (2015). The branding logic behind Google's creation of Alphabet. *Harvard Business Review, 14*(Aug). Retrieved from https://hbr.org/2015/08/the-branding-logic-behind-googles-creation-of-alphabet

Kotler, P., Armstrong, G., Agnihotri, P., & Haque, E. U. (2010). *Principles of Marketing: A South Asian Perspective.* New Delhi: Pearson Education India.

Kotler, P., & Keller, K. L. (2007). *A Framework for Marketing Management* (3rd ed.). New Delhi: Pearson Education Inc.

Kotler, P., & Pfoertsch, W. (2007). Being known or being one of many: The need for brand management for business-to-business (B2B) companies. *Journal of Business and Industrial Marketing, 22*(6), 357–362. doi:10.1108/08858620710780118

Kuhn, K. L., Alpert, F., & Pope, N. K. L. (2008). An application of Keller's brand equity model in a B2B context. *Qualitative Market Research. International Journal (Toronto, Ont.), 11*(1), 40–58.

Kurian, B., & Sharma, S. (2014). Ratan Tata buys into e-jewellery company. *The Times of India.* Retrieved July 25, 2016, from http://timesofindia.indiatimes.com/tech/tech-news/Ratan-Tata-buys-into-e-jewellery-company/articleshow/42200767.cms

Laroche, M., Nepomuceno, M. V., & Richard, M. O. (2010). How do involvement and product knowledge affect the relationship between intangibility and perceived risk for brands and product categories? *Journal of Consumer Marketing, 27*(3), 197–210. doi:10.1108/07363761011038275

Lechner, C. (2002). *Unternehmensnetzwerke: Wachstumsfaktor für Gründer.* Berlin: Springer-Verlag.

Lennartz, E. M., Fischer, M., Krafft, M., & Peters, K. (2015). Drivers of B2B brand strength – Insights from an international study across industries. *Schmalenbach Business Review, 67*(1), 114–137.

Lynch, J., & De Chernatony, L. (2004). The power of emotion: Brand communication in business-to-business markets. *Brand Management, 11*(5), 403–419. doi:10.1057/palgrave.bm.2540185

Mäläskä, M., Saraniemi, S., & Tähtinen, J. (2011). Network actors participation in B2B SME branding. *Industrial Marketing Management, 40*(7), 1144–1152. doi:10.1016/j.indmarman.2011.09.005

McKinsey & Co. (n.d.). *Business Branding Bringing Strategy to Life.* Retrieved May 20, 2016, from https://www.mckinsey.de/sites/mck_files/files/b2b_branding.pdf

McQuiston, D. H. (1989). Novelty, complexity, and importance as causal determinants of industrial buyer behavior. *Journal of Marketing, 53*(2), 66–79. doi:10.2307/1251414

Milgrom, P., & Roberts, J. (1986). Price and advertising signals of product quality. *Journal of Political Economy, 94*(4), 796–821. doi:10.1086/261408

Mitra, S., & Verma, S. (2016, July 28). Paytm, Zomato in Interbrand's breakthrough brands list. Mint.

Morris, M., Schindehutte, M., & Allen, J. (2005). The entrepreneurs business model: Toward a unified perspective. *Journal of Business Research*, *58*(6), 726–735. doi:10.1016/j.jbusres.2003.11.001

Mosley, R. (2015). CEOs need to pay attention to employer branding. *Harvard Business Review*. Retrieved July 25, 2016, from https://hbr.org/2015/05/ceos-need-to-pay-attention-to-employer-branding

Nair, A. A. (2016). *Titan buys majority stake in CaratLane - Strengthens competition with Ratan Tata-backed Bluestone*. Retrieved July 25, 2016, from https://yourstory.com/2016/05/titan-caratlane/

Nanda, P. K. (2016). How IIT-JEE (Advanced) works, from results to rank list. *Live Mint*. Retrieved August 21, 2016, from http://www.livemint.com/Politics/aYn5sugfwlS2RNav35Z6dJ/How-IITJEE-Advanced-works-from-results-to-ranks.html

Narayandas, D. (2005). Building loyalty in business markets. *Harvard Business Review*, *83*(9), 131–139. PMID:16171217

Petkova, A. P., Rindova, V. P., & Gupta, A. K. (2008). How can new ventures build reputation - An exploratory study. *Corporate Reputation Review*, *11*(4), 320–334. doi:10.1057/crr.2008.27

Porter, M. E. (1985). *The Competitive Advantage: Creating and Sustaining Superior Performance*. New York, NY: Free Press.

Rao, Y. (2016). Number of JEE (Main) aspirants shrinks by over 1 lakh in a year. *The Times of India*. Retrieved August 21, 2016, from http://timesofindia.indiatimes.com/home/education/entrance-exams/Number-of-JEE-Main-aspirants-shrinks-by-over-1-lakh-in-a-year/articleshow/50632885.cms

Rode, V., & Vallaster, C. (2005). Corporate branding for startups: The crucial role of entrepreneurs. *Corporate Reputation Review*, *8*(2), 121–135. doi:10.1057/palgrave.crr.1540244

Schumpeter, J. (1936). *Theory of Economic Development*. Cambridge, MA: Harvard University.

Sethuraman, R., Tellis, G. J., & Briesch, R. A. (2011). How well does advertising work: Generalizations from meta-analysis of brand advertising elasticities. *JMR, Journal of Marketing Research*, *48*(3), 457–471. doi:10.1509/jmkr.48.3.457

Srivastava, M. (2015). Nasscom's top 10 hottest startups. *Live Mint*. Retrieved August 22, 2016, from http://www.livemint.com/Companies/hreuaBUAKKosM5YkKXrJtL/Nasscoms-top-10-hottest-startups.html

Steenkamp, J. B. (2014). How global brands create firm value: The 4V model. *International Marketing Review*, *31*(1), 5–29. doi:10.1108/IMR-10-2013-0233

Stinchcombe, A. L. (1968). *Constructing Social Theories*. New York, NY: Harcourt, Brace & World.

Sweeney, B. (2002, September). B2B brand management. Brand Strategy, 32.

Timmons, J. A. (1999). *New Venture Creation (5ᵗʰ ed.)*. Boston: McGraw-Hill.

Vargo, S. L., & Lusch, R. F. (2004). Evolving to a new dominant logic for marketing. *Journal of Marketing*, *68*(1), 1–17. doi:10.1509/jmkg.68.1.1.24036

Vargo, S. L., & Lusch, R. F. (2008). Service-dominant logic: Continuing the evolution. *Journal of the Academy of Marketing Science*, *36*(1), 1–10. doi:10.1007/s11747-007-0069-6

Venkataraman, R. (2015). Startup stories - We went without salary for 2 yrs. *The Times of India*. Retrieved August 22, 2016, from http://epaperbeta.timesofindia.com/Article.aspx?eid=31806&articlexml=STARTUP-STORIES-We-went-without-salary-for-2-10102015021050&utm_source=Social%20media&utm_medium=sm&utm_campaign=TOI%20news

Ward, M. R., & Lee, M. J. (2000). Internet shopping, consumer search and product branding. *Journal of Product and Brand Management*, *9*(1), 6–20. doi:10.1108/10610420010316302

KEY TERMS AND DEFINITIONS

Branding: The act or process of creating and establishing a brand.

Branding Models: Constructs that have been tested and proposed that explain the logic of the brand's architecture whether in a B2B or B2C context.

Brands: A combination of a name; logo; design; color; graphic etc. that is used to differentiate a product/service or company/organization among other products or companies for the benefit of both internal and external stakeholders of the organization.

Startups: Companies that have been established by independent founders and those that are not subsidiaries of existing companies and are less than five years old.

ENDNOTE

[1] Sarees in the Indian subcontinent refer to a traditional women's garment, consisting of 6 to 11 yards of fabric wrapped around the waist and then draped over the upper half of the torso complementing a stitched blouse for the upper body. Sarees vary in their length based upon the different subcultures and regions of India where women belonging to different ethnic groups wear it in different styles. They are worn across all age groups with equal felicity and are only differentiated by their vividness of color and design wherein older age group women may eschew certain designs/colors construed as too young or inappropriate.

There is a whole eco-system of designs, colors, fabrics and weaves as far as making sarees are concerned, ranging from machine made to hand-woven sarees. Almost each state of India has its own language of sarees, as this piece of cloth has almost mythical powers and sensibility within the Indian culture. For instance a white saree traditionally is the mark of widow-hood and is never worn by brides in Hindu weddings, whereas red is the color of fertility and is frequently the color of wedding sarees. This garment is symbolically also presented to deities in many rituals and usually is the mark of a girl's coming of age in the Indian culture.

This research was previously published in Global Entrepreneurship and New Venture Creation in the Sharing Economy edited by Norhayati Zakaria and Leena Ajit Kaushal, pages 54-74, copyright year 2018 by Business Science Reference (an imprint of IGI Global).

Chapter 10
Fuzzy Time Series:
An Application in E-Commerce

Ali Karasan
Yıldız Technical University, Turkey

İsmail Sevim
Yıldız Technical University, Turkey

Melih Çinar
Yıldız Technical University, Turkey

ABSTRACT

In this chapter, we are planning to make a comparison between conventional Time Series Models and Fuzzy Time Series Models by an application in an e-commerce company. Future sales of furniture will be predicted. The performance of different models and forecasting periods are going to be analyzed to discuss advantages and disadvantages of each method. MAE is chosen as performance indicators of each model and forecasting period combination. As a conclusion to this chapter, generic strategies for prediction in an e-commerce company will be formulated in consideration of these indicators.

1. INTRODUCTION

"Forecasting is about predicting the future as accurately as possible, given all of the information available, including historical data and knowledge of any future events that might impact the forecasts" (Hyndman & Athanasopoulos, 2014). On the other hand, "digital marketing is the marketing which aims to promote brands and reach customers by using all advertisement segments in an electronic medium" (Kahraman et. al, 2015).

This chapter introduces an application of fuzzy time series for a furniture company which makes sells via online. Time series is a part of forecasting methods and such a vague environment like we have, using time series with fuzzy methods is the most appropriate way for forecasting. So in this framework, we search the Scopus database for forecasting, fuzzy time series and e-commerce, then give the obtained review results in tabular and graphical forms.

DOI: 10.4018/978-1-5225-5187-4.ch010

Our chapter is organized as follows. We would like to introduce a mixed way of forecasting and digital marketing, an application of e-commerce for possible solutions with fuzzy time series. Section 2 presents digital marketing. Section 3 presents forecasting and its characteristics. Section 4 presents fuzzy logic. Section 5 presents fuzzy time series and includes a brief literature review about it. Rest of the chapter starts with the Singh's method, follow as Hwang-Chen- Lee's method, regression analysis, and double exponential smoothing using Holt's Method then ends with a conclusion.

2. DIGITAL MARKETING

The Digital Marketing Institution's (DMI) definition for digital marketing is "The use of digital technologies to create an integrated, targeted and measurable communication which helps to acquire and retain customers while building deeper relationships with them".

Digital Marketing's definition for digital marketing is "Digital Marketing is a sub-branch of traditional Marketing and uses modern digital channels for the placement of products e.g. downloadable music, and primarily for communicating with stakeholders e.g. customers and investors about the brand, products, and business progress" (Royle & Laing, 2014).

The concepts "digital marketing" and "e-commerce" are often misused interchangeably. The synonyms to digital marketing are e-marketing, online marketing, or web-marketing and it is related to e-commerce in that manner digital marketing is the tool supporting e-commerce process with supplementary ways such as email marketing, search engine marketing, and social media marketing. Section 6 introduces methods that what we are going to use and includes Singh's method.

Some areas of digital marketing can be sorted as below:

- Advanced Search Engine Optimization (SEO),
- Advertising Support,
- Brand Management,
- Campaign Management,
- Competition Tracking,
- Digital Public Relations,
- E-Commerce,
- Event Management,
- Export Marketing,
- Impact Analysis,
- Mobile Marketing,
- Social Media Management,
- Training,
- Web Analytics, and
- Web Content.

3. FORECASTING

Before we start an extent properties and components of time series and fuzzy time series, we mention forecasting briefly with a list of characteristics' that a decision maker must understand the plan and manage his or her decisions on it effectively for the company's future. Forecasts are made to guide decisions in a variety of fields. This list is given for where forecasts are used and in return diversity of decisions aided by forecasts.

1. Operations planning and control,
2. Economics,
3. Marketing,
4. Financial asset management,
5. Financial risk management,
6. Business and government budgeting,
7. Risk management,
8. Elections,
9. Accidents, and
10. Traffics.

3.1 Characteristics of Forecasts

Companies and managers should take into consideration the some characteristics of forecasts while taking some actions for the future strategies. For being explanatory and more understandable, we use Chopra's and Nahmias' books as a reference explaining of them. Characteristics of the forecast are taken from Nahmias' (2009) book is given with explanations in Table 1.

As in Nahmias' book refers, Chopra and Meindl (2007) determine the same things as properties. It can be shown in Table 2.

Mary Ann Anderson et al (2013) also indicate that in addition to those characteristics:

Table 1. Characteristics of forecasts that were taken from Nahmias' book

1. Forecasts are usually wrong.	Inflexible and sensitive planning system, unexpectable conditions, not included criteria while forecasting may lead too far from results which are anticipated from managers.
2. A good forecast is usually more than a single number.	As Nahmias says a good forecast has not only results but also some measure of expected forecast error.
3. For a good forecasting, aggregation is usually more correct.	"On a percentage basis, the error made in forecasting sales for an entire product line is generally less than the error made in forecasting sales for an individual item."
4. "The longer the forecast horizon, the less accurate the forecast will be."	This one is quite vague. In a high fuzziness environment, one can predict tomorrow's value of the stock market value more accurately than next year's value.
5. "Forecasts should not be used to the exclusion of known information."	If the company is planning a special promotional sale, so that the demand will probably be higher than normal. This information must be annually factored into the forecast.

Table 2. Characteristics of forecasts that were taken from Nahmias' book

1. "Forecasts are always wrong and should thus include both the expected value of the forecast and a measure of forecast error."
2. "Long-term forecasts are usually less accurate than short-term forecasts; that is, long-term forecasts have a larger standard deviation of error relative to the mean than short-term forecasts."
3. "Aggregate forecasts are usually more accurate than disaggregate forecasts, as they tend to have a smaller standard deviation of error relative to the mean."
4. "In general, the farther up the supply chain a company is (or the farther it is from the consumer), the greater is the distortion of information it receives. One classic example of this is the bullwhip effect, in which order variation is amplified as orders move farther from the end customer. As a result, the farther up the supply chain, an enterprise is, the larger is the forecast error. Collaborative forecasting based on sales to the end customer helps upstream enterprises reduce forecast error."

- "If a simple technique yields acceptable accuracy, don't use a more advanced technique",
- Select a forecasting technique that makes good use of the available data,
- There is no single best forecasting technique.

3.2 Elements of a Forecast and Forecasting Methods

A company must be enlightened about numerous factors that are related to forecasting of the future strategies. Some of these factors are listed below:

- Past demand and sales,
- State of the economy,
- Planned price discounts and raises,
- Actions against to competitors,
- Interest rates,
- Inflation rates, and
- Country's environmental conditions.

Francis X. Diebold (1998) clarify six considerations basis for successful forecasting;

- Decision Environment and Loss Function,
- Forecast Aim,
- Forecast Expression,
- Forecast Horizon,
- Information Data Set, and
- Method and Its Complexity.

In light of the foregoing, we must choose the way we will study. There are four types of forecasting where are listed below as Chopra and Meindl (2007) refers;

- **Qualitative:** "Qualitative forecasting methods are primarily subjective and depend on human judgment. They are most appropriate when little historical data is available or when experts have market intelligence that may affect the forecast." This method can be useful and right to accurate when a company joins a new market or develop a new strategy that has no historical data.

- **Causal:** Causal forecasting methods pretend to something that the decision maker wants to find out is highly correlated with certain environmental factors (the state of the economy, interest rates, stock marketing, accidents, etc.). "Causal forecasting methods find this correlation between demand and environmental factors and use estimates of what environmental factors will be to forecast future demand." For example, current account deficit is strongly correlated value of the import. Current account deficit of a country can be reduced by raising the volume of its exports relative to the volume of imports.

- **Simulation:** "Simulation forecasting methods imitate the consumer choices that give rise to demand to arrive at a forecast." Using simulation, a government can combine time-series and causal methods to answer such questions as What will be the impact of local services on vote increases? What will be the impact of a skyscraper construction on urban environment? In a different field with simulation, many facilities' layout plans are imitated to find most productive one. In a conclusion, simulation is distinctly from the other methods and gives us to see results with a way of imitating real word processes.

- **Time Series:** "In these forecasting methods, historical demand is used to make a forecast. They are supported by the hypothesis which event of past demand is a good index of future demand. When the elementary demand motive doesn't differ considerably from one year to the next, these methods are most proper. These are the most easiest approaches to implementing and can serve as a good starting point for a demand forecast." We will use this information as a starting point and build on it with a way of fuzziness.

3.3 Time Series

Therewithal we will go with Time Series and its properties after on. Time series methods are often called naive methods, as they require no information other than the past values of the variable being predicted. Time series is a collection of observations of some economic or physical phenomenon drawn at a discrete point in time. The idea is that information can be inferred from the pattern of past observations and can be used to forecast future values of the series. (Nahmias, 2009)

In time series analysis the goal is to isolate the patterns that arise most often. These include the following as Nahmias (2009) refers;

Trend: *Trend refers to the disposition of a time series to exhibit a stable pattern of rises or decreases. Distinguishing between linear trend (the pattern described by a straight line) and nonlinear trend (the pattern described by a nonlinear function, such as a quadratic or exponential curve). When the pattern of the trend is not specified, it is generally understood to be linear.*

Seasonality: *A seasonal pattern is one that repeats at fixed intervals. In time series, generally thinking of the pattern repeating every year, although daily, weekly, and monthly seasonal patterns are common as well. Fashion wear, ice cream, sunglasses, tanning cream, and heating oil exhibit a yearly seasonal pattern. Consumption of electricity exhibits a strong daily seasonal pattern.*

Cycles: *Cyclic variation is similar to seasonality, except that the length and the magnitude of the cycle may vary. One associates cycles with long-term economic variations (that is, business cycles) that may be present in addition to seasonal fluctuations.*

Randomness: *A pure random series is one in which there is no recognizable pattern to the data. One can generate patterns purely at random that often appear to have structure. An example of this the methodology of stock market chartists who impose forms on random patterns of stock market price data. On the other side of the coin, data that appear to be random could have a very definite structure. Truly random data that fluctuate around a fixed mean form what is called a horizontal pattern.*

4. FUZZY LOGIC

Fuzzy Logic was firstly presented in 1965 by Lotfi A. Zadeh who is a professor of computer science.

While in Boolean logic, there are only two possibilities about the truth values of variables (They might only be '0' or '1'), in Fuzzy logic, a form of many-valued logic, the truth values of variables might be any real number between '0' and '1'. We can say that concept of partial truth, in which the truth value might range between thoroughly true and thoroughly false is solved by means of Fuzzy logic.

There are numerous fields used Fuzzy logic such as robotics, artificial intelligence, optimization, image processing, control theory and thousands of researchers has published a lot of scientific publications (articles, papers, research papers etc.) about Fuzzy logic and Fuzzy Sets. When viewed from this aspect, Fuzzy logic is very useful and fruitful topic for researchers and presents important contributions. Some of these significant contributions of Fuzzy logic was expressed by Lotfi A. Zadeh as the following: (Zadeh, 2008)

1. *FL-generalization. Any bivalent-logic-based theory, T, may be FL-generalized, and hence upgraded, through addition to T of concepts and techniques drawn from fuzzy logic. Examples: fuzzy control, fuzzy linear programming, fuzzy probability theory and fuzzy topology.*
2. *Linguistic variables and fuzzy if–then rules. The formalism of linguistic variables and fuzzy if–then rules is, in effect, a powerful modeling language which is widely used in applications of fuzzy logic. Basically, the formalism serves as a means of summarization and information compression through the use of granulation.*
3. *Cointensive precisiation. Fuzzy logic has a high power of cointensive precisiation. This power is needed for a formulation of cointensive definitions of scientific concepts and cointensive formalization of human-centric fields such as economics, linguistics, law, conflict resolution, psychology, and medicine.*
4. *NL-Computation (computing with words). Fuzzy logic serves as a basis for NL-Computation, that is, computation with information described in natural language. NL-Computation is of direct relevance to mechanization of natural language understanding and computation with imprecise probabilities. More generally, NL-Computation is needed for dealing with second-order uncertainty, that is, uncertainty about uncertainty, or uncertainty for short.*

In summary, progression from bivalent logic to fuzzy logic is a significant positive step in the evolution of science. In large measure, the real-world is a fuzzy world. To deal with fuzzy reality what is needed is fuzzy logic. In coming years, fuzzy logic is likely to grow in visibility, importance, and acceptance.

5. FUZZY TIME SERIES

Fuzzy Time Series (FTS) is a quite new approximation and it is used for finding a solution linguistic time series data problems.

5.1 Definition

Let $Y(t)$ $(t=0,1,2,...)$, a subset of real numbers, be the universe of discourse on which fuzzy sets $f_i(t)$ $(i=1,2,...)$ are defined and $F(t)$ is a collection of $f_i(t)$ $(i=1,2,...)$. Then $F(t)$ is called a Fuzzy Time Series defined on $Y(t)$ $(t=0,1,2,...)$. (Song & Chissom, 1993)

Fuzzy time series methods comprise of three steps, respectively, as the following:

- Fuzzification,
- Identification of fuzzified relations,
- Defuzzification.

A search in the SCOPUS database for the concept "fuzzy time series" gives 4409 papers, it in their titles, abstract and keywords. We analysis 49 of them in detail and only give 33 in below table as a literature review. We will give this review as fuzzy time series and its application area in Table 3. Contextually, Table 3 shows a brief literature review to introduce our framework.

Figure 1 shows the publications that we are examining with respect to subject area, and the distribution is in that way: 24 of the papers are related to computer science (24 papers); engineering (22 papers); mathematics (13 papers); environmental sciences (7 papers); decision sciences (5 papers); social science (5 papers); business, management and accounting (3 papers); other areas (11 papers).

Table 3 illustrates the countries that published the furthest number of fuzzy time series papers. The distribution is given in Table 4.

6. FORECASTING FURNITURE SALES USING SINGH'S METHOD (SINGH, 2008)

6.1 Forecasting Method

It is hard to find a trend or a cycle component in most of the time series data of real world problems and this fact makes conventional time series methods unsuitable for forecasting. Thus, using fuzzy time series is necessary for many real life situations. (Singh, 2008) proposes a fuzzy time series forecasting method to forecast enrollments of Alabama University. Steps of the algorithm of the method are given as:

Table 3. A brief literature reviews about fuzzy time series

Researchers	Problem Definition	Analysis Method	Disadvantages of the Proposed Method	Advantages of the Proposed Method
Wong et. al (2010)	Forecasting the amount of Taiwan export	Comparison of traditional forecasting methods (ARIMA and Vector ARMA) with fuzzy time series models (Two-factor time-variant model, Heuristic model, and Multivariate fuzzy time series Markov model).	Larger forecasting errors in longer experiment time period.	More accurate in the limited information and urgent decision-making circumstances.
Reuter & Möller (2010)	Necessity of predetermining process model to simulate and forecast time series possessing fuzzy random characteristics	Artificial neural networks	Deciding the parameters of artificial neural network is a challenging process.	"Neural networks for fuzzy time series neither need a predetermined process model nor any prior knowledge of the random characteristics to simulate and forecast time series with fuzzy data."
Hwang & Oh (2010)	Predicting the daily and weekly open, high, low, and close prices of the Korea Composite Stock Price Index.	The information used in traditional candlestick chart analysis was newly employed as input variables. A multi-input-multi-output model is decomposed into many multi-input single output models.	Decomposition strategy may cause a loss of valuable information.	The stock market trend can be forecasted based on the predicted open, high, low, and close values. The daily predicted KOSPI information will be useful in trading future prices.
Hadavandi et. al (2010)	Stock price prediction	"Integrated approach based on genetic fuzzy systems (GFS), artificial neural networks (ANN), a hybrid artificial intelligence method called clustering-genetic fuzzy system (CGFS)"	It incurred high computational complexity and lacked stability.	The results of the proposed method showed that forecasting accuracy of CGFS outperforms the rest of approaches regarding MAPE evaluation, and CGFS can be used as a suitable forecasting tool to deal with stock price forecasting problems.
Huang et. al (2011)	To improve forecasting models under fuzzy fluctuations	Fuzzy time series and particle swarm optimization	Comparison with the other models is insufficient due to the low number of selected models and their types.	"Proposed AFPSO model gets higher forecasting accuracy than any existing models at all. It also performs best for fuzzy time series with various orders in training and testing phases, respectively."
Bahrepour et. al (2011)	FOREX forecasting	Self-organizing map method and fuzzy time series	"This hybrid algorithm also requires more computation. While this limitation is not severely hampering for the considered example, since decisions are made only on a daily basis here, it can become a limiting factor when the fast decision and adaptation are required."	"Results indicate that the proposed method surpasses the two earlier studies by providing more accurate prediction."
Oztaysi & Bolturk (2012)	Performance analysis of fuzzy methods on demand forecasting.	Comparison of fuzzy time series, fuzzy regression, adaptive network-based fuzzy inference system and fuzzy rule based system.	"The temporal patterns were defined by rigid regions that were hard to adjust when there is noise in phase space."	Hwang, Chen, Lee's Method outperforms Singh's Method.
Ge et. al (2013)	Forecast university enrollments	Integrated fuzzy time series with the exponential smoothing method	"The temporal patterns were defined by rigid regions that were hard to adjust when there is noise in phase space."	"The empirical analysis shows that the proposed model reflects the fluctuations in fuzzy time series better and provides better overall forecasting results."

continued on following page

Table 3. Continued

Researchers	Problem Definition	Analysis Method	Disadvantages of the Proposed Method	Advantages of the Proposed Method
Singh & Borah (2013)	An efficient time series forecasting model	Mean-Based Discretization(MBD) approach	1. "Apply the proposed model in different regions of temperature data set and check its accuracy and performance with different sizes of intervals and orders." 2. "To test the performance of the model for different types of financial, stocks and marketing data set." 3. This study determines a weight for each FLRs based on the "IBWT". However, Artificial Neuron Networks and Genetic Algorithm may be the feasible alternatives for determining the weight. 4. This study performs defuzzification operation based on the "IBDT". However, researchers can employ Artificial Neuron Networks as an alternative for defuzzification operation, and compare the forecasted results with the presented ones in this paper.	Empirical analyzes signify that the proposed model have the robustness to handle one-factor time series data set very efficiently than the conventional fuzzy time series models.
Petr Dostal (2013)	Companies don't share all the details of their applications. Therefore, information about companies is vague.	Use of fuzzy logic for forecasting purposes.	The temporal patterns were defined by rigid regions that were hard to adjust when there is noise in phase space.	Fuzzy approaches can be used as a support for a decision making on the stock market.
Pandey et. al (2013)	Forecasting for diffusion of innovation by analyzing Tata Nano Car sales in India	Comparison of four fuzzy time series forecasting models and Bass model.	Methods have computational complexity.	All of the four fuzzy time series forecasting models give more accurate results than Bass model where Singh's Algorithm is the most accurate model.
Wang & Xiong (2014)	Forecast the daily wind speed in Hainan province	The first part, "the hybrid model has three steps: an initial ARMA model, outlier detection, and cubic spline interpolation. The second part, a hybrid forecasting model is used to estimate the forecasting model, and the hybrid model is composed of an ARMA model and a bivariate fuzzy time-series model."	Despite the number of observation sites that can useable, they only use at four observation sites in Hainan for daily wind speed forecasting. Due to the a low number of data they have been lacked stability.	"Numerous studies have been conducted to improve the accuracy of wind speed forecasting, but few studies have attempted to improve the forecasting accuracy by removing the outliers in the original wind speed data set that seriously affect the construction and forecasting ability of the models." "Across the population will lead to the greatest preventive impact on fatal traffic injuries among young people and fatal non-traffic injuries among older people."
Ramli et. al (2014)	Early warning system for predicting currency crisis	"AHP to get weights of indicators and ARIMA to forecast the individual indicator and finally by using fuzzy optimization theory to compute the general risk-based relative membership grade."	Founded results show that from a combination of ARIMA and fuzzy optimization models are quite poor especially in predicting future crises.	Proposed method constructed an early warning system by using fuzzy optimization for assessing various currency crisis risks and ARIMA models to forecast individual EWS indicators.
Sadaei et. al (2014)	Multilayer stock forecasting	Fuzzy time series	The method is used for stock market forecasting purposes. In short, although presenting a new model is not a definite proposition because not everyone will agree on the principles followed.	The results show that the proposed model can be considered as a standard systematic model whereby it is possible to develop stock predictions by using FTS.
Marszałek et. al (2014)	To predict movement direction of futures contract on WIG20	Fuzzy time series model	It often generated a false-positive prediction.	Proposed method's representation of financial data using the concept of the ordered fuzzy candlestick can be very useful and allows the construction the forecasting models with more relevant information about the modeled process.

continued on following page

Table 3. Continued

Researchers	Problem Definition	Analysis Method	Disadvantages of the Proposed Method	Advantages of the Proposed Method
Jiang et. al (2015)	Alcohol consumption and fatal injuries in Australia before and after major traffic safety initiatives	ARIMA model	The traditional method needs a large amount of sample data and long-term historical data and also, this study has no certain solutions that can be used in the subject area.	"Study has presented analyzes of what the magnitude and distribution of the reduction in injury mortality might be per liter less of per capita alcohol consumption, suggesting that reducing alcohol consumption."
Wang et. al (2015)	Water quality prediction	Cloud model and fuzzy forecasting	In the proposed method, there are still limitations needed to improve such as the efficient method of employing the approximate periodicity of the water quality parameters.	A fuzzy time series prediction model was applied to generate the computation rule and calculate the predicted value. Compared with the traditional models, it represented the historical numerical data as linguistic value and predicted the water quality parameter based on the fuzzy logical relationship groups, which can better handle the uncertain dataset.
Ismail et. Al (2015)	Electric Load Forecasting	Fuzzy Time Series (FTS) model	More options in selecting the appropriate model to be developed for analyzing future time series data.	A straightforward approach is introduced that is easier to follow. In this forecasting model, authors also make use of the differencing approach to smoothen and to achieve better forecast results.
Prema & Rao (2015)	Necessity of finding an appropriate model for short-term prediction of solar irradiance	Moving Average, Exponential Smoothing, and Decomposition Models are compared.	When the beginning date of past data gets earlier, forecasting error increases.	Decomposition model is more accurate with limited information.
Yi & Chan (2015)	Assess the nonlinear and delayed effects of temperatures on cause-specific and age-specific mortality	A Quasi-Poisson model combined with a distributed lag non-linear model	It incurred high computational complexity and lacked stability.	Allows simultaneous estimation of the non-linear effects across lags.
Kuo et. al (2015)	Fuzzy time series forecasting models usually do not use a learning mechanism to extract valuable information from historical data.	"Evolutionary fuzzy forecasting model in which a learning technique for a fuzzy relation matrix is designed to fit the historical data."	Evolutionary models may not work well for some instances.	"The method can naturally smooth the defuzzification process, thus obtaining better results than many other fuzzy time series forecasting models."
Kocak (2015)	Lack of usage of Moving Averages variables in fuzzy time series models	Autoregressive Moving Averages (ARMAs) models that are based not only on the lagged values of the time series (AR variables) but also on the lagged values of the error series (MA variables).	Identification and estimation can be badly distorted by outlier effects.	Since ARMA models are based on AR and MA variables, they are more realistic than AR models.
Chan et. al (2015)	Test the effectiveness of fuzzy time series forecasting system in a supply chain experiencing disruptions	Discrete event simulation based on the popular beer game model is used.	If tiers are higher, fuzzy time series forecasting gets inferior.	If tiers are not high, fuzzy time series forecasting outperforms classic time series models such as ARIMA.
Baş et. al (2015)	To propose a new hybrid method	Fuzzy time series and a new hybrid forecasting method	"Confidence intervals for the forecasts can not be obtained because the proposed method does not include a stochastic approach. Second, inputs of the network cannot be determined by taking advantage of statistical hypothesis tests. Having the input choice made by the stochastic method rather than by trial and error and obtaining confidence intervals for forecasts is an important step and will constitute the main objective of our future work."	"The application of the proposed method reveals that the proposed method has good forecasting performance. In addition, the proposed method is the first hybrid approach of a fuzzy-time-series method and an autoregressive method. With this hybrid method, a network approach that can model both linear and nonlinear structures in time series was proposed. Applying a fuzzy-time-series method within a network structure allows a connection between ANNs and fuzzy-time-series methods to be established."

continued on following page

Table 3. Continued

Researchers	Problem Definition	Analysis Method	Disadvantages of the Proposed Method	Advantages of the Proposed Method
Telfer et. al (2015)	To obtain relative search engine traffic for terms relating to foot and ankle pain and common treatments	A time series analysis of internet search terms	The proposed method has not enough stability and robustness.	The proposed method may provide insights into some conditions at population levels.
Moosa et. al (2015)	In food insecure countries	A structural time series approach	"A question was raised by an anonymous referee about the possibility of multicollinearity arising from the correlation between the trend and the explanatory variable. This is unlikely to be the case because the trend is not a variable but rather a time series component that is equivalent to the intercept term and a deterministic time trend in a conventional regression equation. In any case, when the correlation coefficient between the trend and the explanatory variable is calculated, it turns out to be statistically insignificant."	"The model does exceptionally well in out-of-sample forecasting."
Lee et. al (2015)	To examine effects of particulate matter	A multicity time-series	They used PM 2.5 concentrations from a single monitoring station for several cities, which may have created a larger exposure measurement error.	Results indicate that stringent air quality regulations are necessary for the East Asia region, as the region continues to produce large amounts of PM emissions with minimal regulation.
D'Urso et. al (2015)	Classifying time series	Autoregressive model, Robust fuzzy C-medoids clustering	The disadvantage of the method is that optimum model order is not known a priori.	Their robust fuzzy clustering model is more appropriate than standard procedures to analyze air quality data properly, inheriting the features of the theoretical and methodological approaches adopted in the clustering process. In particular: It does not depend on the order in which the time series are presented, except when equivalent solutions exist, which very rarely occurs in practice (this is not the case for many other algorithms present in literature).
Davenport et. al (2015)	To analyze grain prices	Time series	A major disadvantage of CBC is that the distance matrices can change quickly. Changes in dissimilarity values should only be interpreted substantively if they persist through time.	The method allows identifying markets where price behavior is either different from other markets in a country or region
Bessec et. al (2016)	Forecasting electricity spot prices in France	Comparison of linear regressions, Markov-switching models, threshold models with a smooth transition and also different combinations of these models.	"The temporal patterns were defined by rigid regions that were hard to adjust when there is noise in phase space."	Markov-switching models give most accurate results but the pooling forecasts.
Cheng et. al (2016)	Forecasting the Taiwan stock exchange capitalization weighted stock index (TAIEX)	The method contains fuzzy time series, fuzzy logical relationships, the particle swarm optimization techniques, the K-means clustering algorithm, and similarity measures.	Metaheuristic nature of the method may deteriorate the performance of forecasting for some instances.	Forecasts of TAIEX predicted by the proposed method are more accurate than the predictions of existing models.

Figure 1. Fuzzy time series publications with respect to subject area

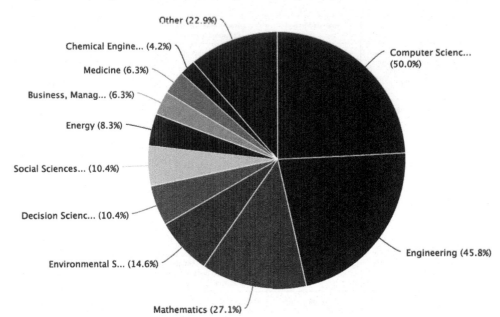

Table 4. Furthest number of fuzzy time series papers with respect to the countries

Country/Territory	Documents
China	11
Malaysia	6
Taiwan	6
India	5
Turkey	4
Iran	4
United States	3
Australia	2
Germany	2
Indonesia	2

1. Let D be a time series data, D_{min} be the minimum value of D, and, D_{max} be the maximum value of D. Then define the universe of discourse (U),

$$U = \left[D_{min} - D_1, D_{max} + D_2 \right]$$

where D_1 and D_2 are two suitable nonnegative numbers.

2. Partition U into equal length of intervals: $u_1, u_2, u_3, \ldots, u_m$. A number of intervals must be equal to the numbers of linguistic variables: $A_1, A_2, A_3, \ldots, A_m$.

3. Construct the fuzzy sets A_i in accordance with the intervals in the previous step and apply the triangular membership rule to each interval $i = 1, 2, \ldots, m$ in each A_i.

4. Fuzzify the historical data and establish the fuzzy logical relationships by the rule:

Let A_i be the fuzzified figure of period n, and let A_j be the fuzzified figure of period n+1, then the fuzzy logical relation is shown as $A_i \to A_j$. Note that A_i is the current state and A_j is the next state.

5. Forecast.

6.1.1 Rules for Forecasting

Notation will be used in the algorithm are defined as

- $\left[*A_j \right]$: Corresponding interval u_j for which membership in A_j is Supremum. (i.e. 1)

- $L\left[*A_j \right]$: The lower bound of interval u_j.

- $U\left[*A_j \right]$: The upper bound of interval u_j.

- $l\left[*A_j \right]$: The length of interval u_j whose membership in A_j is Supremum. (i.e. 1)

- $M\left[*A_j \right]$: The midvalue of interval u_j having Supremum value in A_j.

For $A_i \to A_j$:

Let A_i be the fuzzified figure of period n,

Let A_j be the fuzzified figure of period $n+1$,

Let E_i be the crisp figure of period n,

Let E_{i-1} be the crisp figure of period $n-1$,

Let E_{i-2} be the crisp figure of period $n-2$, and

Let F_j be the crisp forecasted figure of period $n+1$.

This order of three model uses figures of periods $n-2$, $n-1$ and n for framing rules to implement on fuzzy logical relation, $A_i \to A_j$. The method forecasts the figures of period $n+1$ by utilizing actual figures of $n-2$, $n-1$ and n.

6.1.2 Computational Algorithm

Let K be the number of elements in a time series data. Forecasting algorithm of Singh's Method:

```
for k=3:K
R=0;
S=0;
```

```
D(k)=||(E(k)-E(k-1))|-|(E(k-1)-E(k-2))||;
X(k)=E(k)+D(k)/2;
XX(k)=E(k)-D(k)/2;
Y(k)=E(k)+D(k);
YY(k)=E(k)-D(k);
P(k)=E(k)+D(k)/4;
PP(k)=E(k)-D(k)/4;
Q(k)=E(k)+2*D(k);
QQ(k)=E(k)-2*D(k);
G(k)=E(k)+D(k)/6;
GG(k)=E(k)-D(k)/6;
H(k)=E(k)+3*D(k);
HH(k)=E(k)-3*D(k);
if X(k)>=L[*A(k+1)] & X(k)<=U[*A(k+1)] then
        R=R+X(k);
        S=S+1;
endif
if XX(k)>=L[*A(k+1)] & XX(k)<=U[*A(k+1)] then
        R=R+XX(k);
        S=S+1;
endif
if Y(k)>=L[*A(k+1)] & Y(k)<=U[*A(k+1)] then
        R=R+Y(k);
        S=S+1;
endif
if YY(k)>=L[*A(k+1)] & YY(k)<=U[*A(k+1)] then
        R=R+YY(k);
        S=S+1;
endif
if P(k)>=L[*A(k+1)] & P(k)<=U[*A(k+1)] then
        R=R+P(k);
        S=S+1;
endif
if PP(k)>=L[*A(k+1)] & PP(k)<=U[*A(k+1)] then
        R=R+PP(k);
        S=S+1;
endif
if Q(k)>=L[*A(k+1)] & Q(k)<=U[*A(k+1)] then
        R=R+Q(k);
        S=S+1;
endif
if QQ(k)>=L[*A(k+1)] & QQ(k)<=U[*A(k+1)] then
        R=R+QQ(k);
        S=S+1;
```

```
endif
if G(k)>=L[*A(k+1)] & G(k)<=U[*A(k+1)] then
        R=R+G(k);
        S=S+1;
endif
if GG(k)>=L[*A(k+1)] & GG(k)<=U[*A(k+1)] then
        R=R+GG(k);
        S=S+1;
endif
if H(k)>=L[*A(k+1)] & H(k)<=U[*A(k+1)] then
        R=R+H(k);
        S=S+1;
endif
if HH(k)>=L[*A(k+1)] & HH(k)<=U[*A(k+1)] then
        R=R+HH(k);
        S=S+1;
endif
F(k+1)=(R+M(*A(k+1)))/(S+1);
endfor
```

6.2 Application

Sales figures of an online furniture company are analyzed to show the forecasting ability of Singh's Method. Monthly sales of Product-ES3 belongs to the period 01/01/2014-04/30/2015 are given in Table 5.

Steps of the forecasting process:

1. $D_{min} = 1$ and $D_{max} = 68$. Let $D_1 = 0$ and $D_2 = 2$. Then $U = [1,70]$.

2. Let us decide that there are 7 intervals have equal length. Then intervals are given in Table 6.

Fuzzy sets (Linguistic Variables) and corresponding definitions are given in Table 7.

3. Membership grades to fuzzy sets defined in the previous step are

$$A_1 = 1/\mu_1 + 0.5/\mu_2 + 0/\mu_3 + 0/\mu_4 + 0/\mu_5 + 0/\mu_6 + 0/\mu_7,$$
$$A_2 = 0.5/\mu_1 + 1/\mu_2 + 0.5/\mu_3 + 0/\mu_4 + 0/\mu_5 + 0/\mu_6 + 0/\mu_7,$$
$$A_3 = 0/\mu_1 + 0.5/\mu_2 + 1/\mu_3 + 0.5/\mu_4 + 0/\mu_5 + 0/\mu_6 + 0/\mu_7,$$
$$A_4 = 0/\mu_1 + 0/\mu_2 + 0.5/\mu_3 + 1/\mu_4 + 0.5/\mu_5 + 0/\mu_6 + 0/\mu_7,$$
$$A_5 = 0/\mu_1 + 0/\mu_2 + 0/\mu_3 + 0.5/\mu_4 + 1/\mu_5 + 0.5/\mu_6 + 0/\mu_7,$$
$$A_6 = 0/\mu_1 + 0/\mu_2 + 0/\mu_3 + 0/\mu_4 + 0.5/\mu_5 + 1/\mu_6 + 0.5/\mu_7,$$
$$A_7 = 0/\mu_1 + 0/\mu_2 + 0/\mu_3 + 0/\mu_4 + 0/\mu_5 + 0.5/\mu_6 + 1./\mu_7.$$

Table 5. Monthly sales of Product-ES3

#	Period	#Sold
1	01/01/2014-01/31/2014	1
2	02/01/2014-02/28/2014	2
3	03/01/2014-03/31/2014	3
4	04/01/2014-04/30/2014	3
5	05/01/2014-05/31/2014	8
6	06/01/2014-06/30/2014	6
7	07/01/2014-07/31/2014	10
8	08/01/2014-08/31/2014	22
9	09/01/2014-09/30/2014	32
10	10/01/2014-10/31/2014	29
11	11/01/2014-11/30/2014	33
12	12/01/2014-12/31/2014	36
13	01/01/2015-01/31/2015	59
14	02/01/2015-02/28/2015	49
15	03/01/2015-03/31/2015	61
16	04/01/2015-04/30/2015	68

Table 6. Intervals

	Interval
u_1	1-10
u_2	11-20
u_3	21-30
u_4	31-40
u_5	41-50
u_6	51-60
u_7	61-70

Table 7. Fuzzy sets and definitions

Fuzzy Sets	Definition
A_1	
A_2	
A_3	Average Sales
A_4	
A_5	
A_6	Excellent Sales
A_7	Extraordinary Sales

4. Fuzzified sales figures of Product-ES3 is given in Table 8.

5. For forecast the 15th period, variable values can be seen in Table 9 - note that $k = 14$, $L\left[*A(15)\right] = 61$, $U\left[*A(15)\right] = 70$, and $M\left[*A(15)\right] = 65$.

By using values in Table 5, $R = 62$, and $S = 1$. Thus,

Table 8. Linguistic variables of Product-ES3 sales

#	Period	#Sold	Sales in Linguistic Variables
1	01/01/2014-01/31/2014	1	A_1
2	02/01/2014-02/28/2014	2	A_1
3	03/01/2014-03/31/2014	3	A_1
4	04/01/2014-04/30/2014	3	A_1
5	05/01/2014-05/31/2014	8	A_1
6	06/01/2014-06/30/2014	6	A_1
7	07/01/2014-07/31/2014	10	A_1
8	08/01/2014-08/31/2014	22	A_3
9	09/01/2014-09/30/2014	32	A_4
10	10/01/2014-10/31/2014	29	A_3
11	11/01/2014-11/30/2014	33	A_4
12	12/01/2014-12/31/2014	36	A_4
13	01/01/2015-01/31/2015	59	A_6
14	02/01/2015-02/28/2015	49	A_5
15	03/01/2015-03/31/2015	61	A_7
16	04/01/2015-04/30/2015	68	A_7

Table 9. Variable values for forecast of 15th period

Variable	Value	Is Value ∈ [61, 70] ?
D(14)	13.00	-
X(14)	55.50	No
XX(14)	42.50	No
Y(14)	62.00	Yes
YY(14)	36.00	No
P(14)	52.25	No
PP(14)	45.75	No
Q(14)	75.00	No
QQ(14)	23.00	No
G(14)	51.17	No
GG(14)	46.83	No
H(14)	88.00	No
HH(14)	10.00	No

$$F\left(15\right) = \left(62 + 65\right)/\left(1+1\right) = 63.5.$$

Actual and forecasted monthly sales of Product-ES3 are given in Table 10. A comparison of actual and forecasted sales can be seen in Figure 2.

7. FORECASTING FURNITURE SALES USING HWANG, CHEN, LEE'S METHOD (HWANG, CHEN, & LEE, 1998)

7.1 Forecasting Method

Let x be an element of a time series data corresponding to period t, and y be the element corresponding to period $t-1$. Then difference $x-y$ is the variation between period t and $t-1$. (Hwang, Chen, & Lee, 1998) proposes a fuzzy time series forecasting method based on fuzzified variations of a time series data. The fuzzified variation of the historical data between period t and period $t-1$ is as follows:

$$F(t) = u_1/A_1 + u_2/A_2 + \cdots + u_m/A_m$$

where $F\left(t\right)$ denotes fuzzified variation between periods t and $t-1$, u_i is the grade of membership to linguistic variable A_i, m is the number of intervals in universe of discourse - note that $1 \le i \le m$.

Order of proposed model is chosen as a parameter called *window basis*. Let w be the window basis. Then the variation of last year is constitutes the criterion matrix and other w past years are used to construct the operation matrix. Assume that it is intended to forecast the value of period t. Then criterion matrix $C\left(t\right)$ and operation matrix $O^w\left(t\right)$ are built as follows:

Table 10. Actual and forecasted sales of Product-ES3 using Singh's Method

#	Period	Actual Sales	Forecasted Sales
1	01/01/2014-01/31/2014	1	-
2	02/01/2014-02/28/2014	2	-
3	03/01/2014-03/31/2014	3	-
4	04/01/2014-04/30/2014	3	3.15
5	05/01/2014-05/31/2014	8	3.15
6	06/01/2014-06/30/2014	6	6.50
7	07/01/2014-07/31/2014	10	14.00
8	08/01/2014-08/31/2014	22	25.00
9	09/01/2014-09/30/2014	32	34.33
10	10/01/2014-10/31/2014	29	27.25
11	11/01/2014-11/30/2014	33	32.88
12	12/01/2014-12/31/2014	36	33.15
13	01/01/2015-01/31/2015	59	55.00
14	02/01/2015-02/28/2015	49	47.00
15	03/01/2015-03/31/2015	61	63.50
16	04/01/2015-04/30/2015	68	62.60

Figure 2. Comparison of actual and forecasted sales of Product-ES3 by period using Singh's Method

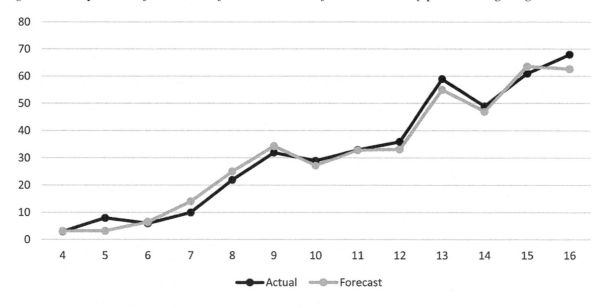

$$C(t) = F(t-1) = [C_1 \quad C_2 \quad \cdots \quad C_m],$$

$$O^w(t) = \begin{bmatrix} F(t-2) \\ F(t-3) \\ \vdots \\ F(t-w-1) \end{bmatrix} = \begin{bmatrix} O_{11} & O_{12} & \cdots & O_{1m} \\ O_{21} & O_{22} & \cdots & O_{2m} \\ \vdots & \vdots & \vdots & \vdots \\ O_{w1} & O_{w2} & \cdots & O_{wm} \end{bmatrix}$$

A relation matrix $R(t)$ is built to calculate the relation between $C(t)$ and $O^w(t)$ and

$$R(t) = O^w(t) \otimes C(t)$$

where

$$R(t) = \begin{bmatrix} O_{11} \times C_1 & O_{12} \times C_2 & \cdots & O_{1m} \times C_m \\ O_{21} \times C_1 & O_{22} \times C_2 & \cdots & O_{2m} \times C_m \\ \vdots & \vdots & \vdots & \vdots \\ O_{w1} \times C_1 & O_{w2} \times C_2 & \cdots & O_{wm} \times C_m \end{bmatrix} = \begin{bmatrix} R_{11} & R_{12} & \cdots & R_{1m} \\ R_{21} & R_{22} & \cdots & R_{2m} \\ R_{31} & R_{32} & \cdots & R_{3m} \\ R_{w1} & R_{w2} & \cdots & R_{wm} \end{bmatrix}$$

where

$$R_{ij} = O_{ij} \times C_j, 1 \le i \le w, 1 \le j \le m$$

and x is the multiplication operator. Then we get fuzzified forecasted variation between period t and $t-1$ where

$$F(t) = \Big[\max \big(R_{11}, R_{21}, \cdots, R_{w1} \big) \cdots \max \big(R_{w1}, R_{22}, \cdots, R_{w2} \big) \cdots \max \big(R_{1m}, R_{2m}, \cdots, R_{wm} \big) \Big]$$

7.2 Application

Step by step calculations of forecasted monthly sales of Product-ES3 belongs to the period 01/01/2014-04/30/2015 are given as follows:

1. Monthly sales of Product-ES3 and variations between consecutive periods are given in Table 11. Assume that variation between 6th and 7th period is needed. Then $variation = 10 - 6 = 4$. Minimum increase D_{min} and maximum increase D_{max} in Product-ES3 sales, and two suitable nonnegative numbers D_1 and D_2 must be determined to define the universe of discourse. $D_{min} = -10$ and $D_{max} = 23$. Let $D_1 = 0$ and $D_2 = 2$. Then the universe of discourse

Table 11. Actual and forecasted sales of Product-ES3 using Singh's method

#	Period	Actual Sales	Variations
1	01/01/2014-01/31/2014	1	-
2	02/01/2014-02/28/2014	2	1
3	03/01/2014-03/31/2014	3	1
4	04/01/2014-04/30/2014	3	0
5	05/01/2014-05/31/2014	8	5
6	06/01/2014-06/30/2014	6	-2
7	07/01/2014-07/31/2014	10	4
8	08/01/2014-08/31/2014	22	12
9	09/01/2014-09/30/2014	32	10
10	10/01/2014-10/31/2014	29	-3
11	11/01/2014-11/30/2014	33	4
12	12/01/2014-12/31/2014	36	3
13	01/01/2015-01/31/2015	59	23
14	02/01/2015-02/28/2015	49	-10
15	03/01/2015-03/31/2015	61	12
16	04/01/2015-04/30/2015	68	7

$$U = \left[D_{\min} - D_1, D_{\max} + D_2 \right] = [-10, 25].$$

2. The universe of discourse U must be partitioned into some number of intervals have even length. Let interval length be equal to 5. Then number of intervals is equal to 7. Intervals are given in Table 12.
3. Fuzzy sets and linguistic variables on the universe of discourse U must be defined. Linguistic variables represented by fuzzy sets are described in Table 13.

Fuzzy sets on the universe of discourse U is as follows:

$$A_1 = 1 / u_1 + 0.5 / u_2 + 0 / u_3 + 0 / u_4 + 0 / u_5 + 0 / u_6 + 0 / u_7,$$

$$A_2 = 0.5 / u_1 + 1 / u_2 + 0.5 / u_3 + 0 / u_4 + 0 / u_5 + 0 / u_6 + 0 / u_7,$$

$$A_3 = 0 / u_1 + 0.5 / u_2 + 1 / u_3 + 0.5 / u_4 + 0 / u_5 + 0 / u_6 + 0 / u_7,$$

$$A_4 = 0 / u_1 + 0 / u_2 + 0.5 / u_3 + 1 / u_4 + 0.5 / u_5 + 0 / u_6 + 0 / u_7,$$

$$A_5 = 0 / u_1 + 0 / u_2 + 0 / u_3 + 0.5 / u_4 + 1 / u_5 + 0.5 / u_6 + 0 / u_7,$$

Table 12. Intervals

	Interval
u_1	(-10)-(-5)
u_2	(-5)-0
u_3	0-5
u_4	5-10
u_5	10-15
u_6	15-20
u_7	20-25

Table 13. Linguistic variables represented by fuzzy sets

Fuzzy Sets	Definition
A_1	Too Big Decrease
A_2	Big Decrease
A_3	Decrease
A_4	No Change
A_5	Increase
A_6	Big Increase
A_7	Too Big Increase

$$A_6 = 0/u_1 + 0/u_2 + 0/u_3 + 0/u_4 + 0.5/u_5 + 1/u_6 + 0.5/u_7,$$

$$A_7 = 0/u_1 + 0/u_2 + 0/u_3 + 0/u_4 + 0/u_5 + 0.5/u_6 + 1/u_7.$$

4. Sales of Product-ES3 must be fuzzified. If the variation between period t and $t-1$ is p where $p \in u_j$, and if there is a value represented by A_k in which the maximum membership value occurs at u_j, then p is translated to A_k. The fuzzified variations of sales of Product-ES3 is given in Table 14.

5. A suitable window basis w must be chosen. Let $w = 2$, and $t = 7$. Then the criterion matrix $C(7)$ is fuzzy variation of 6th period. Thus

$$C(7) = \begin{bmatrix} 0.5 & 1 & 0.5 & 0 & 0 & 0 & 0 \end{bmatrix}.$$

The operation matrix

$$O^2(7) = \begin{bmatrix} Fuzzy\ variation\ of\ period\ 5 \\ Fuzzy\ variaton\ of\ period\ 4 \end{bmatrix} = \begin{bmatrix} A_4 \\ A_3 \end{bmatrix}$$

Table 14. Fuzzified variations of sales of Product-ES3

#	Period	Actual Sales	Variations	Fuzzified Variations
1	01/01/2014-01/31/2014	1	-	-
2	02/01/2014-02/28/2014	2	1	A_3
3	03/01/2014-03/31/2014	3	1	A_3
4	04/01/2014-04/30/2014	3	0	A_3
5	05/01/2014-05/31/2014	8	5	A_4
6	06/01/2014-06/30/2014	6	-2	A_2
7	07/01/2014-07/31/2014	10	4	A_3
8	08/01/2014-08/31/2014	22	12	A_5
9	09/01/2014-09/30/2014	32	10	A_5
10	10/01/2014-10/31/2014	29	-3	A_2
11	11/01/2014-11/30/2014	33	4	A_3
12	12/01/2014-12/31/2014	36	3	A_3
13	01/01/2015-01/31/2015	59	23	A_7
14	02/01/2015-02/28/2015	49	-10	A_1
15	03/01/2015-03/31/2015	61	12	A_5
16	04/01/2015-04/30/2015	68	7	A_4

$$O^2(4) = \begin{bmatrix} 0 & 0 & 0.5 & 1 & 0.5 & 0 & 0 \\ 0 & 0.5 & 1 & 0.5 & 0 & 0 & 0 \end{bmatrix}.$$

Then the relation matrix

$$R(7) = O^2(7) \otimes C(7) = \begin{bmatrix} 0 & 0 & 0.5 & 1 & 0.5 & 0 & 0 \\ 0 & 0.5 & 1 & 0.5 & 0 & 0 & 0 \end{bmatrix} \otimes \begin{bmatrix} 0.5 & 1 & 0.5 & 0 & 0 & 0 & 0 \end{bmatrix}$$

$$R(7) = \begin{bmatrix} 0 & 0 & 0.25 & 0 & 0 & 0 & 0 \\ 0 & 0.5 & 0.5 & 0 & 0 & 0 & 0 \end{bmatrix}.$$

Then fuzzified forecasted variation of 7th period

$$F(7) = \begin{bmatrix} 0 & 0.5 & 0.5 & 0 & 0 & 0 & 0 \end{bmatrix}.$$

6. Fuzzified forecasted variations must be defuzzified. If the grades of membership of the fuzzified forecasted variation have only one maximum u_i, then the forecasted variation is equal to midpoint of u_i, m_i . If there are more than one maximum in the grades of membership of the fuzzified forecasted variation, then the forecasted variation is equal to the average of the midpoints of intervals have maximum grade. For example, forecasted variation of 7th period is equal to $[(-2.5) + 2.5] / 2 = 0$. Note that if all membership grades are equal to 0, then forecasted variation is equal to 0 .

7. Forecasted sales must be calculated. The forecasted sales of a period t is equal to forecasted variation of period t plus sales of period $t - 1$. For instance forecasted sales of 7th period is equal to 6, sales of 6th period, plus 0, forecasted variation of 7th period. Then forecasted sales of 7th period is 6 .

Actual and forecasted sales of Product-ES3 for all periods are given in Table 15 (Window basis $w = 2$). Also a curve compares actual and forecasted sales can be found in Figure 3.

8. FORECASTING FURNITURE SALES USING LINEAR REGRESSION ANALYSIS

8.1 Linear Regression Analysis (Taylor III, 2010)

Linear regression is a forecasting method measures the relationship between two variables. One of these variables is called dependent where the other one is called independent. Relationship is shown in the form of a linear equation:

Table 15. Actual and forecasted sales of Product-ES3 using Hwang, Chen, Lee's Method

#	Period	Actual Sales	Forecasted Sales
1	01/01/2014-01/31/2014	1	-
2	02/01/2014-02/28/2014	2	-
3	03/01/2014-03/31/2014	3	-
4	04/01/2014-04/30/2014	3	-
5	05/01/2014-05/31/2014	8	5.50
6	06/01/2014-06/30/2014	6	13.00
7	07/01/2014-07/31/2014	10	6.00
8	08/01/2014-08/31/2014	22	12.50
9	09/01/2014-09/30/2014	32	29.50
10	10/01/2014-10/31/2014	29	44.50
11	11/01/2014-11/30/2014	33	36.50
12	12/01/2014-12/31/2014	36	33.00
13	01/01/2015-01/31/2015	59	38.50
14	02/01/2015-02/28/2015	49	66.50
15	03/01/2015-03/31/2015	61	46.50
16	04/01/2015-04/30/2015	68	78.50

Figure 3. Comparison of actual and forecasted sales of Product-ES3 by period using Hwang, Chen, Lee's Method

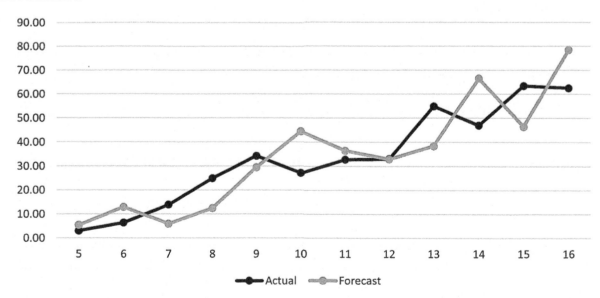

$y = a + bx.$

where y is dependent variable, a is intercept, b is slope, and x is independent variable. The slope and the intercept must be calculated to develop the linear equation given below. By using the following least squares formulas:

$$b = \frac{\sum xy - n\overline{xy}}{\sum x^2 - n\overline{x}^2},$$

$$a = \overline{y} - b\overline{x}.$$

where $\overline{x}$ is the mean of the x data and $\overline{y}$ is the mean of the y data. Once linear equation is developed, forecasts of periods can be calculated by using the equation.

8.2 Application

Monthly sales of Product-ES3 is given in Table 1. For sales data, an independent variable is a period number and the dependent variable is actual sales of Product-ES3. Thus, the data to be used in linear regression analysis can be given as Table 16.

By using least squares formulas, an intercept a and slope b is found -13.375 and 4.6765, respectively. Thus linear equation is

$$y = 4.6765x - 13.375.$$

Assume that forecasted sales of 12th period is needed. If $F(t)$ is the forecasted sales of period t, then $F(12)$ is equal to y where $x = 12$. Therefore

$$F(12) = 4.6765 \times 12 - 13.375 = 42.743.$$

Actual and forecasted sales of Product-ES3 for all periods are given in Table 17. Also, a curve compares actual and forecasted sales can be found in Figure 4.

Table 16. Sales data in terms of dependent and independent variables for linear regression analysis

x	1	2	3	4	5	6	7	8	9	10	11	12	13	14	15	16
y	1	2	3	3	8	6	10	22	32	29	33	36	59	49	61	68

Table 17. Actual and forecasted sales of Product-ES3 using linear regression analysis

#	Period	Actual Sales	Forecasted Sales
1	01/01/2014-01/31/2014	1	-8.70
2	02/01/2014-02/28/2014	2	-4.02
3	03/01/2014-03/31/2014	3	0.65
4	04/01/2014-04/30/2014	3	5.33
5	05/01/2014-05/31/2014	8	10.01
6	06/01/2014-06/30/2014	6	14.68
7	07/01/2014-07/31/2014	10	19.36
8	08/01/2014-08/31/2014	22	24.04
9	09/01/2014-09/30/2014	32	28.71
10	10/01/2014-10/31/2014	29	33.39
11	11/01/2014-11/30/2014	33	38.07
12	12/01/2014-12/31/2014	36	42.74
13	01/01/2015-01/31/2015	59	47.42
14	02/01/2015-02/28/2015	49	52.10
15	03/01/2015-03/31/2015	61	56.77
16	04/01/2015-04/30/2015	68	61.45

Figure 4. Comparison of actual and forecasted sales of Product-ES3 by period using linear regression analysis

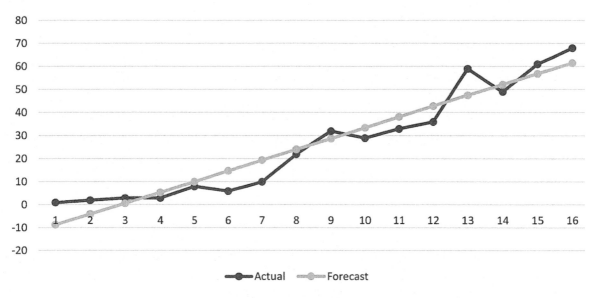

9. FORECASTING FURNITURE SALES USING DOUBLE EXPONENTIAL SMOOTHING USING HOLT'S METHOD

9.1 Double Exponential Smoothing Using Holt's Method (Nahmias, 2009)

Holt's method is a version of double exponential smoothing developed to forecast time series follow a linear trend. Two smoothing constants α and β must be determined for forecasting, α is for the value of time series (intercept) and β is for the trend (slope). Method uses two equations to calculate S_t as the value of intercept at period t and G_t as the value of the slope at period t. These two equations are as follows where D_t is the actual figure of period t:

$$S_t = \alpha D_t + (1 - \alpha)(S_{t-1} + G_{t-1}),$$

$$G_t = \beta(S_t - S_{t-1}) + (1 - \beta)G_{t-1}.$$

If the current period is t and figures of τ periods after from period t is needed to be forecasted, then following formula is used for forecasting:

$$F_{t,t+\tau} = S_t + \tau G_t.$$

Four parameters must be defined before applying Holt's method formulas: α, β, S_0 and G_0. There are two rules for α and β:

1. $\alpha, \beta \in [0,1]$,
2. $\beta \leq \alpha$.

The first rule is obligatory. However latter one is not an obligation but recommended for stability. There is no certain rule for choosing S_0 and G_0 One option can be choosing intercept and slope of a linear regression equation as S_0 and G_0, respectively. This strategy is used in application of this method in this study.

9.2 Application

Monthly sales of Product-ES3 may be found in Table 5. Assume that for sales data $\alpha = \beta = 0.8$, $S_0 = -13.375$, $G_0 = 4.6765$, and $\tau = 1$ (Note that S_0 is equal to interception value of linear regression analysis and G_0 is equal to slope value of linear regression analysis).

For forecasting sales of 1st period:

$$S_1 = 0.8 \times 1 + (1 - 0.8) \times (-13.375 + 4.6765) = -0.9397,$$

$$G_1 = 0.8 \times \left(-0.9397 + 13.375\right) + \left(1 - 0.8\right) \times 4.6765 = 10.88354 ,$$

$$F_{1,1} = -0.9397 + 1 \times 10.88354 = 9.94384 .$$

Actual and forecasted sales of Product-ES3 for all periods are given in Table 18. Also, a curve compares actual and forecasted sales can be found in Figure 5.

10. CONCLUSION

It is well-known that main advantage of e-commerce companies over traditional "brick-and-mortar" retailers is a substantial reduction in infrastructure related costs. The number of e-commerce companies has been increased since the 1990s. Developments in internet technologies and electronic payment methods enable e-commerce companies to reach many customers around the world. Therefore, these companies serve more people than traditional companies. However, this constitutes a problem: Forecasting demand accurately. Selling different types of products, serving customers from all around the world and different cultures, and possibility to gain new customers day by day make forecasting the customer demand a challenging problem. Thus, forecasting methods work properly for traditional retailers may not forecast demands of e-commerce companies accurately.

Table 18. Actual and forecasted sales of Product-ES3 using Double Exponential Smoothing Using Holt's Method

#	Period	Actual Sales	Forecasted Sales
1	01/01/2014-01/31/2014	1	9.94
2	02/01/2014-02/28/2014	2	9.39
3	03/01/2014-03/31/2014	3	5.99
4	04/01/2014-04/30/2014	3	3.40
5	05/01/2014-05/31/2014	8	9.82
6	06/01/2014-06/30/2014	6	7.06
7	07/01/2014-07/31/2014	10	11.59
8	08/01/2014-08/31/2014	22	28.76
9	09/01/2014-09/30/2014	32	42.27
10	10/01/2014-10/31/2014	29	34.08
11	11/01/2014-11/30/2014	33	34.95
12	12/01/2014-12/31/2014	36	38.20
13	01/01/2015-01/31/2015	59	70.56
14	02/01/2015-02/28/2015	49	55.23
15	03/01/2015-03/31/2015	61	65.46
16	04/01/2015-04/30/2015	68	74.73

Figure 5. Comparison of actual and forecasted sales of Product-ES3 by period using double exponential smoothing using Holt's method

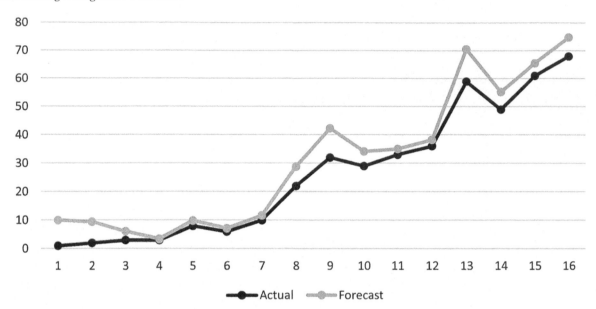

Different kinds of techniques are used for forecasting. Forecasting methods can be grouped into four categories as qualitative, casual, simulation, and time series. Each group has its own pros-and-cos and it is said that there is not a method works best for all situations. Qualitative methods are preferred when no historical data exists where causal methods are used when two or more variables are thought to be correlated. Simulation methods incorporate time series and causal relations into models to imitate consumer choices. Fuzzy set theory can help forecasters to incorporate human intuition and experience into forecasting models while handling uncertainty.

In this study, a brief literature review about fuzzy time series is given in discussions about the relation between digital marketing and e-commerce, fuzzy set theory and fuzzy time series forecasting methods. One causal model, one-time series method, and two different fuzzy time series forecasting methods are compared for a product sold by an e-commerce company of furniture sales. Mean absolute error (MAE) is used as performance measure where $MAE = \dfrac{1}{n}\sum_{i=1}^{n}\left|f_i - y_i\right|$ where n is the number of elements in a dataset, y_i is the value of ith element of the dataset, and f_i is the forecasted value of ith element of the dataset. Singh's method has a MAE value of 2.61 where Hwang, Chen, Lee's method, Linear Regression Analysis, and double exponential smoothing using Holt's method have MAE values 13.01, 9.17, and 6.28 respectively. Note that lower MAE values are preferred among others.

As future study given Product-ES3 sales data may be analyzed by other fuzzy time series forecasting methods to compare the accuracy of each method. Also superiority of fuzzy time series forecasting models over conventional time series methods may be studied by comparison of fuzzy and conventional methods.

REFERENCES

Bahrepour, M., Akbarzadeh-T, M. R., Yaghoobi, M., & Naghibi-S, M. B. (2011). An adaptive ordered fuzzy time series with application to FOREX. *Expert Systems with Applications*, *38*(1), 475–485. doi:10.1016/j.eswa.2010.06.087

Bas, E., Egrioglu, E., Aladag, C. H., & Yolcu, U. (2015). Fuzzy-time-series network used to forecast linear and nonlinear time series. *Applied Intelligence*, *43*(2), 343–355. doi:10.1007/s10489-015-0647-0

Bessec, M., Fouquau, J., & Meritet, S. (2016). Forecasting electricity spot prices using time-series models with a double temporal segmentation. *Applied Economics*, *48*(5), 361–378. doi:10.1080/0003 6846.2015.1080801

Bolturk, E., Oztaysi, B., & Sari, I. U. (2012, November). Electricity consumption forecasting using fuzzy time series. In *Computational Intelligence and Informatics (CINTI), 2012 IEEE 13th International Symposium on* (pp. 245-249). IEEE. doi:10.1109/CINTI.2012.6496768

Chan, F. T., Samvedi, A., & Chung, S. H. (2015). Fuzzy time series forecasting for supply chain disruptions. *Industrial Management & Data Systems*, *115*(3), 419–435. doi:10.1108/IMDS-07-2014-0199

Cheng, S. H., Chen, S. M., & Jian, W. S. (2016). Fuzzy time series forecasting based on fuzzy logical relationships and similarity measures. *Information Sciences*, *327*, 272–287. doi:10.1016/j.ins.2015.08.024

Chopra, S., & Meindl, P. (2007). Supply chain management. In *Strategy, planning & operation* (pp. 265-275). Gabler.

D'Urso, P., De Giovanni, L., & Massari, R. (2015). Time series clustering by a robust autoregressive metric with application to air pollution. *Chemometrics and Intelligent Laboratory Systems*, *141*, 107–124. doi:10.1016/j.chemolab.2014.11.003

Davenport, F., & Funk, C. (2015). Using time series structural characteristics to analyze grain prices in food insecure countries. *Food Security*, *7*(5), 1055–1070. doi:10.1007/s12571-015-0490-5

Deng, W., Wang, G., & Zhang, X. (2015). A novel hybrid water quality time series prediction method based on cloud model and fuzzy forecasting. *Chemometrics and Intelligent Laboratory Systems*, *149*, 39–49. doi:10.1016/j.chemolab.2015.09.017

Diebold, F. X. (1998). *Elements of forecasting*. South-Western College Publ.

Dostál, P. (2013). Forecasting of Time Series with Fuzzy Logic. In Nostradamus 2013: Prediction, Modeling, and Analysis of Complex Systems (pp. 155-161). Springer International Publishing. doi:10.1007/978-3-319-00542-3_16

Efendi, R., Ismail, Z., & Deris, M. M. (2015). A new linguistic out-sample approach of fuzzy time series for daily forecasting of Malaysian electricity load demand. *Applied Soft Computing*, *28*, 422–430. doi:10.1016/j.asoc.2014.11.043

Ge, P., Wang, J., Ren, P., Gao, H., & Luo, Y. (2013). A new improved forecasting method integrated fuzzy time series with the exponential smoothing method. *International Journal of Environment and Pollution, 51*(3-4), 206–221. doi:10.1504/IJEP.2013.054030

Hadavandi, E., Shavandi, H., & Ghanbari, A. (2010). Integration of genetic fuzzy systems and artificial neural networks for stock price forecasting. *Knowledge-Based Systems, 23*(8), 800–808. doi:10.1016/j.knosys.2010.05.004

Huang, Y. L., Horng, S. J., He, M., Fan, P., Kao, T. W., Khan, M. K., & Kuo, I. H. et al. (2011). A hybrid forecasting model for enrollments based on aggregated fuzzy time series and particle swarm optimization. *Expert Systems with Applications, 38*(7), 8014–8023. doi:10.1016/j.eswa.2010.12.127

Huarng, K. (2001). Heuristic models of fuzzy time series for forecasting. *Fuzzy Sets and Systems, 123*(3), 369–386. doi:10.1016/S0165-0114(00)00093-2

Hwang, H., & Oh, J. (2010). Fuzzy models for predicting time series stock price index. *International Journal of Control, Automation, and Systems, 8*(3), 702–706. doi:10.1007/s12555-010-0325-2

Hwang, J. R., Chen, S. M., & Lee, C. H. (1998). Handling forecasting problems using fuzzy time series. *Fuzzy Sets and Systems, 100*(1), 217–228. doi:10.1016/S0165-0114(97)00121-8

Hyndman, R. J., & Athanasopoulos, G. (2014). *Forecasting: principles and practice*. OTexts.

Ismail, Z., Efendi, R., & Deris, M. M. (2015). Application of Fuzzy Time Series Approach in Electric Load Forecasting. *New Mathematics and Natural Computation, 11*(3), 229–248. doi:10.1142/S1793005715500076

Javedani Sadaei, H., & Lee, M. H. (2014). Multilayer stock forecasting model using fuzzy time series. *The Scientific World Journal*. PMID:24605058

Jiang, H., Livingston, M., & Room, R. (2015). Alcohol consumption and fatal injuries in Australia before and after major traffic safety initiatives: A time series analysis. *Alcoholism, Clinical and Experimental Research, 39*(1), 175–183. doi:10.1111/acer.12609 PMID:25623416

Kahraman, C., Yazıcı, I. & Karaşan, A. (2015). *A Literature Survey on the Usage of Fuzzy MCDM Methods for Digital Marketing*. doi: 10.4018/978-1-4666-8808-7.ch001

Kocak, C. (2013). First-order ARMA type fuzzy time series method based on fuzzy logic relation tables. *Mathematical Problems in Engineering*.

Kuo, I. H., Horng, S. J., Kao, T. W., Lin, T. L., Lee, C. L., & Pan, Y. (2009). An improved method for forecasting enrollments based on fuzzy time series and particle swarm optimization. *Expert Systems with Applications, 36*(3), 6108–6117. doi:10.1016/j.eswa.2008.07.043

Marszałek, A., & Burczyński, T. (2014). Modeling and forecasting financial time series with ordered fuzzy candlesticks. *Information Sciences, 273*, 144–155. doi:10.1016/j.ins.2014.03.026

Mary Ann Anderson, M. S. E., Anderson, E. J., & Parker, G. (2013). *Operations Management for Dummies*. John Wiley & Sons.

Moosa, I. (2015). The effect of oil prices on stock prices: A structural time series approach. *International Journal of Global Energy Issues*, *38*(4-6), 232–241. doi:10.1504/IJGEI.2015.070261

Nahmias, S. (2009). *Production and operations analysis* (International Edition). McGraw-Hill.

Pandey, P., Kumar, S., & Shrivastav, S. (2013). Forecasting using Fuzzy Time Series for Diffusion of Innovation: Case of Tata Nano Car in India. *National Academy Science Letters*, *36*(3), 299–309. doi:10.1007/s40009-013-0140-4

Prema, V., & Rao, K. U. (2015). Development of statistical time series models for solar power prediction. *Renewable Energy*, *83*, 100–109. doi:10.1016/j.renene.2015.03.038

Ramli, N. A., & Ismail, T. (n.d.). *Application of Fuzzy Optimization and Time Series for Early Warning System in Predicting Currency Crisis*. Academic Press.

Reuter, U., & Möller, B. (2010). Artificial neural networks for forecasting of fuzzy time series. *Computer-Aided Civil and Infrastructure Engineering*, *25*(5), 363–374. doi:10.1111/j.1467-8667.2009.00646.x

Singh, P., & Borah, B. (2013). An efficient time series forecasting model based on fuzzy time series. *Engineering Applications of Artificial Intelligence*, *26*(10), 2443–2457. doi:10.1016/j.engappai.2013.07.012

Song, Q & Chissom, B. S. (1993). Forecasting enrollments with fuzzy time series-Part I. *Fuzzy Sets and Systems, 54*, 1–9. doi:0165-0114/93/$06.001

Song, Q & Chissom, B. S. (1993). Forecasting enrollments with fuzzy time series-Part II. *Fuzzy Sets, and Systems, 62*, 1–8. doi:0165-0114/94/$07.00

Song, Q., & Chissom, B. S. (1993). Forecasting enrollments with fuzzy time series-Part I. *Fuzzy Sets and Systems*, *54*(1), 1–9. doi:10.1016/0165-0114(93)90355-L

Taylor, B. W. III. (2010). *Introduction to Management Science* (10th ed.). Upper Saddle River, NJ: Prentice Hall.

Telfer, S., & Woodburn, J. (2015). Let me Google that for you: a time series analysis of seasonality in internet search trends for terms related to foot and ankle pain. *Journal of Foot and Ankle Research*, *8*(1), 1-10.

Wang, J., & Xiong, S. (2014). A hybrid forecasting model based on outlier detection and fuzzy time series–A case study on Hainan wind farm of China. *Energy*, *76*, 526–541. doi:10.1016/j.energy.2014.08.064

Wong, W. K., Bai, E., & Chu, A. W. C. (2010). Adaptive time-variant models for fuzzy-time-series forecasting. Systems, Man, and Cybernetics, Part B: Cybernetics. *IEEE Transactions on*, *40*(6), 1531–1542.

Yi, W., & Chan, A. P. (2015). Effects of temperature on mortality in Hong Kong: A time series analysis. *International Journal of Biometeorology*, *59*(7), 927–936. doi:10.1007/s00484-014-0895-4 PMID:25179530

Zadeh, L. A. (1965). Fuzzy Sets. *Information and Control*, 8(3), 338–353. doi:10.1016/S0019-9958(65)90241-X

Zadeh, L. A. (1968). Fuzzy algorithms. *Information and Control*, 12(2), 94–102. doi:10.1016/S0019-9958(68)90211-8

Zadeh, L. A. (1973). Outline of A New Approach to the Analysis of-of Complex Systems and Decision Processes. *IEEE Transactions on Cybernetics*, 3(1), 28–44. doi:10.1109/TSMC.1973.5408575

Zadeh, L. A. (2002). Is there a need for fuzzy logic. *Information Sciences*, 178(13), 2751–2779. doi:10.1016/j.ins.2008.02.012

This research was previously published in the Handbook of Research on Intelligent Techniques and Modeling Applications in Marketing Analytics edited by Anil Kumar, Manoj Kumar Dash, Shrawan Kumar Trivedi, and Tapan Kumar Panda, pages 258-290, copyright year 2017 by Business Science Reference (an imprint of IGI Global).

Chapter 11
Branding Through Sponsorship–Linked Marketing:
A Case of Chinese Sports Apparel and Equipment Brand "Li Ning"

Luke Lunhua Mao
University of New Mexico, USA

James Zhang
University of Georgia, USA

ABSTRACT

The essence of sponsorship is reciprocity. Whereas sport organizations and event promoters have increasingly relied on sponsors' resources and financial support to stage their events, many companies have also been vigorously seeking sponsorship opportunities to actualize their marketing goals, such as enhancing brand equity. This research examines the impacts of sponsorship-linked marketing activities on perceived consumer-based brand equity elements (i.e., brand loyalty, perceived quality, and brand awareness/associations) of the sponsor. This was done through a case study of how sponsorship-linked marketing strategy has shaped the development of Li Ning Company Limited, a Chinese sports apparel and equipment company. Results show that the branding effectiveness of sponsorship directly depends on event quality, perceived event-brand congruency, and brand experience, but not level of sports involvement.

INTRODUCTION

Sponsorship-linked marketing is the "orchestration and implementation of marketing activities for the purpose of building and communicating an association (link) to a sponsorship" (Cornwell, 1995, p. 15). Research findings have suggested that most companies invest in sport sponsorships in an effort to achieve branding goals, such as increasing brand awareness and enhancing brand image (Cornwell & Maignan, 1998; Walliser, 2003). Many corporate marketing managers have perceived sponsorship as an effective vehicle to enhance brand equity (Cornwell, Roy, & Steinard, 2001). In fact, corporate in-

DOI: 10.4018/978-1-5225-5187-4.ch011

vestments on sponsorship have increased rapidly over the past two decades. The number of U.S.-based companies spending more than $ 15 million on sponsorship grew from 85 in 2005 to over 100 in 2013 (IEG, 2014), with worldwide sponsorship expenditure projected at $ 53.3 billion in 2013 (IEG, 2013). Companies of various backgrounds have actively involved in sponsorship-linked marketing (IEG, 2014). The top U.S. based sponsors, among many others, include Anheuser-Busch, PepsiCo, General Motors, Coca-Cola, Nike, and Visa (IEG, 2014). The magnitude of sponsorship can also be manifested by The Olympic Partners (TOP) program. For instance, the twelve TOP sponsors of the Beijing Olympic Games contributed $866 million in cash, goods, and/or services for the 2008 Olympic Games (IOC, 2009). The average expenditure for each TOP sponsor exceeded $ 60 million.

With the prevalence of sponsorship-linked marketing, the evaluation of its effectiveness has attracted much scholarly interest. Researchers have proposed various theoretical explanations in an attempt to demystify the black box of the branding function of event sponsorship, including mere exposure (Zajonc, 1968), low involvement processing (Pham, 1991), image transfer (Gwinner, 1997), consumer inference (Pracejus, 1998), brand-event-dual-route (Martensen et al., 2006) and associative learning (Mao, Zhang, Connaughton et al. 2013). For instance, the central theme of mere exposure theory is that when an individual is repeatedly exposed to a stimulus, the mere exposure is capable of creating a positive attitude or preference for this stimulus, which is independent of cognition system (Zajonc, 1980). The image transfer theory, assuming that the cumulative interpretation of meanings or associations attributed to events is "transferrable" to sponsoring brands, by paring a brand with an event. Whereas mere exposure effects just take advantage of event as a vehicle for exposure, the effects of image transfer is typically moderated by the degree of function and/or image similarities between event and brand (Gwinner & Bennett, 2008; Kamins & Gupta, 1994; McDaniel & Heald, 2000). Therefore, sports apparel and equipment companies, such as Nike, Adidas, Wilson, and Speedo, have an innate advantage of using sports sponsorship and athlete endorsement to promote their brands due to their natural links (i.e., function and image similarities) with sports. Sponsorship resource is typically regarded by these companies as their distinct competitive advantage (Amis, Pant, & Slack, 1997).

Most existing studies on sponsorship have taken the prevailing effects-measurement perspective, which essentially are empirically driven (Olkkonen, 2001). A case study based on more detailed and longitudinal descriptions may offer an alternative approach to delineate the picture of the phenomenon. At issue is how a company may adopt sponsorship-linked marketing to enhance brand equity. The development of the Chinese sports apparel and equipment company, Li Ning (itself is also a brand), is a case that provides insight of how a company gradually learns to position and market its brand by using sponsorship-linked marketing. The goal of this case is to show how sports sponsorship-linked marketing has helped Li Ning to raise brand awareness and establish brand image in its domestic market—China during different stages of development, and how it plans to use sponsorship marketing strategy to gain entry into western markets that are predominated by international industrial leaders (e.g., Nike, Adidas, and others). The case is structured as follows. First, we briefly introduce the company (brand) of Li Ning. We then discuss the managerial dilemma confronted in current stage of development, followed by an investigation of its sponsorship practices in building its brand equity. Third, to corroborate the section on "Li Ning and its sponsorship-linked marketing practice", a survey study was also conducted and discussed. Finally, we summarize its successful experience and propose caveats and suggestions for future development.

LI NING AND ITS SPONSORSHIP-LINKED MARKETING

Theoretically sponsorship-linked marketing works for a company's branding strategy (Cornwell et al., 2001; Keller, 1993), it comes with costs. It often requires financial and human resources investment, as well as committed responsibilities. Empirically, it is very difficult to evaluate the true effects of sponsorship due to sponsorship contracts are always not publicly observable, and the effects are confounded by other marketing activities, such as advertising, sales promotion, or publicity (Pham, 1991). The case of Li Ning may shed light on how sponsorship-linked marketing strategy may work for a sport apparel company in an emerging market.

Development of Li Ning and Its Strengths

Li Ning Company Limited, is a major Chinese athletic company which makes athletic shoes and sporting goods. Li Ning, the major brand of the company, was founded in 1991 by and named after Mr. Li Ning, the Chinese legendary gymnast who won 6 medals at the Los Angles Olympic Games in 1984. Through over 20 years' development, the company underwent several rounds of reform (Yu, 2008). The company has seen an explosive growth in shoe sales in the past several years. In 2009, the company's total revenue broke the threshold of $1 billion for the first time and reached $1.25 billion. The company was listed in Hong Kong Stock Exchange Market in 2004. In January 2010, Li Ning opened its U.S. headquarters and flagship store in Portland, Oregon. The company manufactures and sells branded products targeting for consumers engaging in sporting activities such as running, basketball, badminton, football, tennis, and fitness. As of 2010, Mr. Li Ning remains the Chairman of the Board of Directors (Li Ning Company Limited, 2011).

The growth of Li Ning has a dynamic interaction with the strengths associated with its brand name. Firstly, Li Ning's branding strength lies with the name of its creator. Mr. Li Ning, as a heroic athletic star, has been known as the "prince of gymnastics" and recognized as one of the most influential athlete in China. The Li Ning brand was founded in 1991 when China was for the first time to host an international sporting event-- the 11th Asian Games. Taking advantage of Mr. Li Ning's reputation and the event, the Li Ning brand was able to be made known to the public expeditiously (Yu, 2008). In particular, in early 1990s, international brands such as Nike and Adidas had just begun to pilot China's market and had not fully assaulted the market. This gave Li Ning a golden opportunity to grow and it soon became the number one sports product brand in China in terms of reputation and sales (Cheng, 2002). The brand name "Li Ning" and the brand logo resembling the initials of "LN" therefore have been widely recognized in mainland China's market (Yu, 2008; Moore, 2008).

Secondly, the brand "Li Ning" has relative strong product category association due to the success and impact of Mr. Li Ning as an athletic icon. The brand itself has an innate link with sports performance and athletic spirit which many of Li Ning's competitors may have taken many years to forge and a substantive fortune to communicate to the market. In addition, Li Ning is also associated with the belief of "nationality", and has an emotional appeal of "kinship" or "affinity". In China, athletes are national assets because they have been traditionally financially supported by the country (Riordan & Jones, 1999). In a collectivism culture like China, a high performance athlete in the grassroots' mind represents the national pride and national spirit of excellence (Xu, 2006). Therefore, the association Li Ning has naturally embedded is a distinctive asset for the brand.

Branding Ling Ning: Weakness

Despite the advantages associated with the brand name, Li Ning has encountered many branding difficulties during its stages of development, such as establishing unique brand associations. Marketing gurus have advocated that each product must tirelessly communicate a single distinctive benefit to its consumers (Kotler & Keller, 2006). In a society where consumers are faced with overloading information, the brand must own a simple, focused position in the prospect's mind, usually a benefit associated with the product category (Aaker, 1996; Kotler & Keller, 2006; Shugan, 1980). Although Li Ning has pioneering advantage in the brand association of "athletic performance" in China, the association is not unique and has been undermined by company's unclear strategy during early period of development (Yu, 2008). First, the brand association is not distinctive. Most high profile sports brands, apparel brand Nike, tennis brand Wilson, or outdoor brand The North Face, share these associations. In addition, due to competitors' high spending on contracting high performance athletes to represent their products, Li Ning's brand associations have been overshadowed. Second, the social economic development stage of China's society overall has shaped Li Ning's development strategy. In early days, Li Ning had been selling clothes and shoes for casual wearing rather than for sports. At that time, sport was just a flamboyant concept rather than lifestyle. Chinese people used to wear Li Ning on any occasion. Further, due to the constraints of technology and expertise, Li Ning had not established the image of "professional sports products" brand (PwCC, 2002).

Li Ning understands the importance of youth market. However, the majority of youth in China nowadays are dreaming of the coolness of Nike. The brand personality Li Ning has been cultivating were "grassroots", "affinity", "national", but not "energetic", "coolness", or "rebellious" that most younger generations of Chinese want to be (PwCC, 2002). The story the Li Ning has been telling is no longer resonated in younger Chinese culture. Although Li Ning has a higher market share in 2nd and 3rd tier cities, we suspect that the brand loyalty is rather low among young consumers. Actually, it is reported that 50% of Li Ning's consumers are 35 years old or above (PwCC, 2002). They are more interested in international brands, but due to availability and affordability, they may have chosen Li Ning as a substitute. Given any opportunity, these consumers may switch to other brands.

Branding Ling Ning: Challenges

The global market for athletic footwear has grown in the last decades, but the market is cooling down with a reduced growth rate. From 2003 to 2004, the market for athletic apparel and footwear grew by almost $7.5 billion, 12%. Between 2004 and 2005, however, it grew by less than $4 billion; in percentage terms, the 6% growth was only half as high as growth a year earlier. Furthermore, in 2007, global footwear sales reached $44.4 billion, a mere 2% increase from 2006. The international market have been dominated by traditional high profile brands—Nike, Adidas, Reebok, Puma, etc. (Wikinvest, 2009).

In fact, Li Ning produces shoes and sportswear, largely for the Chinese market (Li Ning Company Limited, 2014). While the global and European athletic footwear market has been slowing down, the market for athletic footwear in China has grown at double-digit rates since 2000 (Wikinvest, 2009). China's increasing wealth and rising middle class led the Chinese market for retail goods to reach over $232 billion in 2006, with growth expected to be at least 15% annually (Wikinvest, 2014). For example, Nike's sales in China increased by 50% on a currency-neutral basis in 2008, particularly because of higher footwear sales (Nike, 2009). Li Ning also increased by over 50% in 2008, with total revenue reached

$983 million (Li Ning Company Limited, 2009). In China's sports apparel market, Li Ning takes a lead in second and third tier cities where consumers have limited accession to Nike and Adidas, and Li Ning has absolute distribution advantages (PwCC,2002). However, in the most profitable metropolitan markets, Li Ning can hardly compete with Nike and Adidas. Those international high profile brands have already established high entry barriers to defend their market share. These barriers include efficiency of global production, advanced channel management, innovation and designing, experience and expertise, and most importantly brand personality (PwCC, 2002). In second and third tier cities, Li Ning is facing fierce competition with other international brands, Chinese domestic brands, and unbranded products because in this market, the entry barriers are relatively easy to overcome.

Li Ning's Sponsorship-Linked Marketing Strategy

Since the birth of the brand, Li Ning has been active in sponsoring sports events in China, mainly by sponsoring national teams, individual athletes, the event organizers, or the event itself (li-ning.com, 2014). In fact, Li Ning made its début appearance through sponsoring the Beijing Asian Games in 1992. Li Ning applied to be the exclusive provider of sportswear for the Asia torch relay with five million yuan (less than one million US dollars) with the support of a state-owned enterprise, *jianlibao*, which the Li Ning brand was affiliated with. It is clear that in earlier years, Li Ning took a rather opportunistic approach to sponsorship (Yu, 2008). The purpose of the sponsorship activities was to raise brand awareness and notify the mass Chinese that Li Ning founded a brand under his name.

Over the years, Li Ning has aggressively used sponsorship deals, particularly with athletes and sports teams, both at home and abroad, to raise its profile. In 2006 the company signed "strategic collaborations" contracts with the National Basketball Association, the Association of Tennis Professionals, the China University Basketball Association, and the China University Football League. It also signed sponsorship deals with the Chinese national teams and the Sudan track and field team. The company provided apparel for the Argentina national basketball team at international events including the 2008 Summer Olympic Games and 2012 Summer Olympic Games (Li Ning, 2007). A similar deal was made with the Swedish Olympic Committee (China Daily, 2007). Since at least 2004, both the men's and women's Spanish National Basketball Team have been equipped by Li Ning. Li Ning is an official marketing partner of the American National Basketball Association and has sponsorship deals with at least six players: Baron Davis of the Los Angeles Clippers, Shaquille O'Neal of the Boston Celtics, Damon Jones of the Milwaukee Bucks, José Calderón of the Toronto Raptors, Evan Turner of the Philadelphia 76ers, and Dwyane Wade of the Heat (Li-ning.com, 2014). In 2006, O'Neal signed a five-year deal with Li Ning, reportedly worth US$1.25 million (China Daily, 2006). Six years later, Dwyane Wade signed a ten-year deal with Li Ning, reportedly worth US$60 million, the largest deal made by the company, and the highest profile signing of an American sports star by a Chinese company (Beam, 2014).

With the growth of company and accumulative experience in marketing, the company realizes that brand awareness is no longer as imperative an issue as it was in the earlier days. As discussed, the major difficulty lies with Li Ning's brand personality and acceptance by younger consumers. Since 2000, Li Ning has made tremendous efforts to promote their brands among the younger generation through sponsoring / initiating youth sports events, such as China University Football League, Chinese Youth Basketball Events, and etc. Besides sponsoring events, the company is also actively seeking for endorsement of athletic stars, in particular the NBA star players who have tremendous influences on the Chinese youth. For example, Shaquille O'Neal of the Boston Celtics has a personality that is inconsistent with traditional Li Ning brand personality. However, by aligning with the "Shark", it seems that Li Ning aimed at changing its brand image to catering the culture of the younger generation. The appeal of O'Neal to the younger generation is what Li Ning was missing. In 2010, Li Ning signed the Philadelphia 76ers rookie, Evan Turner, to represent its products. It is reported to be a 3-year deal worth around $12 million dollars (phillystylemag.com, 2010). How Li Ning will leverage the values of Evan Turner bringing to the brand is still an open question. Turner will wear Li Ning's shoes for both home and away games. It is expected that the signing of Turner will expose the brand to the world-wide NBA fans; and the publicity of Turner will bring "free" publicity to the brand. More importantly, by associating the brand with Turner, Li Ning would expect that sports fans will transfer their affection from their star player to the sponsored brand (Gwinner, 1997; Mao et al., 2013); the performance of Turner will enhance Li Ning's perceived brand quality in consumer's mind; and Turner's star power and personality can cultivate a preferable brand personality among younger consumers.

In summary, Li Ning has primarily relied on sponsorship-linked marketing strategy to brand its products. However, to evaluate the effects of these marketing efforts is a formidable task for professionals and researcher. In recent years, researchers have proposed various sponsorship communication theories or models to explain the effects of sponsorship, such as low-involvement communication model (Pham, 1991), image transfer model (Gwinner, 1997), and associative learning theory (Mao et al., 2013). In order to gain some insights into how consumers respond to Li Ning's sponsorship-linked marketing activities, a theoretical framework was firstly developed based on a review of literature and a survey study was subsequently conducted to test the findings from the first stage.

BRANDING AND BRAND EQUITY

Traditionally, two approaches or paradigms have been used to study brand equity. One is a financially based approach for estimating the value of a brand in terms of asset valuation (Kapferer, 2008; Keller, 1993). The other is strategy-based customer-oriented approach for improving marketing productivity (Keller, 1993), focusing on the relationship between customers and the brand (Kapferer, 2008). Following a customer orientation approach, frameworks developed by Aaker (1991, 1996) and Keller (1993) have often been adopted for studying brand equity. In Aaker's seminal brand equity framework, brand equity comprises five elements:

1. Brand awareness,
2. Perceived quality,
3. Brand associations,
4. Brand loyalty, and
5. Other proprietary brand assets.

Aaker (1996) later expanded the span of the concept and proposed the Brand Equity 10 as a systematic measure to evaluate brand equity across products and markets with both financial and distribution indicators. Keller's (1993) consumer-based brand equity, somewhat different from Aaker's model, is based on the premise that the brand resides in the minds of individual consumers as a cognitive construal (Heding, Knudtzen, & Bjerre, 2009) and focuses solely on the brand's relationship with its consumers (Batra, Myers, & Aaker, 1997). In Keller's conceptualization, consumer-based brand equity is "the differential effect of brand knowledge on consumer response to the marketing of the brand" (p. 2), and brand knowledge comprises brand awareness (e.g., brand recall and recognition) and brand image (i.e., a set of associations linked with the brand's attributes, benefits, or attitudes toward it). As such, consumers' familiarity and knowledge of a brand in terms of favorability, strength, and uniqueness determine a brand's equity. Comparatively speaking, Aaker's (1996) framework is essentially more comprehensive and incorporates a wide range of customer-based brand equity dimensions.

The awareness, associations, perceived quality, and loyalty dimensions represent consumers' perceptions of a brand. Awareness is related to the strength of a brand in consumer's memory reflected by consumers' ability to recall or recognize the brand under different conditions (Keller, 1993). Brand awareness plays an important role in consumers' decision-making as it can affect perceptions and attitudes, and in some context, it can drive brand choice and even loyalty (Aaker, 1996). Aaker divided brand associations into eleven categories, which include product attributes, intangibles, customer benefits, relative price, use/application, user/customer, celebrity/person, lifestyle/personality, product class, competitors, and country/geographic area. Brand associations lead to brand image and thus establish a solid network of brand knowledge (Keller, 1993). Perceived quality is consumer's subjective judgment about a product's overall excellence or superiority based on personal product experiences, unique needs, consumption situations, and other factors (Yoo et al., 2000; Zeithaml, 1998). As one of the key dimensions of brand equity, perceived quality provides a surrogate variable for other more specific elements of brand equity (Aaker, 1996). Brand loyalty is a deeply held commitment to purchase a preferred product or service in the future (Oliver, 1997) and is the core dimension of brand equity (Aaker, 1996). It is generally comprised of behavioral and attitudinal loyalty (Kaynak, Salman, & Tatoglu, 2008), suggesting that loyal customers hold favorable attitudes and thus routinely purchase a particular brand. Drawn from Aaker and Keller's conceptualizations of brand equity, Yoo and Donthu (2001) developed a multi-dimensional consumer-based brand equity scale (MBE). This measure was developed through rigorous measurement procedures, and it exhibited sound psychometric properties. Its generalizability has been examined across multiple samples drawn from Koreans, Korean American, and American populations (Yoo, Donthu, & Lee, 2000).

Factors Affecting Branding Effects

Martensen et al. (2007) proposed that two routes can influence the branding effectiveness of sponsorship-linked marketing, namely brand route and event route. Brand route represents the default psychological state of a consumer towards a brand; whereas, event route refers to the consumer's involvement, emotions, and attitude towards an event and their transfer into a sponsoring brand. Furthermore, as image transfer theory suggested, perceived brand-event congruence (Becker-Olsen & Simmons, 2002; McDaniel, 1999; Speed & Thompson, 2000) is a major factor that links event route and brand route and thus has a significant influence on branding effects.

The event route is a major concern of this study as it is under volitional control of sponsorship marketing managers. In particular, the quality of an event to be sponsored is crucial to the success of sponsorship-linked marketing and thus a major decision factor of marketing managers – the conceptual model accordingly highlights event quality as a core determinant. How to evaluate the quality of event itself is a formidable task for researchers, and is beyond the scope of this paper. We construe the quality of event as a subjective evaluation associated with consumers' event involvement, emotions intrigued by the event and event attitudes. Although all these three factors had been investigated in the regard of sponsorship effects evaluation (Hansen, Halling, & Christensen, 2006; McDaniel, 1999), they were not systematically conceptualized as indicators of event quality. In this paper, we have constructed a second order index called the Event Quality Index (EQI) which comprised involvement, emotions, and event attitude to measure event quality. Furthermore, we acknowledge the importance of brand route and perceived brand-event congruency in evaluating the branding effects. Without controlling the influence of existing brand experience and perceive brand-event congruency, we may commit omitted variables bias (Wooldridge, 2009). In this investigation, we have also included sports involvement, as it is a key characteristic of the target market of Li Ning's products, active sports participants and followers. The main purpose of the survey study was to investigate the influence of event quality, perceived brand-event congruence, prior brand experience, and sports involvement, on the branding effects of Li Ning's sponsorship-linked marketing.

METHOD

Based on a comprehensive review of literature, we developed a questionnaire including the following sections:

1. An index of event quality that consists of involvement, emotional responses, and attitude toward the event,
2. Prior brand experiences and perceived brand-event congruency,
3. Perceived branding effects of the event to be sponsored by Li Ning, and
4. Sport/event involvement and background information.

Stimulus

Three diverse sporting events of different magnitudes and market environments were purposefully selected as stimulus to measure the branding effects of Li Ning's sponsorship-linked marketing. They are a hallmark mega event (i.e., 2008 Beijing Olympic Games), a popular national major sport league with high achievement in international competitions (i.e., Chinese Basketball Association), and a notorious national major sport league with low achievement in international competitions (i.e., Chinese Soccer League). The two leagues and one event represented the primary sport properties in China at the time of data collections and they vary drastically in event magnitude, event participants, event spectators, television viewership, and national and social significance.

Branding Effects

The major dependent variable is branding effectiveness. It is operationalized in accordance with Aaker's conceptualization. Measurement of branding effectiveness was based on a modified application of the multidimensional brand equity measure (MBE) developed by Yoo and Donthu (2001). MBE contains 10 items on Likert five-point scale. This measure incorporates three dimensions of brand equity: brand awareness/associations, perceived quality, and brand loyalty. This section was preceded with the following statement: 'If Li Ning athletic shoe brand decides to sponsor Event X, to what extent will your evaluation of the following aspects of the brand be changed?'

The Yoo and Donthu's (2001) consumer-based brand equity scale was validated in literature. As the questions were modified and translated into Chinese in this study, exploratory factor analyses were executed to analyze the dimensionality of the perceived change of brand equity. The dimensions generated in this study generally matched with Yoo and Donthu's original dimensions: brand awareness/ association, brand royalty, and perceived quality. 63.7% to 66.7% of total variances were explained by this three-factor extraction. The rotated component matrix is presented in Table 1. All dimensions except "perceived quality" in CBA data (0.65) were higher than the generally recommended lower threshold of .70 for Cronbach's alpha (Nunnally & Bernstein, 1994), and the perceived quality generally exceeded the minimum criterion 0.6 (Bagozzi & Yi, 1988; Malhotra and Birks, 2006) for satisfactory internal consistency reliability. Summary scores for each dimension therefore were used in further analysis.

Event Quality Index

Event Quality Index (EQI) was comprised of the following components: involvement, emotions, and event attitude. Zaichkowsky's (1994) Personal Involvement Inventory (PII) was adopted to measure the consumers' involvement with an event. This 10-item short version of PII contains items on a 7-point semantic-differential scale. PII and its revised versions have been repeatedly used in sport marketing studies (Martensen *et al.*, 2007; McDaniel, 1999). A measure of 20 statements assessing personal feelings developed by Hansen et al. (2005, 2006) was chosen to assess emotional responses to the broadcast viewing of Beijing Olympic Games. This measure had been tested in several sport event settings (Hansen et al., 2006; Hansen, Martensen, & Christensen, 2005; Martensen et al., 2007). The 20 items were measured on a 4-point Likert scale (4 = very strong feeling to 1 = no feeling). Attitude toward the event was measured by 3 items measured on a 7-point semantic-differential scale, which was adopted from Muehling and Laczniak (1988). The measures adopted in this study were context and domain free in nature; therefore, they could be used to measure the involvement with, attitudes towards, and feelings about other events and to compare different events.

For the involvement variables, an identical two-factor pattern emerged across all the three groups based on an eigenvalue equal to or greater than 1.0, explaining a total of 54.4% to 60.3% of variances (Table 1). An examination of content interpretability was conducted by comparing current results with Zaichkowsky's (1994) results. In Zaichkowsky's research, affective dimension included "interesting, exciting, appealing, fascinating, and involving", and cognitive dimension included "important, relevant, means a lot to me, valuable, and needed". Three items (important, interesting, and relevant) in the current study did not fit in with original conceptualization, hence were not used for further analysis. The 20 items of emotional responses first generated different patterns of dimensionality across three groups. Both Olympic Game and CSL data sets generated three factors, while CBA data set generated two factors, which is rather reasonable as emotions are not as simple as just positive and negative (Bagozzi et al., 1999; Richins, 1997). For the Olympic data, the item "worry" alone turned out to be the third factor, and the item "hope" had a tendency of double loading; and the item of "surprising" in CSL data had high loadings on all the three e factors. As mentioned, a two-factor solution to emotional responses has been commonly used by researchers (Martensent et al., 2004). Hence factor analyses fixing number of factors at two were conducted to further check the pattern congruency among three groups. A clear pattern of positive-negative emotions was then generated across all three groups, with 47.5% to 53.4% of total variances explained. The rotated component matrix is presented in Table 1. The internal reliability for positive involvement, cognitive involvement, positive emotions, negative emotions, and attitude construct

Table 1. Solutions of factor analyses of variables associated with branding effects

Variable	Olympic (N=556)					CBA (N=615)					CSL (N=621)				
	M	SD	1	2	3	M	SD	1	2	3	M	SD	1	2	3
I consider myself to be loyal to X	.39	.68			.69	.40	.23	.83			.68	.13		.69	
X would be my first choice	.19	.81			.75	.31	.26	.79			.81	.18		.75	
I will not buy other brands if X is available at the store	.09	.75			.66	-.15	.17	.64			.75	.17		.66	
The likely quality of X is extremely high	.35	.23	.76		.24	.78	.19		.80		.23	.76			.78
The likelihood that X would be functional is very high	.23	.18	.86			.79	.26		.84		.18	.86			.79
I can recognize X among other competing brands	.53	.30		.66		.18	.57			.53	.30	.40	.66		
I am aware of X	.73	.12		.73		.11	.72			.73	.12	.30	.73		
Some characteristics come to my mind quickly	.82	.13		.66		.29	.72			.82	.13	.12	.66		
I can quickly recall the symbol or logo of X	.71	.24		.78		.22	.74			.71	.24	.26	.78		
I have difficulty in imagining X in my mind	.73	.31		.72		.07	.73			.73	.31	.23	.72		
Eigen value			2.88	2.02	1.77	2.79	1.69	1.68	2.69	2.02	1.66	2.88	2.02	1.77	2.79
% variance explained			28.70	2.20	17.70	27.90	16.90	16.80	26.90	2.10	16.60	28.70	2.20	17.70	27.90

were higher than the generally recommended lower threshold of .70 for Cronbach's alpha (Nunnally & Bernstein, 1994). As emotional responses are discrete in nature, we converted the positive emotions and negative emotions to a ratio scale based on the following equation – Emotional Ratio= (Summary of Positive Emotions)/ (Summary of Negative Emotions). To construct an event quality index, the cognitive involvement, affective involvement, emotional ratio, and attitude then model in a second order CFA model. The second order event quality model fits the data well (RMSEA=.094, CFI=.99, SRMR=.018).

Brand Experience, Perceived Brand-Event Congruence, and Sport Involvement

To measure prior brand experience, two follow-up questions about familiarity and likeability with the brand on a Likert 5 point scale were asked to those respondents who answered 'yes' to the question 'have you ever used/owned Li Ning product.' The perceived event-brand congruence of each brand with Olympic Games was also assessed by adopting 2 items adopted from Gwinner's (1999) representing functional-based similarity and image-based similarity, respectively. These items were "It is likely that (participants) in the (event name) use (brand name) during the (event name)," and "The (event name) and (brand name) have a similar image" (Gwinner & Eaton, 1999, p. 50). Three items of sports involvement was adapted from Orlick's (1974) Primary and Secondary Sport Involvement scale. Participants rated the frequency with which they take part in any sport activities, and the frequency with which they watch sport on television. They also reported how much they like sports on a Likert 5-point scale. In addition, a demographic information section included the following variables: gender, age, education level, and residency. These items were phrased in a multiple-choice response format.

Participants and Procedures

Research participants ($N = 803$) were students in two comprehensive universities that are located in a metropolitan coastal city and a mid-sized city of China respectively. Because both universities accept students from all over China, a wide range of geographical representations among the respondents were further ensured. Given that university students are a predominant segment of spectators and TV viewers of sporting events in China and they are also an important market segment of Li Ning's products, studying a student sample for the research questions was deemed relevant and appropriate.

Following the institutional approval for the conduct of this study, instructors of general physical education classes with the university was contacted and asked for support and cooperation with the data collection process. The physical education classes were a part of the general education curriculum of the university; thus, students in these classes represented a wide range of academic majors and disciplines. With the support of an instructor, test administration was usually conducted right before or during a class. Participation in the study was voluntary although a small notebook was used as an incentive for those who completed the questionnaire. Generally, it took an individual approximately 20 minutes to complete the questionnaire. All responses were anonymous and confidentiality was ensured.

A total of 1002 copies of questionnaires (i.e., 334 copies each set) were distributed to those who were willing to participate in the study and 803 copies were returned with completed responses, representing a valid response rate of 80.1%. The completion of each questionnaire was checked before rewarding a respondent with a notebook. Of all respondents, 63.6% were female and 36.4% were male. In terms of geographic locations where they mostly lived before 16 years old, 10% grew up in large size cities, 12.3% in medium size cities, 41.7% in small towns, 34.2% in countryside, and the remaining 1.8% in other countries or multiple urbanity settings.

Data Analyses

SPSS 17.0 was utilized to calculate descriptive statistics for variables in each of the sections and Cronbach's alpha coefficients for each construct. As most scales were adopted from existing literature, the validity and reliability of them have been tested. We confirm these psychological constructs (i.e., involvement, emotions, attitude, and brand equity) through a series of confirmatory factor analysis before we proceeded to construct a summary score for each variable. Items that were not loaded highly on the construct were eliminated for further analysis. To compare different variables, all summary data were mean-centered.

Mplus 5.21 (Muthén & Muthén, 2009) program was used to conduct an SEM analysis to examine the proposed structural relationships among sports involvement, event quality, perceived congruency, brand experience and the branding effectiveness variables. We have primarily used the robust maximum likelihood (MLR) method. Multiple Goodness-of-Fit (GOF) indices were chosen to evaluate model fit according to the suggestions made by several scholars (Hu & Bentler, 1998, 1999; McCallum & Austin, 2000), including chi-square per degree of freedom (or the scaled ML chi-square, Satorra-Bentler chi-square, when using MLR method), the Root Mean Square Error of Approximation (RMSEA), Tucker and Lewis Reliability Coefficient (TLI), Bentler's Comparative Fit Index (CFI), and the weighted root mean square residual (WRMR, or SRMR, the standardized root mean square residual when using MLR method). Hu and Bentler (1999) suggested that RMSEA values less than .05 indicate a close fit, between .05 and .08 indicate an acceptable fit, and greater than .10 indicate a poor fit. Because RMSEA has been identified as the best performing index for WLSMV estimate (Yu, 2002), it is our primary index to determine model fit. The TLI (Tucker & Lewis, 1973), also known as the non-normed fit index, penalizes for model complexity. The criterion for goodness of fit by TLI traditionally was .90 (Kline, 2005). A rule of thumb for the CFI index is that researcher's model has a reasonable fit when a value is larger than .90 (Hu & Bentler, 1999). Following the adequacy of the overall measurement model, we proceeded to examine the hypothesized relations among eight latent variables. This step allowed us to test the following:

1. Relationship between attitude toward event and the branding effectiveness of sponsorship (i.e., brand loyalty, perceived quality, and brand awareness/associations), and
2. Relationship among involvement, emotions, and attitude. Same GOF indices as the CFA were adopted in evaluating the structural model.

RESULTS

Descriptive Statistics

Among all 803 respondents, 244 completed the Olympic questionnaire, 278 completed CBA questionnaire and 281 completed CSL questionnaire. The sport involvement level overall did not differ among three groups ($F=1.74, p=0.18$). Their experience with Li Ning's products had some differences. The CSL group had a significantly higher percentage (48.1%) of respondents who had used Li Ning's products while the Olympic group (37%) had the least product usage rate. As a result, the three groups significantly differ in brand familiarity ($F=18.11, p<.01$). But brand favorability measure had no significant difference among three groups ($F=2.38, p<.09$). Descriptive statistics for the sport involvement, event quality, perceived congruency, brand experience and branding effects are presented in Table 2. As expected, all three sources for event quality differ significantly among three events, with Beijing Olympic Games having highest composite score and China Soccer League having lowest composite score. Both the perceived functional congruency and image congruency between event and the brand also differed cross three groups ($F=6.02$, p<.01, and $F=82.99$, p<.01 respectively).Not surprisingly, different events showed significantly different branding effects. Beijing Olympic Games had the highest value to create brand equity while the CSL had the least value. Figure 1 presents the branding effects of sponsoring different sports properties. Sponsoring CSL even may cause a decrease of brand loyalty because consumer's negative emotional and attitudinal reaction to the event may have transferred to the sponsored brand. Sponsorship-linked marketing announcement had different effects on elements of brand equity, with perceived quality having the highest boosting effect and brand loyalty the least.

Data Screening and Reduction

To further examine the measurement property of the psychological state and brand equity variables, exploratory factor analyses (EFA) with principal component extraction and a varimax rotation technique were conducted for the 10 involvement, 20 emotions, and 10 brand equity variables, respectively. The

Table 2. Descriptive statistics for sponsorship-linked marketing and perceived consumer-based brand equity variables

Variable	Olympic (N=244)		CBA (N=278)		CSL (N=281)		Pooled (N=803)	
	M	SD	M	SD	M	SD	M	SD
Sport Involvement	0.52	0.81	0.54	0.80	0.37	0.80	0.47	0.81
Love sports/exercise	-0.45	1.10	-0.39	1.08	-0.46	1.05	-0.43	1.08
Sports participation	-0.03	0.71	-0.15	0.76	-0.15	0.79	-0.11	0.76
Sports event fellowship								
Event Quality								
Event Involvement	1.95	1.11	0.19	1.09	-0.57	1.28	0.46	1.56
Emotional Surplus	2.80	1.02	1.46	0.72	0.99	0.64	1.70	1.10
Event Attitude	2.48	1.05	0.86	1.28	-0.23	1.49	0.97	1.69
Perceived Congruency								
Functional congruency	0.74	0.82	0.57	0.84	0.48	0.96	0.59	0.88
Image congruency	0.78	0.85	0.32	0.91	-0.28	1.05	0.25	1.04
Brand Experience								
Previous use (%)	37%		44.5%		61.8%		48.1%	
Familiarity	-0.14	1.05	0.17	0.93	0.37	0.97	0.15	1.00
Favorability	0.25	0.74	0.35	0.71	0.38	0.75	0.33	0.73
Branding Effect								
Brand Loyalty	0.21	0.66	0.19	0.64	-0.07	0.82	0.10	0.72
Perceived Quality	0.76	0.82	0.65	0.80	0.40	0.85	0.59	0.83
Brand Association/Awareness	0.71	0.74	0.62	0.72	0.39	0.74	0.57	0.75

Kaiser-Meyer-Olkin (KMO) measure of sampling adequacy (Kaiser, 1974) for the involvement, emotions, and brand equity across three groups were greater than .85, indicating that the samples were adequate for factor analyses. Bartlett Test for Sphericity was significant at .01 level, indicating that the hypothesis of variance and covariance matrix of the variables as an identity matrix was rejected; therefore, conducting the factor analyses was appropriate.

For the involvement variables, an identical two-factor pattern emerged across all the three groups based on eigenvalue equal to or greater than 1.0, explaining a total of 54.4% to 60.3% of variances. An examination of content interpretability was conducted by comparing current results with Zaichkowsky's (1994) results. In Zaichkowsky's research, affective dimension included "interesting, exciting, appealing, fascinating, and involving", and cognitive dimension included "important, relevant, means a lot to me, valuable, and needed". Three items (important, interesting, and relevant) in the current study did not fit in original conceptualization, hence were not used for further analysis.

The 20 items of emotional responses first generated different patterns of dimensionality across three groups. Both the Olympic Game and CSL data sets generated three factors, while the CBA data set generated two factors, which is rather reasonable as emotions are not as simple as just positive and negative (Bagozzi et al., 1999; Richins, 1997). For the Olympic data, the item "worry" alone turned out to be the third factor, and the item "hope" had a tendency of double loading; and the item of "surprising" in CSL data had high loadings on all the three factors. As mentioned, a two-factor solution to emotional responses has been commonly used by researchers (Martensent et al., 2004). Hence factor analyses fixing the number of factors at two were conducted to further check the pattern congruency among three groups. A clear pattern of positive-negative emotions was then generated across all three groups, with 47.5% to 53.4% of total variances explained. The rotated component matrix is presented in Table 1.

Cronbach's alpha was calculated to measure internal consistency of obtained factors (Cronbach, 1951). A total of 11 items were eliminated for parsimony as they did not significantly contribute to the reliability. Table 5 depicted the results of internal reliability based on reduced items.

Path Modeling

To further explore the impacts of different variables on the branding effects. A structural model relating four independent variables to dependent variables were modeled through a path model based on the correlation matrix presented in Table 3. The model was assessed by using the Maximum Likelihood estimate in Mplus 5.21. Figure 2 presents the conceptual model. The values of Goodness-of-Fit indices suggested the resulting model has a close fit: $\chi2/df = 2.02$, RMSEA=.036, CFI=.985, TLI=.969, SRMR=.024. Event quality, functional congruency, image congruency and brand favorability are significantly predictive of all three elements of the branding effects. Brand familiarity was only significantly predictive of brand loyalty while not predictive of brand quality and association. The sport involvement variable is not predictive of any of the three elements of branding effects. Table 4 summarizes the results of the path coefficients.

DISCUSSION

In today's extremely competitive and dynamic business climate, companies are striving to sustain long-lasting development by strategically positioning and differentiating themselves from competitors in the

Figure 1. Branding effects of sponsoring different sports properties

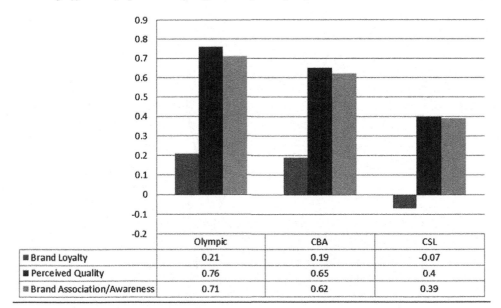

	Olympic	CBA	CSL
■ Brand Loyalty	0.21	0.19	-0.07
■ Perceived Quality	0.76	0.65	0.4
■ Brand Association/Awareness	0.71	0.62	0.39

Table 3. Correlation matrix for the sponsorship-linked marketing and perceived consumer-based brand equity constructs

	LS	SP	EF	EI	EM	EA	FC	IC	BU	Bfam	Bfav	Lo	Qu	As
Love Sport	1													
Sport Participation	0.264	1												
Event Followship	0.317	0.186	1											
Involvement	0.127	0.007	0.148	1										
Emotion	0.068	-0.048	0.034	0.643	1									
Attitude	0.087	0.015	0.056	0.779	0.617	1								
Functional Congruency	0.153	0.126	0.174	0.188	0.118	0.189	1							
Image Congruency	0.089	0.051	0.065	0.49	0.429	0.442	0.37	1						
Usage	-0.011	-0.026	-0.163	0.169	0.159	0.201	-0.027	0.098	1					
Familiarity	0.126	0.125	0.24	-0.191	-0.169	-0.184	0.197	-0.059	-0.336	1				
Favorability	0.185	0.14	0.23	-0.029	-0.059	-0.025	0.349	0.065	-0.266	0.475	1			
Loyalty	0.115	0.039	0.106	0.296	0.191	0.253	0.294	0.407	0.027	0.111	0.237	1		
Quality	0.132	0.03	0.109	0.257	0.184	0.238	0.254	0.311	0.044	0.042	0.202	0.433	1	
Association	0.148	0.004	0.074	0.279	0.159	0.301	0.295	0.339	0.044	0.075	0.202	0.522	0.526	1

marketplace. Brands are one of the few assets available to a company that can provide a long-lasting competitive advantage (Bharadwaj, Varadarajan, & Fahy, 1993; Kapferer, 2008). Brands can distinguish products, provide legal protection for companies, signal a certain level of quality, increase the probability of brand choice, command premium price from loyal consumers, facilitate business forecasting, and gain greater market share (Kotler & Keller, 2006; Yoo, Donthu, & Lee, 2000). The power of a brand lies

Figure 2. Structural equation model

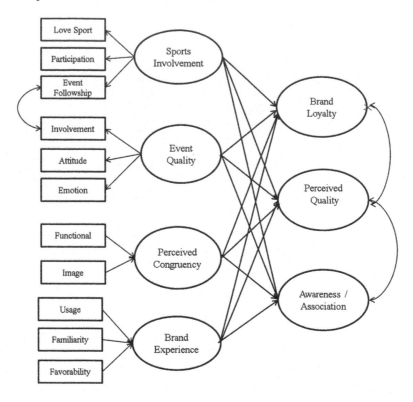

with its brand equity as well as customer's subjective and intangible assessment of the brand (Kotler & Keller, 2006). Therefore, branding effectiveness of sponsorship can be conceptualized as the influence of sponsorship related marketing on the enhancement of brand equity.

The purpose of this research is to examine the impacts of sponsorship-linked marketing activities on perceived consumer-based brand equity elements. It is done through an empirical investigation of how sponsorship-linked marketing strategy has influenced the positioning and branding of Li-Ning. This study firstly reviewed the history and strategy of Li-Ning's sponsorship-linked marketing practice. It shows how sports sponsorship-linked marketing has helped Li-Ning to raise brand awareness and establish brand image in its domestic market—China during different stages of development, and how it plans to use sponsorship-linked marketing strategy to gain entry into international markets that are predominated by international industrial leaders.

A conceptual framework linking factors of sponsorship effectiveness (i.e., event quality, brand experience, perceived event-brand congruency and sport involvement) to brand equity elements (i.e., brand loyalty, perceived quality, and brand awareness/associations) is then developed based on a comprehensive review of literature. As the quality of an event to be sponsored is crucial to the success of sponsorship-linked marketing and thus a major decision factor of marketing managers, the conceptual model accordingly highlights event quality as a core determinant. Accordingly, we have constructed a second order formative index called the Event Quality Index (EQI), which comprised the following reflective components: involvement, emotions, and event attitude. We further acknowledge the importance of brand experience, brand-event congruency, and sports involvement, which have been frequently addressed in literature,

Table 4. Summary of structural model including path coefficient values and model fit indices

Hypothesized Path	β	se	t	p
Brand Loyalty				
Sport Involvement → Brand Loyalty	0.01	0.05	0.21	0.83
Event Quality → Brand Loyalty	0.15	0.04	3.58	0.00
Functional Congruency → Brand Loyalty	0.08	0.04	2.28	0.02
Image Congruency → Brand Loyalty	0.28	0.04	7.16	0.00
Brand Usage → Brand Loyalty	0.04	0.03	1.20	0.23
Brand Familiarity → Brand Loyalty	0.08	0.04	1.94	0.05
Brand Favorability → Brand Loyalty	0.17	0.04	4.31	0.00
Perceived Quality				
Sport Involvement → Perceived Quality	0.07	0.05	1.37	0.17
Event Quality → Perceived Quality	0.15	0.04	3.38	0.00
Functional Congruency → Perceived Quality	0.09	0.04	2.26	0.02
Image Congruency → Perceived Quality	0.17	0.04	4.16	0.00
Brand Usage → Perceived Quality	0.05	0.04	1.26	0.21
Brand Familiarity → Perceived Quality	-0.02	0.04	-0.41	0.68
Brand Favorability → Perceived Quality	0.16	0.04	3.92	0.00
Association/Awareness				
Sport Involvement → Association / Awareness	0.02	0.05	0.34	0.73
Event Quality → Association / Awareness	0.20	0.04	4.52	0.00
Functional Congruency → Association / Awareness	0.13	0.04	3.46	0.00
Image Congruency → Association / Awareness	0.17	0.04	4.22	0.00
Brand Usage → Association / Awareness	0.04	0.04	1.24	0.21
Brand Familiarity → Association / Awareness	0.05	0.04	1.17	0.24
Brand Favorability → Association / Awareness	0.14	0.04	3.41	0.00

GOF indices: $\chi2/df = 2.02$, RMSEA=.036, CFI=.985, TLI=.969, SRMR=.024.

thus have been included in the model. A questionnaire is developed and administered to college students (N=803) who are a major segment of sports products consumers.

The survey investigation reveals that sport involvement is not predictive in our model. It means that no matter you are a sport fan or not, sponsoring an event will have an impact on the perceptions of the consumers. However, sport involvement may still remain a relevant factor as it may well influence the frequency of brand exposure, which our model did not consider. Not surprisingly, quality of event as defined by its involvement and also emotional and attitudinal characteristics is significantly predictive of branding effects. Sponsoring a low quality event as CSL has double sided effects: on the one hand, it can raise brand awareness /associations or even perceived quality; but on the other hand, it may hurt brand loyalty. As low quality event is often less expensive; depending on the tactical purposes of the company (e.g., merely increase brand awareness), it may be appropriate for a company to sponsoring lower profile events. Conforming to previous study, congruency is also significantly predictive of branding effects.

The brand experience is also related to branding effects. Interestingly, however, brand familiarity is not significantly predictive of perceived quality. It may suggest that consumers rely on their cognition when they are familiar with brands.

There were several limitations in this study. Foremost, as a case study, an issue is how the practices by Li Ning Company will be generalizable to other companies. Mr. Li Ning had been an icon in Chinese society that goes beyond the realm of sport; and Li Ning brand was the very first brand created in China that named after a celebrity athlete. The political and economic climate in China had consequential influence on the development of the brand and the company. We suspect that the success of Li Ning can be replicated in today's China. On the other hand, the practices of sponsorship-link marketing of Li Ning proffer insights about how a company in emerging economy may utilize sponsorship to position or reposition its brand, and build its brand equity. Second, the dearth of research in China's sport markets and the lack of sound existing measures to evaluate the constructs proposed in this study were another limitation of this study. Although the measures, adopted from relevant disciplines, achieved adequate reliability and validity evidence after eliminating 15 items, it signals further efforts needed to tailor those existing measures from other disciplines or develop original measures focusing on the sport phenomenon. In summary, this study makes a first step in understanding China's sport marketplace for sponsorship. These findings invite future research on the relationship between the management of sponsorship marketing and the development of brand equity.

REFERENCES

Aaker, D. A. (1991). *Managing brand equity: Capitalizing on the value of a brand name*. The Free Press.

Aaker, D. A. (1996). *Building strong brands*. New York: Free Press.

Aaker, D. A. (1996). Measuring brand equity across products and markets. *California Management Review*, *38*(Spring), 102–120. doi:10.2307/41165845

Amis, J., Pant, N., & Slack, T. (1997). Achieving a sustainable competitive advantage: A resource based view of sport sponsorship. *Journal of Sport Management*, *11*(1), 80–96.

Batra, R., Myers, J. G., & Aaker, D. A. (1997). *Advertising management* (5th ed.). Prentice Hall.

Beam, C. (2012). Dwyane Wade and Li Ning: Can an American superstar save a Chinese sneaker company? *ESPN The Magazine*. Retrieved from http://espn.go.com/nba/story/_/id/10781332/miami-heat-dwyane-wade-new-face-chinese-sneaker-company-li-ning-espn-magazine

Becker-Olsen, K., & Simmons, C. J. (2002). When do social sponsorships enhance or dilute equity? Fit, message source, and the persistence of effects. *Advances in Consumer Research. Association for Consumer Research (U. S.)*, *29*(1), 287–289.

China Daily. (2006). *Li Ning goes global*. Retrieved from http://www.chinadaily.com.cn/bizchina/2006-08/15/content_664979.htm

China Daily. (2007). *Li Ning to sponsor foreign team*. Retrieved from http://www.chinadaily.com.cn/bizchina/2007-05/21/content_5415104.htm

Cornwell, T. (1995). Sponsorship-linked marketing development. *Sport Marketing Quarterly, 4*(4), 13–24.

Cornwell, T. B. (2008). State of the art and science in sponsorship-linked marketing. *Journal of Advertising, 37*(3), 41–55. doi:10.2753/JOA0091-3367370304

Cornwell, T. B., & Maignan, I. (1998). An international review of sponsorship research. *Journal of Advertising, 27*(1), 1–21. doi:10.1080/00913367.1998.10673539

Cornwell, T. B., Roy, D. P., & Steinard, E. A. (2001). Exploring managers' perceptions of the impact of sponsorship on brand equity. *Journal of Advertising, 30*(2), 41–51. doi:10.1080/00913367.2001.10673636

Gwinner, K. (1997). A model of image creation and image transfer in event sponsorhsip. *International Marketing Review, 14*(2/3), 145–158. doi:10.1108/02651339710170221

Gwinner, K., & Bennett, G. (2008). The impact of brand cohesiveness and sport identification on brand fit in a sponsorship context. *Journal of Sport Management, 22*(4), 410–426.

Gwinner, K. P., & Eaton, J. (1999). Building brand image through event sponsorship: The role of image transfer. *Journal of Advertising, 28*(4), 47–57. doi:10.1080/00913367.1999.10673595

Hansen, F., Halling, J., & Christensen, L. B. (2006). Choosing among alternative parties to be sponsored for supporting brand strategies, based upon emotional responses. *Journal of Consumer Behaviour, 5*(6), 504–517. doi:10.1002/cb.199

Hansen, F., Martensen, A., & Christensen, S. R. (2005). Modelling emotional and attitudinal responses as drivers of sponsorship value. *International Journal of Sports Marketing & Sponsorship, 7*(1), 75–80.

Heding, T., Knudtzen, C. F., & Bjerre, M. (2009). *Brand management: Research, theory and practice*. Abingdon, UK: Routledge. doi:10.4324/9780203996171

Hu, L., & Bentler, P. (1999). Cutoff criteria for fit indexes in covariance structure analysis: Conventional criteria versus new alternatives. *Structural Equation Modeling, 6*(1), 1–55. doi:10.1080/10705519909540118

IEG. (2013). *2013 sponsorship outlook: Spending increase is double-edged sword*. Retrieved from http://www.sponsorship.com/iegsr/2013/01/07/2013-Sponsorship-Outlook--Spending-Increase-Is-Dou.aspx

IEG. (2014). *Who spent the most on sponsorship in 2013: IEG's top spenders list*. Retrieved from http://www.sponsorship.com/IEGSR/2014/05/27/Who-Spent-The-Most-On-Sponsorship-In-2013--IEG-s-T.aspx

IOC. (2009). *International Olympic Committee marketing report Beijing 2008*. IOC.

Kamins, M., & Gupta, K. (1994). Congruence between spokesperson and product type: A matchup hypothesis perspective. *Psychology and Marketing, 11*(6), 569–586. doi:10.1002/mar.4220110605

Kaynak, E., Salman, G. G., & Tatoglu, E. . (2008). An integrative framework linking brand associations and brand loyalty in professional sports. *Journal of Brand Management*.

Keller, K. L. (1993). Conceptualizing, measuring, and managing customer-based brand equity. *Journal of Marketing, 57*(1), 1–22. doi:10.2307/1252054

Kotler, P., & Keller, K. L. (2006). *Marketing management* (12th ed.). Person Prentice Hall.

Kotler, P., & Keller, K. L. (2009). *Marketing management* (13th ed.). Upper Saddle River, NJ: Pearson Prentice Hall.

Li Ning Company Limited. (2007). *Li Ning forges cooperation with Argentina National basketball team makes further strides in brand internationalization.* Retrieved from http://www.lining.com/eng/media/press_popup.php?file=inside-3_1_24.html

Li Ning Company Limited. (2009). *2008 annual report.* Retrieved from http://www.irasia.com/listco/hk/lining/annual/

Li Ning Company Limited. (2011). *2010 annual report.* Retrieved from http://www.irasia.com/listco/hk/lining/annual/

Li Ning Company Limited. (2014). *About Li Ning.* Retrieved from http://www.li-ning.com.cn/english_test/news/about_intro2.html

Mao, L. L., & Zhang, J. J. (2013). Impact of consumer involvement, emotions, and attitude toward beijing olympic games on branding effectiveness of event sponsors. *Sport, Business, and Management International Journal (Toronto, Ont.), 3*(3), 226–245.

Mao, L. L., Zhang, J. J., Connaughton, D. P., Holland, S., & Spengler, J. O. (2013). An associative learning account of branding effects of sponsorship. *Journal of Customer Behaviour, 12*(1), 25–51. doi:10.1362/147539213X13645550618489

Martensen, A., Gronholdt, L., Bendtsen, L., & Jensen, M. J. (2007). Application of a model for the effectiveness of event marketing. *Journal of Advertising Research, 47*(3), 283–301. doi:10.2501/S0021849907070316

Martensen, A., & Hansen, F. (2004). *Modelling emotional and attitudinal evaluations of major sponsors.* Academic Press.

McCracken, G. (1989). Who is the celebrity endorser? Cultural foundations of the endorsement process. *The Journal of Consumer Research, 16*(3), 310–321. doi:10.1086/209217

McDaniel, S. R. (1999). An investigation of match-up effects in sport sponsorship advertising: The implications of consumer advertising schemas. *Psychology and Marketing, 16*(2), 163–184. doi:10.1002/(SICI)1520-6793(199903)16:2<163::AID-MAR6>3.0.CO;2-Y

McDaniel, S. R., & Heald, G. R. (2000). Young consumers' responses to event sponsorship advertisements of unhealthy products: implications of schema-triggered affect theory. *Sport Management Review, 3*(2), 163–184. doi:10.1016/S1441-3523(00)70084-2

Muehling, D., & Laczniak, R. (1988). Advertising's immediate and delayed influence on brand attitudes: Considerations across message-involvement levels. *Journal of Advertising*, *17*(4), 23–34. doi:10.1080/00913367.1988.10673126

Muthén, L. K., & Muthén, B. O. (2009). Mplus user's guide (4th ed.). Los Angeles, CA: Muthén & Muthén.

Nike. (2009). *Nike 10-K 2009*. Retrieved from http://www.wikinvest.com/stock/Nike_(NKE)/Filing/10-K/2009/F46739126

Oliver, R. L. (1997). *Satisfaction: A behavioral perspective on the consumer*. New York, NY: McGraw-Hill.

Olkkonen, R. (2001). Case study: The network approach to international sport sponsorship arrangement. *Journal of Business and Industrial Marketing*, *16*(4), 309–329. doi:10.1108/EUM0000000005503

Orlick, T. D. (1974). An interview schedule designed to assess family sports environment. *International Journal of Sport Psychology*, *5*(1), 13–27.

Pham, M. T. (1991). The evaluation of sponsorship effectiveness: A model and some methodological considerations. *Gestion*, *2000*(4), 47–65.

Phillystylemag.com. (2010). *10 questions with Evan Turner*. Retrieved from http://phillystylemag.com/personalities/articles/10-questions-with-sixers-star-evan-turner

PwCC. (2002). *Strategic report on Li Ning Company Ltd*. Li Ning Company Limited Internal Report.

Riordan, J., & Jones, R. (1999). *Sport and physical education in China*. London: E & FN Spon.

Shugan, S. M. (1980). The cost of thinking. *The Journal of Consumer Research*, *7*(2), 99–111. doi:10.1086/208799

Speed, R., & Thompson, P. (2000). Determinants of sports sponsorship response. *Journal of the Academy of Marketing Science*, *28*(2), 227–238. doi:10.1177/0092070300282004

Tucker, L., & Lewis, C. (1973). A reliability coefficient for maximum likelihood factor analysis. *Psychometrika*, *38*(1), 1–10. doi:10.1007/BF02291170

Walliser, B. (2003). An international review of sponsorship research: Extension and update. *International Journal of Advertising*, *22*(1), 5–40.

Wikinvest. (2009). *Nike(NKE)*. Retrieved from http://www.wikinvest.com/stock/Nike_(NKE)/Asia_Pacific_Region

Wikinvest. (2014). *Rise of China's middle class*. Retrieved from http://www.wikinvest.com/concept/Rise_of_China%27s_Middle_Class

Wooldridge, J. M. (2009). *Introductory econometrics: A modern approach* (4th ed.). South-Western.

Xu, X. (2006). *Modernizing China in the Olympic spotlight: China's national identity and the 2008 Beijing Olympiad.* Oxford, MA: Blackwell Publishing.

Yoo, B., Donthu, N., & Lee, S. (2000). An examination of selected marketing mix elements and brand equity. *Journal of the Academy of Marketing Science, 28*(2), 195–211. doi:10.1177/0092070300282002

Yu, C. (2002). *Evaluating cutoff criteria of model fit indices for latent variable models with binary and continuous outcomes.* Los Angeles, CA: University of California Los Angeles.

Yu, L. (2008). *Li Ning - The heart of the champion.* Beijing, China: China Citic Press.

Zajonc, R. (1980). Feeling and thinking: Preferences need no inferences. *The American Psychologist, 35*(2), 151–175. doi:10.1037/0003-066X.35.2.151

ADDITIONAL READING

Amis, J., & Cornwell, T. (2005). *Global sport sponsorship.* Oxford: Berg.

Amis, J., Slack, T., & Berrett, T. (1999). Sport sponsorships as distinctive competence. *European Journal of Marketing, 33*(3/4), 250–272. doi:10.1108/03090569910253044

Beck-Burridge, M., & Walton, J. (2002). *Sport sponsorship and brand development:The subaru and jaguar sotries.* Basingstoke: Palgrave Macmillan.

Becker-Olsen, K. (2003). Questioning the name game: An event study analysis of stadium naming rights sponsorship announcements. *International Journal of Sports Marketing & Sponsorship, 5*(3), 181–192.

Chien, P. M., Cornwell, T. B., & Pappu, R. (2011). Sponsorship portfolio as a brand-image creation strategy. *Journal of Business Research, 64*(2), 142–149. doi:10.1016/j.jbusres.2010.02.010

Close, A. G., Finney, R. Z., Lacey, R. Z., & Sneath, J. Z. (2006). Engaging the consumer through event marketing: Linking attendees with the sponsor, community, and brand. *Journal of Advertising Research, 46*(4), 420–433. doi:10.2501/S0021849906060430

Close, A. G., & Kahle, L. R. (2011). *Consumer behavior knowledge for effective sports and event marketing.* New York: Routledge.

Cornwell, T. B. (2008). State of the art and science in sponsorship-linked marketing. *Journal of Advertising, 37*(3), 41–55. doi:10.2753/JOA0091-3367370304

Cornwell, T. B., & Maignan, I. (1998). An international review of sponsorship research. *Journal of Advertising, 27*(1), 1–21. doi:10.1080/00913367.1998.10673539

Cornwell, T. B., Weeks, C. S., & Roy, D. P. (2005). Sponsorship-linked marketing: Opening the black box. *Journal of Advertising, 34*(2), 21–42. doi:10.1080/00913367.2005.10639194

Crompton, J. L. (2004). Conceptualization and alternate operationalizations of the measurement of sponsorship effectiveness in sport. *Leisure Studies, 23*(3), 267–281. doi:10.1080/0261436042000183695

Drengner, J., Gaus, H., & Jahn, S. (2008). Does flow influence the brand image in event marketing? *Journal of Advertising Research, 48*(1), 138–147. doi:10.2501/S0021849908080148

Henseler, J., Wilson, B., Götz, O., & Hautvast, C. (2007). Investigating the moderating role of fit on sports sponsorship and brand equity. *International Journal of Sports Marketing & Sponsorship, 8*(4), 321–329.

Johar, G. V., & Pham, M. T. (1999). Relatedness, prominence, and constructive sponsor identification. *JMR, Journal of Marketing Research, 36*(3), 299–312. doi:10.2307/3152078

Keller, K. L. (1993). Conceptualizing, measuring, and managing customer-based brand equity. *Journal of Marketing, 57*(1), 1–22. doi:10.2307/1252054

Kotler, P., & Keller, K. L. (2006). *Marketing management* (12th ed.). New Jersey: Person Prentice Hall.

Lacey, R., Close, A. G., & Finney, R. Z. (2010). The pivotal roles of product knowledge and corporate social responsibility in event sponsorship effectiveness. *Journal of Business Research, 63*(11), 1222–1228. doi:10.1016/j.jbusres.2009.11.001

Masterman, G. (2007). *Sponsorship: For a return on investment.* London: Butterworth-Heinemann.

Meenaghan, T. (2001). Sponsorship and advertising: A comparison of consumer perceptions. *Psychology and Marketing, 18*(2), 191–215. doi:10.1002/1520-6793(200102)18:2<191::AID-MAR1005>3.0.CO;2-C

Pham, M. T. (1991). The evaluation of sponsorship effectiveness: A model and some methodological considerations. *Gestion, 2000*(4), 47–65.

Skinner, B., & Rukavina, V. (2003). *Event sponsorship.* John Wiley & Sons.

Sneath, J. Z., Finney, R. Z., & Close, A. G. (2005). An imc approach to event marketing: The effects of sponsorship and experience on customer attitudes. *Journal of Advertising Research, 45*(4), 373–381. doi:10.1017/S0021849905050440

Van Osselaer, S. J., & Alba, J. W. (2000). Consumer learning and brand equity. *The Journal of Consumer Research, 27*(1), 1–16. doi:10.1086/314305

Yoo, B., & Donthu, N. (2001). Developing and validating a multidimensional consumer-based brand equity scale. *Journal of Business Research, 52*(1), 1–14. doi:10.1016/S0148-2963(99)00098-3

Yoo, B., Donthu, N., & Lee, S. (2000). An examination of selected marketing mix elements and brand equity. *Journal of the Academy of Marketing Science, 28*(2), 195–211. doi:10.1177/0092070300282002

KEY TERMS AND DEFINITIONS

Brand Association: Images and symbols associated with a brand in a sophisticated and interconnected fashion.

Brand Awareness: The extent to which a brand is recognized or recalled by consumers under different conditions.

Brand Loyalty: Consumer's behavioral and attitudinal commitment to purchase a preferred products or services in the future.

Branding Effects: Perceived enhancement of elements of brand equity as a result of sponsorship-linked marketing communication.

Event Quality: Event consumers' subjective evaluation associated with consumers' event involvement, emotions intrigued by the event, and event attitudes.

Perceived Event-Brand Congruency: Perceived relevance between a brand and an event based on consumer's judgment of the fit between the functions and images of both parties.

Perceived Quality: Consumer's subjective judgment about a product's overall excellence.

Sponsorship-Linked Marketing: Marketing activities designed and implemented by using sponsorship as an integrated communication platform.

This research was previously published in Emerging Trends and Innovation in Sports Marketing and Management in Asia edited by Ho Keat Leng and Noah Yang Hsu, pages 44-65, copyright year 2015 by Business Science Reference (an imprint of IGI Global).

Chapter 12
Consuming "Innovation" in Tourism:
Augmented Reality as an Innovation Tool in Digital Tourism Marketing

Azizul Hassan
The Cardiff Metropolitan University, UK

Roya Rahimi
University of Wolverhampton, UK

ABSTRACT

Upon understanding definition, features, application analysis of innovation and relevant theory of the Diffusion of Innovations, this study suggests Augmented Reality (AR) as a technological innovation. AR is an advanced stage of virtual reality that merges reality with computer simulated imageries in the real environment. This chapter synthesizes AR as an emerging and potential technology of digital tourism marketing and management. The aim of this analytical approach based chapter is to understand innovation from tourism product or services consumption perspective. Relevant evidences are also included on lenses of marketing, digitalization and innovation consumption. Results outline that, technology consumption is gradually reshaping and getting supported by the availability and accessibility of electronic formats as AR as a technological innovation. This symbolizes that the consumption of technological innovation as AR offers freedom to select, purchase and recommend in relation to the theory of Diffusion of Innovations by Rogers (1962).

INTRODUCTION

Tourism is the world's largest industry that continuously contributing global economy. The economic and market structures of countries across the world are diverse that necessitates technology application to cater growing demands of both consumers and businesses. Technology application in tourism is said as linked with Information and Communication Technology (ICT). ICT has been continuously contrib-

DOI: 10.4018/978-1-5225-5187-4.ch012

uting business activities including tourism. The extended roles and capacities of ICT are also diverging traditional means of technology adoption in tourism. ICT has witnessed a sharp rise of up gradation over the last few decades where, innovations in ICT have contributed largely. This is thus significant that, ICTs in present days are more innovative than ever before that simultaneously affecting the tourism enterprises. The attachment of innovative natured technologies is adopted by both traditional and electronic tourism enterprises. On the other side, the gradual excellence of technology has given rise to innovative technologies as Augmented Reality (AR). AR is seen as blending computer simulations of digital imageries in a real environment (Dadwal & Hassan, 2015; Jung et al., 2015). The growing demand is one of the key reasons to introduce and adopt technological innovation as AR in the particular area of digital marketing.

Innovation is expressed through creativity or excellence and thus the process is simultaneously well balanced with product or service development. Through all of these, innovation is responsible for both of application and maintenance the use and application of technological standards. The outcome of technological innovations can appear in diverse forms and in numerous forms. The term invention as followed by innovation is more focused on the society and the human being. These can also generate both positive and negative effects those can have immense effects on both of the humans and the society, itself. Innovations normally widens in more areas through their adoption and application. However, in tourism this is well manageable with destination management, service or product development. Technological innovation relates interests and general understanding of the general academia. Still, studies related to innovation show conceptual directions to develop general marketing approaches in tourism (Buhalis & Law, 2008; Hassan, 2012a, Hassan 2013b; Hassan & Rahman, in press; Hassan & Rahman, 2015; Hassan & Iankova, 2014). Thus, the development of innovation researches in tourism is critical and challenging from many perspectives. This becomes more evident with the involvement of internet supported technologies those are adopted in diverse forms by numerous agents having active presence in tourism marketing.

Upon understanding this theory, definition, features and application analysis of innovation suggests AR as a technological innovation. This study considers AR as an innovation and relies on the Diffusion of Innovations Theory of Rogers (1962). Thus the aim of this chapter is to critically explain the consumption of technological innovation. AR is the example of such innovation relying on digital format as Internet. Rapid digitalization helps expanding tourism product or service markets as well as increasing consumption capacities. Relevant evidences and examples are also been presented to support arguments.

INNOVATION IN TOURISM

A number of researches outlines that, technologies of innovative nature surely are affecting tourism trade (Hassan & Dadwal, in press; Hassan & Donatella, in press; Hassan, 2015; Azim & Hassan, 2013a; Azim & Hassan, 2013b). Innovation is a relatively an uncommon concept that mostly relates to technological excellences. According to Sarker (2007), the word 'Innovation' is derived from the Latin word 'in+novare' that means to make new, to renew or to alter. Sarker (2007) also suggests that, theoretically innovation is intertwined with entrepreneurship that supports unlocking opportunities of a new market leading to enhanced efficiency and economic growth. Finally, Sarker (2007) defines innovation as about to have or apply a new idea or even applying other people's idea in novel and new ways. From a general understanding, innovation refers to the process of advancement as concerned with application of updated technologies (Dodgson & Gan, 2010). Such technological innovations have expanded to more areas of human lives through their adoption and application. The adoption and consumption of a specific technology that can be termed as an innovation is not attached to a single factor rather, an accumulation of diverse factors generated from different perspectives. A consumer's capacities can vary in terms of spending, knowledge and interests to use technologies. From this perspective, innovation refers to a process that is attached more with application and use than planning or manufacturing (Fahrer, 2012).

In general, innovation is not attached with a single factor rather, an accumulation of diverse factors and artefacts of different perspectives. Innovation in a more applied understanding resembles its relatedness with science or arts and the application of theoretical understanding into practice for the well-being of the entire human being. Also, this is more related with the process of offering diverse social benefits. Innovations can appear in many types where, technological gadgets can replace the position of existing applications or machines, or even the entire systems (Penn State, 2013).

Innovation as the core of technological advancements can have applications in several business areas where, tourism sector can become a valid example for this. The online and web based technologies are demanding more priorities, in terms of their access and nature of uses in travel and tourism sector (Morrison, 2013). However, tourism service sector visibly renders better prospects to serve the entire innovation adoption process and thus to ensure better business profitability. In tourism, the offers and demands of services or products remain immense and are changing constantly. However, the application of technological innovation at least can support the innovation process to reach a certain stage of development that otherwise would remain difficult to reach. This is more understandable that, innovations can be beneficial for the entire tourism market development mainly through their non-conventional features. From consumer perspective, these situations in turn can emphasize more on developing services or products innovations for tourism. This creates more spaces for the application of technological innovation to support the tourists from harms across destinations in the world. Innovation can become a part of tourism strategy development towards embracing different market situations and abilities to adopt in diverse market conditions (Chang & Cheung, 2001). The relevance and requirement of tourism product or service innovations remains as a requisite for the comprehensive development of tourism industry in different countries across the world. These patterns and approaches always remain as challenging those need to be updated in accordance with both existing and potential demands. In a dynamic tourism market place where, the level and rhythm of competition are fierce and the involvement of competitors is strong, this is less likely that marketers can exist in competition without adopting valid sets of technological innovations. Enterprises ranging from medium to small scale has to adopt and apply technological innovations in accordance with their given capacities and limitations (Olsson & Väänänen-Vainio-Mattila, 2013). In case, when technological innovations are not adopted in an expected form and volume, the acceptability and validity of tourism market dynamics turn as less effective. This claim becomes evident not only for big scale in tourism enterprises but also, for small and medium scale enterprises, indeed.

Innovation Consumption

The general understanding of technological innovation consumption involves common practices and thus to attempt to apply the knowledge gathered so far (Yu & Tao, 2009). This is more aligned with product or service betterment through a way that concentrates on tourism market development through increased participation of parties or stakeholders. Innovation consumption is an important area while discussing innovation. Innovation consumption of a certain technology, product or service relies on users' habit, behaviour or consumption pattern (Shavininia, 2003). Innovation in a more applied understanding resembles its relatedness with science and technology and its theoretical motive to be placed into practice for well-being of the humans (McMeekin, 2002). Through all of the understandings, innovation is viewed to maintain and apply an updated technological standard.

Firm based innovation is playing crucial roles in technology application in tourism. One of the key examples of firm based innovation is the involvement of many firms to develop AR. The reshaping of AR is also hugely contributed by tourism firms aiming to bring further excellences in this sector. The outcome of a technological innovation can appear in diverse forms and in numerous areas. Technological innovation involves general practices and the attempt to apply such knowledge for human kind. Thus, from user acceptance and consumption perspective for a technology, the term invention as followed by innovation is more focused on the society and the human being (Swann, 2009). This is more related with the process of offering diverse benefits for users. Technological innovation relates to the understanding of general academic paradigms and shifting trends of knowledge to benefit both concepts and marketing approaches. The development of tourism marketing is critical and challenging from many perspectives. Marketing in tourism can appear in a type; where, technological gadgets can replace the existing applications or machines, or even the systems (Francesconi, 2012). Such trend of replacement becomes more evident with the involvement and support of internet that is adopted in diverse forms by numerous active agents of tourism marketing. Innovation is viewed as creativity or excellence and as a process that simultaneously balances well with product or service development and consumer use. However in tourism, the use of technology is seen as well managed in destinations across the world through effective management, service or product development (Hall & Allan, 2008). Innovation consumption in tourism is more aligned with product or service betterment that concentrates on tourism market development through increased participation of consumers, tourists, parties or stakeholders (Cox & Rigby, 2013).

Market based innovation is getting more attention and development over the last few decades. Tourism market is passing through so many changes and is getting familiar with so many technologies that, this is very often difficult to identify the nature and types of technologies those can be viewed as innovations (SAS Institute Inc., 2015). Tourism industry is also experiencing growing demands, modifications or developments and these are mostly technology supported. Such things in common can consequence to dramatic changes in the global tourism marketplace. For example, tourism industry has been passing through many unexpected situations and many of them can be viewed as fully undesired like war and attack on tourists (Conrady & Buck, 2011). Certain incidents as and accidents necessitate the demand and application of technological innovation for ensuring tourist safety. Lack of security and war issues can have negative effects on the growth of tourism business in certain countries of the world. Unexpected situations aggregate when life risks of tourists are also involved (Mihart, 2012). These create more crises in many areas of tourism industry and thus the improvement of existing situation becomes more critical and essential to get rid of ill effects of such incidents. Technological innovation adoption thus becomes necessary to minimize risks of such unexpected situations.

Augmented Reality (AR)

AR by name might appear as something that emerges from a different planet. However, the technology has been in use for quite a long time under different label of virtual reality. AR is thus seen as an advanced format of an earlier technology to concentrate on creating bridge between reality and augmentation. This technology is a visibly a blend of reality and computer generated simulation related to improve users' visual and motion capacities. Several types of AR technologies exist to cater demands of diverse consumer bases in visitor management, in museums, destination image formation or even in tourism related education (Hassan & Ramkissoon, in press; Hassan, 2013; Hassan, in press; Hassan & Sharma, in press; Hassan& Jung, in press; Shabani & Hassan, 2015; Hassan & Shabani, 2015). However, in general mobile AR is viewed as an advanced form to address increasing and multi-fold demands of tourists. The technology relies on using a mixed set of sensors for measuring 'data' from surroundings of a mobile device user for visualizing relevant information on mobile phone display as based on that specific perspective (Azim & Hassan, 2013). The data of such measurement can be anything but, depends on sensor capacities of the mobile phone or a particular electronic gadget. Thus, this is relevant to view AR as a medium to display a user's surroundings on either a mobile phone or any other electronic device. This is normal that the capacities and accessibilities of certain electronic gadgets can vary in accordance with the make and also considering market potentials. However, in general almost all Smartphones are more or less equipped with technologies those tend to support AR to meet increasing consumer demands. Still, this is a bit confusing to which degree or level a technological device can become able to support AR in both applications and device hardware.

AR brings changes in both the ways general users interact with a specific technology. Following advancements, this technology offers added benefits to general consumer bases and creates more opportunities to become popular within diverse consumer bases. AR is actually makes technology easier to reach and access with ensuring better outcomes. In many cases, future potentials of AR become visibly more reliable as developments of this technology have been made in recent times. In case more sensors are added in Smartphones, the capacities of AR are expected to reach a content level (Kounavis et al., 2012). For example, a user walks down a trendy shopping district and looks for an exclusive brand cloth. A particular brand stays in the user's mind and unexpectedly, the user cannot find that brand store. The user then starts using AR app using Smartphone's camera to get street image that stays ahead. AR overlays name of each store in streets that sells cloths of that particular brand. Then provides information of that particular and directs. Also, the user points Smartphone's camera on a specific store and gets information about products or brands those are carried in that store. The user then clicks the button and gets information about business hours of that particular store and plan shopping in accordance. AR technology tends to perform symmetrically both inside and outside the store to make shopping easier and comfortable for shoppers and users.

With the input of computer generated sound, information, graphics, video or GPs data, AR provides a live view in a real world or physical environment. The origin and development of AR is less questionable and clear. In particular, the existence of this technology cannot be less than decades. Boeing (2015) confirms that during the 1990s, this technology was used by the leading aircraft manufacturer Boeing. This time, AR was used with head mounted displays to support aircraft wiring assembly. This is one of the most complex jobs in aircraft manufacturing and the person who was in responsible for his job had a screen in front of them. The screen was overlaid with data showing the exact place to put the wires followed by identifying right colours and the functions of these wires and so on. However, the technology has been gradually changing over the years and these days this technology is no longer a complex technical task. AR has been turned as a relatively easier technology to be accessed by the general users and mass populations through using computer devices or mainly Smartphones. Several apps in Smartphones allow users to get familiar and access to AR technology. By using specific apps and phone's camera, AR technology allows users are entertained. For example, a user place the phone camera on a distant mountain and the app simultaneously overlays name of that mountain on the phone screen. The user then touches the button and gets detailed information about that particular mountain, its natural fauna, elevation and related information. This is not a miracle and technology brings information to users. AR apps in Smartphones use the phones in built digital compass, motion sensors and GPS to detect the positioning of that user. This particular technology is advancing rapidly on the basis of recent technological inventions. AR makes technology application livelier to the users through its diverse applications.

The Diffusion of Innovation Theory

Due to the unavailability of required number of literature, critical discussions about the Diffusion of Innovation Theory can hardly be elaborated and widened to understand academic stances related to this theory. As because there are shortage of relevant and sufficient number of literature, focuses are also need to be made on both core and peripheral research areas of technological innovation diffusion from tourism marketing contexts. The development of a critical understanding of technological innovation depends on sound academic knowledge. This requires critical understanding of discussed subject matters that entirely depends on both subjective and objective awareness of a researcher in tourism. For a relatively new researcher within the academic paradigm of tourism marketing, technological innovation can become an interest topic. Theoretically, technological innovation is attached with diffusion and can be assumed as a subject matter for further checks in terms of its application and acceptability.

The Diffusion of Innovation theory by Rogers (1962) is a widely popular concept for other knowledge areas including marketing, information technology and so on. But for tourism, its application is widely limited related to technology adoption. This is obvious that this theory of Rogers (1962) however, can make appeal to business entrepreneurs and tourism products or service consumers, symmetrically. This theory developed in 1962 but, there has been a long way to understand its application in recent tourism market structures. There are almost no scopes to ignore the importance and relevancy of technological innovation diffusion as an interesting subject area in tourism research. The application of technological innovation with their effective application have been left as understudied and unexplored for a long time. This is a key fact of tourism marketing that deserves proper attention both from the academic and practical senses. This is evident from the lack of available literatures those have concentrated on these study areas. A proper review of literature sometimes becomes impossible due to the unavailability of literatures in these identified areas. The adoption of technology through numerous innovations is brought to consumers through tourism enterprises. These enterprises cannot be identified as traditional rather they are more focused into technology and its purposeful application. Even almost every aspects of technology adoption become valid in the current tourism marketing context. Still, this is very unlikely that technological innovation diffusion gets sufficient focus from the concerned academics and researchers. Technological innovation diffusion can appear as a valid and promising research topic of tourism marketing. Also, in a world where, technology as an essential element deserves to be widely available and accessible in almost every spheres of human livelihood there are very low space to ignore the importance of technology in practical life. Thus, technological innovation diffusion as part of a research and study deserves due attention and particularly from academic tourism marketing perspective. Each aspects of the Diffusion of Innovation theory by Rogers (1962) require proper attention, discussion, description, critics and application from tourism research perspectives. This is particularly important to allow fellow researchers to advance further research in this defined knowledge area.

Following the Diffusion of Innovation theory by Rogers (1962), an innovation by the nature needs to be will matched and harmonized with the existing values or norms of a specific society. This should help to allow innovation to create specific type of impacts, in accordance. An innovation should create link between the innovators, practitioners and users, simultaneously. This should also benefit a society in terms of advancements and well performance. Also, the diffusion of a specific technological innovation has to be well accepted by the specific industry. Tourism industry in particular can be an example where, there are still lots of spaces left to improve and accelerate the patterns of both diffusion or adaption of innovations. Innovations need to be simple to use and their adaption should also be well documented, in terms of their applications and potentials. A simpler characteristic of innovation increases the chances for better affectivity and thus to create further opportunities for getting more popular. Relatively, newer types of innovations demand skills and knowledge transfer to turn them as more prepared for substantial use in practical grounds. The other feature of innovation is the triability that is, innovations demand experimentation in limited capacities. This is crucial because, previous trials offer innovations to generate better results and thus to turn them as more capable to match with demands of both of the existing and potential customer bases. The later feature is observation that is; innovations are required to be well adapted by individuals. Better outcomes of an innovation can produce the better acceptability of individuals, groups or customers. Possible results of innovations can encompass both visual and non-visual aspects. As the visual results of an innovation can have better capacities to attract certain number of individuals or customers. Visible results of an innovation can act as a way to spread the features of an innovation to allow them to create more interests among the friends, relatives or family members.

Features of the Diffusion of Innovation theory by Rogers (1962) can raise interests among a considerable number of customers, individuals or groups. These can also help to identify the weaknesses of an innovative product or service and thus to offer some sort of suggestions to improve them to reach a certain limit of betterment. The Diffusion of Innovation theory by Rogers (1962) is affecting tourism industry and has managed to create interests within certain individuals or customers. This theory has also become able to stimulate researchers to focus on identified individuals or customer base's demand fulfilment. This is thus very important to understand the limit or boundaries of the working capacities of this theory. The contexts or working spaces of this theory can vary and also can raise specific disputes among the target audiences. In the particular scene of tourism industry, outcomes of this theory thus lie within the entire tourism industry. This is evident that, innovations in tourism are taking place in terms of technologies and their applications. There are also elaborated credentials to outline the potentials of this theory that is; this theory may not have similar affectivity in every situation where, the variables vary over the years, places or circumstances. This is also essential to end any unexpected situations or circumstances those can have negative impacts on the entire tourism industry. Later discussion in this chapter is aimed to view augmented reality as an innovation in digital tourism marketing based on the above critical analysis of the Diffusion of Innovation theory by Rogers (1962).

Augmented Reality as an Innovation

On the basis of the Diffusion of Innovation theory by Rogers (1962), AR can be defined as an innovation. This questionable to identify the similarities between AR with mobile phone or other electronic devices followed by the contexts of its usage. Although AR is seen as an innovation but, its application has been present from the sixties, in terms of physical interaction of a certain technology with the humans. AR blends with virtual reality and offers multiple features including sound, visuals and physical sensations.

The technology interacts in real time on the grounds of these three diverse aspects. These three different aspects can be viewed as stimuli. Different industries have utilized AR technology in different times but, the aeronautical industry becomes the pioneer to advance this specific type technology. Boeing is the leading player of this technology's global popularization followed by the unprecedented development of research initiatives in this specific technology. During the 90s, Boeing developed a special type AR goggle for engineers in wire harness assembly process. However, recent time's developments have witnessed AR to accumulate both visual data visualization as well as the local environment. Later on, several other industries have initialized the technology to certain limits covering entertainment and others.

Recent researches in tourism have explored different approaches of tourism by using AR for enhancing tourist experiences as a technological innovation. This technology has been viewed as more beneficial for the development of tourism and related research. Even followed by recent popularity of AR, there has been very low number of researches to identify AR as an innovation in tourism. The recent penetration of mobile, portable and wearable smart devices has in fact brought revolution in defining technological innovation in tourism. This has resulted the rise of demands of personalised items as smartphone devices to meet increasing demands of customers. The technology has offered various types functions to users those are mostly concerned with technological innovation development. Also, AR as a non-traditional technology has been placed in diverse technological gadgets ranging from mobile phone devices, recently developed Smartphones and wearable devices as Smart watches and many other devices those are expected to appear in the near future.

Countries across the world have applied or started applying AR in tourism. The European countries are way too forward in such endeavours. The Natural History Museum, the British Museum or even the Manchester museum in the United Kingdom has applied AR technology. France has applied the technology in many areas of tourism operation including Museum. The Louvre Museum is the basic example. Germany has applied AR in city based tourism where, the most prominent example in Berlin. Visitors in the Acropolis Museum in Greece have experienced AR. Numerous examples of AR application have been witnessed in countries many countries.

This technology has been expanded to mobile devices thus giving rise to mobile AR technology. AR has offered users with benefits of applying situational information that are based on their movements. Recently developed applications are mostly attached with identifying and offering information of user movements like sensor or positioning information to help users materializing desired outcomes. The increasing number of mobile phone users has actually expanded the entire market of AR application leaving more spaces for involving more users. Friendly attitudes of users towards a specific technological device have widened the boundaries of a specific technology use as AR. User friendly feature of this technology has been experiencing fierce competition in terms of experience sharing and advertising in mobile phone and wearable devices. AR has been appearing as a promising element of advertisement to create more interests among diverse consumer bases. Also, traditional mobile AR applications are getting attached with advertisements to offer the augmenting Point of Interest (POI) service (Juniper Research, 2015). However, this service relies on the positioning system of both user and their surroundings.

AR has prospects to offer in situ and essential information. Still, mainly due to the satellites' margin error, this technology has a sort of limitation to offer concrete and prompt information to the users. Also, the gross rate of failure to provide straightforward and accurate information in relation to real and visible information can be judged as crucial to get more concentration. This is evident that AR applications are interesting and capable to generate fun or entertainment. Still, the proper development of this technology deserves more attention from the authorities concerned to make it profitable and benefit generating. The both way communication between AR application and users need proper attention to reduce the error margin those are caused by satellites. Thus, the satellite positioning denotes importance to increase functionalities of AR technology. The technology offers both promises and prospects but, the accessibility and complex nature of usability restricts its mass use leaving it more sophisticated and less demanding in every parts of the world.

Not only in tourism but also in different other areas of marketing AR technology have been applied. One of the popular examples of such application that has been influenced by digital marketing strategies is IKEA. According to IKEA (2015), the world's leading furniture brand IKEA determines to address this issue in their 2014 catalogue. Following this catalogue application, users can be able to superimpose a specific product straightaway from the catalogue to a specific area of their home or office to check its match or position in the given room or office space. Thus a customer can be able to see and feel a desired furniture item without even going to an IKEA store or spending time. However, innovation is a relatively uncommon concept in the tourism academia and particularly related to technology application. The features of innovation are diverse and depend on certain backgrounds to adopt. In order to be termed as 'innovation' in tourism, a technology application followed by the use of gadgets as Smartphones or computers needs to be workable in a complex market system. Also, such technological innovation needs to be unique, technically excellent and risk minimized features with its user friendliness (Abernathy & Clark, 2007). The presentation of a novel technological innovation in tourism needs to be apparently prospective for marketing. Thus, an innovation in tourism typically has to be new and focused towards serving diverse consumer demands.

Digital Marketing in Tourism

Digital tourism denotes the marketing of services or products by using digital channels (Holloway, 2004). Internet stands as the key platform of such type marketing to reach consumers. In principal, the basic objective of digital marketing remains as to introduce, promote or marketing of brands on different forms of Internet supported media (Middleton et al., 2009). In tourism, digital marketing in most cases can hardly expand over the use of Internet to reach target consumers for marketing purposes (McCabe, 2013). Digital marketing in tourism remains as the most reliable and measurable Integrated Marketing Communication (IMC) component in tourism (Morrison, 2013).

The conventional types of marketing strategies can in many cases show less affectivity and this is why, the adoption of innovation becomes more powerful. The management of tourism destination can become less effective without using technological innovations on the base of their along innovative applications (Mariaani et al., 2014). This becomes specifically important when, destinations mostly rely on conventional technological processes (Turban et al., 2008). Typically, the management of tourism destinations is based on theoretical aspects and less likely to involve any form of dynamism of products or services development. In certain cases, existing strategies attached with destination marketing can become less effective followed by relatively poor capabilities to produce better outcomes and avoiding complexities. In a complex and more advanced market structure, the relevancy and adaptation level of technology can vary in relation to their capacities and the demand of situations.

Information technology is becoming amalgamated with manufacturing turning as more capable to offer product or service betterment for a specific industry, as a whole.

Product or service innovation has relatively more importance in tourism to fully exploit the capacities of technology adoption to represent technological advancements of improvements.

Increasing number of tourists is facilitating the process of innovation adoption through their wider forms of roles and abilities. Also, there are many cases those appear as aggravated and irrelevant when an increasing demand to meet diverse types of consumers is related. The trends and features of tourist bases across the world are constantly changing followed by the increasing number of ageing tourists (Yang, 2004).

The capacities to offer a memorable tourism experience are crucial and are influenced by the application of technological innovation into practice. Innovations need to be market demand driven than only focusing on using advanced technologies (Candela & Figini, 2012). The adoption and application of innovations mainly can then lead to fulfil the requirements of customers with the space for creating more opportunities. Technological innovation in tourism can improve the common market place.

Global marketing approaches in tourism are potential and the level of such potentials become less valid when, innovations cannot be applied at their expected pattern. This is very common that over the years almost every developed country in the world have passed through economic advancements based on technological innovations (Michopoulou & Buhalis, 2013). Such developments are mostly viewed as more effective towards creating opportunities for socio-economic development. Innovation creates roadmap for creating a specific industry to be featured as more wealthy. Such industry in a country therefore can become beneficial for serving demands of huge consumer bases. The existing market patterns in tourism in developed countries do not always support niche markets. Still, these markets are relevant for benefitting entire tourism market structures across the world to reach the optimum level. To ensure this, effective participation and involvement of both existing and potential customers is essential. These examples are viewed as replicable for other nations those are termed as developing nations (Wynne et al., 2001). The emergence of new markets can have huge impacts on the existing tourism market structure by both generating and supporting increased number of tourists. Brazil, India or China are example and expected to be major players of global tourism in coming years.

Augmented Reality Consumption in Digital Tourism Marketing

AR is actually a game changer for a business enterprise that relies on digital platforms as Internet. Business enterprises related to sports or entertainment has closer interaction with AR as well as with social media. The increasing popularity of AR can be actually viewed as the start of a potential technology application aimed to dominate the future technology world. This is expected that over the next few years AR is not only leaving huge effects on the existing technology led lifestyle but also; create scopes to interact with the whole world mainly by wearable technological gadgets (Breeze, 2014; Buchholz, 2014).

The involvement of social elements to AR is an interesting fact to be considered for the general development of this particular technology. For example in a busy crowd or meeting, a general pedestrian needs to reach home quickly (Mitropoulos & Tatum, 2008). In reality he is lost in the crowd and fails to identify the shortest route to escape from such crowd. AR application is brought in use and the app shows the direction of crowd with exits to reach home within the shortest possible time. This example has been brought in reality by a San Francisco based start-up company named CrowdOptic. Invention of this company allows users to identify the exact direction to which peoples' crowd pointing their phones. By using the app developed by CrowdOptic, users can then become able to invite others to see the displays of those phones. Again, in busy and big racing track at a NASCAR race many visitors could not see the track. These spectators then point their phones towards a distant track, get relevant photos with videos those closer viewers were watching and gathered (AR blog, 2015).

According to inc (2015), a recent research shows that by the end of 2015, approximately 2.5 billion AR applications should be downloaded per year and expects to generate a minimum of US $ 1.5 billion as revenue. Several agencies and entrepreneurs become involved with developing and using AR to serve specific purposes. AR can be viewed as passed its infancy stage and becoming more mature. 3Pillar Global is a company that builds applications mostly AR for reputed companies as PBS and CARFAX. 3Pillar builds an attractive app for the Ballston Business Improvement District that allows attendants at the Taste of Arlington event to pose for pictures with DC sports celebrities virtual version as the Washington Capitals' Alex Ovechkin, DC United's Chris Pontius and the Washington Wizards' John Wall. Such approach in a sense can be featured as great to promote a specific event on the way this is moves on and allows the experiences live longer even after the attendees go back home. David DeWolf, the Chief Executive Officer of 3Pillar Global identified three specific ways within which AR supports customer experiences to change expected interactions with the physical environment. These three ways as mentioned above are innovative.

The first innovative way is to support physical product purchase. If a company is aimed to sell physical products as decorative items or furniture the most difficult barrier appears before them is their ability to visualize how the product would look or fit in a desired space as the consumer's home or office. According to AR-Media (2015), AR as technology can work both inside and outside of store or place. For example, a customer tends to purchases a specific product from a warehouse that is massive in size. Out of hundreds of products, the customer's demand to buy a tiny item of a plant is visibly very difficult. The customer tend to find assistants but could not find one and then wanderer from aisles to aisles and still could not find the desired plant item. The customer then brings augmented reality technology in use on the basis of built app in Smartphone. The customer tells the Smartphone the actual plant name and details. The customer then pans around the Smartphone camera and have the AR app activated. As the customer moves inside the store a small arrow on the Smartphone screen starts directing from one aisle to the other and thus showing the exact place where the plant is displayed. Thus, both visibly and practically, AR makes life easier as well as customary shopping patterns of the users (Azuma, 1997).

The second innovative way is to get engaged with customers in novel ways. Turning a general customer as loyal for years cannot be simple job. This requires clear engagement both before and afterwards purchases. Customer relationship management is a more theoretical notion that has been placed as an interesting subject matter for years. J. Walter Thompson (2015) affirms that, Johnson & Johnson's is mainly a leading medical equipment and toiletries product manufacturer. This company has expanded operation across the world by both adopting dynamic marketing strategies and using technology applications. One of its products, Band-Aid Magic Vision becomes a good example for following customer relationship. AR application for this product is simply innovative in a way that engages an important target market with a consumer package goods company. The target market is defined as two to eight year old consumers. The time when a user points the camera of their device that is mostly a Smartphone a t a braded Band-Aid, they can see video messages from Muppets characters. These Muppets characters are commonly viewed as popular. This is one of the basic ways to maintain customer engagement even after making purchases.

The third innovative way is to enhance on-site customer experiences. According to Prote (2015), Bacon technology and AR is used in the Peter Paul Rubens Museum in Antwerp. These technologies widen user experiences by offering an interactive guide that is virtual and provides added information on their surroundings relying the location. Such application benefits visitors by providing extra information about the museum's art work, interactive games and guided tour services. A business that ensures the presence of a brick-and-mortar, similar applications can be used to capitalize possibilities of both in- store and direct marketing.

A changed purchase and consumption patterns exists to accept and gradually direct marketing initiatives for tourism. Gartner (2013) expects that, on the basis of continual technological advancements, general public will be highly accepting the AR technologies in 2014. However, AR applications as marketing instruments are still subject of further explanation where, technology for mass consumer base cannot be always readily available (Yovcheva et al., 2012). Recently developed technological gadgets are harnessing such technologies those the users have not experienced in their previous use. One of such examples is that AR tends to become a popular means of entertainment and have started to expand in other relevant areas as education (Shen et al., 2011).

CONCLUSION

This conceptual chapter mainly concentrates on aspects technology innovation consumption in tourism marketing with AR as an example. AR is seen as an innovative technology that is emerging in marketing. In tourism, innovation is a common word and mostly related to technological excellences and from a more general understanding, innovation refers to the process of advancement that is concerned with the improvement of technological applications. From a more tourism conceptual perspective, innovation refers to a process that is attached with both planning and manufacturing of an idea at the same time. This is involved with the development of ideas, placing ideas into action, examining, experimentation and the manufacturing of a specific product or service. Thus, these features can clearly outline AR as a technological innovation. AR is also outlined by something that is not existed or that is more in advanced form than present. This chapter confirms the introduction and presence of technological innovation as AR in different activities of consumption. The wider availability of technology through many types of innovations has made both commercialization and marketing easier than ever before. In particular, this chapter considers the case of AR as example to outline a shift from conventional to non-conventional. On the basis of Rogers (1962), the Diffusion of Innovations Theory, the chapter identifies AR as an innovation. In addition citing many examples of consumption, behaviour this study defines AR as a valid tool of technology supported marketing. The chapter proposes that a clear understanding of technological innovation consumption is required to learn gradual or potential changes. Technology application expands the capacities of consumers allowing them more freedom for marketing. The changing patterns of tourism product or service consumers' behaviour, attitude or perception about particular technological innovation consumption requires more attention from both academics and practitioners. This is obvious that the capacities of AR to appear as a marketing instrument are convincing as well as challenging. Innovation as a notion has been mostly popularised by Rogers (1962) through the 'Diffusion of Innovations' theory. Basic limitations of this chapter are the lack of available literature and absence of primary data. These two concerns can be seen as key drawbacks of this particular chapter. Future research areas can cover more technological innovations those can potentially be viewed as emerging to dominate future market settings.

REFERENCES

Abernathy, W., & Clark, K. B. (2007). Innovation: Mapping the winds of creative destruction. *Research Policy*, *14*(1), 3–22. doi:10.1016/0048-7333(85)90021-6

AR-Media. (2015). *Augmented reality and the future of printing and publishing opportunities and perspectives*. Retrieved from: http://www.inglobetechnologies.com/docs/whitepapers/AR_printing_white-paper_en.pdf

Augmented Reality Blog. (2015). *How augmented reality can revolutionize the hospitality industry*. Retrieved from: http://www.augmentedrealitytrends.com/augmented-reality/hospitality-industry.html

Azim, R., & Hassan, A. (2013). Impact analysis of wireless and mobile technology on business management strategies. *Journal of Information and Knowledge Management*, *2*(2), 141–150.

Azim, R., & Hassan, A. (2013a). *Understanding Recent Wireless and Mobile Technological Changes for Business Management Practises*. The 6th International Conference on Business Market Management (BMM). The University of Bamberg. Available at: http://bit.ly/Ns5u1C

Azim, R., & Hassan, A. (2013b). *Analysing the impact of mobile and wireless technology on Business Management Strategies*. The 6th International Conference on Business Market Management (BMM). The University of Bamberg. Available at: http://bit.ly/Ns5u1C

Azuma, R. (1997). A survey of augmented reality. *Presence (Cambridge, Mass.)*, *6*(4), 355–385. doi:10.1162/pres.1997.6.4.355

Boeing. (2015). *Boeing's working on augmented reality, which could change space training, ops*. Retrieved from: http://bit.ly/1SquO89

Breeze, M. (2014). *How augmented reality will change the way we live*. Retrieved from: http://tnw.co/1nEDN6O

Buchholz, R. (2014). *Augmented reality: New opportunities for marketing and sales*. Retrieved from: http://bit.ly/1nMCLYO

Buhalis, D., & Law, R. (2008). Progress in information technology and tourism management: 20 years on and 10 years after the internet-The state of eTourism research. *Tourism Management*, *29*(4), 609–623. doi:10.1016/j.tourman.2008.01.005

Candela, G., & Figini, P. (2012). *The economics of tourism destinations*. Berlin: Springer. doi:10.1007/978-3-642-20874-4

Chang, M. K., & Cheung, W. (2001). Determinants of the intention to use Internet/ WWW at work: A confirmatory study. *Information & Management*, *39*(1), 1–14. doi:10.1016/S0378-7206(01)00075-1

Conrady, R., & Buck, M. (2011). *Trends and issues in global tourism 2011*. London: Springer. doi:10.1007/978-3-642-17767-5

Cox, D., & Rigby, J. (2013). *Innovation policy challenges for the 21st century*. New York: Routledge.

Dadwal, S., & Hassan, A. (2015). The Augmented Reality Marketing: A Merger of Marketing and Technology in Tourism. In N. Ray (Ed.), *Emerging Innovative Marketing Strategies in the Tourism Industry* (pp. 78–96). Hershey, PA: IGI Global. doi:10.4018/978-1-4666-8699-1.ch005

Dodgson, M., & Gan, D. (2010). *Innovation: a very short introduction*. Oxford, UK: Oxford University Press. doi:10.1093/actrade/9780199568901.001.0001

Fahrer, N. (2012). *Innovation and other useless things: a jump-start for discussions*. New York: Norman Fahrer.

Francescon, S. (2012). *Generic integrity and innovation in tourism texts in English*. Academic Press.

Gartner Incorporated. (2014). *Gartner technology research*. Retrieved from: http://gtnr.it/1nvU5Bb

Hall, M. C., & Allan, W. (2008). *Tourism and innovation*. Oxon, UK: Routledge.

Hassan, A. (2012a). Key Components for an Effective Marketing Planning: A Conceptual Analysis. *International Journal of Management & Development Studies*, 2(1), 68–70.

Hassan, A. (2012b). Rationalization of Business Planning Through the Current Dynamics of Tourism. *International Journal of Management & Development Studies*, 2(1), 61–63.

Hassan, A. (2013). Perspective Analysis and Implications of Visitor Management - Experiences from the Whitechapel Gallery, London. *Anatolia: An International Journal of Tourism and Hospitality Research*. DOI: 10.1080/13032917.2013.797916

Hassan, A. (2015). The Customization of Electronic Word of Mouth: An Industry Tailored Application for Tourism Promotion. In S. Rathore & A. Panwar (Eds.), *Capturing, Analyzing and Managing Word-of-Mouth in the Digital Marketplace* (pp. 61–75). Hershey, PA: IGI Global.

Hassan, A. (in press). Destination Image Formation: The Function Analysis of Augmented Reality Application. In M. Khosrow-Pour (Ed.), *The Encyclopaedia of Information Science and Technology* (4th ed.). Hershey, PA: IGI Global.

Hassan, A., & Dadwal, S. (in press). Search Engine Marketing – An Outlining of Conceptualization and Strategic Application. In W. Ozuem & G. Bowen (Eds.), *Competitive Social Media Marketing Strategies*. Hershey, PA: IGI Global.

Hassan, A., & Donatella, P. S. (in press). Google AdSense as a Mobile Technology in Education. In J. L. Holland (Ed.), *Handbook of Research on Wearable and Mobile Technologies in Education*. Hershey, PA: IGI Global. doi:10.4018/978-1-5225-0069-8.ch011

Hassan, A., & Iankova, K. (2012). Strategies and Challenges of Tourist Facilities Management in the World Heritage Site: Case of the Maritime Greenwich, London. *Tourism Analysis*, 17(6), 791–803. doi:10.3727/108354212X13531051127348

Hassan, A., & Jung, T. (in press). Augmented Reality as an Emerging Application in Tourism Education. In D. H. Choi, A. Dailey-Hebert, & J. S. Estes (Eds.), *Emerging Tools and Applications of Virtual Reality in Education*. Hershey, PA: IGI Global.

Hassan, A., & Rahman, M. (2015). Macromarketing Perspective in Promoting Tourism: The Case of the Buddhist Vihara at Paharpur. *Tourism Spectrum*, *1*(2), 13–19.

Hassan, A., & Rahman, M. (in press). World Heritage Site as a Label in Branding a Place. *Journal of Cultural Heritage Management and Sustainable Development*.

Hassan, A., & Ramkissoon, H. (in press). Augmented Reality for Visitor Experiences. In J. N. Albrecht (Ed.), *Visitor Management*. Oxfordshire, UK: CABI.

Hassan, A., & Shabani, N. (2015). *eMarketing Adoption in Tourism and Hospitality Industry in London: Industry Analysis and Some Narratives*. The 4th International Interdisciplinary Business-Economics Advancement Conference (IIBA). Available at: http://bit.ly/1BQqGnI

Hassan, A., & Sharma, A. (in press). Wildlife Tourism: Technology Adoption for Marketing and Conservation. In M. A. Khan & J. K. Fatima (Eds.), *Wilderness of Wildlife Tourism*. Waretown: Apple Academic Press, Inc.

Holloway, J. C. (2004). *Marketing for tourism*. Essex, UK: Pearson Education Limited.

IKEA. (2015). *2014 IKEA Catalogue Comes To Life with Augmented Reality*. Retrieved from: http://bit.ly/1uQHR86

inc. (2015). *3 smart ways augmented reality is changing the customer experience*. Retrieved from: http://www.inc.com/eric-holtzclaw/using-augmented-reality-to-enhance-the-customer-experience.html

Jung, T., Chung, N., & Leue, M. (2015). The determinants of recommendations to use augmented reality technologies: The case of a Korean theme park. *Tourism Management*, *49*, 75–86. doi:10.1016/j.tourman.2015.02.013

Juniper Research. (2015). *Mobile augmented reality IFx1 2013-2018*. Retrieved from: http://www.juniperresearch.com/researchstore

Kounavis, C. D., Kasimati, A. E., & Zamani, E. D. (2012). Enhancing the tourism experience through mobile augmented reality: Challenges and prospects. *International Journal of Engineering Business Management*, *4*, 1–6.

Marcello, M., Baggio, M. R., Buhalis, D., & Longhi, C. (2014). Tourism management, marketing, and development: volume I: the importance of networks and ICTs. New York: Palgrave McMillan.

McCabe, M. (2013). *The Routledge handbook of tourism marketing*. New York: Routledge.

Mcmeekin, A., Tomlinson, M., Green, K., & Walsh, V. (2009). *Innovation by demand: an interdisciplinary approach to the study of demand and its role in innovation (new dynamics of innovation and competition MUP)*. Manchester, UK: Manchester University Press.

Michopoulou, E., & Buhalis, D. (2013). Information provision for challenging markets: The case of the accessibility requiring market in the context of tourism. *Information & Management*, *50*(5), 229–239. doi:10.1016/j.im.2013.04.001

Middleton, V. T. C., Fyall, A., Morgan, M., & Ranchhod, A. (2009). *Marketing in travel and tourism*. Oxford, UK: Butterworth Heinemann.

Mihart, C. (2012). Impact of Integrated Marketing Communication on Consumer Behaviour: Effects on Consumer Decision – Making Process. *International Journal of Marketing Studies*, *4*(2), 121–129. doi:10.5539/ijms.v4n2p121

Mitropoulos, P., & Tatum, C. B. (2008). Forces driving adoption of new information technologies. *Journal of Construction Engineering and Management*, (September-October), 340–348.

Morrison, A. M. (2013). *Marketing and managing tourism destinations*. Oxon, UK: Routledge.

Okazaki, S. (2005). Mobile advertising adoption by multinationals: Senior executives' initial responses. *Internet Research*, *15*(2), 160–180. doi:10.1108/10662240510590342

Olsson, T., & Väänänen-Vainio-Mattila, K. (2013). Expected User Experience of Mobile Augmented Reality Services. *Personal and Ubiquitous Computing*, *17*(2), 287–304. doi:10.1007/s00779-011-0494-x

Penn State. (2013). *Factors identified that influence willingness to use new information technology*. Retrieved from: http://news.psu.edu/story/267639/2013/03/07/science-and-technology/factors-identified-influence-willingness-use-new

Prote. (2015). *iBeacon*. Retrieved from: http://bit.ly/1embSQh

Rogers, M. E. (1962). *Diffusion of Innovations*. New York: Free Press.

Salvadori, N., & Balducci, R. (2005). *Innovation, unemployment, and policy in the theories of growth and distribution*. Cheltenham, UK: Edward Elgar Publishing. doi:10.4337/9781845428167

Sarker, S. (2007). *Innovation, market archetypes and outcome: An integrated framework*. New York: Physica-Verlag.

SAS Institute Inc. (2015). *Digital marketing-what is it and why it matters*. Retrieved from: http://bit.ly/1cRj6SG

Shabani, N., & Hassan, A. (2015). *Innovative Technology Diffusion in Hospitality: Concept and Industry Perspective*. The 5th International Interdisciplinary Business-Economics Advancement Conference (IIBA). Available at: http://bit.ly/1BQqGnI

Shavinina, L. V. (2003). *The international handbook on innovation*. Oxford, UK: Elsevier Science Limited.

Shen, Y., Ong, S. K., & Nee, A. Y. C. (2011). Vision-based hand interaction in augmented reality environment. *International Journal of Human-Computer Interaction*, *27*(6), 523–544. doi:10.1080/10447318.2011.555297

Swan, G. M. P. (2009). *The economics of innovation: an introduction*. Cheltenham, UK: Edward Elgar Publishing.

Turban, E., McLean, E. R., & Wetherbe, J. C. (2008). *Information technology for management*. John Wiley and sons, Inc.

Werthner, H., & Klein, S. (1999). *Information technology and tourism - a challenging relationship*. Vienna: Springer-Verlag. doi:10.1007/978-3-7091-6363-4

Wynne, C., Berthon, P., Pitt, L., Ewing, M., & Napoli, J. (2001). The impact of the Internet on the distribution value chain- the case of the South African tourism industry. *International Marketing Review*, *18*(4), 420–431. doi:10.1108/EUM0000000005934

Yang, C. C. (2004). Exploring factors affecting the adoption of mobile commerce in Singapore. *Telematics and Informatics*, *22*(3), 257–277. doi:10.1016/j.tele.2004.11.003

Yovcheva, Z., Buhalis, D., & Gatzidis, C. (2012). Smartphone augmented reality applications for tourism. *e-Review of Tourism Research*, *10*(2), 63-66.

Yu, C.-S., & Tao, Y. H. (2009). Understanding business-level innovation technology adoption. *Technovation*, *29*(2), 92–109. doi:10.1016/j.technovation.2008.07.007

ADDITIONAL READING

Gartner Incorporated. (2014). Gartner Technology Research. Retrieved from: http://Online.gartner.com/technology/home.jsp> (accessed: the 29th September, 2014).

Herbst, I., Braun, A.-K., Mccall, R., & Broll, W. (2008). TimeWarp: Interactive time travel with a mobile mixed reality game. Retrieved from: http://citeseerx.ist.psu.edu/viewdoc/download;jsessionid=7001C F82F69CEA5001A5B74F7C8CD1B9?doi=10.1.1.368.5238&rep=rep1&type=pdf (accessed: the 01st January, 2015).

Jung, T., & Han, D. (2014). Augmented reality (AR) in urban heritage tourism. e-Review of Tourism Research, p. 1.

Marketing Society. (2015). Pepsi pushes augmented reality to the MAX. Retrieved from: https://www.marketingsociety.com/the-library/pepsi-pushes-augmented-reality-max (accessed: the 01st January, 2015).

Preexamples (2015). Paddy Power augmented reality campaign brings the Queen's face on £10 note to life. Retrieved from: http://bit.ly/1CRur13 (accessed: the 09th January, 2015).

prweb (2011). Digital frontiers media uses augmented reality to market St. Pete/Clearwater tourism with miles media. Retrieved from: http://www.prweb.com/releases/2011/03/prweb5141134.htm (accessed: the 01st January, 2015).

Seo, B.-K., Kim, K., & Park, J. (2011). Augmented reality-based on-site tour guide: A study in Gyeongbokgung. *Lecture Notes in Computer Science*, *6469*, 276–285. doi:10.1007/978-3-642-22819-3_28

Social Media and Games Law Blog. (2015). Recently in augmented reality category. Retrieved from: http://www.socialgameslaw.com/augmented-reality/ (accessed: the 01st February, 2015).

Spencer, A. J., Buhalis, D., & Moital, M. (2011). A hierarchical model of technology adoption for small owner-managed travel firms: An organizational decision-making and leadership perspective. *Tourism Management*, *33*(5), 1195–1208. doi:10.1016/j.tourman.2011.11.011

Suh, Y., Shin, C., Woo, W., Dow, S., & MacIntyre, B. (2011). Enhancing and evaluating users' social experience with a mobile phone guide applied to cultural heritage. *Personal and Ubiquitous Computing*, *15*(6), 649–665. doi:10.1007/s00779-010-0344-2

Sung, J., & Cho, K. (2012). User experiences with augmented reality advertising applications: Focusing on perceived values and telepresence based on experiential learning theory. *Lecture Notes in Electrical Engineering*, *182*, 9–15. doi:10.1007/978-94-007-5086-9_2

Total Immersion. (2015). The Future of augmented reality. Retrieved from: http://www.t-immersion. com/augmented-reality/future-vision (accessed: the 01st January, 2015).

KEY TERMS AND DEFINITIONS

Augmented Reality: Augmented reality is an advanced stage of virtual reality that merges reality with computer simulated imageries in the real environment.

Digital Tourism Marketing: The non-conventional form of marketing that involves electronic platform mainly the Internet for operation.

Innovation: From a general understanding, innovation refers to the process of advancement as concerned with application of updated technologies.

This research was previously published in Global Dynamics in Travel, Tourism, and Hospitality edited by Nikolaos Pappas and Ilenia Bregoli, pages 130-147, copyright year 2016 by Business Science Reference (an imprint of IGI Global).

Chapter 13

Conceptualizing and Measuring Content Marketing in Luxury Firms:
An Exploratory Analysis

Elisa Rancati
University of Milan – Bicocca, Italy

Niccolo Gordini
University of Milan – Bicocca, Italy

Alexandru Capatina
University Dunarea de Jos of Galati, Romania

ABSTRACT

Luxury marketing has gone through some major changes over the past couple of decades. The power is moving away from luxury firms to luxury consumers, who are playing a more significant role than ever before. These challenges in global markets have sparked a growing interest by practitioners and academics in the content marketing and in the metrics to measure its impact on luxury firm performance. However, the literature is still fragmented. Trying to fill this gap, this chapter has two main objectives. Firstly, it reviews the existing literature on content marketing and the main metrics used. Secondly, it analyses the degree of use and effectiveness of content marketing strategies, tools and metrics on a sample of 218 luxury firms. The results of the study revealed that content marketing is seen by luxury firms as marketing communications strategy that provides valuable and helpful information to a clearly defined target audience with the aim to increase sales.

DOI: 10.4018/978-1-5225-5187-4.ch013

INTRODUCTION

The introduction of digital technology and the spread of the Internet have led to radical changes in the way luxury firms meet the expectations and interests of its stakeholders (Okonkwo, 2010; Mosca, 2008, 2010, 2012) and in corporate communication (Okonkwo, 2007). In digital luxury, compared to conventional one, marketing has focused on the content. Content is one of the main competitive factor of e-marketing mix model (Lauterborn, 1990) that offer the optimal value to the online customer. The contents of a luxury brand's website are significant in sustaining the brand's image. The corporate, product and services information provided on the website should be up-to-date and highly interesting (Okonkwo, 2007). "Content is king" is, in fact, one of the most popular slogan in the digital economy. Focus on content involves analyzing new communication models, very different than the usual format used by luxury firms. Content marketing (CM) attracts potential consumers and increases their engagement and empowerment (Kucuk & Krishnamurthy, 2007) through the creation, dissemination and sharing of free content, relevant, meaningful, valuable and able to inspire confidence in existing and potential customers. However, although CM is an up-to-date and hot concept it is actually as old as any other marketing initiative, but CM is still in the beginning phase as not all companies are making the most of it (Pulizzi, 2012). Despite the great attention CM is getting, literature is still fragmented. Many of the marketing journal articles focus on social media and digital marketing tools, and the changes these tools bring to marketing, but do not discuss the topic of content marketing itself. Several authors (Kaplan & Haenlein, 2010; Henning-Thurau, Malthouse, Friege, Gensler, Lobschat, Rangaswamy & Skiera, 2010, 2013; Wymbs, 2011; Weinberg & Pehlivan, 2011) focus on social media and digital marketing, and most do not even mention CM. A recent study (Rowley, 2008) suggests that there is a need for further research in the area of digital CM. Thus, clearly more academic attention is required in the field of CM. A few more contributions (Keyes, 2006; Rowley, 2008; Pulizzi & Barrett, 2009; Halvorson, 2010; Handley & Chapman, 2010; Gunelius, 2011; Lieb, 2011) try to define CM, and, above all, to measure its impact on luxury firms performance. Consequently, this chapter theoretically and empirically examines the evolution of the concept of CM in luxury firms. In doing so, this chapter especially contributes to the research on luxury goods marketing in two ways. First, authors review the literature about the concept of CM and the main metrics used for its measurement. Second, authors analyze the degree of use and effectiveness of CM strategies and metrics by a sample of 218 luxury firms. Actually, the findings of this study suggest that CM as opposed to the conventional communication strategies leads to significantly higher value creation.

In the remainder of this chapter background reviews existing literature on CM concept and metrics. This is followed by an empirical analysis of 214 luxury firms. Sampling, data collection and findings are outlined. The chapter concludes with a discussion, managerial implications and directions for further research.

BACKGROUND

This paragraph as a whole provides a review of the literature, which this research is based on. Although CM is the main subject of this study, it is crucial to explain the broader field which CM is part of in order to fully understand the theme of this research. Firstly, CM is a tool of integrated marketing communications (Keller, 2009; Ewing, 2009), which is the base of the marketing literature where authors find CM.

Secondly, the concept of digital marketing (Hauer, 2012) is essential for CM as most of the CM tools today are digital. After these two important concepts have been discussed in the light of marketing literature, the concept of CM is tackled from a few different perspectives; e.g. concept itself, content and channels.

The Concept of Content Marketing

The use of the content as a marketing strategy has recently undergone a deep evolution thanks to the spread of digital communications and social networks. The digital dimension, in particular, has led to the birth of terms such as digital CM (Rakic, Beba & Mira, 2014) that focus on the changes that technological innovation has produced on creation, delivery and content management. Consequently, in recent years, studies on CM (Keyes, 2006; Pulizzi & Barrett, 2009; Halvorson, 2010; Handley & Chapman, 2010, 2012; Gunelius, 2011; Lieb, 2011; Nelli, 2012; Jefferson & Tanton, 2013; Rahimia & Hassanzadeh 2013) are significantly increased without reaching a clear and unique definition of this concept and of metrics for its measurement. Thus, the trying to systematize the literature review on this topic seems particularly relevant. In particular, the review, according to other recent systematic reviews within the management field (Newbert, 2007), focused only on double peer-reviewed journals articles, regardless of their impact factor. The computer based research was performed in August 2015 by using the academic journals within the Ebsco-Host database. Choosing the most suitable research keywords mostly derived from the reading of leading journals articles and books on CM. Authors have conducted a 5 phase research. In the first phase authors have researched papers that contain in their abstract the keyword CM, selecting 382 articles. In the second phase, the relevance of the articles was ensured by requiring that the articles selected in the previous phase also contained at least one of the following keywords (concept* or definition or theor* or framework) in their abstract. The asterisk at the end of a keyword allowed for different suffixes (e.g. theory or theoretical). This phase outputted 110 papers. In the third step the 110 articles' relevance was ensured by requiring that those articles also contained at least one of the following three keywords (literature reviews or background or synthesis) in their abstract. This phase outputted 26 articles. In the fourth step, these 26 papers were further scanned by reading all their abstracts and texts, thus controlling their connection with the research topic. This phase output-ted 3 articles. Finally, in the last phase, the snowballing technique (Atkinson & Flint, 2004; Iacobucci & Churchill, 2010) was adopted for integrating the results from the previous phase with papers, book chapters or books, relevant to our research topics, but not found in the EBSCO-Host database. This phase outputted 23 papers and books as shown in Table 1.

Distinctive Features of Content Marketing

After analyzing these 23 papers and books, it has been possible to identify three pillars that characterize CM: 1) contents; 2) customers engagement and 3) goals. Only a synergistic vision of all these elements enables an understanding of the sources of competitive advantage generated by the CM. This definition raises a particular interest as it allows you to focus on a fundamental question for the survival of the company: which contents are able to create a competitive and long-lasting (content longevity) advantage, generating higher performance than competitors? Literature identifies the creation and sharing of unique content, meaningful, valuable, dynamic and relevant to the competitors one of the load-bearing characteristics for competitive advantage. The proposed content must: 1) be able to generate interest, involving, but also informing and educating the customer; 2) express all those values that identify the

Table 1. Studies regarding the concept of CM

Author	Paper/Book	Definition
Chaffey D., Mayer R., Johnston K., Ellis-Chadwick F. (2000)	Internet marketing, Pearson Education, Edinburgh.	Content is the design, text and graphical information that forms a web page. Good content is the key to attracting customers to a web site and retaining their interest or achieving repeat visits.
Keyes J. (2006)	Knowledge management, business intelligence and content management, Auerbach Publications, Broken South Parken.	CM is usually focus on intranet-based or internet-based corporate content, including data and knowledge bases.
Pulizzi J., Barrett N. (2009)	Get content. Get customers, McGraw Hill, New York	CM is a marketing technique of creating and distributing relevant and valuable content to attract, acquire, and engage a clearly defined and understood target audience – with the objective of driving profitable customer action. CM is owning, as opposed to renting media. It's marketing process to attract and retain customers by consistently creating and curating content in order to change or enhance a consumer behavior.
Halvorson K. (2010)	Content strategy for the web, New Riders, Berkeley	Content strategy is the practice of planning for the creation, delivery, and governance of useful, usable content.
Handley A., Chapman C.C. (2010)	Content Rules, John Wiley, New York	CM is anything an individual or an organization creates and/or shares to tell their story. What it isn't: A warmed-over press release served as a blog post. It is conversational, human and doesn't try to constantly sell to you. It also isn't a tactic that you can just turn on and off and hope that will be successful. It has to be a mindset that is embraced and encouraged. You've got to start thinking like a publisher and use that to plan and execute your entire marketing plan which content of any variety should be a part.
Gunelius S. (2011)	Content Marketing for Dummiers, Wiley, New York	CM is the process of indirectly and directly promoting a business or brand through value-added text, video, or audio content both online and offline. It can come in long-form (such as blogs, articles, e-books, and so on), short-form (such as Twitter updates, Facebook updates, images, and so on), or conversational-form (for example, sharing great content via Twitter or participating in an active discussion via blog comments or through an online forum).
Lieb R. (2011)	Content Marketing: think like a publisher. How to use content to market online and in social media, Que Publishing, Indianapolis.	CM, in other words, is nothing new. Companies having been creating and distributing content for many years, both to attract new business and to retain existing customers. However, here's the point of differentiation from more traditional forms of marketing and advertising: using content to sell isn't selling. It isn't advertising. It isn't push marketing, in which messages are sprayed out at groups of consumers. Rather, it's a pull strategy—it's the marketing of attraction. It's being there when consumers need you and seek you out with relevant, educational, helpful, compelling, engaging, and sometimes entertaining information.
Cashman J., Treece M. (2012)	Content marketing essentials for small business, Create Space Independent Publishing Platform, London.	CM is the process of creating video, articles, e-books, how-to-guides, social media updates, picture galleries, infographs, webinars, or other forms of media about your business or brand. Creating content, posting it on your website, then promoting it via social media.
Crestodina A. (2012)	Content chemistry: an illustrated handbook for content marketing, Orbit Media Studios, New York.	CM is the art and science of pulling your audience toward your business. It is based on the concept that there are relevant prospects looking for your product or service right now. Content marketers create and promote useful, relevant information with the goal of attracting and engaging website visitors, and then converting those visitors into leads and customers. Content marketing is sensitive to the behaviors and psychology of potential buyers.

continued on following page

Table 1. Continued

Author	Paper/Book	Definition
Jefferson S., Tanton S. (2013)	Valuable content marketing, Kogan Page, New York.	CM as it the approach has become known is the focus of the most successful marketing today – driving results for all kind of companies and a real differentiator for independent firms and small businesses. CM is an approach that puts your clients first. It's about sharing information that is relevant and valuable to those who buy your services, so people choose to come to you.
Clay B., Newland M. (2014)	Content marketing strategies for professionals, Create Space Independent Publishing Platform, North Charleston.	CM achieves business objectives by strategically creating and sharing content.
Didner P. (2014)	Global content marketing, Mc-Graw Hill, New York.	CM is the process of creating video, articles, e-books, how-to-guides, social media updates, picture galleries, infographs, webinars, or other forms of media about your business or brand. Creating content, posting it on your website, then promoting it via social media.
Fishbein M. (2014)	Growth hacking with content marketing, Create Space Independent Publishing Platform, London.	CM, social media marketing and growth hacking are cheap, efficient and effective!
Gordini N., Rancati E. (2014)	Content marketing e creazione di valore. Aspetti definitori e metriche di misurazione, Giappichelli, Turin.	CM is a marketing strategy associated with creating, communicating, distributing, and exchanging content in digital communication that has value for the firm.
Holliman G., Rowley J. (2014)	Business to business digital content marketing: marketers' perception of best practice, Journal of research in Interactive Marketing	Digital CM is the activity associated with creating, communicating, distributing, and exchanging digital content that has value for customers, clients, partners, and the firm and its brands.
Lancaster C. (2014)	Content marketing: turn content into powerful marketing tool, Pogo Book Publishing, London.	CM is used to sell something, but at the same time, you need to educate, encourage and help the targeted audience so they can realize the need and importance of that information in their life.
Lilly M.C. (2014)	Content marketing essentials for small business, Create Space Independent Publishing Platform, London.	Though it goes by many names, CM is defined as publishing content that empowers, engages, educates, and connects readers. To explore it much further, there are five pillars of CM: editorial based (otherwise known as long-form, it is content that tells both a relevant and valuable story. The point of editorial content is to be informative, educational, and/or entertaining); marketing-based (businesses have marketing and sales objectives that they seek to accomplish, and this is no different when it comes to content. Businesses on line have an underlying goal with the content they publish); behavior driven (content seeks to maintain or alter a reader's/consumer's behavior. Having relevant and valuable content accomplishes this); multi-platform (this means that content comes in a variety of media, including print, digital, audio, video, events, etc. It can, but does not necessarily have to be, connected across all platforms); targeted (like all good marketing, knowing your audience is key to having a successful strategy. Know your audience down to the particulars)
Pulizzi J. (2014)	Epic content marketing. Mc Graw Hill, London.	CM is the marketing and business process for creating and distributing valuable and compelling content to attract, acquire, and engage a clearly defined and understood target audience – with the objective of driving profitable customer action. A CM strategy can leverage all story channels (print, online, in-person, mobile, social, and so on); be employed at any and all stages of the buying process, from attention-oriented strategies to retention and loyalty strategies; and include multiple buying groups.

continued on following page

Table 1. Continued

Author	Paper/Book	Definition
Ramos M. (2014)	Content Marketing: insider's secret to online sales and lead generation. One Night Expert Publishing New York	CM is a marketing technique that uses high-quality, relevant content to educate, engage, and acquire your target customer. CM is not just creating content for the sake of producing content: its objective is always sales. The true potential of CM lies in its ability to provide a conversion path for your leads to follow on their own schedule and at their convenience.
Rotsztein B. (2014)	Content marketing ideas, Creative force publishing, London.	The term "CM" is a catch-all that means different things to different people. Its meaning comes down to a matter of perspective. The author defines CM as the creation and distribution of editorial content used to achieve visibility, credibility and conversions.
Slater V. (2014)	Content marketing: recycling and reuse. How your best online content can engage and attract new customers, i30 Media Corporation, New York	CM is a dynamic way to get customers. It is the process of sharing expertise and knowledge online to attract potential customers and establish a relationship with them. CM has to be focused on creating, publishing, and sharing suitable content. However, many CM often overlook a readily available source of content – articles, case studies, blog, posts, videos, images, and other assets that were created years before yet still have the potential to draw new customers.
Van Lieshout L. (2014)	Content marketing for professionals. CreateSpace Independent Publishing platform, London.	CM is any marketing that involves the creation and sharing of media and publishing content in order to acquire and retain customers. This information can be presented in a variety of formats, including news, video, white papers, e-books, infographics, case studies, how-to guides, question and answer articles, photos, etc. CM has been defined in multiple ways. The meaning of the term depends a lot on the purpose and context. One of the most used definition states that CM is the technique of creating and distributing relevant and valuable content to attract, acquire and engage a clearly defined target audience in order to drive profitable customer action. CM creates interest in a product through educational, entertaining or informative material. Successful CM relies on providing "consistent, high-quality content that solves people's problems".
Jarvinen J., Taiminen H. (2015)	Harnessing marketing automation for B2B content marketing, Industrial Marketing Management	CM is a new paradigm that leads potential buyer to interact with their company.

Source: Our Elaboration

company in terms of uniqueness, consistency, quality and relevance; 3) be pro-active, that is able to evolve over time: the company must push the community and every visitor to interact, edit content, stimulate conversation, improve and enrich the information (Fantini, 2013). The second basic element of the CM is the consumer engagement. CM encompasses all forms of content that add value to consumers, directly or indirectly thereby promoting a business, brand, product, or services. It occurs both online and offline, but the free and simple tools of the social web have opened up the ability for companies of all sizes to compete alongside one another, not for market share but for voice and influence (Gunelius, 2011). The centrality of consumer's role is therefore reflected in the content management system, creating a logical customer centric based on research of a constant adaptation of content to the needs and preferences of customers. On the other hand, customers are increasingly participating in the process of creating value through frequent interactions with the company (value co-creation). This leads implicitly to abandon the traditional concept of the market as a physical exchange of goods and services, separate from the concept of value. The reasons for the occurrence of this model must first be sought in the technological process: Internet, in particular, has accelerated the process of democratization of consumption, making the final customer more and more informed, interconnected with the company and with other customers, and thus more central. Transferring power to customers (customer empowerment) becomes inevitable to allow CM to co-create value through constant dialogue between customers and businesses. Customers can shop provide content is to contribute to company or product-specific discussions forums or communities (Chaffey, Mayer & Johnson, 2000). According to this definition, then, the distinctive characteristics of the CM not only exist on the types of content produced, but in the fact that they add value for customers and potential than competitors, attracting them, creating empowerment and involving (engagement). In this regard, social networks play a key role, being the main meeting place with users, where conversations and exchange of opinions multiply and information is the starting point for each interaction. CM means to produce quality content (Handley & Chapman, Lieb, Jefferson & Tanton, Rose & Pulizzi). When a user posts a message, that user is effectively adding content about the product being discussed, as several authors argue that the Web is a pull medium where the customer decides which content to view (Hoffman, Novak & Yung, 2010). Finally, the third element relates to the objectives pursued by the CM that does not lead back to the single action of operational marketing, but concern the creation, capture, delivery, customization and management of content across an organization. Luxury firms use digital CM to support the implementation of multiple business objectives, such as brand awareness, attraction of customers, creating the leads, maintaining of customer relationships/loyalty (Rakic, Beba & Mira, 2014). According with literature review and with the three main features identified in this study the authors define the CM in luxury firms as a tool to share content, but also to create value and high returns and financial means of the customers distribution, attraction, involvement, acquisition and retention.

Content Marketing Formats

CM strategies enable real commitment of the target group and create an authentic relation with the group (Rancati & Gordini, 2015). CM formats are numerous and articulated. Understanding that different people have very different learning capabilities, seeing, hearing, knowing, it's fundamental for luxury firms try to get the most value from every piece of content by reusing the content in different formats (Jefferson & Tanton, 2013). There are four different groups of CM formats: print, digital, social and live.

Print formats are relevant, well-written and well-designed print publications can make a dramatic impression on company's audience (Pulizzi & Barrett, 2009). There are four categories of print format: magazines, newsletters, white papers and reports.

Today, with news technologies and Internet, there are different options and it is easier for companies connect with customers and clients (Jennifer & Tanton, 2013). Thanks to user-friendly Web tools are easy to get started and to add an additional Web presence. Many of these tools enable companies to begin an ongoing dialogue with them prospects and will improve acquisition and retention. (Pulizzi & Barrett, 2009). Digital formats analysed in the literature are websites, microsites, digital magazines, e-newsletters, FAQ, video, photo-gallery, storytelling, podcast, webinar and mobile App. Social formats are social network and blogs. The main benefits for companies in the use of social media are efficiency: social media used to achieve business objectives allow to implement strategies much more efficient than traditional media and allow a significant reduction of costs in the search for information (Kazim & Karahan, 2011); awareness of the brand: the spread of the brand easier thanks to the large number of users connected to social media; create community: social media enable companies to combine users, far apart geographically, thanks to shared interests by creating groups where users can express their thoughts (Weber, 2009); word of mouth: users through word of mouth become major players in the content's distribution business. Blog represents the earliest form of social media. Live formats are events. In the last twenty years, corporate events, conventions and presentations have begun to be rationally incorporated by companies within the strategies of communication and dissemination of business content. These tools have thus become effective methods able to spread content and information about company, consolidating the company's image at the various stakeholders and establish relations with the territory (Nelli, 2012).

Content Marketing Metrics

Define the CM as a value added activity with a significant relationship on firm performance requires the development and adoption of appropriate system of metrics (Giachetti et al., 2013). Hovewer, CM is one of the many revolutionary aspects of the web is that we are now able to measure with some precision how people interact with our content online (Halvorson, 2010), the identification of such system is a complex, sophisticated and under constant revision, activity, which assumes the simultaneous use of different measurement methodologies. Marketing metrics literature has often been criticized for its limited diagnostic capacity, for its attention to the short term, for the excessive number of different indexes not comparable, for the lack of attention to the creation of shareholder value (Doyle, 2000). All these issues bring to define the marketing metrics as one of the aspects of marketing more "resistant to conceptualization, definition or application" (Bonoma & Clark, 1988). CM cannot be measured with a single metric, because no one metric can successfully or satisfactorily explain whether company goal is achieving. Instead, companies need to create an array of metrics. It is possible to summarize CM metrics in four main categories: consumption, sharing, lead generation e sales (Linn, 2012; Gordini & Rancati, 2014; Rancati & Gordini, 2014; Rancati & Gordini, 2015a; Rancati & Gordini, 2015b). These four categories, independent but at the same time strictly related to each other, allow companies to measure the contribution of the three pillars of CM to value creation, identifying any gap between the results obtained and planned and, consequently, implementing corrective actions in order to achieve the goals. Consumption metrics help marketing manager to measure brand awareness and website traffic generated by the content. This category help to measure the effect of the first pillar of CM. Consumption metrics are the most fundamental type of content metrics and they are generally easy to measure through Google Analytics or similar. Some of the more prominent consumption metrics are: page views, video views, document views, downloads; social chatter; visitors; visitors returns; time on page. These metrics may also be combined each other by providing more specific information such as, for example, the page views/visitor or the number of pages viewed by each visitor. Sharing metrics measure the level of content sharing by consumers with their network of people with a direct and significant impact on the engagement. Thus, these metrics are a useful tool for the measurement of the second pillar of the CM. Examples of sharing metrics are likes, shares, tweets, +1; email forwards; inbound links. These metrics are extremely useful for measuring the diffusion and the sharing of content amongst a large number of consumers and their network of people. However, these metrics do not provide any information on the real economic return generated by the CM. Lead generation metrics create a list of potential contacts interested in the products or services offered by the company. Through these metrics the companies obtain information and data included in a specific database that will be used to contact potential consumers and turn them into actual customers. A few crucial examples of these metrics are: form completions &

downloads; email subscriptions; blog subscriptions; blog comments; conversion rate. The sales metrics help marketers to measure the impact of CM on firm performance, finding out how CM impacts customer acquisition and sales goals. Example of these metrics are online and offline sales; customer retention; cost saving; content marketing ROI.

RESEARCH METHODOLOGY

To understand how luxury firms perceive CM and measure its effects on performance, the authors have administered an online questionnaire to the marketing manager. The authors selected a sample of 800 luxury firms covering a broad range of luxury consumer goods (wine and spirits, perfume and cosmetics, fashion and accessories) and luxury durable goods (watches, cars, yachts, jewelry, home design). Authors relied on four well established luxury brand rankings, namely Brand Networks (2014), Brandz (2014), Interbrand (2014), and World Luxury Association (2012) as well as Okonkwo's (2010) list of best practice luxury brand websites to select luxury firms for the sample. The questionnaire consists of 20 items divided into two sections: the first, consisting of 5 multiple choice items, allows to reach general info about the sample (e.g. gender and the age of the respondent, size, business sector, geographical area). The second, consisting of 15 items measured by a Likert scale, analyze: 1) the use of CM and how marketers rate the effectiveness of their organization's use of CM; 2) the main goals of CM strategies; 3) the main tactics used by CM to achieve goals; 4) the amount of total marketing budget in CM and 5) the knowledge and the use of the four categories of metrics previously examined. The initial response rate to this survey was 24% (132 firms). To increase the number of respondents, a follow-up was sent out. The final response rate was 28% (224 firms). In addition, authors have performed checks for potential nonresponse biases by dividing our respondents into early and late respondents. This procedure is performed under the assumption that late respondents are more similar in nature to non-respondents than early respondents. No statistical differences between the early and late respondents had observed, which suggests that nonresponse bias was not a major problem (Kanuk & Berenson, 1975). Finally, we have eliminated all questionnaires with missing data, obtaining a final sample of 218 luxury firms. Table 2 shows our sample.

Table 2. Composition of the sample

	Percentage	Number of Luxury Firms
Cars	16%	34
Watches	14%	31
Home design	9%	20
Jewellery	12%	26
Yachts	12%	26
Fashion and accessories	20%	44
Perfume and cosmetics	11%	24
Wine and spirits	6%	13

Source: Our Elaboration

FINDINGS

Results have been analyzed first at aggregate level and, then, according to the typology of the luxury goods, that is luxury consumer goods and luxury durable goods.

Results show a good use of CM between luxury firms (Table 3). 85% of our sample has claimed to know and use tools of CM in carrying out their activities. In analyzing how marketers rate their organization's use of CM, results show that respondents consider CM to be very effective in 25% of cases, effective in 55%, low effective in 9% and not at all effective in 11% of the cases. The effectiveness is measured by asking respondents if they believe the tools of CM effective and efficient for easier achievement of corporate objectives and increased performance.

When the analysis is conducted by typology of luxury goods, results show that both firms operating in luxury consumer goods sector and in luxury durable goods sector consider CM a very effective tool. Noteworthy, luxury consumer goods make a wider use of CM compared to durable goods.

Among top goals of CM (Table 4), content marketers cite brand awareness (90%), customer acquisition (75%) and sales (78%) as the main goals for content marketing in luxury industry. Other goals are customer retention/loyalty (50%), lead generation and lead management/nurturing (respectively 54% and 42%), website traffic (30%) and thought leaders (45%).

By type of luxury goods (Table 4), the firms of luxury consumer goods primarily use CM for brand awareness, customer acquisition and lead generation, whilst the firms of luxury durable goods for sales and customer retention.

Although at the aggregate level, 85% of luxury firms use CM and 25% considers it useful or very useful in achieving better performance, only 58% carefully plan a content marketing strategy, based, for example, on industry trends, company characteristics, profile of individual decision makers, analysis of content strategies of competitors. These data are confirmed analyzing the sample for typology of luxury goods (Table 5). In particular, firms of luxury durable goods tend to not adopt a well-planned CM strategy

Table 3. Percentage of luxury brands respondents using content marketing and how marketers rate the effectiveness of their organization's use of content marketing

	Use (%)	Effectiveness (%)			
		Very Effective	**Effective**	**Low Effective**	**Not at All Effective**
OVERALL	85%	25%	55%	9%	11%
Luxury Durable Goods					
Cars	15%	9%	30%	28%	33%
Watches	17%	12%	40%	30%	18%
Home design	8%	10%	32%	30%	28%
Jewelry	9%	10%	27%	33%	30%
Yachts	11%	8%	32%	42%	18%
Luxury Consumer Goods					
Fashion and accessories	22%	10%	41%	34%	15%
Perfume and cosmetics	12%	14%	38%	28%	20%
Wine and spirits	6%	8%	28%	40%	24%

Source: Our Elaboration

Table 4. Goals pursed by CM

GOALS	Brand awareness	Customer acquisition	Sales	Customer retention/ loyalty	Lead generation	Lead management/ nurturing	Website Traffic	Thought leadership
OVERALL	**90%**	**75%**	**78%**	**50%**	**54%**	**42%**	**30%**	**45%**
Luxury Durable Goods								
Cars	12%	12%	16%	15%	10%	6%	9%	11%
Watches	13%	11%	22%	21%	18%	13%	13%	17%
Jewelry	11%	12%	18%	15%	11%	10%	9%	8%
Home design	10%	12%	15%	16%	12%	11%	4%	14%
Yachts	12%	10%	14%	15%	5%	8%	10%	8%
Luxury Consumer Goods								
Fashion and accessories	25%	22%	12%	15%	25%	14%	11%	12%
Perfume and cosmetics	28%	24%	14%	18%	18%	22%	15%	14%
Wine and spirits	19%	16%	6%	7%	16%	10%	7%	9%

Source: Our Elaboration

Table 5. Factors influencing the adoption of a well-planned CM strategy for type of luxury goods

	Industry Trends	Company Characteristics	Profile of Individual Decision Makers	Analysis of Content Strategies of Competitors	No Strategy
Luxury Durable Goods					
Cars	23%	10%	18%	14%	35%
Watches	18%	12%	16%	14%	40%
Home design	18%	6%	18%	13%	45%
Jewelry	21%	13%	15%	12%	39%
Yachts	22%	15%	15%	10%	38%
Luxury Consumer Goods					
Fashion and accessories	20%	18%	12%	26%	24%
Perfume and cosmetics	21%	16%	16%	25%	22%
Wine and spirits	16%	17%	22%	27%	18%

Source: Our Elaboration

or, in alternative, a strategy based on industry trends and profile of individual decision makers. Firms of luxury consumer goods, instead, tend to make a wider use of a well-planned CM strategy, principally based on industry trends and analysis of content strategies of competitors.

In addition, only 43% of luxury firms have a human resource specifically dedicated to oversee CM activities, whilst outsource CM activities. Breaking down this figure by typology of goods, our results show that firms make a more extensive use of human resources specifically dedicated to CM in the fashion and accessories, perfume and cosmetics.

The figures and tables below examine at the aggregate level and for each typology of luxury goods, 1) the most used CM tools to achieve the goals outlined above (Figure 1 and Table 6), 2) the most used platforms of the most used tool (social media content) (Figure 2 and Table 7) and 3) how firms judge these platforms in terms of usefulness and effectiveness (Figure 3 and Table 8).

As shown in Figure 1, to achieve their objectives, the firms in the sample mainly use the following tools: social media content (96%), blogs (84%), eNewletters (79%), articles on the website of the company (77%), video (75%), infographics (71%) or online presentations (70%). The videos, infographics and online presentation, in which luxury firms operating in the fashion and accessories take percentages greater than or equal to 90%, are instead recorded in other sectors lower values (respectively 72%, 60%, 57%, 54%, 46%, 41%, 32%).

Table 6 confirms the findings obtained at the aggregate level, demonstrating that for both types of luxury goods, the most used tools to achieve the objectives analyzed above are: social media, blogs, the eNewletters, the articles on the website of the company, videos, infographics and online presentations.

Analyzing the intensity with which respondents make use of the various platforms that constitute the social media (the tool most widely used), most of them makes a very significant use of Twitter (93%), Facebook (90%), Linkedin (87%), Slideshares (81%) or Google + (81%), i.e. the platforms most popular,

Figure 1. The most used content marketing tools

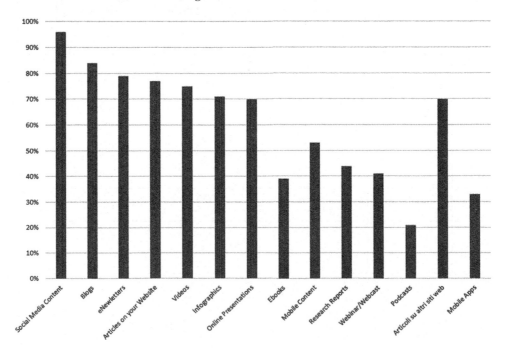

Table 6. The most used tools of content marketing for type of luxury goods

	Social Media	Blogs	eNews	Articles on own website	Videos	Infographics	Online presentations	Ebooks	Mobile content	Research reports	Webinars/ Webcasts	Podcasts	Articles on other website	Mobile Apps
Luxury Durable Goods														
Cars	11%	8%	7%	8%	6%	9%	4%	6%	6%	12%	12%	5%	2%	4%
Watches	13%	10%	9%	3%	7%	7%	7%	9%	8%	8%	7%	9%	1%	2%
Home design	9%	6%	3%	8%	11%	2%	7%	2%	10%	8%	8%	7%	4%	15%
Jewellery	6%	4%	2%	9%	8%	3%	3%	5%	11%	6%	10%	12%	12%	9%
Yachts	8%	6%	4%	11%	5%	6%	9%	8%	10%	8%	8%	6%	7%	4%
Luxury Consumer Goods														
Fashion and accessories	12%	6%	8%	3%	9%	1%	6%	3%	9%	5%	9%	4%	7%	18%
Perfume and cosmetics	11%	9%	7%	8%	7%	8%	6%	8%	9%	7%	4%	5%	4%	7%
Wine and spirits	7%	3%	8%	8%	12%	9%	8%	2%	8%	8%	9%	4%	10%	4%

Source: Our Elaboration

Figure 2. The most used social media platforms

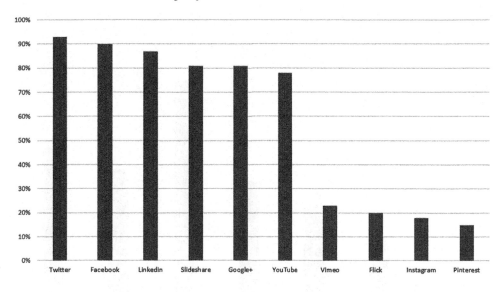

Table 7. The most used social media platforms for type of luxury goods

	Twitter	Facebook	Linkedin	Slideshare	Google +	YouTube	Vimeo	Flick	Instagram	Pinterest
Luxury Durable Goods										
Cars	58%	71%	59%	30%	29%	45%	12%	7%	5%	9%
Watches	56%	72%	58%	26%	23%	49%	11%	8%	13%	17%
Home design	52%	74%	58%	27%	27%	34%	12%	9%	12%	13%
Jewellery	16%	18%	16%	7%	10%	49%	12%	7%	12%	14%
Yachts	10%	11%	9%	13%	12%	30%	10%	9%	6%	10%
Luxury Consumer Goods										
Fashion and accessories	67%	67%	69%	41%	30%	45%	11%	9%	7%	9%
Perfume and cosmetics	69%	63%	62%	49%	34%	46%	10%	11%	12%	14%
Wine and spirits	68%	62%	65%	41%	33%	32%	13%	9%	8%	9%

Source: Our Elaboration

Figure 3. Percentage of total marketing budget spent on content marketing activities by luxury firms

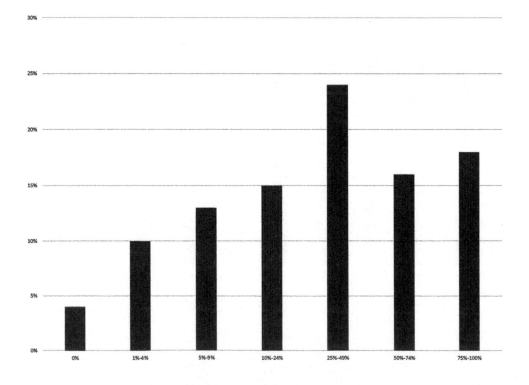

Table 8. Percentage of total marketing budget spent on content marketing activities for type of luxury goods

	99%-75%	74%-50%	49%-25%	24%-10%	9%-5%	4%-1%	0%	I do Not Know
Luxury Durable Goods								
Cars	5%	19%	10%	9%	16%	12%	15%	11%
Watches	16%	21%	14%	9%	7%	8%	18%	7%
Home design	15%	18%	9%	14%	11%	9%	13%	11%
Jewelry	12%	19%	10%	12%	11%	9%	10%	17%
Yachts	9%	15%	10%	12%	13%	13%	12%	16%
Luxury Consumer Goods								
Fashion and accessories	16%	30%	16%	15%	9%	6%	2%	6%
Perfume and cosmetics	19%	25%	13%	11%	8%	7%	9%	8%
Wine and spirits	10%	20%	9%	10%	10%	11%	14%	16%

Source: Our Elaboration

easy to use, and that do not need huge investments or advanced skills which would require a resource specifically dedicated to CM, as demonstrated by previous results (Figure 2).

Figure 3 analyzes the 2013 investment in CM activities, calculated on the total expenditures of communication. Results confirm that the interest of luxury firms in CM is constantly growing and how companies are increasingly willing to invest in these activities a significant part of their budget.

When the analysis is conducted by typology of luxury goods (Table 8) results shows that firms of luxury consumer goods invest more in CM activities than firms of durable goods. In particular, firms of fashion and accessories are those who spend most of their budget in CM activities of CM, followed by companies in the perfume and cosmetics.

Finally, we have analyzed whether the firms use the four categories of metrics previously analyzed both at the aggregate level and for type of luxury goods (Table 9). In agreement with the literature, our results show: 1) an extensive use of consumption (on average 87% of the sample) and sharing (on average 75%) metrics, i.e. metrics that measures the returns of the activities of publishing and sharing, that are easily calculable in terms of both time and cost and that do not require high skills and competencies; 2) an average use of lead generation metrics (on average 54%); and 3) a low use of sales metrics (on average 31%), i.e. metrics that give a clear economic quantification of the strategies of CM. The analysis conducted for type of luxury goods confirms these data. In particular, firms of durable goods mainly use consumption and sharing metrics, whilst firms of consumer goods also use lead generation and sales metrics.

These results show, both at the aggregate and disaggregated level, a very significant use of consumption and sharing metrics rather than lead generation or sales metrics, allowing us to make some considerations that should lead luxury firms to rethink the role of the CM.

In fact, the greater use of consumption and sharing metrics compared to the others two categories show how luxury firms consider CM. The great importance given to consumption and sharing metrics highlights that, especially for firms of durable goods, CM is still considered simply as a activity of publishing and sharing content, without recognizing, therefore, at CM a key role into value creation process. The prevalent use of these two categories of metrics may be due to their ease of use, to their low cost and to the fact that they do not require high skills and competencies. However, in increasingly dynamic and hyper competitive market, CM must be considered as a value creation strategy and not only as a strategy for publishing and sharing contents.

DISCUSSION AND CONCLUSION

The picture that emerges from the analysis is interesting: the CM permeates the activities of most of the luxury firms. However, despite this positive result, luxury firms are yet too anchored to a reductive concept of CM which qualifies it as a tool for publication and sharing of content, and not as a key factor for value creation. At the conclusion of this study it is, therefore, possible to trace the three main trends for luxury firms:

1. In the aggregate the luxury firms demonstrate a good use of the CM, shall evaluate them positively oriented and invest a significant portion of their budget to boost such activities. At the same time, however, does not take careful planning of these decisions, do not invest on the training of human resources and make extensive use of metrics designed to measure aspects of publishing and content sharing rather than a metric to assess the 'economic impact of CM sign, this, that you have not yet realized the strategic importance of this tool for the acquisition of a lasting competitive advantage;
2. The field of activity affecting the use of the tools of CM. On a one hand, results show that the luxury firms operating in the fashion and accessories, watches and perfume and cosmetics use CM, find it very effective and efficient to achieve their objectives; adopt a well-planned CM strategy, have human resources specifically dedicated to CM activities; invest more than 50% of their budget for communication costs in activities of CM; also begin to use metric to measure economic aspects of CM;
3. Opposite trend reversed, however, there is the luxury firms of wine and spirits sectors, cars, yachts, jewelery, home design. In particular these companies: they record the almost total lack of careful planning strategies CM and use of lead generation and sales metrics; to recognize such instruments a low level of utility; use mainly to familiar tools and easy to use (such as Facebook or Twitter) that do not require dedicated human resources or huge investments, but can be managed internally by the entrepreneur or by a member of the company responsible for other functions.

To sum up our results suggest that: 1) luxury firms show a very good use of CM, rate it effective, allocate between the 50% to 75% of their total marketing budget to CM. However, they don't develop a documented and planned content strategy and not investing on the training of human resources dedicated to CM activities. This is a first evidence that luxury firms do not recognize yet a strategic role to value creation at CM; 2) luxury firms make an extensive use of metrics designed to measure aspects related to the publication and sharing of content, but, at the same time, a low use of metrics to evaluate the economic-financial impact of the CM strategies and tactics. This is a further evidence that luxury firms do not have yet fully understood the centrality of CM to obtain and sustain a competitive advantage. Thus, these two results suggest that luxury firms do not have still recognized the strategic role of CM in the value creation process.

Table 9. Percentage of usage of the four categories of metrics at aggregate level and for type of luxury goods

Metrics	Use (%)	Luxury Durable Goods					Luxury Consumer Goods		
		Cars	Watches	Home Design	Jewelry	Yachts	Fashion and Accessories	Perfume and Cosmetics	Wine and Spirits
Consumption Metrics	Average	Average	Average	Average	Average	Average	Average	Average	Average
	81%	12%	15%	11%	13%	10%	21%	12%	6%
Page views	76%	10%	17%	11%	12%	12%	22%	10%	6%
Visitors	82%	16%	12%	12%	6%	11%	24%	12%	7%
Video views	84%	12%	15%	11%	14%	14%	18%	13%	3%
Time on page	82%	7%	17%	9%	16%	13%	19%	12%	7%
Document views	81%	11%	15%	12%	15%	11%	20%	11%	5%
Downloads	79%	8%	16%	7%	13%	15%	25%	8%	8%
Page views/visitor	82%	19%	15%	11%	10%	5%	23%	13%	4%
Visitors returns	85%	15%	13%	10%	15%	6%	22%	14%	5%
Time on page/ visitors	75%	11%	19%	12%	15%	4%	20%	11%	8%
Sharing Metrics	Average	Average	Average	Average	Average	Average	Average	Average	Average
	67%	16%	15%	11%	12%	10%	22%	10%	5%
Likes, share, tweets, +1, retweets, pins	79%	18%	18%	11%	11%	6%	21%	9%	6%
Mail forward	64%	16%	15%	11%	12%	9%	24%	8%	5%
Inbound Links	58%	13%	12%	10%	14%	14%	21%	13%	3%
Lead-Generation Metrics	Average	Average	Average	Average	Average	Average	Average	Average	Average
	48%	14%	15%	10%	11%	9%	23%	12%	7%
Form completions	61%	15%	15%	8%	11%	9%	24%	8%	10%
RSS feed	58%	14%	16%	11%	10%	5%	20%	15%	9%
Blog Comments	55%	11%	14%	8%	13%	13%	21%	15%	5%
Email subscription	52%	14%	14%	10%	8%	8%	28%	10%	8%
Newsletter subscription	45%	15%	17%	7%	8%	9%	29%	10%	5%
Qualitative feedback dai consumatori	42%	11%	14%	11%	12%	11%	20%	11%	10%
Blog subscription	39%	13%	19%	14%	9%	9%	17%	15%	4%
Conversion rate	35%	20%	8%	9%	14%	8%	23%	15%	3%
Sales Metrics	Average	Average	Average	Average	Average	Average	Average	Average	Average
	36%	15%	15%	8%	12%	11%	23%	11%	6%
Offline sales	81%	19%	14%	10%	11%	10%	23%	8%	5%
Online sales	72%	12%	17%	9%	10%	16%	20%	11%	5%
Customer retention	15%	11%	16%	6%	15%	11%	24%	10%	7%
Cost saving	8%	15%	15%	4%	12%	10%	25%	13%	6%
Content Marketing ROI	6%	18%	14%	10%	11%	9%	22%	11%	5%

Source: Our Elaboration

The results of our study suggest some managerial implications to develop the debate on the CM as a strategy to increase performance and create value. In particular, CM managers should 1) quit the idea of the CM as a simple tactic to publish and share content; 2) begin to carefully plan CM strategies, using human resource dedicated to this activity; 3) increase the use of economic-financial metrics (i.e. lead generation and sales metrics) to properly assess the impact of CM on value creation.

LIMITATIONS AND FURTHER RESEARCH DIRECTIONS

The main limitations of the study are:

1. The small size of the sample. Furthermore, global luxury firms for the sample were selected from Brand Networks (2014), Brandz (2014), Interbrand (2014), and World Luxury Association (2012) as well as Okonkwo's (2010). As there is no official listing of the best global luxury firms who do CM, the sample could have also been constructed of another set of luxury firms. However, the sample of global luxury firms analyzed are all involved in CM and were therefore able to contribute interesting results to this study;

2. The exploratory analysis cannot rely on statistical inference (Dubois & Gadde, 2002). Therefore, another researcher might have had different conclusions from the same data as no descriptive statistical conclusions can be made. Reliability and validity are used to evaluate this research (Iacobucci & Churchill, 2010). The first dimension refers to the extent to which the measure or procedure generates the same results: many similarities were found both between this research and between the studies found in the literature (Gordini & Rancati, 2014), not in luxury markets. In addition, the concept of CM is variable as mentioned earlier and in a few years the perceptions of CM might be different even within the luxury firms. Thus, even though a repeated study might not draw exactly identical conclusions, similar findings would most probably be found in this period of time. The second dimension used to evaluate research agree with the goal of this study: get a corporate perspective on CM in luxury firms;

3. The perspective of the luxury firm was selected and studied due to the research gap rising from the literature and empirical data. However, CM can and should be studied from the customer perspective as well. CM has so far gained fairly little academic attention, further research could be conducted in order to examine the concept of CM from a customer point-of-view. Based on the current literature and also on the findings of this study, customer has a very central role in CM. Thereby, more information is definitely needed from consumer and customer perspective. Previous studies in luxury firms confirm that customer understanding is a difficult, yet one of the most important aspects of CM (for example in webatmosphere). Although CM is a great tool to engage with customer, luxury firms still have to use time on speculating which are the important themes and contents that should be discussed. Thus, research, insight and tools should be developed in order to make it easier for luxury firms to actually figure out what are the contents and stories that the customer needs and wants (storytelling).

Moreover, based on this research, the role of customers in luxury content creation is expected to increase. Consumers make their own meanings of brands they use in their daily lives and that they are in fact co-creators of the brand stories (Gensler, Völckner, Liu-Thompkins & Wiertz, 2013). In fact, for some luxury firms it is valuable to reduce their own branding efforts and rely more on the consumer-generated brand stories, because if the story is told by a consumer instead of the company, it can be perceived as clearer and more reliable (Gensler, Völckner, Liu-Thompkins & Wiertz, 2013). Therefore, the interrelations between the role of consumer in CM and the luxury brand perception might create and interesting foundation for future research. Furthermore, another intriguing future research theme could be to examine the effects of CM on intangible assets in luxury firms for example. One of the main objectives of luxury firms competition in global markets is to increase sales and build strong brand using online and offline communication tools. For example, a study could be conducted, maybe even with these same luxury firms, to see whether their CM efforts actually make a difference in brand perception in customer perspective. Finally, this study show many differences in the ways CM is used. Some luxury firms found it to be a great tool to increase awareness and arouse interest whereas others emphasized it to be very effective in engaging the customers. Thus, further research could be developed to find out whether CM is more suitable for luxury firms objectives.

REFERENCES

Atkinson, R., & Flint, J. (2004). *Snowball Sampling. The SAGE Encyclopedia of Social Science Research Methods*. London: SAGE Publications.

Bonoma, T. V., & Clark, B. H. (1988). *Marketing Performance Assessment*. Boston: Harvard Business School Press.

Cashman, J., & Treece, M. (2012). *Content marketing essentials for small business*. London: Create Space Independent Publishing Platform.

Chaffey, D., & Ellis-Chadwick, F. (2012). *Digital Marketing–Strategy, Implementation and Practice*. Edinburgh: Pearson Education Limited.

Chaffey, D., Mayer, R., Johnston, K., & Ellis-Chadwick, F. (2000). *Internet marketing*. Edinburgh, UK: Pearson.

Clay, B., & Newland, M. (2014). *Content marketing strategies for professionals*. North Charleston: Create Space Independent Publishing Platform.

Crestodina, A. (2012). *Content chemistry: an illustrated handbook for content marketing*. New York: Orbit Media Studios.

Damian, R. & Calvin, J (2013). *Marketing digitale: trarre il massimo vantaggio da e-mail, siti web, dispositivi mobili, social media e PR online*. Bergamo: Tecniche nuove.

Didner, P. (2014). *Global content marketing*. New York: Mc-Graw Hill.

Doyle, P. (2000). *Value-Based Marketing*. Chichester, UK: Wiley.

Dubois, A., & Gadde, L. E. (2002). Systematic combining: An abductive approach to case research. *Journal of Business Research*, *55*(7), 553–560. doi:10.1016/S0148-2963(00)00195-8

Fantini, M. (2013). *Content Marketing, image, notorietè, conquete, fidelisation: boostez voster webmarketing par la contenu*, Paris: Eni editions Peterson E.T.

Fishbein, M. (2014). *Growth hacking with content marketing*. London: Create Space Independent Publishing Platform.

Foglio, A. (2013). *Il marketing comunicativo dell'impresa: dalla pubblicità alla comunicazione offline e online al consumatore*. Milan: Angeli.

Gensler, S., Völckner, F., Liu-Thompkins, Y., & Wiertz, C. (2013). Managing Brands in the Social Media Environment. *Journal of Interactive Marketing*, *27*(4), 242–256. doi:10.1016/j.intmar.2013.09.004

Giachetti, C., Spadafora, E., & Bursi, T. (2013). Internazionalizzazione, performance delle imprese e crisi economiche: i produttori di piastrelle di ceramica del distretto di Modena e Reggio Emilia. *Mercati e competitività*, *2*, 37-58.

Gordini, N., & Rancati, E. (2014). *Content marketing e creazione di valore. Aspetti definitori e metriche di misurazione*. Turin: Giappichelli.

Gunelius, S. (2011). *Content Marketing for Dummies*. New York: Wiley.

Halvorson, K. (2010). *Content strategy for the web*. Berkeley, CA: New Riders.

Handley, A., & Champman, C. C. (2012). *Content marketing: fare business con i contenuti per il web*. Milan: Hoepli.

Handley, A., & Chapman, C. C. (2010). *Content Rules*. New York: John Wiley & Sons.

Hauer, C. (2012). Marketing in the Digital Age. *Editors' Bulletin*, *7*(3), 77–79.

Hennig-Thurau, T., Malthouse, E. C., Friege, C., Gensler, S., Lobschat, L., Rangaswamy, A., & Skiera, B. (2010). The Impact of New Media on Customer Relationships. *Journal of Service Research*, *13*(3), 311–328. doi:10.1177/1094670510375460

Henning-Thurau, T., Hofacker, C., & Bloching, B. (2013). Marketing the Pinball Way: Understanding How Social Media Change the Generation of Value for Consumers and Companies. *Journal of Interactive Marketing*, *27*(4), 237–241. doi:10.1016/j.intmar.2013.09.005

Holliman, G., & Rowley, J. (2014). Business to business digital content marketing. *Journal of Research in Interactive Marketing*, *8*(4), 269–293. doi:10.1108/JRIM-02-2014-0013

Iacobucci, D., & Churchill, G. A. (2010). Marketing Research: Methodological Foundations (10th ed.). Mason, OH: South Western Cengage Learning.

Jarvinen, J., & Taiminen, H. (2015). (in press). Harnessing marketing automation for B2B content marketing. *Journal of Industrial Marketing Management*. doi:10.1016/j.indmarman.2015.07.002

Jefferson, S., & Tanton, S. (2013). Valuable Content Marketing. How to make quality content the key of your business success, London: Kogan Page: London.

Kanuk, L., & Berenson, C. (1975). Mail Surveys and Response Rates: A Literature Review. *JMR, Journal of Marketing Research*, *12*(4), 440–453. doi:10.2307/3151093

Kanuk, S. U., & Krishnamurthy, S. (2007). An analysis of consumer power on the Internet. *Technovation*, *27*(1-2), 47–56. doi:10.1016/j.technovation.2006.05.002

Kaplan, A. M., & Haenlein, M. (2010). Users of the world unite! The challenges and opportunities of Social Media. *Business Horizons*, *53*(1), 59–68. doi:10.1016/j.bushor.2009.09.003

Kazim, K., & Karahan, F. (2011). To be or not to be in Social Media Arena as the Most Cost Efficient Marketing Strategy after the Global Recession. *Procedia: Social and Behavioral Sciences*, 24.

Keller, K. L. (2009). Building on strong brands in a modern marketing communications environment. *Journal of Marketing Communications*, *15*(2-3), 139–155. doi:10.1080/13527260902757530

Keronen, K., & Tanni, K. (2013). *Johdata Asiakkaasi Verkkoon*. Helsinki: Talentum Media Oy.

Keyes, J. (2006). *Knowledge management, business intelligence and content management. Broken South Parken*. Auerbach Publications. doi:10.1201/9781420013863

Kucuk, S. U., & Krishnamurthy, S. (2007). An Analysis of Consumer Power on the Internet. *Technovation*, *27*(1/2), 47–56. doi:10.1016/j.technovation.2006.05.002

Lancaster, C. (2014). *Content marketing: turn content into powerful marketing tool*. London: Pogo Book Publishing.

Lauterborn, R. (1990). *New marketing litany: 4Ps passé; 4Cs take over*. New York. *Advertising Age*.

Lieb, R. (2011). *Content Marketing: think like a publisher. How to use content to market online and in social media*. Indianapolis, IN: Que Publishing.

Lilly, M. C. (2014). *Content marketing essentials for small business*. London: Create Space Independent Publishing Platform.

Linn, M. (2012). *A Field Guide to the 4 Types of Content Marketing Metrics*. Retrieved 15 November 2014 from www.contentmarketinginstitute.com

Malthouse, E. C., Haenlein, M., Skiera, B., Wege, E., & Zhang, M. (2013). Managing Customer Relationships in the Social Media Era: Introducing the Social CRM House. *Journal of Interactive Marketing*, *27*(4), 270–289. doi:10.1016/j.intmar.2013.09.008

Mosca, F. (2008). Market-driven management in fashion and luxury industries. *Symphonya. Emerging Issues in Management*, *1*, 53–78.

Mosca, F. (2010). *Marketing dei beni di lusso*. Milano: Pearson.

Mosca, F. (2012). *Product concepts and heritage per i beni ad elevato valore simbolico*. Turin: Giappichelli.

Nelli, R. P. (2012). *Branded Content Marketing*. Milan: Vita e Pensiero.

Newbert, S. L. (2007). Empirical research on the resource-based view of the firm: An assessment and suggestions for future research. *Strategic Management Journal, 28*(12), 121–146. doi:10.1002/smj.573

Okonkwo, U. (2007). *Luxury fashion branding*. Hampshire, UK: Palgrave. doi:10.1057/9780230590885

Okonkwo, U. (2010). *Luxury online*. Hampshire, UK: Palgrave. doi:10.1057/9780230248335

Parikh, A., & Deshmukh, S. (2013). Search Engine Optimization. *International Journal of Engineering Research & Technology, 2*(11), 324–348.

Prandelli, E., & Verona, G. (2011). *Vantaggio competitivo in Rete: dal Web 2.0 al Cloud Computing*. Milan: McGraw-Hill.

Pulizzi, J. (2012). The Rise of Storytelling as the New Marketing. *Publishing Research Quarterly, 28*(2), 116–123. doi:10.1007/s12109-012-9264-5

Pulizzi, J. (2012). *Six Useful Content Marketing Definitions*. Retrieved 21 February 2015 from http://contentmarketinginstitute.com/2012/06/contentmarketing-definition/

Pulizzi, J. (2014). *Epic content marketing*. London: Mc Graw Hill.

Pulizzi, J., & Barrett, N. (2009). *Get content. Get customers*. New York: McGraw Hill.

Rahimia, F., & Hassanzadeh, J. (2013). The impact of website content dimension and e-trust on e-marketing effectiveness: The case of Iranian commercial saffron corporations. *Information & Management, 50*(5), 240–247. doi:10.1016/j.im.2013.04.003

Rakic, R., Beba, R., & Mira, R. (2014). Digital Content Marketing for organizations as buyers. *Ekonomika. Journal of Economic Theory and Practice and Social Issues, 1*, 109–123.

Ramos, R. (2014). *Content Marketing: insider's secret to online sales and lead generation*. Expert Publishing.

Rancati, E., & Gordini, N. (2014). Content marketing metrics: Theoretical aspects and empirical evidence. *European Scientific Journal, 10*(34), 92–104.

Rancati, E. & Gordini N. (2015a). Gli strumenti di misurazione delle strategie di content marketing: un confronto tra imprese italiane e inglesi. *Mercati e competitività, 1*, 45-74.

Rancati, E., & Gordini, N. (2015b), Content marketing: conceptualizing and measuring. Evidence from a sample of Italian firms. In *Proceedings of the 44th EMAC Conference: Collaboration in Research*.

Rose, R., & Pulizzi, J. (2011). *Managing Content Marketing. The real-world guide for creating passionate subscribers to your brands*. Cleveland, OH: CMI Books.

Rotsztein, B. (2014). *Content marketing ideas*. London: Creative Force Publishing.

Rowley, J. (2008). Understanding digital Content Marketing. *Journal of Marketing Management, 24*(5-6), 517–540. doi:10.1362/026725708X325977

Ryan, D., & Jones, C. (2009). *Understanding Digital Marketing – Marketing Strategies for engaging the digital generation.* London: Kogan Page Limited.

Scott, M. D. (2014). *Le nuove regole del marketing. Come usare social media, video online, app mobile, blog, comunicati stampa e marketing virale per raggiungere i clienti.* Milan: Hoepli.

Slater, V. (2014). *Content marketing: recycling and reuse. How your best online content can engage and attract new customers.* New York: i30 Media Corporation.

Van Lieshout, L. (2014). *Content marketing for professionals.* London: CreateSpace Independent Publishing Platform.

Venkatesh, R., & Chatterjee, R. (2006). Bundling, Unbundling, and pricing of multiform products: The case of magazine content. *Journal of Interactive Marketing, 20*(2), 54–78. doi:10.1002/dir.20059

Vescovi, T. (2007). *Il marketing e la Rete. La gestione integrata del Web nel business, Comunicazione, E-commerce, sales management, business to business.* Milan: Il Sole 24 Ore.

Weinberg, B. D., & Pehlivan, E. (2011). Social spending: Managing the social media mix. *Business Horizons, 54*(3), 275–282. doi:10.1016/j.bushor.2011.01.008

Winer, R. S. (2009). New Communications Approaches in Marketing: Issues and research directions. *Journal of Interactive Marketing, 23*(2), 237–256. doi:10.1016/j.intmar.2009.02.004

Wymbs, C. (2011). Digital marketing: The time for a new "academic major" has arrived. *Journal of Marketing Education, 33*(2), 93–106. doi:10.1177/0273475310392544

ADDITIONAL READING

Rahimia, F., & Hassanzadeh, J. (2013). The impact of website content dimension and e-trust on e-marketing effectiveness: The case of Iranian commercial saffron corporations. *Information & Management, 4,* 124–145.

Savar, A. (2013). *Content to Commerce: Engaging Consumers Across Paid, Owned and Earned Channels, New Jersey.* Somerset: Wiley.

Zahay, D. (2014). Beyond interactive marketing. *Journal of Research in Interactive Marketing, 8*(4), 32–46. doi:10.1108/JRIM-08-2014-0047

KEY TERMS AND DEFINITIONS

Consumption Metrics: Measurement of brand awareness and website traffic generated by the content.

Content Marketing: The marketing and business process for creating and distributing valuable and compelling content to attract, engage, acquire, educate and connect a clearly defined target audience with the objective of driving profitable consumer action and creating firm value.

Lead Generation Metrics: Measurement of number of leads generated.

Sales Metrics: Measurement of the impact of CM on firm performance, finding out how CM impacts customer acquisition and sales goals.

Sharing Metrics: Measurement of the level of content sharing by consumers with their network of people with a direct and significant impact on the engagement.

This research was previously published in Global Marketing Strategies for the Promotion of Luxury Goods edited by Fabrizio Mosca and Rosalia Gallo, pages 109-132, copyright year 2016 by Business Science Reference (an imprint of IGI Global).

Chapter 14
Building Academic Branding:
The Digital Branding as Academic Footprint

Ruth Matovelle Villamar
Escuela Superior Politécnica del Litoral, Ecuador

ABSTRACT

Nowadays, many professionals of different areas of expertise have found themselves at the needs to incorporate in the digital world, their personal digital branding as a result of entrepreneurship projects, or as a crisis of business sectors. A different phenomenon occurs in the academic field; the researchers are forced to incorporate themselves in the digital field. The research professors have a responsibility to society, popularizing science, this represents to value their own work and contribute to its visibility, and the starting point is to have "digital academic Branding. This chapter explains step-by-step techniques that develop a digital academic branding, starting from an interior analysis of the academic up to the formulation of the visual and conceptual brand; it is important is to make in a sequential manner every one of the activities described here.

INTRODUCTION

This chapter is the result of the synthesis and reorder of ideas, from different authors, plus the academic experience of the author. This model of brand building does not intend to create an industrialized model or series making, on the contrary its objective is to enhance their individuality. It seeks to show clearly the steps to follow to discover and create your personal brand, using basic indications, methodologies and theories used in the business, psychological and communicational field.

Starting from an interior analysis of the academic up to the formulation of the visual and conceptual brand. The importance of this chapter is to make in a sequential manner every one of the activities described here, rest assured that the result would be entirely satisfactory. Welcome to the world of personal branding.

DOI: 10.4018/978-1-5225-5187-4.ch014

BACKGROUND

Nowadays, colleges and universities have a fundamental roll in the human and social development, channeled primarily through the investigations made by their teacher-researchers. In recent years there has been an increase in the number of arguments supporting reforms to create socially responsible scientists, considering the need to democratize knowledge and provide expert advice and plural to the democratic institutions and the general public, thus increasing the capacity to discuss and finally meet the expectations of citizens. (Vessuri, 2010).

This leads us to think then that the researcher not only has to develop a task of research, but is also relevant his task as a communicator of: the scientific community interested in his field of work; to the media and citizens.

New technologies have contributed to the awareness of many communicators that previously limited themselves to encourage scientific knowledge from more minority plots (research department). This is generating real networks of scientific communication and research teams are increasingly aware of the need to explain what they do to their peers, but also the general public. (Sapiña, 2013).

The 2.0 environment offers a variety of platforms and scientific networks broadcasting scientific work and publications, the most important is to know and select the appropriate ones for each particular researcher. But if the center of everything is the disclosure, what role does personal branding do in this? Well a fundamental role is the starting point for disclosure.

Having a digital academic branding allows the academic to be identified by its target, it places you as an expert in a specific field, facilitates the search for other researchers to disseminate the work done, in order to establish new partnerships and attract funding.

The academic success of their digital branding, will contribute greatly to the success of your academic institution, which will be reflected in the positions in rankings that measure the quality of the IES1.

HOW TO CREATE A PERSONAL DIGITAL BRANDING

The author Marcos (2009), assures that the creation of a personal brand, "has to do with the creation and keeping up the credibility" and reassures that the best personal brands are the ones that are authentic, under any aspect of what they are and do strengthens the set, these "have a visibility based on placement, contact consistently regardless of the medium used" (Marcos 2009). A brand built from ideologies, placing dreams instead of real values can be compared as building a fictional character in a play, which could eventually be found out.

Since 1996, different authors have written about how to construct a Brand, there are many books dedicated to this subject. Nowadays, this can be seen from a simple point of view, focus the principles of branding to the people, but the current job goes beyond that, this chapter addresses the issue from a deeper and personal vision aimed to the academic researchers. I have developed a scheme to work on brand building, made of 4 phases: Know yourself; your personality, place it on your brand; express your thoughts; express your emotions and finally build your academic branding.

Figure 1.
Source: Author, 2015

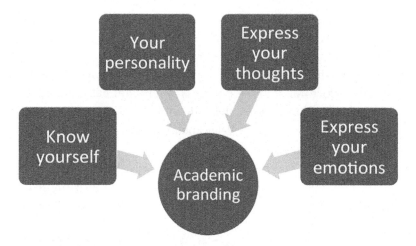

Know Yourself

The first step to knowing yourself, is to perform the technique Swot(Strengths, Weaknesses, Opportunities and Threats). This technique currently has a high degree of applicability in the business field, but can also be used in the personal field, that is called Personal SWOT specifically focused on the human being. This will evaluate the strengths and opportunities of a person just as their weaknesses and threats that revolve their environment. Originated by Albert S Humphrey in the 1960s, SWOT Analysis is as useful now as it was then. You can use it in two ways - as a simple icebreaker helping people get together to "kick off" strategy formulation, or in a more sophisticated way as a serious strategy tool (Swot Analysis, 2011).

This will be a self conscience exercise, one should be fair enough to yourself, and place the corresponding information no matter what it is, if the reader finds it very difficult, he or she can ask help from someone of their trust. The focus will be specifically on the academic role, it is required to have at hand a lot of information: a list of research conducted throughout his career, published articles, training events, debates, all the congresses where he or she has participated in, a list of places where they usually go on vacation, list tasks often performed on weekends, etc.

Now take a pencil and a blank sheet of paper, divide it into four sections and place the following titles: Strengths, Weaknesses, Opportunities and Threats, next do a breathing exercise and fill in each division the information required:

- **Strengths:** Identify the best you do as an academic, example: write, speak in public, participate in debates, research, etc., if you have any difficulty you can help yourself answering the following questions: What do you do better than anyone else?; What was the reason you were asked to participate in a project?; What are your strengths recorded in the evaluations that the institution where you work made to you?

- **Weaknesses:** Identify in what specific activity you are not doing too well, how would you like, maybe you do not like to participate in conferences with a large public, or debates, tv, radio or other interviews, if you have any difficulties you can help yourself answering the following questions: In which of my professional activities I feel uncomfortable?; Which are the factors where you have the lowest scores in your professional evaluations?
- **Opportunities:** Identify what you consider may arise along the way and you can take advantage of: a scholarship, a postdoctoral study, a congress where you can participate, etc., if you have trouble you can help yourself answering the following questions: What benefits can come if I study to work for an innovating project?; What mentions or awards can I apply in the university that helps me create new partnerships?.
- **Threats:** Identify what could affect your academic development that can come from an external agent. If you have trouble you can help yourself answering the following questions?; Which obstacles do you confront?; Can any of your weaknesses put in serious jeopardy your job?.

Once you have finished filling out the four variables, the reader will already have his first instrument.

Identify Relevant and Sustainable Differential Values

A valuable person is a person that has interior values and that lives by it. Therefore a man is worth what his values are worth and the way he lives them (Ardilla & Orozco)

The "*El libro de los valores*", by the authors Ardilla & Orozco mentions that the values are fundamental beliefs that help us decide, appreciate and choose some things over others, we acquire them during the process of growing and are influenced by the environment that surrounds us and mostly by the family. They are a guideline for formulating goals and personal or collective purposes and reflect our interests, feelings and most important convictions.

Several authors have written about this exciting topic from different perspectives and areas of knowledge, but a general acceptance is that these are classified into seven values: biological, sensitive, aesthetic, intellectual, economic, moral and religious.

The quality of our lives depends much on the values we have, what makes us unique and different. With this in mind, it is necessary to make a self-analysis and identify your values, just as in the previous section be sincere and objective, to make this process easier below is a chart with a list of values (both work and personal) (Metcalf & Palmer, 2011), select the ten that are most important to you—as guides for how to behave, or as components of a valued way of life. Feel free to add any values of your own to this list.

Upon completion of this activity, the reader now has his second instrument of the process.

Establish Where You're Headed and Your Role in the Future

The best way to do this activity is to do it in an atmosphere of meditation in a personal space, without interruptions.

The mission is about our reason of being in life, it is about the human need of identifying and expressing our purpose in life.

Figure 2.
Source: http://www.metcalf-associates.com/

Personal Values Checklist		
Achievement	Fast-paced work	Pleasure
Advancement and promotion	Financial gain	Power and authority
	Freedom	Privacy
Adventure	Friendships	Public service
Arts	Having a family	Recognition
Autonomy	Health	Relationships
Challenge	Helping other people	Religion
Change and variety	Honesty	Reputation
Community	Independence	Security
Compassion	Influencing others	Self-respect
Competence	Inner harmony	Serenity
Competition	Integrity	Sophistication
Cooperation	Intellectual status	Spirituality
Creativity	Leadership	Stability
Decisiveness	Location	Status
Democracy	Love	Time away from work
Economic security	Loyalty	Trust
Environmental stewardship	Meaningful work	Truth
	Money	Volunteering
Effectiveness	Nature	Wealth
Efficiency	Openness and honesty	Wisdom
Ethical living	Order (tranquility/stability)	Work quality
Excellence		Work under pressure
Expertise	Peace	Other: _____
Fame	Personal development/learning	
Fast living		

Understand that the personal mission is about answering the following questions: * who am I?* who do I want to be? Who do I want to be in the future?* Why am I here?* Am I successful? Why or why not?

For many of the readers it may seem unnecessary the elaboration of the mission, because of the day by day activities it helps the fulfillment, but it results very interesting to make this self-analysis by answering all the questions in the previous paragraph, and with this make the mission. The result of this exercise may bring many surprises, it may come up that your daily work does not contribute in anything your mission, or on the contrary it rectifies it.

The vision is about what we want to achieve in the long term, the place where we want to be after several years, it is the mark the academic wants to leave as his legacy, it is important to establish it in a maximum of two lines projecting yourself in a period of at least 15 years.

The mission and the vision are closely related and to write a personal vision, we must consider the mission.

By finishing this activity, the reader now has his third instrument of the process.

Your Personality Should be Shown on Your Brand

An identity is a self-definition, implicitly, that a human being should be able to develop in the course of his conversion to adulthood and continue redefining throughout his life (Erikson, 1950)

To build an identity three dimensions should be considered: The personality the brand builds while it communicates, the message of all you have to say and the expressions to be used so they can be understood.

Brand personality is defined formally here as "The set of human characteristics associated with a brand " (Aaker, 1997). In contrast to "product-relate attributes" which tend a serve a utilitarian function for consumers, brand personality tends to serve a symbolic or self-expressive function (Keller, 1993).

Conducting a review of authors on the construct Brand, (Bailey II & Schechter, 1994,) and (Grossman, 1994), refer to the brand only for it's tangible elements, defining it by it's most basic expression, on the other hand is the point of view, (Kapferer, 1992; Fournier, 1998; Aaker D., 1996; Sweeney & Brandon, 2006), in which the emotional, symbolic and intangible elements of the Brand are predominant. In these symbolic elements the personality of the Brand, the way the Brand reinforces the identity of the consumers and the ability of the brands to represent the consumers before others are included (Schlesinger Díaz & Cervera, 2008).

These authors conclude that the brand has a personality that is perceived by the consumers, whether it represents a product a tangible or intangible commodity, since the topic of this book is centered around personal academic branding, the Brand that we should define belongs to a human being, whom already has an established personality, following is a list of elements that help establish the personality of the Brand:

1.   Country of origin.
2.   Sector of activity.
3.   Style of communication.
4.   Image of spokesman.
5.   Image of the users.

Country of Origin

The country of origin of the academic will carry to the Brand those prototypical features of the image representing the citizen of that country, just like Roobert Govers explains it in his book titled "Place branding: Glocal, virtual and physical identities, constructed, imagined and experienced" where he affirms:

The identities of the places are constructed by historical, political, religious and cultural discourses, also through local knowledge and the inevitable interference of power struggles. The real identity of places is managed by the realization of the group of unique features and / or group of meanings existing in a place and its culture at a particular moment in time (Govers & Go, 2009)

The reader must now identify the values and positive traits that transmits the Brand of his country, and place them in a contribution under this name.

Sector of Activity

The organizations working in the same sector must necessarily share values because the category requires it, the same way and for the same reasons some general personality traits are shared (Avalos, 2013).

The claim of Avalos is quite successful at present time by the way the global markets behave, this is the fundamental reason why sectorial brands are made, their creation is focused primarily towards the industrial area, this solidifies the placement of the industry mainly to search, maintain and strengthen its presence in international markets.

But, is this the same behavior in the field of higher education? An immediate answer would be to think that this field is appropriately represented by its sectorial Brand bonded with the country Brand, and the combination of both elements will help us see certain glimpses of the sector's quality.

The other answer would be no, a sectorial Brand can not represent the sector, since it has special particular characteristics and as a result it is necessary to implement a different methodology. Precisely this has been the worldwide way and today in the academic field what prevails in first instance is the reputation earned by the school's Brand in particular.

The publications showing the lists of institutions of higher education or programs supposedly in order of their quality are part of the current landscape of higher education systems in many countries. As in many cases, this phenomenon has appeared with a lot of anticipation in the United States but, at least from the decade of 1990 it has expanded all over the world (Martínez Rizo, 2011).

Currently there are many rankings that measure the academic quality of Universities all over the world, some of these are:

The Academic Ranking of World Universities (ARWU) was first published in June 2003 by the Center for World-Class Universities (CWCU), Graduate School of Education (formerly the Institute of Higher Education) of Shanghai Jiao Tong University, China, and updated on an annual (Academic Ranking Of World Universities, s.f.).

The Times Higher Education World University Rankings 2014-2015 list the best global universities and are the only international university performance tables to judge world-class universities across all of their core missions - teaching, research, knowledge transfer and international outlook. (The World University Rankings, s.f.).

Nowadays the Shanghai Ranking is the most widely accepted ranking among academics, as it is stated in Salinas Torres and Docampo in their article entitled "The new Highly cited researchers list from Thomson Reuters and the Shanghai: Spain's position and university map", in which it is mentioned that this ranking has currently become a "performance measurement tool of national and worldwide university", joining the competition among institutions to climb positions, are causing universities to pay more attention to the variables that make up the different scores of the ranking (Torres & Docampo, 2013).

The measurements have evolved, now it is not enough to only measure the quality of the universities, works are now being done at a more detailed level, It aims to identify the potential of researchers who work in these institutions, we will discuss more about this topic in the following chapters, for now we will mention the Highly Cited Researcher (HCR), made by Thomson-Reuters, they publish an annual list of heighted cited researchers openly available on the site http://highlycited.com.

The importance of the HCR is that from 2012 Thomson-Reuters incorporates this as a component of the Academic Ranking of World Universities (ARWU)- Ranking of Shanghái, which has turned the highly cited researchers into a "solid asset for their universities and has generated, just like in the style of great sport leagues, recruitments with clear intentions to quickly scale positions in the ranking" (Torres salinas & Docampo, 2013).

After the broad explanation of how the sector transmits and shares values and personality traits towards academic branding, the reader should identify in an impartial way the values that the identity of the institution of higher education transmits and place them in a section entitled "values of the sector",

Figure 3.
Source: http://highlycited.com/

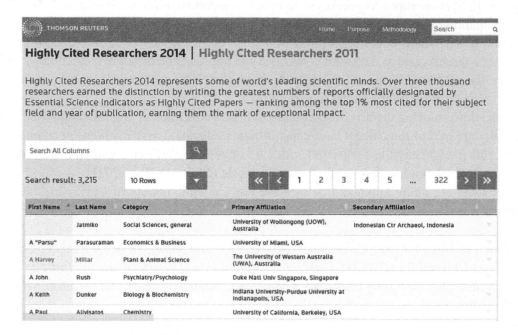

as an additional exercise the reader can idealize what are the values they wish to reach and place them here, keeping in mind "my goal institution" at where they would like to work at a near time.

Establish Your Style of Communication

Each person has their own style of communication, the ones that let us establish relationships with other people creating a link with other persons, this process flows through the components of social abilities (behavioral, cognitive, and physiological).

Monjas (1993) defines social skills as "specific behaviors or social skills required to competently perform a task of interpersonal nature, involving a set of learned and acquired behaviors and not a personality trait. They are a group of complex interpersonal behaviors that come into interaction with other people".

Rich and Schroeder (1976) state that this set of behaviors are closely linked to the physical and psychological characteristics of the individual, and the degree of awareness that has the communication process. While more aware the person is about the process and their own social skills, he will be able to control, change or improve those weak components, avoiding they act against him.

The reader should ask himself or herself now what are my social abilities? What are my weak components? to answer these questions it is necessary to look at the social abilities and their components, however I must anticipate that there are many authors who have written about this concept, so it has a lot of definitions with different approaches, shown here is the theory presented by (Caballo, 1998)

The components that constitute the social abilities are three:

The behavioral components classify themselves into:

Figure 4.
Source: Author, 2015.

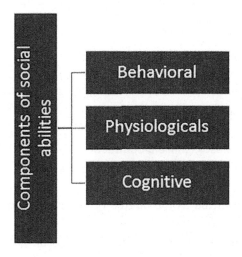

Figure 5.
Source: Author, 2015.

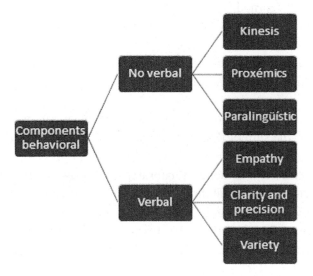

- Non verbal
  - Within the Kinesis[2] we can distinguish the body posture, eye contact and gestures.
  - Proxemics[3] concerns the appropriate use of space.
  - In the paralinguistic we can differentiate the volume and tone of voice, inflection, speed and fluency in speech and silence.
- Verbal
  - Empathy. The skilled person transfers his empathy with the expressions used.
  - Clarity and precision.

○ Variety. The unskilled people have a smaller variety of subjects for use in the conversation, minor expressions of interest to the interlocutor, the more utterances of interest to oneself and excessive self-revelation.

The physiological components refer to:

- The pulse.
- Blood pressure and blood flow.
- The electrodermal responses (sweating).
- The electromyographic responses (muscle contraction).
- Breathing (depth and frequency).

In practice this is what is identified as the degree of anxiety that occurs at the time the person is interacting.

The Cognitive components may be the cause why a person can fail when displaying a socially responsible behavior, they are:

- Lack of acquisition or learning the skill: it is possible that a certain type of skill is never acquired, or has been inadequately learned.
- Failure to use the ability in certain situations: sometimes a social skill is shown in some situations and not in others.
- Influence of situational variables: people learn what social skills should be strengthened in certain situations and adapt their behavior accordingly.

Communication styles could then be described in terms of the components of social skills used by the individual. This gives us the sum of three main styles (Vander Hofstadt, 2003):

- **Assertive Communication:** It is the most natural, straightforward style. It is used by people with self-esteem and security in them, that through communication seek to raise issues that are satisfactory for all, without resorting to manipulation or pretense.
- **Aggressive Communication:** It is the style of who seek to achieve its objectives without worrying about the satisfaction of the other. Often they use strategies like the feeling of guilt, intimidation or anger.
- **Passive Communication:** It is the style used by people who avoid confrontation and attention. To do so they respond passively, without getting involved in the issue or showing conformity with whatever arises.

Features that identify each style of communication.

The reader now should identify from the given list their social skills and communication style. This is a really easy exercise if you really know your "inner self", if instead you have got confused with the information, take your time and read again in detail the information provided in this section, than look closely your daily actions one by one at the moment of communicating and interacting with your environment, you can ask for help from a friend but sincere in the information he will provide you. When you have the required information place it in a section under the name "Social abilities and communication styles".

Figure 6.
Source: http://www.slideshare.net/ ; Steven M. Gerson & Sharon J. Gerson.

Characteristics of Communication Styles (adapted from Sherman, 2001)			
Characteristics	**Aggressive**	**Passive**	**Assertive**
Mottoes and Beliefs	"Everyone should be like me." "I am never wrong."	"Don't make waves." "Don't disagree."	"I have rights, and so do others."
Communication Style	Close minded Poor listener	Always agrees Hesitant	Active listener States ideas directly
Characteristics	Domineering Bullying	Apologetic Does not express self	Confident Non-judgmental
Behavior	Puts others down Bossy	Asks permission unnecessarily A fence sitter	Firm Action oriented
Non-verbal Cues	Points with jabbing finger Frowns	Looks down Slouches	Direct eye contact Confident and relaxed posture
Verbal Cues	"Don't ask why. Just do it." Verbal abuse	"I'll try to do what you suggest. . . ."	"I choose to. . . ." "What are my options?"
Confrontation and Problem Solving	Must win arguments Threatens	Avoids or postpones Needs supervision	Negotiates Confronts problems when they occur
Feelings Felt	Anger Hostility	Powerlessness	Enthusiasm Well being
Effects	Wastes time and energy micromanaging Provokes others	Loses self esteem Builds dependent relationships	Achieves self esteem and confidence

After this broad explanation the reader with full security can answer the questions posed at the beginning of this subject and enter them in the corresponding section.

- What are your social skills?
- What is your communication style?

Image of Spoke: Man

The use of what is technically called spoke-man or spokesman for the Brand consists of choosing a specific person with certain associated values, to represent the brand and transfer its aesthetics, values and attitudes to this, it is the common procedure that is used in the business world, but how does it work in the academic branding?, the answer is very simple, you are the Brand and the only authorized spokesman to represent it.

Therefore, nothing has to be done in this section, just place here the values that you identified in section 2 of this chapter.

Image of Brand Users

The image we have of brand users is perhaps one of the strongest determinants of personality because it is mediated; the experience is personal and direct, proving to be one of the basic techniques in brand management (Avalos, 2013). You can also experience a backlash towards the expected, you can rule out a brand when you see that a person we do not like is using it.

Turning to the family level, which plays a large component in the formation of the personality of the individual in the growth stage, some have to feel familiar with some proverbs, which are proverbial[4] sayings or phrases used in Spanish since the Middle Ages and have come down to us through oral tradition, the well known phrase "Tell me who you walk with and I'll tell you who you are." You can guess the likes and hobbies of someone by their friends and environments they frequent. Similarly, this proverb warns of the great influence on the behavior or customs on someone the companies of the rest, whether good or bad.

The statements from the business and family point of view about the users of the brand, gives us a space to think about who are our colleagues, that we frequent, and therefore identify us. What values am I achieving to transmit through my fellow researchers, the circle that surrounds me as a professional, is the circle that I really want to be in?

After these reflections, which certainly could be considered more philosophical, we can clearly identify the values that identify the users of my brand, and place them in a section entitled "values of my users"

This activity certainly has resulted strenuous, little by little enter each of the elements that conform the personality, which is the result of a combination of situational conditions moderated by hereditary and environmental factors, which often goes unnoticed by the individual.

Now you have the fourth element of this process, the same that has sub elements represented in the Figure 7.

Express Your Thoughts

The speech is a linguistic message in the broadest and deepest sense, it brings to light all the values and brand promises. All speeches converge towards the establishment and operation of the brand universe. The expression of values through contents (meanings) and forms (significant) ensures cohesion and coherence, or must, at all times.

The speech of the brand is made up by: taglines or slogans, stories, anecdotes and short stories and voice tone.

Figure 7.
Source: Author.

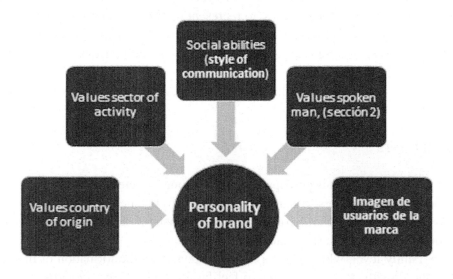

Taglines of Slogans

It is a phrase that immediately follows the logo, generally it synthesizes the concept or essence of the brand promise, this should consider the following features:

1. Be short.
2. Separate itself from the competition.
3. Be unique and original.
4. Capture the essence of the brand and it's placement.
5. Have an easy pronunciation and easy to remember.
6. Motivate an emotional response.

They can be imperative, descriptive, superlative, provocative, specific, here are some examples, from renowned scientists for their presence in the social networks:

Example 1: The scientist Ben Goldacre, cited by Science magazine as a "star" scientist in Twitter with about 409.196 followers (July 10/2015), British physician, academic and science writer. As of March 2015, he is a Senior Clinical Research Fellow at the Centre for Evidence-Based Medicine based at Nuffield Department of Primary Care Health Science, University of Oxford, has the slogan "Bad Science". (Figure 8)

Example 2: Brian Edward Cox, cited by Science magazine as a "star" scientist in Twitter with about 1'611.000 of followers (July 10/2015), is an English physicist, and professor of particle physics in the School of Physics and Astronomy at the University of Manchester, has a slogan made up of questions that clearly conveys the essence of his brand. (Figure 9)

Surely right now you are wondering what is the essence of the brand? Or how do I build my slogan?, well now is the time to use the material produced in section 3 of this chapter, read what you wrote and try to consolidate all of this in a slogan, or multiple slogans, which clearly conveys what you want to

Figure 8.
Source: https://www.facebook.com

Figure 9.
Source: https://www.facebook.com

achieve in life, the reason for your existence, how do you want to be remembered, in other words the mark you want to leave imprinted.

Tone of Voice

A tone of voice both embodies and expresses the brand's personality and set of values. It's about the people that make up the brand – the things that drive them, their loves and hates, and what they want to share with the world. (Cummings, 2015)

A brand's tone of voice should be distinctive, recognizable and unique. This may seem like a tall order until we consider the use of our own language in everyday life. We all employ language - both written and spoken - in our own way. Of course, culture and dialect are the most significant factors dictating our approach to words. But within these, we each have our own idiosyncrasies, favorite expressions, inflections, pace and so forth.

Therefore you should only be "yourself", when you answer questions or write messages spreading your academic work.

Now you can prepare the elements of section five, the "Speech", slogans, at least two expressions that determine your tone of voice.

Express Your Emotions

"Expression" according to the Royal Academy of Language is the representation with words or with other external symbols, of a thought, an idea, or a feeling. In his book Brand Sense, Lindstrom defines the term as:

We store our values and emotions in memory banks for each sense — image, sound, smell, taste, and touch. Events, moods, feelings, and even products in our lives are continuously imprinted in our memories, from the second we wake to the moment we sleep. However, most advertising messages that we're exposed to on a daily basis come to us through only two of the five senses: sight and sound (Lindstrom, 2005)

In this section we shall especially work with these two senses: sight and sound, since the personal brand principally develops online. The sight is the most powerful of our senses and comparatively has the ability of a wider range of subtlety. The elements that could be grouped under this item are the following:

- **Graphic**: Look for a graphic where you can permeate your professional vision (use the instrument prepared in subparagraph 3), and represent you appropriately, consider every detail, if there isn't a graphic that meets your expectations, look for a graphic designer and ask him to design one for you.
- **Objects**: Each object used in your visual communication, whether in imagery as in the information being shared should carefully support your ethical values.
- **Actors and Clothing**: The outfit faithfully reflects your personality, this clearly conveys the values of your country of origin, the values of the institution you represent and your personal tastes for colors and designs.

Example 1: Let's review again the scientist Brian Edward Cox, but now analyzing the existing visual elements on his Twitter profile image, carefully look at Figure 10:

Figure 10.
Source: https://twitter.com/profbriancox

His facial expression detonates strength, force, his fist conveys power, aggressiveness willing to discover new challenges, and he fears nothing. The objects that complement the scene: the helmet, uniform and motorcycle harmoniously complement each other to convey that: adventure, courage, ability.

Example 2: Neil deGrasse Tyson, cited by Science magazine as a "star" scientist on Twitter with about 3'952.599 of followers (July 10/2015), born October 5, 1958 is an American astrophysicist, cosmologist, author, and science communicator. Since 1996, he has been the Frederick P. Rose Director of the Hayden Planetarium at the Rose Center for Earth and Space in New York City., watch carefully each of the elements involved in the picture captured from his Twitter account shown in Figure 11:

What first stands out is his look, it's a happy look, denotes comfort, friendliness, which articulated with his face gesture invites to an open and emotional dialogue. His clothing gives a space of formality, who likes the nightlife, celebrate with friends, the background photo complements this interpretation, it's like you want to come see the sunrise? Do not forget his passion is being a cosmologist.

Example 3: Richard Dawkins, cited by Science magazine as a "star" scientist on Twitter with about 1'211.218 followers (July 10/2015), born March 26, 1941, is an English ethologist, evolutionary biologist,[3] and writer. He is an emeritus fellow of New College, Oxford,[4] and was the University of Oxford's Professor for Public Understanding of Science from 1995 until 2008 (Figure 12)

The image speaks of nature, quickly my mind takes me to the habitat, I can hear the birds and feel the warmth of the sun, transmitted by the cool clothes worn by the protagonist of the image. The word "RELIGION" is strongly emphasized as a label on the shirt, this one word evokes the religious values this scientist surely has, on the other hand his gaze triggers that he wants to see beyond the obvious.

Figure 11.
Source: https://twitter.com/neiltyson

Figure 12.
Source: https://twitter.com/richarddawkins

These three examples to which I have applied a simple visual analysis, helps to convey to the reader everything what an image can say, each element combines an important role in this. There may also be different interpretations of a same image, depending on the degree of experiences, maturity and perspective of the person who makes it, what is difficult is to change the visual cues that establish a context in the image.

In the hearing aspect we can group: sounds, music and broadcasting voice in the online environment, we are talking about the background music we might have in the background of our resources, or some video that we may have made to present them in several selected informative formats.

To this section a little more time has to be dedicated in taking care of every element that will make up your profile, it would be good to ask for help from a photographer friend to make some good shots and we have the sixth instrument.

BUILD YOUR ACADEMIC BRANDING

In the previous sections, the material has focused on getting the essence of the brand and its value proposition that carries out your personality as a valuable human being with whom it is worth sharing, focusing mainly on your professional talent. Now what's left is to develop the visual brand, which shall transmit all this at a glance, it is important to remember the words of the author Schwabel on personal branding, to be psychologically ready in preparing the remaining steps:

The personal brand describes the process by which the person and the businessmen differentiate and stand out among a multitude, identifying and expressing their proposal of unique value, whether it be professional, that later promote on different platforms, with a message and a consistent image that let's them reach a specific goal. This way, people can be recognized more and more as experts in their field, build up a reputation and credibility, further his career and improve your self-confidence. (Schwabel, 2009)

The logo is your own name, which has identified you since you where born, as simple as that, in sight that a personal branding is being formulated. The most appropriate now is to make a broad search on the internet of your name, with the intention to find homonyms, if that were the case write down on a sheet of paper these repetitions, to have a clear position of the situation.

If they are many repetitions, than you would have to add to your logo differential elements, for example: for the field "Names" use the name that less repeats itself, and the most repeated abbreviate it or omit it, in many contexts in a world wide level it is indifferent if a person uses his first or second name; for the field of "last names" it is obligatory to place the first one, if you have many repetitions of this one, in the conjunction add your middle name as a differentiator, on the other hand if your first last name is not too common, forget about placing your second last name because it will visually overload your brand. If you are one of the lucky persons in the world without any homonyms, congratulations, you automatically already have added a unique value and differentiator.

Refining the name, now it's time to decide about the typography, about this topic there are many scientific definitions that could be of great help at the moment of selecting the ideal letter type, but I do not wish to not mention Massimo Vignelli "was, is, the most important and influential designer of the last third of the 20th century and beginning of the 21st, the golden age which the classic design culminates" (Corazón, 2014), with one of his most famous phrases.

In the new computer age the proliferation of typefaces and type manipulations represents a new level of visual pollution threatening our culture. Out of thousands of typefaces, all we need are a few basic ones, and trash the rest. So come and see a few basic typefaces (Vignelli, 2010)

Select the typography with your best criteria for your logo, once this has been done you now have your logo.After finishing this chapter, you must have a total of 7 inputs, allowing you to create any profile on the selected digital formats:

1. A unique name, with a letter type that represents your values and homonym free.
2. A list of professional strengths (personal SWOT).
3. 10 values that identify you as an individual.
4. Mission and Vision.
5. Personality (country values, sector values, social abilities, personal values and finally an image of the users of the brand).
6. The speech, represented by a slogan that transmits your mission and vision.
7. Photographs creating in context, in which the brand is developed, in which each element has a meaning that represents the personality of the brand: expression, environment, position of the hands, eye sight, clothing, complementary elements, etc.

With this material you are ready to open your profile and present your personal academic digital branding.

FUTURE RESEARCH DIRECTIONS

This problem, about the imminent need that the academic researchers should have a digital presence with a unique value, makes space to see future research directions, that allow to correctly direct the actions of the researchers. One of the questions to answer would be: does the academic require a previous communicational work to the present surroundings to strengthen his reputations before formulating the academic branding online? Or failing that, they get better results for example, for his acceptance in competitive opportunities, the academic start their way to become brands versus those who hasn't.

CONCLUSION

This chapter enfasized that to create your academic branding, it is neccessary first to know oneself, which will let you quickly identify your value proposition. Also, you should know which is your current role and future one, in other words, dream, establishing the goals you wish to reach, without forgetting to transmit the values, personality and feelings through expressions and speech, elements that should be reflected by the visual Brand, therefore building an authentic personal Brand.

Personal branding does not focus on the outer side of the person, it is not an image consulting, it is not the way we dress or our appearance. Personal Branding is the set of elements that goes from the inside of the person and how he transmits it, these elements are the ones that will make us be perceived as valuable and reliable professionals, which automatically transforms in their footprint, as explained by Andrés Pérez, "personal branding is about leaving a mark in other people. If that mark you left is well defined and you communicate it effectively, you will influence on their emotions" (Perez, 2014).

Los Academics researches have the responsibility to leave an academic mark, which contributes to the recognizing of the institution of higher education they represent and a commitment to society in disseminating the science. They should also function successfully at virtual organizations, in highly integrated social networks, virtual (professional) communities and virtual laboratories / e-science, resulted from research, so it is necessary to have one academic branding.

It is important to point out that to obtain and academic mark it demands a lot of work, time, dedication, patience and persistence, you cannot reach it from one day to another; it is a process that it's results will be shown on a long term. Therefore a good communicational strategy is required and a plan to acquire visibility of the brand that complements your career as a researcher. There is much to do to make an academic footprint, the following chapters are the guide to the management and fluidity of online academic reputation. Good luck!

REFERENCES

Aaker, D. (1996). *Building Strong Brands*. New York: The free press.

Aaker, J. (1997). Dimensions of brand personality. *JMR, Journal of Marketing Research*, *34*(3), 347. doi:10.2307/3151897

Ardilla, & Orozco. (n.d.). *El libro de los valores*. El tiempo.

Avalos, C. (2013). *La marca identidad y estrategia*. Argentina: La Crujía.

Bailey, I. I. I., & Schechter, A. (1994). The corporation as brand: An identity dilemma. *Chief Executive*, *98*, 42–45.

Caballo, V. (1998). *Manual de evaluacion y entrenamiento de las habilidades sociales*. Madrid: Siglo XXI de España.

CorazónA. (2014). *El País*. Retrieved from http://cultura.elpais.com/

Cummings, H. (2015). *Finding Your Brand's voice*. Retrieved from https://www.distilled.net/t

Erikson, E. (1950). *Childhood and society*. New York: Norton.

Fournier, S. (1998). Consumers and their brands: Developing Relationship theory in consumer research. *The Journal of Consumer Research*, *24*(4), 343–373. doi:10.1086/209515

Govers, R., & Go, F. (2009). *Place branding: Glocal, virtual and physical identities, constructed, imagined and experienced*. Hampshire: Palgrave Macmillan. doi:10.1057/9780230247024

Grossman, G. (1994). Carefully crafted identity can build brand equity. *The Public Relations Journal*, *50*, 18–21.

Kapferer, J. (1992). *Startegic Brand Management*. Kogan.

Keller, K. (1993). Conceptualizing, measuring, and managing customer- based brand equity. *Journal of Marketing*, *57*(1), 1–22. doi:10.2307/1252054

Lindstrom, M. (2005). *Brands Sense. Build Powerful Brands through Touch, Taste,Smell, Sight and Sound*. New York: The Free Press.

Marcos, T. (2009). *Como crear y mantener una marca personal*. Madrid.

Martínez Rizo, F. (2011). Los rankings de universidades: una visión crítica. *Revista de la educación superior*.

Metcalf, M., & Palmer, M. (2011). *Innovative Leadership Fieldbook*. Tucson, AZ: Integral Publishers.

Monjas, M. (1993). *Programa de enseñanza de habilidades de interacción social. Para niños y niñas en edad escolar*. Valladolid: MIMC.

Perez, A. (2014). *Marca Pesonal para Dummies*. Barcelona: Wiley Publishing.

Rich, A., & Schroeder, H. (1976). *Research issues in assertiveness training*. Academic Press.

Sapiña, L. (2013). *Aprender a divulgar la ciencia*. Metode.

Schlesinger Díaz, M., & Cervera, A. (2008). Estudio comparativo entre personalidad de marca ideal vs. percebida. *Innovar*, 31.

Schwabel, D. (2009). *Me 2.0: A Powerful way to Achieve Brand Success*. New York: Kaplan Publishers.

Sweeney, J., & Brandon, C. (2006). Brand personality: Exploring the potential to move from factor analytical to circumplex models. *Psychology and Marketing, 23*(8), 639–663. doi:10.1002/mar.20122

Swot Analysis. (2011). Retrieved from http://www.washington.edu/

The World University Rankings. (n.d.). Retrieved from www.timeshighereducation.co.uk

Torres Salinas, D., & Docampo, D. (2013). The new Highly cited researchers list from Thomson Reuters and the Shanghai: Spain´s position and university map. *El profesional de la Información*, 265.

Vander Hofstadt, C. (2003). *El libro de las habilidades de comunicación*. Academic Press.

Vessuri, H. (2010). *El rol de la investigación en la Educación Superior*. Academic Press..

Vignelli, M. (2010). The Vignelli canon. New York: Academic Press.

ENDNOTES

[1]   Higher Education Institution.

[2]   Kenesis, the movement of an organism in response to a stimulus, as light.

[3]   Proxemics, Sociology, Psychology. the study of the spatial requirements of humans and animals and the effects of population density on behavior, communication, and social interaction.

[4]   Proverbial, it is a short, pithy and witty statement that conveys an instructive message, prompting the intellectual and moral reflection.

This research was previously published in Digital Tools for Academic Branding and Self-Promotion edited by Marga Cabrera and Nuria Lloret, pages 31-51, copyright year 2017 by Information Science Reference (an imprint of IGI Global).

Chapter 15
Destination Brand–Building of Cultural Heritage Tourism

Xing Huibin
Hebei University, China

Azizan Marzuki
Universiti Sains Malaysia, Malaysia

Stella Kostopoulou
Aristotle University of Thessaloniki, Greece

ABSTRACT

Hebei province is a one of the most typically representative cultural destinations in China with abundant high-quality cultural heritage resources rooting from its more than 4000-year history. However, Hebei has still not evolved into a distinctive cultural brand in the tourism market even though lots of funds have been allocated and invested in tourism. The question thus is how to gradually build a successful cultural tourism brand vital to Hebei province. This paper first extracts the successful components from previous studies, and using France as the most celebrated cultural destination with the largest international tourism arrivals, comparisons are then made with Hebei from the perspective of destination branding of cultural tourism. Finally, given the practical conditions of Hebei and actual tourism needs of segment market, the paper proposes a conceptual brand-building model of Hebei cultural tourism.

INTRODUCTION

Cultural heritage has become increasingly one of the main attractions in tourist destinations, whether tangible parts or intangible ones (Bowitz & Ibenbolt, 2009) such as historical, artistic, scientific or lifestyle, etc. (Silberberg, 1995). Hebei province, located in the East-North of China (see Figure 1), has many kinds of wonderful cultural heritage resources. According to the 3rd National Survey of Cultural Relics China in 2009, there are more than 33,000 immovable cultural relics in Hebei, including 3 world cultural heritages and 168 key cultural relic protection sites at national level, ranked third by amount in China. Additionally, there are 930 cultural heritage units under the provincial protection or above,

DOI: 10.4018/978-1-5225-5187-4.ch015

ranked second in China. Besides, 3,780 sites are protected under the city or county. Moreover, there are 89 museums and memorial halls of different types with more than 900 thousand pieces of collections, including nearly 80,000 precious antiques. Thus, Hebei province tops the country in quantity and type of cultural heritages, of which many heritages have already been well known at home and abroad, such as Zhaozhou Bridge, East and West Mausoleum of the Qing Dynasty, Mountain Resort, etc. These abundant and high-quality cultural heritage resources provide great potential for Hebei's tourism industry.

Based on the rich cultural heritage resources, the cultural industry in Hebei enjoys rapid development with 31.7% of average annual increase from 2004 to 2009. In 2013, the increased value of Hebei's cultural industry reached up to95 billion RMB with more than 30% of average annual growth and account for 3.25% in GDP. In 2014, the cultural industry brought 112 billion RMB increased value with 20% growth rate.

Currently, relying on the cultural heritage resources (revolutionary Taihang culture, grand Great Wall culture, Yan and Zhao culture, pan-capital culture, and Bohai culture), Hebei has achieved rapid tourism development. In 2014, Hebei received 0.315billion domestic and foreign visitors in total and the total tourism income achieved 256.149 billion RMB, increasingly respectively by 16.15% and 27.43%. Additionally, protection of cultural resources in Hebei Province has recently been given major boosts with, for example, 0.2 billion Yuan allocation for protection of Shanhai Pass Great Wall, 3 billion Yuan for the restoration of ancient town of Shanhai Pass, 0.6 billion Yuan for protection of Chengde Mountain Resort and neighboring temple cultural relics,9.8 billion Yuan for the construction of Chengde Royal Historical and Cultural City, more than 100 billion Yuan for the construction of cultural tourism blocks such as Old Tangshan Street and Canal Cultural Street, and 100 billion Yuan for the construction of Great Xibaipo Revolutionary Cultural Base.

Generally, tourism branding has become one of the most characteristic tourist resource and product in tourist destinations, and also the source for keeping the vitality of tourist products and sustainable

Figure 1. The location of Hebei Province

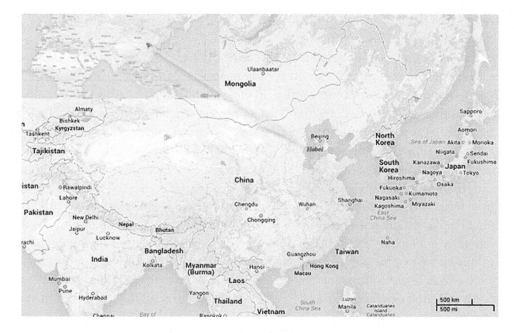

tourism charm especially for the comparative intangible cultural product. It follows therefore that cultural tourism brand-building should be given more attention especially for cultural-based tourist destinations like Hebei. From 2010, 10 key tourism brand strategies have been implemented in Hebei, of which 5 of them aim directly to cultural heritages, i.e. historical and cultural tourism brand, folk customs and art tourism brand, festival tourism brand, revolutionary tourism brand, and rural tourism brand. Besides, another 5 tourism brands (leisure vacationing, ecological, commercial marine, and experience) are also closely related to the tourism surroundings established by cultural tourism. Moreover, authorities in Hebei are really concerned about tourism brand-building especially in recent years. From 2012, 3.3 billion RMB of special funds have been allocated to 4A destinations to upgrade the destination quality and marketing publicity, together with 0.3 billion RMB of financial subsidies from the government. In total, Hebei province received 41 billion RMB of tourism investment in 2013and 35 billion RMB in 2014. However, the huge financial allocation and investments have not transformed Hebei into the expected success in terms of tourism brand-building. There is still no distinctive cultural tourism brand specific to Hebei, and this has had a negative influence towards the increase of added value of the cultural tourism industry and the sustainable development of Hebei tourism.

Undoubtedly, there are still some existing problems and barriers that restrict the sustainable development of cultural tourism in Hebei. It is thus necessary to select one successful destination to make a comparison with Hebei's cultural tourism to recognize its current situation for the effective strategy and measures of development in the future. Since 2005 until 2014, France has always been the top tourist destination in international tourist arrivals, mostly attributable to its charming cultures. Cultural tourism resources in France are concentrated especially in Paris and its suburban areas and some other cultural centers, and these "cultures" have furthermore endowed its tourism industry with long-lasting charm. Additionally, its scientific and effective cultural heritage management has brought great success in terms of the tourism industry. France is therefore considered the appropriate selection as the case to carry out the comparison with Hubei on cultural tourism.

LITERATURE REVIEW

Brand is a consistent system mainly combining characters, images or emotions that consumers recall or experience which sustainably attracts customers and maintains their loyalty (Rooney, 1995; Simeon, 2006). The brand should provide customers with a distinctive and unique attraction differentiating from other brands of the competitors (Qi, et al., 2011). Branding is now recognized increasingly as one of the very important successful foundations in modern society. Generally, brand owners can increase their profit 50 folds if a good brand is built successfully (Fan, 2006). This is especially true for tourism (Medway & Warnaby, 2008). Tourism has become the largest service industry, offering 255 million jobs and generating 9% of the world GDP (WTTC, 2013). Tourism, as a service industry, offers mostly wonderful experiences to tourists without visible and tangible products unlike other industrial sectors (Blain et al., 2005). Additionally, more dependent customers are more likely to be unfamiliar with the destination they are seeking (Lee & Ganesh, 1999). Also, most tourists select destinations mainly by relying on the brand partly as most are new places without them having previous experiences and information. Cultural heritages, as one of the biggest attractions in tourism, seem more inaccessible to tourists without the related knowledge. Tourist destinations, especially based on cultural heritages, should therefore focus more attention towards brand building.

Tourism brand is difficult to be recognized clearly due to its higher complexity of general components and emotional interpretation (Balakrishnan, 2009; Fan, 2006; Meenaghan, 1995). The official academic research on destination branding began in the late 1990s, which analyzed the tourism brand of Croatia and Wales (Dosen et al., 1998; Pritchard and Morgan, 1998), although earlier literatures have mentioned the related terms, such as destination positioning (Woodside, 1982), and destination slogans (Pritchard, 1982). Until 2004, destination branding, as an explicit academic term, appeared in a journal article by Morgan, Pritchard, and Pride (2004). Thereafter, the research becomes gradually diversified, including case studies, conceptual paper, web content analysis, and research-based paper (Pike, 2009). However, after 20 years, researches on brand-building (Hankinson, 2005; Pike, 2005) in tourism academia are still few although there have been fruitful academic achievements on destination brand images especially on leisure tourism (Walmsley & Young, 1998; Qu, et al., 2011).

The conceptual studies on destination brand focus mainly on the brand development, such as technology's role (Palmer, 2002), contextualization (Morgan and Prichard, 2002; Ryan, 2002), success factors (Gilmore, 2002), structure (Gnoth, 2007), model (Kotler and Gertner, 2002; Hankinson, 2007; Balakrishnan, 2009; García, et al., 2012), etc. In academia, five components are involved in the related case studies namely, vision & stakeholder, target market & product portfolio, positioning & differentiation, communication, and feedback & response (see Table 1.). Further, destination brand loyalty can be affected by self-congruence, brand identification and lifestyle-congruence (Ekinci et al., 2013). Based on reviews of previous studies, Balakrishnan (2009) proposed a brand-building framework from the market strategy perspective, which mainly consists of version, customer targeting, stakeholder management, product portfolio positioning/differentiation, brand components, communication, and feedback. In 2012, Garcia, et al. designed a brand assessment model mixing two dimensions: destination brand and destination image from the stakeholders' perspective, which has similarities with Marzano and Scott (2009), focusing on social power in destination branding process. However, in tourism academia, studies on brand-building on cultural tourism have not appeared so far, though cultural heritages have become more important tourism resources.

Moreover, in cultural studies, some scholars involve brand-building. Most of the literatures in this field concentrated on fashion culture or popular culture (Ko & Lee, 2011; Simeon, 2006), rather than cultural heritages or cultural tourism. In all, this paper focuses on the brand-building model of cultural tourism which has not been fully captured in academia.

METHODOLOGY

In this research, the comparative method is the main study methodology. Comparative method, consisting of observational unit (used in collection and data analysis) and explanatory unit (used to explain the pattern of results obtained), is commonly treated as the basis of all scientific ideas and scientific researches (Swanson, 1971). In social science, all research methods are related to comparative in a broad sense (Smelser, 1976). Typically, the method, as a core method, is commonly used in the comparative social science related to the cross-societal differences and similarities (Easthope, 1974). Besides cross-societal researches, it is also widespread in the case-oriented studies. Additionally, the comparative method has become a centre for empirical social science because it can provide a better way to interpret and assess the cases (Ragin, 1994). Specifically, the comparative method is superior in many ways, as it mainly

Table 1. Main components of destination brand-built in existing studies

Components	Sub-Components
Vision and stakeholder	Vision, mission, heritage and culture, people and values, philosophy; Country of origin/reputation/ credibility of brand (destination) name, tourism quality
Target market and product portfolio	History heritage; Culture, ambience and experience, entertainment, dining; Business tourism; Main economic activity, economic development and industrial environment; External profile; Accessibility; Affordability; pricing; People characteristics; Social/quality of life/welfare; International reputation; Health; Education; Visiting family and friends; Retail, local handicrafts; Rest and recreation; Sports; Special occasions; events; Religious tourism; Experience, and exploration, natural wonders, climate
Positioning and differentiation	Tangible and functional elements: Name, logo, trade mark, graphics; Symbols; Slogan, adjectives; Colors; Service delivery process/servicescape; Postcards, pictures, movies, ads – images information; Buildings architecture, facilities, places of interest, Scenery & attributes; Souvenirs, shopping items; Heroes and heroines; Functionality; Ingredient/associated brands, sponsorships, events
	Intangible and symbolic elements: Perceptions of image; Service satisfaction; Personality of place, culture, heritage, ambience; Relationship, bond, familiarity, interaction and empathy; Relevance, representational & self-image congruence; Personal and social values, self-personality & lifestyle, self-expression; Needs (physiological & safety & relationship & self-esteem and fulfillment needs); Emotions/mood/senses; Legends; Image/roles of people associated with service delivery or destination; Occasion association, experiences, ambience; Perception of others perception (WOM, public relations, publicity); Value/expense perceptions; Association with other brands
Marketing	Newspapers, televisions, magazines and radios; Internet & Virtual sites; word-of-mouth & Recommendations; Smart device ads; Event marketing & Embedded ads
Feedback and response	Brand Netnography; word of mouth; souvenirs; License management

The table is amended based on the study by Balakrishnan, 2009.

includes non-combination, sufficient explanations, the flexible boundary of samples, and system analysis. However, so far, it is still very limited used in social science.

Ragin (1994) classified comparative method into two sorts: case-oriented comparative method and variable-oriented comparative method. The former is suited to determine invariant patterns by using small cases, while the latter is best suited to analyze the correlations among variables (See Table 2.). In variable-oriented approaches, statistical procedures decompose the original cases into values on variables, while the cases just become anonymous in the process. In cases-oriented approaches, the cases keep their complex units and are capitalized, even if the variables are mentioned in the analysis process (Porta, 2008). Undoubtedly, the two methods have both good features and limitations. For example, Smelser (1976) argued that case-oriented comparative method was inferior to the statistical method due to the smaller cases and limited variety if there was a shortage of quantitative analysis inside. Table 2 indicates the two comparative methods, which are increasingly complementary and should be combined so that the best features of the two methods can be integrated. Additionally, it should be noted that the requirements of the synthetic strategy are two: large cases and strict logic of experimental design (Ragin, 1994).

Balakrishnan (2009) pointed out that the conceptual model of tourism brand-building should be extracted from achievements of previous studies in the theory and successful experiences in practice based on the destination context, which is the main methodology in the paper. The study adopts mainly case-oriented comparative method between Hebei and France which is the most successful case in the world. France is ratednumber1 in international tourism and best known as the cultural destination in the world. France is thus selected as the study case to extract the successful experiences in the cultural tourism branding aspect to provide valuable reference to Hebei's cultural tourism requirements.

Table 2. The comparison between case-oriented strategy and variable-oriented strategy

Case-Oriented Comparative Method	Variable-Oriented Comparative Method
Focusing on combinations of characteristics	Focusing on the correlations among variables
To reveal invariant patterns	To assess probabilistic relationships and explain variation
Insensitive to the frequency distribution of cases	Sensitive to the statistic data
Extensive dialogue between ideas and the data	Testing hypothesis derived from theories
Regarding cases as a whole unit	Discomposing phenomenon into variables
Easy to examine the causal complexity	Difficult to examine the causal complexity
Complexity over generality	Generality over complexity
Revealing the historical condition	Testing hypotheses of general theories
Small sample size	Big sample size
To be very familiar with the cases	Lower level of familiarity with the cases

The table is amended on the opinions in "Comparative Method: Moving beyond Qualitative and Quantitative Strategies" (Ragin, 1994)

Comparison Between Hebei and France

France, covering a land of 551,000 km², connects the English Channel in the north end, the Atlantic Ocean in the west, and the Mediterranean Sea in the south. With higher terrains in the southeast and lower in the northwest, central France consists of the central plateau and ancient hills, while most of France enjoy a temperate climate. Since 2005 until 2012, France has always been the top tourist destination in international tourist arrivals attributed mostly to its charming cultures. In 2012, France received 83 million international tourists which were far more thanthe60 million of local citizens, and was ranked number 1 by international tourist arrivals. France correspondingly obtained €35.8 billion from international tourism, which ranked third in the world and produced over 7% of France's GDP (UNWTO, 2013). The tourism trade in France achieved a surplus of nearly €13 billion in 2012up rom €7.5 billion in 2011, heading the list of all industries in France (France Diplomatie, 2013). Tourism in France provides more than 1 million job opportunities, 4 times of that in the automotive industry and 1.5 times that in agriculture and agricultural product processing industry. In 2020, tourist income of France is expected tohit€49 billion, which will catapult the country to become the first and largest destination by international tourism revenue in the world. Cultural tourism resources in France are concentrated, especially in Paris and its suburban areas and some other cultural centers, and these "cultures" have furthermore endowed its tourism industry with long-lasting charm. Additionally, its scientific and effective cultural heritage management has brought great success to its tourism industry.

On the other hand, Hebei province has a weaker brand of cultural tourism, though there are abundant cultural heritage resources. It is therefore significant for Hebei to borrow and emulate the successful experiences on brand-building of cultural tourism from France. Specifically; the differences between the two areas mainly exist at six aspects: industrial chain of tourism, market strategy, festivals, tourist souvenirs, planning & management, and cultural protection (see Table 3).

Table 3. Comparison of brand-building of cultural tourism between Hebei and France

Items of Comparison	Hebei	France
Industrial chain of tourism	Lower driving power for other industries	Promoting related industries' development, such as agriculture, education, catering service, etc.
Market strategy	Traditional marketing	Extending new market positively
Festivals	No influential festival	Many festivals and activities based on the traditional cultures
Tourist souvenirs	Higher homophily	Distinctive souvenirs rooting at local cultures
Planning and management	Multiple management	Management system with distinct responsibility
Cultural protection	Few funds on protection	Protection is the centre

Industrial Chain of Tourism

In Hebei, despite the long history and abundant cultural tourism resources, most of the local cultural tourism products are developed in a static way, which has failed to form a complete industrial chain, while the development of many excellent cultural tourism resources has remained at the superficial level, and its potentials have not been further explored. In major sections of the tourism industry, such as dining, accommodation, transportation, sightseeing, shopping and entertainment, cultural factors have not been given due attention or been developed systematically; this has not added value nor improve the attractions of the cultural tourism industry, thereby creating an unfavourable cultural atmosphere of the tourism industry, and unable to cultivate and nurture cultural tourism brands.

Comparatively, French cultural tourism products are not limited to architecture and art, but also encapsulatemany fields, such as agriculture and education. "Great planning" of their cultural heritage has been advocated by previous French presidents, and the heritage sites have been revitalized through functional replacement. These originally-designed and high-quality "presidential projects" have brought France a great number of tourist resources characterized by the spirit of the times. For example, Orsay Museum in Paris was transformed from an abandoned railway station, and has already become one of the top three art museums together with Louvre Museum and The Pompidou Center. Original bathing pools were maintained in the museum of Roubaix, which was reformed on the basis of bath houses, where a gallery was constructed around the bath house. There are also many themed museums in France for example, ecotourism museum in Alsace and a motor museum in Mulhouse. Meanwhile, cultural and educational tourism activities have been organized annually for teenagers. More than 600 science-related festivals a year have contributed not only to tourism development, but also the popularization of scientific knowledge and research fruits. Additionally, vacationing tour for global millionaires have driven local catering services and real estate, as well as the high-end leisure industries such as golf.

Market Strategy

In the case of Hebei, promotion of cultural tourism depends mainly on newspaper, TV and promotional fairs without fully encouraging the public to participate in tourism propagation and promotion. In France's case, in view of the developed market (such as Europe, North America and Japan with a great many tourists and great purchasing power), new economic entities (such as China, Brazil and Russia) and business tourist market, diversified in-depth tourist routes have been invented, and the infiltration into and marketing of tourism segment markets have been strengthened under the guidance of tourism slogan and identification of "meeting in France", so as to enhance the influence of French tourism. China has now become the biggest Asian inbound market with Brazilians and Russians having an increasing share recently.

French tourism services are also considered very distinguishing, which is another marketing feature. On summer holidays, tourism departments of all wine-producing regions cooperate with vineyard owners and launch characteristic tourism programs such as "tour in wine country", "wine tasting in chateau". Tourists can visit wine cellars and vineyards, taste various wines and can find the invitation signboard of vineyards anytime when driving in wine-producing regions. Special dishes are also the favorites of tourists, for example, goose liver in southwest France, raw oysters in Brittany and fish soup in Marseilles. French restaurants are famous for elegant designs and outstanding artistic atmosphere, and almost all restaurant owners pay attention to the historical inheritance; this also extends to menu design and environment setting, so tourists will not only enjoy the delicacy, but also enjoy wonderful ambience. In addition, the catering and hotel industries have also developed novel ideas to attract tourists, for example, "renting Paris houses for weekend" to enable couples from other regions or countries to experience classic "Paris sentiment" while obtaining economic benefits.

Tourism Festivals

In Hebei, with the exception of the Wuqiao International Acrobatics Festival, there is no influential cultural tourism festival. Festivals, on the other hand, are very important attractions in France, which celebrates various festivals with passion and quality. Each district has its own festival, which is always related to certain events, such as the harvest festival, and according to the scale of the host location, French festivals fall into two categories: festivals in large buildings or plazas in central cities, for example, in museum, school or factory; and festivals in small towns or countryside. Tourism activities in these small towns are always organized on the basis of local natural conditions and cultural features, especially for tourists and such festivals are found everywhere at any time, for example, the "Grape Festival" in all wine-producing towns, "Classical Music Festival" in the suburbs of Paris, "Choir Festival" in central mountainous areas, "Hiking Pilgrimage Festival" before or after religious festivals in the neighborhood of ancient churches, and "Forest Camping Festival" in golden fall.

Moreover, folk customs are better demonstrated in festivals hosted by small towns far away from famous scenic areas, and are always held on weekends and organized by local volunteers which greatly reduces the cost, which therefore translates to affordable pricing, attracting considerable tourists even in the off season. Some towns even become famous for their characteristic and unique festivals, and these become annual events in the local areas. For example, Deauville, a small town with only 4,500 residents, hosts 10 festivals annually, with each festival attracting tens of thousands of tourists, and 70% of the town's total income comes from tourism industry. The tourism industry in Deauville has now matured systematically, and the Tourism Office has taken over responsibility for the organization and coordination of events.

Souvenirs for Tourists

In Hebei, the tourism souvenirs are almost identical to other regions, without much innovation, and include mainly telescopes, wooden swords, toys, faked antiques, mountain specialties, bracelets, paper fans, stone carvings, bamboo products and other tourist necessities. More specifically, destination managers and operators have only a faint awareness of souvenir development and pay more attention on service hardware in the destinations like infrastructure, rather than souvenirs. Consequently, there is no developed tourism souvenir chain due to the lack of designers, producers and distributors. Further, the souvenir quality in Hebei is generally poor, partly because most of the souvenirs are provided from locals without formal production workplace, special skills or education and innovation consciousness.

In France, there are diverse and varied styles of tourist souvenirs, in addition to such "standard souvenirs" as building models of the Eiffel Tower and Arch de Triomph, postcards and key chains. There are also goods and ornaments such as sculptures, swords, firelocks, china wares, arras, refrigerator posters, coasters, lighters, T-shirts, dolls, paper knifes, wine stoppers and so on. All of these souvenirs are characterized by outstanding features of French cultures, for example, chinaware painted with Claude Monet's The Water Lily, coasters painted with the streetscape of Champs Elysées, refrigerator posters in the shape of burgundy bottle or baguette, arras with the pattern of the Versailles Garden, wallets with the pictures of Notre Dame de Paris, umbrellas painted with portrait of the Mona Lisa, and lavender-shaped pendants. Beyond these, cheese, sausage and blue porcelain are also special products of France.

French tourist souvenirs are always also designed in a novel way, which fully shows the romantic personality of the French people. For example, the model of the Eiffel Tower bends like the symbol of Omega, the mysterious Mona Lisa becomes a homely woman, the adjutant bird (symbol of Alsace) always appears as fantasy characters, and Saint-Exupery's "The Little Prince" is always applied on traditional chinaware. Furthermore, the real attractions of French tourism souvenirs lies in their elegance, hence crudely-made products are hardly ever found in the market. "Soft fire makes sweet malt" is an outstandingly unique feature of the French production, and even refrigerator posters and key chains priced at about €1 are delicately made and packed, so tourists are willing to buy as gifts, let alone arras and blue porcelain worth hundreds of Euros. Scenery pictures and postcards are also elegantly designed with text explanation in many languages, are also reasonably priced and have a profound cultural connotation, thus becoming one of the most popular tourism souvenirs in France.

Planning and Management

In Heibei, because of the diverse cultural tourism resources, development of the cultural tourism industry involves multiple authorities in tourism, cultural relics, culture, architecture and even religion. Additionally, departments related to business administration, municipal administration, planning, price, health and public security also have certain administrative power over the development of the industry. These departments discharge their own duties independently, and rarely communicate or coordinate with other departments. Therefore, without full cognition of cultural tourism and a unified authority, relevant policies and measures made by these departments even conflict with each other, which to a great extent offsets the positive effects brought about by cultural tourism development and make integration of local cultural tourism resources and integrated building of tourism brands more difficult.

In France, Cultural tourism resources are assessed and managed by the Ministry of Culture and Bureau of Historic Relics, and its cultural tourism industry is operated by French Tourist Authority for France Travel & Tourism. All of these departments have well-defined power and responsibility, cooperate closely and bring their superiority into full play to co-manage the cultural tourism industry. In addition, experts and scholars of different disciplines gather in 36,000 industry associations or management branches and are important forces in promoting the sustainable development of cultural tourism. Furthermore, the

French Tourist Authority for France Travel & Tourism makes long-term, medium-term and short-term development plans of the tourism industry together with departments, enterprises, experts and scholars of various fields.

Cultural Protection

In Hebei, cultural protection has not been implemented effectively in practice, though government and operators have gradually realized its importance. The creation of a cultural tourism atmosphere has not been given due attention in the construction of urban software and hardware, with municipal funds having been devoted to mainly construction of urban infrastructure, greening and lighting, but less towards creating a cultural atmosphere. In addition, there is no cultural atmosphere indicator to judge the 'star' level of particular scenic areas (spots); the areas (spots) are thus only willing to invest in the improvement and standardization of such infrastructure such as roads, dining services, stores and hotels, but not in the exploration of cultural connotations.

In France, in terms of urban planning, ancient images of the downtown areas in all French cities must be maintained, and the "heritage houses" are protected and repaired regularly by municipal governments according to their architectural characteristics and styles. According to the *Malraux Act*, all construction and repair activities in historic districts have to be assessed and approved by "State Architects". Moreover, height, layout, color and construction plan of new buildings around these heritage houses must be approved by the relevant departments. As for cultural relics far away from the downtown areas, the protection focuses more on maintaining their original images, and no extra buildings or railings are set outside, with only a plate or a wooden pavilion used to introduce the relics or mysteries related to the relics. Green spaces around the relics are built into nature reserves where house construction, tree cutting or hunting activities are all prohibited. The Bureau of Historic Relics is responsible for the protection and maintenance of cultural heritage, and made and passed the first modern act for cultural heritage protection—*Law of Historic Relics Protection*. Civil protection organizations, investors, scholars, local residents and handicraftsmen are all encouraged to protect the cultural heritage.

Model Building

Cultural tourism brand building in Hebei should be established not only on its practical development condition and situation, but also on the preferences and needs of tourists mainly from Beijing, Tianjin and Hebei. Although many cultural tourism resources in Hebei can be considered national or world-class cultural products, such as the East and West Mausoleum of the Qing Dynasty, they are still less competitive in terms of popularity and quality compared to the Palace Museum and Badaling Great Wall in nearby regions. Therefore, from the perspective of complementary principle, Hebei should fully consider the tourist preference of its segment market(Beijing, Tianjin, and Hebei)in building the cultural tourism brand. Moreover, cultural tourism, as one of the specialized tourism sector, needs to coordinate with the images defined by the overall tourism planning of Hebei and other specialized plans in terms of brand building. Correspondingly, this paper proposes that Hebei should cultivate and build the tourism brand of "Cultural Leisure Happy Hebei" with the support of the current revolutionary tourism, leisure tourism and folk tourism (see Figure 2), so as to form a distinctive and characteristic cultural tourism image in the tourism market of Beijing, Tianjin and local areas, as well as to integrate and drive the development of multiple cultural tourism resources in Hebei.

Tourism Product

Hebei should integrate its cultural tourism resources on the basis of the diverse folk customs, revolutionary relics and long-lasting leisure and body-building traditions, and create a favorable tourism atmosphere centred around "Cultural Recreation and Enjoy Touring in Hebei" by exploring more participatory projects such as cultural festivals and designing culture-themed tourism lines. In addition, all regions and scenic areas in Hebei should design more unique cultural tourism commodities and relevant tourism derivatives according to its own cultural features and characteristics of visitors from Beijing, Tianjin and local areas, consolidated under the unified image of its cultural tourism.

Tourism Marketing

Cultural tourism marketing has to use not only traditional marketing modes, but also follow inherent laws of cultural transmission. The cultural tourism of Hebei should establish a stereo marketing and promotion system, consider behavioral and consumption features of visitors from its target markets and integrate multiple marketing modes such as festival marketing, online marketing, conference marketing, virtual marketing, experience marketing and event marketing, on the basis of traditional planar and three-dimensional media, coordinate scenic areas (spots) and authorities, unify logos and propagation themes, and build its own cultural tourism brand (Figure 2).

Figure 2. Brand-building model of cultural tourism in Hebei

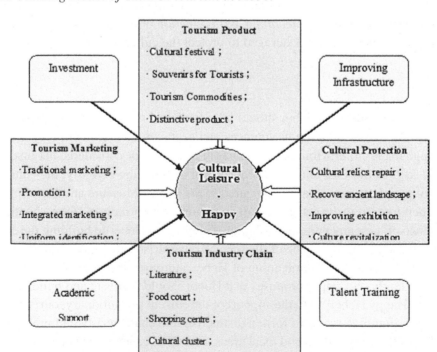

Tourism Industry Chain

In terms of the industry chain, cultural themes should be introduced in all sections of the tourism indus-try, such as dining, accommodation, transportation, shopping and entertainment; cultural connotations should be reflected in product design, project development, environment layout, marketing and promo-tion to improve the added cultural value of the local tourism industry. From the perspective of horizontal expansion, new situations of economic and social development should be taken into consideration to further expand the industrial chain of cultural tourism, and broaden the economic sphere by venturing into the publishing, dining, business, film and television industry.

Cultural Protection

An authentic and unique culture is the foundation for the sustainable development of cultural tourism. The local government should thus promulgate relevant laws and regulations, and also preferential poli-cies for cultural protection and enhance the protection of cultural heritage inheritors. Within the cradles of unique cultures, such as Weixian County, paper-cutting courses can be arranged in elementary and middle schools to cultivate successors of the cultural heritage and create the unique characteristic cultural atmosphere. For important cultural tourism relics, ancient images should be restored or maintained by following the principles of "doing as much as the resources permit, repairing the old like the old, and financing from multiple channels", while relevant cultural exhibition halls should be built and upgraded, and environment layouts and exhibits on display should be able to showcase the theme of cultural tour-ism. Furthermore, local communities are encouraged to participate in the management and supervision of cultural protection, and by establishing a stereo protection mechanism, safeguarding and inheritance of cultural tourism resources should be enhanced effectively.

Safeguarding Measures

Cultural tourism brand building is a systematic project in need of support and assistance of multiple departments. In view of the current cultural tourism development in Hebei, more efforts should be de-voted in the following 4 aspects. First, a series of cultural academic symposia and exchange activities with domestic and international influence can be organized by inviting experts, government offices and industry leaders, and several influential cultural forums can be formed in the academic circle and tourist circle via market operation[4]. Second, by attracting government financial support and inviting investments, offering preferential policies and business marketing, more domestic and international en-terprises will be attracted to invest in the local cultural tourism industry, and also more supports should be given to local tourism enterprises to expand the scale and enhance the strength. Third, traditional culture classes and elective courses can be offered to pupils and middle school students, and relevant professions arranged in universities, to create an atmosphere of respecting and loving local cultures. Moreover, inter-disciplinary design and management talents should be cultivated for the local cultural tourism industry, staff in local scenic areas (spots) should be adequately trained, and more talents at-tracted from other regions to improve the team quality of the cultural tourism industry. Fourth, tourism infrastructure should be improved constantly, design of tourism facilities innovated and tourism func-tions further improved according to consumption needs of tourist markets, as well as to ensure proper consideration to potential visitors.

CONCLUSION

Cultural tourism brand building is extremely important for provinces such as Hebei with its abundant cultural tourism resources. On the basis of local cultural tourism development, this paper introduced the experience of other domestic cultural tourism brands, considered psychological needs of visitors from Beijing, Tianjin and local areas, established the model of cultural tourism brand building for Hebei and proffered concrete measures. This model is also a valuable reference for brand cultivation and development of tourist destinations in China, especially those mainly catering for domestic visitors.

ACKNOWLEDGMENT

Thanks for the supports from National Social Science Fund Project of China in 2014(14CGL074).

REFERENCES

ASKCI. (2013). *Analysis of development situation of Hebei cultural industry*. Retrieved 8th March 2014 from http://www.askci.com/news/201311/12/1217290151146.shtml

Balakrishnan, M. S. (2009). Strategic branding of destinations: A framework. *European Journal of Marketing, 43*(5/6), 611–629. doi:10.1108/03090560910946954

Balakrishnan, M. S., Nekhili, R., & Lewis, C. (2011). Destination brand components. *International Journal of Culture. Tourism and Hospitality Research, 5*(1), 4–25.

Blain, C., Levy, S. E., & Ritchie, J. B. (2005). Destination branding: Insights and practices from destination management organizations. *Journal of Travel Research, 43*(4), 328–338. doi:10.1177/0047287505274646

Doen, D., & Prebeac, D. (1998). The importance of branding in the development of marketing strategy of Croatia as tourist destination. *Acta Turistica, 10*(2), 110–127.

Easthope. (1974). *A history of social research method*. London: Longmann.

Ekinci, Y., Sirakaya-Turk, E., & Preciado, S. (2013). Symbolic consumption of tourism destination brands. *Journal of Business Research, 66*(6), 711–718. doi:10.1016/j.jbusres.2011.09.008

Fan, Y. (2006). Branding the nation: What is being branded? *Journal of Vacation Marketing, 12*(1), 5–14. doi:10.1177/1356766706056633

France Diplomatie. (2013). *France, the world's leading tourist destination*. Retrieved 8th March 2014 from http://www.diplomatie.gouv.fr/en/coming-to-france/facts-about-france/one-figure-one-fact/article/france-the-world-s-leading-tourist

García, J. A., Gómez, M., & Molina, A. (2012). A destination-branding model: An empirical analysis based on stakeholders. *Tourism Management, 33*(3), 646–661. doi:10.1016/j.tourman.2011.07.006

Gilmore, F. (2002). A country-can it be repositioned? Spain-the success story of country branding. *The Journal of Brand Management, 9*(4-5), 4–5.

Gnoth, J. (2007). The structure of destination brands: Leveraging values. *Tourism Analysis, 12*(5-6), 5–6.

Hankinson, G. (2005). Destination brand images: A business tourism perspective. *Journal of Services Marketing, 19*(1), 24–32. doi:10.1108/08876040510579361

Hankinson, G. (2007). The management of destination brands: Five guiding principles based on recent developments in corporate branding theory. *Journal of Brand Management, 14*(3), 240–254. doi:10.1057/palgrave.bm.2550065

Ko, E., & Lee, S. (2011). Cultural heritage fashion branding in Asia. *Advances in Culture. Tourism and Hospitality Research, 5*, 89–109. doi:10.1108/S1871-3173(2011)0000005008

Kotler, P., & Gertner, D. (2002). Leveraging export brands through a tourism destination brand. *Journal of Brand Management, 9*(4/5), 249–261. doi:10.1057/palgrave.bm.2540076

Lee, D., & Ganesh, G. (1999). Effects of partitioned country image in the context of brand image and familiarity: A categorization theory perspective. *International Marketing Review, 16*(1), 18–41. doi:10.1108/02651339910257610

Lei, W. (2012). Cultural Tourism Enlightenment from France for Hebei Province, China. *Journal of Landscape Research, 4*(12), 59–61.

Lei & Chen. (2013). Research on Brand Construction of Cultural Tourism in Hebei Province. *Journal of Landscape Research, 5*(10), 21-22, 26.

Ma, Y. (2014). *Hebei increases the special fund of tourism up to 0.3 billion.* Retrieved 8 March 2014 http://www.zgsxzs.com/a/20140226/594924_2.html

Marzano, G., & Scott, N. (2009). Power in destination branding. *Annals of Tourism Research, 36*(2), 247–267. doi:10.1016/j.annals.2009.01.004

Medway, D., & Warnaby, G. (2008). Alternative perspectives on marketing and the place brand. *European Journal of Marketing, 42*(5/6), 641–653. doi:10.1108/03090560810862552

Meenaghan, T. (1995). The role of advertising in brand image development. *Journal of Product and Brand Management, 4*(4), 23–34. doi:10.1108/10610429510097672

Morgan, N., & Pritchard, A. (2002). Contextualizing destination branding. In N. Morgan, A. Pritchard, & R. Pride (Eds.), *Destination branding: Creating the unique destination proposition* (pp. 10–41). Oxford, UK: Butterworth-Heinemann.

Morgan, N., Pritchard, A., & Pride, R. (2004). *Destination branding: Creating the unique destination proposition.* Butterworth-Heinemann Ltd.

Palmer, C. (1999). Tourism and the symbols of identity. *Tourism Management, 20*(3), 313–321. doi:10.1016/S0261-5177(98)00120-4

Pike, S. (2005). Tourism destination branding complexity. *Journal of Product and Brand Management, 14*(4), 258–259. doi:10.1108/10610420510609267

Pike, S. (2009). Destination brand positions of a competitive set of near-home destinations. *Tourism Management, 30*(6), 857–866. doi:10.1016/j.tourman.2008.12.007

Pritchard, A., & Morgan, N. (1998). 'Mood marketing'—The new destination branding strategy: A case study of 'Wales' The Brand. *Journal of Vacation Marketing, 4*(3), 215–229. doi:10.1177/135676679800400302

Pritchard, G. (1982). Tourism promotion: Big business for the states. *The Cornell Hotel and Restaurant Administration Quarterly, 23*(2), 48–52. doi:10.1177/001088048202300220

Qu, H., Kim, L. H., & Im, H. H. (2011). A model of destination branding: Integrating the concepts of the branding and destination image. *Tourism Management, 32*(3), 465–476. doi:10.1016/j.tourman.2010.03.014

Ragin, C. (1994). *Comparative Method: Moving beyond Qualitative and Quantitative Strategies*. Berkeley, CA: University of California Press.

Rooney, J. A. (1995). Branding: A trend for today and tomorrow. *Journal of Product and Brand Management, 4*(4), 48–55. doi:10.1108/10610429510097690

Ryan, C. (2002). The politics of branding cities and regions: The case of New Zealand. In N. Morgan, A. Pritchard, & R. Pride (Eds.), *Destination branding: Creating the unique destination proposition* (pp. 66–86). Oxford, UK: Butterworth-Heinemann.

Simeon, R. (2006). A conceptual model linking brand building strategies and Japanese popular culture. *Marketing Intelligence & Planning, 24*(5), 463–476. doi:10.1108/02634500610682863

Smelser, N.J. (1976). *Comparative methods in the social sciences*. Englewood Cliffs, NJ: Prentice-Hall.

Swanson, G. (1971). Frameworks for comparative research: Structural anthropology and the theory of action. In I. Vallier (Ed.), Comparative methods in sociology: Essays on trends and applications, (pp. 141-202). Academic Press.

UNWTO. (2012). *2012 Tourism highlights*. Madrid: UNWTO.

Walmsley, D. J., & Young, M. (1998). Evaluative images and tourism: The use of personal constructs to describe the structure of destination images. *Journal of Travel Research, 36*(3), 65–69. doi:10.1177/004728759803600307

Woodside, A. G. (1982). Positioning a province using travel research. *Journal of Travel Research, 20*(3), 2–6. doi:10.1177/004728758202000301

KEY TERMS AND DEFINITIONS

Cultural Commoditisation: The drive toward putting a monetary value on aspects of a culture.

Cultural/Heritage Tourism: When tourists travel to a specific destination in order to participate in a cultural or heritage-related event.

Destination: A destination is a geographical area consisting of all the services and infrastructure necessary for the stay of a specific tourist or tourism segment.

Environmental Stewardship: The practice of ensuring natural resources are conserved and used responsibly in a way that balances the needs of various groups.

International Tourism: International tourism comprises inbound tourism plus outbound tourism, that is to say, the activities of resident visitors outside the country of reference, either as part of domestic or outbound tourism trips and the activities of non-resident visitors within the country of reference on inbound tourism trips.

This research was previously published in Opportunities and Challenges for Tourism and Hospitality in the BRIC Nations edited by Mohinder Chand Dhiman, pages 175-190, copyright year 2017 by Business Science Reference (an imprint of IGI Global).

Chapter 16
The Roles of Corporate Marketing Strategies and Brand Management in the Global Retail Industry

Kijpokin Kasemsap
Suan Sunandha Rajabhat University, Thailand

ABSTRACT

This chapter explores the roles of corporate marketing strategies and brand management in the global retail industry, thus describing the concepts of marketing strategy, international retail marketing strategy, retail marketing mix, and internationalization; the relationship between corporate marketing strategies and internationalization; the challenges of retail marketing mix in the fashion retail industry; the overview of brand management; and the significance of brand management in the global retail industry. The implementation of corporate marketing strategies and brand management is critical for modern organizations that seek to serve suppliers and customers, increase business performance, strengthen competitiveness, and achieve continuous success in global business. Therefore, it is necessary for modern organizations to examine their corporate marketing strategies and brand management applications, create a strategic plan to regularly check their practical advancements, and rapidly respond to the corporate marketing strategies and brand management needs of customers in the global retail industry.

INTRODUCTION

The rapidly evolving consumer needs and habits are bringing radical change to the world's retail industry (Manasseh, Muller-Sarmiento, Reuter, von Faber-Castell, & Pallua, 2012). The ability to internationalize has become a competitive necessity for many small and medium-sized enterprises (SMEs), enabling their survival and access to larger markets (Dutot, Bergeron, & Raymond, 2014). Marketing must be elevated to a higher level of consciousness. An important step in the internationalization process of emerging economy firms is the shift from exports to foreign direct investment (Gaur, Kumar, & Singh, 2014).

DOI: 10.4018/978-1-5225-5187-4.ch016

Retail internationalization is measured in terms of both exporting and foreign purchasing (Hessels & Parker, 2013). Concerning the international nature of retailing (Bianchi & Ostale, 2006), and corporate and consumer responses toward the issue of globalization (Alden, Steenkamp, & Batra, 2006), there has been little consideration of how international retailers may implement retail marketing strategies abroad, or of how these may compare with those domestically implemented.

Creating and maintaining a good brand relationship is necessary for brand management in emerging markets (Kasemsap, 2014a). From the retailer's perspective, retail brands represent equity that can have a significant impact on a retailer's differentiation and competitive superiority (Lymperopoulos, Chaniotakis, & Rigopoulou, 2010). Brand management function needs a partial rethinking since brand managers have to perform the traditional tasks while addressing new challenges (Brexendorf & Daecke, 2012). Corporate brands are strategic assets for organizations, but it is difficult to understand the value added by corporate brand name changes because they often occur simultaneously with business restructuring initiatives (Kalaignanam & Bahadir, 2013).

Business practitioners and researchers have struggled for many years to understand the role of marketing in describing business performance differences between firms (Morgan, 2012). Organizations strive to establish a relationship between brands and consumers (Neudecker, Hupp, Stein, & Schuster, 2012). Strong brand names facilitate competitive advantage (Lee & Back, 2010), increase organizational cash flow (Miller & Muir, 2004), and provide premium price, profitability, and loyalty for customers (Madden, Fehle, & Fournier, 2006).

The strength of this chapter is on the thorough literature consolidation of corporate marketing strategies and brand management in the global retail industry. The extant literatures of corporate marketing strategies and brand management in the global retail industry provide a contribution to practitioners and researchers by describing a comprehensive view of the functional applications of corporate marketing strategies and brand management in the global retail industry to appeal to different segments of corporate marketing strategies and brand management in the global retail industry in order to maximize the business impact of corporate marketing strategies and brand management in the global retail industry.

Background

In the late 1980s, a new wave of international retail activity had begun to build (Alexander & Doherty, 2010). The consumer society that had emerged in the 1980s increasingly generated retailers capable of addressing the challenge of international marketing activity either because of their increasing market orientation (Piercy & Alexander, 1988), their operational size (Treadgold, 1988) or their brand strength (Alexander, 1990; Williams, 1992). It is widely recognized that today's retail environment is highly competitive and that it is essential for retailers to gain some form of differential advantage (Swoboda, Haelsig, Morschett, & Schramm-Klein, 2007).

Regarding corporate marketing strategies, the retailers try to position their stores in such a way that they obtain a defendable and sustainable market position (Oppewal & Timmermans, 1997). Morschett, Swoboda, and Schramm-Klein (2006) applied Porter's framework to develop competitive strategies in retailing (i.e., cost leadership strategy, product differentiation strategies, and focus strategy). The aims of cost leadership strategy are to minimize investment in store design and reduce customer service (Skallerud & Grønhaug, 2010). Other marketing strategies are the economy of scale and the negotiation power over suppliers of products (Ellis & Kelly, 1992). Large firms possess more financial and human resources and higher economy of scale levels (Sun & Lee, 2013). A differentiation strategy implies differentiating the retail offer from its competitors (Davis, 1992). The purpose of differentiation strategy is to adjust certain features more directly to the specific needs of the chosen customer segments (Skallerud & Grønhaug, 2010).

Brands are the sources of organizational value (Brexendorf & Daecke, 2012). Branding is recognized as a key component of marketing strategy (Kent, 2003; Ailawadi & Keller, 2004; Burt & Davies, 2010). Branding within retail settings has been associated with private label brand produced by retailers (Burt & Davies, 2010), thus enabling competitive advantage in the form of superior profit margins, economy of scale, market segmentation, and differentiation. Competing retail brand perspectives have emerged in the retail literature, which embrace the combinations of tangible and intangible service, product, and multi-sensory brand elements as an organized brand strategy (Kent, 2003; Burt & Davies, 2010).

CORPORATE MARKETING STRATEGIES AND BRAND MANAGEMENT IN THE GLOBAL RETAIL INDUSTRY

This section describes the concepts of marketing strategy, international retail marketing strategy, retail marketing mix, and internationalization; the relationship between corporate marketing strategies and internationalization; the challenges of retail marketing mix in the fashion retail industry; the overview of brand management; and the significance of brand management in the global retail industry.

Concept of Marketing Strategy

Global conditions challenge traditional views of management, marketing, and economics (Maglio, Nusser, & Bishop, 2010). Formulating consistent marketing strategies is a difficult task, but successfully implementing them is more challenging (Prange & Schlegelmilch, 2009). Ethical corporate marketing transcends the domains of corporate social responsibility, business ethics, stakeholder theory and corporate marketing (Balmer, Powell, & Greyser, 2011). A vast majority of marketing theory and research has focused on relativism and idealism in order to understand ethical behavior (Rawwas, Arjoon, & Sidani, 2013). Organizations with a large customer base earn higher profits in global marketing (Schmidt, 2013). Organizational culture has a positive impact on marketing-related decision making (Yarbrough, Morgan, & Vorhies, 2011).

Marketing strategy can be defined as an organization's integrated pattern of decisions that specify its crucial choices concerning products, markets, marketing activities and marketing resources in the creation, communication, and delivery of products that offer value to customers in exchanges with the organization and enables organization to achieve specific objectives (Varadarajan, 2010). Marketing strategists should create, maintain, and arrest the decrease of ambiguous resource competences that lead to competitiveness and performance (Hansen, McDonald, & Mitchell, 2013). Marketing segmentation and positioning have been at the essence of marketing management (Cornelius, Wagner, & Natter, 2010). The consideration of strategic customers, who can delay a purchase to take advantage of a future discount, has dramatically increased (Gonsch, Klein, Neugebauer, & Steinhardt, 2013).

Information technology has altered the growth of retail trade sector in the affluent economies (Watson, 2011). Technology has the ability to influence marketing and supply chain practice (Richey, Tokman, & Dalela, 2010). Kasemsap (2014b) suggested that the emergence of social media has a strong and positive influence on the development of modern communication and business growth. Social media utilization contributes to brand performance, retailer performance, and consumer–retailer loyalty (Rapp, Beitelspacher, Grewal, & Hughes, 2013). Social media has transformed the traditional marketing communication, resulting in organizations evolving their customer approach and integrating social media into their marketing strategies (Cvijikj, Spiegler, & Michahelles, 2013). Together with regular retail channels, firms can distribute products through Internet (Hu & Li, 2012). Retail channels need to reallocate their shelf spaces while keeping up their total profit margins (Fadıloğlu, Karaşan, & Pınar, 2010). In information-intensive environments, many firms send their customers to other affiliates' websites in order to generate additional sales for their marketing affiliates (Akcura, 2010).

Considerable research explores advertising's role in influencing consumer perceptions and behavior (Hughes, 2013). A consciousness that grows beyond solving small, immediate problems to addressing long-term, large problems that goes beyond individual customer satisfaction and short-term financial performance to encompass total value creation system (Webster & Lusch, 2013). Both managers and investors are increasingly concerned with the impact of advertising spending on shareholder returns (Luo & de Jong, 2012). Marketing communication tools can play a major role in conveying an organization's corporate social responsibility (CSR) messages and communicating a socially responsible image (Jahdi & Acikdilli, 2010). CSR and corporate reputation have positive effects on industrial brand equity and brand performance (Lai, Chiu, Yang, & Pai, 2010). Many organizations utilize online brand communities to support the launch of their new products (Gruner, Homburg, & Lukas, 2014).

Marketing capabilities are the significant drivers of organizational performance (Vorhies, Orr, & Bush, 2011). In terms of business challenges, intense competition, complexity of managing multiple markets and coordinating marketing strategy, a host of risk elements, and the sheer difficulty of managing geographic, cultural, and political barriers are among factors which obstruct organizational success in global marketplace (Cavusgil & Cavusgil, 2012). Marketing strategy decisions are informed by the characteristics of organization, product offering, target customers, industry, and macro environment, among other factors (Varadarajan, 2011). The natures of business disciplines of marketing, strategic management, and operations are recognized as controllable functions within an organization from which strategies can be enacted to affect an organization's stakeholders (Cronin, Smith, Gleim, Ramirez, & Martinez, 2011).

Concept of International Retail Marketing Strategy

Retail internationalization research has been concerned primarily with understanding its scope, scale and its motivations and directions at a strategic level (Doherty, 2000). Economies also benefit from foreign operations of domestic firms because these activities promote socio-economic development, increase employment, and generate spillover effects such as societal prosperity and assistance for local industries to boost productivity (Pinho & Martins, 2010). Treadgold (1991) described how retailers progress through a process of retail internationalization. Treadgold's (1991) model has been criticized in the context of technological, economic and political developments to enhance retail internationalization in modern business (Alexander & Myers, 2000; Hutchinson, Quinn, & Alexander, 2006).

Salmon and Tordjman (1989) identified the three strategic approaches for internationalization dependent on a retailer's trading characteristics and internal capabilities; the international investment, global and multi-national models. Each of the three strategies is defined by the essence of goods sold by the retailer, the degree of market involvement it desires, the extent and nature of operational control demanded, and the retailer's corporate experience. Each of the three strategies is characterized by the international retailer's foreign market entry method, its organization and management of non-domestic businesses, the store formats they operate from, their branding and consumer communications, and the product ranges they sell (Salmon & Tordjman, 1989; Dawson, 1994).

Literature on the internationalization of SMEs identifies location in a geographic cluster of networked firms as a source of competitive advantage (Brown, McNaughton, & Bell, 2010). Marketing concept and strategic marketing management are recognized as corporate management philosophies driven by the needs and capabilities of larger organizations (Gilmore, Kraus, O'Dwyer, & Miles, 2012). Marketers experience high distribution costs in distributing rural market with widely dispersed population (Velayudhan, 2014). Retail strategy and consumer behavior influence the coexistence of local stores and central retail locations (Velayudhan, 2014). In the global retail industry, the distance between retail stores and the distance between customers and retail stores influence the shopping behavior (Lee & Pace, 2005). Retailers locate close to each other to take advantage of agglomeration factors and certain retailers locate close to consumers to profit from proximity advantage (Mejia & Benjamin, 2002).

Levy and Weitz (2012) defined retail positioning as the decision and implementation of a retail marketing mix to create an image of the retailer in customer's mind related to its competitors. Achieving differentiation is one of the main objectives of retail marketing and is central to the marketing and branding concept, with the assumption that higher levels of differentiation from the competitor lead to the higher marketing profitability (Buzzell & Gale, 1987; Davies, 1992). Differentiating the product is considered important in firms' strategies and productivity growth (Kato, 2012). Differentiation and successful positioning of retailers are the results of the overall image of the retail store and the personality of the store in the consumer's mind (Davies, 1992). Retailers should distinguish themselves from their competitors in order to be successful in the global retail industry (Dennis, Murphy, Marsland, Cockett, & Patel, 2002).

Retailers' entry timing is jointly influenced by the economic conditions of foreign markets, cultural distance, and entry mode (Cai & Wang, 2010). Dynamic processes of interaction and knowledge exchange are shaped by vendor mobility as well as collaborative and competitive forces (Beckie, Kennedy, & Wittman, 2012). The strategic alliance between manufacturer and retailer can effectively achieve desired channel coordination (Hong, Wang, Wang, & Zhang, 2013). Retailers and suppliers must work to integrate marketing activities and supply chain processes both within and across organizations to effectively serve consumer at retail shelf and increase market share (Waller, Williams, Tangari, & Burton, 2010).

Concept of Retail Marketing Mix

Many franchise-based retail outlets offer both the franchisor-owned brand and brands of competitors or independent suppliers (Rajab, Kraus, & Wieseke, 2013). Retailers seek to develop products and brands, promote them and distribute them by adopting a retail marketing strategy. Retail marketing exists as a distinctive off-shoot of the wider marketing strategy literature and shares many of the same antecedents (McGoldrick, 2002). The origins of the term marketing mix may be traced to Culliton (1948), defined by McCarthy (1964) as the classic 4P framework (i.e., product, price, place, and promotion) which remains one of the keystones of marketing theory and practice (Smith & Taylor, 2004; Kotler & Armstrong, 2006). In addition, the 4P model has to be adapted according to the nature of the industry and the factors contingent to the activity of the business (Gronroos, 1994; Rafiq & Ahmed, 1995).

The retailers simultaneously determine purchase time (i.e., lead time) and order quantity (Wang, Wang, Ye, Xu, & Yu, 2013). The price of products and the manufacturing firms' profits are affected by the competition style established in retail market (Ishikawa, 2010). Producers' pricing policies tend to be influenced more by the level of market concentration in retail industries than by competitors' price movements (Michis & Markidou, 2013). Retailers gain bargaining power through lower wholesale prices on imitated national brands (Meza & Sudhir, 2010).

Managers need to understand how customers view commercial relationships with retail staff or other social actors in retailing (Keeling, Keeling, & McGoldrick, 2013). Retailers reserve the right to verify the availability at competitor location (Nalca, Boyaci, & Ray, 2010). Consumers rely on consumer reviews when making decisions about which products and services to purchase online (Malbon, 2013). Marketing competitors seek to match or exceed the price cuts of their marketing rivals while responding to promotions (Volpe, 2013). Online video is a famous form of marketing promotion (Hsieh, Hsieh, & Tang, 2012). However, price promotions cause the significant amounts of waste in packaged goods retailing (Breiter & Huchzermeier, 2010).

The market is progressively saturated, price sensitive, and commoditized (Deloitte, 2013). An effective innovation regarding demand pull and technology push should focus on both the final users/consumers' needs and expectations and the retailers/employees' needs and expectations (Pantano & Viassone, 2014). Marketing innovations make product and process innovations more successful (Schubert, 2010). The presence of a larger quantity of retail goods considerably attracts customers (Parthasarathi, Sarmah, & Jenamani, 2011). Product complexity affects competition and consumers in retail markets (Sitzia & Zizzo, 2011). Competent management of marketing activity is required to create a retail offer that fits with the expectations of the targeted customer segments (Darling, 2001). By combining the retail mix activities, an overall positioning of retail offer may be achieved (Skallerud & Grønhaug, 2010).

Walters and Laffy (1996) identified the four marketing activities that are integrated and parts of the retail mix. The first marketing activity is related to merchandise decisions (i.e., the core merchandise policy, branding, assortment profiles, and merchandise extension). The second marketing activity is related to store format and environment (i.e., profile of the outlet, space allocation, visual merchandising, design, and atmosphere). The third marketing activity is related to customer service (i.e., product services, service products, and personnel services). The fourth and last marketing activity is related to customer communications (i.e., advertising, in-store displays, and visual merchandising). Contributing to brand image is advertising, the purpose of which is to sell the establishment, attract customers to the premises, and sell goods (Jefkins & Yadin, 2000). Cooperative advertising is a key incentive offered by a manufacturer to influence retailers' promotional decisions (Chutani & Sethi, 2012).

The 4P framework has been considered inappropriate for retail industries on account of its production-orientated as opposed to marketing-orientated view (Gronroos, 1994). Below are the characteristics of marketing mix framework regarding retail settings.

1. **Product Quantity:** Retailers sell small quantities of items on a frequent basis (Dibb, Simkin, Pride, & Ferrell, 2006).
2. **Product Assortment:** Retailers offer a greater range of products than do manufacturers (Kent & Omar, 2003).
3. **Convenience:** Retailers provide superior services in terms of location, payment and credit facilities, merchandise range and after-sales support (Levy & Weitz, 2012).

4. **Product Sourcing:** Retailers buy products from often varied and geographically distant suppliers (Kent & Omar, 2003).
5. **Variety of Sales Channels:** Retailers may sell products through stores, mobile shops, mail-order or electronic channels (Levy & Weitz, 2012).
6. **Additional Selling:** Retailers can sell additional services and goods to compliment their prime activities (Fernie, Fernie, & Moore, 2003).
7. **Target Customers:** Retailers should adapt different marketing types of consumer to gain competitive advantage (Kent & Omar, 2003).

Marketing value creation is the core purpose of economic exchange in retail sector (Dean & Rolland, 2012). The importance of managing product categories effectively is increasing (Liu & McGoldrick, 1996). Adding value for the consumer is brand image, the perception of the brand identity as interpreted by consumers (Keller, 1993). This is of value to a retailer as it assures the organization of sales and on-going customer loyalty (Kent & Omar, 2003) and enables them to justify higher selling prices (Levy & Weitz, 2012).

Concept of Internationalization

Internationalization refers to the mobilization of human, material, technological, and organizational resources for international markets (Spowart & Wickramasekera, 2012). Internationalization brings about greater uncertainty and complexity in the environmental and strategic context of SMEs (Westhead, Wright, & Ucbasaran, 2004). Internationalization is considered as a learning strategy (Calza, Aliane, & Cannavale, 2013). The internationalization of a firm is the outward movement of its operations and the process of mobilization, accumulation, and development of a specific set of resources in order to achieve greater performance (Dutot et al., 2014). Knowledge is not only a key influence on foreign operations, but also an important outcome of the internationalization process (Aulakh, 2009).

Internationalization process can vary related to research and development (R&D) innovation, network, technology,and human resources (Raymond & St-Pierre, 2013). Internationalization is jointly linked to globalization and growth (Ruzzier, Hisrich, & Antoncic, 2006). Internationalization is a successful strategy for firms in emerging economies to access and explore vast opportunities at the global level and to build their competitive advantage (Luo & Tung, 2007; Guillen & Garcia-Canal, 2009). Expanding sales to different markets offers learning opportunities that cut across industry or geography and are independent of the actions of foreign firms (Ellis, Davies, & Wong, 2011). As firms extend their scope of international activities or enter diverse foreign markets, they encounter different consumer needs, rival practices, new testing grounds for their products, and engage in exploratory learning (Aulakh, 2009). However, internationalization tends to be a double-edged sword because the theory-based predictions of the effect of internationalization on organizational performance are not unilaterally positive or negative (Chung, Lee, Beamish, Southam, & Nam, 2013).

Relationship Between Corporate Marketing Strategies and Internationalization

In a globalized and hypercompetitive world, organizations have to internationalize in order to enlarge their potential markets, and to reach higher levels of efficiency (Calza et al., 2013). Rapid change in the global business environment during the last few decades has had a strong impact on the internationalization process of many firms around the world (Uner, Kocak, Cavusgil, & Cavusgil, 2013). Global and regional retailers should realize that consumers' perceptions are country specific (To, Tam, & Cheung, 2013). Recent cases in retailing reflect that ethics have a major impact on brands and performance, in turn, demonstrating that brand owners, employees, and consumers focus on ethical values (Biong, Nygaard, & Silkoset, 2010). In today's retail markets, products display opaque pricing that provides no information about the allocation of retail proceeds among marketing agents who bring the products to market (Carter & Curry, 2010). Organizations have to learn new resources and systematic ways to combine the new and existing marketing resources (Calza et al., 2013).

There exist various forms of internationalization strategies for SMEs (Kotabe & Helsen, 2010). Six basic forms of partnership can be identified: exportation, subcontracting, outsourcing, offshoring, strategic alliance, and joint venture (Dutot et al., 2014). Root (1994) indicated that these strategies can be classified into three categories: the first one is called export entry mode (i.e., exportation only). The second one is the contractual entry mode (i.e., transfer of technological or human skills, strategic alliances, subcontracting). The third one is the investment entry mode (i.e., joint-venture, sole venture or foreign direct investment which includes wholly owned subsidiary). Organization chooses the strategy based on its requirements, its resources, the complexity of operation, and its profitability (Ruzzier & Konecnik, 2006). The international activities of SMEs have different levels of complexity (Dutot et al., 2014).

Marketing concepts apply to all forms of exchange concerning goods, services, places, and ideas (Achrol & Kotler, 2012). Marketing capabilities improve customer satisfaction and employee fulfillment which may increase financial indicators (Cruz-Ros, Cruz, & Perez-Cabanero, 2010). Marketing activity refers to the pervasiveness of promotion expenditures and number of retail outlets per capita in a country (Sirgy, Yu, Lee, Wei, & Huang, 2012). Cooperative advertising plays a strategically important role in marketing programs (Yan, 2010). Marketing channel structure is critical in determining both who benefits and the mechanism by which this benefit occurs (Xiao, Palekar, & Liu, 2011). All marketing channel members achieve higher advertising efforts and profit level in the cooperative case rather than in the non-cooperative case (Zhou & Lin, 2014). A higher compatibility of a product with online marketing leads to a higher advertising effort for online channel by manufacturer, an enhanced steady state for demand of brand as well as greater sales in the steady state through online channel (Sayadi & Makui, 2014).

The growing numbers of large retailers have internationalized to emerging markets (Moser, Schaefers, & Meise, 2012). Retail internationalization is important in global business (Doherty, 2007; Wigley & Moore, 2007). When organizations invest abroad, they have to employ new people, integrate new organizational units within their structure, enlarge their stakeholders, and adapt to different environments. Internationalization poses the big marketing challenges in modern organizations. Entering a new market implies the necessity to work within a different culture context. The practical internationalization has been confined to the food-retailing sector (Palmer & Quinn, 2003). The different rules, different behaviors, and different social norms can make coordination difficult, and can significantly impact on communication and organizational image (House, Hanges, Javidan, Dorfman, & Gupta, 2004).

Brouthers and Xu (2002) stated that pursuing a low-price strategy to compete at the international level weakens a firm's performance because profits tend to be smaller under extremely fierce price-based competition. Excessive internationalization increases governance and coordination costs associated with managing export operations, spread management resources across various markets, and increase management's information-processing needs (Aulakh, Kotabe, & Teegen, 2000; Chung, Lu, & Beamish, 2008), which can induce challenges for managers (Xiao, Jeong, Moon, Chung, & Chung, 2013). Managers need to develop a well-rounded appreciation of international expansion that views internationalization not only as a source of additional income, but also an important platform for marketing learning, capability enhancement and organizational renewal (Ibeh & Kasem, 2014).

Salesperson learning has the potential to contribute to the competitive advantage of the organization by increasing its capacity for organizational learning (Bell, Menguc, & Widing, 2010). Learning about new marketplace allows organizations to use their resources, to discover new ones, and to combine them in order to improve their competitiveness (Tung, 1998; Jun, Gentry, & Hyun, 2001). Organizations have to acquire market-knowledge both to coordinate the activity well, and to attract new customers in the global marketplace (Calza et al., 2013).

Learning motivation leads to the learning transfer in modern organizations (Kasemsap, 2013a). Organizational learning, knowledge management, and knowledge-sharing behavior positively affect organizational performance in global business (Kasemsap, 2013b). Kasemsap (2013c) explained that knowledge management practically leads to better job performance. Empowering leadership, team cohesion, and knowledge-sharing behavior are effectively correlated with team performance (Kasemsap, 2013d). Kasemsap (2014c) stated that perception of learning is favorably related to perceived training transfer in the digital age. Academic efforts to create new social networks should be implemented in order to minimize the lack of knowledge (Kasemsap, 2014d). Leaders of global businesses should provide training and provide the necessary information and communication technology skills for all employees to enhance their knowledge in modern business (Kasemsap, 2014e).

Organizations capture new knowledge generated by frontline employees in addressing productivity-quality tradeoffs during customer interactions and transform it into updated knowledge for frontline use (Ye, Marinova, & Singh, 2012). Organizations can internalize service experience knowledge by aggregating learned rules from organization's retail stores (Lin, Po, & Orellan, 2011). Information sharing shifts power upstream which enhances the manufacturer's incentive to bear costs to increase retail demand (Mittendorf, Shin, & Yoon, 2013). Knowledge is a key aspect of internationalization: organizations need to learn how to be competitive in different markets, as well as how to transfer their technology and practical application in order to delocalize their activities in the cheaper marketplace.

Challenges of Retail Marketing Mix in the Fashion Retail Industry

A change in product preference due to fashion trends is the main reason why the demand of fashion industry shows more variations than other industries (Wang, Gou, Sun, & Yue, 2012). Many retailers are in the process of adjusting their logistics operations to their specific requirements against the backdrop of raising pressure in a highly competitive environment (Kuhn & Sternbeck, 2013). Consumption is a central component of many peoples' lives (Ganglmair-Wooliscroft & Lawson, 2012). Consumption is deeply intertwined with social relations and norms (Carrigan, Moraes, & Leek, 2011). The increasing diversity of consumers' demand represents a challenge for retail stores (Walter, Battiston, Yildirim, & Schweitzer, 2012). Firms from different sectors can be expected to differ in philanthropic approach due to differences in public relations exposure (Amato & Amato, 2012). As luxury goods are more than any other products bought for what they mean, beyond what they are, multi-sensory experiences of luxury brands gain more and more relevance in creating superior customer-perceived value (Wiedmann, Hennigs, Klarmann, & Behrens, 2013).

The retail distribution sector is facing a difficult time as the current landscape is characterized by ever-increasing competition (Roig-Tierno, Baviera-Puig, & Buitrago-Vera, 2013). Regulation in retail sector has a considerable influence on firms' efficiency (Suarez & de Jorge, 2010). Retailers' competition drives retail prices lower (Mills, 2013). Prices tend to rise faster when costs rise, relative to the rate at which prices drop when costs fall (Hofstetter & Tovar, 2010). The pricing strategy is considered as one of the five most important priorities in retail management (Fassnacht & Husseini, 2013). Extant pricing strategies assume that all brands in the market are included while setting prices (Pancras, 2010). Coordination beyond simple knowledge of price will be beneficial for improving overall profits (Li, Nukala, & Mohebbi, 2013). The low-priced and medium-priced store brands are able to build individual store brand loyalty and store loyalty among customers (Yang & Wang, 2010).

Product design is defined as important to fashion retailers according to the relationship between fashion products and consumers' need for utility and self-image (Wigley, Moore, & Birtwistle, 2005). Retail shelf space allocation problem is recognized in marketing literature (Gajjar & Adil, 2010). A product's shelf location has a significant impact on sales for retail perspectives (Russell & Urban, 2010). To expand market and financial performance, firms should seek to generate meaningful product innovations through a moderate level of relative R&D power, particularly when their environments are characterized by high competitive intensity (Stock & Reiferscheid, 2014).

Fashion firms are recognized among the successful international retailers (Doherty, 2007; Wigley & Moore, 2007), reflecting in the marketing literature, with various studies focusing on the examples of fashion retailer internationalization (Wigley & Moore, 2007), and emphasizing internationalization among fashion retailers (Hutchinson et al., 2006). Fashion firms focus on the importance of branding (Moore, Fernie, & Burt, 2000), the range and ease of market entry methods (Dawson, 1994), and the potential for off-shore manufacturing (Sparks, 1996). The seasonal sales periods require the mark-down and promotions in order to shift slow-selling goods, but these must be managed toward better marketing profitability (Jackson & Shaw, 2006). The seasonality of fashion retailing and the sensitivity to customer demand require quick turnover of product ranges (Christopher & Peck, 2004).

Fashion retailers manage their pricing strategy, brand image, and market performance. When making order decisions the retailer only examines the price ratio and the fluctuation size of random demand, rather than the channel cost and the retailer's marketing efficiency (Liu, Lei, & Liu, 2014). The retailers operate in the same consumer market in which they compete in prices for consumer demand (Ouardighi, Jørgensen, & Pasin, 2013). Fashion retailers should expand product ranges in order to generate sales revenue, and gain competitive advantage through market attendance. Fashion retailers should improve and maintain the positive relationships with their customers in global retail markets (Sheridan, Moore, & Nobbs, 2006). Fashion retailers should develop the highly sophisticated, distinctive and focused brand identities in retail settings (Harrow, Lea-Greenwood, & Otieno, 2005).

Overview of Brand Management

The concept of brand can be traced back to product marketing where the role of brand and brand management has been primarily to create differentiation and preference for a product or service in the mind of the customer (Knox & Bickerton, 2003). Marketing lacks comprehension on the increasingly important segment of mature consumers concerning their behavior and respective reasons for certain behavior (Helm & Landschulze, 2013). The strong brand influences consumers' perception and brand loyalty focuses on the variables of marketing mix (Yoo, Donthu, & Lee, 2000). Consumers' perceptions of other consumers' product reviews affect brand buying intentions through two intervening variables: product-related attitudes and brand-related attitudes (Bartikowski & Walsh, 2014). Branding is a powerful mean of distinction (Pappu, Quester, & Cooksey, 2005). Brands play a central role in marketing, thus attracting the attention of academicians and practitioners (Brodie, Glynn, & Little, 2006; Erdem, Swait, & Valenzuela, 2006).

One of the major challenges for brand managers in the twenty-first century is to comprehend the relations between loyalty and its antecedents (Taylor, Celuch, & Goodwin, 2004). Business managers increasingly seek to develop brand loyalty through sponsorship activities (Masodier & Merunka, 2012). Staff behavior has an effective impact on brand success (Engel, Tran, Pavlek, Blankenberg, & Meyer, 2013). Branding supports the opportunity of brand extension (Yasin, Nasser Noor, & Mohamad, 2007). Building brand equity is considered as an important part of brand building (Pappu et al., 2005). Brand equity refers to the incremental utility or added value which brand adds to the product (Chen & Chang, 2008). Brand equity is an appropriate metric for evaluating the long-run impact of marketing decision (Atilgan, Aksoy, & Akinci, 2005).

Kasemsap (2014f) indicated that the dimensions of customer value, customer satisfaction, and brand loyalty have mediated positive effect on customer relationship management (CRM) performance in the social media age. Corporate brands are exposed to a wide variety of corporate publicity, which may elicit unexpected consumer responses and requires more academic attention (Xi & Peng, 2010). Brand trust is positively correlated with brand loyalty (Singh, Iglesias, & Batista-Foguet, 2012). Brand attitudes are determined by advertising content for innovative brands (Barone & Jewell, 2014). A favorable online brand experience is important for strengthening the consumers' brand relationship in a digital world (Simon, Brexendorf, & Fassnacht, 2013). The success of new product extension is an increasing function of parent brand's quality and the degree of fit between parent brand and new product extension (Carter & Curry, 2013).

Significance of Brand Management in the Global Retail Industry

In the global retail industry, branding can be especially important in influencing customer perceptions, as well as in motivating store choice and loyalty (Ailawadi & Keller, 2004; Hartman & Spiro, 2005). Customer loyalty has become a major concern for retail stores across the globe (Thomas, 2013). Retail brand can be perceived as an emotional connection between customer and organization (Kozinets, Sherry, DeBerry-Spence, Duhachek, Nuttavuthisit, & Storm, 2002). A better understanding of retail brand management techniques is required from the perspectives of consumers and practitioners (Ailawadi & Keller, 2004). Retail branding has moved beyond product-based explanations of retail brand distinctiveness to a more corporate store-based level (Burt & Davies, 2010). The development of retail brand thinking persists in line with the wider debate presented within the brand management field (Louro & Cunha, 2001).

Brand valuation has a significant positive effect on consumers' perceived value (Lin, 2013). As the retailers have continued to develop and promote such brands, consumers' perceptions of such brands have steadily improved and retail brands have become part of the accepted repertoire of consumer choice (Baltas, 2003). Appropriate management of brand equity leads to the increase in loyalty, to decrease the risk of marketing activity and marketing crisis, flexible response to price fluctuations, more business support and cooperation, high effectiveness of marketing communications, licensing opportunities, additional opportunities for brand extension, more attraction and support from investors (VanAuken, 2005), greater profit margins (Kim & Kim, 2005), increasing the ability to attract good employees (DelVecchio, Jarvis, Klink, & Dineen, 2007), protecting of potential competitors which enter during outsourcing (Lim & Tan, 2009).

Brand equity is the result of consumers' perception (Yasin et al., 2007). Brand equity sources include consumers' brand awareness and strong, favorable and unique brand associations. The first step in creating brand equity is to develop a brand identity (Aaker, 1996; Keller, 2003), achieved through a unique set of brand associations that a firm aspires to create or maintain (Aaker, 1996). There are many empirical researches about the dimensions of brand equity (i.e., brand awareness, brand association, perceived brand quality and brand loyalty) and overall brand equity (Yasin et al., 2007). High brand awareness is a signal of brand quality that assists consumers in making purchase decisions in the global retail industry (Yoo et al., 2000).

Brand awareness can be viewed as an antecedent of brand loyalty (Yoo et al., 2000). Brand awareness plays a special role in driving brand equity in business markets (Davis, Golicic, & Marquardt, 2008). Brand name and brand awareness explain a significant amount of the variation in brand equity in industrial firms (Davis et al., 2008). Consumer's satisfaction has positively influenced loyalty (Ismail, Hasnah, Ibrahim, & Mohd Isa, 2006). When consumers are satisfied with brand, they are more likely to recommend the product to others, are less likely to switch to other alternative brands (Bennett & Rundle-Thiele, 2004). Brand loyalty is considered as a desired outcome of publishing a brand, or brand equity (Van Riel, De Mortanges, & Streukens, 2005; Cater & Cater, 2009). Van Riel et al. (2005) stated that there is a positive relationship between industrial brand equity and brand loyalty.

The importance of brand associations is highlighted in several studies as the brand association can positively influence consumer choice, preferences, purchase intention, and brand extensions' acceptance (Yoo et al., 2000). Perceived brand quality has significant impact on customer satisfaction and brand loyalty (Nguyen, Barrett, & Miller, 2011). Hong-Youl and Kang-Hee (2012) stated that perceived quality have direct impact on brand loyalty and satisfaction. Yoo et al. (2000) showed the perceived brand quality has a positive relationship with a brand that is distributed with a good brand image. Branding enables organizations to achieve competitive advantage through building higher value perception of customers to get a higher price premium (Hsiao & Chen, 2013).

Brand equity is an antecedent of brand loyalty (Taylor et al., 2004). A brand that receives high attention from customers will have a competitive advantage (Nguyen et al., 2011). Managers of international brands design the marketing programs able to communicate distinctive associations with their brands in order to create high brand awareness in building high consumer perception of the brand's perceived value, thus leading to an increase in brand loyalty in the global retail industry (Nguyen et al., 2011). Keller (2003) stated that a positive brand equity can lead to more revenue, lower costs and higher profits, tending customer to seek new distribution channels, marketing communications effectiveness, and success in developing brand and selling licensing opportunities (Atilgan et al., 2005).

FUTURE RESEARCH DIRECTIONS

The strength of this chapter is on the thorough literature consolidation of corporate marketing strategies and brand management in the global retail industry. The extant literatures of corporate marketing strategies and brand management in the global retail industry provide a contribution to practitioners and researchers by describing a comprehensive view of the functional applications of corporate marketing strategies and brand management in the global retail industry to appeal to different segments of corporate marketing strategies and brand management in the global retail industry in order to maximize the business impact of corporate marketing strategies and brand management in the global retail industry. The classification of the prevailing literature in the domains of corporate marketing strategies and brand management will provide the potential opportunities for future research. Future research direction should broaden the perspectives in the implementation of corporate marketing strategies and brand management to be utilized in the knowledge-based organizations.

Practitioners and researchers should recognize the applicability of a more multidisciplinary approach toward research activities in implementing corporate marketing strategies and brand management in terms of knowledge management-related variables (i.e., knowledge-sharing behavior, knowledge creation, organizational learning, learning orientation, and motivation to learn). It will be useful to bring additional disciplines together (i.e., strategic management, marketing, finance, and human resources) to support a more holistic examination of corporate marketing strategies and brand management in order to combine or transfer existing theories and approaches to inquiry in this area.

CONCLUSION

This chapter explored the roles of corporate marketing strategies and brand management in the global retail industry, thus describing the concepts of marketing strategy, international retail marketing strategy, retail marketing mix, and internationalization; the relationship between corporate marketing strategies and internationalization; the challenges of retail marketing mix in the fashion retail industry; the overview of brand management; and the significance of brand management in the global retail industry. To be the successful global retailers, the ability to apply and adjust the retail marketing mix elements and retail brand strategy concerning specific target-market conditions and a wider global marketing strategy, is functionally important in retail settings. The successful global retailing requires both strategic and tactical initiatives, both taking into account company capabilities.

The global retailers should manage retail marketing mix elements and retail brand strategy in order to achieve better marketing outcomes within actionable business architecture. However, the level of manipulation of each in specific markets may be varied within the bounds set by the company's wider strategy. While some retail marketing mix elements and retail brand strategy should be maintained at a consistent level around the world, specific retail marketing mix elements and retail brand strategy may be adapted to suit the local market conditions. Product design and brand image in the retail brand strategy are attributed as being the most important factors, with variables tangible to consumers (i.e., pricing, advertising, product range, shelf space, and customer relationships), supporting these marketing factors in the global marketplace.

Retail marketing mix elements and the associated responsibility for their management tasks should be delegated to foreign markets management. Concerning retail internationalization literature, in order to be successful in the global retail industry, the global retailers should adopt a multinational approach. The overall brand image and product design in retail brand strategy should globally remain consistent and be supported by generally uniform store environment. Corporate marketing strategies should adapt pricing, advertising and product range in each local market, thus performing in the development of managerial structures and roles in retail settings.

The implementation of corporate marketing strategies and brand management is critical for modern organizations that seek to serve suppliers and customers, increase business performance, strengthen competitiveness, and achieve continuous success in global business. Therefore, it is necessary for modern organizations to examine their corporate marketing strategies and brand management applications, create a strategic plan to regularly check their practical advancements, and rapidly respond to the corporate marketing strategies and brand management needs of customers in the global retail industry. Applying corporate marketing strategies and brand management will greatly improve market performance and reach business goals in retail settings.

REFERENCES

Aaker, D. A. (1996). Measuring brand equity across products and markets. *California Management Review*, *38*(3), 102–120. doi:10.2307/41165845

Achrol, R. S., & Kotler, P. (2012). Frontiers of the marketing paradigm in the third millennium. *Journal of the Academy of Marketing Science*, *40*(1), 35–52. doi:10.1007/s11747-011-0255-4

Ailawadi, K. L., & Keller, K. L. (2004). Understanding retail branding: Conceptual insights and research priorities. *Journal of Retailing*, *80*(4), 331–342. doi:10.1016/j.jretai.2004.10.008

Akcura, M. T. (2010). Affiliated marketing. *Information Systems and e-Business Management*, *8*(4), 379-394.

Alexander, N. (1990). Retailers and international markets: Motives for expansion. *International Marketing Review*, *7*(4), 75–85. doi:10.1108/02651339010142797

Alexander, N., & Doherty, A. M. (2010). International retail research: Focus, methodology and conceptual development. *International Journal of Retail & Distribution Management*, *38*(11-12), 928–942.

Alexander, N., & Myers, H. (2000). The retail internationalisation process. *International Marketing Review*, *17*(4-5), 334–353. doi:10.1108/02651330010339888

Amato, L. H., & Amato, C. H. (2012). Retail philanthropy: Firm size, industry, and business cycle. *Journal of Business Ethics*, *107*(4), 435–448. doi:10.1007/s10551-011-1048-x

Atilgan, E., Aksoy, S., & Akinci, S. (2005). Determinants of the brand equity: A verification approach in the beverage industry in Turkey. *Marketing Intelligence & Planning*, *23*(3), 237–248. doi:10.1108/02634500510597283

Aulakh, P. S. (2009). Revisiting the internationalization—Performance relationship: Implications for emerging economy firms. *Decision*, *36*(2), 25–39.

Aulakh, P. S., Kotabe, M., & Teegen, H. (2000). Export strategies and performance of firms from emerging economies: Evidence from Brazil, Chile, and Mexico. *Academy of Management Journal*, *43*(3), 342–361. doi:10.2307/1556399

Balmer, J. M. T., Powell, S. M., & Greyser, S. A. (2011). Explicating ethical corporate marketing. Insights from the BP deepwater horizon catastrophe: The ethical brand that exploded and then imploded. *Journal of Business Ethics*, *102*(1), 1–14. doi:10.1007/s10551-011-0902-1

Baltas, G. (2003). A combined segmentation and demand model for store brands. *European Journal of Marketing*, *37*(10), 1499–1513. doi:10.1108/03090560310487211

Barone, M. J., & Jewell, R. D. (2014). How brand innovativeness creates advertising flexibility. *Journal of the Academy of Marketing Science*, *42*(3), 309–321. doi:10.1007/s11747-013-0352-7

Bartikowski, B., & Walsh, G. (2014). Attitude contagion in consumer opinion platforms: Posters and lurkers. *Electronic Markets*, *24*(3), 207–217. doi:10.1007/s12525-013-0149-z

Beckie, M. A., Kennedy, E. H., & Wittman, H. (2012). Scaling up alternative food networks: Farmers' markets and the role of clustering in western Canada. *Agriculture and Human Values*, *29*(3), 333–345. doi:10.1007/s10460-012-9359-9

Bell, S. J., Menguc, B., & Widing, R. E. (2010). Salesperson learning, organizational learning, and retail store performance. *Journal of the Academy of Marketing Science*, *38*(2), 187–201. doi:10.1007/s11747-009-0149-x

Bennett, R., & Rundle-Thiele, S. (2004). Customer satisfaction should not be the only goal. *Journal of Services Marketing*, *18*(7), 514–523. doi:10.1108/08876040410561848

Bianchi, C. C., & Ostale, E. (2006). Lessons learned from unsuccessful internationalization attempts: Examples of multinational retailers in Chile. *Journal of Business Research*, *59*(1), 140–147. doi:10.1016/j.jbusres.2005.01.002

Biong, H., Nygaard, A., & Silkoset, R. (2010). The influence of retail management's use of social power on corporate ethical values, employee commitment, and performance. *Journal of Business Ethics*, *97*(3), 341–363. doi:10.1007/s10551-010-0523-0

Breiter, A., & Huchzermeier, A. (2010). The new logic of truly efficient retail promotions. *International Commerce Review*, *9*(1-2), 36–47. doi:10.1007/s12146-010-0052-x

Brexendorf, T. O., & Daecke, N. (2012). The brand manager – Current tasks and skill requirements in FMCG companies. *Marketing Review St. Gallen*, *29*(6), 32–37. doi:10.1365/s11621-012-0175-9

Brodie, R. J., Glynn, M. S., & Little, V. (2006). The service brand and the service-dominant logic: Missing fundamental premise or the need for stronger theory. *Marketing Theory*, *6*(3), 363–379. doi:10.1177/1470593106066797

Brouthers, L. E., & Xu, K. (2002). Product stereotypes, strategy and performance satisfaction: The case of Chinese exporters. *Journal of International Business Studies*, *33*(4), 657–677. doi:10.1057/palgrave.jibs.8491038

Brown, P., McNaughton, R. B., & Bell, J. (2010). Marketing externalities in industrial clusters: A literature review and evidence from the Christchurch, New Zealand electronics cluster. *Journal of International Entrepreneurship*, *8*(2), 168–181. doi:10.1007/s10843-010-0053-y

Burt, S., & Davies, K. (2010). From the retail brand to the retailer as a brand: Themes and issues in retail branding research. *International Journal of Retail & Distribution Management, 38*(11-12), 865–878.

Buzzel, R. D., & Gale, B. T. (1987). *The PIMS principles*. New York, NY: Free Press.

Cai, R., & Wang, Y. (2010). An empirical study on the timing of big retailers' initial internationalization: Influence of the target market and entry-mode choice. *Frontiers of Business Research in China, 4*(4), 608–629. doi:10.1007/s11782-010-0113-0

Calza, F., Aliane, N., & Cannavale, C. (2013). Cross-cultural bridges in European firms' internationalization to Islamic countries: The key role of cultural competence. *EuroMed Journal of Business, 8*(2), 172–187. doi:10.1108/EMJB-07-2013-0038

Carrigan, M., Moraes, C., & Leek, S. (2011). Fostering responsible communities: A community social marketing approach to sustainable living. *Journal of Business Ethics, 100*(3), 515–534. doi:10.1007/s10551-010-0694-8

Carter, R. E., & Curry, D. J. (2010). Transparent pricing: Theory, tests, and implications for marketing practice. *Journal of the Academy of Marketing Science, 38*(6), 759–774. doi:10.1007/s11747-010-0189-2

Carter, R. E., & Curry, D. J. (2013). Perceptions versus performance when managing extensions: New evidence about the role of fit between a parent brand and an extension. *Journal of the Academy of Marketing Science, 41*(2), 253–269. doi:10.1007/s11747-011-0292-z

Cater, B., & Cater, T. (2009). Relationship-value-based antecedents of customer satisfaction and loyalty in manufacturing. *Journal of Business and Industrial Marketing, 24*(7-8), 585–597. doi:10.1108/08858620910999457

Cavusgil, S. T., & Cavusgil, E. (2012). Reflections on international marketing: Destructive regeneration and multinational firms. *Journal of the Academy of Marketing Science, 40*(2), 202–217. doi:10.1007/s11747-011-0287-9

Chen, C. F., & Chang, Y. (2008). Airline brand equity, brand preference, and purchase intentions: The moderating effects of switching costs. *Journal of Air Transport Management, 14*(1), 40–42. doi:10.1016/j.jairtraman.2007.11.003

Christopher, M., & Peck, H. (2004). *Marketing logistics*. Oxford, UK: Butterworth-Heinemann.

Chung, C. C., Lee, S. H., Beamish, P. W., Southam, C., & Nam, D. (2013). Pitting real options theory against risk diversification theory: International diversification and joint ownership control in economic crisis. *Journal of World Business, 48*(1), 122–136. doi:10.1016/j.jwb.2012.06.013

Chung, C. C., Lu, J., & Beamish, P. W. (2008). Multinational networks during times of economic crisis versus stability. *Management International Review, 48*(3), 279–295. doi:10.1007/s11575-008-0016-x

Chutani, A., & Sethi, S. P. (2012). Cooperative advertising in a dynamic retail market oligopoly. *Dynamic Games and Applications, 2*(4), 347–375. doi:10.1007/s13235-012-0053-8

Cornelius, B., Wagner, U., & Natter, M. (2010). Managerial applicability of graphical formats to support positioning decisions. *Journal für Betriebswirtschaft, 60*(3), 167–201. doi:10.1007/s11301-010-0061-y

Cronin, J. J., Smith, J. S., Gleim, M. R., Ramirez, E., & Martinez, J. D. (2011). Green marketing strategies: An examination of stakeholders and the opportunities they present. *Journal of the Academy of Marketing Science*, *39*(1), 158–174. doi:10.1007/s11747-010-0227-0

Cruz-Ros, S., Cruz, T. F. G., & Perez-Cabanero, C. (2010). Marketing capabilities, stakeholders' satisfaction, and performance. *Service Business*, *4*(3-4), 209–223. doi:10.1007/s11628-009-0078-2

Culliton, J. W. (1948). *The management of marketing costs*. Boston, MA: Harvard University Press.

Cvijikj, I. P., Spiegler, E. D., & Michahelles, F. (2013). Evaluation framework for social media brand presence. *Social Network Analysis and Mining*, *3*(4), 1325–1349. doi:10.1007/s13278-013-0131-y

Darling, J. R. (2001). Successful competitive positioning: The key for entry into the European consumer market. *European Business Review*, *13*(4), 209–221. doi:10.1108/EUM0000000005535

Davies, G. (1992). The two ways in which retailers can be brands. *International Journal of Retail & Distribution Management*, *20*(2), 24–34. doi:10.1108/09590559210009312

Davis, D. F., Golicic, S. L., & Marquardt, A. J. (2008). Branding a B2B service: Does a brand differentiate a logistics service provider? *Industrial Marketing Management*, *37*(2), 218–227. doi:10.1016/j.indmarman.2007.02.003

Davis, G. (1992). Positioning, image and the marketing of multiple retailers. *International Review of Retail, Distribution and Consumer Research*, *2*(1), 13–34. doi:10.1080/09593969200000002

Dawson, J. (1994). The internationalisation of retailing operations. *Journal of Marketing Management*, *10*(4), 267–282. doi:10.1080/0267257X.1994.9964274

Dean, A. M., & Rolland, S. E. (2012). Using an age-based lens to test the antecedents of value in retail. *der markt. International Journal of Marketing*, *51*(2-3), 85–100.

Deloitte. (2013). *Keeping promises putting customers at the heart of retail financial services*. London, UK: Deloitte.

DelVecchio, D., Jarvis, C. B., Klink, R. R., & Dineen, B. B. (2007). Leveraging brand equity to attract human capital. *Marketing Letters*, *18*(3), 149–164. doi:10.1007/s11002-007-9012-3

Dennis, C., Murphy, J., Marsland, D., Cockett, T., & Patel, T. (2002). Measuring image: Shopping centre case studies. *International Review of Retail, Distribution and Consumer Research*, *12*(4), 355–373. doi:10.1080/09593960210151153

Dibb, S., Simkin, L., Pride, W. M., & Ferrell, O. C. (2006). *Marketing: Concepts and strategies*. Boston, MA: Houghton Mifflin.

Doherty, A. M. (2000). Factors influencing international retailers market entry mode. *Journal of Marketing Management*, *16*(1), 223–245. doi:10.1362/026725700785100514

Doherty, A. M. (2007). The internationalisation of retailing: Factors influencing the choice of franchising as a market entry method. *International Journal of Service Industry Management*, *18*(2), 184–205. doi:10.1108/09564230710737826

Dutot, V., Bergeron, F., & Raymond, L. (2014). Information management for the internationalization of SMEs: An exploratory study based on a strategic alignment perspective. *International Journal of Information Management, 34*(5), 672–681. doi:10.1016/j.ijinfomgt.2014.06.006

Ellis, B., & Kelly, S. (1992). Competitive advantage in retailing. *International Review of Retail, Distribution and Consumer Research, 2*(2), 381–396. doi:10.1080/09593969200000014

Ellis, P., Davies, H., & Wong, A. (2011). Export intensity and marketing in transition economies: Evidence from China. *Industrial Marketing Management, 40*(4), 593–602. doi:10.1016/j.indmarman.2010.10.003

Engel, J., Tran, C., Pavlek, N., Blankenberg, N., & Meyer, A. (2013). The impact of friendliness on brand perception. *Marketing Review St. Gallen, 30*(6), 82–95. doi:10.1365/s11621-013-0302-2

Erdem, T., Swait, J., & Valenzuela, A. (2006). Brands as signals: A cross country validation study. *Journal of Marketing, 70*(1), 34–49. doi:10.1509/jmkg.2006.70.1.34

Fadılolu, M. M., Karaşan, O. E., & Pınar, M. C. (2010). A model and case study for efficient shelf usage and assortment analysis. *Annals of Operations Research, 180*(1), 105–124. doi:10.1007/s10479-008-0497-9

Fassnacht, M., & Husseini, S. E. (2013). EDLP versus Hi–Lo pricing strategies in retailing—A state of the art article. *Journal of Business Economics, 83*(3), 259–289. doi:10.1007/s11573-012-0648-y

Fernie, J., Fernie, S., & Moore, C. M. (2003). *Principles of retailing*. Oxford, UK: Butterworth-Heinemann.

Gajjar, H. K., & Adil, G. K. (2010). A piecewise linearization for retail shelf space allocation problem and a local search heuristic. *Annals of Operations Research, 179*(1), 149–167. doi:10.1007/s10479-008-0455-6

Ganglmair-Wooliscroft, A., & Lawson, R. (2012). Subjective wellbeing and its influence on consumer sentiment towards marketing: A New Zealand example. *Journal of Happiness Studies, 13*(1), 149–166. doi:10.1007/s10902-011-9255-9

Gaur, A. S., Kumar, V., & Singh, D. (2014). Institutions, resources, and internationalization of emerging economy firms. *Journal of World Business, 49*(1), 12–20. doi:10.1016/j.jwb.2013.04.002

Gilmore, A., Kraus, S., O'Dwyer, M., & Miles, M. (2012). Editorial: Strategic marketing management in small and medium-sized enterprises. *The International Entrepreneurship and Management Journal, 8*(2), 141–143. doi:10.1007/s11365-011-0175-2

Gonsch, J., Klein, R., Neugebauer, M., & Steinhardt, C. (2013). Dynamic pricing with strategic customers. *Journal of Business Economics, 83*(5), 505–549. doi:10.1007/s11573-013-0663-7

Gronroos, C. (1994). From marketing mix to relationship marketing: Towards a paradigm shift in marketing. *Journal of Management Decision, 32*(2), 4–20. doi:10.1108/00251749410054774

Gruner, R. L., Homburg, C., & Lukas, B. A. (2014). Firm-hosted online brand communities and new product success. *Journal of the Academy of Marketing Science, 42*(1), 29–48. doi:10.1007/s11747-013-0334-9

Guillen, M. F., & Garcia-Canal, E. (2009). The American model of the multinational firm and the "new" multinationals from emerging economies. *The Academy of Management Perspectives, 23*(2), 23–35. doi:10.5465/AMP.2009.39985538

Hansen, J. M., McDonald, R. E., & Mitchell, R. K. (2013). Competence resource specialization, causal ambiguity, and the creation and decay of competitiveness: The role of marketing strategy in new product performance and shareholder value. *Journal of the Academy of Marketing Science, 41*(3), 300–319. doi:10.1007/s11747-012-0316-3

Harrow, C., Lea-Greenwood, G., & Otieno, R. (2005). The unhappy shopper a retail experience: Exploring fashion fit and affordability. *International Journal of Retail & Distribution Management, 33*(4), 298–309. doi:10.1108/09590550510593220

Hartman, K., & Spiro, R. (2005). Recapturing store image in customer-based store equity: A construct conceptualization. *Journal of Business Research, 58*(8), 1112–1120. doi:10.1016/j.jbusres.2004.01.008

Helm, R., & Landschulze, S. (2013). How does consumer age affect the desire for new products and brands? A multi-group causal analysis. *Review of Managerial Science, 7*(1), 29–59. doi:10.1007/s11846-011-0072-7

Hessels, J., & Parker, S. C. (2013). Constraints, internationalization and growth: A cross-country analysis of European SMEs. *Journal of World Business, 48*(1), 137–148. doi:10.1016/j.jwb.2012.06.014

Hofstetter, M., & Tovar, J. (2010). Common knowledge reference price and asymmetric price adjustments. *Review of Industrial Organization, 37*(2), 141–159. doi:10.1007/s11151-010-9261-9

Hong, X., Wang, J., Wang, D., & Zhang, H. (2013). Decision models of closed-loop supply chain with remanufacturing under hybrid dual-channel collection. *International Journal of Advanced Manufacturing Technology, 68*(5-8), 1851–1865. doi:10.1007/s00170-013-4982-1

Hong-Youl, H., & Kang-Hee, P. (2012). Effects of perceived quality and satisfaction on brand loyalty in China: The moderating effect of customer orientation. *African Journal of Business Management, 6*(22), 6745–6753.

House, R. J., Hanges, P. J., Javidan, M., Dorfman, P. W., & Gupta, V. (2004). *Culture, leadership and organizations: The GLOBE study of 62 societies.* Thousand Oaks, CA: Sage.

Hsiao, Y. C., & Chen, C. J. (2013). Branding vs. contract manufacturing: Capability, strategy, and performance. *Journal of Business and Industrial Marketing, 28*(4), 317–334. doi:10.1108/08858621311313910

Hsieh, J. K., Hsieh, Y. C., & Tang, Y. C. (2012). Exploring the disseminating behaviors of eWOM marketing: Persuasion in online video. *Electronic Commerce Research, 12*(2), 201–224. doi:10.1007/s10660-012-9091-y

Hu, W., & Li, Y. (2012). Retail service for mixed retail and e-tail channels. *Annals of Operations Research, 192*(1), 151–171. doi:10.1007/s10479-010-0818-7

Hughes, D. E. (2013). This ad's for you: The indirect effect of advertising perceptions on salesperson effort and performance. *Journal of the Academy of Marketing Science, 41*(1), 1–18. doi:10.1007/s11747-011-0293-y

Hutchinson, K., Quinn, B., & Alexander, N. (2006). SME retailer internationalisation: Case study evidence from British retailers. *International Marketing Review, 23*(1), 25–53. doi:10.1108/02651330610646287

Ibeh, K., & Kasem, L. (2014). Internationalization's effect on marketing learning: A study of Syrian firms. *Journal of Business Research*, *67*(5), 680–685. doi:10.1016/j.jbusres.2013.11.027

Ishikawa, T. (2010). Effects of retail market structure and production conditions on firm's location selections of fragmented production process. *Jahrbuch für Regionalwissenschaft*, *30*(2), 91–103. doi:10.1007/s10037-010-0044-4

Ismail, I., Hasnah, H., Ibrahim, D. N., & Mohd Isa, S. (2006). Service quality, client satisfaction, and loyalty towards audit firms. Perceptions of Malaysian public listed companies. *Managerial Auditing Journal*, *22*(7), 738–756.

Jackson, T., & Shaw, D. (2006). *The fashion handbook*. Oxon, UK: Routledge.

Jahdi, K. S., & Acikdilli, G. (2010). Marketing communications and corporate social responsibility (CSR): Marriage of convenience or shotgun wedding? *Journal of Business Ethics*, *88*(1), 103–113. doi:10.1007/s10551-009-0113-1

Jefkins, F., & Yadin, D. (2000). *Advertising*. London, UK: Financial Times/Prentice-Hall.

Jun, S., Gentry, J. W., & Hyun, Y. J. (2001). Cultural adaptation of business expatriates in the host marketplace. *Journal of International Business Studies*, *32*(2), 369–377. doi:10.1057/palgrave.jibs.8490958

Kalaignanam, K., & Bahadir, S. C. (2013). Corporate brand name changes and business restructuring: Is the relationship complementary or substitutive? *Journal of the Academy of Marketing Science*, *41*(4), 456–472. doi:10.1007/s11747-012-0321-6

Kasemsap, K. (2013a). Practical framework: Creation of causal model of job involvement, career commitment, learning motivation, and learning transfer. *International Journal of the Computer, the Internet and Management*, *21*(1), 29-35.

Kasemsap, K. (2013b). Synthesized framework: Establishing a causal model of organizational learning, knowledge management, knowledge-sharing behavior, and organizational performance. *International Journal of the Computer, the Internet and Management*, *21*(2), 29-34.

Kasemsap, K. (2013c). Innovative framework: Formation of causal model of organizational culture, organizational climate, knowledge management, and job performance. *Journal of International Business Management & Research*, *4*(12), 21–32.

Kasemsap, K. (2013d). Strategic business management: A practical framework and causal model of empowering leadership, team cohesion, knowledge-sharing behavior, and team performance. *Journal of Social and Development Sciences*, *4*(3), 100–106.

Kasemsap, K. (2014a). The role of brand management in emerging markets. In I. Samanta (Ed.), *Strategic marketing in fragile economic conditions* (pp. 167–184). Hershey, PA: IGI Global. doi:10.4018/978-1-4666-6232-2.ch009

Kasemsap, K. (2014b). The role of social media in the knowledge-based organizations. In I. Lee (Ed.), *Integrating social media into business practice, applications, management, and models* (pp. 254–275). Hershey, PA: IGI Global. doi:10.4018/978-1-4666-6182-0.ch013

Kasemsap, K. (2014c). Constructing a unified framework and a causal model of occupational satisfaction, trainee reactions, perception of learning, and perceived training transfer. In S. Hai-Jew (Ed.), *Remote workforce training: Effective technologies and strategies* (pp. 28–52). Hershey, PA: IGI Global. doi:10.4018/978-1-4666-5137-1.ch003

Kasemsap, K. (2014d). The role of social capital in higher education institutions. In N. Baporikar (Ed.), *Handbook of research on higher education in the MENA region: Policy and practice* (pp. 119–147). Hershey, PA: IGI Global. doi:10.4018/978-1-4666-6198-1.ch007

Kasemsap, K. (2014e). The role of social networking in global business environments. In P. A. C. Smith & T. Cockburn (Eds.), *Impact of emerging digital technologies on leadership in global business* (pp. 183–201). Hershey, PA: IGI Global. doi:10.4018/978-1-4666-6134-9.ch010

Kasemsap, K. (2014f). The role of brand loyalty on CRM performance: An innovative framework for smart manufacturing. In Z. Luo (Ed.), *Smart manufacturing innovation and transformation: Interconnection and intelligence* (pp. 252–284). Hershey, PA: IGI Global. doi:10.4018/978-1-4666-5836-3.ch010

Kato, A. (2012). Productivity, returns to scale and product differentiation in the retail trade industry: An empirical analysis using Japanese firm-level data. *Journal of Productivity Analysis*, *38*(3), 345–353. doi:10.1007/s11123-011-0251-1

Keeling, K., Keeling, D., & McGoldrick, P. (2013). Retail relationships in a digital age. *Journal of Business Research*, *66*(7), 847–855. doi:10.1016/j.jbusres.2011.06.010

Keller, K. L. (1993). Conceptualizing, measuring, and managing customer-based brand equity. *Journal of Marketing*, *57*(1), 1–22. doi:10.2307/1252054

Keller, K. L. (2003). *Strategic brand management: Building, measuring, and managing brand equity.* Upper Saddle River, NJ: Pearson Education.

Kent, T. (2003). 2D3D: Management and design perspectives on retail branding. *International Journal of Retail & Distribution Management*, *31*(3), 131–421. doi:10.1108/09590550310465503

Kent, T., & Omar, O. (2003). *Retailing.* Basingstoke, UK: Palgrave Macmillan.

Kim, H. B., & Kim, W. G. (2005). The relationship between brand equity and firms' performance in luxury hotels and chain restaurants. *Tourism Management*, *26*(4), 549–560. doi:10.1016/j.tourman.2004.03.010

Knox, S., & Bickerton, D. (2003). The six conventions of corporate branding. *European Journal of Marketing*, *37*(7-8), 998–1016. doi:10.1108/03090560310477636

Kotabe, M., & Helsen, K. (2010). *Global marketing management.* New York, NY: John Wiley & Sons.

Kotler, P., & Armstrong, G. (2006). *Principles of marketing.* Englewood Cliffs, NJ: Prentice-Hall.

Kuhn, H., & Sternbeck, M. G. (2013). Integrative retail logistics: An exploratory study. *Operations Management Research*, *6*(1-2), 2–18. doi:10.1007/s12063-012-0075-9

Lai, C. S., Chiu, C. J., Yang, C. F., & Pai, D. C. (2010). The effects of corporate social responsibility on brand performance: The mediating effect of industrial brand equity and corporate reputation. *Journal of Business Ethics*, *95*(3), 457–469. doi:10.1007/s10551-010-0433-1

Lee, J. S., & Back, K. J. (2010). Reexamination of attendee-based brand equity. *Tourism Management*, *31*(3), 395–401. doi:10.1016/j.tourman.2009.04.006

Lee, M. L., & Pace, R. K. (2005). Spatial distribution of retail sales. *The Journal of Real Estate Finance and Economics*, *31*(1), 53–69. doi:10.1007/s11146-005-0993-5

Levy, M., & Weitz, B. A. (2012). *Retailing management*. New York, NY: McGraw-Hill.

Li, X., Nukala, S., & Mohebbi, S. (2013). Game theory methodology for optimizing retailers' pricing and shelf-space allocation decisions on competing substitutable products. *International Journal of Advanced Manufacturing Technology*, *68*(1-4), 375–389. doi:10.1007/s00170-013-4735-1

Lim, W. S., & Tan, S. J. (2009). Using brand equity to counter outsourcing opportunism: A game theoretic approach. *Marketing Letters*, *20*(4), 369–383. doi:10.1007/s11002-009-9071-8

Lin, F. R., Po, R. W., & Orellan, C. V. C. (2011). Mining purchasing decision rules from service encounter data of retail chain stores. *Information Systems and e-Business Management, 9*(2), 193-221.

Lin, W. B. (2013). Factors affecting high-involvement product purchasing behavior. *Quality & Quantity*, *47*(6), 3113–3133. doi:10.1007/s11135-012-9707-2

Liu, H., Lei, M., & Liu, X. (2014). Manufacturer's uniform pricing and channel choice with a retail price markup commitment strategy. *Journal of Systems Science and Systems Engineering*, *23*(1), 111–126. doi:10.1007/s11518-014-5239-8

Liu, H., & McGoldrick, P. J. (1996). International retail sourcing: Trends, nature, and processes. *Journal of International Marketing*, *4*(4), 9–33.

Louro, M., & Cunha, P. (2001). Brand management paradigms. *Journal of Marketing Management*, *17*(7-8), 849–875. doi:10.1362/026725701323366845

Luo, W., & de Jong, P. J. (2012). Does advertising spending really work? The intermediate role of analysts in the impact of advertising on firm value. *Journal of the Academy of Marketing Science*, *40*(4), 605–624. doi:10.1007/s11747-010-0240-3

Luo, Y., & Tung, R. L. (2007). International expansion of emerging market enterprises: A springboard perspective. *Journal of International Business Studies*, *38*(4), 481–498. doi:10.1057/palgrave.jibs.8400275

Lymperopoulos, C., Chaniotakis, I. E., & Rigopoulou, I. D. (2010). Acceptance of detergent-retail brands: The role of consumer confidence and trust. *International Journal of Retail & Distribution Management*, *38*(9), 719–736. doi:10.1108/09590551011062457

Madden, T. J., Fehle, F., & Fournier, S. (2006). Brands matter: An empirical demonstration of the creation of shareholder value through branding. *Journal of the Academy of Marketing Science*, *34*(2), 224–235. doi:10.1177/0092070305283356

Maglio, P. P., Nusser, S., & Bishop, K. (2010). A service perspective on IBM's brand. *Marketing Review St. Gallen*, *27*(6), 44–48. doi:10.1007/s11621-010-0098-2

Malbon, J. (2013). Taking fake online consumer reviews seriously. *Journal of Consumer Policy*, *36*(2), 139–157. doi:10.1007/s10603-012-9216-7

Manasseh, T., Muller-Sarmiento, P., Reuter, H., von Faber-Castell, C., & Pallua, C. (2012). Customer inspiration – A key lever for growth in European retail. *Marketing Review St. Gallen, 29*(5), 16–21. doi:10.1365/s11621-012-0159-9

Masodier, M., & Merunka, D. (2012). Achieving brand loyalty through sponsorship: The role of fit and self-congruity. *Journal of the Academy of Marketing Science, 40*(6), 807–820. doi:10.1007/s11747-011-0285-y

McCarthy, E. J. (1964). *Basic marketing*. Homewood, IL: Irwin.

McGoldrick, P. J. (2002). *Retail marketing*. London, UK: McGraw-Hill.

Mejia, L. C., & Benjamin, J. D. (2002). What do we know about the determinants of shopping center sales? Spatial vs. non-spatial factors. *Journal of Real Estate Literature, 10*(1), 3–26.

Meza, S., & Sudhir, K. (2010). Do private labels increase retailer bargaining power? *Quantitative Marketing and Economics, 8*(3), 333–363. doi:10.1007/s11129-010-9085-9

Michis, A. A., & Markidou, A. G. (2013). Determinants of retail wine prices: Evidence from Cyprus. *Empirical Economics, 45*(1), 267–280. doi:10.1007/s00181-012-0616-y

Miller, J., & Muir, D. (2004). *The business of brands*. Chichester, UK: John Wiley & Sons.

Mills, D. E. (2013). Countervailing power and chain stores. *Review of Industrial Organization, 42*(3), 281–295. doi:10.1007/s11151-012-9364-6

Mittendorf, B., Shin, J., & Yoon, D. H. (2013). Manufacturer marketing initiatives and retailer information sharing. *Quantitative Marketing and Economics, 11*(2), 263–287. doi:10.1007/s11129-013-9132-4

Moore, C., Fernie, J., & Burt, S. (2000). Brands without boundaries: The internationalization of the designer retailer's brand. *European Journal of Marketing, 34*(8), 919–937. doi:10.1108/03090560010331414

Morgan, N. A. (2012). Marketing and business performance. *Journal of the Academy of Marketing Science, 40*(1), 102–119. doi:10.1007/s11747-011-0279-9

Morschett, D., Swoboda, B., & Schramm-Klein, H. (2006). Competitive strategies in retailing – An investigation of the applicability of Porter's framework for food retailers. *Journal of Retailing and Consumer Services, 13*(4), 275–287. doi:10.1016/j.jretconser.2005.08.016

Moser, R., Schaefers, T., & Meise, J. K. (2012). Consumer preferences for product transparency in emerging markets – Lessons learned from India. *Marketing Review St. Gallen, 29*(3), 22–27. doi:10.1365/s11621-012-0133-6

Nalca, A., Boyaci, T., & Ray, S. (2010). Competitive price-matching guarantees under imperfect store availability. *Quantitative Marketing and Economics, 8*(3), 275–300. doi:10.1007/s11129-010-9080-1

Neudecker, N., Hupp, O., Stein, A., & Schuster, H. (2012). Is your brand a one-night stand? Managing consumer-brand relationships. *Marketing Review St. Gallen, 30*(6), 22–33. doi:10.1365/s11621-013-0297-8

Nguyen, T. D., Barrett, N. J., & Miller, K. E. (2011). Brand loyalty in emerging markets. *Marketing Intelligence & Planning, 29*(3), 222–232. doi:10.1108/02634501111129211

Oppewal, H., & Timmermans, H. (1997). Retailer self-perceived store image and competitive position. *International Review of Retail, Distribution and Consumer Research, 7*(1), 41–59. doi:10.1080/095939697343120

Ouardighi, F. E., Jørgensen, S., & Pasin, F. (2013). A dynamic game with monopolist manufacturer and price-competing duopolist retailers. *OR-Spektrum, 35*(4), 1059–1084. doi:10.1007/s00291-012-0300-9

Palmer, M., & Quinn, B. (2003). The strategic role of investment banks in the retailer internationalisation process: Is this venture marketing? *European Journal of Marketing, 37*(10), 1391–1408. doi:10.1108/03090560310487167

Pancras, J. (2010). A framework to determine the value of consumer consideration set information for firm pricing strategies. *Computational Economics, 35*(3), 269–300. doi:10.1007/s10614-009-9193-3

Pantano, E., & Viassone, M. (2014). Demand pull and technology push perspective in technology-based innovations for the points of sale: The retailers evaluation. *Journal of Retailing and Consumer Services, 21*(1), 43–47. doi:10.1016/j.jretconser.2013.06.007

Pappu, R., Quester, P. G., & Cooksey, R. W. (2005). Consumer-based brand equity: Improving the measurement – Empirical evidence. *Journal of Product and Brand Management, 14*(3), 143–154. doi:10.1108/10610420510601012

Parthasarathi, G., Sarmah, S. P., & Jenamani, M. (2011). Supply chain coordination under retail competition using stock dependent price-setting newsvendor framework. *Operations Research, 11*(3), 259–279. doi:10.1007/s12351-010-0077-z

Piercy, N., & Alexander, N. (1988). The status quo of marketing organisation in UK retailers: A neglected phenomenon of the 1980s. *Service Industries Journal, 8*(2), 155–175. doi:10.1080/02642068800000027

Pinho, J. C., & Martins, L. (2010). Exporting barriers: Insights from Portuguese small and medium-sized exporters and non-exporters. *Journal of International Entrepreneurship, 8*(3), 254–272. doi:10.1007/s10843-010-0046-x

Prange, C., & Schlegelmilch, B. B. (2009). The role of ambidexterity in marketing strategy implementation: Resolving the exploration-exploitation dilemma. *BuR - Business Research, 2*(2), 215-240.

Rafiq, M., & Ahmed, P. K. (1995). Using the 7Ps as a generic marketing mix: An exploratory survey of UK and European marketing academics. *Journal of Marketing Intelligence & Planning, 13*(9), 4–15. doi:10.1108/02634509510097793

Rajab, T., Kraus, F., & Wieseke, J. (2013). Resolving conflict over salespeople's brand adoption in franchised channels of distribution. *Review of Managerial Science, 7*(4), 443–473. doi:10.1007/s11846-012-0091-z

Rapp, A., Beitelspacher, L. S., Grewal, D., & Hughes, D. E. (2013). Understanding social media effects across seller, retailer, and consumer interactions. *Journal of the Academy of Marketing Science, 41*(5), 547–566. doi:10.1007/s11747-013-0326-9

Rawwas, M. Y. A., Arjoon, S., & Sidani, Y. (2013). An introduction of epistemology to business ethics: A study of marketing middle-managers. *Journal of Business Ethics, 117*(3), 525–539. doi:10.1007/s10551-012-1537-6

Raymond, L., & St-Pierre, J. (2013). Strategic capability configurations for the internationalization of SMEs: A study in equifinality. *International Small Business Journal, 31*(1), 82–102. doi:10.1177/0266242610391325

Richey, R. G., Tokman, M., & Dalela, V. (2010). Examining collaborative supply chain service technologies: A study of intensity, relationships, and resources. *Journal of the Academy of Marketing Science, 38*(1), 71–89. doi:10.1007/s11747-009-0139-z

Roig-Tierno, N., Baviera-Puig, A., & Buitrago-Vera, J. (2013). Business opportunities analysis using GIS: The retail distribution sector. *Global Business Perspectives, 1*(3), 226–238. doi:10.1007/s40196-013-0015-6

Root, F. R. (1994). *Entry strategies for international markets*. New York, NY: Lexington Books.

Russell, R. A., & Urban, T. L. (2010). The location and allocation of products and product families on retail shelves. *Annals of Operations Research, 179*(1), 131–147. doi:10.1007/s10479-008-0450-y

Ruzzier, M., Hisrich, R. D., & Antoncic, B. (2006). SME internationalization research: Past, present, and future. *Journal of Small Business and Enterprise Development, 13*(4), 476–497. doi:10.1108/14626000610705705

Ruzzier, M., & Konecnik, M. (2006). The internationalization strategies of SMEs: The case of the Slovenian hotel industry. *Journal of Contemporary Management Issues, 11*(1), 17–35.

Salmon, W., & Tordjman, A. (1989). The internationalisation of retailing. *International Journal of Retailing, 4*(2), 3–16.

Sayadi, M. K., & Makui, A. (2014). Feedback Nash Equilibrium for dynamic brand and channel advertising in dual channel supply chain. *Journal of Optimization Theory and Applications, 161*(3), 1012–1021. doi:10.1007/s10957-013-0479-1

Schmidt, R. C. (2013). Price competition and innovation in markets with brand loyalty. *Journal of Economics, 109*(2), 147–173. doi:10.1007/s00712-012-0296-2

Schubert, T. (2010). Marketing and organisational innovations in entrepreneurial innovation processes and their relation to market structure and firm characteristics. *Review of Industrial Organization, 36*(2), 189–212. doi:10.1007/s11151-010-9243-y

Sheridan, M., Moore, C. M., & Nobbs, K. (2006). Fast fashion requires fast marketing. *Journal of Fashion Marketing and Management, 10*(3), 301–315. doi:10.1108/13612020610679286

Simon, C., Brexendorf, T. O., & Fassnacht, M. (2013). Creating online brand experience on Facebook. *Marketing Review St. Gallen, 30*(6), 50–59. doi:10.1365/s11621-013-0299-6

Singh, J. J., Iglesias, O., & Batista-Foguet, J. M. (2012). Does having an ethical brand matter? The influence of consumer perceived ethicality on trust, affect and loyalty. *Journal of Business Ethics, 111*(4), 541–549. doi:10.1007/s10551-012-1216-7

Sirgy, M. J., Yu, G. B., Lee, D. J., Wei, S., & Huang, M. W. (2012). Does marketing activity contribute to a society's well-being? The role of economic efficiency. *Journal of Business Ethics, 107*(2), 91–102. doi:10.1007/s10551-011-1030-7

Sitzia, S., & Zizzo, D. J. (2011). Does product complexity matter for competition in experimental retail markets? *Theory and Decision, 70*(1), 65–82. doi:10.1007/s11238-009-9163-1

Skallerud, K., & Grønhaug, K. (2010). Chinese food retailers' positioning strategies and the influence on their buying behaviour. *Asia Pacific Journal of Marketing and Logistics, 22*(2), 196–209. doi:10.1108/13555851011026944

Smith, P. R., & Taylor, J. (2004). *Marketing communications.* London, UK: Kogan Page.

Sparks, L. (1996). Reciprocal retail internationalisation: The southland corporation, Ito-Yokado and 7-Eleven convenience stores. In G. Akehurst & N. Alexander (Eds.), *The internationalisation of retailing* (pp. 57–96). London, UK: Frank Cass.

Spowart, M., & Wickramasekera, R. (2012). Explaining internationalisation of small to medium sized enterprises within the Queensland food and beverage industry. *International Journal of Business and Management, 7*(6), 68–80. doi:10.5539/ijbm.v7n6p68

Stock, R. M., & Reiferscheid, I. (2014). Who should be in power to encourage product program innovativeness, R&D or marketing? *Journal of the Academy of Marketing Science, 42*(3), 264–276. doi:10.1007/s11747-013-0354-5

Suarez, C., & de Jorge, J. (2010). Efficiency convergence processes and effects of regulation in the nonspecialized retail sector in Spain. *The Annals of Regional Science, 44*(3), 573–597. doi:10.1007/s00168-008-0270-7

Sun, K. A., & Lee, S. (2013). Determinants of degree of internationalization for U.S. restaurant firms. *International Journal of Hospitality Management, 33*, 465–474. doi:10.1016/j.ijhm.2012.11.006

Swoboda, B., Haelsig, F., Morschett, D., & Schramm-Klein, H. (2007). An intersector analysis of the relevance of service in building a strong retail brand. *Managing Service Quality, 17*(4), 428–448. doi:10.1108/09604520710760553

Taylor, S., Celuch, K., & Goodwin, S. (2004). The importance of brand equity to customer loyalty. *Journal of Product and Brand Management, 13*(4), 217–227. doi:10.1108/10610420410546934

Thomas, S. (2013). Linking customer loyalty to customer satisfaction and store image: A structural model for retail stores. *DECISION, 40*(1-2), 15–25. doi:10.1007/s40622-013-0007-z

To, W. M., Tam, J. F. Y., & Cheung, M. F. Y. (2013). Explore how Chinese consumers evaluate retail service quality and satisfaction. *Service Business, 7*(1), 121–142. doi:10.1007/s11628-012-0149-7

Treadgold, A. (1988). Retailing without frontiers. *Retail and Distribution Management, 16*(6), 8–12. doi:10.1108/eb018382

Treadgold, A. (1991). The emerging internationalisation of retailing: Present status and future challenges. *Irish Marketing Review, 5*(2), 11–27.

Uner, M. M., Kocak, A., Cavusgil, E., & Cavusgil, S. T. (2013). Do barriers to export vary for born globals and across stages of internationalization? An empirical inquiry in the emerging market of Turkey. *International Business Review, 22*(5), 800–813. doi:10.1016/j.ibusrev.2012.12.005

Van Riel, A. C. R., De Mortanges, C. P., & Streukens, S. (2005). Marketing antecedents of industrial brand equity: An empirical investigation in specialty chemicals. *Industrial Marketing Management, 34*(8), 841–847. doi:10.1016/j.indmarman.2005.01.006

VanAuken, B. (2005). *The brand management checklist: Proven tools and techniques for creating winning brands*. London, UK: Kogan Page.

Varadarajan, R. (2010). Strategic marketing and marketing strategy: Domain, definition, fundamental issues and foundational premises. *Journal of the Academy of Marketing Science, 38*(2), 119–140. doi:10.1007/s11747-009-0176-7

Varadarajan, R. (2011). Marketing strategy: Discerning the relative influence of product and firm characteristics. *AMS Review, 1*(1), 32–43. doi:10.1007/s13162-011-0003-4

Velayudhan, S. K. (2014). Outshopping in rural periodic markets: A retailing opportunity. *International Journal of Retail & Distribution Management, 42*(2), 151–167. doi:10.1108/IJRDM-07-2013-0136

Volpe, R. J. (2013). Promotional competition between supermarket chains. *Review of Industrial Organization, 42*(1), 45–61. doi:10.1007/s11151-012-9352-x

Vorhies, D. W., Orr, L. M., & Bush, V. D. (2011). Improving customer-focused marketing capabilities and firm financial performance via marketing exploration and exploitation. *Journal of the Academy of Marketing Science, 39*(5), 736–756. doi:10.1007/s11747-010-0228-z

Waller, M. A., Williams, B. D., Tangari, A. H., & Burton, S. (2010). Marketing at the retail shelf: An examination of moderating effects of logistics on SKU market share. *Journal of the Academy of Marketing Science, 38*(1), 105–117. doi:10.1007/s11747-009-0146-0

Walter, F. E., Battiston, S., Yildirim, M., & Schweitzer, F. (2012). Moving recommender systems from on-line commerce to retail stores. *Information Systems and e-Business Management, 10*(3), 367-393.

Walters, D., & Laffy, D. (1996). *Managing retail productivity and profitability*. London, UK: Palgrave MacMillan.

Wang, J., Wang, L., Ye, F., Xu, X., & Yu, J. (2013). Order decision making based on different statement strategies under stochastic market demand. *Journal of Systems Science and Systems Engineering, 22*(2), 171–190. doi:10.1007/s11518-013-5217-6

Wang, K., Gou, Q., Sun, J., & Yue, X. (2012). Coordination of a fashion and textile supply chain with demand variations. *Journal of Systems Science and Systems Engineering, 21*(4), 461–479. doi:10.1007/s11518-012-5205-2

Watson, B. C. (2011). Barcode empires: Politics, digital technology, and comparative retail firm strategies. *Journal of Industry, Competition and Trade, 11*(3), 309–324. doi:10.1007/s10842-011-0109-2

Webster, F. E., & Lusch, R. F. (2013). Elevating marketing: Marketing is dead! Long live marketing! *Journal of the Academy of Marketing Science, 41*(4), 389–399. doi:10.1007/s11747-013-0331-z

Westhead, P., Wright, M., & Ucbasaran, D. (2004). Internationalization of private firms: Environmental turbulence and organizational strategies and resources. *Entrepreneurship & Regional Development, 16*(6), 501–522. doi:10.1080/0898562042000231929

Wiedmann, K. P., Hennigs, N., Klarmann, C., & Behrens, S. (2013). Creating multi-sensory experiences in luxury marketing. *Marketing Review St. Gallen, 30*(6), 60–69. doi:10.1365/s11621-013-0300-4

Wigley, S., & Moore, C. M. (2007). The operationalisation of international fashion retailer success. *Journal of Fashion Marketing and Management, 11*(2), 281–296. doi:10.1108/13612020710751437

Wigley, S., Moore, C. M., & Birtwistle, G. (2005). Product and brand: Critical success factors in the internationalization of a fashion retailer. *International Journal of Retail & Distribution Management, 33*(7), 531–544. doi:10.1108/09590550510605596

Williams, D. (1992). Motives for retailer internationalization: Their impact, structure, and implications. *Journal of Marketing Management, 8*(3), 269–285. doi:10.1080/0267257X.1992.9964196

Xi, Y., & Peng, S. (2010). The effects of two kinds of corporate publicity on customer-brand relationship. *Frontiers of Business Research in China, 4*(1), 73–100. doi:10.1007/s11782-010-0004-4

Xiao, S. S., Jeong, I., Moon, J. J., Chung, C. C., & Chung, J. (2013). Internationalization and performance of firms in China: Moderating effects of governance structure and the degree of centralized control. *Journal of International Management, 19*(2), 118–137. doi:10.1016/j.intman.2012.12.003

Xiao, Y., Palekar, U., & Liu, Y. (2011). Shades of gray—The impact of gray markets on authorized distribution channels. *Quantitative Marketing and Economics, 9*(2), 155–178. doi:10.1007/s11129-011-9098-z

Yan, R. (2010). Cooperative advertising, pricing strategy and firm performance in the e-marketing age. *Journal of the Academy of Marketing Science, 38*(4), 510–519. doi:10.1007/s11747-009-0171-z

Yang, D., & Wang, X. (2010). The effects of 2-tier store brands' perceived quality, perceived value, brand knowledge, and attitude on store loyalty. *Frontiers of Business Research in China, 4*(1), 1–28. doi:10.1007/s11782-010-0001-7

Yarbrough, L., Morgan, N. A., & Vorhies, D. W. (2011). The impact of product market strategy-organizational culture fit on business performance. *Journal of the Academy of Marketing Science, 39*(4), 555–573. doi:10.1007/s11747-010-0238-x

Yasin, N., Nasser Noor, M., & Mohamad, O. (2007). Does image of country-of-origin matter to brand equity? *Journal of Product and Brand Management, 16*(1), 38–48. doi:10.1108/10610420710731142

Ye, J., Marinova, D., & Singh, J. (2012). Bottom-up learning in marketing frontlines: Conceptualization, processes, and consequences. *Journal of the Academy of Marketing Science, 40*(6), 821–844. doi:10.1007/s11747-011-0289-7

Yoo, B., Donthu, N., & Lee, S. (2000). An examination of selected marketing mix elements and brand equity. *Journal of the Academy of Marketing Science, 28*(2), 195–211. doi:10.1177/0092070300282002

Zhou, M., & Lin, J. (2014). Cooperative advertising and pricing models in a dynamic marketing channel. *Journal of Systems Science and Systems Engineering, 23*(1), 94–110. doi:10.1007/s11518-013-5221-x

ADDITIONAL READING

Abratt, R., & Kleyn, N. (2011). Corporate identity, corporate branding and corporate reputations: Reconciliation and integration. *European Journal of Marketing, 46*(7-8), 1048–1063.

Aggerholm, H. K., Andersen, S. E., & Thomsen, C. (2011). Conceptualising employer branding in sustainable organizations. *Corporate Communications: An International Journal, 16*(2), 105–123. doi:10.1108/13563281111141642

Allaway, A. W., Huddleston, P., Whipple, J., & Ellinger, A. E. (2011). Customer-based brand equity, equity drivers, and customer loyalty in the supermarket industry. *Journal of Product and Brand Management, 20*(3), 190–204. doi:10.1108/10610421111134923

Batra, R., Ahuvia, A., & Bagozzi, R. P. (2012). Brand love. *Journal of Marketing, 76*(2), 1–16. doi:10.1509/jm.09.0339

Cairns, P., Quinn, B., Alexander, N., & Doherty, A. M. (2010). The role of leadership in international retail divestment. *European Business Review, 22*(1), 25–42. doi:10.1108/09555341011008990

Carpenter, J. M., & Balija, V. (2010). Retail format choice in the US consumer electronics market. *International Journal of Retail & Distribution Management, 38*(4), 258–274. doi:10.1108/09590551011032081

Chen, Y. M., & Su, Y. F. (2012). Do country-of-manufacture and country-of-design matter to industrial brand equity? *Journal of Business and Industrial Marketing, 27*(1), 57–68. doi:10.1108/08858621211188966

Choo, H. J., Moon, H., Kim, H., & Yoon, N. (2012). Luxury customer value. *Journal of Fashion Marketing and Management, 16*(1), 81–101. doi:10.1108/13612021211203041

D'Andrea, G. (2010). Latin American retail: Where modernity blends with tradition. *International Review of Retail, Distribution and Consumer Research, 20*(1), 85–101. doi:10.1080/09593960903497864

Dogerlioglu-Demir, K., & Tansuhaj, P. (2011). Global vs. local brand perceptions among Thais and Turks. *Asia Pacific Journal of Marketing and Logistics, 23*(5), 667–683. doi:10.1108/13555851111183084

Dwivedi, A., & Merrilees, B. (2013). Brand extension feedback effects: Towards a mediated framework. *Journal of Consumer Marketing, 30*(5), 450–461. doi:10.1108/JCM-01-2013-0414

French, A., & Smith, G. (2013). Measuring brand association strength: A consumer based brand equity approach. *European Journal of Marketing, 47*(8), 1356–1367. doi:10.1108/03090561311324363

Ha, H. Y., John, J., Janda, S., & Muthaly, S. (2011). The effect of advertising spending on brand loyalty in services. *European Journal of Marketing, 45*(4), 673–691. doi:10.1108/03090561111111389

Hollebeek, L. D. (2011). Demystifying customer brand engagement: Exploring the loyalty nexus. *Journal of Marketing Management, 27*(7-8), 785–807. doi:10.1080/0267257X.2010.500132

Hur, W. M., Ahn, K. H., & Kim, M. (2011). Building brand loyalty through managing brand community commitment. *Management Decision, 49*(7), 1194–1213. doi:10.1108/00251741111151217

Juntunen, M., Saraniemi, S., Halttu, M., & Tahtinen, J. (2010). Corporate brand building in different stages of small business growth. *Journal of Brand Management, 18*(2), 115–133. doi:10.1057/bm.2010.34

Kaufmann, H. R., Vrontis, D., Czinkota, M., & Hadiono, A. (2012). Corporate branding and transformational leadership in turbulent times. *Journal of Product and Brand Management, 21*(3), 192–204. doi:10.1108/10610421211228810

Konecnik Ruzzier, M. (2012). Developing brand identity for Slovenia with opinion leaders. *Baltic Journal of Management, 7*(2), 124–142. doi:10.1108/17465261211219778

Kuikka, A., & Laukkanen, T. (2012). Brand loyalty and the role of hedonic value. *Journal of Product and Brand Management, 21*(7), 529–537. doi:10.1108/10610421211276277

Kumar, R. S., Dash, S., & Purwar, P. C. (2013). The nature and antecedents of brand equity and its dimensions. *Marketing Intelligence & Planning, 31*(2), 141–159. doi:10.1108/02634501311312044

Lindgreen, A., Beverland, M., & Farrelly, F. (2010). From strategy to tactics: Building, implementing, and managing brand equity in business markets. *Industrial Marketing Management, 39*(8), 1123–1125. doi:10.1016/j.indmarman.2010.02.018

Liu, F., Li, J., Mizerski, D., & Soh, H. (2012). Self-congruity, brand attitude, and brand loyalty: A study on luxury brands. *European Journal of Marketing, 46*(7-8), 922–937.

Lloyd, S., & Woodside, A. (2013). Corporate brand-rapture theory: Antecedents, processes, and consequences. *Marketing Intelligence & Planning, 31*(5), 472–488. doi:10.1108/MIP-04-2013-0064

Mann, B. J. S., & Kaur, M. (2013). Exploring branding strategies of FMCG, services and durables brands: Evidence from India. *Journal of Product and Brand Management, 22*(1), 6–17. doi:10.1108/10610421311298650

Marzocchi, M., Morandin, G., & Bergami, M. (2013). Brand communities: Loyal to the community or the brand? *European Journal of Marketing, 47*(1-2), 93–114. doi:10.1108/03090561311285475

Mishra, A., & Ansari, J. (2013). A conceptual model for retail productivity. *International Journal of Retail & Distribution Management, 41*(5), 348–379. doi:10.1108/IJRDM-03-2013-0062

Mitchell, R., Hutchinson, K., & Bishop, S. (2012). Interpretation of the retail brand: An SME perspective. *International Journal of Retail & Distribution Management, 40*(2), 157–175. doi:10.1108/09590551211201883

Mourad, M., Ennew, C., & Kortam, W. (2011). Brand equity in higher education. *Marketing Intelligence & Planning*, *29*(4), 403–420. doi:10.1108/02634501111138563

Nam, J., Ekinci, Y., & Whyatt, G. (2011). Brand equity, brand loyalty and customer satisfaction. *Annals of Tourism Research*, *38*(3), 1009–1030. doi:10.1016/j.annals.2011.01.015

Paswan, A., Pineda, M. D. S., & Ramirez, F. C. S. (2010). Small versus large retail stores in an emerging market – Mexico. *Journal of Business Research*, *63*(7), 667–672. doi:10.1016/j.jbusres.2009.02.020

Pike, S., Bianchi, C., Kerr, G., & Patti, C. (2010). Consumer-based brand equity for Australia as a long-haul tourism destination in an emerging market. *International Marketing Review*, *27*(4), 434–449. doi:10.1108/02651331011058590

Pillai, A. (2012). Corporate branding literature: A research paradigm review. *Journal of Brand Management*, *19*(4), 331–343. doi:10.1057/bm.2011.43

Prasad, C. J., & Aryasri, A. R. (2011). Effect of shopper attributes on retail format choice behaviour for food and grocery retailing in India. *International Journal of Retail & Distribution Management*, *39*(1), 68–86. doi:10.1108/09590551111104486

Quintal, V., & Phau, I. (2013). Brand leaders and me-too alternatives: How do consumers choose? *Marketing Intelligence & Planning*, *31*(4), 367–387. doi:10.1108/02634501311324852

Ramkrishnan, K. (2010). The competitive response of small, independent retailers to organized retail: Study in an emerging economy. *Journal of Retailing and Consumer Services*, *17*(4), 251–258. doi:10.1016/j.jretconser.2010.02.002

Rindell, A., & Strandvik, T. (2010). Corporate brand evolution: Corporate brand images evolving in consumers' everyday life. *European Business Review*, *22*(3), 276–286. doi:10.1108/09555341011040976

Saini, G. K., & Sahay, A. (2014). Comparing retail formats in an emerging market - Influence of credit and low price guarantee on purchase intention. *Journal of Indian Business Research*, *6*(1), 48–69. doi:10.1108/JIBR-03-2013-0026

Sathish, D., & Raju, V. D. (2010). The growth of Indian retail industry. *Advances in Management*, *3*(7), 15–19.

Schnittka, O., Sattler, H., & Zenker, S. (2012). Advanced brand concept maps: A new approach for evaluating the favorability of brand association networks. *International Journal of Research in Marketing*, *29*(3), 265–274. doi:10.1016/j.ijresmar.2012.04.002

Spence, M., & Essoussi, L. H. (2010). SME brand building and management: An exploratory study. *European Journal of Marketing*, *44*(7-8), 1037–1054. doi:10.1108/03090561011047517

Stahl, F., Heitmann, M., Lehmann, D. R., & Neslin, S. A. (2012). The impact of brand equity on customer acquisition, retention, and profit margin. *Journal of Marketing*, *76*(4), 44–63. doi:10.1509/jm.10.0522

Valette-Florence, P., Guizani, H., & Merunka, D. (2011). The impact of brand personality and sale promotions on brand equity. *Journal of Business Research*, *64*(1), 24–28. doi:10.1016/j.jbusres.2009.09.015

KEY TERMS AND DEFINITIONS

Brand Management: The process of maintaining, improving, and promoting a brand.

Brand Strategy: The long-term marketing support for a brand, based on the definition of the characteristics of the target consumers.

Branding: The process involved in creating a unique name and image for a product in the consumers' mind, mainly through advertising campaigns with a consistent theme.

Competitive Advantage: A superiority gained by an organization when it can provide the same value as its competitors but at a lower price, or can charge higher prices by providing greater value through differentiation.

Corporate Strategy: The overall scope and direction of a corporation and the way in which its various business operations work together to achieve particular goals.

Marketing: The management process through which goods and services move from concept to the customer.

Marketing Mix: A planned mix of the controllable elements of a product's marketing plan commonly termed as 4Ps: product, price, place, and promotion.

Marketing Strategy: An organization's strategy that combines all of its marketing goals into one comprehensive plan.

Retailing: The commercial transaction in which a buyer intends to consume the good or service through personal, family, or household use.

This research was previously published in Successful Technological Integration for Competitive Advantage in Retail Settings edited by Eleonora Pantano, pages 310-339, copyright year 2015 by Business Science Reference (an imprint of IGI Global).

Chapter 17
The Role of Value Co-Creation on Brand Image:
A Conceptual Framework for the Market Performance of SMEs in Malaysia

Pravina Jayapal
Universiti Sains Malaysia, Malaysia

Azizah Omar
Universiti Sains Malaysia, Malaysia

ABSTRACT

The proliferation of SMEs in Malaysia shows that a better understanding on this SMEs are needed. Even though the SME market is booming, these SMEs face difficulties in sustaining in the constantly evolving marketplace. In order to continuously flourish in this industry, the firms should understand the role of value co-creation in improving their market performance. The lack of value co-creation implementation has been found to act as a barrier for these SMEs. Moreover, SMEs are identified to have issues in establishing a strong brand image through value co-creation. Therefore, the book chapter develops a conceptual framework to improve the understanding on the contribution of value co-creation in the development of stronger brand image and greater market performance.

INTRODUCTION

The existence of Small Medium Enterprises (SMEs) plays an important role in the socioeconomic development of the country. In recent years, the SMEs in Malaysia have been continuously booming. According to SME Corp. Malaysia, among the business entities in Malaysia, approximately 97.3% are SMES based on the year 2014, which contributed about 33.1% towards the Gross Domestic Product (GDP) and 57.5% of employment (Rosley, 2015). Up to the year 2015, the Malaysian government has allocated RM11.34 billion towards the development of these SMEs (SME Annual Report, 2015). This allocation is expected to boost the productivity as well as encourage new businesses to embark into the

DOI: 10.4018/978-1-5225-5187-4.ch017

SME industry. The major focus of these firms is to improve their market performance which depends on the capability and ability of the SMEs' market orientation. Thus, firms have come up with various strategies in order to improve their market performance. One of the recent strategies of firms are collaborating with customers in terms of value co-creation.

Firms have evolved from the goods-dominant logic (G-D) which focuses solely on the activities performed by the company to the service dominant logic (S-D), giving importance to the involvement of the consumers in the process chain and the relationship between the firms and consumers. Value co-creation has been identified to provide various benefits to the firms as well as consumers. According to Badurdeen and Liyanage (2011), value co-creation contributes to the betterment and sustainability of the products whereby, firms get to understand and meet the consumers' needs and preferences. Therefore, firms are able to modify and implement the decision making process which is more efficient and saves time and resources (Chen et al., 2012). This shows that value co-creation is able to encourage competitive advantage and improve its market performance.

One of the organization that successfully practice value co-creation is IKEA, one of the popular retail furniture company in the world. In IKEA, consumer value is implemented through the co-creation of personalized customer experiences in the store itself in terms of testing and trying the home design which are available. Different themes of rooms are provided based on the customers' preferences. Moreover, IKEA also uses value co-creation where consumers are required to conduct their own assembly operation. By doing so, IKEA manages to have high turnover of products while consumers benefit from the lower cost. Another company that uses value co-creation is LEGO. LEGO has an online platform called Lego Ideas which allow Lego users to come up with their own ideas and share them here. Other users are allowed to vote on these ideas and the ideas which are the most popular will receive a small amount from the net revenue from LEGO. Since the G-D logic has transitioned into the S-D logic, SMEs are also moving into the value co-creation process in order to sustain within their highly competitive industry. Value co-creation is vital for SMEs as it would be able to train them to utilize their limited resources efficiently and effectively while sustaining their brand in the marketplace.

In addition, value co-creation also plays a role in the field of new product development. Here, consumers come into the picture in providing useful information and ideas on the products and services that they need and want. These products and services might not be available in the market currently but is considered to be useful in the nearest future. Therefore, the firms which practice value co-creation would have the competitive advantage of introducing a new product which will meet the demand of consumers. However, even though SMEs have difficulties in terms of budget and resources, investing in product development would benefit the firm in terms of sustainability and increase in sales revenue. Through value co-creation, SMEs can expect to have more involvement in the product development which will subsequently improve their brand image.

In the current business world, the brand image of the organization plays an important role. Brand image is defined as the combinations of different brand names in terms of the brands' characteristics (Keller, 1993). Brands are an important asset for every firm because it determines the value of the particular firm and drives the entire marketing activity of the firm. Moreover, the brand serves as a competitive advantage for the firm. For SMEs, creating a strong brand image would ensure its sustainability in the marketplace. Having a strong brand image would help the SME in terms of spending lesser budget on promotions of the brand. This is because brands which are reputable, trusted and well known provide assurance and confidence to consumers in purchasing its products.

Building a good business image takes a long time to establish and it can be further improved by identifying the strengths and overcoming the weaknesses of the particular brand. SMEs which are able to establish their brand among customers will have many advantages. Consumers would trust and purchase the products which are provided by firms with the positive brand image. Moreover, a well communicated brand image would be able to help consumers to recognize the needs and wants that can be satisfied by the brand as well as distinguishing it from its competitor brands (Huang & Cai, 2015). As mentioned in previous literature, brand image has a positive impact on the firms' market performance in terms of customer satisfaction, customer loyalty, market share, expanding into a new market and customer retention. However, establishing and creating a well-known brand consumes a lot of time and fund. SMEs have been identified to face problem in maintaining their brand image. To gain the trust of customers as well as retaining them, SMEs would have make sure that the quality of the products manufactured and sold is consistent and reliable. Positive brand image requires the hard work of every actors of the firm to maintain it.

As we know, value co-creation requires a huge amount of investment and expertise to be created and implemented within the firms' process chain. Larger firms have been successfully implementing value co-creation by interacting with their customers. Technology plays an important role in value co-creation in terms of having access to latest resources, knowledge on systems and new products, supply chain management and keeping track of the competitors (Möller & Törrönen, 2003). As been expected, technology implementation and advancement has been continuously taking place within the larger firms.

SMEs on the other hand, encounter difficulties in survival and growth in value co-creation because of the lack of financial strength (Desouza & Awazu, 2006). Moreover, SMEs need to compete in gaining the knowledge on value co-creation and implementing it to enhance their competitive advantage. Having limited resources such as capital, labour force and land serves as its major hurdle. In order to improve their market performance, efficient use of resources is required (Desouza & Awazu, 2006). Other than that, SMEs have been facing issues in the field of technology and value co-creation. The advancement of technology has provided various ways for consumers to communicate with firms such as the Internet, social networks, emails and websites (Hoyer et al., 2010). Realizing on the importance of technology in improving business performance as well as creating a strong brand image, SMEs in Malaysia are beginning to embark into the Internet. However, the lack of budget has held them back in pursuing their business activities in the online platform. Moreover, with the vast growth of technology, SMEs will soon be forced to take up the online environment for their business activities especially through value co-creation. Having a strong brand image could help SMEs in establishing themselves in the industry. However, this brand image needs the hard work and perseverance of the firms.

A strong brand image is achieved only when the customers have a better impression of the firms' brand and are more confident to associate with it. As more customers purchase products from the firm, strong brand image would be established. Firms believe that brand image acts as a guide to the identity of the brand, targeted market and benefits that it has to offer to customers. The improvement of the firms' brand image results in more profit and better market performance. However, the problem arises when the SMEs need to implement and develop their brand image. In order to do so, the brand needs to be known, communicated and shared which will be efficient with the help of value co-creation between the firm and customers (Payne et al., 2009).

Payne et al. (2009) further added that even though scholars have been focusing on the service-dominant logic area, very few have embarked into the role of brand in value co-creation. Other studies also agree that previous literature has only been indirectly discussing branding in the value co-creation context (Brodie et al., 2006). Moreover, Vargo and Lusch (2004) also briefly pointed out on the concept of branding in their paper. Bell and Loane (2010) stressed that many studies have focused on huge companies with strong brand while limited attention have been given to SMEs and their value co-creation. Only a few recent studies have begun to investigate on the branding of SMEs. Gilmore et al. (1999) and Merrilees (2007) also supports that there is considerable quantity of SMEs studies in the marketing literature but only a limited number embarks into branding. This is because SMEs are also facing problems in establishing and sustaining brand image (Mäläskä et al., 2010). This creates a need for studies on branding within SMEs in Malaysia.

In addition, more research on the effects of value-co-creation on firm's performance are required (Hoyer et al., 2010) as SMEs have been booming and gaining importance in the Malaysian business market. Mäläskä et al. (2010) further supported that actors of a business are considered to be useful in providing information and advice on improving the brand image of the SMEs which will eventually increase the firm's profit and sales. However, how the brand image of SMEs can enhance the market performance through integrating consumers into the value chain has remains unclear. Thus, this study proposes that the application of value co-creation with consumers of SMEs in Malaysia will have a positive impact on brand image which in turn leads to a higher level of market performance. Based on these issues, the objective of this study is to propose a conceptual framework on the relationship between value co-creation, brand image and market performance.

BACKGROUND

Value Co-Creation

Over the years, many definitions of value have emerged within the literature (Sánchez-Fernández & Iniesta-Bonillo, 2007). Value was initially being conceptualized as unidimensional but later on evolved into a multi-dimensional construct. Value has a vast range of definitions, i.e. value as a symbolic meaning, value added concept (Woodruff & Flint, 2006), relativistic preference experience (Holbrook, 1999) and value-in-use (Vargo & Lusch, 2004). According to Moore et al. (2014), consumer value is what the consumers want or believe that they would gain from the purchase of a product or service. These values might differ between consumers as different consumers have different value propositions from the same product or purchase. For example, one consumer might emphasize on the functionality of product while another would consider the design and colour. This study uses the definition of Ulaga and Eggert (2006), which describes value co- creation as the value which exists between the firm and the customer as well as produced from the relationship between them.

Based on previous literature, value and value creation are divided into two categories which are: "value-in-exchange" and "value-in-use" (Vargo & Lusch, 2008). Value-in-exchange is related to the goods-dominant logic (G-D) (Lin et al., 2010). Based on Vargo and Lusch (2008), value-in exchange refers to the value which is quantifiable whereas, value-in-use is heterogeneous because the definition varies according to individuals. According to the G-D approach, value is created by the activities which are executed by the firm alone such as designing the products, creating manufacturing processes, developing the marketing cues and controlling the sales without the involvement of the consumers (Prahalad, 2004), which later leads to the distribution of value into the market in the form of goods exchange and monetary transactions (Vargo et al., 2008). The role of both actors are distinct whereby the firms act as the value producer and distributor while consumers are the end users of the value. However, from the 1980s, literature started to focus on different areas within the marketing field such as market orientation, relationship marketing, service marketing, quality management and brand relationship (Smit et al., 2007). Later on, the goods-dominant logic started to reflect limitations which urged firms to question the approach and begin venturing into a new solution for better market performance, reaching diverse markets and fulfil customers' needs and wants (Tanev et al., 2011).

The evolvement of the market can be identified through the introduction of value co-creation. Value co-creation represents the S-D logic from the previous G-D logic in terms of products and services personalization (Vargo & Lusch, 2008). The S-D logic was beginning to be utilized when the exchange of products was replaced with exchange of intangible products such as knowledge and expertise. S-D logic is associated with the value-in-use whereby service refers to individual usage of the knowledge and skills in order to provide value to others (Vargo & Lusch, 2008). According to Barrett et al. (2015), the S-D logic is conceptualized as the process of utilizing an individual's resources for the benefit of others. The process of co-creation is frequently expressed in the literature as dyadic, two-way, continuous, voluntary, active, open and voluntary (Zwass, 2010). According to S-D logic, firms cannot provide value, however they can only give value proposition. This is because the consumers will be the ones deciding on the final value of the product or service (Vargo & Lusch, 2008). S-D logic offers a suitable framework to explain creative exchange forms (Lusch & Vargo, 2014). As the logic of branding has moved from a firm-centric to a collective, value co-creation activity, SDL and branding related research can boost and inform each other (Payne et al., 2009)

Recently, firms marketing strategy evolved into collaboration with customers and working hand-in-hand with their partners for improving their market performance. Some of the areas studied were customer and market orientation, value and supply chain management, relationship marketing, network analysis, quality management, services marketing and resource management (Vargo & Lusch, 2004) (As displayed in Figure 1). The transformation works in understanding the needs and wants of market, customizing the products and services offered and co-creating with the stakeholders to improve their market performance (Payne et al., 2008).

These changes have played a major impact on the firm's organizational structure and its daily activities. Consumers opinions and ideas became important inputs that could help the firms' market performance tremendously (Payne et al., 2008). Other stakeholders such as employees, stockholders and government organizations also play a role as the co-creator of value, but the value is decided by the consumers (As displayed in Figure 2). Therefore, it can be assumed that the firm and consumer relationship has changed by the involvement of all other actors of the value co-creation who work together in creating the value which is favourable to the consumers (Vargo & Lusch, 2008).

From the value co-creation perspective, Grönroos (2011) and Korkman et al. (2010) claimed that consumers are the ones who create value and it is supported by the communication between the customer and firms. Various benefits could be experienced by firms as well as consumers through value co-creation in terms of product development, consumers communicate with the firm on the suitable design for the product, production activities, logistics as well as consumption behaviour. Other than that, through communication with customers, firms are able to introduce new product or service which are needed (Lin et al., 2010). Value co-creation is important because firms identify and acknowledge the customers' value creation and this approach gives priority to the activities which are co-created as a result of a business relationship rather than the activities performed by the firm on its own. Hence, the S-D logic transformed from consumers to co-creators of value, value chain to value network, product

Figure 1. The evolution of marketing
Source: Vargo and Lusch (2004).

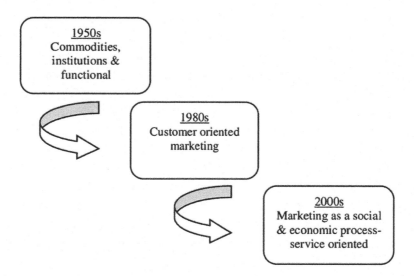

Figure 2. Value co-creators in a business organization

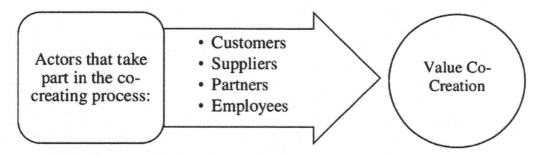

value to network value, simple co-operation or competition to complex co-opetition, individual firm strategy to strategy in relation to the total value ecology (Juscius & Jonikas, 2013).

The significance of consumers in the value co-creation process is undeniable. Prahalad and Ramaswamy (2001) described that consumers represent a new source of competitive advantages. They further introduced the DART model in order to reduce the traditional information imbalance between consumers and the firm. It also acts as a foundation for the value co-creation process (Prahalad, 2004). Four components have been found to act as the building blocks in describing the interaction between consumers and firms. These factors are dialogue (D), access (A), risk-benefits (R) and transparency (T) (DART). This DART model has been found to assist in value co-creation by creating innovation strategies and providing a system for value co-creation. Numerous literatures have explained the relationship between these four factors and value co-creation. Dialog (D) refers to the communication between both parties which is essential in value co-creation. Dialog assist in the interactivity, commitment, capability and willingness of both parties in engaging with each other (Prahalad, 2004). For example, firms will be required to be transparent on the financial statements and information sharing which are confidential to the organization. Moreover, dialogue helps in understanding the emotional, social and cultural needs of consumers. Other than that, it develops trust between the stakeholders and firms which enables them to share information and ideas that are important to them. It also assists consumers and firms to communicate and work together in improving the product or services that are provided by the firm (Taghizadeh et al., 2016).

However, dialogue will only be fruitful when consumers are given the access and transparency to the firm's information. By providing access and being transparent to the stakeholders, it will provide a better understanding and develop honest relationship between both parties. Through the advancement of technology, consumers are able to gather information about the firm through stakeholders and online community of other consumers which is easily and conveniently accessible these days. Consumers who have the exact information about the brand and firm would be able to have a stronger bond with the organization which will provide more satisfaction and loyal consumers. The dialog, access and transparency results in risk-assessment which is the trade-off between the risks and benefits involved in the value co-creation process.

Access is defined as how alliances provide strength to consumers in gaining knowledge and information through value co-creation (Spena et al., 2012). According to Islam et al. (2015), access portrays the facilities and information that are available for consumers. Risk assessment describes the likelihood of risk to consumers. The stakeholders who go through value co-creation require firms to provide them with details on the risks that they might be exposed to and this makes them more responsible in dealing with the possible risks (Prahalad & Ramaswamy, 2013). Other than that, risk assessment also relates to the evaluation of the risks and advantages that the stakeholders will obtain through value co-creation (Islam et al., 2015). Lastly, transparency helps in providing shared information on the products, technologies available in the firm and business systems (Prahalad & Ramaswamy, 2013).

DART model has been focusing on the interaction facets of the value co-creation activity. Moreover, the dimensions explained by this model would be able to provide a better way of decision making after evaluating the risk and benefits of the value co-creation (Prahalad & Ramaswamy, 2004). It also helps in simplifying the value co-creation process. In addition, Skaržauskaitė (2013) also supported that the usage of DART model would enable firms to engage better with their consumers. Through the DART model, firms can co-create mutual values and improve on their current collaborations too. Other than that, the firm would be able to learn about the consumer's behaviour directly through the consumer's feedback on their preferences. Therefore, it is agreeable that the DART model provides a guideline which eases the firms in value co-creation with their consumers. By practising the DART model, SMEs would be able to have a proper guideline in developing and monitoring their innovation strategies. The transformation to value co-creation is deemed important for every SMEs in order to them to sustain in the marketplace. Ramaswamy and Gouillart (2010) mentioned that value co-creation is a process building the activities of the firm with the stakeholders which is in contrast to the traditional way of creation whereby firm carries the responsibility of building the firm solely and wait for the stakeholders to come to them. As a result, firms are open to more business advantages, growth and more opportunities towards innovation. Therefore, firms need to change their approach in terms of the firms' practices and management if they would want to adapt to the value co-creation environment (Ramaswamy, 2009).

BRAND IMAGE

Brand image is an important component in the marketing field. Different definitions and conceptualizations have emerged from past literatures. Kotler (2001) defined image as "the set of beliefs, ideas, and impression that a person holds regarding an object". Low and Lamb (2000) stated that brand image represents consumers' attachment on the rational or emotional aspects of a brand. Brand plays its role during the decision making process of consumers whereby it helps in differentiating products and services. Moreover, Ataman and Ülengin (2003) explained brand image as to how consumers' choose between brands after the information gathering in the buying decision making process. Brand image represents the perceptions, beliefs and expectations of consumers on a brand based on the value that it can provide to them and the firm (Nandan, 2005). Besides that, brand image also refers to the stakeholder's idea or perception of the brand. In the organization perspective, some studies have provided differing definitions for brand image. Besides that, Vukasovic (2009) claimed that brand image is the overall perception and associations that the consumer has in his/ her mind. This book chapter uses the widely used definition of brand image from Keller (1993) which describes brand image as the perception of consumers on a particular brand which is developed through brand association in the consumer's memory and experiences. It was further added that the brand image within consumers are from the experiences that they have been through when purchasing or using the product.

The various definition and concepts of brand image was found to be possible due to the lack of the foundation theory which explains the brand image in detail (Dobni & Zinkhan, 1990). Brand image has been used interchangeably with terms such as brand identity. However, Aaker (1996) had clarified on the differences between these two concepts. "Brand identity is a unique set of brand associations that the brand strategist aspires to create or maintain", whereby the brand identity is the idea that firms want the consumers to relate the brand to. It further explains on the assurance of what the brand provides to the consumers. However, brand image represents the way the brand is perceived by the consumers which has been developed through the consumers past experience or memories.

Apéria and Back (2004) claimed that brand image is derived through the mental image or the way that the brand is perceived by the consumers. This is because brand image is mainly influenced by those who consume the final brand which are the end users. Thus, it is understood that brand image is formed from the way stakeholders interpret the signs that are deriving through the firm's products or services (Aaker, 2003). Brand image is found to be highly influenced by symbolic interpretations that are gained through the product's characteristics or the benefit that the consumers perceive to receive when consuming the product. By understanding brand image, SMEs are able to identify the strength and weakness of their brand as well as the perception of consumers towards their brand. This is because brand image differs based in the consumer's perception. Therefore, brand image is an essential component that SMEs need to focus on.

In the organizational perspective, brand image determines the reputation of a particular firm (Mudambi, 2002). According to Kapferer (2012), brand image comprises of the name of the product, logo, physical attributes and functionality. Leek and Christodoulides (2011) explained brand image as "a combination of stakeholders" evaluation of the firms' ability to reach their desired goals and expectations which should also parallel with the brand identity. Brand image is different than brand identity in the sense that identity represents the firms' values and culture (Michel & Rieunier, 2012) while brand image describes the mental image of the firm and goes beyond the status and identity (Schmitt, 2012).

There are different ways to identify the brand image of a firm or product. Ataman and Ülengin (2003) provided further clarification that brand image is commonly portrayed through the name of the product, the attributes and exterior of the product such as the design and packaging, the functionality which helps in determining the consumer's choice of brand. These aspects are examined by the consumers during the information searching process before purchasing a product or service. Aaker (1991) explained that brand image is significant in assisting consumer in processing information, providing valid reason for purchase, distinguishing the brand from its competitors' and ensuring consumers feel happy and satisfied at the end of the purchase. For SMEs, patenting their brand name, logo and trademark would be able to improve their brand image. By having a strong brand image, SMEs would be able to compete with their competitors as well as other established brands.

However, a particular brand image might be favourable to only a certain group of consumers. This is because brand image can be formed from the information that a consumer receives from their social group or through the positive relationship that the consumer has developed with the firm and its brand. Through branding, firms can produce, cultivate and innovate their products or services. Based on this, SMEs can market the product to the targeted customers by segmenting their market. These consumers will continuously be loyal to the brand and brand switching is unlikely to take place. This can be done through understanding the needs of each target market and deciding which target market will be suitable for their brand. The inability to focus on the right consumer market might lead to less sales revenue and profit margin. As a result, the brand will not be able to sustain with the competing brands due to their lack of knowledge on the consumers buying behaviour. Therefore, having a strong and successful brand image is important to firms especially SMEs.

A successful brand should be able to attract its targeted consumers based on its distinct attributes and benefits (Jalilvand & Samiei, 2012; Keller, 1993). Attributes refer to characteristics of a brand that describes a brand. It focuses on the product-related attributes and non-product-related attributes. Product-related attributes describe the characteristics of the product which helps in delivering the function of the product while non product-related attributes describes the external aspects of the product or service (Keller, 1993). Besides that, benefits describe the values that consumers see in a particular brand or product and how the brand can add value to their life. For example, what a consumer perceives about a brand and what they can gain when they purchase the brand. These brands have such a strong brand image that when features such as high quality or price saving are mentioned, consumers could immediately associate it with a particular brand. This displays the success of the firm in positioning its brand. This distinctiveness is able to set the brand apart from the competing brand (Webster & Keller, 2004). The benefits have been divided into the components in previous studies namely, functional, experiential and symbolic benefits. Functional represents the intrinsic advantages of the product such as the quality and price. Experiential discusses the feelings and emotional characteristics that consumers feel when utilizing the product while symbolic benefits refer to the need for self-expression and social approval. SMEs are able to attract customers through any of these benefits. Therefore, sufficient planning and emphasis should be provided to the brand image in order to secure a permanent position within their targeted group of customers.

According to Hsieh et al. (2004), a strong brand image is displayed when consumers could satisfy their needs with it and able to distinguish it from other competing brand which increases the probability of consumer's purchase behaviour. A particular brand image might be favourable to only a certain group of consumers. Therefore, SMEs have to segment their market in order to identify their target market. This can be done through understanding the needs of each target market and deciding which target market will be suitable for their brand. The inability to focus on the right consumer market might lead to less sales revenue and profit margin. The brand will also not be able to sustain with the competitive brand due to their lack of knowledge on the consumers buying behaviour.

Furthermore, Solomon et al. (2009) suggested the use of marketing strategies and marketing mix to ensure a strong brand image. This could help in the product positioning for the suitable targeted market. Customers who are receiving the brand have the power to determining their perceptions of brand image. Kapferer (2012) supported that the sender-receiver model relies on perception of the customers on brand, product and firm. Moreover, Bengtsson and Servais (2005) mentioned that brand image is related to the relationship between all the actors related to a firm. In addition, Keller (1993) stressed on the importance of positive brand image among firms to encourage the loyalty of consumers. It is also understood that favourable brand image leads to positive impression on the brand which enables firms to charge premium prices for their products. This is because the consumers are loyal to the particular brand and would encourage positive word-of-mouth to others (Dennis et al., 2007).

Strong brand images need time to be established. Firms have to build a long term relationship with customers if they would want to retain their customers and create brand loyalty. The value for the particular brand can be determined by the strength of the bond with its customers (Nandan, 2005). Through value co-creation, firms are able to establish a strong bond with customers. Leek and Christodoulides (2011) supported this by explaining that firms require skills and ability to understand the needs of the customers through active communication in order to provide better product or service. By doing so, the firms will be more trustworthy and reliable. Therefore, customers' confidence, satisfaction and loyalty will increase which leads towards better market performance.

Additionally, Ojasalo et al. (2008) suggested that brand image can also be built by developing a good relationship with their business partners. The business partners also play an important role in the establishment of a strong brand image. They are able to promote the brand to other actors in the network which helps in promoting the brand. Moreover, actors in the business system will start developing their trust on the brand based on the positive word-of-mouth from the partners. Therefore, partners act as the intermediaries between the firm and other players in the business chain.

Besides that, brand image is significant due to it being the deciding factor when a consumer decides whether the particular brand is suitable for themselves or vice versa. This will later on affect the next decision making and buying behaviour of the consumer and subsequently brand equity. According to Keller (1993), brand equity is described as the distinctive differences of brand knowledge towards consumer's reaction the marketing of the particular brand. Strong brand image would be able to provide better brand position which helps in standing out from the competing brand, improving the market performance as well as shaping the brand equity of the product which will determine the future of the brand and the firm (Bian & Moutinho, 2011; Keller, 1993). Research on brand image has begun as early as the 1950s which signifies the important role that it plays in businesses. However, there is a lack of clarity and agreement on the conceptualization of brand image. Therefore, a comprehensive understanding on brand image is absent.

MARKET PERFORMANCE

In the dynamic business world, firms have to constantly compete with each other to create its unique competitive advantage and improve its market performance to sustain in the market. This is also found to be relevant in the SME industry. Most of the SMEs are striving to appear unique in the eyes of their customers and achieve higher market shares. Market performance can be determined by many different aspects such as image, customer satisfaction, customer loyalty and ability to attract new customers (Storey & Easingwood, 1999). Based on Laukkanen et al. (2013), market performance is defined as the firm's success in gaining new customers and maintaining existing ones. Other than that, Griffin and Page (1993) identified that profitability, revenue of sales and market share can also determine market performance. This book chapter describes firms' market performance through the number of products or services that are successfully sold, customer loyalty, new customers, attaining the targeted market share and growth rate (Homburg et al., 2010).

Even though performance measures such as customer satisfaction, customer acceptance and degree of competitive advantage is found to be useful if applied, in the practical world, it is seldom utilized (Griffin & Page, 1993). The development in market performance is possible through creating new products and services while constantly understanding the demand and evolvement of the consumers' needs and wants. This serves as an issue in SMEs due to the lack of funding and facilities. Firms try their best to identify, understand and satisfy the needs and wants of consumers. However, firms that are able to meet the needs of the consumers remain at the top of their industries. For SMEs, it is important for them to be able to sustain their consumers in terms of their satisfaction and loyalty. Those consumers who are loyal would spread word of mouth which would help in gaining new consumers. As it is known, maintaining existing customers cost lesser than acquiring new ones (Storbacka et al., 1994). Nevertheless, successful firms are those that could gain new customers and maintaining their existing ones.

The market performance of the firm is very important in order for the firm to sustain in the business. One of the way to increase market performance is by co-creating with customers. By doing so, customers get to express their needs and preferences while the firms will be able to serve the customers better. The fulfilment of the consumers' needs would improve sales of the firms' products as well as provide satisfaction for consumers which leads towards brand loyalty as well as recommendation to other consumers (Mokhtar et al., 2014), As the competition between SMEs are stiff, having the co-creation with customers serves as a competitive advantage for these organizations. Therefore, the SMEs that are practicing value co-creation would be able to perform better in the market compare to their competitors.

However, in order to achieve higher market performance, SMEs are trying to embark in new innovations to promote their brand to potential customers. Through technology, SMEs are able to reach their customers faster and it appears to be more convenient for the firm as well as the customers. being able to penetrate into the Internet and social media helps firms to bring their brand to the next level of innovation while increasing their market performance. Customers are also feeling comfortable with the new approach due to the ease of communicating and co-creating with firms through the new platform.

PROPOSED RESEARCH MODEL

Research focusing on branding have been found to give little importance to brand relationships and co-creation. This was supported by Arnould et al. (2006) who suggested that more research should be conducted on branding within the service-dominant logic (S-D). Moreover, Keller and Lehmann (2006) also emphasized on the relationship between brand and customer experience. Customer experience which falls under value-co creation is deemed to be related to brand image. In addition, Beverland et al. (2007) described value to be present when there is a mutual understanding between the firms and its stakeholders. Value co-creation can be identified in activities such as co-designing, co-production, co-production and co-branding. Hence, the incorporation of value co-creation in every process of the firm helps in the enhancement of its brand image. As an example, Intel improved its brand image by collaborating with its manufacturers and assemblers as well as displaying its logo clearly on the products that are promoted.

In addition, with value co-creation, firms are able to influence the rest of the stakeholders, and the stakeholders in turn are also utilizing this opportunity to communicate with firms (Håkansson & Snehota, 2006). Value co-creation acts as a way for the firm and its stakeholders to work together in providing a positive and enhance brand image for the company (Mäläskä et al., 2010). Thus, the brand image is influenced by the value co-creation process. Subsequently, various literatures have been found the influence of different stakeholders on brand image such as consumers (Merrilees, 2007), employees (Wong & Merrilees, 2005), resellers (Ojasalo et al., 2008) and business partners (Beverland et al., 2007).

Besides that, as SMEs have limited resources, other stakeholders assist and provide guidance on the business strategies of these SMEs. By focusing on value co-creation, the stakeholders are able to give suggestions on the firms operation and brand image which will be very useful to these SMEs (Mäläskä et al., 2010). In addition, Ojasalo et al. (2008) supported that branding in SMEs can be improved through the value co-creation with other stakeholder, thereby creating a supportive brand relationship.

Other than that, studies on brand has been found to be focusing on value co-creation recently (Hatch & Schultz, 2010). Another study by Ind and Coates (2013) also justified that brands should be built through value co-creation. Moreover, Merz et al. (2009) explains that brands are now being created through collaboration with stakeholders and the firm itself. Ojasalo et al. (2008) further described that the internal and external stakeholders of the firm play an important role in the brand's success. The commitment of the stakeholders is essential since SMEs have limited resources to establish their brand through huge branding activities. These stakeholders could assist by providing their knowledge and expertise in improving the SMEs brand image. Therefore, it is proposed that:

P1: Value co-creation is positively related to brand image.

Other than that, according to previous scholars, there is a positive, significant relationship between brand image and customer loyalty (Esch et al., 2006; Zins, 2001) Customer loyalty, satisfaction and purchase behaviour are often found as a measurement for market performance (Kim et al., 2009). Thus, brand image is a positive predictor to market performance. Moreover, Wong and Merrilees (2008) seconded that a strong brand image would be able to create a good reputation for the brand and encourage product purchase which will satisfy the needs and wants of the consumer. Strong brand image also leads towards more satisfaction and continuous satisfaction and consequently towards consumer loyalty. When consumers are satisfied, they would repeat their purchase, as well as introduce the particular brand to other consumers. Rundle-Thiele et al. (2005) further added that brand image plays a role in influencing consumer's satisfaction which later develops into loyalty. This word of mouth recommendation by existing consumers are able to reduce the cost of the firm in acquiring new consumers. As a result of the positive brand image, the sales, market share and profit of the firm will increase.

Furthermore, Park et al. (1986) explained that well communicated brand image is able to distinguish the brand from its competing brands, helps in positioning the brand and improves the brand's market performance. When the brand image of the firm is strong, the firm will be able to reduce the cost in establishing their brand among consumers. They only need to sustain the brand image that they have created. Besides that, Malhotra et al. (1999) found that brand image is related to market performance such market share and sales. This leads to the next proposition:

P2: Brand image is positively related to market performance.

In addition, value co-creation is deemed essential for the firm to sustain in the continuously evolving business world. Lusch and Harvey (1994) found that the strong bond between consumers and firms resulted in higher revenue and better financial stability for the firm. Coopetition approach has been identified to lead to better market performance (Grant & Baden-Fuller, 2004). Ahuja (2000) also supported that the capability of the firm increases when collaboration with partners take place. Coopetition benefits the firm in terms of joining forces for a certain technology or innovation that would help improve the market performance of each of the players involved in the co-creation activity. Besides that, value co-creation would also help in gathering the resources which could assist in the betterment of the firms performance (Ritala, 2012). Those firms that are not able to sustain a strong brand image are likely to be left behind by their competitors (Laukkanen et al., 2013).

According to Prahalad (2004), value co-creation has been predicted to influence the market performance of the firm. Through value co-creation, the firm would gain competitive advantages compared to the other firms (Payne et al., 2008). By having the competitive advantage, the firm has already secured loyal consumers who would continue purchasing the product. However, the firm needs to have the knowledge and capability to sustain these consumers. This is only possible through understanding the needs of consumers which can be performed effectively through value co-creation. By implementing value co-creation, firms will gain many advantages. One of the advantage is the increase in production and reduction in cost of production. The reduction of cost is possible for the firm in terms of gaining information from consumers in new product development which costs lesser compared to through their employees and market researchers (Evans & Wolf, 2005). Therefore, the employment cost will be reduced and firms would also receive valuable details on the latest need of the consumer market from the consumer itself which will be more reliable.

Next, the firm would be able to improve its efficiency. This would be through the improvement of the product value, innovation ideas for new products and fulfilling the needs and wants of consumers (Hoyer et al., 2010). Therefore, firms would be able to cater the needs of consumers earlier than their competitors. When they are able to receive the new ideas from consumers in advance, therefore, they have the advantage of satisfying this need before other firms (Sawhney et al., 2005). Value co-creation has also been found to significantly influence the firm's performance in terms of the reduced product and service turnover, increase in employee and consumer satisfaction, sales revenue and profit (Hoyer et al., 2010; Vega-Vazquez et al., 2013).

Besides, value co-creation gives the firms the competitive advantage in embarking into innovation. Innovation is important if the firm wants to remain in the market for long term. According to Prahalad and Ramaswamy (2013), firms that are successful in value creating innovation and are able to protect their innovation from being replicated by their competitors would perform better in the market. When the firm dominates the market, it would be hard for other firms to compete with them. This is further supported by Taghizadeh et al. (2016) who claimed when consumers co-create with the firms in the process of innovation, a stronger bond is formed between the firm and its customers. It was also added that innovation has the ability to improve the market performance of the firm. Firms that have been continuously providing innovative products would create a positive image for the firm.

From the stakeholders perspective, Ritter and Gemünden (2003) stated that firms do not have the power to control the stakeholders and the market. However, the stakeholders have the ability to influence and change the market as well as determining the firm's success or failure. The value co-creation between the stakeholders and firm serves as a great way for the stakeholders to convey their needs to the firms. This interdependency between all the players in the market is able to determine future of the firm (Mäläskä et al., 2010). Therefore, the next proposition is recommended:

P3: Value co-creation is positively related to market performance.

As a contribution to the existing theory, a concept of the value co-creation was proposed. In this study, value co-creation is studied in relation to brand image which incorporates all stakeholders that co-create an SME's brand identity and image, both directly and indirectly which in turn increases its market performance. In this respect, a firm's capability to acquire resources through exchange with the actors in its brand co-creation will have a significant impact on its brand success and market performance. Furthermore, Tung (2012) explained that in terms of product innovation, consumers would be able to have a wide range of products to select from which will ensure better market performance as well as consumer satisfaction. Therefore, this explains the next proposition which is:

P4: Brand image mediates the relationship between value co-creation and market performance.

Based on the findings and models from prior studies, a conceptual model on the influence of value co-creation towards market performance is proposed in Figure 3. The Figure 3 proposes that the market performance is influenced by value co-creation and brand image.

PROPOSED METHODOLOGY

This research will utilise the quantitative research method to collect the data as suggested by Creswell and Clark (2011). Self- administered questionnaire will be distributed to Malaysian SMEs via purposive sampling. The respondents will consist of business owners of SMEs operating in Malaysia. The inclusion criteria for the organisations are (1) the organization must have less than 150 employees for the manufacturing sector and less than 50 employees for the service sector, and (2) the organization must be a stand-alone firm, not a franchise or part of a larger organization. The survey will be designed in two languages namely English and Malay.

Figure 3. Proposed conceptual model

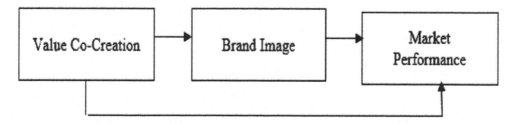

The instruments that will be utilized for this study are adapted from Ulaga and Eggert (2006) for value co creation, brand image from Keller (1993) and Homburg et al. (2010) for market performance. The data will be analysed using the Partial Least Squares (PLS) 3.0.

STUDY IMPLICATIONS

The primarily purpose of this study was to contribute to the body of knowledge in the importance of value co-creation for SMEs. This study also hopes sought to provide better understanding on the theoretical and practical understanding of the role of brand image in improving the market performance of SMEs which has been understudied especially in Malaysia. By conducting this research, we will be able to understand how crucial value co-creation and brand image are for SMEs. By engaging in value co-creation, firms will be able to understand the needs of consumers better as they will be able to communicate and share their preferences. Other than that, this study will also provide SMEs with the importance of value co-creation in new product development and advancement. The feedback and suggestions that are received from the consumers could help in enhancing the product's quality as well as its brand image. The improved product would be able to satisfy the consumers better and attract new ones too.

Brand image is crucial for firms especially SMEs. By establishing a strong brand image, firms will be able to penetrate their target market easily. Brand image is built by gaining the trust and loyalty of consumers which require lots of time and effort. In order to achieve this, firms have to put in consistent and continuous effort. Firms should also understand that consumer's brand image perception differs among individual. Therefore, providing a personalized and more variety of products would be able to cater the needs of the consumers.

Stakeholders are also an important actor in the value co-creation process. The inputs and ideas from these stakeholders would be useful for the firm in improving their business. Firms should utilize the expertise, knowledge as well as experiences of these stakeholders to flourish in their business. In the context of SMEs whereby resources are known to be limited, firms are able to use the stakeholders to their advantage. Some of the ways of collaborating includes joint recognition, training workshops and developing a positive relationship with suppliers.

Moreover, this study would be able to provide an interconnection between value co-creation, brand image and market performance which has been scarcely studied in the past. As all the actors in a SME collaborate, communicate and co-create, better products could be manufactured. These products which are good in functional and experiential factors would be able to attract more consumers. Therefore, a strong brand image has been formed. This strong brand image will further lead to consumer satisfaction, repurchase and loyalty. Consumers who are loyal will introduce these products to new consumers. This explains the importance of having a strong brand image. The successful brand will then lead to better sales, more revenue and profit.

FUTURE RESEARCH DIRECTIONS

This research reveals that various studies have been conducted on value co-creation, brand image and market performance. However, studies on value co-creation within SMEs remain scarce. SMEs particularly in Malaysia have not been investigated thoroughly by researchers. As a result, the current proposed research model is expected to further explore SMEs market performance. Future studies could be carried out by expanding the current model through adding relevant variables to better explain market performance. Furthermore, future study could re-examine the relationships among the constructs in the existing model in different contexts. Other than that, with the increasing popularity social media, further research could be carried out on the impact of social communities on SMEs market performance. A focused and systematic effort on this proposed framework can lead to a meaningful impact on the market performance of SMEs in Malaysia.

CONCLUSION

The objective of the book chapter was to review and propose a framework on the influence of value co-creation and brand image on market performance. The framework shown in Figure 3 gives an overview of the factors influencing market performance. The proposed framework is believed to help researchers to identify the role and importance of value co-creation on the market performance of SMEs. The authors propose that the practice of value co-creation is able to improve the image of the brand which consequently enhances the market performance of SMEs.

The study also proposes a framework that could be utilised further in future studies. As explained, value co-creation explains that customers and other actors in the value chain are given the priority in assisting the firm on its products and services. The authors suggest that communication and the strong bond between customers and the firm is important for the firm to better understand the needs and wants of the customers. By co-creating value, firms would be able to enhance their brand image and reputation. When the brand image is strong, it would lead towards more purchase, as well as increase in customer satisfaction. Customers' who are satisfied will continue purchasing the brand which will result in customer loyalty. This would further improve the firm's market performance.

SMEs need to be studied further to improve the knowledge that the market has on this industry. Understanding the SMEs is deemed important because of the increasing number of SMEs in Malaysia. These SMEs have the knowledge to implement the value co-creation. However, the problem that they face is in terms of the monetary support. Due to this, very few SMEs are involved in value co-creation activities. SMEs should expand their business into the value co-creation system in order to increase their market performance and sustain in the market. The government and financial institutions should provide the help needed for these SMEs to invest in value co-creation activities. By doing so, the SMEs would be able to compete with their competitors as well as larger firms.

REFERENCES

Aaker, D. (1991). *Managing brand equity*. New York: The Free Press.

Aaker, D. (1996). Measuring brand equity across products and markets. *California Management Review*, *38*(3), 102–120. doi:10.2307/41165845

Aaker, D. (2003). The power of the branded differentiator. *MIT Sloan Management Review*, *45*(1), 83.

Ahuja, G. (2000). Collaboration networks, structural holes, and innovation: A longitudinal study. *Administrative Science Quarterly, 45*(3), 425–455. doi:10.2307/2667105

Apéria, T., & Back, R. (2004). *Brand relations management: bridging the gap between brand promise and brand delivery*. Copenhagen Business School Pr.

Arnould, E. J., Price, L. L., & Malshe, A. (2006). Toward a cultural resource-based theory of the customer. In R. F. Lusch & S. L. Vargo (Eds.), The service-dominant logic of marketing: Dialog, debate and directions (pp. 320-333). M. E. Sharpe.

Ataman, B., & Ülengin, B. (2003). A note on the effect of brand image on sales. *Journal of Product and Brand Management, 12*(4), 237–250. doi:10.1108/10610420310485041

Badurdeen, F., & Liyanage, J. P. (2011). Sustainable value co-creation through mass customisation: A framework. *International Journal of Sustainable Manufacturing, 2*(2-3), 180–203. doi:10.1504/IJSM.2011.042151

Barrett, M., Davidson, E., Prabhu, J., & Vargo, S. L. (2015). Service innovation in the digital age: Key contributions and future directions. *Management Information Systems Quarterly, 39*(1), 135–154.

Bell, J., & Loane, S. (2010). 'New-waveglobal firms: Web 2.0 and SME internationalisation. *Journal of Marketing Management, 26*(3-4), 213–229. doi:10.1080/02672571003594648

Bengtsson, A., & Servais, P. (2005). Co-branding on industrial markets. *Industrial Marketing Management, 34*(7), 706–713. doi:10.1016/j.indmarman.2005.06.004

Beverland, M., Lindgreen, A., Napoli, J., Ballantyne, D., & Aitken, R. (2007). Branding in B2B markets: Insights from the service-dominant logic of marketing. *Journal of Business and Industrial Marketing, 22*(6), 363–371. doi:10.1108/08858620710780127

Bian, X., & Moutinho, L. (2011). The role of brand image, product involvement, and knowledge in explaining consumer purchase behaviour of counterfeits: Direct and indirect effects. *European Journal of Marketing, 45*(1/2), 191–216. doi:10.1108/03090561111095658

Brodie, R. J., Glynn, M. S., & Little, V. (2006). The service brand and the service-dominant logic: Missing fundamental premise or the need for stronger theory? *Marketing Theory, 6*(3), 363–379. doi:10.1177/1470593106066797

Chen, L., Marsden, J. R., & Zhang, Z. (2012). Theory and Analysis of Company-Sponsored Value Co-Creation. *Journal of Management Information Systems, 29*(2), 141–172. doi:10.2753/MIS0742-1222290206

Creswell, J., & Clark, V. (2011). *Designing and Conducting Mixed Methods Research* (2nd ed.). Sage Publications Inc.

Dennis, C., King, T., & Martenson, R. (2007). Corporate brand image, satisfaction and store loyalty: A study of the store as a brand, store brands and manufacturer brands. *International Journal of Retail & Distribution Management, 35*(7), 544–555. doi:10.1108/09590550710755921

Desouza, K. C., & Awazu, Y. (2006). Knowledge management at SMEs: Five peculiarities. *Journal of Knowledge Management*, *10*(1), 32–43. doi:10.1108/13673270610650085

Dobni, D., & Zinkhan, G. M. (1990). In search of brand image: A foundation analysis. *Advances in Consumer Research. Association for Consumer Research (U. S.)*, *17*, 110–119.

Esch, F.-R., Langner, T., Schmitt, B. H., & Geus, P. (2006). Are brands forever? How brand knowledge and relationships affect current and future purchases. *Journal of Product and Brand Management*, *15*(2), 98–105. doi:10.1108/10610420610658938

Evans, P., & Wolf, B. (2005). Collaboration rules. *IEEE Engineering Management Review*, *33*(4), 50–57. doi:10.1109/EMR.2005.27015 PMID:16028820

Gilmore, A., Carson, D., O'Donnell, A., & Cummins, D. (1999). Added value: A qualitative assessment of SME marketing. *Irish Marketing Review*, *12*(1), 27.

Grant, R. M., & Baden-Fuller, C. (2004). A knowledge accessing theory of strategic alliances. *Journal of Management Studies*, *41*(1), 61–84. doi:10.1111/j.1467-6486.2004.00421.x

Griffin, A., & Page, A. L. (1993). An interim report on measuring product development success and failure. *Journal of Product Innovation Management*, *10*(4), 291–308. doi:10.1016/0737-6782(93)90072-X

Grönroos, C. (2011). Value co-creation in service logic: A critical analysis. *Marketing Theory*, *11*(3), 279–301. doi:10.1177/1470593111408177

Håkansson, H., & Snehota, I. (2006). No business is an island: The network concept of business strategy. *Scandinavian Journal of Management*, *22*(3), 256–270. doi:10.1016/j.scaman.2006.10.005

Hatch, M. J., & Schultz, M. (2010). Toward a theory of brand co-creation with implications for brand governance1. *Journal of Brand Management*, *17*(8), 590–604. doi:10.1057/bm.2010.14

Holbrook, M. B. (1999). *Consumer value: a framework for analysis and research*. Routledge. doi:10.4324/9780203010679

Homburg, C., Klarmann, M., & Schmitt, J. (2010). Brand awareness in business markets: When is it related to firm performance? *International Journal of Research in Marketing*, *27*(3), 201–212. doi:10.1016/j.ijresmar.2010.03.004

Hoyer, W. D., Chandy, R., Dorotic, M., Krafft, M., & Singh, S. S. (2010). Consumer cocreation in new product development. *Journal of Service Research*, *13*(3), 283–296. doi:10.1177/1094670510375604

Hsieh, M.-H., Pan, S.-L., & Setiono, R. (2004). Product-, corporate-, and country-image dimensions and purchase behavior: A multicountry analysis. *Journal of the Academy of Marketing Science*, *32*(3), 251–270. doi:10.1177/0092070304264262

Huang, Z. J., & Cai, L. A. (2015). Modeling consumer-based brand equity for multinational hotel brands–When hosts become guests. *Tourism Management*, *46*, 431–443. doi:10.1016/j.tourman.2014.07.013

Ind, N., & Coates, N. (2013). The meanings of co-creation. *European Business Review*, *25*(1), 86–95. doi:10.1108/09555341311287754

Islam, M. A., Agarwal, N. K., & Ikeda, M. (2015). Conceptualizing value co-creation for service innovation in academic libraries. *Business Information Review*, *32*(1), 45–52. doi:10.1177/0266382115573155

Jalilvand, M. R., & Samiei, N. (2012). The effect of electronic word of mouth on brand image and purchase intention: An empirical study in the automobile industry in Iran. *Marketing Intelligence & Planning*, *30*(4), 460–476. doi:10.1108/02634501211231946

Juscius, V., & Jonikas, D. (2013). Integration of CSR into Value Creation Chain: Conceptual Framework. *The Engineering Economist*, *24*(1), 63–70.

Kapferer, J.-N. (2012). *The new strategic brand management: Advanced insights and strategic thinking* (5th ed.). Kogan Page.

Keller, K. L. (1993). Conceptualizing, measuring, and managing customer-based brand equity. *Journal of Marketing*, *57*(1), 1–22. doi:10.2307/1252054

Keller, K. L., & Lehmann, D. R. (2006). Brands and branding: Research findings and future priorities. *Marketing Science*, *25*(6), 740–759. doi:10.1287/mksc.1050.0153

Kim, E. Y., Knight, D. K., & Pelton, L. E. (2009). Modeling brand equity of a US apparel brand as perceived by Generation Y consumers in the emerging Korean market. *Clothing & Textiles Research Journal*, *27*(4), 247–258. doi:10.1177/0887302X08327085

Korkman, O., Storbacka, K., & Harald, B. (2010). Practices as markets: Value co-creation in e-invoicing. [AMJ]. *Australasian Marketing Journal*, *18*(4), 236–247. doi:10.1016/j.ausmj.2010.07.006

Kotler, P. (2001). *A framework for marketing management*. Upper Saddle River, NJ: Prentice-Hall.

Laukkanen, T., Nagy, G., Hirvonen, S., Reijonen, H., & Pasanen, M. (2013). The effect of strategic orientations on business performance in SMEs: A multigroup analysis comparing Hungary and Finland. *International Marketing Review*, *30*(6), 510–535. doi:10.1108/IMR-09-2011-0230

Leek, S., & Christodoulides, G. (2011). A literature review and future agenda for B2B branding: Challenges of branding in a B2B context. *Industrial Marketing Management*, *40*(6), 830–837. doi:10.1016/j.indmarman.2011.06.006

Lin, Y., Wang, Y., & Yu, C. (2010). Investigating the drivers of the innovation in channel integration and supply chain performance: A strategy orientated perspective. *International Journal of Production Economics*, *127*(2), 320–332. doi:10.1016/j.ijpe.2009.08.009

Low, G. S., & Lamb, J. C. W. Jr. (2000). The measurement and dimensionality of brand associations. *Journal of Product and Brand Management*, *9*(6), 350–370. doi:10.1108/10610420010356966

Lusch, R. F., & Harvey, M. G. (1994). Opinion: The Case for an Off-Balance-Sheet Controller. *Sloan Management Review*, *35*(2), 101.

Lusch, R. F., & Vargo, S. L. (2014). *The service-dominant logic of marketing: Dialog, debate, and directions*. New York: Routledge.

Mäläskä, M., Saraniemi, S., & Tähtinen, J. (2010). *Co-creation of Branding by Network Actors.* Paper presented at the 10th annual EBRF conference on Co-Creation as a Way Forward, Co-creation of Branding by Network Actors.

Malhotra, N. K., Peterson, M., & Kleiser, S. B. (1999). Marketing research: A state-of-the-art review and directions for the twenty-first century. *Journal of the Academy of Marketing Science, 27*(2), 160–183. doi:10.1177/0092070399272004

Merrilees, B. (2007). A theory of brand-led SME new venture development. *Qualitative Market Research: An International Journal, 10*(4), 403–415. doi:10.1108/13522750710819739

Merz, M. A., He, Y., & Vargo, S. L. (2009). The evolving brand logic: A service-dominant logic perspective. *Journal of the Academy of Marketing Science, 37*(3), 328–344. doi:10.1007/s11747-009-0143-3

Michel, G., & Rieunier, S. (2012). Nonprofit brand image and typicality influences on charitable giving. *Journal of Business Research, 65*(5), 701–707. doi:10.1016/j.jbusres.2011.04.002

Mokhtar, S. S. M., Yusoff, R. Z., & Ahmad, A. (2014). Key elements of market orientation on Malaysian SMEs performance. *International Journal of Business and Society, 15*(1), 49.

Möller, K. K., & Törrönen, P. (2003). Business suppliers value creation potential: A capability-based analysis. *Industrial Marketing Management, 32*(2), 109–118. doi:10.1016/S0019-8501(02)00225-0

Moore, K., Berger, P. D., & Weinberg, B. D. (2014). *Issues for Exploration of Differing Values among Sub-groups of Young-Adult Consumers* (Vol. 1). Global Journal of Business and Social Science.

Mudambi, S. (2002). Branding importance in business-to-business markets: Three buyer clusters. *Industrial Marketing Management, 31*(6), 525–533. doi:10.1016/S0019-8501(02)00184-0

Nandan, S. (2005). An exploration of the brand identity–brand image linkage: A communications perspective. *The Journal of Brand Management, 12*(4), 264–278. doi:10.1057/palgrave.bm.2540222

Ojasalo, J., Nätti, S., & Olkkonen, R. (2008). Brand building in software SMEs: An empirical study. *Journal of Product and Brand Management, 17*(2), 92–107. doi:10.1108/10610420810864702

Park, C. W., Jaworski, B. J., & MacInnis, D. J. (1986). Strategic brand concept-image management. *Journal of Marketing, 50*(4), 135–145. doi:10.2307/1251291

Payne, A., Storbacka, K., Frow, P., & Knox, S. (2009). Co-creating brands: Diagnosing and designing the relationship experience. *Journal of Business Research, 62*(3), 379–389. doi:10.1016/j.jbusres.2008.05.013

Payne, A. F., Storbacka, K., & Frow, P. (2008). Managing the co-creation of value. *Journal of the Academy of Marketing Science, 36*(1), 83–96. doi:10.1007/s11747-007-0070-0

Prahalad, C. K. (2004). The cocreation of value. *Journal of Marketing, 68*(1), 23.

Prahalad, C. K., & Ramaswamy, V. (2001). The value creation dilemma: New building blocks for co-creating experience. *Harvard Business Review, 18*(3), 5–14.

Prahalad, C. K., & Ramaswamy, V. (2004). Co-creation experiences: The next practice in value creation. *Journal of Interactive Marketing, 18*(3), 5–14. doi:10.1002/dir.20015

Prahalad, C. K., & Ramaswamy, V. (2013). *The future of competition: Co-creating unique value with customers*. Harvard Business Press.

Ramaswamy, V. (2009). Leading the transformation to co-creation of value. *Strategy and Leadership*, *37*(2), 32–37. doi:10.1108/10878570910941208

Ramaswamy, V., & Gouillart, F. J. (2010). *The Power of Co-Creation: Build It with Them to Boost Growth, Productivity, and Profits* (1st ed.). New York: Free Press.

Ritala, P. (2012). Coopetition strategy–when is it successful? Empirical evidence on innovation and market performance. *British Journal of Management*, *23*(3), 307–324.

Ritter, T., & Gemünden, H. G. (2003). Network competence: Its impact on innovation success and its antecedents. *Journal of Business Research*, *56*(9), 745–755. doi:10.1016/S0148-2963(01)00259-4

Rosley, F. (2015). Faster SME Growth. *The Star*. Retrieved from http://www.thestar.com.my/business/business-news/2015/10/19/faster-sme-growth/

Rundle-Thiele, S., Russell-Bennett, R., & Dann, S. (2005). The Successful Preperation and Development of Future Marketing Professionals: A Recommended Methodological Framework. *Journal for Advancement of Marketing Education*, *7*, 27–35.

Sánchez-Fernández, R., & Iniesta-Bonillo, M. Á. (2007). The concept of perceived value: A systematic review of the research. *Marketing Theory*, *7*(4), 427–451. doi:10.1177/1470593107083165

Sawhney, M., Verona, G., & Prandelli, E. (2005). Collaborating to create: The Internet as a platform for customer engagement in product innovation. *Journal of Interactive Marketing*, *19*(4), 4–17. doi:10.1002/dir.20046

Schmitt, B. (2012). The consumer psychology of brands. *Journal of Consumer Psychology*, *22*(1), 7–17. doi:10.1016/j.jcps.2011.09.005

Skaržauskaitė, M. (2013). Measuring and managing value co-creation process: overview of existing theoretical models. *Socialnės Technologijos,* (1), 115-129.

Smit, E., Bronner, F., & Tolboom, M. (2007). Brand relationship quality and its value for personal contact. *Journal of Business Research*, *60*(6), 627–633. doi:10.1016/j.jbusres.2006.06.012

Solomon, M. R., Bamossy, G., Askegaard, S., & Hogg, K. (2009). *Consumer Behaviour: A European Perspective* (4th ed.). Prentice Hall.

Spena, T. R., Caridà, A., Colurcio, M., & Melia, M. (2012). Store experience and co-creation: The case of temporary shop. *International Journal of Retail & Distribution Management*, *40*(1), 21–40. doi:10.1108/09590551211193586

Storbacka, K., Strandvik, T., & Grönroos, C. (1994). Managing customer relationships for profit: The dynamics of relationship quality. *International Journal of Service Industry Management*, *5*(5), 21–38. doi:10.1108/09564239410074358

Storey, C., & Easingwood, C. J. (1999). Types of new product performance: Evidence from the consumer financial services sector. *Journal of Business Research*, *46*(2), 193–203. doi:10.1016/S0148-2963(98)00022-8

Taghizadeh, S. K., Jayaraman, K., Ismail, I., & Rahman, S. A. (2016). Scale development and validation for DART model of value co-creation process on innovation strategy. *Journal of Business and Industrial Marketing, 31*(1), 24–35. doi:10.1108/JBIM-02-2014-0033

Tanev, S., Bailetti, T., Allen, S., Milyakov, H., Durchev, P., & Ruskov, P. (2011). How do value co-creation activities relate to the perception of firms' innovativeness? *Journal of Innovation Economics & Management,* (1), 131-159.

Tung, J. (2012). A study of product innovation on firm performance. *International Journal of Organizational Innovation (Online), 4*(3), 84.

Ulaga, W., & Eggert, A. (2006). Value-based differentiation in business relationships: Gaining and sustaining key supplier status. *Journal of Marketing, 70*(1), 119–136. doi:10.1509/jmkg.2006.70.1.119

Vargo, S. L., & Lusch, R. F. (2004). Evolving to a new dominant logic for marketing. *Journal of Marketing, 68*(1), 1–17. doi:10.1509/jmkg.68.1.1.24036

Vargo, S. L., & Lusch, R. F. (2008). Service-dominant logic: Continuing the evolution. *Journal of the Academy of Marketing Science, 36*(1), 1–10. doi:10.1007/s11747-007-0069-6

Vargo, S. L., Maglio, P. P., & Akaka, M. A. (2008). On value and value co-creation: A service systems and service logic perspective. *European Management Journal, 26*(3), 145–152. doi:10.1016/j.emj.2008.04.003

Vega-Vazquez, M., Ángeles Revilla-Camacho, M., & Cossío-Silva, J., F. (2013). The value co-creation process as a determinant of customer satisfaction. *Management Decision, 51*(10), 1945–1953. doi:10.1108/MD-04-2013-0227

Vukasovic, T. (2009). Searching for competitive advantage with the aid of the brand potential index. *Journal of Product and Brand Management, 18*(3), 165–176. doi:10.1108/10610420910957799

Webster, F. E., & Keller, K. L. (2004). A roadmap for branding in industrial markets. *The Journal of Brand Management, 11*(5), 388–402. doi:10.1057/palgrave.bm.2540184

Wong, H. Y., & Merrilees, B. (2005). A brand orientation typology for SMEs: A case research approach. *Journal of Product and Brand Management, 14*(3), 155–162. doi:10.1108/10610420510601021

Wong, H. Y., & Merrilees, B. (2008). The performance benefits of being brand-orientated. *Journal of Product and Brand Management, 17*(6), 372–383. doi:10.1108/10610420810904112

Woodruff, R. B., & Flint, D. J. (2006). Marketing's service-dominant logic and customer value. In R. F. Lusch & S. L. Vargo (Eds.), *The service-dominant logic of marketing: Dialog, debate, and directions* (pp. 183–195). New York: Taylor and Francis.

Zins, A. H. (2001). Relative attitudes and commitment in customer loyalty models: Some experiences in the commercial airline industry. *International Journal of Service Industry Management, 12*(3), 269–294. doi:10.1108/EUM0000000005521

Zwass, V. (2010). Co-creation: Toward a taxonomy and an integrated research perspective. *International Journal of Electronic Commerce, 15*(1), 11–48. doi:10.2753/JEC1086-4415150101

KEY TERMS AND DEFINITIONS

Brand Image: The perception of consumers on a particular brand based on the characteristics of the brand itself and the consumer's experience.

Goods-Dominant Logic: An approach whereby the process chain activities are solely planned by the firm.

Market Performance: The performance of a firm which can be measured through sales revenue, market share, profitability, competitive advantage, customer satisfaction and loyalty.

Service-Dominant Logic: An approach which focuses on the customer's involvement and communication with the firm in the process chain activities.

Small-Medium-Enterprise (SME): A stand-alone firm which has lesser than 150 employees.

Value Co-Creation: The value which results from the collaboration of all stakeholders and the firm.

Value-In-Exchange: Value that is gained from the trade-off between cost and benefits of a product/ service.

Value-In-Use: Value that consumers perceive to obtain from consumption of a product or service.

This research was previously published in the Handbook of Research on Small and Medium Enterprises in Developing Countries edited by Noor Hazlina Ahmad, T. Ramayah, Hasliza Abdul Halim, and Syed Abidur Rahman, pages 185-207, copyright year 2017 by Business Science Reference (an imprint of IGI Global).

Chapter 18
Co–Creating Brand Value Through Social Commerce

Yichuan Wang
Auburn University, USA

Nick Hajli
Newcastle University, UK

ABSTRACT

This chapter looks at the opportunities of social commerce for branding. The chapter examines social commerce constructs and their impact on brand development. The results of this empirical study show that both social factors and social commerce constructs have positive effects on co-creating brand value intention. This study also highlights the moderating effect of privacy concern between social commerce constructs and co-creating brand value. Contribution of this chapter is the combination of social media, social commerce, and social support in branding strategies, which produce co-creating brand value strategies. The chapter also provides practical implications for the market to develop co-creating brand value strategies through social commerce.

INTRODUCTION

In the social media era, consumers have empowered to exert an influence on brands through various social media platforms, such as social networking sites (SNSs) and online forums. Recent estimates from a report show that on SNSs such as Facebook, clicking on the "like" button by a user is worth $174.17 for a brand page - a 28 percent increase since 2010 (Scissons, Kalehoff, & Laufer, 2013). This implies that a significant brand value is facilitated by online consumers' tendencies (Naylor, Lamberton, & West, 2012). Social commerce, the powerful combination of customer-oriented social computing technologies and the rising social networking effect in an online environment, has been portrayed as a means of managing a brand (Gensler, Volckner, Liu-Thompkins, & Wiertz, 2013; Yadav, de Valck, Hennig-Thurau, Hoffman, & Spann, 2013). Social commerce creates an environment where consumers are turned into brand ambassadors by leveraging a series of collective, co-creational processes with other consumers in a virtual manner (Holt, 2003; Cayla & Arnould, 2008). Such an environment might have the potential to

DOI: 10.4018/978-1-5225-5187-4.ch018

not only influence consumers' intentions and behavior to adopt a brand through social interactions and relationships but also increase companies' sales growth and brand values (Gensler et al., 2013; Pentina, Gammoh, Zhang, & Mallin, 2013).

Although the existing branding literature is abundant in the field of marketing management, understanding whether brands can co-create with consumers through social commerce remains a research question that still requires attention. Previous studies considering the context of social commerce have found that a lack of social capital is the predominant reason why online customers hesitate to make decisions to purchase products (Liang, Ho, Li, & Turban, 2011). Some researchers have denoted to study whether social capital factors will affect customers' intentions to co-creation in branding (Hajli, 2015; Hajli et al., 2014; Kim & Park, 2013; Liang et al., 2011). Nevertheless, this path of effects has not been studied explicitly in the literature. Thus, drawing on social support theory and relationship marketing theory, the first purpose of this study is to examine the inter-relationships among relationship quality and social support on co-creating brand value intentions in the social commerce environment.

Social commerce constructs such as forums and communities, ratings and reviews, and referrals and recommendations are important elements for these social capital factors (Hajli, 2015). With the constructs of social commerce serving as a construct, it not only increases the understanding of social commerce constructs per se and its impact on members' intention but also differentiates social commerce from other online business environments (Hajli, 2013; Kim & Park, 2013). Thus, there is a need to empirically examine the impacts of these social commerce constructs (Ba & Pavlou, 2002; Hajli, 2013; Hajli, Lin, Featherman, & Wang, 2014). In this regard, the second purpose of this study is to treat the social commerce constructs as an antecedent variable, which is causally related to the effect of relationship quality and social support, which in turn, the intention to co-creation in branding.

Privacy is a mounting concern as the amounts of voluntary disclosure of personal information become available in SNSs (Yadav & Pavlou, 2014). Prior research has generally explored the effects of privacy concerns being treated as an independent variable directly to affect the intention-related constructs and behavioral reactions, especially to individuals' acceptance of social networking services and their intentions to purchase online (Shin, 2010). Additionally, Smith, Dinev, & Xu (2011) suggest that privacy concern is a context-sensitive factor that should take into account the impacts of particular contexts. This is of special importance for social commerce, given the very nature of social network that expects and encourages information disclosure. Based on the above, the third purpose of this study is to examine the relationship between social commerce contrasts and co-creating brand value moderated by privacy concern.

To this end, this raises to our research questions: *firstly whether consumers' intention to co-create brand value can be facilitated by increasing social support and relationship quality in social commerce environment and second whether privacy concerns moderates the relationship between social commerce constructs and co-creating brand value intention.* To address this, our theoretical framework is grounded in social support theory, relationship marketing theory, and the influences of social commerce characteristics, privacy concern. The next section reviews the existing literature and develops the theoretical model and associated hypotheses for this research. Sections 3 and 4 describe the research methodology and present the results of our analysis. Finally, Section 5 discusses the contributions of this study and implications for management scholars and practitioners.

Conceptual Framework

To understand the complexity of brand management in the social commerce era, we theoretically anchor our work in social support theory and relationship marketing theory. We argue that social commerce constructs will affect community members' perceptions, which may increase their social supports from other members and perceive relationship quality toward platforms by interactions with other members. In this regards, by using social commerce platforms, members are willing to co-create a brand with others by sharing their information and providing voluntary supports to others and trust other members' behaviors.

We propose an adapted social commerce conceptual model as shown in Figure 1. This model empirically examines the relationship among social commerce constructs, relationship quality, social support, and co-creating in branding intention, and also proposes to test the moderating role of privacy concerns. Our research model can be theorized as follows. With the use social commerce platforms and communications, when consumers in a brand page of SNSs perceive emotional and informational support, it would be natural for them to trust other members, to satisfy their needs and to make commitment to this page. This, in turn, constructs a strong brand by obtaining these co-creating values. However, the relationship between social commerce constructs and consumers' intention to co-creating in branding will moderate by their privacy concerns. We describe each of them and explain the linkage among the constructs in detail next.

Social Commerce Constructs

Social commerce is defined as a new type of e-commerce which uses of Web 2.0 and social technologies to support consumers' interactions in which they acquire the services and products in an online context (Liang & Turban, 2011). Social commerce can be viewed as the delivery of e-commerce via social media (Liang et al., 2011). Consumers enabled by social media are distinct from e-commerce contexts,

Figure 1. Research model

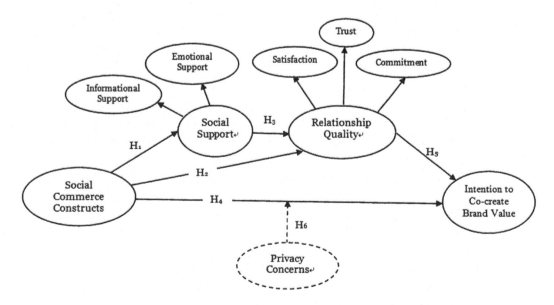

because they can have social interactions with other individuals by social technologies (Park, Lee, & Han, 2007). For example, social media technologies such as really simple syndication (RSS), asynchronous JavaScript and XML (AJAX), or application program interface (APIs) provide online members an interactive system which allows them to make connections with platforms and other. This, in turn, has not only sociability and relationships with e-vendor and other consumers but also social communication on group-purchasing platforms (Pelaez, Yu, & Lang, 2013).

Previous studies related to social commerce research has been focused on the adoption of social commerce (e.g., Madhavaram & Appan, 2010; Zhou, Zhang, & Zimmermann, 2013), and consumer behavior in the context of social commerce (e.g., Shin, 2013; Ng, 2013). However, the constructs of social commerce are noticeably absent from these articles. Only Kim & Park's (2013) study has demonstrated the effects of various constructs of social commerce, such as reputation, size, and information quality on consumer trust toward social commerce and trust performance. In this study, the social commerce constructs we used are related to social platforms and social communication channels, which are forums and communities, ratings and reviews, and referrals and recommendations (Hajli, 2013; Hajli, 2014; Pelaez et al., 2013). Companies use these constructs to communicate with customers and to enable customers to communicate with each other, which is a new channel to accomplish customer relationship management.

Forums and communities, social platforms where allows customers to take part in group discussion and sharing information, are developed by online vendors. These platforms give consumers the opportunity to gain more product knowledge prior to their decision to buy. The other constructs, ratings and reviews, and referrals and recommendations, are associated with social communication. These communication channels provide customers to reassure each other through information exchange and experiences, thereby increasing their confidence and consequent willingness to purchase (Han & Windsor, 2011). For example, SNSs community members can access to browse friends' product reviews and recommendations in a brand page, where there is an emotional aspect that adds a personal touch to the decision-making process of buying (Hajli, 2013). Thus, each of the three methods captures a unique set of constructs but all together reflects the more complete picture of social commerce that impacts social capital factors.

Social Support

The concept of social support is derived from social support theory. Social support theory has been proposed to explain how social relationships influence the cognitions, emotions, and behaviors (Lakey & Cohen, 2000). This theory emphasizes that supportive behavior can contributes to health by protecting people from the adverse effects of stress and promoting self-esteem and self-regulation (Lakey & Cohen, 2000). Social support is defined as "the social resources that persons perceive to be available or that are actually provided to them by non-professionals in the context of both formal support groups and informal helping relationships" (Gottlieb & Bergen, 2010). Social support has been thoroughly investigated in psychology, sociology and health studies. Social support can be regarded as the measures how an individual experiences the feeling of being cared for, responded to and facilitated by people in their social groups (Cobb 1976; House, 1981). The social supportive resources can be emotional and informational. From social commerce perspective, emotional support is defined as "providing messages that involve emotional concerns such as caring, understanding, or empathy" (Liang et al., 2011). Informational support refers to "providing messages, in the form of recommendations, advice, or knowledge that could be helpful for solving problems" (Liang et al., 2011).

Based on the social support theory, these sources of social support are fundamental elements to form a social relationship network by interactions in social commerce community. This theory stresses that the effects of social support cannot be separated from relationship processes that often co-occur with support (Lakey & Cohen, 2000, p. 29). Similar, the formation of social support mechanisms must be linked with interpersonal process and constructs (Lakey & Cohen, 2000). Following this logic, we theoretically tie two theories (i.e., social support and relationship marketing theories) together and examine the impact of social support on relationship quality.

Relationship Quality

Relationship marketing theory has showed the effects of network and cooperation with customers by elaborating the roles of commitment and trust (Morgan & Hunt, 1994). The central theme of this theory is a focus on relationship quality dimensions that comprise trust, commitment, and satisfaction (Garbarino & Johnson, 1999; Palmatier, Dant, Grewal, & Evans, 2006). Relationship quality is defined as the intensity and tightness of a relationship, which plays a pivotal role in influencing customer loyalty (Palmatier et al., 2006). Relationship quality is included with three constructs: trust, satisfaction, and commitment (Garbarino & Johnson, 1999; Palmatier et al., 2006). Trust is defined as "a willingness to rely on an exchange partner in word-of-mouth that has confidence (Moorman, Deshpande, & Zaltman, 1993, p. 82)." Commitment is defined as a desire to maintain a relationship (Moorman et al., 1993; Morgan & Hunt, 1994). Satisfaction refers to a customer's overall emotional evaluation of the performance of a service/product provider (Gustafsson, Johnson, & Roos, 2005). Liang et al. (2011) has applied relationship perspective as a lens to elucidate the role of relationship quality in the social media context and study their impacts toward online consumers' purchasing intentions. Thus, relationship quality can be a predictor of social commerce community member intention to co-creating in branding.

Intention to Co-Create Brand Value

The notion of co-creating brand value is stemmed from Vargo & Lush (2004). Vargo & Lush (2004), arguing that the value can be facilitated by a co-creation process where the customers are turned into an active player. Recently, Cayla & Arnould (2008) suggest that the construction of brands is through reaching the collective consensus on a brand's meaning among the members of social brand communities. These members share their brand experiences (e.g., using experience) collectively and deliver the sensory, emotional, cognitive, behavioral and relational value to others, which is a process of co-creating value (Schmitt, 2003). Based on these earlier works, we defined co-create brand value as the intention to co-create the value of the brand and co-construct unique branding experiences through the exchange of information and knowledge with other customers (Prahalad & Ramaswamy, 2004; Vargo & Lusch, 2004). Recently, Gensler et al. (2013) stress that once online consumers have intentions to co-brand, they are willing to devote their time and effort to providing the shopping experiences and information about brands as well as encouraging others to purchase. Thus, in this study, co-creating in branding is a powerful outcome for assessing social commerce performance that can be accelerated by social commerce constructs and relationship quality.

Privacy Concern

Users disclose their personal information to online platforms when they register for an online forum as a member or request for more information from the website. Not surprisingly, online member are reluctant to engage in social activities when they feel insecurity about information privacy (Vijayasarathy, 2004). Privacy concerns in an online context refer to the users' subjective views of fairness toward information privacy (Malhotra, Kim, & Agarwal, 2004). Indeed, most users' privacy concerns are derived from social networking sites per se (Shin, 2010). For example, some SNSs may expose members' information to cooperative third-party communities that seek to offer a personalized and tailored online service. Such privacy concerns have resulted in online members' negative actions, such as being less willing to release personal information, reducing the intention to use online services, and in which the members do not trust others (Bélanger, Hiller, & Smith, 2002). Thus, we treat privacy concern as a moderator between social commerce constructs and co-creating in branding.

Hypotheses Development

The Effect of Social Commerce Constructs on Social Support

With the emergence of Web 2.0 and social relationships commanding a more prominent position in online technologies, social support has become of interest and relevance. For instance, Twitter is a good example in which members of communities regularly provide social support for others (Gruzd, Wellman, & Takhteyev, 2011). Such social interactions on SNS show that they have the ability to influence other members and to help each other (Gruzd et al., 2011). This is of special interest when it comes to customer recommendations, which are considered as a vital source of information for showing consumer supports toward online communities.

Through social commerce constructs, users are more likely to receive online social support. Online users have indicated that social support is one of the main reasons for joining online communities (Ridings & Gefen, 2004). The supports that people receive in online communities can be both informational and emotional support (Hajli, 2014; Riding & Gefen, 2004). Bagozzi & Dholakia (2002) indicate that members of online communities participate in different group activities and support other members through their social interactions and communications in the platform. They use social technologies, such as social media, online communities and other Web 2.0 applications, to support other members by their experience and information sharing (Hajli & Lin, 2014). Information, which is created by other consumers, is a new kind of word-of-mouth recommendation used in traditional markets (Park et al., 2007). This leads to the following hypothesis.

Hypothesis 1: The effect of social commerce constructs is positively associated with the user's social support in a social networking site.

The Effect of Social Commerce Constructs on Relationship Quality

In the context of social commerce, social technologies, such as the customer review mechanism in Amazon.com, offer opportunities to enhance social interactions among the website's users. Through this mechanism customers are willing to maintain a robust relationship with other consumers and e-venders, in order to obtain a wealth of information, thereby making their appropriate purchasing decisions. However, information related to the identity of reviewers has an effect on community members' perceptions (Chris, Anindya, & Batía, 2008). This issue has been raised as a result of fake ratings and reviews produced by third parties. Fake information will lead to customers' possessing an incorrect judgment about purchasing, resulting in lower commitment and satisfaction toward E-vendors. E-vendors have to consider whether to take actions to persuade reviewers to give more information about their identity (Chris et al., 2008), to assure consumers about the authenticity of ratings and reviews. Therefore, social commerce constructs can support businesses to establish trust, satisfaction, and commitment. Based on the above we propose that:

Hypothesis 2: The effect of social commerce constructs is positively associated with the user's relationship quality in a social networking site.

Users in a social commerce platform may believe that relationship quality can be guaranteed if they feel that people in online communities would provide substantial support to them (Liang et al., 2011). This implies that strong perceptions of social support in communities will influence users' behavior so that they may be willing to have more connections with others, thereby enhancing the relationship quality. Thus, this leads to the following hypothesis.

Hypothesis 3: The effect of social support is positively associated with the user's relationship quality in a social networking site.

The Effects of Social Commerce Constructs on Co-Creating Brand Value

Traditionally, companies engage the customers in the brand activities by strengthening their store image (Chien, Yu, Wang, & Kuo, 2014). When it comes to social commerce, however, from the standpoint of practitioners, there is a consensus that a brand development is inextricably linked with the power of social media. Such a power will help companies establish not only closer customer relationships, but also robust brand communities where customers are able to communicate with others and share their enthusiasm for the brands. According to Lithium Technologies Company's investigation, 74% of online consumers prefer to engage with the brand through social media after purchasing products, because they feel a sense of trust with the brand, like an insider with the brand, and have strong affection from the communities (CMO Council, 2011).

Previous research showed a clear consensus that the notion of co-creating brand values has been highlighted in the social commerce context (e.g., Gensler et al. 2013). For example, Gensler et al. (2013) provide an overview of managing brands in the social media environment. They indicate that the rise of social media strengthens the dynamic interactions within online communities that make it possible for consumers to communicate consumer-generated brand stories with others and to co-create brand's linking values, resulting in development of a successful brand in the marketplace. This implies that the construction of brands can be accelerated through repeated interactions with other consumers on the SNSs where they communicate the brand meanings and share the brand perceptions and experiences (Pentina et al., 2013; Vargo & Lusch, 2004). Based on this literature, co-creating brand value intention was selected as the outcome variable to evaluate the effects of social commerce constructs in our research model. This leads to the following hypothesis.

Hypothesis 4: Social commerce constructs are positively associated with the user's intention to co-create brand value in a social networking site.

The Effect of Relationship Quality on Co-Creating Brand Value

Research on relationship perspective has focused on the formation of actual partnerships between customers and service providers in the real world. It is also certain that an active relationship with high quality would raise the likelihood of positive customer interactions and foster the formation of brand loyalty (Fournier, 1998). For example, Fournier (1998) developed a model of relationship quality in the context of consumer product, showing that relationship stability can be facilitated by a robust relationship quality with customers. He also empathized that consumers with high levels of commitment are most likely to dedicate to a brand that fosters relationship stability with a brand.

However, with the technology advancement in social commerce, interactive relationships in online communities become anonymous, impersonal, and automated (Wang & Emurian, 2005). People are willing to participate in forums and communities, share their experiences and knowledge, and leave their advices and recommendations for other members as they perceive strongly the feelings of trust, satisfaction, and commitment in this community (Hajli, 2014). Pentina et al. (2013) demonstrate the effect of brand relationship quality in the social media context based on brand-related marketing theories. Their findings reveal the role of brand relationship quality in enhancing the likelihood of consumer recommendation to others and the intentions to continue using the SNSs and brands. It could be argued that, a successful business model based on social commerce should take serious consideration on how to boost relationship quality to encourage online consumers to co-create in community branding. This leads to the following hypothesis.

Hypothesis 5: Relationship quality is positively associated with the user's intention to co-create brand value in a social networking site.

The Moderating Role of Privacy Concerns

Prior research has indicated that SNSs are plagued by rising users' privacy concerns. For example, Shin (2010) developed a framework model of SNS acceptance. Shin's results confirmed a significant effect of perceived privacy on online users' trust, attitude, in turn, impacting on their intention. Cha (2011) considered privacy concerns as a dimension underlying perceived characteristics of online shopping. Surprisingly, their results showed that the effects of privacy concerns did not influence their intentions to purchase. Based on this literature, the effects of privacy concerns as an independent variable that directly affect the intention-related constructs and behavioral reactions has been explored. It worths noting that Bélanger & Crossler (2011) and Smith et al. (2011) have highlighted the privacy paradox, which describes that individuals' intentions are inconsistent with their behavior reactions as they face the privacy issue. This implies that individuals may be concerned about their privacy being encroached upon, but their actual behavior may not represent thoroughly (Bélanger & Crossler, 2011). A potential reason is that privacy decision processes are influenced by bounded rationality (Acquisti & Grossklags, 2005), which means that individuals' protection intention and behavior is depended on the different extent and intensity of their privacy concern. We propose that the privacy concern may be a moderator in the relationship between social commerce constructs and intentions to co-creating brand value. This leads to the following hypothesis.

Hypothesis 6: The relationship between social commerce constructs and co-creating brand value intention is moderated is by user's privacy concerns in a social networking site.

Research Methodology

Sample Frame and Data Collection

This study employed a survey to collect primary data from the social networking sites in United States. The sample population for this study is the online users who have involved in at least one social networking site. Data was collected by an electronic questionnaire in January, 2014 (One month period). A pilot study with 10 students and 5 MIS researchers was used to make sure the questions and wordings and clearly understand by respondents. This pilot exercise was to debug the instrument (Bell, 2010).

Potential participants were identified from band pages of social networking sites for this survey. The design of online-based survey is flexible and can be beneficial in terms of the cost and time. The questionnaire, which was sent by email, requested people to participate in the survey. We selected our samples from brand pages on Facebook. Finally, we received 207 useable responses. From 1000 invitation we received 230, indicating 23% respond rate.

Of the respondents of e-survey, 52.2% were male and 46.4% were female (with 3 missing value); 67.1% were White, 12.3% were Black or African American, and 20.6% were Asian (with 3 missing value); 4.9% received a Graduate level degree, 85.4% received a Bachelor degree, and 9.7% were enrolled in college or less. The age range of the sample was predominately above 30 (94.3%), with less subjects who were under 30 (2.4%) (3.3 were missing).

Measurement Development

All items (see the Appendix) are adapted from literature and modified as needed for this study. All items used a seven-point Likert scale (ranging from 1="strongly disagree" to 7="strongly agree"). This detailed description has been cut off due to the word limits.

Results

We will look at reliability and validity of our research first and then we will discuss structural model using PLS analysis.

Reliability and Validity

Using SEM-PLS enables us to look at the reliability through composite reliability (CR) as shown in Table 1. CR measures internal consistency scores (Gefen, Rigdon, & Straub, 2011; Hair, Black, Babin, & Anderson, 2010), which in our research along with Cronbach's alpha exceed 0.70, as a good test for reliability (Nunnally & Bernstein, 1994).

Table 1. Quality criteria and square of correlation between latent variables

Constructs	AVE	CR	CB	RC	SE	SI	PC	RQ	RS	SCC	SS	RT
CB	.83	.94	.92									
RC	.83	.94	.17	.92								
SE	.73	.89	.07	.07	.86							
SI	.82	.93	.10	.06	.06	.92						
PC	.56	.82	-.06	-.00	-.06	-.06	.75					
RQ	.54	.91	.18	.86	.06	.11	-.05	.74				
RS	.81	.93	.15	.53	.02	.09	-.09	.81	.89			
SSC	.57	.78	.03	.10	.08	.10	.10	.14	.12	.76		
SS	.56	.80	.12	.08	.53	.88	-.08	.12	.08	.12	.75	
RT	.74	.90	.19	.56	.06	.13	-.03	.81	.48	.12	.14	.87

Legend: CR: composite reliability; CB: intention to co-create brand value; RC: commitment; SE: emotional support; SI: informational support; PC: privacy concern; RQ: relationship quality; RS: satisfaction; SCC: social commerce constructs; RT: trust; SS: social support. (N=207; Cronbach's alpha on diagonal)

Investigating on convergent validity by measuring discriminant validity and divergent validity is the second step of the test of validity and reliability of our results. First we report average variance extracted (AVE), shown on Table 1. To have achieve convergent validity, AVE need to be more than 0.50 (Kline, 2010). Table 1 also shows that this research has convergent validity by having value of more than 0.50 for each constructs. The next step was to look at discriminant validity. We compare and report the square of the correlations among research latent variables with the AVE in Table 1. This assessment is reported by other researchers (Chin, 1998). An alternative approach to test both convergent validity and discriminant validity is the examination of factor loading. Each indicator should have a factor loading greater than on any other factor. We report factor loadings as it is shown in the Appendix there is no cross loading among constructs.

Structural Model

Using Smart-PLS software to analyze our model, we found all paths of to be positive at the standard level of 0.05. First we look at R^2s. Model fits or R^2s accounts for 36%, 31%, and 35% of the variance in co-creating brand value intention, relationship quality, and social support. R^2s showed an acceptable level of explanation as model fits are in a good level, indicating that co-creating brand value was affected by relationship quality and social commerce constructs. In addition, the results suggested that social support was affected by social commerce constructs.

We also examined the path coefficients as shown in Figure 2 to report the relationship among constructs of our model. Overall, all our proposed hypotheses are supported. According to the results, both relationship quality (0.404) and social commerce constructs (0.302) have positive effects on co-creating brand value intention. However, the effect of relation quality is stronger. Social commerce constructs and social support positively affect relationship quality (0.208 v.s. 0.302) highlighting the stronger effect of social support on relationship quality. Social commerce constructs also positively affect social support (0.209) and its most influence is on co-creating brand value intention (0.309 v.s. 0.209 and 0.208). Fi-

Figure 2. Results of the PLS Analysis

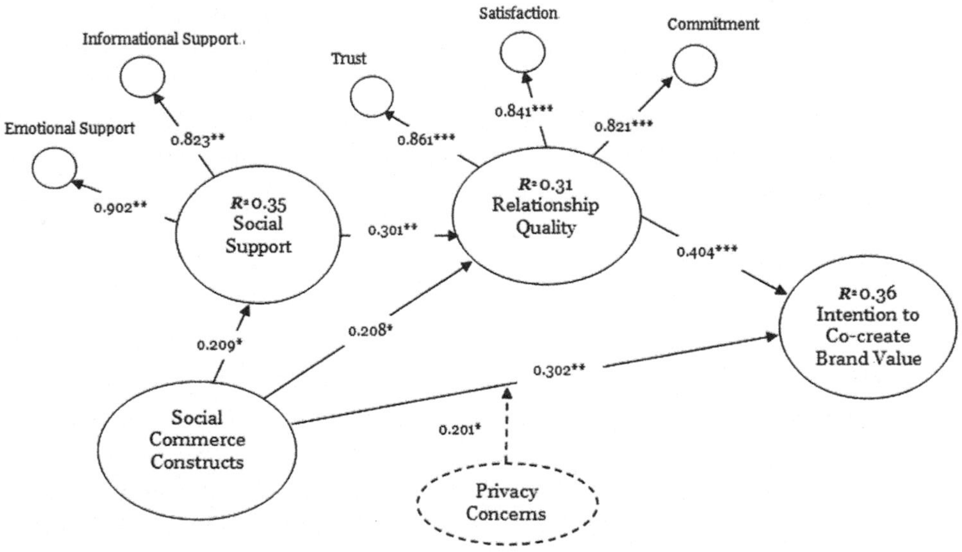

* Path coefficient <.05; ** path coefficient <.01; *** path coefficient <.001.

nally, this research confirms the moderating effect of privacy concern (0.201) between social commerce constructs and co-creating brand value.

Discussion

The central theme of our research is to advance the marketing and brand management literature by understanding how social commerce Constructs enable online communities to have better co-creative customer values through the perspectives of social support, relationship quality, and privacy concerns. The argument is that in social commerce era businesses have the opportunity of co-creation of value with customers instead of co-creation of value for customers. Co-creation in brand development is an example of that. As such this research proposed a research framework using social support theory from social-psychology, relationship marketing from marketing field, and social commerce constructs from information systems stream to investigate on a new concept of co-creating in branding. The empirical evidence supports our three key findings. First, we found that the impacts of social commerce Constructs positively affect social support, relationship quality, and co-creating brand value intention. This finding highlights the role of social media in attracting consumers to social commerce constructs and facilitating their social interaction with their peers to co-create value. This value can develop social support and relationship marketing. Developing a supportive environment creates value for the businesses and co-creating brand value is one of these values.

Second, data indicated that social support positively correlates with relationship quality, in turn, co-creating brand value intention. The results is highlighting social interaction of consumers in social networking sites produce informational support and emotional support. This supportive environment developed by sharing of information, knowledge, and experiences among consumers. This is very helpful, particularly for firms launching a new product and brand and need to "put customers at work" to develop their new brand.

Finally, it showed that social commerce constructs indirectly influence co-creating brand value intention, an impact that is moderated by the effects of privacy concerns. This part of our results shows that privacy is a challenging issue in social networking sites and working on trust-building plans can help the businesses to develop a new brand. The findings particularly contribute to a growing interest of both academics and managers to understand a facilitator of successful social commerce. Based on these findings, we offer some insights regarding theoretical and managerial implications in the remainder of this section.

Theoretical and Managerial Implications

Brand in social commerce community is the newest brand research area in the fields of information system and marketing. Studies in these domains are scarce in interpreting the formation of brand community in SNSs. Developing social commerce literature and extending typology of social commerce is theoretical contribution of present research. By integrating theories from social-psychology, information systems and marketing to increase an understanding of social commerce, this study has provided the insights in the field of social commerce. This also can be a theoretical foundation for this track. The study developed a new theory by borrowing social support theory and relationship marketing theory, proposing a new model given the new concepts in social commerce. This research borrowed constructs from information technology tools of social commerce, which show that information systems is a reference discipline for predicting consumer behavior in an online context.

Moreover, social support theory shows that information systems need to investigate other theories from different disciplines such as sociology or psychology as the social relationships of people and their interconnectivity are forcing changes in many business plans. The results bring together theories in IS, sociology and marketing for customer behavior studies. The research also introduces social commerce constructs for the first time and discusses how these constructs can influence trust and intention to buy in a social commerce environment. SCCs have been explained by the social support theory and how social support theory can be applied to studies of online behavior.

This research also has some practical implications. Using social media and social commerce constructs can be a practical tool for marketing management to develop a new brand. Co-creation of value with consumers instead of co-creation of value for customers through social commerce constructs is a unique strategy of developing a new brand by this paper. Therefore, marketing managers can think about the opportunities that social interaction of consumers may offer to businesses to develop a new brand.

CONCLUSION

Our primary research objective was to unravel the relationships among social commerce constructs, social support, relationship quality, and co-creating brand value intention. We indicated that social commerce might reveal windows of opportunities for creating brand values with customers. Co-creating brand value through social commerce is a new opportunity for businesses to develop a new brand. This study also shows that privacy concerns play an important moderating role in the relationship between social commerce constructs and co-creating brand value intention. These findings challenge researchers and managers to rethink how and why social commerce affect consumers' intention to co-create in branding through the lens of social support and relationship quality. Consequently, the contributions of this study provide new insights into marketing and brand management literature by proposing an initial model of social commerce.

REFERENCES

Acquisti, A., & Grossklags, J. (2005). Privacy and rationality in individual decision making. *IEEE Security and Privacy*, *3*(1), 26–33. doi:10.1109/MSP.2005.22

Ba, S., & Pavlou, P. A. (2002). Evidence of the effect of trust building technology in electronic markets: Price premiums and buyer behavior. *Management Information Systems Quarterly*, *26*(3), 243–268. doi:10.2307/4132332

Bagozzi, R. P., & Dholakia, U. M. (2002). Intentional social action in virtual communities. *Journal of Interactive Marketing*, *16*(2), 2–21. doi:10.1002/dir.10006

Bélanger, F., & Crossler, R. E. (2011). Privacy in the digital age: A review of information privacy research in information systems. *Management Information Systems Quarterly*, *35*(4), 1017–1041.

Bélanger, F., Hiller, J., & Smith, W. J. (2002). Trustworthiness in electronic commerce: The role of privacy, security, and site attributes. *The Journal of Strategic Information Systems*, *11*(3/4), 245–270. doi:10.1016/S0963-8687(02)00018-5

Bell, J. (2010). *Doing your research project*. New York, NY: McGraw-Hill International.

Cayla, J., & Arnould, E. J. (2008). A cultural approach to branding in the global marketplace. *Journal of Interactive Marketing*, *16*(4), 88–114.

Cha, J. (2011). Exploring the Internet as a unique shopping channel to sell both real and virtual items: A comparison of factors affecting purchase intention and consumer characteristics. *Journal of Electronic Commerce Research*, *12*(2), 115–132.

Chien, S., Yu, C., Wang, Y., & Kuo, P. L. (2014). Improving the quality perception of private brands using co-branding: The role of brand equity and store image. *International Journal of Management and Sustainability*, *3*(9), 540–551.

Chin, W. W. (1998). Commentary: Issues and opinion on structural equation modeling. *Management Information Systems Quarterly*, *22*(1), vii–xvi.

Chris, F., Anindya, G., & Batía, W. (2008). Examining the relationship between reviews and sales: The role of reviewer identity disclosure in electronic markets. *Information Systems Research*, *19*(3), 291–313. doi:10.1287/isre.1080.0193

Cobb, S. (1976). Social support as a moderator of life stress. *Psychosomatic Medicine*, *38*(5), 300–314. doi:10.1097/00006842-197609000-00003 PMID:981490

Council, C. M. O. (2011). *Variance in social brand experience*. CMO Council.

Fournier, S. (1998). Consumers and their brands: Developing relationship theory in consumer research. *The Journal of Consumer Research*, *24*(4), 343–373. doi:10.1086/209515

Garbarino, E., & Johnson, M. S. (1999). The different roles of satisfaction, trust, and commitment in customer relationships. *Journal of Marketing*, *63*(2), 70–87. doi:10.2307/1251946

Gefen, D., Rigdon, E. E., & Straub, D. (2011). An update and extension to SEM guidelines for administrative and social science research. *Management Information Systems Quarterly*, *35*(2), iii–xiv.

Gensler, S., Volckner, F., Liu-Thompkins, Y., & Wiertz, C. (2013). Managing brands in the social media environment. *Journal of Interactive Marketing*, *27*(4), 242–256. doi:10.1016/j.intmar.2013.09.004

Gottlieb, B. H., & Bergen, A. E. (2010). Social support concepts and measures. *Journal of Psychosomatic Research*, *69*(5), 511–520. doi:10.1016/j.jpsychores.2009.10.001 PMID:20955871

Gruzd, A., Wellman, B., & Takhteyev, Y. (2011). Imagining Twitter as an imagined community. *The American Behavioral Scientist*, *55*(10), 1294–1318. doi:10.1177/0002764211409378

Gustafsson, A., Johnson, M. D., & Roos, I. (2005). The efects of customer satisfaction, relationship commitment dimensions, and triggers on customer retention. *Journal of Marketing*, *69*(4), 210–218. doi:10.1509/jmkg.2005.69.4.210

Hair, J. Jr, Black, W., Babin, B., & Anderson, R. (2010). *Multivariate data analysis: with readings* (7th ed.). Upper Saddle River, NJ: Pearson Education Inc.

Hajli, M.M., Shanmugam, M., Hajli, A., Khani, A.H., & Wang, Y. (2014). Health care development: integrating transaction cost theory with social support theory. *Informatics for Health and Social Care*. doi:10.3109/17538157.2014.924950

Hajli, M. N. (2013). A research framework for social commerce adoption. *Information Management & Computer Security*, *21*(3), 144–154. doi:10.1108/IMCS-04-2012-0024

Hajli, M. N. (2014). The role of social support on relationship quality and social commerce. *Technological Forecasting and Social Change*, *87*, 17–27. doi:10.1016/j.techfore.2014.05.012

Hajli, M. N., & Lin, X. (2014). Developing tourism education through social media. *Tourism Planning & Development*, *11*(4), 405–414. doi:10.1080/21568316.2014.883426

Hajli, N. (2015). Social commerce constructs and consumer's intention to buy. *International Journal of Information Management*, *35*(2), 183–191. doi:10.1016/j.ijinfomgt.2014.12.005

Hajli, N., Lin, X., Featherman, M. S., & Wang, Y. (2014). Social word of mouth: How trust develops in the market. *International Journal of Market Research*, *56*(5), 673–689. doi:10.2501/IJMR-2014-045

Han, B. O., & Windsor, J. (2011). User's willingness to pay on social network sites. *Journal of Computer Information Systems*, *51*(4), 31–40.

Holt, D. B. (2003). *Brands and branding*. Boston, MA: Harvard Business School Publishing.

House, J. S. (1981). *Work stress and social support*. Reading, MA: Addison-Wesley.

Kim, S., & Park, H. (2013). Effects of various characteristics of social commerce (S-Commerce) on consumers' trust and trust performance. *International Journal of Information Management, 33*(2), 318–332. doi:10.1016/j.ijinfomgt.2012.11.006

Kline, R. B. (2010). *Principles and practice of structural equation modeling* (3rd ed.). New York: The Guilford Press.

Lakey, B., & Cohen, S. (2000). Social support theory and measurement. In S. Cohen, L. Underwood, & B. Gottlieb (Eds.), *Measuring and intervening in social support*. New York: Oxford University Press.

Liang, T. P., Ho, Y. T., Li, Y. W., & Turban, E. (2011). What drives social commerce: The role of social support and relationship quality. *International Journal of Electronic Commerce, 16*(2), 69–90. doi:10.2753/JEC1086-4415160204

Liang, T. P., & Turban, E. (2011). Introduction to the special issue social commerce: A research framework for social commerce. *International Journal of Electronic Commerce, 16*(2), 5–14. doi:10.2753/JEC1086-4415160201

Madhavaram, S., & Appan, R. (2010). Potential implications of web-based marketing communications for consumers implicit and explicit brand attitudes: A call for research. *Psychology and Marketing, 27*(2), 186–202. doi:10.1002/mar.20326

Malhotra, N. K., Kim, S. S., & Agarwal, J. (2004). Internet users' information privacy concerns (IUIPC): The construct, the scale, and a causal model. *Information Systems Research, 15*(4), 336–355. doi:10.1287/isre.1040.0032

Moorman, C., Deshpande, R., & Zaltman, G. (1993). Factors affecting trust in market relationships. *Journal of Marketing, 57*(1), 81–101. doi:10.2307/1252059

Morgan, R. M., & Hunt, S. D. (1994). The commitment-trust theory of relationship marketing. *Journal of Marketing, 58*(3), 20–38. doi:10.2307/1252308

Naylor, R. W., Lamberton, C. P., & West, P. M. (2012). Beyond the "Like" button: The impact of mere virtual presence on brand evaluations and purchase intentions in social media settings. *Journal of Marketing, 76*(6), 105–120. doi:10.1509/jm.11.0105

Ng, C. S. P. (2013). Intention to purchase on social commerce websites across cultures: A cross-regional study. *Information & Management, 50*(8), 609–620. doi:10.1016/j.im.2013.08.002

Nunnally, J. C., & Bernstein, I. H. (1994). *Psychometric theory*. New York, NY: McGraw-Hill.

Palmatier, R. W., Dant, R. P., Grewal, D., & Evans, K. R. (2006). Factors influencing the effectiveness of relationship marketing: A meta-analysis. *Journal of Marketing, 70*(4), 136–153. doi:10.1509/jmkg.70.4.136

Park, D. H., Lee, J., & Han, I. (2007). The effect of on-line consumer reviews on consumer purchasing intention: The moderating role of involvement. *International Journal of Electronic Commerce, 11*(4), 125–148. doi:10.2753/JEC1086-4415110405

Pelaez, A., Yu, M. Y., & Lang, K. R. (2013). Social buying: The effects of group size and communication on buyer performance. *International Journal of Electronic Commerce, 18*(2), 127–157. doi:10.2753/JEC1086-4415180205

Pentina, I., Gammoh, B. S., Zhang, L., & Mallin, M. (2013). Drivers and outcomes of brand relationship quality in the context of online social networks. *International Journal of Electronic Commerce, 17*(3), 63–86. doi:10.2753/JEC1086-4415170303

Prahalad, C. K., & Ramaswamy, V. (2004). Co-creation experiences: The next practice in value creation. *Journal of Interactive Marketing, 18*(3), 5–14. doi:10.1002/dir.20015

Ridings, C.M., & Gefen, D. (2004). Virtual community attraction: Why people hang out online. *Journal of Computer-Mediated Communication, 10*(1).

Schmitt, B. H. (2003). *Customer experience management*. New York: John Wiley.

Scissons, M., Kalehoff, M., & Laufer, R. (2013). The value of a Facebook fan 2013: Revisiting consumer brand currency in social media. New York: Syncopse.com.

Shin, D. H. (2010). The effect of trust, security and privacy in social networking: A security-based approach to understand the pattern of adoption. *Interacting with Computers, 22*(5), 428–438. doi:10.1016/j.intcom.2010.05.001

Shin, D. H. (2013). User experience in social commerce: In friends we trust. *Behaviour & Information Technology, 32*(1), 52–67. doi:10.1080/0144929X.2012.692167

Smith, H. J., Dinev, T., & Xu, H. (2011). Information privacy research: An interdisciplinary review. *Management Information Systems Quarterly, 35*(4), 989–1015.

Stewart, K. A., & Segars, A. H. (2002). An empirical examination of the concern for information privacy instrument. *Information Systems Research, 13*(1), 36–49. doi:10.1287/isre.13.1.36.97

Vargo, S., & Lusch, R. F. (2004). Evolving to a new dominant logic for marketing. *Journal of Marketing, 68*(1), 1–17. doi:10.1509/jmkg.68.1.1.24036

Vijayasarathy, L. R. (2004). Predicting consumer intentions to use online shopping: The case for an augmented technology acceptance model. *Information & Management, 41*(6), 747–762. doi:10.1016/j.im.2003.08.011

Wang, Y. D., & Emurian, H. H. (2005). An overview of online trust: Concepts, elements, and implications. *Computers in Human Behavior, 21*(1), 105–125. doi:10.1016/j.chb.2003.11.008

Yadav, M. S., de Valck, K., Hennig-Thurau, T., Hoffman, D. L., & Spann, M. (2013). Social commerce: A contingency framework for assessing marketing potential. *Journal of Interactive Marketing, 27*(4), 311–323. doi:10.1016/j.intmar.2013.09.001

Yadav, M. S., & Pavlou, P. A. (2014). Marketing in computer-mediated environments: Research synthesis and new directions. *Journal of Marketing, 78*(1), 20–40. doi:10.1509/jm.12.0020

Zhou, L., Zhang, P., & Zimmermann, H. D. (2013). Social commerce research: An integrated view. *Electronic Commerce Research and Applications, 12*(2), 61–68. doi:10.1016/j.elerap.2013.02.003

KEY TERMS AND DEFINITIONS

Co-Create Brand Value: Refers to the intention to co-create the value of the brand and co-construct unique branding experiences through the exchange of information and knowledge with other customers.

Privacy Concern: Refers to the users' subjective views of fairness toward information privacy.

Relationship Quality: Refers to the intensity and tightness of a relationship among people.

Social Commerce: Refers to the use of Web 2.0 and social technologies to support consumers' interactions in which they acquire the services and products in an online context.

Social Support: Is defined as the social resources that persons perceive to be available or that are actually provided to them by non-professionals in the context of both formal support groups and informal helping relationships.

This research was previously published in the Handbook of Research on Integrating Social Media into Strategic Marketing edited by Nick Hajli, pages 17-34, copyright year 2015 by Business Science Reference (an imprint of IGI Global).

APPENDIX

Table 2. Constructs and items with factor loading

Codes	Scales	Factor Loading
Social Support (Adapted from Liang et al., 2011)		
Emotional Support		
SE1	When faced with difficulties, some people on my favorite social networking site are on my side with me.	0.84
SE2	When faced with difficulties, some people on my favorite social networking site comforted and encouraged me.	0.86
SE3	When faced with difficulties, some people on my favorite social networking site listened to me talk about my private feelings.	0.89
SE4	When faced with difficulties, some people on my favorite social networking site expressed interest and concern in my well-being.	0.87
Informational Support		
SI1	On my favorite social networking site, some people would offer suggestions when I needed help.	0.87
SI2	When I encountered a problem, some people on my favorite social networking site would give me information to help me overcome the problem.	0.95
SI3	When faced with difficulties, some people on my favorite social networking site would help me discover the cause and provide me with suggestions.	0.91
Relationship Quality (Adapted from Liang et al., 2011)		
Commitment		
RC1	I am proud to belong to the membership of my favorite social networking site.	0.91
RC2	I feel a sense of belonging to my favorite social networking site.	0.93
RC3	I care about the long-term success of my favorite social networking site.	0.89
Satisfaction		
RS1	I am satisfied with using my favorite social networking site.	0.89
RS2	I am pleased with using my favorite social networking site.	0.88
RS3	I am happy with my favorite social networking site.	0.93
Trust		
RT1	The performance of my favorite social networking site always meets my expectations.	0.80
RT2	My favorite social networking site can be counted on as a good social networking site.	0.89
RT3	My favorite social networking site is a reliable social networking site.	0.89
Intention to Co-Create Brand Value (New Items)		
CB1	I am willing to provide my experiences and suggestions when my friends on my favorite social networking site want my advice on buying something from a brand.	0.94
CB2	I am willing to buy the products of a brand recommended by my friends on my favorite social networking site.	0.94
CB3	I will consider the shopping experiences of my friends on my favorite social networking site when I want to shop a brand.	0.85

Codes	Scales	Factor Loading
Social Commerce Constructs (Adapted from Hajli, 2013)		
SCC1	I will ask my friends on forums and communities to provide me with their suggestions before I go shopping from a brand.	0.73
SCC2	I am willing to recommend a product of a brand that is worth buying to my friends on my favorite social networking site.	0.81
SCC3	I am willing to share my own shopping experience of a brand with my friends on forums and communities or through ratings and reviews.	0.93
SCC4	I would like to use people online recommendations to buy a product from a brand.	0.83
Concern for Information Privacy (Stewart and Segars, 2002)		
PC1	It usually bothers me when my favorite social networking site asks me for personal information.	0.74
PC2	When my favorite social networking site asks me for personal information, I sometimes think twice before providing it.	0.85
PC3	It bothers me to give personal information to so many people.	0.86
PC4	I am concerned that my favorite social networking site is collecting too much personal information about mc.	0.82

Chapter 19
Pre–Purchase User Perceptions of Attributes and Post– Purchase Attitudes in Building Successful Online Retail Promotional Strategies

Sajad Rezaei
Taylor's University – Lakeside, Malaysia

Rona Chandran
Taylor's University – Lakeside, Malaysia

Yoke Moi Oh
Taylor's University – Lakeside, Malaysia

ABSTRACT

As a critical feature of the human experience, attitude plays an important role which is essential in implementation of effective online retail strategies. The purpose of this chapter is to conceptualize consumer's pre-purchase user perceptions of attributes and post-purchase attitudes in building successful online retail promotional strategy in emerging economies-Malaysia. The chapter proposes an integrative conceptual framework toward implementation of effective promotional strategy which includes usage expediency, trustworthiness, price awareness, navigation design, experiential gratification and electronic word-of-mouth (EWOM). The chapter argues that pre-purchase user perceptions of attributes and post-purchase user perceptions of attitudes are important concept in promoting successful online retail website. Theoretical implications of chapter are further discussed.

DOI: 10.4018/978-1-5225-5187-4.ch019

INTRODUCTION

The demand of services is increasing and the companies are responding with a rage of promotional strategies to effectively meet new demands of its customers. The organization in Ems markets has already commenced on the trend of using internet and e-commerce models. The Ems has huge population and infrastructure challenges. The most of retailing in Ems or least developed countries is still as unorganized sector. In such market the role and significance of E-commerce is still explored, but has shown huge potential. E-Commerce is traditionally described as a form of transaction that enables the firm/retailer and the purchaser/procurer to interact electronically rather than through physical exchanges or direct physical contact (Yu, Guo, Guo, & Huang, 2011). Originally, the term E-Commerce was applied to the implementation of transactions through electronic applications such as electronic data exchange (Valaei, Rezaei, Ismail, & Oh, 2016). However, with the arrival of the Internet in the mid 1990's, E-commerce started to mainly refer to the sales of goods and services on the Internet and primarily using electronic payment methods (Carmona et al., 2012). Most of online retail companies are endeavoring to increase channel synergies by enabling customers to purchase products via the Internet medium and then collect the goods at the firm's available local stores (Mahar, Salzarulo, & Daniel Wright, 2012; Rezaei, Emami, & Valaei, 2016). Hence, promoting successful online retailing according to user perceptions of E-Commerce attributes and post-purchase attitudes of users is important. There are many reasons why firms are considering E-Commerce as their core business activities/model (Rezaei, Amin, Moghaddam & Mohamed, 2016). E-Commerce has the great potential to change the way people and firm interact which each other and offers efficiencies and effective ways in the form of decreasing the operational and procedure cost, development of market access and information (Ashworth, Schmidt, Pioch, & Hallsworth, 2006; Lee, Lee, Kim, & Lee, 2003). In fact, E-retail as a channel signifies a great opportunity to reduce the firm's expenses, expand the channels to several market segments, and grow and boost loyal customers, connecting with strong new business models and potential global market development (Ashworth et al., 2006; Lee et al., 2003). E-Commerce is no longer considered as a threat to firms in the retail industry, and it is a significant phenomenon (Wrigley & Currah, 2006). E-commerce businesses models provide numerous benefits compared to offline retail and other operators (Lu & Liu, 2013), although there are some barriers for consumers wanting to perform a B2C transaction in E-Commerce (Yu et al., 2011).

Consequently, as a critical feature of the human experience, attitude plays an important role in practical applications in social research (Piotrowski and Guyette, 2010). Specifically, customers in retail stores pose a certain behaviour (Reitberger et al., 2007). The marketing strategist's challenge to the behavioural scientist is to construct a more specific model of the mechanism in the black box i.e. psychology behaviour (Kotler, 1965a). Therefore, the experiential need to keep consciousness changed is responsible for a great deal of consumer consumption behaviour (Mihaly Csikszentmihalyi, 2000), which makes the experience of flow as one of the most powerful manifestations of complexity at the consumers intrapersonal level (Csikszentmihalyi, 2004). Therefore, the purpose of this study is to identify pre-purchase user perceptions of attributes and post-purchase user perceptions of attitudes in promoting successful online retailing website. This study proposes an integrative conceptual framework toward implementation of effective promotional strategy which includes usage expediency, trustworthiness, price awareness, navigation design, experiential gratification and electronic word-of-mouth (EWOM). This study concludes that promoting successful online retailing could be achieved through pre-purchase user perceptions of attributes and post-purchase attitudes (See Figure 1).

BACKGROUND

The Internet is an identical and powerful marketing and sales tool. This tool has been successfully used by a range of companies to promote their products and services both in developed and emerging markets. The Internet currently operates as the arbitrator medium between customer and service provider (Mohseni, Jayashree, Rezaei, Kasim & Okumus, 2016). Using the internet sagaciously for online retailing not only helps to promote online retail businesses but develops a brand identity for the retailer which is beneficial in strengthening and expending ones business and sales. Effective online retailing websites helps retailers build their image, attract new customers, and generate a pool of loyal customers (Stacey, 2015; Rezaei, Ali, Amin, Jayashree, 2016). An increasing number of customers utilizing Web 2.0 instruments for example weblogs, consumer review site, online forum, social network sites, and so forth to express their own views and also transfer product information (Cheung & Thadani, 2012). Social network services are easily accessible for consumers via online; therefore, individuals can share their shopping experience with others (Lee et al., 2013). WOM is related to casual conversation between customers with regards to products or services (Dierkes, Bichler, & Krishnan, 2011). Although WOM has long been seen as having essential impact on purchaser attitude, intention and also behaviour, not much attention has given on how organisations can handle this phenomenon (Williams & Buttle, 2011).

There are however some basic guidelines that online retailer should pay attention to in order to enhance their business and sales (Alavi, Rezaei, Valaei, & Ismail, 2016). Browntape, India's leading e-commerce solutions experts, have listed that online retailers who run webstores should focus on upselling and cross selling their products, revive sales of abandon carts and maximize benefits from social media such as Instagram, face book and even creating one's own web page or Apps (browntape.com). Online retailers should also aim to exceed customer expectation to provide good service quality (Soloman & Stuart, 2003; Zeithaml, 1998) because good service quality ensures successful business (Yapp, Tanakinjal & Sondoh, 2014). Therefore it is important for retailers to be aware of their customer's expectations to enable them to exceed those expectations. Various bottlenecks ranging from infrastructure, technology, internet availability, risk perceptions, cost of internet, and past habits of the consumers are still needs to be managed.

Main Focus of Chapter

Past research mostly investigated factors that contributes to online consumer attitudes and behavior regarding intention, acceptance and adoption level of online shopping and an IS (Information system), while a few studies have been conducted on post-adoption online retailing (Taylor & Strutton, 2010). Taylor and Strutton (2010) established the distinction between pre-purchase perception of attributes, pre purchase perception of attitudes and post purchase user attitudes. Previous studies (e.g., Gardial, Clemons, Woodruff, Schumann, & Burns, 1994; Ofir & Simonson, 2007; Woodruff, Cadotte, & Jenkins, 1983) revealed that there are important differences between post-purchase thoughts versus those from both pre-purchase and satisfaction. Factors that influence intention to use the IT and IS have been discussed by scholars in the last decades (Dholakia et al., 2010; Huh & Kim, 2008; Liu, Ja-Chul, Yung-Ho, & Sang-Chul, 2012). Therefore, this study proposes an integrative conceptual framework towards implementation of effective promotional strategy which includes usage expediency, trustworthiness, price awareness, navigation design, experiential gratification and EWOM (See Figure 1). To effectively promote reatiling or any service online the organisations needs to manage the whole process from pre-purchase, during purchase and post purchase effectively.

Figure 1. Conceptual research framework

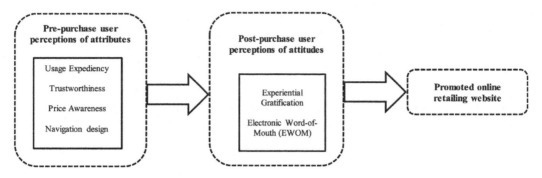

Solution and Recommendation

Pre-Purchase User Perceptions of Attributes

Gardial et al. (1994) distinguished pre-purchase from post-purchase attitudes and behaviors of online shoppers. Previous studies has applied TAM construct as a main variable to examine human behavior in different context. Cyr, Head, and Ivanov (2006) in mobile loyalty, Li and Yeh (2010) in mobile trust and Hassanein and Head (2007) explored consumer attitudes towards online shopping in social context by using PU as a central variable. An analysis of experienced e-shoppers includes PU and PEOU to determine the impact of self-efficacy in E-shopping (Hernandez, Jimenez, & Jose Martin, 2009). Pavlou (2003) deployed PU as a construct to explore consumer's acceptance of E-Commerce. Ooi, Sim, Yew, and Lin (2011) used PEOU construct as control variable in broadband adoption in Malaysia. Thus, in this study we examine PUU, convenience motivation and experiential value as pre-purchase user perceptions of attributes. If the consumers don't have positive perceptions about usefulness, eas of use or positive social norms, they may not use online purchase, and the process may stops= at the beginning itself.

Usage Expediency and Trustworthiness

"Convenience is the ability to reduce consumers' non-monetary costs (i.e., time, energy and effort) when purchasing or using goods and services" (Chang & Polonsky, 2012, p. 107). As the online retailing sector quickly grows, providing more convenient Internet shopping features to consumers is becoming an important subject to online marketers (Cho & Schwarz, 2012). Sohn (2000) has listed trustworthiness as the most important dimension out of five dimensions of service quality. Trustworthiness influences the online purchaser's perception of the overall quality service provided (Rezaei, 2015). It also increases confidence to pursue online purchasing. Trustworthiness is achieved through online services that are reliable and secure. This is achieved by means of strict policies enhanced with up to date online security technologies (Cai & Jun, 2003). Ernst and Young (2001) have suggested that online it is the responsibility of the webstore or online retailers to convince purchasers that they online transactions are secure by providing clear guidelines and evidence to their claims. However a study conducted in Australia found that only 33% of the small medium businesses have standard risk management operating procedures in the event that there is a security breach.

The most employed security measure was the provision of a physical address and phone number which was in place for 58% of the business (Stancombe Research & Planning, 2012) which logically serve more as a reaction to a security breech than a prevention measure. The spatial distance between the business and the consumer makes trust a key component in web based B2C (Lanford, 2006; Rezaei & Amin, 2013). The trustworthiness of an on line business can be increased by a professional web interface. A carefully designed web page with no errors, attractive, suitable and quality graphics and animation and great presentation has proven to increase trustworthiness. Although web site design can be very subjective based on industry but the fundamental guidelines discussed are relevant.

Price Awareness

One of the main reasons online business are able to take over the traditional business strategies is the fact that consumers are awareness of the price difference between products offered on webstores and physical stores. The general assumption is that products obtained via online purchase is cheaper that off line purchase due to the absence of many overhead costs. E-commerce is also believed to be frictionless in comparison to physical stores (Pan, Ratchfold & Shankar, 2001). A study conducted by Stancombe Research & Planning (2012), for the NSW Fair Trading on the Australian consumers' and businesses' attitudes towards online shopping and their knowledge of security precautions, found that the main reason consumers shopped online was because of the cheaper prices and the discounts offered on line. On the other hand the research discovered that the main reason retailers chose to do online business was due to the higher was a wider pool of customers (39%), effective sales procedures (18%), and cost effectiveness (16%). The ability to offer better prices to customers was only mentioned as a reason for online retailing by 1/3 of the respondents. Therefore it is important for online retailers to have knowledge about the price awareness and underlying expectations of getting a better deal when shopping online (Daliri, Rezaei & Ismail, 2014; Amin, Rezaei & Abolghasemi, 2014).

Navigation Design

Navigation design is an important aspect of B2C retailers because shoppers at webstores develop their opinions about the business within just few seconds of navigation (Awad, 2004). Investment in an attractive, functional, practical, convenient, secure, and fuss free web design would contribute to high levels of customer satisfaction and improve the quality of service offered (Rezaei, Amin & Ismail, 2014). A study conducted on the Fortune 500 B2C products and service pages found that successful on line retails owned websites that took an average of two mouse clicks and 74 seconds to navigate from the cooperate homepage to shopping pages (Zhao, Truell & Alexander, 2006). This provided a convenient and pleasant shopping experience to their customers that increased and sustained their number of return customers. Besides that, online retailers should strive to improve the "Stickiness" of their webpages. Kim and LaRose (2002) have defined sticky websites as websites that are able to attract a great volume of frequent and repeat customers who spend long hours on the website and visit many pages. Sticky websites are able to keep customers engrossed that they divert from their original intention of visiting the site and they are willing to diverge from their set standards of browsing efficiency. A sticky website should offer a gratifying online shopping experience. Among navigation features that are identified as necessary are interactivity and effective features (Rezaei & Ismail, 2014). An interactive on line shopping site would reduce transaction time and search cost. Ideally, e-commerce retailers should strive to improve on the three main dimensions of an effective interactive website which are the degree of control a user has, the level of interaction offered and the connectedness (Zhao, Truell & Alexander; 2006; Rezaei & Ghodsi 2014). A convenient and satisfying navigation experience directly increases the trustworthiness of the B2C online retailer.

Post-Purchase User Perceptions of Attitudes

According to Thong *et al.* (2006), there is less research undertaken regarding post-adoption environment where consumers and users decide whether to continue or discontinue usage of an information technology and information system. Continued intention and usage of the information technology and information system is considered as a research issue in these fields (Hsu, Yen, Chiu, & Chang, 2006). Post-purchase theory development and research are still at an early stage (Gardial et al., 1994). Studying drivers of individuals' repatronage intention, attitude and behavior is important because of the significant influence of continued usage on profitability of an IS firm such as online retailers (Hannah & Lybecker, 2010; Khalifa & Limayem, 2003; Pingjun & Bert, 2005; Thong et al., 2006; Valvi & Fragkos, 2012; van Raaij, Strazzieri, & Woodside, 2001). The high cost of acquiring customers during early transactions forces them to understand consumer repatronage intention (Srinivasan, Anderson, & Ponnavolu, 2002). Thus, examining consumers' patronage intention and behaviors has valuable implication for the retailers in order to implement multiple levels' strategy (Liao, Chen, & Lin, 2011).

Experiential Gratification

A key component of a firm in the competitive market is to differentiate by means of creating unique customer experiences (Walls, 2012). According to Woodruff (1997) customer satisfaction management usually fails "as experience grows with the company", at which point organizations start to have problems. Customer experience is conceptualized as the total direct and indirect customer response to the firm (Lemke, Clark, & Wilson, 2011). This experience roots from the interactions between a firm's customer, product, the firm itself or part of its business which lead to a reaction (Verhoef et al., 2009). An experience is a real offering like service, good, or commodity (Addis & Holbrook, 2001; Davis & Hodges, 2012; Pine & Gilmore, 1998). Traditionally, Pine and Gilmore (1998; 2000) distinguished experiences as with services, goods, and commodities. Importantly, value is considered as the center of the "experiences of consumers" (Iyanna, Bosangit, & Mohd-Any, 2012) and experiential marketing incorporates senses, feelings, thoughts, and related aspects of consumption that effects consumers' evaluation of experiences (Hausman, 2011). Many restaurants use reviewing sites such as TripAdvisor or last minute dot com etc to enhance their marketing effectiveness.

Electronic Word-of-Mouth (EWOM)

For decades, WOM has been recognized as a key influencer in consumer decision-making, with studies showing its impact on individuals to be greater than advertising (Nguyen & Romaniuk, 2014). EWOM takes place in a more complex computer-mediated context, whereas traditional WOM typically happens in a face to face/ one-on-one context (King, Racherla, & Bush, 2014). WOM also takes place within a variety of online environments (known as EWOM), allowing information exchanges to be immediately available to a multitude of people and institutions (Kim, Sung, & Kang, 2014). EWOM can be comparatively speedy, a casual strategy for expressing views and also involved in merchandise distribution using other customers that are geographically spread (Verhagen, Nauta, & Feldberg, 2013). It actually, plays a critical role in illustrating consumer's attitude and behavior in the direction of a particular product or service (Lee, Noh, & Kim, 2013).

Therefore, the WOM behavior which was previously operating traditionally, but currently comes with an automated element, is causing a large study stream of EWOM (King et al., 2014). Unlike conventional interpersonal communication, where the credibility of opinion providers is considered critical, EWOM facilitates information sharing without face-to-face interaction (Kim et al., 2014). Previous reports have discovered that customers understand WOM as far more dependable and also persuasive compared to traditional marketing, for instance art print ads, private promoting and also TV marketing (Cheung & Thadani, 2012). Online WOM plays an important role in electronic commerce as the consumers consider these consumer-generated reviews (Gu, Tang, & Whinston, 2013). EWOM platforms support collections of people in forming specialized, non-geographically bound consumer communities (King et al., 2014). The shift toward E-Commerce is undeniable even though WOM has received considerable attention from researchers and theorists of late (Eisingerich, Chun, Liu, Jia, & Bell, 2014). However the companies should note that there are two kind of word of mouth communications, one being Positive WOM and other as negative WOM. In online environment is is vey difficult to control either positive or negative reviews or eWOM. Also some studies has indicated that negative WOM spreads faster and may increase more doubts than a positive e WOM. Hence the organization has to effectively manage eWOM campaigns. The core is that the customer needs should be at the core of product or service design. All other things will fit in right direction, if the company is customer need oriented.

CONCLUSION

Based on the research conceptual framework and the literature on the mentioned components, it is highly advisable for online business retailers to give due consideration to the elements in the framework to promote their on line businesses. The identified elements are usage expediency, trustworthiness, price awareness, navigation design, experiential gratification and electronic word-of-mouth (EWOM). Online business owners should be aware of the importance of these elements and its contribution towards understanding consumer behavior and the company's continuing growth and success. Retailers are trying to build unique experiences for customers that will enhance their shopping value and help differentiating their stores from other competitors (Sands, Oppewal, & Beverland, 2009). However, literature on the definition and empirical investigation of retail focusing on the stimulus of experiences is lacking (Bäckström & Johansson, 2006). Most companies realize the importance of consumer experience in building positioning strategy (Shobeiri, Laroche, & Mazaheri, 2013) specifically in online shopping environment when consumers' attitudes would change when their shopping experience changes (Zhang, Xu, Ye, & Wang, 2012). According to Yang, Mao, and Peracchio (2012), although some consumers spend less time for shopping activities, they are pursuing delightful experiences. Therefore, to remain competitive, retailers should invest considerable resources in creating a positive dynamic experience amongst their customers in order to build and maintain strong relationships with customers (Lindsey-Mullikin & Munger, 2011).

Gardial et al. (1994) distinguished pre-purchase from post-purchase attitudes and behaviours of online shoppers. Previous studies applied TAM construct as a main variable to examine human behaviour in different context. Cyr et al. (2006) in mobile loyalty, Li and Yeh (2010) in mobile trust and Hassanein and Head (2007) explored consumer attitudes towards online shopping in social context by using PU as a central variable. An analysis of experienced e-shoppers includes PU and PEOU to determine the impact of self-efficacy in e shopping (Hernandez et al., 2009b). Pavlou (2003) deployed PU as a construct to explore consumer's acceptance of E-Commerce. Ooi et al. (2011) used PEOU construct as control variable in broadband adoption in Malaysia. Thus, in this study we examine PUU, convenience motivation and experiential value as pre-purchase user perceptions of attributes. Research has shown that a staggering number of 88% of online shoppers actually abandon their shopping carts midway due to the overwhelming number of steps that the purchaser had to perform in a transaction, feelings of insecurity due to too much of personal and financial information that was requested and finally failure to receive immediate assistance when required (Zhao, Truell & Alexander, 2006; Amin, Rezaei & Tavana, 2015). This has clearly indicated that the main criteria to enhance the online shopping experience and satisfaction could be to reduce the navigation time and number of clicks.

Therefore, a well-designed website that displays three main dimensional images of the products will make the website looks more professional and consequentially create a positive riffle effect on the overall trustworthiness of the webstore (Kamari & Kamari, 2012; Rezaei, 2015; Moghaddam, Rezaei & Amin, 2015). Kamari and Kamari (2012) have also stated the importance of the real life presence of a company. According to them the physical existence of on online B2C retailer increases their trustworthiness. This is because customers will be convinced to make purchases from the webstores that actually physically exists in the real world which they are able to see and relate as compared to a webstore that only exists in the cyberspace.

REFERENCES

Addis, M., & Holbrook, M. B. (2001). On the conceptual link between mass customisation and experiential consumption: An explosion of subjectivity. *Journal of Consumer Behaviour*, *1*(1), 50–66. doi:10.1002/cb.53

Alavi, S. A., Rezaei, S., Valaei, N., & Wan Ismail, W. K. (2016). Examining shopping mall consumer decision-making styles, satisfaction and purchase intention. *International Review of Retail, Distribution and Consumer Research*, *26*(3), 272–303. doi:10.1080/09593969.2015.1096808

Amin, M., Rezaei, S., & Abolghasemi, M. (2014). User satisfaction with mobile websites: The impact of perceived usefulness (PU), perceived ease of use (PEOU) and trust. *Nankai Business Review International*, *5*(3), 258–274. doi:10.1108/NBRI-01-2014-0005

Amin, M., Rezaei, S., & Shajari Tavana, F. (2015). Gender differences and consumers repurchase intention: The impact of trust propensity, usefulness and ease of use for implication of innovative online retail. *International Journal of Innovation and Learning*, *17*(2), 217–233. doi:10.1504/IJIL.2015.067409

Ashworth, C. J., Schmidt, R. Ä., Pioch, E. A., & Hallsworth, A. (2006). An approach to sustainable fashion e-retail: A five-stage evolutionary strategy for Clicks-and-Mortar and Pure-Play enterprises. *Journal of Retailing and Consumer Services*, *13*(4), 289–299. doi:10.1016/j.jretconser.2005.08.018

Awad, E. M. (2004). *Electronic commerce: From vision to fulfillment*. Upper Saddle River, NJ: Prentice Hall.

Bäckström, K., & Johansson, U. (2006). Creating and consuming experiences in retail store environments: Comparing retailer and consumer perspectives. *Journal of Retailing and Consumer Services, 13*(6), 417–430. doi:10.1016/j.jretconser.2006.02.005

Cai, S., & Jun, M. (2003). Internet users perceptions of online service quality: A comparison of online buyers and information searchers. Managing Service Quality, 13(6), 504-519.

Carmona, C. J., Ramírez-Gallego, S., Torres, F., Bernal, E., del Jesus, M. J., & García, S. (2012). Web usage mining to improve the design of an e-commerce website: OrOliveSur.com. *Expert Systems with Applications, 39*(12), 11243–11249. doi:10.1016/j.eswa.2012.03.046

Chang, Y.-W., & Polonsky, M. J. (2012). The influence of multiple types of service convenience on behavioral intentions: The mediating role of consumer satisfaction in a Taiwanese leisure setting. *International Journal of Hospitality Management, 31*(1), 107–118. doi:10.1016/j.ijhm.2011.05.003

Cheung, C. M. K., & Thadani, D. R. (2012). The impact of electronic word-of-mouth communication: A literature analysis and integrative model. *Decision Support Systems, 54*(1), 461–470. doi:10.1016/j.dss.2012.06.008

Cho, H., & Schwarz, N. (2012). I Like Your Product When I Like My Photo: Misattribution Using Interactive Virtual Mirrors. *Journal of Interactive Marketing, 26*(4), 235–243. doi:10.1016/j.intmar.2012.03.003

Csikszentmihalyi, M. (2004). Stalking a New World Order. *New Literary History, 35*(2), 339–348. doi:10.1353/nlh.2004.0029

Cyr, D., Head, M., & Ivanov, A. (2006). Design aesthetics leading to m-loyalty in mobile commerce. *Information &amp. Management, 43*(8), 950–963. doi:10.1016/j.im.2006.08.009

Daliri, E., Rezaei, S., & Ismail, W. K. W. (2014). Online social shopping: The impact of attitude, customer information quality, effectiveness of information content and perceived social presence. *International Journal of Business Environment, 6*(4), 426–450. doi:10.1504/IJBE.2014.064995

Davis, L., & Hodges, N. (2012). Consumer shopping value: An investigation of shopping trip value, in-store shopping value and retail format. *Journal of Retailing and Consumer Services, 19*(2), 229–239. doi:10.1016/j.jretconser.2012.01.004

Dholakia, U. M., Kahn, B. E., Reeves, R., Rindfleisch, A., Stewart, D., & Taylor, E. (2010). Consumer Behavior in a Multichannel, Multimedia Retailing Environment. *Journal of Interactive Marketing, 24*(2), 86–95. doi:10.1016/j.intmar.2010.02.005

Dierkes, T., Bichler, M., & Krishnan, R. (2011). Estimating the effect of word of mouth on churn and cross-buying in the mobile phone market with Markov logic networks. *Decision Support Systems, 51*(3), 361–371. doi:10.1016/j.dss.2011.01.002

Eisingerich, A. B., Chun, H.E. H., Liu, Y., Jia, H., & Bell, S. J. (2014). Why recommend a brand face-to-face but not on Facebook? How word-of-mouth on online social sites differs from traditional word-of-mouth. *Journal of Consumer Psychology*, (0). doi:10.1016/j.jcps.2014.05.004

Ernst & Young. (2001). *Global Online Retailing*. Available at www.ey.com/global/ vault.nsf/US/2001_Retail_Study/$file/GOR.pdf

Gardial, S. F., Clemons, D. S., Woodruff, R. B., Schumann, D. W., & Burns, M. J. (1994). Comparing Consumers Recall of Prepurchase and Postpurchase Product Evaluation Experiences. *The Journal of Consumer Research*, *20*(4), 548–560. doi:10.1086/209369

Gu, B., Tang, Q., & Whinston, A. B. (2013). The influence of online word-of-mouth on long tail formation. *Decision Support Systems*, *56*(0), 474–481. doi:10.1016/j.dss.2012.11.004

Hannah, B., & Lybecker, K. M. (2010). Determinants of Recent Online Purchasing and the Percentage of Income Spent Online. *International Business Research*, *3*(4), 60–71. doi:10.5539/ibr.v3n4p60

Hassanein, K., & Head, M. (2007). Manipulating perceived social presence through the web interface and its impact on attitude towards online shopping. *International Journal of Human-Computer Studies*, *65*(8), 689-708. doi: 10.1016/j.ijhcs.2006.11.018

Hausman, A. (2011). Attribute satisfaction and experiential involvement in evaluations of live musical performance: Theory and managerial implications for services. *Journal of Retailing and Consumer Services*, *18*(3), 210–217. doi:10.1016/j.jretconser.2010.11.001

Hernandez, B., Jimenez, J., & Martin, J. (2009). The impact of self-efficacy, ease of use and usefulness on e-purchasing: An analysis of experienced e-shoppers. *Interacting with Computers*, *21*(1-2), 146–156. doi:10.1016/j.intcom.2008.11.001

Hsu, M.-H., Yen, C.-H., Chiu, C.-M., & Chang, C.-M. (2006). A longitudinal investigation of continued online shopping behavior: An extension of the theory of planned behavior. *International Journal of Human-Computer Studies*, *64*(9), 889–904. doi:10.1016/j.ijhcs.2006.04.004

Huh, Y. E., & Kim, S.-H. (2008). Do early adopters upgrade early? Role of post-adoption behavior in the purchase of next-generation products. *Journal of Business Research*, *61*(1), 40–46. doi:10.1016/j.jbusres.2006.05.007

Iyanna, S., Bosangit, C., & Mohd-Any, A. A. (2012). Value evaluation of customer experience using consumer generated content. *International Journal of Management & Marketing Research*, *5*(2), 89–102.

Kamari, F., & Kamari, S. (2012). Trust in electronic commerce: A new model for building online trust in b2c. *European Journal of Business Management*, *4*(10), 125–134.

Khalifa, M., & Limayem, M. (2003). Drivers of Internet shopping. *Communications of the ACM*, *46*(12), 233–239. doi:10.1145/953460.953505

Kim, E., Sung, Y., & Kang, H. (2014). Brand followers retweeting behavior on Twitter: How brand relationships influence brand electronic word-of-mouth. *Computers in Human Behavior*, *37*(0), 18–25. doi:10.1016/j.chb.2014.04.020

Kim, J., & LaRose, R. (2002). *What makes e-commerce websites "Sticky?": Interactivity and impulsivity in online browsing behavior*. Paper submitted to Communication and Technology Division 53rd Annual Conference of the International Communication Association.

King, R. A., Racherla, P., & Bush, V. D. (2014). What We Know and Dont Know About Online Word-of-Mouth: A Review and Synthesis of the Literature. *Journal of Interactive Marketing*, *28*(3), 167–183. doi:10.1016/j.intmar.2014.02.001

Kotler, P. (1965). Behavioral models for analyzing buyers. *Journal of Marketing, 29*(4), 37–45. doi:10.2307/1249700

Lanford, P. (2006). *E-Commerce: A Trust Perspective*. Auburn University.

Lee, H. G., Lee, S. C., Kim, H. Y., & Lee, R. H. (2003). Is the internet making retail transactions more efficient? Comparison of online and offline CD retail markets. *Electronic Commerce Research and Applications, 2*(3), 266–277. doi:10.1016/S1567-4223(03)00030-9

Lee, S.-H., Noh, S.-E., & Kim, H.-W. (2013). A mixed methods approach to electronic word-of-mouth in the open-market context. *International Journal of Information Management, 33*(4), 687–696. doi:10.1016/j.ijinfomgt.2013.03.002

Lemke, F., Clark, M., & Wilson, H. (2011). Customer experience quality: An exploration in business and consumer contexts using repertory grid technique. *Journal of the Academy of Marketing Science, 39*(6), 846–869. doi:10.1007/s11747-010-0219-0

Li, Y.-M., & Yeh, Y.-S. (2010). Increasing trust in mobile commerce through design aesthetics. *Computers in Human Behavior, 26*(4), 673–684. doi:10.1016/j.chb.2010.01.004

Liao, S.-H., Chen, Y.-J., & Lin, Y.-T. (2011). Mining customer knowledge to implement online shopping and home delivery for hypermarkets. *Expert Systems with Applications, 38*(4), 3982-3991. doi:10.1016/j.eswa.2010.09.059

Lindsey-Mullikin, J., & Munger, J. L. (2011). Companion Shoppers and the Consumer Shopping Experience. *Journal of Relationship Marketing, 10*(1), 7–27. doi:10.1080/15332667.2011.549385

Liu, F., Ja-Chul, G., Yung-Ho, S., & Sang-Chul, L. (2012). How to attract Chinese online game users: An empirical study on the determinants affecting intention to use Chinese online games. *Asian Journal on Quality, 13*(1), 7–21. doi:10.1108/15982681211237798

Lu, Q., & Liu, N. (2013). Pricing games of mixed conventional and e-commerce distribution channels. *Computers & Industrial Engineering, 64*(1), 122–132. doi:10.1016/j.cie.2012.09.018

Mahar, S., Salzarulo, P. A., & Wright, D. (2012). Using online pickup site inclusion policies to manage demand in retail/E-tail organizations. *Computers & Operations Research, 39*(5), 991–999. doi:10.1016/j.cor.2011.06.011

Marketing Techniques to Promote Your Online Retail Business. (2015). Retrieved from http://browntape.com/5-marketing-techniques-to-promote-your-online-retail-business/

Moghaddam, H. A., Rezaei, S., & Amin, M. (2015). Examining job seekers perception and behavioural intention toward online recruitment: A PLS path modelling approach. *Journal for Global Business Advancement, 8*(3), 305–325. doi:10.1504/JGBA.2015.071331

Mohseni, S., Jayashree, S., Rezaei, S., Kasim, A., & Okumus, F. (2016). Attracting tourists to travel companies websites: The structural relationship between website brand, personal value, shopping experience, perceived risk and purchase intention. *Current Issues in Tourism*, 1–30. doi:10.1080/13683500.2016.1200539

Nguyen, C., & Romaniuk, J. (2014). Pass it on: A framework for classifying the content of word of mouth. *Australasian Marketing Journal*, 22(2), 117–124. doi:10.1016/j.ausmj.2013.12.014

Ofir, C., & Simonson, I. (2007). The Effect of Stating Expectations on Customer Satisfaction and Shopping Experience. *JMR, Journal of Marketing Research*, 44(1), 164–174. doi:10.1509/jmkr.44.1.164

Ooi, K.-B., Sim, J.-J., Yew, K.-T., & Lin, B. (2011). Exploring factors influencing consumers behavioral intention to adopt broadband in Malaysia. *Computers in Human Behavior*, 27(3), 1168–1178. doi:10.1016/j.chb.2010.12.011

Pan, X., Racthford, B. T., & Shankar, V. (2001). *Why aren't the prices on the same item the same at Me.com and You.com? Drivers of price dispersion among e-tailers*. Retrieved from https://www.researchgate.net/publication/242445825_Why_Aren't_the_Prices_of_the_Same_Item_the_Same_at_Mecom_and_Youcom_Drivers_of_Price_Dispersion_Among_e-Tailers_Xing_Pan_Brian

Pavlou, P. A. (2003). Consumer Acceptance of Electronic Commerce: Integrating Trust and Risk with the Technology Acceptance Model. *International Journal of Electronic Commerce*, 7(3), 101–134.

Pine, I. I. B. J., & Gilmore, J. H. (1998). Welcome to the experience economy. *Harvard Business Review*, 76(4), 97–105. PMID:10181589

Pine Ii, B. (2000). Satisfaction, sacrifice, surprise. *Strategy and Leadership*, 28(1), 18–23. doi:10.1108/10878570010335958

Pingjun, J., & Bert, R. (2005). Customer intention to return online: Price perception, attribute-level performance, and satisfaction unfolding over time. *European Journal of Marketing*, 39(1), 150–174.

Piotrowski, C., & Guyette, J. R. W. (2010). The case for the semantic differential in organizational and business research. *Journal of Instructional Psychology*, 37(4), 337–339.

Reitberger, W., Obermair, C., Ploderer, B., Meschtscherjakov, A., & Tscheligi, M. (2007). Enhancing the shopping experience with ambient displays: A field study in a retail store. In B. Schiele, A. Dey, H. Gellersen, B. Ruyter, M. Tscheligi, R. Wichert, & A. Buchmann et al. (Eds.), *Ambient intelligence* (Vol. 4794, pp. 314–331). Springer Berlin Heidelberg. doi:10.1007/978-3-540-76652-0_19

Rezaei, S. (2015). Segmenting consumer decision-making styles (CDMS) toward marketing practice: A partial least squares (PLS) path modeling approach. *Journal of Retailing and Consumer Services*, 22, 1–15. doi:10.1016/j.jretconser.2014.09.001

Rezaei, S., Ali, F., Amin, M., & Jayashree, S. (2016). Online impulse buying of tourism products: The role of website personality, utilitarian and hedonic web browsing. *Journal of Hospitality and Tourism Technology*, 7(1), 60–83. doi:10.1108/JHTT-03-2015-0018

Rezaei, S., & Amin, M. (2013). Exploring online repurchase behavioural intention of university students in Malaysia. *Journal for Global Business Advancement*, 6(2), 92–119. doi:10.1504/JGBA.2013.053561

Rezaei, S., Amin, M., & Ismail, W. K. W. (2014). Online repatronage intention: An empirical study among Malaysian experienced online shoppers. *International Journal of Retail & Distribution Management*, 42(5), 390–421. doi:10.1108/IJRDM-03-2012-0026

Rezaei, S., Amin, M., Moghadam, M., & Mohamed, N. (2016). *3G post adoption users experience with telecommunications services: a partial least squares (PLS) path modelling approach.* Nankai Business Review International. doi:10.1108/NBRI-01-2016-0007

Rezaei, S., Emami, M., & Valaei, N. (2016). *The moderating impact of product classification on the relationship between online trust, satisfaction, and repurchase intention. In Encyclopedia of E-Commerce Development, Implementation, and Management* (p. 1692). IGI Global.

Rezaei, S., & Ghodsi, S. S. (2014). Does value matters in playing online game? An empirical study among massively multiplayer online role-playing games (MMORPGs). *Computers in Human Behavior, 35,* 252–266. doi:10.1016/j.chb.2014.03.002

Rezaei, S., & Ismail, W. K. W. (2014). Examining online channel selection behaviour among social media shoppers: A PLS analysis. *International Journal of Electronic Marketing and Retailing, 6*(1), 28–51. doi:10.1504/IJEMR.2014.064876

Sands, S., Oppewal, H., & Beverland, M. (2009). The effects of in-store themed events on consumer store choice decisions. *Journal of Retailing and Consumer Services, 16*(5), 386–395. doi:10.1016/j.jretconser.2009.05.001

Shobeiri, S., Laroche, M., & Mazaheri, E. (2013). Shaping e-retailers website personality: The importance of experiential marketing. *Journal of Retailing and Consumer Services, 20*(1), 102–110. doi:10.1016/j.jretconser.2012.10.011

Sohn, C. S. (2000). *Customer Evaluation of Internet Base Service Quality and Intention to Re-Use Internet Base Services* (Unpublished Dissertation). Southern Illinois University, Carbondale, IL.

Soloman, M. R., & Stuart, E. W. (2003). Marketing: Real People, Real Choices. The IUP Journal of Marketing Management, 13(2).

Srinivasan, S. S., Anderson, R., & Ponnavolu, K. (2002). Customer loyalty in e-commerce: An exploration of its antecedents and consequences. *Journal of Retailing, 78*(1), 41–50. doi:10.1016/S0022-4359(01)00065-3

Stacey, H. (2015). *How online retailers can promote their content better.* Retrieved from https://www.ometria.com/blog/ecommerce-content-promotion

Stancombe Research & Planning. (2012). *Consumer and SMB Attitudes to Online Shopping and Awareness of Security Measures (Research Executive Summary); New South Wales.* Retrieved from http://www.fairtrading.nsw.gov.au/pdfs/Consumers/Executive_summary_consumer_and_smb_attitudes_to_online-shopping_and_awareness_of_security_measures.pdf

Taylor, D. G., & Strutton, D. (2010). Has e-marketing come of age? Modeling historical influences on post-adoption era Internet consumer behaviors. *Journal of Business Research, 63*(9–10), 950–956. doi:10.1016/j.jbusres.2009.01.018

Thong, J. Y. L., Hong, S.-J., & Tam, K. Y. (2006). The effects of post-adoption beliefs on the expectation-confirmation model for information technology continuance. *International Journal of Human-Computer Studies, 64*(9), 799–810. doi:10.1016/j.ijhcs.2006.05.001

Tshin, Y. H., Tanakinjal, G. H., & Sondoh, S. L., Jr. (2014). The key dimensions of online service quality: Study of consumer perceptions. Journal of Marketing Management, 13(2), 7-18.

Valaei, N., Rezaei, S., Ismail, W. K. W., & Moi, O. Y. (2016). (in press). Cultural effect on attitude toward online advertising and online brands: Applying Hofstede's cultural factors to Internet marketing. *International Journal of Internet Marketing and Advertising.*

Valvi, A., & Fragkos, K. (2012). Critical review of the e-loyalty literature: A purchase-centred framework. *Electronic Commerce Research*, 1–48. doi:10.1007/s10660-012-9097-5

van Raaij, W. F., Strazzieri, A., & Woodside, A. (2001). New developments in marketing communications and consumer behavior. *Journal of Business Research*, *53*(2), 59–61. doi:10.1016/S0148-2963(99)00075-2

Verhagen, T., Nauta, A., & Feldberg, F. (2013). Negative online word-of-mouth: Behavioral indicator or emotional release? *Computers in Human Behavior*, *29*(4), 1430–1440. doi:10.1016/j.chb.2013.01.043

Verhoef, P. C., Lemon, K. N., Parasuraman, A., Roggeveen, A., Tsiros, M., & Schlesinger, L. A. (2009). Customer experience creation: Determinants, dynamics and management strategies. *Journal of Retailing*, *85*(1), 31–41. doi:10.1016/j.jretai.2008.11.001

Walls, A. R. (2012). A cross-sectional examination of hotel consumer experience and relative effects on consumer values. *International Journal of Hospitality Management*, (0). doi:10.1016/j.ijhm.2012.04.009

Williams, M., & Buttle, F. (2011). The Eight Pillars of WOM management: Lessons from a multiple case study. *Australasian Marketing Journal*, *19*(2), 85–92. doi:10.1016/j.ausmj.2011.01.001

Woodruff, R. B. (1997). Customer value: The next source for competitive advantage. *Journal of the Academy of Marketing Science*, *25*(2), 139–153. doi:10.1007/BF02894350

Woodruff, R. B., Cadotte, E. R., & Jenkins, R. L. (1983). Modeling Consumer Satisfaction Processes Using Experience-Based Norms. *JMR, Journal of Marketing Research*, *20*(3), 296–304. doi:10.2307/3151833

Wrigley, N., & Currah, A. (2006). Globalizing retail and the new e-conomy: The organizational challenge of e-commerce for the retail TNCs. *Geoforum*, *37*(3), 340–351. doi:10.1016/j.geoforum.2005.06.003

Yang, X., Mao, H., & Peracchio, L. A. (2012). Its Not Whether You Win or Lose, Its How You Play the Game? The Role of Process and Outcome in Experience Consumption. *JMR, Journal of Marketing Research*, *49*(6), 954–966. doi:10.1509/jmr.10.0083

Yu, X., Guo, S., Guo, J., & Huang, X. (2011). Rank B2C e-commerce websites in e-alliance based on AHP and fuzzy TOPSIS. *Expert Systems with Applications*, *38*(4), 3550–3557. doi:10.1016/j.eswa.2010.08.143

Zeithaml, V. (1998). Consumer Perceptions of Price, Quality and Value: A MeansEnd Synthesis of Evidence. *Journal of Marketing, 52*(3), 2-22. 24.

Zhang, L., Xu, Y., Ye, B., & Wang, Q. (2012). Exploring Differences of Consumers' Perceived Factors in Shopping Online: The Effects of Shopping Experience and Gender. In D. Jin & S. Lin (Eds.), *Advances in Electronic Engineering, Communication and Management* (Vol. 1, pp. 639–646). Springer Berlin Heidelberg. doi:10.1007/978-3-642-27287-5_104

Zhao, J. J., Truell, A. D., & Alexander, M. W. (2006). User-Interface Design Characteristics of "Fortune 500" B2C E-Commerce Sites and Industry Differences. *Delta Pi Epsilon Journal*, *48*(1), 43–55.

KEY TERMS AND DEFINITIONS

Convenience: "The ability to reduce consumers' non-monetary costs (i.e., time, energy and effort) when purchasing or using goods and services" (Chang & Polonsky, 2012, p. 107).

E-Commerce: A term refers to a wide variety of Internet-based business models. Typically, an e-commerce strategy incorporates various elements of the marketing mix to drive users to a Web site for the purpose of purchasing a product or service" (American Marketing Association, 2016).

Post-Purchase Evaluation: The evaluation of a product or service after consumption. This may involve remorse as well as the feeling of satisfaction or dissatisfaction.

Price Awareness: The price awareness refers to the individual's ability to remember prices in the marketplace.

Retailing: "A set of business activities carried on to accomplishing the exchange of goods and services for purposes of personal, family, or household use, whether performed in a store or by some form of non-store selling" (American Marketing Association, 2016).

Sticky Websites: Websites that are able to attract a great volume of frequent and repeat customers who spend long hours on the website and visit many pages (Kim and LaRose, 2002).

This research was previously published in Promotional Strategies and New Service Opportunities in Emerging Economies edited by Vipin Nadda, Sumesh Dadwal, and Roya Rahimi, pages 164-183, copyright year 2017 by Business Science Reference (an imprint of IGI Global).

Chapter 20
Online Brand Expansion Towards the Offline Setting:
Which Way to Go?

Rafael Bravo
Universidad de Zaragoza, Spain

Leif E. Hem
Norwegian School of Economics, Norway

José M. Pina
Universidad de Zaragoza, Spain

ABSTRACT

Brand extension and brand alliances are two possible strategies to expand the brand towards different product categories. In this chapter, the authors focus on brands that are well-known for their online services launching offline products. They analyse the results of these strategies in terms of their effects on parent brand image and under different conditions of initial brand image and perceived fit. In order to meet these aims, an empirical study was conducted to 407 undergraduates in a Spanish University. Data are analysed through multivariate analysis of variance. Main results lead us to conclude that: (1) the effects of extensions and alliances are mainly negative on the online brand image, (2) the impact is focused specially on the functional and emotional dimensions of brand image, (3) the effect is more negative for online brands with higher image than for online brands with lower image, and (4) the effect is more negative in the case of an alliance with an offline brand with low image than in the case of an alliance with an offline brand with high image or in a brand extension. This work covers some gaps in the previous literature in online branding. The authors apply concepts and theories used in brand extensions and alliances literature in an offline setting by delving into the differences of these effects on the brand image dimensions. The results obtained in this work may help brand practitioners expand their brands towards different product categories.

DOI: 10.4018/978-1-5225-5187-4.ch020

INTRODUCTION

The rise of the Internet and its applications to almost every device has made the online and offline settings to become more and more closely connected. Consumers have both online and offline identities and they move continuously from one to another (Rau, 2004). In this context, companies with traditional offline business have looked at the Internet as a necessary way for surviving. However, this connection offline-online goes a step further, and companies with online brands have also started to look at the offline context.

As an example, Google has launched its own phones and tablets (Nexus) that have been made in collaboration with different manufacturers as LG, HTC or Samsung (Chen, 2012). The launch of phones or tablet devices may confuse consumers who linked the image of Google exclusively with the online setting, but this combined online-offline strategy can be perfectly in line with its corporate brand identity. Thus, Google states that its mission is *"to organize world's information and make it universally accessible and useful"*. Therefore, the launch of this type of offline products is perfectly aligned with this goal to provide information accessibility.

Two strategies that may allow an online company to go offline are brand extensions and brand alliances. However, the launch of new products and the association with other partner brands in an alliance may change the consumer perception of a brand image (Loken & John, 1993; Delgado & Hernández, 2008). The success of a new launch can not only be measured by its sales figures or its benefits, but also by the impact that the new launch has on the parent brand. In the previous literature, there are works that deals with offline brands launching new online services (Horppu, Kuivalainen, Tarkiainen & Ellonen, 2008; Boshoff, Schlechter & Ward, 2009). However, the expansion of an online brand going offline has not been analysed yet. In the same sense, much of the work in the brand extension and brand alliance literature has focused on the acceptance of the new product and consumer intention to purchase, while lesser attention has received the effect of these strategies on the parental brand image (Völckner, Sattler & Kaufmann, 2008; Pina, Iversen & Martinez, 2010). Thus, in the present work we will try to fill these gaps giving answer to the following questions:

- Are these strategies of brand extensions and alliances to reach an offline setting harming or strengthening the parental online brand image?
- Focusing on the variation in the online brand image:
- Is it more effective to develop these strategies for an online brand with low image or for an online brand with high image?
- Does the fit between the online brand and the offline product category play an important role in this decision?
- What type of strategy is best to reach the offline category, extensions or alliances?; and in the latter, with which type of ally?

The conclusions of this work may help companies such as Dell, that is a company that used a direct sales distribution from its beginnings, and afterwards it expanded its distribution to retail stores. However, moving from selling online to distribute through retail stores may also entail risks that need to be thoroughly analysed (Lawton, 2008). This movement must be carefully implemented in order to avoid risks, and the control of the offline brand experience is considered as the key for its success (Davis, 2007).

The analysis of the effects that the new launch has on the parental brand image is of main importance to determine the success of the strategy (Aaker, 1991; Keller, 1993). In fact, the parent brand image can be diluted even in successful brand expansions in terms of attitude towards the new launch (Farquhar, 1989, Kardes & Allen, 1991, Völckner *et al.,* 2008). The cost of introducing a new brand may be prohibitely high (Yorkston, Nunes & Matta, 2010), and therefore leveraging brand image and transferring brand associations between online and offline settings are hot topics in the literature (Kwon & Lennon, 2009). For these reasons, feedback effects on the parental brand image may be more important to consider than the own acceptance of the new product.

Finally, much of the research has studied either brand extensions or brand alliances independently, but comparatively few works have compared both strategies empirically (James, 2006; Besharat, 2010; Marin & Ruiz, 2010). From the managerial perspective, to know which strategy is best, and under which conditions, is of great relevance in order to launch new products. Indeed, there is a lack of consensus on the literature regarding the suitability to use one strategy or the other. Some works point at the preference of an extension strategy when the brand image and reputation is high, indicating that brand alliance is appropriate when moving to a distant product category. However, in practice we may see that brand extensions are far more common than brand alliances, and there are examples of successful brand extensions even in relatively distant categories (Marin & Ruiz, 2010).

For the above reasons, this work delves into the effects that the new offline launch has on the parental online brand image, and it analyses them under different conditions of brand image and perceived fit. Comparisons between two strategies: extensions and alliances will be made, and within the latter, differences between alliances with and offline brand with high image and alliances with an offline brand with low image will also be studied.

In the following section we review the literature and develop a series of hypotheses. Then, the methodology and the results obtained are presented. The paper finishes with the conclusions of the study, and with the implications and limitations that give shape to new lines of research.

CONCEPTUAL BACKGROUND

From the online branding literature, different factors have been proved to affect the consumer perception of a brand. Thus, Kierzkowski *et al.* (1996) point at the importance of five factors to determine success in the digital framework:

1. To attract users,
2. To engage users' interests and participation,
3. To retain users,
4. To learn about their preferences, and
5. To relate back to users to provide customised interactions.

Among these strategies, Teo and Tan (2002) found empirical evidence that both the implementation of strategies to attract customers and to relate to customers have positive effects on online brand equity, and this in turn have a positive effect on financial growth. Recently, Vernuccio *et al.* (2012) have also studied the determining factors of attitude towards an online brand. These authors point at three main factors: interactivity, personalization and trust. From a consumer-based brand equity perspective, Rios

& Riquelme (2010) highlight the importance of functionality, fulfillment of the promise and customer service support.

However, literature on this field is not clear regarding the specific effect that expansion strategies such as brand extensions or alliances may entail in the consumer perception of the online brand. Brand extensions and brand alliances are two growth strategies commonly used in the marketplace. Specifically, brand extension refers to a situation "whereby a current brand name is used to enter a completely different product class" (Aaker & Keller, 1990, pp. 27), while a brand alliance is defined as "the short or long term association or combination of two or more individual brands, products and/or other distinct proprietary assets" (Simonin & Ruth, 1998, pp. 30). Focusing on these strategies as two ways to launch a new product, we can say that the main goal is to favor the consumer acceptance of the new product leveraging the equity of the brands (de Chernatony & McDonald, 2003; Keller, 1993). However, this new launch, either as brand extension or as a brand alliance, may also have effects on the parent brand (Milberg, Park & McCarthy, 1997; Balachander & Ghose, 2003).

Concerning their foundations, brand extensions and alliances share many points in common. The literature of both brand extensions and brand alliances point out two reciprocal effects: first, an effect from the parent brand on the new product, and second, a spillover from the new product to the parent brand. These have been usually conceptualized as forward effect and backward or feedback effect, respectively (Milberg, Park & McCarthy, 1997; Balachander & Ghose, 2003). In fact, this literature has developed similar conceptual models for brand extensions and alliances, and the same cognitive theories and variables have been frequently used to explain the consumer's attitude and behavior (Bouten, Snelders & Hultink, 2006; James, 2006; Samuelsen & Olsen, 2012). In general, it can be argued that for both conceptual models, attitude towards the new product, being an extension or an alliance, is determined mainly by two factors:

1. Parent brand information (brand image, attitude, perceived quality, etc.) and
2. Perceived fit.

These factors affect also the parental brand image (Lee & Ulgado, 1993; Simonin & Ruth, 1998). Even if the variables and conceptual models are similar, the consumer response may be different between the strategies.

EFFECTS ON THE ONLINE BRAND IMAGE

Every time consumers get new information from the brand, this information is susceptible to produce changes in their perceptions (Aaker, 1991; Keller, 1993). The launch of a new product marketed under the same brand provides new information for the consumer, and then this new information is added to the previous that the consumers have about the brand, subsequently affecting the consumers' attitude and behavior. This process is usually explained from cognitive theories such as the associative network. Specifically, this theory postulates that the consumer's mind is articulated by a network of associations and beliefs (Anderson, 1983). Thus, every time consumers face information about the brand, new associations may be linked to the brand, and this information may also reinforce or dilute the existing ones. In this sense, the new product may create, reinforce or dilute the associations, causing subsequently an effect on the parent brand. However, the question that still remains is in which direction these effects will take place. To foresee the direction, we may use the categorization and schema-congruence theories. Mainly, these theories postulate that consistency between cognitive elements and similarity among various stimuli may ease consumers' attitude evaluations (Aaker & Keller, 1990; Kamins & Gupta, 1994).

In our particular situation, the consumer will be especially surprised when seeing an online brand out of the online setting. Given that this type of expansion online-offline is not frequent on the marketplace, we may think that this will be particularly noticeable for the consumer. Applying the associative network, it is expected that this new launch offline will affect the consumer perception of the online brand. Moreover, following the theory of the categorization and schema congruence, we may think that this strategy may be initially perceived by the consumer as incoherent. Thus, the scarcity of examples in practice, together with a perception of difficult applicability of the know-how of the online brand company in the offline setting, may lead consumer to believe that going offline is too big a leap for the online brand. Consequently, this perception may trigger a negative attitude by the consumer towards the online brand image. Hence, we hypothesise a negative effect for the online brand expansion (either extension or alliance) towards the offline product category:

H1: The online brand image will be worse after the offline expansion than prior the expansion

The Effects of Online Brand Image and Perceived Fit

Even though we have already hypothesized a negative variation on the online brand image for this expansion, the quantity of this variation may differ depending on the online brand image. A strong brand is characterized by unique, positive, and strong associations while the opposite characterize a weak brand (Keller, 1993). These differences make the consumer to have usually a clearer and more positive image of a strong brand than of a weak brand (Aaker, 1991). Due to these differences, we may also expect different effects when the consumer faces incongruent information about the brand. In the case of a brand with high image, this information will be particularly shocking for consumers, since they thought they knew the brand fairly well (Dickinson & Barker, 2007). On the contrary, incongruent information may have a lesser impact on a weak brand, since consumers are still giving shape to the brand node, and then the information would not be as noticeable as in the former case.

In the situation of an online brand going offline, this perception of lack of congruence can be particularly harmful. Thus, incongruent information caused by a new launch in the offline setting may result in a dilution of previous associations connected with the internet world. These associations are usually the consequence of huge investments and effort, developed throughout the years by the company (Roth, 1994; Kazoleas, Kim & Moffit, 2001; Stern, Zinkhan & Jaju, 2001). As a result, a dilution will damage the strong online brand more than a weak online brand. This is also in line with some managerial practice, where companies with strong brands usually implement more conservative strategies in order to protect the images of their brands, while firms with weak brands may be more proneness to assume higher risks. In consequence, we propose that the variation in the online brand image will be more negative for the stronger online brand than for the weaker one, and thus:

H2: The variation in the online brand image will be more negative in the case of an online brand with high image than in an online brand with low image

Perceived fit is the other most cited factor in the literature on brand extensions and alliances. However, most of the works have focused exclusively on the effects of this variable on consumer perception, attitude and intention to purchase the new product. In online branding, the work by Song *et al.* (2010) explores these relations focusing on an online technology service brand. Empirical results of this study shows that perceived fit has a positive effect on quality perception of an online brand extension. When explaining the expected effects of online-offline expansion on parent brand image, we hypothesized a negative effect on the online brand image because of the consumer perception of incongruence. However, the variation in the online brand image may vary depending on the perceived fit between the online brand and the offline product category. On the basis of the previous cited theories of categorization and schema-congruence, most of the works share the opinion that the lower perception of fit, the more negative effect on the parent brand (Aaker & Keller, 1990; Lafferty, Goldsmith & Hult, 2004; Völkner & Sattler, 2006). Even though this effect has been usually studied in offline settings, the same rationale may be applicable to online brands. In consequence, the perception of low category fit in a distant offline category will have more negative variation in the online brand image than in the high fit. Hence, for online brands going offline through extensions and alliances we may hypothesise:

H3: The variation in the online brand image will be more negative in the case of low fit with the new product than in the case of a high fit

The Effects of Type of Strategy

Finally, differences in relation with the type of strategy are also expected at the light of the previous theories. Extensions and alliances may entail different effects on the online brand image. And in the latter case, differences may also be presumed depending on the image of the brand ally.

Starting with the differences between strategies of brand extension and alliances, brand alliances have been reported to be useful when the value of an extension is questionable (Kumar, 2005; James, 2006). Park, Jun & Shocker (1996) argue that a composite brand may overcome the limitations of a single-brand to reach new markets. Thus, combining two brands with complementary attributes may enable every single brand to extend its name to other products, with greater success than would be possible by a direct extension or sub-branding. Brand alliances may allow potentially to access far markets by capitalising the strength and reputation of each brand (Rao & Ruekert, 1994; Monga & Lau-Gesk, 2007). Therefore, a brand alliance is an interesting strategy to cross over the boundaries of brand extensions, providing an advantage over alternative growth strategies (Desai & Keller, 2002; Monga & Lau-Gensk, 2007).

Besides, differences between extensions and alliances may be also inferred from signaling theory. Two brands may provide more signals of quality about the new product than just one, therefore alliances provide more information than brand extensions. In an alliance, all the partner brands act as signals of the quality of the new product, and this may help to reduce the uncertainty and risk associated with the purchase. In this sense, there are at least two companies that support the new launch, and they are putting their money and reputation at stake. However, this reduction in uncertainty and risk will take place only when the partner brand has a positive contribution in the alliance. This was the case of Orbit whitening gum powered by Crest. Procter & Gamble's brand manager stated that they had been working on bringing its own gum, but they came to the realization that they needed someone who had great experience within the product category (Buss, 2003). This is not only important from the production or distribution point of view, but also from the customer perception perspective. In this scenario, the inclusion of a brand specialized on gums may act as an information signal for the consumer.

In our particular situation, the existence of an offline partner in an alliance may be interpreted by the consumer as a sign of security to buy the new product. In this situation, the consumer may feel that, even though there is a lack of congruency for the online brand moving offline, there is an offline brand that supports the new launch. Therefore, the consumer will feel more trust to the new launch that will foster trust on the new product. This will be especially important when the offline brand is already commercializing products that are similar or in close product categories to the new product launch. As a consequence, the consumer will perceive less congruence in the strategy of brand extension than in the strategy of brand alliances. In the latter, the offline brand may apply its know-how to the production or distribution process, and the online brand may contribute with some added value derived from its reputation and brand image. Contrarily, this is not applicable to the online brand extension, where the consumer may just rely on the online brand. This lack of congruency in the expansion is not eased by an offline ally contributing to fill the gap, and therefore this brand extension strategy may affect more severely the online brand image than in the case of a brand alliance online-offline. In consequence, we propose that:

H4: The variation in the online brand image will be more negative in the case of a strategy of brand extension than in the case of a strategy of brand alliance with an offline brand

In case of choosing the strategy of an alliance, the company should analyze thoroughly the most suitable partner. Consumers' perception of the alliance will depend on the image that each consumer has about every member in the alliance. Regarding differences between the images of the partner brands in an alliance, and based on the associative network theory, there will be a reciprocal transfer of associations where, in general, the brand with the lowest image is winning with the alliance in terms of feedback effects, while the brand with the highest image is loosing in the relationship (Hillyer & Tikoo, 1995; Dickinson & Barker, 2007). Additionally, Levin & Levin (2000) use the foundations of context effects models to explain the transfer of affect between brands in an alliance. From these models, they point at two opposite effects so-called contrast and assimilation. When the evaluation of an object is moving away from the point of reference, a contrast effect is said to occur. On the contrary, when the judgment tends to move towards a contextual anchoring point, the phenomenon is known as assimilation (Meyers-Levy & Sternthal, 1993; Levin, 2002). Assimilation and contrast are co-acting in the consumer's evaluation. However, Levin (2002) found empirical evidence that assimilation effects are stronger in a brand alliance than contrast effects.

Taking the negative effect of the online-offline expansion, we may expect that the online brand will be more damaged when allying with a weak offline brand than in the case of a strong offline partner. Thus, assimilation effects as a consequence of the alliance may result in a transfer of associations from the offline brand. In consequence, the weaker the offline brand, the poorer the associations to be transferred to the online brand. All this lead to think that the variation in the online brand image will be more negative in the case of a brand alliance with a weak offline brand than in the case of an alliance with a strong offline brand, and hence:

H5: The variation in the online brand image will be more negative in the case of an alliance with an offline brand with low image than in the case of an offline brand with high image

METHOD

An empirical analysis was developed in order to reach the goals and test the proposed hypotheses. We chose Internet web-portals, since they offer an ample variety of services. Due to the extendibility of these portals, consumers may perceive coherence if they launch new and untraditional products (van Riel & Ouwersloot, 2005). Selection of offline product categories and brands as well as the selection of a brand image scale were made via two pre-tests. In the first one, online brands and offline category products were selected. In the second pre-test, offline brands were chosen for each offline product category and brand image scale was tested. The criterion was to select two categories with high versus low fit; and to choose two brands with high vs. low brand image both for the Internet portals and for every offline product category. Only well-known brands were chosen in order for respondents to have an established image of the brands, and then to gain reliability in their responses (Low & Lamb, 2000).

A total of 54 and 82 undergraduates participated in the first and second pre-tests respectively. Respondents were asked to indicate their degree of familiarity with different online and offline brands and their perception of image towards each brand through seven-point bipolar scales (familiarity: 1=very unfamiliar, 7=very familiar; brand image: 1=very bad image, 7=very good image). As a result, we removed the brands that were not familiar for the sample (brands with average values in familiarity below 4 in the seven-point scale), and we selected from the familiar brands those with the highest and lowest scores on image. In order to choose two offline product categories with high and low perceived fit, respondents in the first pre-test were asked the following question: do you think it is coherent for (the online brand) to launch (offline product category)? (1=very incoherent, 7=very coherent). Thus, we chose two products with high versus low fit with the Internet portals. The final selection can be seen in Table 1.

Significant differences were found in fit with the online brand between the two offline categories (t=5.25, p<0.001), and also in brand image for the Internet portals (Z=3.945, p<0.001) and for the offline brands in both the low (Z=6.16, p<0.001) and high (Z=7.43, p<0.001) fit categories.

The second pre-test was also used to test the scale of brand image to be applied in the final study. This step was crucial, as this scale had to be suitable to measure brand image online and offline. Thus, the development of the scale was made on the basis of the most cited dimensions and items of brand image on both functional as well as emotional attributes (Aaker, 1991; Aaker, Benet-Martínez & Garolera, 1997; Martínez & Pina, 2009). Since we departed from previous research on brand image in the offline context, respondents in the pre-test were asked to evaluate the online brands (MSN and Yahoo) in order to check its applicability to this type of brands. As a result of these analyses, no particular problems were revealed in the adaption of this scale to the online brand context. Thus, we obtained a preliminary scale composed of 10 items that were grouped along three-dimensions. Given their composition, we called

Table 1. Brands and categories selected in the pretests 1 and 2

Categories		High Brand Image	Low Brand Image
Online	Portal sites	MSN (6.09)	Yahoo (5.19)
Offline	Mobile phones (high coherence: 4.31)	Nokia (6.45)	Alcatel (3.56)
	Plasma TV (low coherence: 3.17)	Sony (6.12)	Pioneer (4.58)

Note. Average values between brackets in 7-point scales. These values refer to coherence in the categories column, and to brand image in the highest and lowest brand image columns.

these dimensions 1) functional, 2) emotional, and 3) commitment. Regarding the latter, this dimension was composed of three items (X takes into account the opinion of consumers", "X has a high commitment with consumers" and "X has good principles in the relationship with consumers"). Although only one of these items refers directly to "commitment", the other two items were related to the involvement the company has with its consumers. This concept of involvement is close to commitment, and there are authors that even consider involvement as conceptually similar to commitment (Gundlach, Achrol & Mentzer, 1995; Ingram, Skinner & Taylor, 2005). In consequence, we decided to label this dimension as "commitment". Composition of the scale can be seen in Table 2.

After these pre-tests, a survey was carried out in a main Spanish city on 419 undergraduates in the year 2008. The use of students is especially suitable in this particular study, given their high level of familiarity with new electronic technologies and the Internet. Thus, the sample of respondents was reported to spend more than 14 hours per week on average on the Internet. Questionnaires were distributed in class, and respondents were asked to fill them in voluntarily and to hand them on the following day. The sample was composed of 56,7% female students and 43,3% male students, age range varies from 18 to 36 and the average was 22 years-old. In total, 12 versions of the questionnaire were developed, one for each single combination of type of online brand (low/high brand image), product category (low/ high fit) and expansion strategy (alliance with an offline brand with low image/alliance with an offline brand with high image/brand extension). Finally 407 valid questionnaires were collected with similar number of responses for each version. The composition of the questionnaire was mainly structured in two parts. In the first one, respondents had to fill in the brand image scale reported in Table 2 for the online brand (and also for the offline brand in case of alliances); in the second part, respondents were asked to fill in again the brand image scale for the online brand after the exposure to the new product. In this second part, respondents were also asked to answer to questions regarding their perception of fit between the online brand and the new product.

The empirical study analysed the image both pre and post the information of the new product is presented to the respondent (hereinafter pre- and post- brand image). Moreover, the work was planned to analyse for differences in type of online brand image, type of fit in the offline product category and

Table 2. Scale composition

Factors	Items	Cronbach's Alpha
Brand image (functional)	X products and services are of high quality	(0.72-0.88)
	Consumers are not disappointed with X	
	X products and services are easy-to-use	
Brand image (emotional)	Its products and services have original designs	(0.80-0.88)
	X transmits a different personality from the competition brands	
	X provides more fun and entertainment than competition	
	Everybody came to like X	
Brand image (commit.)	X takes into account the opinion of consumers	(0.83-0.91)
	X has a high commitment with consumers	
	X has good principles in the relationship with consumers	

Note: X denotes the online brand name, values between brackets refer to the lowest and highest Cronbach's alpha between the pre-online brand image, post-online brand image and offline brand image for the data sample of brand extensions and alliances.

type of strategy for the expansion. Therefore, a mixed between-within experimental design is proposed, where pre- and post- brand image is measured within the same questionnaire, and the conditions of 2 (low/high brand image) x 2 (low/high fit) x 3 (low image ally/high image ally/no ally) were treated in different questionnaires. Similar designs are used in the literature to compare extension and alliance strategies, and to analyse the effects on the parent brand (d'Astous, Colbert & Fournier, 2007; Washburn, Till & Priluck, 2004).

RESULTS

This section has been divided into three main points. In the two first sections we describe the process of validation of the online brand image scale and manipulation checks; the third point is devoted to the hypotheses testing.

Validation of the Online Brand Image Scale

The first step in the empirical analysis was to analyse the properties of the brand image scale. Thus, we proceeded with an exploratory factor analysis with SPSS, and subsequently we validated the results by means of a confirmatory analysis through EQS.

Given that brand image was measured both prior and after the exposure to the new launch, we made the analysis separately for the brand image scale prior and post, and both for the conditions of brand extensions and alliances. In all cases, results showed coherence and the same three-dimensional structure emerged (composition is shown in Table 2). This structure was also similar to the one obtained in pre-test 2 for the same scale. In consequence, we considered in our analysis a three-dimensional structure for the brand image scale, and in line with the composition of the dimensions, we called them functional, emotional and commitment.

In all cases, the item "*X products and services are easy-to-use*" was removed from the scale due to a low individual reliability coefficient, below the common threshold of 0.5 (Hair *et al.*, 2005). No problems of convergent or discriminant validity were found, and the scale was reliable with Cronbach's alpha that ranged from 0.85 to 0.91. These values are over the commonly accepted thresholds in the literature (Hair *et al.*, 2005).

Manipulation Checks

After analysing the properties of the scales, the next step was to confirm that the selected brands and product categories in the study were identified by the sample as high vs. low brand image, both for online and offline brands, and high fit vs. low fit product categories, just as established in the pre-test.

An overall measure for brand image was created for the manipulation checks by computing the mean scores on each dimension in the initial online brand image scale. Results of these analyses show that the pre-image of the online brand considered as high image had certainly a higher brand image than the pre-online brand with low image, and this difference was statistically significant (t=4.38, p<0.05). Analogously, we proceeded for the offline brand, and the image of the offline brands selected to represent the high brand image were statistically higher than the ones chosen for low brand image, both in the mobile category (t=10.88, p<0.05) and in the plasma TV category (t=4.38, p<0.05).

Finally, in relation to the perception of fit, we used a three-item seven-point bipolar scale where respondents were asked for their opinion regarding the new launch made by the online brand (1=not at all logical, 7=very logical, 1=not at all appropriate, 7=very appropriate, 1=not at all coherent, 7=very coherent). These items had been commonly used in the previous literature (Desai & Keller, 2002; Worm & van Durme, 2006). The validation process showed the unidimensionality of the scale, and all the properties of validity and reliability were fulfilled. Similarly, we calculated mean score of the three items to measure the perception of product category fit. Results showed that the product category chosen in the pretest as high fit, were certainly perceived with a higher fit than the category selected as low fit, and this difference was also significant (t=7.158, p<0.05). Thus, manipulation checks confirmed that respondents in each treatment accurately evaluate the image of the selected brands and the product category fit, as proposed on the basis of the results from the pre-tests.

Hypotheses Testing

In order to test for the variation in the online brand image and then contrast hypothesis 1, we studied the differences between the pre and post online brand image. Given that brand image is a multidimensional construct, we proceeded to run a repeated measures MANOVA. In this analysis, the three dimensions of brand image were used as dependent variables, and time (pre and post) was considered as the independent variable. Once the assumptions of this technique were tested, results show a significant effect for time on the combined dependent variables (Wilks' Lambda=0.89, F=16.27, p<0.05). Regarding the effect size, partial eta squared reached a value of 0.11, which can be considered as a moderate-large effect. If we analyse the means prior and after the respondent is exposed to the new launch, we can see in Table 3 that online brand image is lower after the exposure than prior in every dimension. In consequence, we can say that the effect of an online-offline brand expansion on the online brand image is negative. This gives support to hypothesis 1. Following with the analysis in every separate dimension of brand image, we can see that there were significant effects on the functional (F=33.32, p<0.05, partial eta squared=0.08) and emotional dimensions (F=22.51, p<0.05, partial eta squared=0.05), but not in the commitment dimension (F=0.45, p<0.05, partial eta squared=0.01).

The next step was to look for differences in the variation of online brand image according to the three variables that determine the experimental conditions in this study: type of online brand image, type of product category fit and type of strategy. In order to analyse the variation in online brand image, we created new variables which are the differences between pre and post online brand image for each dimension. We called these variables "variation in functional image", "variation in emotional image" and "variation in commitment image". Thus, a three-way between groups MANOVA was considered for the analysis. The new variables: variation in functional image, variation in emotional image and variation

Table 3. Differences between pre- and post-online brand image

Dimensions	Pre-Online Brand Image	Post-Online Brand Image	F	Sig.	Partial Eta Squared
Functional dimension	4.42	4.12	33.32	0.01	0.08
Emotional dimension	4.58	4.35	22.51	0.01	0.05
Commitment dimension	4.14	4.11	0.45	0.50	0.01

in commitment image were used as dependent variables, and type of online brand image (low vs. high), type of product category fit (low vs. high) and type of strategy (extension vs. alliance with offline brand with low image vs. alliance with offline brand with high image) were used as the independent variables. Before running this analysis, we tested for the required assumptions of the MANOVA technique. Correlations between the dependent variables ranged from 0.66-0.69 and no problems of multicolinearity were found. Levene's tests are significant and show no violation of the assumption of equality of variance. It is necessary to highlight that Box's test of equality of covariance matrix was not significant. This can be a consequence of a large sample size, as in our case. In this sense, Tabachnick & Fidell (2007) point out that this test tends to be too strict when the sample size is large. No other problems were found and then we proceeded with the analysis. MANOVA creates a new composite dependent variable which is a linear combination of the three dependent variables. These are the variations in the three dimensions of online brand image. This new variable is used to test the hypothesis proposed.

As seen in Table 4, results show that the type of online brand image has a significant effect on the composite variable (Wilks' Lambda=0.97, F=3.88, $p<0.05$, partial eta squared=0.03). Variation in online brand image was more negative in the case of online brand with high image (M_{funct}=-0.42; M_{emot}=-0.36; M_{commit}=-0.04) than in the case of online brand with low image (M_{funct}=-0.18; M_{emot}=-0.10; M_{commit}=-0.03). In consequence, we can give support to hypothesis 2. When the results for the dependent variables were analysed separately, we verified that significant effects are found in the functional (F=6.27, $p<0.05$, partial eta squared=0.01) and emotional (F=7.47, $p<0.05$, partial eta squared=0.02) image dimensions, but not in the commitment one (F=0.04, $p>0.05$).

In relation to the type of category fit, results show that the effect of this variable on the variation of online brand image is not significant (Wilks' Lambda=0.99, F=0.66, $p>0.05$). Therefore, we reject hypothesis 3. This result was not expected, and in order to analyse the causes, we revised the analysis for each dependent variable separately. Although we found that variation in online brand image was more negative in a low category fit expansion (M_{funct}=-0.35; M_{emot}=-0.29; M_{commit}=-0.09) than in a high category fit expansion (M_{funct}=-0.27; M_{emot}=-0.19; M_{commit}=-0.02), none of the dimensions of brand image had a significant main effect. Nevertheless, we found indirect effects in the functional dimension between type of image and type of fit (F=3.79, $p<0.05$, partial eta squared=0.01) and between type of fit and type of strategy (F=5.27, $p<0.05$, partial eta squared=0.02). As a result, we may think that indirect relations could partly explain the non-significant main effect. Thus, perceived fit had an effect on

Table 4. Determining factors of the variation in online brand image

	Value	F	Sig.	Partial Eta Squared
Intercept	0.89	15.83	0.01	0.11
Image	0.97	3.88	0.01	0.03
Fit	0.99	0.66	0.58	0.01
Strategy	0.95	3.49	0.01	0.03
Image x fit	0.99	1.30	0.28	0.03
Image x strategy	0.98	1.37	0.22	0.01
Fit x strategy	0.97	1.73	0.11	0.01
Image x fit x strategy	0.99	0.38	0.90	0.01

the variation in the functional online brand image through the interactive effects with the type of online brand image and type of strategy variables. This is in line with the previous literature, where empirical works have shown that these effects can be found not only when comparing the direct effect of fit (Lee & Ulgado, 1993; Jun, Mazumdar & Raj, 1999), but also in the interaction effect between brand image and fit (Kim & Lavack, 1996; Jun *et al.*, 1999).

Finally, regarding the type of strategy, results showed a significant main effect of this variable on the variation of online brand image (Wilks' Lambda=0.95, F=3.49, p<0.05, partial eta squared=0.03). Post-hoc comparisons using the Tukey HSD test showed significant differences of 5% in the emotional dimension between the strategies of alliance with an offline brand with low image ($M_{variation}$=-0.53) and alliance with an offline brand with high image ($M_{variation}$=-0.08), and between the strategies of alliance with an offline brand with low image ($M_{variation}$=-0.53) and brand extension ($M_{variation}$=-0.11). Similarly, differences were also found in the commitment dimension both between the strategies of alliance with an offline brand with low image ($M_{variation}$=-0.25) and alliance with an offline brand with high image ($M_{variation}$=0.07), and between the strategies of alliance with an offline brand with low image ($M_{variation}$=-0.25) and brand extension ($M_{variation}$=0.08). In order to complement these analyses and to obtain a composite result for the analysis of brand image to test hypotheses 4 and 5, new MANOVA models were run analogously to compare specifically between the strategies of brand extension and brand alliances, and between the strategies of brand alliance with an offline brand with low image and brand alliance with an offline brand with high image. In the case of the former comparison between extensions and alliances, no significant differences were found and then hypothesis 4 has to be rejected. Regarding the comparison between brand alliance with an offline brand with low image and brand alliance with an offline brand with high image, significant differences were found (F=4.67, p<0.05) and then we can give support to hypothesis 5. In line with the results obtained in the post-hoc analysis, we verified that significant effects were found in the emotional (F=11.77, p<0.05, partial eta squared=0.04) and commitment (F=7.59, p<0.05, partial eta squared=0.03) dimensions of brand image.

Table 5. Summary of the hypotheses and results obtained

Hypothesis	Composite results (sig.)	Support	Direct and indirect effects in brand image dimensions
H1: "The online brand image will be worse after the offline expansion than prior…"	F=16.27 (p<0.01)	Yes	- Functional (F=33.32, p<0.01) - Emotional (F=22.51, p<0.01)
H2: "The variation in the online brand image will be more negative in online brand with high image…"	F=3.88 (p<0.01)	Yes	- Functional (6.27, p<0.01) - Emotional (7.47, p<0.01)

H3: "The variation in the online brand image will be more negative in low fit…"	F=0.66 (p=0.58)	No	- Functional (indirect effects):
			  - image x fit (F=3.79, p<0.01)
			  - fit x strategy (F=5.27, p<0.01)

H4: "The variation in the online brand image will be more negative in brand extension than in alliance"	F=1.61 (p=0.18)	No	
H5: "The variation in the online brand image will be more negative in alliance with low image partner that with high image partner"	F=4.67 (p<0.01)	Yes	- Emotional (F=11.77, p<0.01) - Commitment (F=7.59, p<0.01)

CONCLUSION

The previous findings allow us to extract a series of implications for both academicians and practitioners. From the academic point of view, this research has contributed to fill the gap of research in online branding (Ibeh, Luo & Dinnie, 2005). The applicability of some of the most frequently used theories on extensions and alliances have been proved in this particular case of an online brand going offline. Harvin (2000) suggested that offline brand power is likely to be transferable to the online environment. Similarly Horppu *et al.* (2008) proved this linkage between online-offline settings. In the latter work, consumer experiences and satisfaction in the online setting affect perceptions, attitudes and behaviours towards the brand in the offline context. Our paper has complemented this line of research in online branding, and it has widen the study of effects on the online brand, delving into the differences in brand image dimensions. The division of brand image into its three dimensions allowed us to expand these findings for each component. The online-offline expansion may carry a negative variation in the online brand image. However, there are important differences on the effects on each dimension. These results are in line with those obtained by Mahasuweerachai (2012), who shows that service quality perceptions of hotel brand extensions have an impact on core brand reputation, loyalty and consumer perceptions of future brand extensions. However these effects are different depending on the dimensions of service quality. Thus, our work shows that the least negative variation is found on the commitment dimension. These results lead us to think that the consumer perceives that the online brand may maintain its philosophy of commitment with the consumer in the new offline product, taking into account their opinions, and maintaining the same good principles. However, the consumer hesitates about the online brand ability to manufacture offline products. Differences between the two settings are found to be high especially for the functional dimension, probably because the consumer perceives that the company may hardly transfer its know-how to the new product. Similarly, the consumer also hesitates that the company may take advantage of its experience in the online setting to develop a good design and to maintain the personality of the brand. In general, symbolic attributes have been posited to be easier to stretch in terms of finding links between brand nodes related to functional attributes (Park *et al.*, 1991; Czellar, 2003), this is caused by the more holistic and abstract nature of these attributes, which allows consumers to identify more points of relatedness on symbolic imagery between a parent brand and the new product (Pina *et al.*, 2010).

From the managerial perspective, we may summarize the findings in four main implications. First, we have seen that for an online brand going offline, the effects on the brand image are negative. These results advise against this type of brand expansion, and warn about the damage of brand extension and alliance strategies on the image of the online brand. The consumer may perceive incongruence in an online brand going offline, even if trying to reach a category with some kind of connection Maybe if some strong companies ventured to follow this step, the consumer would start to perceive the expansion online-offline as normal, and then probably the negative effects detected in this work may be reduced or even become positive. As indicated by Corkindale & Belder (2009), a strong brand with high reputation may favor the acceptance of innovations in a product category. Nonetheless, it is important to interpret these results within a context where the consumer has no information about the new product. In a situation where the new product was proved to have a good quality and the company emphasized the benefits of this product through a proper marketing campaign, maybe the consumer proneness to accept the new product would be higher, and then derive in a positive effect for the brand image (Supphellen, Eismann & Hem, 2004). In this sense, the success in Nexus or Kindle tablets may lead consumers to change their perceptions. Bajarin (2012) posits that Amazon has a service first mentality, and therefore there is coherence to move from online services to offline software or even to hardware, just as other companies as Google or Apple do. As indicated by this author, the main goal with these movements is not to make money directly, but to be the best platform for their services. This message is reaching the Amazon customer, and it is generating loyalty and trust.

Second, even though results have evidenced negative variation in the online brand image, these effects vary depending on the dimension of brand image. The variation is not equal on each dimension of brand image, and thus we have seen that the commitment dimension is less vulnerable than the functional or emotional dimensions. This is in line with the work by Landseng & Olsen (2012), where the effect of category fit is especially important in functional alliances. This work also points at the effect of brand concept consistency (see Park, Milberg & Lawson, 1991), and its relevance for expressive brand alliances. Managers may use marketing mix variables such as advertising campaigns to increase perceived brand concept consistency (Mariadoss, Echambadi, Arnold & Bindroo, 2010). Thus, companies may emphasize the main parent brand associations that are transferable to the new product category in order to minimize these negative effects. Nevertheless, there are authors that advice about the difficulty to mitigate negative image feedback effects through advertising, at least in the short term (Völckner *et al.,* 2008). The key to leverage their image in the expansion may be to control its personality and consumer engagement. As pointed by Jarvis (2009), the key of success is to foster user feedback and to involve consumers in the creative process, be they online or offline. In the case of moving towards the offline setting, maybe these companies have to implement actions in a different way as they do, but the core of the strategy of engagement and involvement should remain. As we extracted from the results of our work, the commitment dimension of brand image is the less vulnerable in this expansion online-offline and companies should maintain this high commitment by keeping their engagement with consumers.

Third, differences between low versus high online brand image have evidenced that the online brand with low image has less to lose compared to a brand with a high image. The brand with a low image may be more proneness to put its image at stake than a brand with a high image. This is also in line with the previous literature, where the effects in brand image were more negative for strong brands with high familiarity than for brands with low familiarity (Dickinson & Barker, 2007; Völckner *et al.,* 2008). Müge-Arslan & Korkut-Altuna (2010) even posit that brand expansion to other categories always produces a drop in parent brand image, being category fit high or low. Nevertheless, these authors' study also shows that the dilution on the brand image is higher when the image of the parent brand is strong versus when the parent brand image is weak.

Fourth, when comparing strategies to go offline, results showed that the alliance with an offline brand with low image is the worse option in terms of variation in the online brand image. Overall, no significant differences were found between the strategy of brand extension and the strategy of alliance with an offline brand with high image. Thus, we cannot recommend one specific strategy between brand extensions and alliance with a partner with high image, and we just advise against the strategy of brand alliance with an offline partner with low image. In fact, there is no consensus in the literature whether which strategy, brand extensions or brand alliances, is best. Recently we can find works that either lean towards brand extensions (Samuelsen & Olsen, 2012) or show its preference for brand alliances (Thompson & Strutton, 2012). In any case, previous studies outline that in case of choosing the strategy of brand alliances, the selection of partners should be based in balanced relationships, with similar contributions made from each company (Bucklin & Segupta, 1993). The common rule to select between extensions and alliances should be made at the light of potential benefits for both companies, in terms of risk and organizational contingencies. The ally brand should be selected because of its reputation and ability to contribute with signals of quality in the new product (Leuthesser, Kohli & Suri, 2003; Kumar, 2005). Nevertheless, to choose between a brand extension or a brand alliance strategy is a complex decision. From the general view that brand extensions are suitable for brands with high reputation and brand alliances are interesting when reaching a distant product category (Desai & Keller, 2002; Marin & Ruiz, 2010), we may argue from our results that the decision, in terms of feedback effects on the brand image, also depends on every different scenario and on each specific brand image dimension. Overall, this online-offline strategy would have a lower harm in the alliance with a high brand image partner than in the brand extension or a brand alliance with a low brand image partner for the emotional and commitment dimensions. In fact, as pointed by other authors, the acceptance of the brand extension or the brand alliance would also depend on the type of consumer. Thus, the feedback effects on the brand image for those high involved consumers with high degree of consumer-company identification may be different than for those consumers with low involvement or low degree of consumer-company identification (Marin and Ruiz, 2010). As indicated by Yorkston *et al.* (2010) it is also important to analyse not only the brand personality but also the consumer personality traits.

Regarding limitations and future lines of research, the study covers only certain products and brands, and therefore there is a need to include more categories and a broader spectrum of brands in order to generalize the results. Moreover, further studies should be needed to analyse asymmetric effects on the brand image (Lei, Dawar & Lemmink, 2008). In this work, we have focused on the effects of the online brand. However, differences may arise if we analyse the effects on the offline brand. In addition, even if differences have been found between brand image dimensions, it would be interesting to delve into the nature of these differences conducting an ad hoc study, with products and brands that specially control for functional, emotional and commitment attributes.

Finally, it would be also important to control for the effect of other external factors regarding with the type of consumer or situational variables such as consumer innovativeness or consumer involvement (Bengtsson, 2002; Hem, de Chernatony & Iversen, 2003; Helmig, Huber & Leeflang, 2007). This type of variables may act as moderators or mediators in the relations between the category fit and the brand image. Thus, Chatterjee (2010) recently finds that consumer traits of self-efficacy has an impact on consumer perception of category fit, and this in turn has an effect on consumer intentions to adopt an online brand extension. Category usage would moderate the latter relation. In the same sense and in the case of alliances, it would be interesting to test for the complementarity of brand attributes (Hillyer & Tikoo, 1995; Park *et al.*, 1996; Samu, Krishnan & Smith, 1999) or to analyse the effect of different consumer-related variables in these relations. The work by Myers, Kwon & Forsythe (2013) focuses on cause-brand alliances, and it analyses the specific role of perceived brand motivations and consumer involvement in brand attitude and purchase intentions. Despite the differences with other types of alliances as cobranding and the dissimilarities between the offline and online setting, consumer factors as the level of involvement with a product category or brand may have an impact on the spillover effects derived from the alliance that is worth to study in future research. Gammoh & Voss (2011) also remark this new research avenue, and they add the need to deepen into the factors related with the partner brands relation such as partner similarity, resource complementarity, and relationship commitment.

All in all, it is important to highlight that what really determines the effects on the brand image, is the success or failure of the new product. If the new offline launch gathers the needs of consumers, it provides satisfactory consumer experiences and it leads to brand engagement, then the effects on the online brand could be positive (Rowley, 2009).

In this work, we have tried to shed some light into the strategy of going offline. Despite the negative effects showed in general on the online brand image, the decision of implementing an extension or alliance strategy should be based also on other factors. This is the case of consumer's acceptance of the new product, the desire of the organization to associate itself with a specific partner, the relative implementation cost of each strategy, the risk of a partner's negative behavior and its impact on the host brand image, or the future business plans of the company (d'Astous *et al.*, 2007). Certainly moving from online to offline may entail risks of diluting the brand image, and that is why if online companies want to conquer the offline setting, they have to control more than ever one of the most important assets that they have that is their brand image.

There is a need to delve into the connections of online and offline businesses. The innovativeness of the discussed growth strategies in this particular case, together with the scarcity of research in the topic, makes this line of research a very promising one. The online-offline gap is steadily becoming thinner, and future works should guide brand managers to choose the right strategies to face this gap.

ACKNOWLEDGMENT

Authors want to give thanks for the financial assistance provided through the I+D+I project (Ref: ECO2009-08283) from the Spanish Government, through the GENERES (ref. S-09) project from the Government of Aragon, and from the Norwegian Research Council.

REFERENCES

Aaker, D. A. (1991). *Managing brand equity*. New York: The Free Press.

Aaker, D. A., & Keller, K. L. (1990). Consumer evaluations of brand extensions. *Journal of Marketing*, *54*(1), 27–41. doi:10.2307/1252171

Aaker, J., Benet-Martinez, V., & Garolera, J. (2001). Consumption symbols as carriers of culture: A study of Japanese and Spanish brand personality constructs. *Journal of Personality and Social Psychology*, *81*(3), 492–508. doi:10.1037/0022-3514.81.3.492 PMID:11554649

Anderson, J. R. (1983). A spreading activation theory of memory. *Journal of Verbal Learning and Verbal Behavior*, *22*(3), 261–295. doi:10.1016/S0022-5371(83)90201-3

Bajarin, B. (2012). *What I like about Amazon's kindle strategy*. Retrieved from http://techpinions.com/what-i-like-about-amazons-kindle-strategy/9951

Balachander, S., & Ghose, S. (2003). Reciprocal spillover effects: A strategic benefit of brand extensions. *Journal of Marketing*, *67*(1), 4–13. doi:10.1509/jmkg.67.1.4.18594

Bengtsson, A. (2002). Unnoticed relationships: Do consumers experience co-branded products? *Advances in Consumer Research. Association for Consumer Research (U. S.)*, *29*, 521–527.

Besharat, A. (2010). How co-branding versus brand extensions drive consumers' evaluations of new products: A brand equity approach. *Industrial Marketing Management, 39*(8), 1240–1249. doi:10.1016/j.indmarman.2010.02.021

Boshoff, Shclechter, & Ward. (2009). The mediating effect of brand image and information search intentions on the perceived risks associated with online purchasing on a generically-branded website. *Management Dynamics, 18*(4), 18–27.

Boulton, C. (2007). Google phone: Build it and they will buy it. *eweek.com*. Retrieved from www.eweek.com

Bouten, L. M., Snelders, H. J., & Hultink, H. L. J. (2006). A chip off two old blocks: The influence of fit on evaluation of a cobranded product. In *Proceedings of the European Marketing Academy Conference*. Athens, Greece: EMAC.

Bucklin, L., & Segupta, S. (1993). Organising successful co-marketing alliances. *Journal of Marketing, 57*(2), 32–46. doi:10.2307/1252025

Buss, D. (2003). Happily ever after? *BrandChannel*. Retrieved from http://www.brandchannel.com/features_effect.asp?pf_id=151

Chatterjee, P. (2010). e-Service brand extensions: The role of perceived fit and category usage level on adoption. *Journal of Service Science, 3*(1), 7–13.

Chen, B. X. (2012, November 2). One on one: Google Android director on Nexus strategy. *The New York Times*. Retrieved from http://bits.blogs.nytimes.com/2012/11/02/android-nexus-strategy/

Corkindale, D., & Belder, M. (2009). Corporate brand reputation and the adoption of innovations. *Journal of Product and Brand Management, 18*(4), 242–250. doi:10.1108/10610420910972765

Czellar, S. (2003). Consumer attitude towards brand extensions: An integrative model and research propositions. *International Journal of Research in Marketing, 20*(1), 97–115. doi:10.1016/S0167-8116(02)00124-6

d'Astous, A., Colbert, F., & Fournier, M. (2007). An experimental investigation of the use of brand extension and co-branding strategies in the arts. *Journal of Services Marketing, 21*(4), 231–240. doi:10.1108/08876040710758531

Davis, D. (2007). Dell checks into offline sales with Wal-Mart. *Internet Retailer*. Retrieved from http://www.internetretailer.com/2007/05/25/dell-checks-into-offline-sales-with-wal-mart

de Chernatony, L., McDonald, M., & Wallace, E. (2010). *Creating powerful brands in consumer, service and industrial markets* (4th ed.). Oxford, UK: Butterworth-Heinemann.

Delgado, E., & Hernández, M. (2008). Building online brands through brand alliances in Internet. *European Journal of Marketing, 42*(9/10), 954–976. doi:10.1108/03090560810891091

Desai, K. K., & Keller, K. L. (2002). The effects of ingredient branding strategies on host brand extendibility. *Journal of Marketing, 66*, 73–93. doi:10.1509/jmkg.66.1.73.18450

Dickinson, S., & Barker, A. (2007). Evaluations of branding alliances between non-profit and commercial brand partners: The transfer of affect. *International Journal of Nonprofit and Voluntary Sector Marketing, 12*, 75–89. doi:10.1002/nvsm.291

Farquhar, P. H. (1989). Managing brand equity. *Marketing Research, 1*, 24–33.

Gammoh, B. S., & Voss, K. E. (2011). Brand alliance research: In search of a new perspective and directions for future research. *Journal of Marketing Development and Competitiveness, 5*(3), 81–93.

Gundlach, G. T., Achrol, R. S., & Mentzer, J. T. (1995). The structure of commitment in exchange. *Journal of Marketing, 59*, 78–92. doi:10.2307/1252016

Hair, J. E., Black, W. C., Babin, B. J., & Anderson, R. E. (2005). *Multivariate data analysis* (7th ed.). Upper Saddle River, NJ: Prentice-Hall.

Harvin, R. (2000). In internet branding, the off-lines have it. *Brandweek, 41*(4), 30–31.

Helmig, B., Huber, J. A., & Leeflang, P. S. H. (2007). Explaining behavioral intentions toward co-branded products. *Journal of Marketing Management, 23*(3/4), 285–304. doi:10.1362/026725707X196387

Hem, L., de Chernatony, L., & Iversen, N. M. (2003). Factors influencing successful brand extensions. *Journal of Marketing Management, 19*(7/8), 781–806.

Hillyer, C., & Tikoo, S. (1995). Effect of cobranding on consumer product evaluations. *Advances in Consumer Research. Association for Consumer Research (U. S.), 22*, 123–127.

Horppu, M., Kuivalainen, A., Tarkiainen, A., & Ellonen, H. K. (2008). Online satisfaction, trust and royalty, and the impact of the offline parent brand. *Journal of Product and Brand Management, 17*(6), 403–413. doi:10.1108/10610420810904149

Ibeh, K., Luo, Y., & Dinnie, K. (2005). e-Branding strategies of internet companies: Some preliminary insights from the UK. *Journal of Brand Management, 12*(5), 205–228. doi:10.1057/palgrave.bm.2540231

Ingram, R., Skinner, S. J., & Taylor, V. A. (2005). Consumers' evaluation of unethical marketing behaviors: The role of customer commitment. *Journal of Business Ethics, 62*, 237–252. doi:10.1007/s10551-005-1899-0

James, D. O. (2006). Extension to alliance: Aaker and Keller's model revisited. *Journal of Product and Brand Management, 15*(1), 15–22. doi:10.1108/10610420610650846

Jarvis, J. (2009). *What would Google do?* New York: Harper Collins.

Jun, S. Y., Mazumdar, T., & Raj, S. P. (1999). Effects of technological hierarchy on brand extension evaluations. *Journal of Business Research, 46*, 31–43. doi:10.1016/S0148-2963(98)00025-3

Kamins, M. A., & Gupta, K. (1994). Congruence between spokesperson and product type: A matchup hypothesis perspective. *Psychology and Marketing, 11*(6), 569–586. doi:10.1002/mar.4220110605

Kardes, F. R., & Allen, G. T. (1991). Perceived variability and inferences about brand extensions. *Advances in Consumer Research. Association for Consumer Research (U. S.), 18*, 392–398.

Kazoleas, D., Kim, Y., & Moffitt, M. A. (2001). Institutional image: A case study. *Corporate Communications: An International Journal, 6,* 205–216. doi:10.1108/EUM0000000006148

Keller, K. L. (1993). Conceptualizing, measuring, and managing customer-based brand equity. *Journal of Marketing, 57*(1), 1–22. doi:10.2307/1252054

Kierzkowski, A., McQuade, S., Waitman, R., & Zeisser, M. (1996). Marketing to the digital consumer. *The McKinsey Quarterly, 3,* 5–21.

Kim, C. K., & Lavak, A. M. (1996). Vertical brand extensions: Current research and managerial implications. *Journal of Product and Brand Management, 5*(6), 24–37. doi:10.1108/10610429610152813

Kumar, P. (2005). The impact of co-branding on customer evaluation of brand counter-extensions. *Journal of Marketing, 60*(3), 1–18.

Kwon, W. S., & Lennon, S. J. (2009). Reciprocal effects between multichannel retailers' offline and online brand images. *Journal of Retailing, 85*(3), 376–390. doi:10.1016/j.jretai.2009.05.011

Lafferty, B. A., Goldsmith, R. E., & Hult, G. T. M. (2004). The impact of the alliance on the partners: A look at cause-brand alliances. *Psychology and Marketing, 21*(7), 509–531. doi:10.1002/mar.20017

Landseng, E. J., & Olsen, L. E. (2012). Brand alliances: The role of brand concept consistency. *European Journal of Marketing, 46*(9), 1108–1126. doi:10.1108/03090561211247874

Lawton, C. (2008, March 1). Dell threads carefully into selling PCs in stores. *The Wall Street Journal.*

Lee, M., & Ulgado, F. M. (1993). Service extension strategy: A viable basis for growth? *Journal of Services Marketing, 7*(2), 24–35. doi:10.1108/08876049310038382

Lei, J., Dawar, N., & Lemmink, J. (2008). Negative spillover in brand portfolios: Exploring the antecedents of asymmetric effects. *Journal of Marketing, 72,* 111–123. doi:10.1509/jmkg.72.3.111

Leuthesser, L., Kohli, C. S., & Suri, R. (2003). 2+2 = 5? Framework for using co-branding to leverage your brand. *Journal of Brand Management, 1*(2), 35–47. doi:10.1057/palgrave.bm.2540146

Levin, A. M. (2002). Contrast and assimilation processes in consumers' evaluations of dual brands. *Journal of Business and Psychology, 17*(1), 145–154. doi:10.1023/A:1016256401980

Levin, I. P., & Levin, A. M. (2000). Modeling the role of brand alliances in the assimilation of product evaluations. *Journal of Consumer Psychology, 9,* 43–52. doi:10.1207/s15327663jcp0901_4

Loken, B., & John, D. R. (1993). Diluting brand beliefs: when do brand extensions have a negative impact? *Journal of Marketing, 57,* 71–84. doi:10.2307/1251855

Low, G. S., & Lamb, C. W. (2000). The measurement and dimensionality of brand associations. *Journal of Product and Brand Management, 9*(6), 350–368. doi:10.1108/10610420010356966

Mahasuweerachai, P. (2012). *A study of spillover effects of multiple hotel brand extensions.* (Ph.D. Dissertation). Oklahoma State University, Oklahoma City, OK.

Mariadoss, B. J., Echambadi, R., Arnold, M. J., & Bindroo, V. (2010). An examination of the effects of perceived difficulty of manufacturing the extension product on brand extension attitudes. *Journal of the Academy of Marketing Science, 38*(6), 704. doi:10.1007/s11747-010-0190-9

Marin, L., & Ruiz, S. (2010). Estrategias de marca para nuevos productos ¿Extensión o alianza? *Revista Española de Investigación y Marketing ESIC, 14*(2), 91–111.

Markoff, J. (2010, June 10). Google cars drive themselves in traffic. *New York Times.*

Martínez, E., & Pina, J. M. (2009). Modelling the brand extensions' influence of brand image. *Journal of Business Research, 62*(1), 55–60.

Meyers-Levy, J., & Sternthal, B. (1993). A two-factor explanation of assimilation and contrast effects. *JMR, Journal of Marketing Research, 30*(3), 259–268. doi:10.2307/3172887

Milberg, S. J., Park, C. W., & McCarthy, M. S. (1997). Managing negative feedback effects associated with brand extensions: The impact of alternative branding strategies. *Journal of Consumer Psychology, 6*(2), 119–140. doi:10.1207/s15327663jcp0602_01

Monga, A. B., & Lau-Gesk, L. (2007). Blending co-brand personalities: an examination of the complex self. *JMR, Journal of Marketing Research, 44*, 389–400. doi:10.1509/jmkr.44.3.389

Müge-Arslan, F., & Korkut-Altuna, O. (2010). The effect of brand extensions on product brand image. *Journal of Product and Brand Management, 19*(3), 170–180. doi:10.1108/10610421011046157

Myers, B., Kwon, W. S., & Forsythe, S. (2013). Creating successful cause-brand alliances: The role of cause involvement, perceived brand motivations and cause-brand alliance attitude. *Journal of Brand Management, 20*(3), 205–217. doi:10.1057/bm.2012.34

Northstream. (2010). *The Google phone: Friend or foe.* Retrieved from http://northstream.se/the-google-phone-%e2%80%93-friend-or-foe/

Park, C. W., Jun, S. Y., & Shocker, A. D. (1996). Composite branding alliances: An investigation of extension and feedback effects. *JMR, Journal of Marketing Research, 33*(4), 453–466. doi:10.2307/3152216

Park, C. W., Milberg, S. J., & Lawson, R. (1991). Evaluation of brand extensions: The role of product feature similarity and brand concept consistency. *The Journal of Consumer Research, 18*, 185–193. doi:10.1086/209251

Pina, J. M., Iversen, N. M., & Martinez, E. (2010). Feedback effects of brand extensions on the brand image of global brands: a comparison between Spain and Norway. *Journal of Marketing Management, 26*, 153–176. doi:10.1080/02672570903458789

Rao, A., & Ruekert, R. W. (1994). Brand alliances as signals of product quality. *Sloan Management Review, 36*(1), 87–97.

Rau, P. A. (2004). Online/offline (hybrid) consumers and the attention economy. *Thunderbird International Business Review, 46*(2), 221–226. doi:10.1002/tie.20004

Rios, R. E., & Riquelme, H. E. (2010). Sources of brand equity for online companies. *Journal of Research in Interactive Marketing, 4*(3), 214–240. doi:10.1108/17505931011070587

Roth, M. S. (1994). Innovations in defining and measuring brand image. *Advances in Consumer Research. Association for Consumer Research (U. S.), 21*, 495.

Rowley, J. (2009). Online branding strategies of UK fashion retailers. *Internet Research, 19*(3), 348–367. doi:10.1108/10662240910965397

Samu, S. H., Krishnan, S., & Smith, R. E. (1999). Using advertising alliances for new product introduction: Interactions between product complementarity and promotional strategies. *Journal of Marketing, 63*, 57–74. doi:10.2307/1252001

Samuelsen, B. M., & Olsen, L. E. (2012). The attitudinal response to alternative brand growth strategies. *European Journal of Marketing, 46*(1/2), 177–191. doi:10.1108/03090561211189293

Simonin, B. L., & Ruth, J. A. (1998). Is a company known by the company it keeps? Assessing the spillover effects of brand alliances on consumer brand attitudes. *JMR, Journal of Marketing Research, 35*(1), 30–42. doi:10.2307/3151928

Song, P., Zhang, C., Xu, Y., & Huang, L. (2010). Brand extension of online technology products: Evidence from search engine to virtual communities and online news. *Decision Support Systems, 49*(1), 91. doi:10.1016/j.dss.2010.01.005

Stern, B., Zinkhan, G. M., & Jaju, A. (2001). Marketing images: Construct definition, measurement issues and theory development. *Marketing Theory, 1*(2), 201–224. doi:10.1177/147059310100100203

Supphellen, M., Eismann, O., & Hem, L. (2004). Can advertisements for brand extensions revitalise flagship products? *International Journal of Advertising, 23*, 173–196.

Tabachnick, B. G., & Fidell, L. S. (2007). *Using multivariate statistics* (5th ed.). Upper Saddle River, NJ: Pearson International Education.

Teo, T. S. H., & Tan, J. S. (2002). Senior executive's perceptions of business-to-consumer (B2C) online marketing strategies: The case of Singapore. *Internet Research, 12*(3), 258–276. doi:10.1108/10662240210430937

Thompson, K., & Strutton, D. (2012). Revisiting perceptual fit in co-branding applications. *Journal of Product and Brand Management, 21*(1), 15–25. doi:10.1108/10610421211203079

van Riel, A. C. R., & Ouwersloot, H. (2005). Extending electronic portals with new services: Exploring the usefulness of brand extension models. *Journal of Retailing and Consumer Services, 12*(3), 245–254. doi:10.1016/j.jretconser.2004.07.003

Vernuccio, M., Barbarossa, C., Giraldi, A., & Ceccotti, F. (2012). Determinants of e-brand attitude: A structural modeling approach. *Journal of Brand Management, 19*(6), 500–512. doi:10.1057/bm.2011.59

Völckner, F., Sattler, H., & Kaufmann, G. (2008). Image feedback effects of brand extensions: Evidences from a longitudinal field study. *Marketing Letters, 19*, 109–124. doi:10.1007/s11002-007-9028-8

Völkner, F., & Sattler, H. (2006). Drivers of brand extensions success. *Journal of Marketing*, *70*, 18–34. doi:10.1509/jmkg.70.2.18

Washburn, J. H., Till, B. D., & Priluck, R. (2004). Brand alliance and customer-based brand equity effects. *Psychology and Marketing*, *21*(7), 487–508. doi:10.1002/mar.20016

Worm, S., & van Durme, J. (2006). An empirical study of the consequences of co-branding on perceptions of the ingredient brand. In *Proceedings EMAC Conference*. Athens, Greece: EMAC.

Yorkston, E. A., Nunes, J. C., & Matta, S. (2010). The malleable brand: The role of implicit theories in evaluating brand extensions. *Journal of Marketing*, *74*, 80–93. doi:10.1509/jmkg.74.1.80

This research was previously published in Trends in E-Business, E-Services, and E-Commerce edited by In Lee, pages 69-89, copyright year 2014 by Business Science Reference (an imprint of IGI Global).

Chapter 21
The Functions of the Narrator in Digital Advertising

Nursel Bolat
Ondokuz Mayis University, Turkey

ABSTRACT

Storytelling, which was taken over from traditional advertising, has been continuing existence of it sown in the World of digital advertising. Efficiency of storytelling is intensively used in digital advertisements with the aim of directing attention of consumers to the product and encouraging them to buy product. In digital advertisements, stories are narrated by storytellers. In this study, storytelling in digital advertising and different types of storytellers are examined and traces of storytelling which has existed from past to the present, are followed.

INTRODUCTION

Technological developments are becoming visible within life by increasing day by day, and they continue their influence in virtual reality with access to technology's being fast and cheap. In conjunction with the technological innovations experienced, more people interact with each other in society. The areas of use of the increased communication tools have become widespread when it united with the internet. This new technology activates the audience through positioning them as participants.

With the rapidly evolving technology, communication tools, smart phones, tablets, computers, smart televisions are used both as media of communication and as data banks. In conjunction with this rapid change experienced, digital media are articulated to traditional media. The digital age experienced with digital media puts "people-oriented" view instead of "customer-oriented" view forward. Nowadays, this situation heads people towards setting people-oriented strategies instead of consumer specification.

In the transformation of advertising sector from traditional media to digital media, it is seen that the process of storytelling supported by narrative and visual elements used in traditional media is now used in digital media to a high degree so as to increase sales. Television and print media advertisements requiring large budgets are leaving their place to digital media which need a more modest budget and which can create more effective results. Despite all these, a new, fast-growing, perishable and highly consumed media is faced with.

DOI: 10.4018/978-1-5225-5187-4.ch021

The narrative and storytelling used in the advertising industry are making room for themselves in the digital space with the spread of digital broadcasting. The act of telling has existed since the ancient times of humanity as it is a basic human need. Constantly advancing and changing from telling to narrative forms, it leads to the question of the existence or position of the narrator being one of the main problems. Narrative that exists in the dramas of cinema and television, appears in the advertising sector as the most influential narrative focus of today with its own forms of expression.

In the digital age, in which there are information density and pollution, producers try hard to market their products with storytelling in digital advertising to attract attention to their products. In the advertisements produced for the digital media, digital storytelling of people is used effectively in marketing products.

THE CONCEPT OF DIGITALIZATION AND THE WORLD OF COMMUNICATION

As one of the most important problems of today, information surplus is laid emphasis on. The fact that where people will store so much information that they receive quite rapidly without endeavoring creates uncertainty. Castells describes internet as the "universal, interactive, computerized communications network of the Information Age" (Castells, 2008, p. 465). McLuhan, on the other hand, states that "the information age is to reconstruct the world in our image" (Castells, 2008, p. 465). This is because of the fact that today users are no longer limited to a certain monopoly guidance; they live in a sea of information which is shaped by many people. The positive aspect of this period experienced by digitalization is the removal of monopolization, while the negative aspect is seen as the challenge to reach the correct information among too much information.

When the concept of digitalization is examined, it is seen that it has been addressed as the most important concept of technological progress within the development process seen in a wide area in recent years. Digitalization is defined as the conversion process of analog messages (words, pictures, letters) to signals consisting of different dashes that can be transported from one place to another, processed and stored electronically. Audio, video and text messages can be digitized and easily combined and this feature provides information integration being possible with the new technology. The effects of digitalization make progress far beyond telecommunications. The fact that the sound, image and texts are processed together provides a large multimedia application designed specific to computers. At the same time, digitization process is experienced intensely in all communication tools such as telephones, music players, cameras, radios, televisions and computers (Ormanlı, 2012, pp. 32-33). While increasing the production and efficiency with the latest technologies is targeted, digitalization becomes the focus of communication. While digitization is increasing its prevalence in all communication fields, advertising industry takes its place in this digitization process effectively. In recent years, all brands have become aware of the importance and power of digital technology and social media for the advertising industry.

This is because people can get into contact and interact with the whole world from their whereabouts in the electronic age, they can communicate within the world just like the tribal people communicated with their tribes in the tribal era. So today, the expansion of communication transforms all the world into a single tribe. In this way, people live in a world established on a global scale. Castells calls this electronic age the "network society" as the internet connects people to each other and this changes McLuhan's "global village" definition to a degree. The "surfing" practice (watching several programs at the same time) which is very common, allows the audience to create their own visual mosaics. In today's world, in which communication tools have become connected to each other on a global scale, programs and messages move around in a global network; people live in huts produced globally and distributed locally rather than in a global village (Castells, 2008, p. 457). The digitalized world brings new concepts with it in its own way. This contradiction of terms is not only limited to technological concepts but it also binds societies to certain concepts.

The important developments in digital technology in recent years have brought along different definitions in social structure and between generations. Prensky names the new generation as "digital natives" who extensively use the internet, play virtual games, and are in digital communication with smartphones. He describes the pre-1980 generation as "digital immigrants" in which digital technologies became intense (Prensky, 2001, p. 3). In the period evaluated as the Digital Age, these concepts emerged in accordance with the style and duration of societies' internet use bring along the decomposition of digitalization taking the main effects of the internet on cultural and social structure into account. Among these concepts, digital immigrants and digital natives are seen as the most remarkable ones.

The post-1980 generation using digital tools in every aspect of life and seeing these tools as a part of life, forms the group that creates its own language, that is evaluated by digital natives definition and starts life with today's technology. This new generation emerges as the 21st century children and youngsters placing online media to the center of their lives and performing all their daily works with digital technology (Bilgiç, Duman, Seferoğlu, 2011, p. 2). This group being the generation of the digital age defined as digital natives, involves people who met with technology at young ages. The main language of digital natives is stated as the digital language being the language of computers, video games and internet. These people are considered as experienced and skilled users since they use interactive products intensively.

Considering the digital immigrants, they seem to be people who are not born into a digital world unlike the digital natives, who are in a struggle for finding their way in the digital life without being within the digital life (Palfrey and Gasser, 2008, p. 296). These digital immigrants are faced with many problems within the developing technology. Digital immigrants are making effort to adapt to the use of these new technological developments. Therefore, digital immigrants represent the generation finding themselves entering into a different process with the technological development experienced (Bilgiç, Duman, Seferoğlu, 2011, p. 2). Although these digital immigrants meet with the new technology in their later lives, it is considered that they adapt to new technology in a short time and they are not far away from technology. While the popular technology for digital immigrants is the traditional media, they essentially represent the ones producing digital technology. Therefore, it is an incorrect identification to mark the digital immigrants as digitally unskillful.

THE CHANGING VIEW OF ADVERTISING IN A DIGITALIZING WORLD

Significant changes in production, distribution and marketing are experienced with digital structuring. With this structuring, classic factors of production such as natural resource, capital and labor are being replaced by production with brain power. Serial and single type productions being mass production are turning into a production type having much more variety but the production is in limited numbers. In this period, the system heads towards digitalization from mechanization, agriculture and industry based sector is shifting to service sector. At the same time, production costs fall with technological developments and they provide technology transfer (Yılmaz and Erdem, 2016, p. 161). The process of digitalization which first started in Western societies and began to expand to other societies over time, have also made great progress in marketing field. When considered especially from the perspective of advertising industry, it is seen that digitalization has rapidly begun to dominate the sector.

The Concept of Advertising

According to a classic definition of advertisement, it includes all efforts of promoting a product or service to masses through purchasing space and time from mass media with its payer being apparent (Cetinkaya, 1992, p. 17). The basic functions that advertising bears are giving and announcing information. Its purpose is to convey the brand and specifications of the product to the audience. The more people hear about the product in wide areas, the more the product will have buyers. The more a product's brand and what it is are repeated, the more it will stick in people's minds and the efficiency will last for years (Elden et al, 2005, p. 62). The success of an advertisement is determined by the increase in the number of product or service buyer, in other words it is determined by the increase in sales rate. This requires thinking like a real seller and acting according to that.

Nowadays, advertisements have become one of the most important cultural factors shaping and reflecting our lives. They are omnipresent and ubiquitous making them an indispensable part of people's lives. Advertisements are inevitably encountered everywhere. Advertising sector has a clearly unlimited and autonomous existence covering all media and an enormous power to influence and a structure with a large superstructure (Williamson, 2001, p. 11). With this power to influence, it leads not only the advertisers but also a lot of people. Thus, significant efforts are made to attract attention and influence the target audience.

The impact of advertising objects that are made attractive receives support from their being based on facts. Advertisements continuously address the future buyers throughout the production of meaning process and they instill through embracing the "pleasure hunger" of individuals. Advertisements presenting the attractive images to their consumers' taste, consider determining the position of the individual in society as their duty. The audience or buyer thinks that he/she would in an enviable situation when he/she obtains the product. It is expected that the person using the purchased product will become an object of envy to others (Berger, 1999, p. 134). The types of advertisements that consumers are most affected by, that they believe, and accept without the need for any word, are the ones in which products or services are described, images and photos are used and the production type is shown.

The clear and specific function of advertisements is showing the products fictionalized to create new meaning structures so as to sell something by means of creating demand in consumers and making products become meaningful for the consumer. In this context, advertising gains its value as a meaning-making process. Advertisements make the expressions they take from the world of things meaningful for people. At the end of the day, advertisements clearly establish a vast superstructure depending on an autonomous existence and a tremendous power to influence (Williamson, 2001, p. 12). Day by day, advertising designs increasingly use many variables for the consumers to be affected. These variables include humor, use of famous people, amazing events, entertainment, high standards of living, comfort, peace, advanced technologies and similar items.

Digital Age and Advertising

The digital age is closely connected with the economic field in the development process of the information society. Accordingly, it undergoes a change in the information society and uses knowledge as one of the main factors of production. Within the structure of the information society, it takes economy, information and human capital to forefront. An economic structure based on information production in which new career structurings, new modes of production and social structures are densely observed appears together with the digital age and information society (Çoban, 1997, pp. 57- 58). Today, the e-commerce concept has come forth in information societies concerning production and sale and information consumers can both reach and purchase the products within the framework of this system as well. Advertisements based on sales and marketing which use this process intensively are positioned as the main actors of this new economic field.

According to W. L. Neuman, the use of digital media with sales and marketing purposes shortens geographical distances, removes the obstacles and increases the power of communication accordingly in the digital age. The digital age creates opportunities for the communication speed to increase in advertising and marketing and it also provides many opportunities for interactive communication. This process is said to pave the way for correlating a number of independent communication methods with each other (Bozkurt, 2013, p. 178). Although digital advertising is not a sales method, it is seen as a process of association and communication providing an increase in sales due to the results it obtained. Digital advertising facilitates access to new sources in terms of competitive advantage.

Advertising programs that interact with digital broadcasting are specially prepared from its scenario to its shooting, fiction and broadcasting. Keeping the target audience and all kinds of expectations and information requests of the target audience in mind, programs are organized according to opportunities to access to different communication channels. In this technique, the product to be advertised is prepared with audio-visual presentation, text, graphics, live view supports; detailed information about the product is given and the audience or consumer is even provided with instant access to the product through uploading the payment and purchase information for the sales of the product (Durmaz, 1999, p. 339). The consumer can both reach the product he/she sees on digital media and experience the convenience to buy the product from digital media.

As one of the key technologies in the development of new advertisements, digitalization can transmit any information, audio and video to consumers in a fast and reliable way through data forms consisting of 0 and 1. In this way, the access and impact rate of the advertisement increase and it emerges in the form of a virtual economy in the new economy. The largest reflection of digitalization in new computer-based advertising strategies is the fact that the traditional media are rapidly being replaced by online interactive media that are practiced via the internet. With creative advertisements designed with digital advertising strategies, companies increase both their popularity abstractly and their profit concretely; therefore, consumers are involved in the production and planning stage in the direction they want through forming an interaction with the companies for their products or services interactively (Sahin, Tuna and Tutuncu, 2014, p. 12). To realize the new digital-based creative advertising purposes within the compass of companies' including the customers in the process, the companies offer all the processes of advertising campaigns to their consumers.

Today's mass communication is basically constructed to provide the goods produced be pushed towards consumption areas. This pushing process displays activity in shaping the advertisements as a descriptive feature of mass media (Sener, 1999, p. 40). In addition to traditional media, advertisements now trigger this pushing process through interactive, new and digital media. With the digital age and digital broadcasting, the audience determine their preferences according to their own interests. Today, the audience who can program their own TV channels are exposed to advertisement with their own consent so as to find the product they desire. Besides, advertisements are watched in accordance with the preference of consumers in interactive channels.

Interactive digital advertising media provide advertising information presentation via digital bases, keep sectors engaged in marketing mutually and relatively interactive, and with consumers' use of digital media, marketing takes place. Interactive digital advertising clients can be controlled via advertisements, can provide process from the real-time screen and can be measured in the processes performed. This is because digital advertising has the features of sensitization, customization, personalization and easy targeting. Interactive digital marketing inarguably ranks as the most powerful tool for advertisers (Ming and others, 2009, p. 503). In recent years, together with the development of information technologies, the advertising industry has begun to follow a different path. New technologies are revealing serious structural changes in the traditional advertising and the media used are becoming diversified. Situated in the two different sides of advertising industry, clients and advertising agencies are beginning to use the internet channel with this new technology. The spread of the internet as a result of technological developments, in line with the increase in consumer demand, increases the competition among institutions and organizations set new advertising strategies.

ADVERTISING NARRATIVE AND STORYTELLING IN DIGITAL AGE

Narratology and Digital Age

Narrative is defined as the type of text created through placing a sequence of events associated with each other into a specific space and time with a person's particular point of view (Günay, 2003, p. 156). Porter Abbottis describes narrative simply as a "re-presentation of an event or a series of events" (Abbott 2002, p. 12). According to these definitions, narrative is specified as the explanation of a plot in a certain time period by a narrator with a particular perspective.

While the evolution of narrative studies in recent years should not be presented as a simple story of progress toward a single, unified goal, it provides a critical context that illuminates key developments in research on digital narratives in particular (Page and Thomas, 2011, p. 3). Changes are gone through in the classical narrative with the beginning of the digital narrative which has entered into our lives with the digital process.

Narrative

The narrative is set up in the framework of a story and a narrator. A narrative includes the structure that should take part within the communication process of a "transmitter" and a "receiver". The narrative takes its shape around the desire of people to express themselves being one of the basic human needs and the desire of readers or audience to understand the world. Changes and developments taking place in the world are changing in the context of a dialectical relationship in narratives (Batur, 1979, p. 13). With the emerging technologies, the functions of classic storytelling and narrative are becoming different. While narratives have the function of telling the daily life in general, some narratives serve a function in taking people to other worlds through moving them away from the real life. While traditional narrative structures offer more of a solution to people, digital narratives prefer showing the existing situation rather than offering a solution.

The basic premise of the narrative, whether it is written or oral, is formed by language, it appears in the form of static or dynamic body movements or a regular mixture of all these elements in vision. The narrator and the perspective of the narrator in narratives are important in the process of narrative analysis. In a narrative, the question 'who speaks' takes the person directly to the narrator, while the question "who perceives and sees' shows the perspective. The narrator appears as the vision and sound telling the story in the framework of different perspectives. In digital dynamic advertisements, events, actions, and thoughts that people have are presented to the audience in terms of certain points backed by images and sounds. As the narration is made through the eyes of a person, the features of the narrative is naturally determined as there is an informational field restriction (Sozen, 2008, pp. 578-580). The concepts of narrator and perspective inevitably become the basic elements in the types based on narrative. In a way, the narrator delivers the words the writer needs and he/she is actually involved in the fictional world even though he/she is confused with the writer. The visibility of the presence of the narrator also varies. While some narrators constantly intervene even at the expense of cutting the flow of events, while some of them make themselves completely invisible.

The basis of the development of dramatic events shows a structure based on continuity. The narrative line is constructed according to a perspective that is accepted hypothetically and can rather be considered as the eyes of the audience. The audience is placed in this existing perspective; therefore, the audience has to believe, participate and identify with it for the audience to find their way into this perspective. In short, the audience have to be persuaded to this perspective. At this point, the rationality of the relationships to ensure the continuity of events is important. As long as the audience believes in the course of events, in characters; namely, if he/she does not have doubts about the rationale here, his/her interest in the story intensifies and he/she takes the position within the perspective needing to take the audience in. As a result, the audience gets enthusiastic and excited and it becomes easier to identify with the perspective (Ünal, 2008, p. 134). When the audience are properly communicated and identified with, they abandon themselves to the plot.

Narrator

The narrator is defined as someone living in different periods, being a superhuman infiltrating in the deepest corners of people's minds, created as a personality knowing everything and being everywhere. It may sometimes show up, be vaguely heard and be intermingled with the implicit author. While the narrator is conditionally formed in an inconsistent manner, its type may vary as well. In narratives, the narrator may appear as a personality being everywhere, knowing everything, infiltrating in the deepest corners of characters' souls. The narrator may sometimes display a view explaining too much unnecessary information at first glance. Due to such changes, it is seen that while the participation of the narrator is sometimes intense, it is sometimes completely forgotten. No matter how the narrator is objective, personless and variable, as Schmid noted, the narrator is always situated as a subject having the perspective that it specified so as to pick certain elements from "events" for the "story" it is telling (Schmid, 2003, p. 67). The narrator, chosen and created by the author for the purpose of telling the story as a fictional person, has a feature that does not have a counterpart in the real world just like the heroes of the story. It can transfer the story chronologically or within temporal changes, can hide the thoughts of the characters or tells them clearly. In other words, narrators serve both as the constructive and reflective elements of the narrative world.

In cinema or in advertisements, the narrator is the combination of sound and image telling the story in reference to various perspectives. Events, actions, people and the ideas of these people in the story are presented from certain points of views to readers and viewers via images and voice (Jahn, 2003, p. 10). The term perspective (point of view / focalization) basically refers to two different elements. The first one gives the "physical" position of perspective to "things" while the second one gives the "mental position" a perspective has. The first refers to the distance against narrative and mental position of the narrator, and the second refers to the distance against narrative and mental position of the audience (Chatman, 1990, p. 139).

Storytelling

Storytelling is stated as a form of communication of the collective world. Storytelling draws its strength from the repetition of the story/event told and its being transmitted by different actors. Transmitting or telling a word or an event is experiencing what is told, being within life in the form of breathing with it in a way. Thus, the narrator experiences what he/she has never experienced before and makes it possible for others to experience as well. Storytelling indicates a tradition in terms of its being inherited from generation to generation and a common meaning horizon as it is a collective action. This resulting horizon of meaning heads people towards plurality instead of singularity and provides them to have the experience of the same world. Thus, while storytelling ensures the unity of action and word which is shivering, it also offers the opportunity to achieve a common life, even a common "experience". For this reason, it is seen that storytelling is a "common experience" immanent to the relationship between individuals and that this "common experience" refers to a "common way of thinking" having all the differences (Sütçü, 2013, p. 80). Storytelling advances by adding new lives on the past lives and it transmits this knowledge to others, which makes sense as the most important aspect of storytelling.

Explicitly or implicitly, every real story involves something useful in itself. This usefulness varies according to the story; while some stories teach moral lessons, an advice, a proverb or a thought is manifested from others. But in any case, the storyteller is in the position of a wise person who can give advice to the reader or audience. Today, the fact that 'giving advice' is perceived as something outdated, is seen in conjunction with experience's becoming less and less transferable. That is why people seem to have no advice to give to themselves or to others (Benjamin, 1995, p. 80). In fact, telling a story means both another person's talking on incomplete events and actions and his/her giving meaning to it again. Besides, both the narrator and the audience in storytelling constantly integrate with the stories of hundreds of thousands of people.

The value storytelling contains in itself lies in people's demand and desire to share the human world. Telling, as living through sharing the life in a way, the experience this life brings forth is constructed socially and considered to be associated with present. In other words, narrating something of life is seen as taking the viewpoints of different periods into account and putting them through an order. In this putting in order process, there is a "thought action line" in which thought and reality intertwine and a plural life is manifested in the light of experience. Seeing that storytelling is a way of thinking and acting carried out jointly by the people, "the integrity of the experience" also arises in the forefront in this joint action. In this case, it is said that the experience offered by storytelling is a common life experience (Sutcu, 2013, p. 81). Therefore, storytelling leads to collective action through pointing to a broader way of thinking. Moreover, the emphasis in this joint thinking and acting is not on a singular and limited thinking process, but rather it is on the integrity of thinking based on the experience.

Digital Storytelling

The new social order which emerged with the definition of information age and which has been established through these technologies, defines new concepts and puts them into practice within this framework. The concept of digital storytelling is also emerging as a concept linked with the developments in electronic and digital media. The storytelling tradition, is gaining a different level of life with the partnership of new technologies. With the technologizing process in the world, stories have also begun to be moved into virtual environments and they are told in these platforms. New digital media is developing new formats in accordance with its own structure in storytelling. As digital storytelling has entered into every area of life; so as to support the sharing in labor divisions and communication for obtaining positive results in the business world, it is now tried to be integrated with methods such as combining information based working practices and sharing of stories in this sense with workers connected via virtual platforms. Entertainment and electronic gaming industry, with participants with interactive editing system, focus on storytelling studies via interactive interface designs. Moreover, the education sector is carrying the new digital media into classrooms as an educational tool through universities and schools and is transferring both formal and non-formal education to an online environment as an artistic way of storytelling (Figa, 2004, pp. 34-36). With the rapid changes and digitalization, geographical distances become closer, different life experiences begin to reflect the multi-cultural approaches with digital storytelling. So as to achieve this, the digital storytelling world is being explored via cameras, scanners, computers, softwares, DVDs and the internet.

Many definitions are encountered in the matter of digital storytelling. According to Chung, digital storytelling is defined as multiple presentations of digital based elements such as texts, images, videos and audios conducted in computer environments as a whole (Chung, 2007, pp. 17-22). Digital storytelling in general, seems to be considered as the sharing of a specific story composed by conveying information related to a topic through multimedia tools.

In other words, digital storytelling is telling first person short stories through stimulating the thoughts and feelings of an ordinary person with the support of videos, photos, music, narrative and editing software brought together in a computer in a similar way through using digital tools. These short stories are considered to be used within a certain purpose in focusing on the subject or point of view in a particular format (Capri, 2011, p. 5). Digital storytelling in advertisements attracts more attention when compared with other advertisements. The target audience is more interested in the stories that he/she links to a slice of his/her life and this provides him/her to associate himself/herself with the product itself.

Digital story identifies an individual subject in its studies and prepares a text with the knowledge gained through research done within the framework of the subject. After that, it creates the scenario in conjunction with the text prepared and this scenario is combined through bringing various multimedia elements such as graphics, images, audio, text, video and music together to create a video. The resulting images tell the story with their own language of expression. The videos obtained are seen as short films that can be watched on a computer or web (Robin, 2008, pp. 220-228). In the sector where marketing is getting more and more difficult, advertisers make great efforts to attract the attention of consumers constantly being subject to a product's promotional content and to establish a trust relationship. Therefore, advertisers are trying to reach consumers with digital storytelling rather than with the product itself as they have the aim of establishing relationships between the target audience and the brand with digital storytelling. In doing so, they tell the digital story through a reliable famous person so as to ensure consumer confidence.

As the process of transferring stories to people through using digital tools, the method of "digital storytelling" is emerging as quite a new term. In other words, the digital storytelling being a method of creating stories through using multimedia applications is spreading rapidly although it is quite new. Many brands have embraced the notion that it is an effective way to use digital narrative techniques in their various projects and in the introduction of their branded contents.The two basic differences between digital and traditional storytelling are seen as digital storytelling's being open to interaction and its providing the opportunity to deepen. Pictures taken to make the story interesting are tried to be consolidated through enriching them with digital applications such as sound effects and animation (Günay, 2003). With the digitization process, digital storytelling is gaining importance and interactive storytelling is becoming prominent for the audience.

Storytelling in Digital Advertising

Storytelling in marketing has the feature of investment in terms of the relationship established between the brand and the target audience. Especially in video marketing, the objective is to ensure that the audience focuses on the story rather than the product. So the product is ingratiated passively to the audience and the sales rates are increased. Storytelling has a strong impact on digital campaigns. This is due to the fact that people grow with stories and thus they love stories. In scientific terms, the information in which stories have strong influence outweigh as they touch personal experience. While a story is being told in the digital platform, its being supported by visual elements is stated to be more effective instead of explaining the intended message to people through telling. This situation gives a sense of confidence with the feeling that their problems are understood and it may show how the product solves this problem. Instead of listing the benefits of your product, you should narrate these benefits with stories supported by visual expressions (Williamson, 2001). Digital conversion is in all areas of people's lives, trademarks in the advertising world are focusing on different storytelling processes. It is seen that some specific web sites are becoming mainstream media together with their being used in the process of sharing their stories with the masses in the digital world.

STORYTELLERS IN ADVERTISEMENTS

Voice-Over in Storytelling Advertising

Voice over indicates an invisible person's giving voice to the advertising narrative in commercials. While some voice overs can make the audience listen to the advertising narrative in a relaxing, pleasant, friendly, caringly and warmly way, some of them have insistent, impulsive and aggressive features. For a voice over to be effective in terms of attracting the attention of the audience, it needs to be associated with the product and to give confidence.

Inner Voice in Storytelling Advertising

Advertisement inner voice is a concept in which the presenters narrating the advertising copy and introducing the product are actively involved in commercials. Inner voices in commercials try to draw the viewer's attention to the product through taking place in the film in different characters and personalities. These are mostly referred to as presenters in front of the camera.

Advertisements use a presenter standing in front of the camera in the storytelling of the advertisement and the story meets the audience through this presenter. The speaker conveys the product to the audience by showing or by presenting it to the audience. While conveying the product to the audience, an appropriate scene (living room, kitchen, office, factory, etc.) or a plain background is used. Although it is important to select someone sympathetic and credible as presenter, it is necessary that the presenter does not take precedence over the product (Russell & Lane, 1993, p. 533). When the presenter takes precedence over the product, the product cannot reach the audience desirably and it stays in the background. Inner voices as presenters used in commercials are seen in various forms such as testimonial presenter, vendor presenter, expert presenter, celebrity presenter, user presenter, advertiser presenter, gifted presenter.

Testimonial Presenter

So as to prove the brand promise in the advertisements, brands refer either to scientific results or to consumer's testimony who uses the product or service. Testimonial advertisement is the production technique in which people using a product or service and being satisfied with the product or service are involved in the advertisement. The person using the product recommends it by stating that he/she was satisfied with the product (Aktuğlu, 2006, p. 14). The testimonial presenters indicate that the product has all the features a consumer needs and that people can use this product safely.

Testimony, especially as a production format frequently used in television advertising, is seen in many different forms in commercials. For instance, a presenter appearing in testimonial advertisements talk to the testifier(s) about the product and the testifier(s) share their experience and views about the product with the presenter. Via the presenter, the message reaches the target audience. In another form of testimonial advertising, the testifier or testifiers convey their impressions and experiences directly to the audience (Gülmez, 2016a, p. 123). The audience's testimony stating his/her satisfaction is believed to convince the consumer through developing trust with the messages to purchase the product.

Vendor Presenter

A representative of the product advertised promotes the product and company. This person conveys the product and the company to target audience. Vendor presenter works as an expert in his/her company, but is not a senior manager (Akyol, 2004, p. 15). With his/her knowledge and experience, he/she conveys the properties of the company's product to the target audience.

Expert Presenter

Expert presenter is defined as an individual or a group with a superior knowledge of the sort of product used. An expert presenter refers to someone who has achieved the knowledge, know-how and experience as a result of his works or studies. For example, a dentist in a toothpaste advertisement or a cook in an instant soup advertisement are expert presenters (Gülmez, 2016b, p. 122). Expert presenters ensure that the product is accepted by the consumer through establishing trust in the target audience due to their conveying information as a matter of their profession.

Celebrity Presenters

In the technique known as celebrity using strategy or "star strategy", the objective is to make the product and brand known in a short while through identifying the product with a person or a personality having reputation (Kocabas and Elder, 1997, p. 126). Within the framework of this modern advertising strategy applied, there appears the efforts in drawing the attention from the celebrities to the product and integrating the product with the celebrity in memories.

A loved and famous person's saying nice things about a product can draw attention to the product that has been ignored until that day. But the important thing in the use of a famous person in an advertisement is the power of association that the celebrity reveals in consumers; hence, the image and value that the celebrity evokes in consumers pass to the brand. This process leads many people to buy products and services (Brott and Zyman, 2003, p. 145). Whether the character used in the advertisement is alive or not, is real or a hero created, do not make a difference on the celebrity's taking precedence over the product. Sometimes a character created may take precedence over the product in an advertisement.

There are also many advantages of famous people's taking part in promotional advertisements. According to the research conducted, it is seen that goods or services advertised by famous people are preferred much more than others by consumers (Agrawal, 1993, p. 563). One of the important advantages of narrative stories in advertisements of famous people is that famous people can attract the attention of consumers. It helps to attract the consumer's attention to the advertisement since there is information density and abundance in marketing fields in today's digital age.

Product User Presenter

A person that used the advertised product or service before and was satisfied with that product or service plays in the commercial as the presenter, A person among the audience who used the advertised product or service before describes the characteristics of the product he/she used. The presenter using the product conveys information to the audience about the product such as his/her experience with the product and solutions to problems (Akyol, 2004, p. 16).

Advertiser Presenter

The company owner or manager of the product being advertised is involved in commercials to promote the company's products. The manager or owner of the company provides information about the product to the target audience and this information serves as the guarantee of the product (Akyol, 2004, p. 17). When the viewer or audience receives information directly from the manufacturer, his/her confidence in the product increases and may lead him/her to purchase the product.

Gifted Presenters

In this type of presenter, the product identifies with the presenter. The person believed to promote the product to be advertised best is chosen as the presenter of the advertising film. This presenter's traits such as discourse, facial expression, smile, determination establish an identification between the audience and the presenter. The gifted presenter builds trust with the audience and convinces people to buy the product (Akyol, 2004, p. 17). The audience or target group establishing an identification with the presenter tries to strengthen the association through using the product the presenter uses.

The Narrator in the Digital Advertisements

An epic, creative plot is built so as to make the stories prepared in digital media convincing. In doing so, it creates different characters such as heroes that the audience will identify themselves with and others being quite the opposite of these heroes to create tension. Digital stories are performed in an interactive digital media and the narrator acts as if he/she were living in that moment within the flow of story. The selected story is narrated through emphasizing the viewpoint determined by an epic expression. While there is an epic narrative in digital stories, there are also stories that focuses on a specific topic/point. Digital stories usually comprise images, text, audio and video and their length does not exceed 10 minutes so as not to be boring (Günay, 2003). Moreover, as in analogue advertising, there are presenters in digital advertising as well. Digital advertising appears before consumers with the same presenter typecasting having similar properties with analogue advertising.

CONCLUSION

In marketing and sales practices, it is essential how the promotion is carried out as well as the promotion of the product or service via advertisements. It is aimed that advertisements in which a product or service is promoted impress the consumer's subconscious about the product or service and therefore it requires a marketing strategy according with the product. It is seen that advertising is heading towards the digital media in accordance with today's market conditions. Advertisers who establish their marketing strategy in the digital media are turning onto digital storytelling.

Especially in the digital age, the media ranked at the beginning of the key elements creating digital stories, brings visual and audial qualifications as well as verbal qualification to narrative with digital storytelling differently from traditional storytelling. To perform this visual storytelling, digital stories are richly created with the multimedia facilities in which graphics, moving images, text, audio, animation, photography and images are used as well as compositions such as single-media and multi-media and are presented to customers with music and effects. Besides, digital storytelling ensures people to have knowledge about objects and places through virtual reality that people do not have the chance to see in reality. Complex information is made easier to perceive through visualization via virtual spaces and platforms created in digital media.

No matter how it is defined, as digital or virtual, digital storytelling creates a new line through its narrative structure's forcing technological possibilities. While some narratives comprise a uniform text with technological advances and digital media, a majority of them tell stories combined with rich media that has quite advanced methods and rich distribution networks. These narratives are produced in digital media and these narratives produced can be stored, modified, corrected, indexed, and converted to new usage areas like entertainment and education in media such as computer.

In digital advertisements, the advertising film takes an important place in the product's promotion and sales. However, advertising activities should follow a certain way after being created within the frame of a certain strategy and plan. In the commercials of advertising sector, advertisement narrative is performed by the presenter who might communicate well with the audience and the memorability of the product and brand is tried to be ensured through identifying these presenters with the brand in the advertisement so as to enhance the impact of the narrative and narrator.In digital advertising narrative, the brands use the trustworthiness and image of the people presenting the advertisement as well as their memorability.

While a narrative is performed through transmitting thoughts and feelings to recipients with behavior, gestures and facial expressions; visual elements get involved in the narrative in advertisements. People tell to ensure the communication and while they tell, they make consumers to focus on the advertisement via storytelling. While the narrative develops around an incident, it finds an expression in the advertising copy within the frame of putting different situations and psychological states into words.

The author gives the mission of telling to a narrator in the texts depending on the expression of the advertising copies as part of a story. The audience watching the advertisement comes to know all goings-on via this narrator. This narrator is chosen as the presenter of the advertisement film who can establish an appropriate and accurate connection with the product. Whether the narrator is a celebrity, company owner or an ordinary person, the audience sees the narrator as the hero of the narrative. Brands try to attract attention to their products through selecting these narrative heroes as they think they have the best personality to be presenters for the promotion of their products.

The characteristics of storytelling in digital advertising are transferred from traditional media and the manner of storytelling and the narrators are used in the same way in digital media. Change in digital advertising experienced with technological developments is seen in media's form of reaching the masses and in its feedback rather than in the advertisement's context and narrative. Digital advertisements carry their narratives into effect through presenters being similar with traditional advertisements by preparing their product commercials.

REFERENCES

Aktuğlu, I. K. (2006). Tüketicinin Bilgilendirilmesi Sürecinde Reklam Etiği. *Küresel İletişim Dergisi*, 2, 1–20.

Akyol, M. (2004). *Gelişen Televizyon ve Reklam Filmi Yapım Sürecinde Kullanımı (*Unpublished Master's Thesis). Selçuk University.

Atabek, G. Ş. (2007). İletişim Çalışmalarında Göstergebilimsel Yöntem. Medya Metinleri Çözümleme. Ankara: Siyasal Publication.

Batur, E. (1979). Anlatı Çözümlemesine Kuramsal Bir Yaklaşım. Dilbilim 4. *Dergipark*, 132-146.

Benjamin, W. (1995). Hikaye anlatıcısı. son bakışta aşk'ın içinde. İstanbul: Metis Publication.

Bilgiç, G. H., Duman, D., & Seferoğlu, S. S. (2011). Dijital Yerlilerin Özellikleri ve Çevrim İçi Ortamların Tasarlanmasındaki Etkileri. Malatya: İnönü University.

Boggs, J. M. (1978). *The Art of Watching Films. The Benjamin/Cumming Company.*

Bozkurt, İ. (2013). *Pazarlama İletişiminde Sihirli Dokunuşlar*. İstanbul: Mediacat Publication.

Capri, I. (2011). *Digital Storytelling: The Process and Product Building Community Through New Media* (Master's Thesis). Kent State University.

Castells, M. (2008). *Ağ Toplumunun Yükselişi*. İstanbul: Bilgi University Publication.

Çetinkaya, Y. (1992). *Reklamcılı*. İstanbul: Ağaç Publication.

Chatman, S. (1990). *Coming to Terms-The Rhetoric of Narrative in Fiction and Films*. Cornell University Pres.

Chion, M. (1992). Bir Senaryo Yazmak. İstanbul: Afa Publication.

Chung, S. K. (2007). Art education technology: Digitalstorytelling. *Art Education*, *60*(2), 17–22.

Çoban, H. (1997). *Bilgi Toplumuna Planlı Geçiş: Gelecekten Kaçılamaz: Bilgi Toplumuna Planlı Geçiş İçin Stratejik Planlama ve Yönetim Bilgi Sistemi Uygulaması*. İstanbul: İnkılap.

Durmaz, A. (1999). *Dijital Televizyonun Temelleri*. Eskişehir: Anadolu Üniversitesi Eğitim Sağlık ve Bilimsel Araştırma Çalışmaları Vakfı.

Elden, M., Ulukök, Ö., & Yeygel, S. (2005). *Şimdi Reklamlar*. İstanbul: İletişim Publication.

Figa, E. (2004). The Virtualization of Storiesand Storytelling. *Storytelling Magazine*, *16*(2), 34–36.

Fiske, J. (1999). *Popüler Kültürü Anlamak*. Ankara: Ark Publication.

Friedman, N. (1982). Romanda Görüş Açısı. *Çağdaş Eleştiri, S.7*, 50 – 64.

Gıanettı, L. (1982). *Understanding Movies*. Prentice – Hall. Inc.

Gülmez, E. (2016). Kullanıcı Tanıklığı Ve Uzman Tanıklığı Reklamlarına Yönelik Tutumların Karşılaştırılması, Trabzon. *Karadeniz Teknik Üniversitesi İletişim Araştırmaları Dergisi*, *3*, 12.

Gülmez, E. (2016a). Tanıklı reklam: reklamda "bir bilen"i göstermek. Reklam Diyor ki 1 İçinde, 119-159.

Günay, D. (2003). *Metin Bilgisi*. İstanbul: Multilingual Publication. Retrieved from https://gizobu.wordpress.com/2013/04/13/nedir-bu-digital-storytelling/

Jahn, M. (2003). *A Guide to Narratological Film Analysis*. Retrieved from http://www.unikoeln.de/~ame02/pppf.htm

Kıran, A. & Kıran, Z. (2007). *Yazınsal Okuma Süreçleri*. Ankara: Seçkin Publication.

Kocabaş, F. & Elden, M. (1997). *Reklam ve Yaratıcı Strateji*. İstanbul: Yayınevi Publication.

Küçükerdoğan, R. (2009). *Reklam Nasıl Çözümlenir*. İstanbul: Beta Publication.

Mccracken, G. (1989). Who is celebrityendorser?.Culturalfoundations of the endorsement process. *The Journal of Consumer Research*, *16*(3), 310–321. doi:10.1086/209217

McLuhan, M. & Povers, B. R. (2001). *Global Köy*. Scala Publication.

Ming, J., Sung, C., Charles, B., Edward, S., Tse, W., Lily, S., & Lien, C. (2009). Consumer Attitudesan dİnteractiveDigitalAdvertising. *International Journal of Advertising*, *28*(3), 501–525.

Ormanlı, O. (2012). Dijitalleşme ve Türk Sineması. *TOJDAC*, *2*(2), 32–38.

Page, R., & Thomas, B. (2011). *New Narratives Stories and Storytelling in the Digital Age* (P. B. T. Ruth, Ed.). University of Nebraska Press.

Palfrey, J., & Gasser, U. (2008). Born Digital, Understanding The First Generation of Digital Natives. Basic Books.

Parsa, S. & Parsa, A. F. (2004). *Göstergebilim Çözümlemeleri*. İzmir: Ege Üniversitesi Publication.

Pensky, M. (2001). Digital Natives, Digital Immigrants. *On the Horizon, 9*(5).

Rifat, M. (1999). *Gösterge Eleştirisi*. İstanbul: Kaf Publication.

Rifat, M. (2005). *XX. Yüzyılda Dilbilim ve Göstergebilim Kuramları*, 2. İstanbul: Yapı Kredi Publication.

Robin, B. R. (2008). Digital Storytelling: A Powerful Technology Tool for the 21st Century Classroom, The College of Education and Human Ecology. *The Ohio State University. Theory into Practice, 47*, 220–228. doi:10.1080/00405840802153916

Russell, J. T., & Lane, W. R. (1993). *Kleppner's Advertising Procudure* (12th ed.). Prentice Hall.

Şahin, N., Tuna, N., & Tütüncü, S. İ. (2014). Yeni Ekonomi Sürecinde Bilgi İletişim Teknolojileri (Bit) Tabanlı Reklam Uygulamalarına Yönelik Bir İnceleme. *Uşak Sosyal Bilimler Dergisi. Sayı, 7*(2), 1–25.

Schmid, W. (2003). *Narratologiya*. Retrieved from www.yanko.lib.ru/books/lit/shmid=narratology.htm

Şener, B. (1999). Reklam İçin İnternet, İnternet İçin Reklam. *Marketing Türkiye, 197*, 82.

Şimşek, S., & Uğur, İ. (2001). *Star Stratejisi Ve Uygulamaları*. Konya: Selçuk Sosyal Bilimler Enstitüsü Dergisi.

Sözen, M. (2008). Sinemasal Anlatıda Bakış Açısı Kavramı ve Örnek Çözümlemeler. *Selçuk Üniversitesi Sosyal Bilimler Enstitüsü Dergisi, 20*, 577–595.

Sütçü, Ö. Y. (2013). Ortak Bir Dünya Deneyimi: Hikaye Anlatıcısı. *ETHOS: Felsefe ve Toplum Bilimlerde Diyaloglar, 6*(2), 76-92.

Ünal, Y. (2008). *Dram Sanatı ve Sinema*. İstanbul: Hayalet Yayınları.

Williamson, J. (2001*). Reklamların Dili*. (Ahmet Fethi, Trans). Ankara: Ütopya Publication. Retrieved from www.dijitalajanslar.com/hikaye-anlatiminin-dijital-kampanyalara-etkisi

Yılmaz, R. & Erdem, N. (2016). *150 Soruda Geleneksel ve Dijital Reklamcılık*. Kocaeli: Umuttepe Publication.

ADDITIONAL READING

Aksoy, A. (2005). *Yeni Reklamcılık*. İstanbul. TR: Bilgi Üniversitesi Publication.

Barthes, R. (1972). *Mythologies*. London, UK: Paladin Publications.

Chatman, S. (2008). *Öykü ve Söylem*.(Yaren Ö,. Trans). Ankara. TR: De Ki Publication.

Dyer, G. (2009). *Advertising as communication*. New York, NY: Routledge Publications.

Elden, M. (2016).Reklam ve reklacılık. Istanbul. TR: Say Publications.

Ertike, A. S., & Yılmaz, R. (2011). Reklamcılığın anahtar kavramları. Istanbul. TR: Derin Publications.

Fidler, R. (1997). *Mediamorphosis: Understanding new media*. Thousand Oaks, CA: Sage Publications.

Genette, G. (1980). *Narrative discourse: An essay in method* (J. E. Lewin, Trans.). New York, NY: Cornell University Press. (Original work published 1972)

Greimas, A. J., & Courtés, J. (1983). *Semiotics and language: An analytical dictionary* (L. Christ et al., Trans.). Indiana: Indiana University Press. (Original work published 1979)

Huisman, R. (2009). Advertising narratives. In H. Fulton (Ed.), *Narrative and media* (pp. 285–299). Berlin, DE: Walter de Gruyter.

Jahn, M. (2012). *Anlatıbilim* (B. Dervişcemaloğlu, Trans.). Istanbul, TR: Dergah Publications. (Original work published 2005)

Jakes, D. S., & Brennan, J. (2005). Capturing stories, capturing lives: An Introduction to digital storytelling. Retrieved 15.01. 2015 from http://bookstoread.com/etp/earle.pdf

Karakoyun, F. (2014). Examining the views of elementary school students and pre-service teachers about digital storytelling activities in online environment. Ph.D Thesis. Anadolu University, Institute of Educational Science, Eskişehir: Turkey.

Karimova, G. Z. (2011). 'Interactivity' and advertising communication. *Journal of Media and Communication Studies*, *3*(5), 160–169.

Nguyen, A. T. (2011). *Negotiations and challenges in creating a digital story: The experience of graduate students*. Dissertation (Ed. D.), University of Houston.

Niemi, H., Harju, V., Vivitsou, M., Viitanen, K., Multisilta, J., & Kuokkanen, A. (2014). *DigitalStorytellingfor 21st Century Skills in Virtual Learning Environments*. Creative Education.

Rigel, N. (1993). *Medya Ninnileri*. İstanbul. TR: Publication.

Ryan, M. L. (2009). Narration in various media. In P. Hühn, J. Pier, W. Schmid, & J. Schönert (Eds.), *Handbook of narratology* (pp. 263–281). Berlin, DE: Walter de Gruyter.

Straubhaar, J., & LaRose, R. (1996). *Communications media in the information society*. Belmont, CA: Wadsworth Press.

Taşkıran, N. Ö., & Yılmaz, R. (2015). *Handbook research on effective advertising strategies in the social media age*. Hershey, PA: IGI-Global International Publications.

Topsümer, F., & Elden, M. (2015). *Reklamcılık: Kavramlar, kurumlar, kararlar*. Istanbul, TR: İletişim Publications.

KEY TERMS AND DEFINITIONS

Digital Advertisement: It is used for describing advertisement activities offered in the new media that offers advantages such as being presented in the digital media, having a fast feedback process, having low cost, being in an instant and effective communication with the consumer.

Digital Age: It is used for defining the period in which the development of information and communication technologies redefined the social, economic and scientific change and in which the network society gradually came to light in the history of mankind.

Digital Storytelling: It emerges as a concept being in conjunction with the start of the narrative tradition in electronic and digital media. It is being used with traditional storytelling's entering into internet media with the partnership of new technologies. With the technologizing process, stories have been transferred to visual platforms and used as narratives in advertising and in other areas.

Inner Voice in Advertising: It is defined as presenter's performing the advertising narrative within the advertisement through acting in the commercial film.

Interactivity: Interactive communication is the structuring of the messages interrelatedly and in a way that allows the users to participate. Namely, the interactivity concept describes interaction, sharing and mutual communication.

Narrative: The concept of narrative is used as a whole which appears as the result of real or imaginary incidents' using different indicator systems and their being narrated; in this sense, it is sometimes used synonymously with the term "text". (Rifat, 1999: 15). Thus, it seems possible to tell that every narrative phrase has a unique structure. At the same time narrative is a chain of events occurring in time and space, interconnecting the cause and effect relation.

Narrator: The narrator is an element that the author needs to convey his/her words and despite the fact that he is confused with the author, he completely pertains to the fictional world. Besides, he/she is closely related to real world with his/her strong structure providing the connection between the reader and the author and work. The visibility of the existence of the narrator may vary according to the narrative.

Storytelling: Storytelling is the vocalization of a text, in other words, of a story being in its basic state, conveying it to the audience with a narrative style and a pleasant audition for the audience.

Voice-Over in Advertising: It means that the presenter performs his/her advertising narrative without being in the advertisement.

Section 3
Tools and Technologies

Chapter 22
Augmented Reality as an Emerging Application in Tourism Marketing Education

Azizul Hassan
Cardiff Metropolitan University, UK

Timothy Jung
Manchester Metropolitan University, UK

ABSTRACT

Augmented Reality (AR) as an advanced format of Virtual Reality (VR) becomes widely available in numerous appliances, mainly in mobile devices like Smartphones or wearable devices. As the prospective benefits of this technology are said to be immense, tourism marketing education is believed to experience a comprehensive application of AR in coming years. At present, AR technologies are in use in many academic disciplines including medicine, geography, information technology, computer aided entertainment and many more. Out of all of the recently developed technological advancements, those can be termed as 'Innovations', augmented reality can be considered as a key innovation. As coined, due to easier operational capacities, AR is becoming more popular and better fitting in tourism marketing education systems. This chapter outlines the use of AR, termed as an 'Innovation' as per the 'Diffusion of Innovations' theory of Rogers (1962), to meet tourism marketing education demands. The chapter critically examines relevant cross-country cases to support the arguments made above.

INTRODUCTION

This chapter discusses diverse features and potentials of augmented reality in tourism marketing education and suggests its inclusion in the academic syllabuses to be studied as a key module. Augmented reality (AR), an extension of virtual reality, is an emerging technology that can provide experiences in which real world places and activities are enhanced with computer-generated content, seamlessly mixing and overlapping human perception with two dimensional (2D) and three dimensional (3D) objects (Yuen, Yaoyuneyong, & Johnson, 2011). AR has emerged as an unprecedented use of technology in a number

DOI: 10.4018/978-1-5225-5187-4.ch022

of fields including architecture, construction, military, medical, entertainment, advertising, travel, and marketing. Global brands from different sectors and industries have managed to use AR technology effectively and efficiently, garnering positive responses and support from consumers (Kaufman & Horton, 2015). As a result AR is having an impact on the everyday lives of consumers (Kipper & Rampolla, 2015).

The use of AR in the tourism industry is emerging. As an example, in 2008, Wikitude, a mobile AR software travel guide, was offered as freeware which displays information about the users' surroundings in a mobile camera view, including image recognition and 3D modeling. Tourists traveling in unfamiliar environments naturally require solid sources of data and information; AR applications can meet the demand of personalized, pertinent and rationalized information at a dependable level (Olsson & Väänänen-Vainio-Mattila, 2011). Today, AR applications are being created by tourism organizations all over the world for educational and marketing purposes. Tourism marketing professionals are responsible for advertising and publicizing a variety of goods and services, ranging from tourist sites, lodging establishments, and special events. Positions related to tourism marketing include, but are not limited to, in-house resort marketing representative, tourism specialist for a marketing firm, head of marketing for a resort or cruise line. Students studying to work in the tourism industry must have knowledge and skills in the use of AR in tourism marketing related jobs in order to be competitive in the employment arena.

The purpose of this chapter is to provide an overview of AR applications and platforms, discuss the use of AR applications and platforms within tourism marketing, and to make a case for including AR as a topic of study in institutions of higher education which offer bachelor's and master's degrees in tourism marketing and related programs. Specifically, this chapter is designed to outline augmented reality and its applications in tourism marketing education mainly in three aspects: theoretical, practical, and cross country examples.

BACKGROUND

AR has the potential to incorporate all human senses (sight, sound, taste, smell, touch) into a technological experience (Abernathy & Clark, 2007). AR applications are accelerated mainly by the latest developments in mobile computing, computer graphics, wire-less and sensor technologies. These advances influence and enhance human experiences through providing real time information displays and reviews (Suh, Shin, Woo, Dow, & MacIntyre, 2011). Gartner (2014) expects that, on the basis of continual technological advancements, the general public will be highly accepting the AR technologies. Still, the use of AR application as a tourism marketing tool is developing and may seem futuristic to some individuals (Shen, Ong, & Nee, 2011; Seo, Kim, & Park, 2011). However, AR applications can appear as marketing tools where these are still subject of exploration, where, touristic demand for information source is common (Yovcheva, Buhalis, & Gatzidis, 2012).

AR technology can work on grounds like the Global Positioning System (GPS) and on mobile devices with capacities to add virtual features and to relate them with reality (Azuma, 1997). AR as a medium of displaying requires intensive use of hardware or electronic devices such as camera, display monitors and computing gadgets. The introduction of handheld electronic items like the Smartphone or the smaller version of wearable computers has extended the realms of AR technology (Buchholz, 2014). On the other side, gaming consoles such as the Nintendo DS or similar also are mostly equipped with augmented reality technologies today (Breeze, 2014). The strengths of AR lie in its technological simplicity and capacities to perform as an educational tool.

AR applications used for marketing products may be the most common and popular way that the everyday consumer has been introduced to the concept and practice of augmented reality. AR applications have specifically been used to market brand names in ways that the product becomes memorable to the consumer and subsequently may build brand loyalty. Following are descriptions of three brand name uses of AR for marketing.

Budweiser is one of the world's famous and popular drink brands. As a part of effective marketing, Budweiser brings the Football Association Challenge Cup (FA Cup) directly into the consumers' house by using AR application. The Football Association Challenge Cup is an annual knockout cup competition in English football that is commonly known as the FA Cup in the world (The FA Cup, 2015). The marketing approach of Budweiser is ground breaking and it has managed to immerse AR in conventional marketing strategies. The Budweiser '*Man of the Match*' mobile application enables users to drink from the virtually-generated FA Cup. This application is developed on AR platform of the Aurasma that allows transforming the beer can into a virtual FA Cup trophy as a basic 3D model. Users have to click a selected button of their Smartphone camera for this purpose. Even though this application of AR for marketing can be effective, this entertainment option is limited, and can only be experienced by selected customers (Aurasma, 2015).

High street betting chain Paddy Power® has also made contributions on putting augmented reality into practice. In cooperation with Blippar, Paddy Power developed a special application which turns the Queens face on a £10 bank note into the user's own face. This technology is as simple as to hover on the face of the Queen's and then enjoy. The digital copy of the Queen turns into animation as soon as the Smartphone can recognize the face. The face then moves as interactive and functional that resembles that the Queen is the official sponsor of the Euro 2012 (Preexamples, 2015).

The Muscle Milk® brand has also used AR in marketing. Through the campaign of Shaq the bottle, this company is grabbing the attention of diverse clients and promoters from all over world. The celebration of Shaquille O'Neal was followed by augmented reality application. This initiative took place in the Cleveland market when the muscle milk brand was chosen to market into a new team created with O'Neals joining the team. A special form of AR marker in the shape of a QR code was printed on the back label of each milk bottle. When a webcam was placed on the marker of each bottle, a user could watch the virtual video showing a mini Shaq in Cleveland. Each of the five different flavours of the Muscle Milk® followed five types of videos and these were limited by edition and number (Showcase, 2015).

TOURISM MARKETING

Digital Marketing

Still, no definition of digital tourism marketing has been offered that can be viewed as comprehensive and well accepted. There are still scopes to develop the definition and to turn it into a workable meaning for understanding the central theme and relevancy with existing market structures of tourism (Buhalis & Yovcheva, 2014). In a very general understanding, digital marketing refers to the pattern of marketing that uses technology as the main platform to reach the target bases of consumers. There are numerous techniques of professional practices in tourism marketing and digital marketing that are entirely technology-based. Wider selection of tourism products or services coupled with marketing tactics like branding or promotion is presented before consumers to allow them to reach an agreeable decision of purchase. Internet is the central base of digital tourism while, television, radio or even the mobile telephone devices are used for the purpose. Digital marketing has unparallel dependency on the Internet and thus very often this is termed as Internet marketing (Daim et al., 2012). The use of the Internet is more effective to reach wider consumer segments and, thus, to persuade them to access the available offers, services or products. Unlike conventional patterns of marketing, this Internet-based marketing is more focused; targeted and comprehensive that brings dynamism in marketing and consumer choice enhancements. This also supports consumers to have expanded formats of products or service selection. Technical terms like the search engine marketing (SEM) or search engine optimization (SEO) are quite familiar in digital marketing and have relevancy in numerous platforms of digital media. Other than the SEM or SEO, digital marketing is also relevant in non-mainstream spaces such as the service offers of mobile telephone technologies as the multimedia messaging service (MMS), short messaging service (SMS) or even games (Deighton & Kornfeld, 2007). The central theme of digital marketing is to create a bond between consumers and technology. There is a constant demand that technologies should support human livelihood and thus to create more spaces to understand the demand of tourism product or service consumers. Digital marketing is more engaged in creating and retaining a strong bond between consumers and technology. This pattern of marketing enables business entrepreneurs to become consumer led and also to become more capable to meet the increasing demands of consumers in more manageable ways (Dhir, 2004).

Digital marketing is entirely related to tourism marketing in recent times where, a specific tourism organization uses a digital marketing campaign for branding or marketing (Azim & Hassan, 2013). Other than email, SMS, MMS and social networking, a certain number of advanced options become available for digital marketing. Display supported digital marketing can offer realistic experiences to consumers and thus to select products or services from a more convenient way. The introduction of Smartphones has enabled digital tourism marketers and consumers to reach a mutual standpoint of offerings and accessibilities (Deluna, 2014). Digital marketing is fast, as a message can be shared quickly to numerous consumer bases across the world. However, evidently, digital tourism marketing requires expert knowledge on certain areas and on technical issues to help advancing capacities of both marketers and consumers. The advantages of digital marketing are mostly positive and getting enormous responses from almost all over the world (Wind & Mahajan, 2001). In comparison with direct marketing, digital marketing has specific advantages. These advantages are most similar to digital marketing and come in numerous forms. The main factor of personal attention of consumers is crucial and is related to interaction with customers. Also, digital marketing tends to focus on each of the customers and thus creates more possibilities to generate direct responses. In digital marketing, this is often manageable and possible to create a personalized message to an individual customer (MarketingWeek, 2015). Each customer can be addressed and greeted separately and uniformly. Thus, this promotes personal serviced marketing that is more effective than other conventional forms. Also, digital marketing supports the measurement of responses from customers (i.e. the replies or reactions from messages sent to each of the customers). This is also important to understand the customers and their responses or mindsets. Digital marketing also does not necessarily require specialized forms of knowledge on marketing or technology. This is more customer-tailored and relevant to meet their demands more satisfactorily (Rust, Katherine, & Valarie, 2004). Digital marketing can become an important addition to any existing or potential business evolving in the tourism sector. This helps customers to achieve a target that is more focused to reality and reliability. There is a gap between traditional and digital forms of marketing and this gap is gradually increasing over the years due to the availability of more advanced types of technologies that continuously surpass one another. Digital marketing is a positive and fruitful outcome of the Internet which is supported by diverse forms of technological innovations (Guimaraes, 2012). This is thus convincing that digital marketing continues evolving over the coming years through the adoption of more advanced technological innovations. This is a way to support, promote and expand an existing business or even to reach desired customer bases. Thus, this is important to ensure that the business is getting the maximum exposure from digital forms of marketing, even within a complex pattern of marketing (Hax, 2010). Digital marketing, due to the fact that it does not necessarily require professional expertise and experiences, has very good possibility to gain popularity in tourism.

Digital marketing has become a necessity for today's business world and more supported by technologies than ever before. Also, the tourism sector requires working or practical knowledge in marketing and technology (Mohapatra, 2009). This form of tourism deals with both supply and demand side that involves interests of both marketers and consumers. Digital marketing is beneficial and rewarding in numerous marketing formats and technology applications. Customers normally stay connected with each other on digital platforms. Again, customer response generation relatively becomes more obvious than conventional marketing (Mobile Marketer, 2015). The success and activity of a tourism business enterprise depends on specific marketing factors. These are also related with diverse types of business functionalities including understanding the targeted customer base and becoming able to know their responses in a purposeful manner (Gay, Charlesworth, & Esen, 2007). The success of digital marketing relies on specific strategies or factors. Like conventional marketing approaches, in digital marketing, there are specific goals to reach. In digital marketing, set business goals are wider that target general expansion within the shortest possible time period. The more customers involved with a business enterprise, the more attention from marketers are required to serve their demands more successfully (Rayport & Jaworski, 2004). Digital marketing is particularly important for any business to reach success within the shortest possible timeframe.

AR Uses in Tourism Marketing

As the trend of creating closer interactions between technologies and electronic gadgets, tourism marketing becomes more powerful and it is obvious that AR marketing will gradually contest existing marketing tools. Technologies are dissolving in tourism marketing in faster motions than any other times. This becomes evident from some revolutionary inventions including augmented reality. Technology enhanced marketing strategies are challenging and replacing relatively more rigid theoretical notions. The content, features, and objectives are basically altered by the use of technology in tourism marketing. There are numerous examples, from around the world, of AR being used in an aspect of tourism marketing. Following are examples from six countries, Canada, France, Germany, the Netherlands, Greece, and China.

In Ontario of Canada, the tourism industry witnessed a global event termed as the '2013 Ontario Tourism Summit' that actually gathered academics, scholars, researchers, industry practitioners and AR marketing experts to share their views and ideas. This summit particularly supported general tourism agendas. As an outcome of this summit, experts reached an agreement that mobile devices are becoming reliable for AR marketing and offer enormous potentials to increase the market. The summit concluded that, AR is no longer confined within photo, video, downloads, games or website links. Rather, AR is becoming a powerful marketing tool for tourism (Augmentedmarketing, 2013). In Canada, AR research has already been integrated with academia and Universities like York University and Ryerson University evidently welcomes research programs in AR (augmentedstories, 2015).

In France, AR is being used to promote historic and cultural sites for global audiences. The Louvre -DNP Museum Lab is a specialized research facility designed for AR application development in museums (Louvre -DNP Museum Lab, 2015). The Louvre is now equipped with AR technology enabled displays and devices that offer information about the collections, histories, compilations, and displays with related data and information. Another example from Paris, France involves using Smartphone devices for tourists to download information about historical images. These images are then contrasted with images of the present time in similar places of the city. Users of such applications can travel back as much as one hundred years and view more than two thousands places of interest. These establishments otherwise have to rely on museum attendants or tour operators to convey information to tourists. The AR technology can also help tourists pursue their own areas of interest. Lastly, the Cluny Abbey in Cluny, France has embraced one of the simplest technology displays of AR. In order to promote learning the history, a big size display screen is used to provide tourists with real-life experiences through AR technology. Displays on this screen actually offer tourists historic backgrounds of the city. Therefore, the intervention of AR technology enhances the tourists' experience. On average, millions of tourists make visits and experience this screen to know the past of this city every year. This facility also creates interests among tourists about AR and its application. In general, such interests through AR technology show the huge potentials of AR for tourism marketing. This also demonstrates how AR technology can be diffused for experience generation, sharing, educational and marketing purposes (Digitalmeetsculture, 2015).

In Germany, remarkable advancements in augmented reality application has been jointly offered by the companies Instant Reality and IGD Fraunhofer. These companies have developed a special AR supported photo system that enables tourists to view images of important sites or attractions of Berlin. The exceptional feature that this system offers is to view images of a site or attraction of Berlin in different periods in history. This technological system is supported by wearable or handheld devices such as Smartphones or ultra-mobile personal computer. This technological application allows users to get connected with the central server system and get access to a database of photographs highlighting the city's decade's old growth (Stricker, Pagani, & Zoellner, 2009).

In the Netherlands, the Netherlands Architecture Institute has introduced a free application, Urban Augmented Reality that is available in eight main cities of the country, enabling both the residents and tourists viewing existing urban environment through historic layouts. In order to share views or ideas, tourists can leave their comments on a database linked to it and the public sector policy planners can also then extract themes of such comments and reflect them in public policy frameworks (Caarls, Jonker, Kolstee, Rotteveel, & van Eck, 2009).

In Greece, the process of AR technology application found its way through virtual reconstruction of a prominent ancient temple located in Olympia of Greece. The development of AR technology supported systems is the outcome of many years long research. According to Vlahakis et al. (2002), the development of ArcheoGuide AR system allows tourists to have memorable sensations from tourism marketing education standpoints. Layar is an AR application which uses GPS location to show nearby service facilities on top of the image of a mobile phone's camera. Through the use of Layar, an application that can be downloaded to a Smartphone, a tourist can get the option to point the phone towards the Berlin wall representing a reality based 3D model. In addition, in Seville, Greece the Past View Company has created a program that can offer tourists an entire city tour using AR. The application operates on a type of electronic earphones or video glasses and connects to a Smartphone to present the city's history (Internet-science, 2015).

China, as a global tourism destination with an abundance of tourism resources, is becoming dominant for both present and future tourists. The Yuanmingyuan or the Garden of Perfect Brightness is located in Beijing and was built during the 18th and 19th centuries. During the Anglo-Chinese War, this majestic garden was totally destroyed. However, the attempt to regenerate the garden came into action through the use of both sketches and paintings with little use of photographs or digital formats. However, as soon as AR technology came into practice, a panel of experts of the Beijing Institute of Technology was engaged in creating a reconstruction process of virtual platforms (Wang, Wang, & Fournier, 2000). Facilities for tourists to learn about this garden were supported by numerous initiatives and approaches related to technology use. These included machines that are operated by coins inputted by customers and special facilities like model reconstruction (Lum, 2012).

Most countries in Europe such as Germany, France, Italy, Greece and the United Kingdom with their enriched social, cultural and historic backgrounds are using AR technologies for exhibiting cultural sites for marketing purposes (Hepburn, 2015; Lee, Chung, & Jung, 2015). However, augmented reality can be used in almost all parts of the world, including both technologically developed and under-developed countries by developing technological infrastructures (Neuhofer, Buhalis, & Ladkin, 2013; Jung, Chung, & Leue, 2015).

The use of AR in different marketing areas is immense. In practice, there are numerous examples of brands using augment reality including Topshop Kinect Dressing Rooms, Shisedio Makeup Mirror, American Apparel Colour-Changing App, De Beers 'Forevermark Fitting', IKEA AR Catalogue, Sayduck Furniture Visualizer, IBM App, Converse Shoe Sampler, Burberry Beauty Box, and Moosejaw X-Ray App (Creative Guerrilla Marketing, 2014). This technology becomes a solid platform for creating and maintaining relationship with the public and the general customer base that can be replicated in tourism and can be highlighted in tourism marketing education.

Resistance to AR Marketing

AR can be applied in tourism marketing. Historic establishments can be rebuilt through the use of AR technologies enabling to support experience enhancements and to promote the site. Such regeneration process through images and visuals can be useful for both commercial and prototype educational purposes (Monday, 2015). The demands of tourism learners are diverse and thus relevant learning experience should be offered to satisfy what they seek. If they seek to experience cultural heritage tourism, they should be offered a realistic experience using AR technology (Han, Jung, & Gibson, 2014; Jung & Han, 2014). The rapid advancement of wearable computing, such as Google Glass, adds possibilities of enhancing the learning experience within cultural organizations such as museums and art galleries. A later study by Hassan (2013) in the Whitechapel Gallery of London cited an example of effective technology application in terms of offering learning experience. Another recent study by Leue, Jung, and tom Dieck (2015) reveals specifically that wearable augmented reality application helps visitors see connections between paintings and personalizes their learning experience.

In tourism research, limited theories and models related to technology use have been developed by scholars, researchers or experts. Relevant theories of technology adoption have been mostly applied to understand the pattern of technology adoption by tourism products or service consumers. The Diffusion of Innovation (Rogers, 1962) is an example of those theories or models. However, understanding the relevancy of this theory in AR technology application context is unique. In a simple sense, this theory explains why, how and at what rate a new technology is diffused into a culture. This theory is originally concerned with technologies, artefacts and ideas that normally pass from theory to application stage (Spencer, Buhalis, & Moital, 2012). According to Rogers (2003), sequences that the Diffusion of Innovation Theory follows are: knowledge, persuasion, decision, implementation and confirmation. On the other side, different stages of this theory are: innovators, *early adopters*, early majority, late majority and laggards. The 'Diffusion of Innovations' theory relies on the innovation-decision process that can be seen as valid in diverse cultures. This theory follows that technological innovations are connected through specific channels of the social system and act over a period of time.

Tourism industry is unprecedentedly gaining benefits from technology integration. Arguably, information and communication technologies are required to offer diverse typologies to become beneficial components for tourism marketing in recent times. The involvement of certain features of tourism is also essential in terms of effective use of technologies to make purchase decisions. The world is now better equipped to welcome and apply technological innovations than ever before (McElheran, 2012). Tour guides, travel agents, and tour operators are influenced by the utmost application of technologies; while tourism products or service and consumers are the direct subject of such influences. Results of technology application in tourism can be replicated in similar or emerging market contexts. From the applied viewpoint and most importantly, augmented reality as an innovation is beneficial for the tourism business enterprises, policy planners and business communities for competitive marketing strategy formulations. The basic question stays relevant to delineate consumer and product or service provider to become able to accept augmented reality as innovation. This question also seems as appropriate to explore the position of augmented reality in the Diffusion of Innovation theory. More importantly, concentrations need to be placed to determine the characteristics of augmented reality to incorporate a theory as the Diffusion of Innovation.

Key Practical Challenges to Inclusion of AR

Tourism is the world's leading industry and there are several techniques of professional and practical practices in tourism marketing education where the strategies and patterns are entirely technology-based (World Tourism Organization, 2015). A purposeful selection of tourism products or services coupled with marketing tactics like branding, promotions with augmented reality technology needs to become valid and effective. In fact, this is a real challenge to introduce, support and promote augmented reality in tourism marketing academia. This allows consumers to reach an agreeable decision of purchase that might turn as positive. This chapter suggests two key challenges to apply augmented reality in tourism marketing. In both perspectives of augmented reality and tourism marketing education, the key challenges appear in theory and practice.

In practice, AR is also mostly viewed as a technological innovation and its mass use is mostly restricted. The activities and successes of a tourism business enterprise depend on the selection of specific marketing approaches followed by their effective application (Turban, McLean, & Wetherbe, 2008). In recent times, marketing approaches mostly rely on technologies and to serve the purposes of business enterprises, augmented reality technology can become effective given its proven capacities to attract consumer interests. The greater number of customers that are attracted to a business enterprise, the more opportunities are created for marketing on digital platforms. This requires proper attention of the marketers to each individual customer. Also, setting realistic business targets to ensure that the business is directed towards the desired goal is also important and can be seen as a challenge. The success of digital marketing relies on careful selection of strategies and policies and AR technology application can possibly be a good option. Like unconventional marketing approach, in digital marketing, there have to be specific goals for each individual business enterprise to reach.

TOURISM MARKETING EDUCATION

Tourism marketing education refers to the education that involves tourism marketing in its syllabus. This type of education can support preparing future tourism marketing professionals. Primarily, the use of technologies is crucial. Effective and valid application of technology for professional development including tourism can bring positive outcomes.

Preparing Future Tourism Marketing Professionals

Specific technology like AR is believed to have capacities to create impact among tourism marketing professionals. This impact can lead to influencing consumers. The world is gradually changing and is continuously embracing updated forms of technologies. It is wise to adopt technologies and to apply them effectively for the purpose of marketing (Lewis, Agarwal, & Sambamurthy, 2003). AR marketing, as a type of digital marketing, is relatively more cost effective and can offer better return of investment than traditional forms of marketing (prweb, 2011). AR applications can be useful to develop skills of tourism marketing professionals and can be viewed as a convenient source to create user interests. AR can be an effective means of sales and revenue generation for tourism businesses. This can render possibilities for professionals. AR applications can enhance consumer experiences. In addition, a number of intermediaries and more selectively electronic mediaries (eMediaires) are adopting and using the Internet and AR to reach target customer segments all over the world (Kumar, Venkatesan, & Reinartz, 2006). On the other side, tourists also seek information on their desired services or products on the Internet. Thus, the Internet and in particular AR can be turned into common platforms of marketing. These cost effective and informative platforms are turning as valid and reliable platforms of marketing for tourists. In order to support digital marketing, numerous forms of display patterns are brought to influence a positive form of consumer decision. The Internet is being challenged by the Internet itself in terms of speed, information or accessibility. Visibly, not other platforms can be as reliable and valid for tourism marketing in the most recent tourism marketing contexts. This is termed as unbelievably simple and within the fingertips of customers (Thorpe, Holm, & van den Boer, 2014). Targeted customers are allowed to search for relevant information and thus to get access to it in more convenient ways than ever before with the effective support of AR technology application. This platform is also crucial to promote and make available certain products or services. The conventional types of digital marketing follow e-commerce, website trafficking and e-mail newsletters. All of these types are more conventional and have been in use for a long time. The demand for more advanced forms of digital marketing becomes apparent due to changing choices of consumers and the features of products or services (Song, Liu, & Chen, 2012). The use of AR becomes very effective in terms of getting responses or experiences shared on specific products or services. Blogging is relative less effective than social media but still offers relevant information. Sometimes, information sharing on networking websites becomes critical and thus appears as more capable to offer better service or product qualities with the support of AR technology application. Thus, AR can have a significant role to play to develop skills of marketing professionals in tourism.

In order to prepare more professionals in tourism marketing, marketers need to stress applying technologies for skills development. In tourism, the basic demand to capitalize on technological advancements is to learn operational skills. In many cases, tourism marketers struggle to apply an innovative technology like AR and this can be regarded as a resistance for a relatively new technology such as AR. However, AR, as an innovative technology, is already in use by tourism businesses and marketers. Following the Diffusion of Innovations by Rogers (1962), AR technology can be classified as '*Early Majority*' stage. The basic reason for this categorization is that the tourism marketing and businesses have already advanced significantly to apply AR technology meaning that they are on the '*Early Majority*' stage.

On the other side, government, university and tourism industry should look at the huge potential of AR marketing in tourism and take action to get this included in the academic syllabuses. This can be done by stressing AR technology and include this in both the undergraduate and postgraduate level academic syllabus. Tourism marketing education in almost every country is at the infancy stage with regards to including AR in its academic syllabus. On the other side, skills of the academics also need to reach that desired level to teach AR in tourism marketing education. On the basis of the Diffusion of Innovations theory of Rogers (1962), the present situation of tourism marketing education outlines that AR is an innovative technology at '*Early Adopters*' stage.

Inclusion of AR Applications in Curriculum

Tourism marketing education syllabuses in graduate and postgraduate stage at university level can highlight AR in their academic syllabuses. Numerous evidences and cases from across the world show that the use of AR for marketing purposes is not rare anymore and the number is increasing (Kaufman & Horton, 2015). The effects and influences of augmented reality technology, in particular can hardly be ignored in many areas of tourism marketing. This supports the claim that AR technology needs to be included in tourism marketing education syllabuses. AR as a technology application supports marketing in a unique way that learners need to know. Tourism marketing dynamics outline that the use of AR technologies needs to be widely utilized. This is still a subject matter of consideration both from technology and marketing domains. In the tourism industry, tourists are mostly capable of using AR technologies through their mobile devices like Smartphones. AR is mainly responsible for experience sharing, education and marketing purposes for tourism. This technology can offer experiences of an entire city tour as linked with its basic history, features and related factors. This creates interests in areas of education, marketing and promoting of specific tourist attractions. Unlike conventional tourism marketing education and marketing types, AR marketing is more dependable, target focused and useful. Thus, tourism marketing education evolved as a necessity of today's businesses as solely supported by technological knowledge (Vong, 2015). However, the availability and accessibility of technology are unequal for general learners and consumer segments. There is a strong demand for technological knowledge and use. A comprehensive academic and industry led understanding of tourism digital marketing is yet to be offered. Very often, it is believed that tourism digital marketing has a strong central theme of technology led knowledge and practical application. This possesses capacities to incorporate both existing and future tourism digital marketing. This study cites examples from several countries in the world in terms of AR technology use. Thus, this study advocates AR to be included in tourism marketing education.

Key Theoretical Challenges to Inclusion of AR

The first challenge is theoretical concept on the ground of knowledge exchange and expertise about augmented reality. This challenge is particularly directed for academics, scholars or experts in tourism marketing education. The application of augmented reality in tourism marketing education academia is a challenge. In theory, academic instructors need to possess sufficient knowledge about augmented reality and its application in tourism marketing education. On the other side in particular cases, augmented reality is seen as an element of post modern marketing outlining its relevancies in the marketing academia. Marketing in post modern age is in fact the blend of conventional and modern approaches of marketing. In post modern marketing, consumers typically stay connected and thus the response generation becomes more obvious than conventional marketing (Yang, 2004). Message on services or products pass over within a very short time to numerous consumer bases across the world. Post modern marketing is related with diverse types of business functionalities including identifying the target consumers and becoming able to comprehend their responses in purposeful manners (Petersen & Toop, 1994).

FUTURE DIRECTIONS

The main message of this section is that AR offers features to be included in any tourism marketing education curriculum. The primary reason of such inclusion is its key feature as a technological innovation. Technology is changing the core contents and grounds of tourism marketing education and there is almost no scope left for ignoring the growing importance. Thus, the contribution of technology is gradually increasing in tourism marketing education leaving more impact on both academics and practitioners in these identified grounds. This chapter discusses diverse features and potentials of augmented reality in tourism marketing practice and education and suggests its inclusion in the academic syllabuses to be studied as a key module. Thus, it would be beneficial to include augmented reality in the tourism marketing education syllabus. The very basic benefit that this inclusion can generate is the diversified knowledge of students. On the other side, assigned teachers and researchers in the tourism marketing education discipline would also possibly become aware about the contents and presentations of AR in tourism marketing education. The future of augmented reality as both an academic and research element of tourism marketing education is convincing. Even at present, augmented reality is facing serious challenges but the potentials are enormous to be included in tourism marketing syllabuses across the globe. The key challenge that augmented reality is facing is its complex nature. This technology also requires relevant expertise of concerned academics. The level of knowledge also needs to be well developed to deliver to students. Consequently, this is mostly obvious that augmented reality is expected to manage a strong position in tourism marketing education syllabus in the near future.

The introduction and availability of a technology commonly varies between nations outlining acute differences between nations including the developed and the developing. Technology application cannot be expected to get similar responses in both developed and developing countries across the world. This requires the demand that updated technology needs to be made widely available and particularly for students, academics and researchers. Their involvement and activities would offer positive advancements to view augmented reality as a valid element of tourism marketing education in near future. Thus, this chapter proposes that augmented reality should be offered as an important subject matter of tourism marketing education in the future.

This chapter is a report of thoughts related to AR application in tourism marketing education. This chapter as a report could possibly be converted into comprehensive research supported by empirical data and information. From that perspective, the basic limitation of this chapter is the lack of empirical evidence from respondents through conducting interviews. Primary data and information could possibly enrich contents of this report by highlighting opinions, arguments and justification from user perspectives. This lack is significant in a manner because, a possible interrelationship between academics, students, experts and practitioners related to tourism marketing education could possibly intensify debate and arguments to view augmented reality as an element of an academic syllabus. A balanced interrelatedness between concepts and peoples' ideologies could possibly create a bridge between theories and applications. This is a very generic limitation of this report that needs to be addressed in future research.

CONCLUSION

Conceptually, technology application supports massive consumption across the world where, such consumption patterns are mostly diverse and ever changing. Augmented reality is a computer generated reality but not necessarily fictitious or purely imaginary. Augmented reality supports the reality that is concerned with existing artifacts. Augmented reality as a technology can be termed as innovation on ground of the Diffusion of Innovation Theory (Rogers, 1962). On the basis of the Diffusion of Innovations Theory of Roger's (1962), this study determines position of augmented reality for tourism marketer or business as the '*Early Majority*' and tourism marketing education as the '*Early Adopters*' stage, respectively. Basic logic for this claim is made on the perspective of an emerging trend in tourism marketing education. The very basic reason is that augmented reality as an element of tourism marketing syllabus still remains at the early stage. Academics, students and researchers are still to become fully aware concerning augmented reality in terms of its meaning and application where the technology is not widely available for mass use.

This paper discusses features of augmented reality to be included in the tourism marketing education syllabuses. The features of augmented reality as an advanced form of virtual reality (VR) is interesting and its application values are also relatively high. Recent technological developments of mobile computing, computer graphics, wireless, sensor technologies, Smartphones and wearable devices have created more prospects to view augmented reality as more rewarding. On the other side, global brands are also using this technology for both advertising and marketing purposes. Also, these brands are constantly relying on such technological innovation to create spaces for marketing and connectivity with mass consumers. In addition, global technological appliance manufacturers are constantly aiming to use and develop this technology creating more opportunities for research and employability for students and researchers. These global brands have allowed consumers to view how technological appliances are designed to perform and entertain. Wearable devices like Smartwatches or Smart glasses are also evolving with modifications creating more spaces for general consumers. The development of sensor and visual technologies are also supporting the potentials of augmented reality technology. This thus allows buyers to support and experience what they are going to purchase and how that will look like.

Thus evidently, AR both as a technology and as an innovation has already established the position in consumers' traditional lifestyle. This is visible and evident through the customary use of technological gadgets those are mostly wearable. This chapter cites examples of augmented reality use from several countries of the world including the United Kingdom, Netherlands, Canada, France, Germany, Greece and China to establish the claim of its application.

This chapter outlines the prospects that AR can offer in terms of knowledge, research and practical aspect of employment possibility. Thus, this paper clearly suggests diverse aspects and examples of augmented reality as available and accessible for students, academics and practitioners in tourism marketing. Also, the paper strongly suggests augmented reality to be included in tourism marketing education syllabus to allow students learn about this technology and to become fit for employability. Augmented reality is an excellent and a trendy concept of recent times. This technology is expected to get wider popularity in the near future. Augmented reality shows prospects to turn into a reliable platform in tourism marketing mainly for its increasing capacities.

REFERENCES

Abernathy, W., & Clark, K. B. (2007). Innovation: Mapping the winds of creative distruction. *Research Policy, 14*(1), 3–22. doi:10.1016/0048-7333(85)90021-6

Augmentedmarketing. (2013). *Ontarion Tourism Summit 2013 features interactive print.* Retrieved from http://bit.ly/1CRuwl6

Augmentedstories. (2015). *Education.* Retrieved from: http://augmentedstories.com/education/

Aurasma. (2015). *The drink of champions.* Retrieved from: http://bit.ly/1Fw66vl

Azim, R., & Hassan, A. (2013). Impact analysis of wireless and mobile technology on business management strategies. *Journal of Information and Knowledge Management, 2*(2), 141–150.

Azuma, R. (1997). A survey of augmented reality. *Presence (Cambridge, Mass.), 6*(4), 355–385.

Breeze, M. (2014). *How augmented reality will change the way we live.* Retrieved from http://tnw.co/1nEDN6O

Buchholz, R. (2014). *Augmented reality: new opportunities for marketing and sales.* Retrieved from http://bit.ly/1nMCLYO

Buhalis, D., & Yovcheva, Z. (2014). *Augmented reality in tourism: 10 best practices.* Retrieved from http://bit.ly/1tphods

Caarls, J., Jonker, P., Kolstee, Y., Rotteveel, J., & van Eck, W. (2009). Augmented reality for art, design and cultural heritage—system design and evaluation. *EURASIP Journal on Image and Video Processing, 2009,* 1–16. doi:10.1155/2009/716160

Creative Guerrilla Marketing. (2014). 10 examples of augmented reality in retail. Retrieved from http://bit.ly/OxuyHI

Daim, T. U., Letts, M., Krampits, M., Khamis, R., Dash, P., & Monalisa, M. (2012). IT infrastructure refresh planning for enterprises: A business process perspective. *Business Process Management Journal, 17*(3), 1–16.

Deighton, J. A., & Kornfeld, L. (2007). *Digital interactivity: unanticipated consequences for markets, marketing and consumers.* Boston: Harvard Business School.

Deluna, K. (2014). *10 rockstar examples of augmented reality for 2014.* Retrieved from http://bit.ly/1mIaCib

Dhir, A. (2004). *The digital consumer technology handbook.* Oxford: Elsevier.

Digitalmeetsculture. (2015). Augmented reality: enriching culture. Retrieved from http://bit.ly/1E46st6

Dutra, J.P. (2015). *ARgos – augmented reality in Volos – Greece.* Retrieved from http://bit.ly/1BgTVTw

Edwards, J. (2011). *Digital frontiers media uses augmented reality to market St. Pete/Clearwater tourism with miles media.* Retrieved from http://www.prweb.com/releases/2011/03/prweb5141134.htm

Gartner Incorporated. (2014). *Gartner Technology Research.* Retrieved from: http://Online.gartner.com/technology/home.jsp>

Gay, R., Charlesworth, A., & Esen, R. (2007). *Online marketing: A customer-led approach.* Oxford: Oxford University Press.

Guimaraes, T. (2012). Industry clockspeed's impact on business innovation success factors. *European Journal of Innovation Management, 14*(3), 322–344. doi:10.1108/14601061111148825

Han, D., Jung, T., & Gibson, A. (2014). Dublin AR: Implementing Augmented Reality (AR) in Tourism. In Z. Xiang & I. Tussyadiah (Eds.), *Information and Communication Technologies in Tourism* (pp. 511–523). Wien, New York: Springer International Publishing.

Hassan, A. (2013). Perspective analysis and implications of visitor management - experiences from the Whitechapel Gallery, London. *Anatolia: An International Journal of Tourism and Hospitality Research, 24*(3), 410-426. doi:.10.1080/13032917.2013.797916

Hax, A. C. (2010). *Reinventing your business strategy.* New York: Springer.

Hepburn, A. (2015). *Top 10 augmented reality examples- digital buzz blog.* Retrieved from http://bit.ly/1nXdp6l

Jung, T., Chung, N., & Leue, M. (2015). The Determinants of Recommendations to Use Augmented Reality Technologies - The Case of a Korean Theme Park. *Tourism Management, 49,* 75–86. doi:10.1016/j.tourman.2015.02.013

Jung, T., & Han, D. (2014). Augmented reality (AR) in urban heritage tourism. *e-Review of Tourism Research.*

Kaufman, I., & Horton, C. (2015). *Digital marketing: Integrating strategy and tactics with values: A guidebook for executives, managers & students.* New York: Routledge.

Kipper, G., & Rampolla, J. (2014). *Augmented reality: An emerging technologies guide to AR*. London: Elsevier.

Kumar, V., Venkatesan, R., & Reinartz, W. J. (2006). Knowing what to sell when to whom. *Harvard Business Review*, May, 131–145. PMID:16515161

Lee, H., Chung, N., & Jung, T. (2015). Examining the cultural differences in acceptance of mobile augmented reality: comparison of South Korea and Ireland. In I. Tussyadiah & A. Inversini (Eds.), *Information and Communication Technologies in Tourism* (pp. 477–491). Wien: Springer International Publishing New York. doi:10.1007/978-3-319-14343-9_35

Leue, M. C., Jung, T., & tom Dieck, D. (2015). Google Glass Augmented Reality: Generic Learning Outcomes for Art Galleries. In I. Tussyadiah & A. Inversini (Eds.), Information and Communication Technologies in Tourism (pp. 463-476). Wien: Springer International Publishing.

Lewis, W., Agarwal, R., & Sambamurthy, V. (2003). Sources of influence on beliefs about information technology use: An empirical study of knowledge workers. *Management Information Systems Quarterly*, *27*(4), 657–678.

Louvre -DNP Museum Lab. (2015). *Past presentation*. Retrieved from http://www.museumlab.jp/english/tech/04tech.html

Lum, R. (2012). *10 mind-blowing augmented reality campaigns*. Retrieved from http://bit.ly/1kMP8AD

MarketingWeek. (2015). *Online retail will drive innovation in interactive marketing*. Retrieved from http://bit.ly/1nbpjdM

McElheran, K. S. (2012). *Do market leaders lead in business process innovation? The case(s) of e-business adoption*. Boston: Harvard Business School.

Mobile Marketer. (2015). *Mobile augmented reality to drive $1.5B in revenue by 2015*. Retrieved from http://bit.ly/1nbq32r

Mohapatra, S. (2009). *Business process automation*. New Delhi: PHI Private Limited.

Monday, C. (2015). *5 augmented reality examples worth looking at - ignite social media*. Retrieved from http://bit.ly/1mN1qZD

Neuhofer, B., Buhalis, D., & Ladkin, A. (2013). A typology of technology-enhanced tourism experiences. *International Journal of Tourism Research*. doi:10.1002/jtr.1958

Nordin, S. (2003). *Tourism clustering and innovation- paths to economic growth and development. Ostersund*. European Tourism Research Institute.

Olsson, T., & Väänänen-Vainio-Mattila, K. (2013). Expected User Experience of Mobile Augmented Reality Services. *Personal and Ubiquitous Computing*, *17*(2), 287–304. doi:10.1007/s00779-011-0494-x

Petersen, C., & Toop, A. (1994). *Sales Promotion in Postmodern Marketing*. Aldershot: Gower Publishing Ltd.

Preexamples. (2015). *Paddy Power augmented reality campaign brings the Queen's face on £10 note to life*. Retrieved from http://bit.ly/1CRur13

Rayport, J. F., & Jaworski, B. J. (2004). Best face forward. *Harvard Business Review, 82*(12), 1–12. PMID:15605565

Rogers, M. E. (1962). *Diffusion of innovations*. New York: Free Press.

Rogers, M. E. (2003). *Diffusion of innovations* (5th ed.). New York: Free Press.

Rust, R. T., Katherine, N. L., & Valarie, A. Z. (2004). Return on marketing: Using customer equity to focus marketing strategy. *Journal of Marketing, 68*(1), 109–127. doi:10.1509/jmkg.68.1.109.24030

Seo, B.-K., Kim, K., & Park, J. (2011). Augmented reality-based on-site tour guide: A study in Gyeong-bokgung. *Lecture Notes in Computer Science, 6469*, 276–285. doi:10.1007/978-3-642-22819-3_28

Shen, Y., Ong, S. K., & Nee, A. Y. C. (2011). Vision-based hand interaction in augmented reality environment. *International Journal of Human-Computer Interaction, 27*(6), 523–544. doi:10.1080/1044 7318.2011.555297

Showcase. (2015). *Shaq augmented reality*. Retrieved from http://bit.ly/1BgTZ5F

Song, H., Liu, J., & Chen, G. (2012). Tourism value chain governance- review and prospects. *Journal of Travel Research, 52*(1), 15–28. doi:10.1177/0047287512457264

Spencer, A. J., Buhalis, D., & Moital, M. (2012). A hierarchical model of technology adoption for small owner-managed travel firms: An organizational decision making and leadership perspective. *Tourism Management, 33*(5), 1195–1208. doi:10.1016/j.tourman.2011.11.011

Stricker, D., Pagani, A., & Zoellner, M. (2009). *In-situ visualization for cultural heritage sites using novel augmented reality technologies*. Retrieved from http://bit.ly/192Vg5N

Suh, Y., Shin, C., Woo, W., Dow, S., & MacIntyre, B. (2011). Enhancing and evaluating users' social experience with a mobile phone guide applied to cultural heritage. *Personal and Ubiquitous Computing, 15*(6), 649–665. doi:10.1007/s00779-010-0344-2

TheF. A. Cup. (2015). *About the FA*. Retrieved from http://bit.ly/1GLcZYu

Thorpe, M., Holm, J., & van den Boer, G. (2014). *Discovering the decisions within your business processes using IBM blueworks live*. New York: International Business Machines Corporation.

Turban, E., McLean, E. R., & Wetherbe, J. C. (2008). *Information technology for management*. New Jersey: John Wiley & sons, Inc.

Vlahakis, V., Ioannidis, N., Karigiannis, J., Tsotros, M., Gounaris, M., Stricker, D., Gleue, T., Daehne, P., & Almeida, L. (2002). Archeoguide: An Augmented Reality Guide for Archaeological Sites. *Computer Graphics in Art History and Archaeology, September/October*, 52- 60.

Vong, K. (2015). *How brands are using augmented reality in marketing to engage customers*. Retrieved from http://bit.ly/SrBNTq

Wang, L., Wang, C., & Fournier, C. (2000). Envisioning Yuan Ming Yuan (Garden of Perfect Brightness). *IEEE Computer Graphics and Applications*, *20*(1), 10–14. doi:10.1109/38.814532

Wind, J., & Mahajan, V. (2001). *Digital Marketing: Global Strategies from the World's Leading Experts*. Chichester: John Wiley & Sons.

World Tourism Organization (UNWTO). (2015). *Understanding tourism: basic glossary*. Retrieved from http://bit.ly/1ki2UGS

Yang, C. C. (2004). Exploring factors affecting the adoption of mobile commerce in Singapore. *Telematics and Informatics*, *22*(3), 257–277. doi:10.1016/j.tele.2004.11.003

Yovcheva, Z., Buhalis, D., & Gatzidis, C. (2012). Smartphone Augmented Reality Applications for Tourism. *e-Review of Tourism Research (eRTR)*, *10*(2), 63-66.

Yuen, S., Yaoyuneyong, G., & Johnson, E. (2011). Augmented reality: An overview and five directions for AR in education. *Journal of Educational Technology Development and Exchange*, *4*(1), 119–140.

ADDITIONAL READING

Bridges-to-technology. (2015). *What is Technology Adoption?* Retrieved from http://bit .ly/T5kFnb

Buhalis, D., & Lew, R. (2008). Progress in information technology and tourism management: 20 years on and 10 years after the internet—the state of eTourism research. *Tourism Management*, *29*(4), 609–623. doi:10.1016/j.tourman.2008.01.005

Business Dictionary. (2015). *Consumer buying behaviour*. Retrieved from http://bit.ly/1kICBJX

Candela, G., & Figini, P. (2012). *The economics of tourism destinations*. Berlin, Heidelberg: Springer. doi:10.1007/978-3-642-20874-4

Cantoni, L., & Zheng, X. (2013). *Information and communication technologies in tourism*. Berlin, Heidelberg: Springer.

Change Vision, A. R. M. (2015). *Augmented reality marketing*. Retrieved from http://bit.ly/1gVIqc0

Cooper, C., & Hall, M. C. (2008). *Contemporary tourism: an international approach*. Oxford: Butterworth-Heinemann.

Duffy, J. A. M., & Ketchand, A. A. (1998). Examining the role of service quality in overall service satisfaction. *Journal of Managerial Issues*, *10*, 240–255.

Hassan, A. (2012). Key components for an effective marketing planning: A conceptual analysis. *International Journal of Management & Development Studies*, *2*(1), 68–70.

Hassan, A. (2012). Rationalization of Business Planning Through the Current Dynamics of Tourism. *International Journal of Management & Development Studies*, *2*(1), 61–63.

Hassan, A. (2014). Revising the 'Five - Fold Framework' in Human Resource Management Practices – Insights from a Small Scale Travel Agent. *Tourism Analysis: An Interdisciplinary Journal, 19*(6), 799–805. doi:10.3727/108354214X14146848084400

KarchM. (2015). *Apps*. Retrieved from http://abt.cm/1l48Ojv

Li, N., Buhalis, D., & Zhang, L. (2013). Interdisciplinary research on information science and tourism: A systematic review. *Tourism Tribune, 28*(1), 114–128.

Michopoulou, E., & Buhalis, D. (2013). Information provision for challenging markets: The case of the accessibility requiring market in the context of tourism. *Information & Management, 50*(5), 229–239. doi:10.1016/j.im.2013.04.001

Mihart, C. (2012). Impact of Integrated Marketing Communication on Consumer Behaviour: Effects on Consumer Decision – Making Process. *International Journal of Marketing Studies, 4*(2), 121–129. doi:10.5539/ijms.v4n2p121

Morrison, A. M. (2013). *Marketing and managing tourism destinations*. London: Routledge.

SAS Institute Inc. (2015). *Digital marketing-what is it and why it matters*. Retrieved from http://bit.ly/1cRj6SG

The University of Bradford. (2015). *Effective learning service-introduction to research and research methods*. Retrieved from http://bit.ly/1gUwTpo

Tremblay, P. (1998). The economic organization of tourism. *Annals of Tourism Research, 25*(4), 837–859. doi:10.1016/S0160-7383(98)00028-0

Walters, D. (2002). *Operations strategy*. New York: Palgrave.

Werthner, H., & Klein, S. (1999). *Information technology and tourism - a challenging relationship*. Vienna: Springer-Verlag. doi:10.1007/978-3-7091-6363-4

Wynne, C., Berthon, P., Pitt, L., Ewing, M., & Napoli, J. (2001). The impact of the Internet on the distribution value chain- the case of the South African tourism industry. *International Marketing Review, 18*(4), 420–431. doi:10.1108/EUM0000000005934

Youngdahl, W., & Loomba, A. (2000). Service-driven global supply chains. *International Journal of Service Industry Management, 11*(4), 329–347. doi:10.1108/09564230010355368

KEY TERMS AND DEFINITIONS

Augmented Reality: This technology is generally viewed as the later stage of Virtual Reality. In this technology, a computer generated environment is created where, the humans as users act. This blends augmentation with reality.

Diffusion of Innovation Theory: This theory offered by Rogers in 1962 explains why and how a new technology or idea spreads in a society and at what rate. The theory proposes five stages for such explanation as part of this theory as: innovators, early adopters, early majority, late majority and laggards.

Digital Marketing: Digital marketing represents conducting marketing activities on digital platforms mainly, Internet.

Innovation: Innovation denotes an idea, method or product that is regarded as new.

Tourism Marketing Education: This deals with marketing in tourism education. In more specific understanding, this type education involves marketing aspects in particular grounds of tourism.

This research was previously published in Emerging Tools and Applications of Virtual Reality in Education edited by Dong Hwa Choi, Amber Dailey-Hebert, and Judi Simmons Estes, pages 168-185, copyright year 2016 by Information Science Reference (an imprint of IGI Global).

Chapter 23
Gaining a Continuous Retaining Relationship with Customers in Mobile Sector

Irene Samanta
Technological Educational Institute of Piraeus (TEI), Greece

ABSTRACT

One of the main characteristics of the global economy is the creation of oligopolistic markets. The decisions of those industries are characterised by interactivity. The risk arising from the domination of the power of oligopoly is the previous stage of manipulation of the market. This situation is against the concept of competitiveness and causes an entirely new situation to the customer's disadvantage. Mobile industry which is a typical oligopolistic market in Europe leads us to examine this specific market in Greece. Therefore, the present study examines the factors that influence the relationship marketing strategy of the industry. The research was conducted using a sample of 806 users of mobile phones. The method used for the quantitative analysis is chi-square test, discriminant analysis, which is based on Multivariate Analysis of Variance (MANOVA). The study has indicated that intense competition between mobile phone firms in Greece leads to the manipulation of consumers' behaviour. Also, findings of the current research demonstrate that firms create a unified policy in order to restrain their customers' consuming behaviour to a state of inertia, the customer passively re-buys the same service provider without much thought.

INTRODUCTION

Globalization has created conditions of competition between countries as well as businesses. High competition between companies has presented its results, which are the creation of oligopoly markets, since only few firms can create a competitive advantage in order to survive, in a profitable way (Kyriazopoulos, 2001).

The mobile industry is one of the faster growing industries in the EU and worldwide (Anwar, 2003). During the last several years the adoption of new technology raises in Greece, which can also be seen at the mobile phone industry. The sector operate in a high competitive market, in reference to usage programs,

DOI: 10.4018/978-1-5225-5187-4.ch023

the prices, the width and the quality of the provided services, their consumers' point of view about the network and the quality of customer service. The new technologies market in Greece follows the global trends but through steadily increasing rhythms. Today the broadband services are used mostly for Internet access. The provision of such functions is the next step for the strengthening of the broadband services.

In this competitive market firms, in order to attract new customers, create a unified marketing strategy. This policy has the aim of manipulating the market at the expense of competition, in a way that customers will be restrained in this policy. This results to consumer's inertia in reference to their primary choice. In order to change that situation, drastic alterations should be made in the pricing policy, as well as in the innovation in both products and services and the customer service (Reinartz et al., 2000).

As a result, the market cannot be segmented and the firms apply an undifferentiated marketing strategy. The above situation appears to be applied to the mobile service sector in Greece. The vast majority of Greek users own a mobile phone while the sector is mainly driven by the network operators, who are looking not only to acquire new customers but also to increase and retain their proportion of higher-value subscribers and increase the revenue generated by each customer. The great extent, to which the mobile phone sector has promoted its products and services as well as established, maintained and enhanced the brand image over the past years, reflects the fast changing environment of the industry.

In order to examine the consequences invoked to the market because of high competition of the mobile sector, a primary research was conducted. The results of the research are presented in this paper in a way that covers both theoretical analysis of market competition concepts and aspects. Then it continues with some background information on the mobile sector in Greece. The study also includes applications and practices followed in the mobile service sector. Finally, the research analysis and methodology refers to the factors of relationship marketing and customer retention, as the business drivers of the mobile sector.

The aim of the research is to identify the general trends of the mobile sector in Greece and to examine how the relationship marketing strategy of the sector influences customer retention. Furthermore, the research determines the factors that have an important role concerning the final decision of the consumer, whether to remain with the same firm, or to move to another one.

BACKGROUND

Relationship Marketing Benefits

Relationship Marketing (RM) emphasizes on a long-term interactive relationship between the provider and the customer, leading to long-term profitability. It recognizes that both the customer and the seller can be active. They should see each other as partners in a win to win relationship (Gronroos, 1995). Both the marketing mix theory and RM are – in theory at least – based on the marketing concept, which focuses on customers and their needs. Although the marketing mix and its additions incorporate relationships and interaction to some extent, RM provides a more radical change, a paradigm shift. It seems though that the primary values of marketing mix concerning manipulation have not changed. Marketing techniques change to "trapping" customers, so as to restrain or even punish their escape (Rust et al., 2003). Nevertheless, if expressions like "customer retention" or "zero defection" are treated as referring to mere manipulation, the application of RM will not make a noteworthy contribution. Ideally, RM assumes good will from all parties (Bennet & Barkensjo, 2005). Relationships are seldom completely symmetrical; one party is often the stronger one. This is acceptable to a degree in an imperfect market, but from a welfare perspective it is unacceptable in the long term (Bendall & Powers, 2003). The main dimensions of relationship marketing include trust, commitment and satisfaction. Those three are established as measures of relationship quality.

Relationship attributes including the length or duration of the relationship; structural or social bonds, dependence and inertia relationship termination costs relationship switching costs cooperation commitment. Athanasopoulou (2009) try to observe the negative effects on RM and study the levels of uncertainty, distance and conflict and their effect on various dimensions of RQ.

Relationship marketing, defined as the degree of appropriateness of a relationship to fulfill the needs of the customer (Papassapa & Miller, 2007). It includes several key components reflecting the overall assessment of the strength of a relationship between the firms and consumers (Rust et al., 2003). Previous research conceptualized relationship marketing as a construct consisting of several distinct, though related, dimensions (Jeng & Bailey, 2012). While the exact dimensions making up relationship quality are still debatable, there is, however, a general agreement around the key components of: satisfaction with the service provider's performance, trust in the service provider, and commitment to the relationship with the mobile telecom networks (Dasgupta et al., 2008).

The construct of customer retention focuses on repeat patronage, and it is different from, while closely related to, purchasing behavior and brand loyalty, in that in retention the marketer is seen as having the more active role in the customer-firm relationship (White & Yanamandram, 2007). A number of factors may drive customer retention, such as satisfaction, quality, switching costs (Wolfl, 2005), marketing strategies (Kyriazopoulos, 2001), and customer acquisition (Cronin et al., 2000). This work focuses on the major motivators of cost, quality, and customer experience.

Factors Influence Relationship Marketing

The study took into consideration six elements, which determine the customer relationships and retention, which is the future propensity of a customer to stay with a service provider (White & Yanamandram, 2004). These elements are service quality, customer satisfaction, trust, inertia, indifference, switching barriers to customer retention.

Competition is the act of striving against another force for the purpose of achieving dominance or attaining goals. In order to examine this hypothesis in depth, we see into the factors leading to the state of inertia, in what concerns the consumers' behaviour to change firms, as a result of the manipulation circumstances of the market. The basic hypothesis examined in our study, is:

H1: The higher the level of competition, the higher the level of consumer's behaviour manipulation.

Service Quality

(Zeithmal et al., 1990) offer a conceptual model of service quality which affects particular behaviours that indicate, whether customers will remain loyal to or leave a firm. According to (Cronin, 2000) a research which involved six industries showed that quality service was closely related to the customers' behaviour. In Cronin study service quality did not appear to have a significant (positive) effect on repurchase intentions. Finally, it has been suggested by (Manoj & Sunil, 2011) that he majority of customers simply remains inactive and do not undertake any action following a negative service experience. In our study we define the customer's perception of the service quality point of view as an important factor of the inertia (White & Yanamandram, 2004a; White & Yanamandram, 2007).

H2: Quality service has a direct impact on customer's behavior.

Price Perceptions

Following (Chatura & Jaideep, 2003) barriers as constraints that prevent switching action. (Yanamandram & White, 2006) examines switching barriers as a determinant of customer switching behaviour. Subsequently, (Fraunholz & Kitchen, 2004) develop a model that includes switching costs as an antecedent of customer loyalty. Also they define switching costs as investment of time, money and effort that, in customers' perception, made it difficult to switch. In our study switching barriers are used in order to investigate the case, in which a homogenous pricing policy by the mobile industry results to the customer's behaviour manipulation in the Greek market. Alternatively, the price perceptions of the consumer confine customers in the same service provider, manipulating thus their behaviour (Kim et al., 2009).

H3: Price Perceptions has a direct impact on customer's behaviour.

Inertia

Inertia is the re-buy of the same service provider passively without much thought. The purchase may even be in spite of the consumer having negative perceptions (Seetharaman & Chintagunta, 1998) and reflects a non-conscious process. In this context, the consumer does not think of alternatives. The effect of inertia is to make re-buy respond to marketing variables. This happens because inertia leads the consumers to be more sensitive towards marketing variables, meaning price reductions or other promotional tools; suggested that the impact of inertia on retention would be determined by the competitive structure of the industry (Rust et al., 2003). In this study we define inertia, as an important factor that influences the customer in order to remain loyal in the same service provider (White & Yanamandram, 2004). As a result of this situation, mobile industry manipulates easier the customer's behaviour.

H4: The higher the level of inertia, the higher the probability of customer manipulation

Indifference

Zeelenberg and Pieters (2004) show that given a homogeneous supply and a heterogeneous demand, the satisfaction levels of the customer are reduced. In that way, customers could remain with a service provider for a long time. Furthermore, in the present research indifference can have a significant moderating effect, which linked with inertia can manipulate the customer's behaviour (Sharma et al., 2006).

H5: A customer's indifference switching to another company may increase the probability of retaining that customer.

Customer Satisfaction

Following (Cronin et al. 2000), we conceptualise customer satisfaction to be an evaluation of an emotion; reflecting the degree in which the customer believes the service provider evokes positive feelings (Lam et al., 2004). Numerous studies in the service sector have hypothesized and empirically validated the link between satisfaction and behaviours such as customer retention and word of mouth (Huang & Chiu, 2006). Indeed, this link is fundamental to the marketing concept, which indicates that satisfying customer needs and desires is the key to re-buy the service (Kim et al., 2009).

In the current study the customer's satisfaction constitutes the key factor in order to retain the customers.

H6: The higher the level of satisfaction, the more likely the retention of customer behaviour.

Trust

Following (Chatura & Jaideep, 2003) conceptualise trust based on interpretation of the construct of the commitment-trust theory of customer retention (Wong & Sohal, 2002). Trust could exist at the individual level or at the firm level (Rust et al., 2003). Furthermore, trust could also be thought of as trust in the service itself (Zeithmal et al., 1990). In our study, we look at a customer's trust in the service provider.

H7: The higher the level of trust, the more likely customer retention is.

Switching Barriers

According to (Yanamandram & White, 2004a), switching barriers are the factors which prevent a customer to change company. (Lam et al., 2004) was one of the first to have studied the barriers of change in relation to the customer behaviour. (Manoj and Sunil, 2011) define the costs of change by referring to time, money and the effort which the customer perceives in order to change firm. Since then, (Ramaseshan et al., 2006) among others have tested and confirmed the positive effect of switching barriers on customer retention. In the current study, we look switching barriers as the factitious constrains that a firm defines, in order to inert the customers' behaviour to change service provider (Athanasopoulou, 2009).

H8: The more a customer is becoming aware of switching barriers, the more likely it is to be retaining in a firm.

General Characteristics of the Mobile Sector

The Greek mobile sector is the fastest growing sector in the country, one of the most dynamic sectors of the economy. Currently there are four GSM mobile network operators, while three of them obtained a 3G license with the obligation to launch commercial UMTS (Universal Mobile Telecommunications System) network in year 2011 (Light et al., 2011). According to the announcements of Greek Mobile network operators in April 2011, there were 9.943.730 mobile subscribers. The distribution of mobile subscribers among the network operators as well as their segmentation based on the method of payment (prepay, post pay).

The distribution of mobile subscribers is performed mostly via specialized stores that the mobile firms mostly own, using their brand name. Nonetheless, other retailers are also involved, such as electrical stores. This day by day increasing distribution of mobile industry products from other retailers is justified, given the benefits offered by adding these sales to an existing range of products. Especially, since pre-paid packages come as a boxed solution, there is no necessity of a specialist's knowledge in order to sell it.

The mobile sector follows an advertising strategy in order to encourage existing mobile phone users to upgrade their telephone to newer ones. The use of the mobiles is also promoted not only for direct communication, but also as an information or multimedia tool for social interaction (Dagupta et al., 2008). On the other hand, advertisement focuses only on mobile handsets promotion and subscription upgrade by presenting the benefits of the enhanced mobile telephone and the new packages offered (Turkyilmaz & Ozkan, 2007). In response to a decline in new subscriptions demand, the falling prices and the intensifying competition, mobile network operators and retailers devote increasingly more resources to advertising as well as to other methods of promotion (Eagle & Kitchen, 2000). In the Greek market, advertisement strategies prefer television as medium of advertising. However, different marketing communication tools are used. Figure 1 presents direct advertising spending costs per medium in 2004 and 2011.

MAIN FOCUS OF THE CHAPTER

The present study investigates the extent to which relationship marketing strategy between mobile phone industries influence the consuming attitude of their customers. This leads to the testing of the hypothesis:

H1: The higher the level of relationship marketing strategy, the higher the level of customer retention.

Firstly, we defined the factors that influence and strengthen the customer retention of the firm. Based on the literature review, we develop a framework linking service quality, customer satisfaction, trust, inertia, indifference, switching barriers to customer retention. According to Jeng and Bailey (2012) customer retention is the future propensity of a customer to stay with a service provider. On the other

Figure 1. Direct advertising spending cost per medium
Source: Media services media vest processing

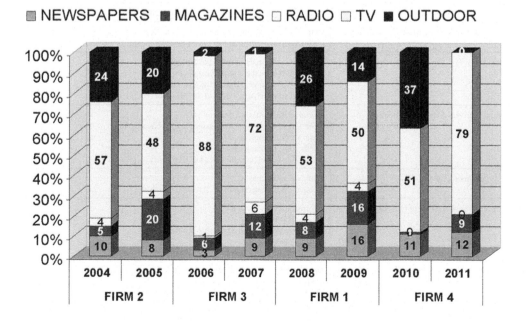

hand (Zeithaml et al., 1990) define the term "future behavioural intentions" in order to describe the construct with the above definition. In our work we follow (Cronin et al., 2000) who treat "behavioural intentions" and "customer retention" as synonymous constructs.

We examine the main effects of each of the independent variables and the simultaneous influence of the above variables on retention. The usage of each parameter related to the customer retention is also analysed. At the development and description of the factors that influence the consuming attitude of the customers the following criteria were taken in mind:

- Every factor examines the customers' attitude from a specific point of view;
- The factors express independently (as much as possible) the customers' attitude (the factors are mutually independent);
- The group of factors covers all the spectrum of the points of consideration that influence the customer retention.

Solutions and Recommendations

For the accomplishment of the research objectives, the questionnaire developed by Cronin, (2000), was used. Modifications were made to the instruments, taking into account the economic environment of Greece, including semantic changes, in order to suit the needs of this study. The questionnaire refers especially to the responders' experiences of the mobile industry. The questionnaire consisted on a variety of questions, concerning different areas of interest. The items of the questionnaire were in the form of statements based on the 5-point Likert – type scale, anchored on 1=totally agree, through 5=totally disagree. The applied questionnaire referred to issues, which are considered essential for the recording of the opinions of respondents. The topics included are (see Table 1).

Table 1. The factors influence customer retention

Factors	Thematic Area
Customer satisfaction as a driver of customer retention	General customer satisfaction from the company Right choosing of the company from the customer
Price Perception as a driver of customer retention	How fix cost charges, seem to the customer How sms charges seem to the customer How variable charges seem to the customer How logical the charges seem to the customer
Switching barriers as a driver of customer retention	Technical difficulties to change firm Difficulty in changing one's number while changing firms Costs a lot to change firm Needs effort to change firm Not able to start a procedure of changing easily
Trust as a driver of customer retention	Company is reliable Company is a pioneer to the progresses
Service quality perceptions as a driver of customer retention	Information for a better use Personnel is helpful Correction measures to a probable problem Personal data security Economic offer packages
Inertia and Indifference as a driver of customer retention	Don't get in the process of changing firm There is no difference between firms There is little difference in the service between firms

Sample Frame

The study was made with the method of private interviews in the area of Greece, referring to young people aged 18-24 years old of the total population of the country, who according to the elements of the national statistical service come to 550000 people. The sample used was the 0.2% of the total population, meaning 1100 young people, whom from we had a 73% response rate (804 people). After excluding some questionnaires because of missing values, in our final analysis we used data coming from 707 people, of whom 73% were women. The research took place from September to November 2010. The sample comes mainly from university areas (68.9% university students). There was a satisfactory representation both of people using post-pay subscription packages and people using pay-as-you-go packages, according to the market share of every mobile phone industry in Greece. It should also be stated that 50% of the total sample concerns people who are subscribers to a particular firm for more than two years, fact that in combination with their young age, shows that probably it isn't the responders who define the relationship with the mobile industries, but their parents. There is a similar behaviour of the sample as far as their preferences are concerned (same percentage agree or disagree to the questions).

The phase of the data processing includes a set of interactive procedures, in order to explore and mine the data and acquire knowledge concerning the behaviour of the customers. Two different approaches were applied.

Typical statistical analyses were used, such as descriptive frequency analysis and cross tabulation, in order to picture the customer behaviour concerning the main characteristics of the sample and the behaviour and preferences on the examined points of view. Also, chi-square test was used in order to determine differences and similarities among the different groups of customers, as well as to assess the attitudes of the customers related to their intention to change mobile phone firm. Figure 2 shown these simple and descriptive statistical techniques provide a medium that allows us to picture the general trends of the sample behaviour and discover or pose more complicated questions.

The second approach concerns discriminant analysis (Tabachmick & Fidel, (1989), an analytical technique from the field of the multivariate data analysis. Discriminant Analysis, which is based on Multivariate Analysis of Variance (MANOVA), provides a technique to construct a model (based on a set of known situations) that can discriminate the different behaviours expressed in a variable or question (called dependent variable) and explain this, taking into consideration a set of quantitative or categorical variables (called independent variables or predictors). The goal is to discover the dimension or dimensions along which the groups are different, and to construct functions able to support the classification

Figure 2. Data process and data mining

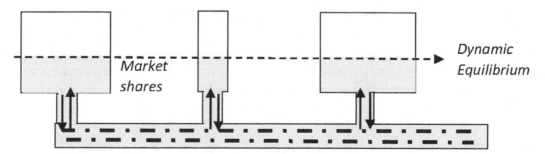

451

of the cases and consequently to predict group membership. The significance and utility of discriminant analysis are:

- To determine which are the independent variables or predictors, reflecting the discrimination of the different groups as well as to assess their importance;
- To construct classification functions, which provide a mean to predict group membership of new cases from its values on the predictors.

The simplest form of classification functions (a classification function is estimated for every group) is:

$$C_j = c_{j0} + c_{j1}X_1 + c_{j2}X_2 + \ldots + c_{jp}X_p$$

where $j=1,2,3,\ldots,k$ are the different groups related to the depended variable and $X_1, X_{2,\ldots,} X_p$ the raw scores of a case on the predictors and c_{ji}, $i=1,2, \ldots, p$ the classification coefficient. The classification coefficient is found from the mean of the p predictors and the pooled within-group variance-covariance matrix. In matrix form is represented as follow:

$$C_j = W^{-1} M_j$$

where W is the within-group covariance matrix and M_j is the matrix of the means of the p predictors for group j.

The constant for group j (c_{j0}) is calculated as follow:

$$c_{j0} = (-1/2)C_j M_j$$

A case is grouped according to its scores, coming from the classification functions. A new case is grouped in the group where the higher score was calculated or the score is close to the mean of the scores for this group of the known situations.

The adequacy of the assessed classification model can be examined through a set of indexes which is the same used in MANOVA. The most important used are the Wilks' Lamda and the approximate F ratio (Tabachmick & Fidel, 1989) while in practice the success of discriminant analysis is determined by the success rate of predictions of memberships of the known cases on the depended variable.

There are three main types of discriminant function analysis:

- The first is the Direct Discriminant Function Analysis where all predictors enter at once and has many similarities with the way ANOVA is used;
- The second is the Hierarchical Descriminant Analysis where the predictors enter to the analysis gradually in an order determined by the researchers;
- The third is the Stepwise Discriminant Function Analysis, also used in this research project, which includes techniques that allow the reducing of the number of predictors, selecting the ones that are significant for the examined case without reflecting population differences.

Descriptive Statistics

Descriptive statistics refer to seven areas of interest, analyzing each one of them. The following (Table 2) shows the frequencies of our variables.

The results given in Table 2 indicate that consumers, in a percentage of 66.8, show that they are satisfied of their company, showing in this way their trust towards their operator. Opinions of the responders concerning price perceptions seem to be similar, the ones who agree versus to the ones who disagree. They consider the charges of the SMS as well as the fixed charges to be high enough, though an important percentage (28.9%) seems to be indifferent to the pricing policy of the mobile industries. The barriers, which the consumer has to overcome while trying to change firm, consist mainly on technical difficulties and much less on the cost of this procedure (70.8%).

The perceptions of the responders related to the total of the services provided by the mobile phone industry seems to be of no importance for them. This means that the communicative policy of the industry hasn't succeeded in giving them attractive messages. The majority, however, acknowledges the facility with which they can turn to the industry's services when needed, though they don't feel that their company can always take correction measures in case of difficulties.

Nevertheless the 64% of the sample consider their firm to be reliable and pioneer of the sector. This combination of reliability and innovation affects their level of trust. Finally, a significant percentage shows that there is no difference between firms, having as a result a lower possibility for a customer to change firm. The fact that the answers of the sample are equally dispersed is also observed in the question of whether they would change firm in the next six months. This attitude indicates a dynamic equilibrium that has been achieved between the two greatest industries in Greece, in reference to the gaining or losing customers.

Discriminant Analysis

From the analysis of all the dependent variables concerning the behaviour of the consumers and their retention to a specific mobile phone industry, we were finally driven to a model of six significant parameters, which play a very important role and explain the desire and thus the final decision of the consumer, whether to remain at the same company or to change (Table 3), (Table 4), (Table 5). A 78,5% of original grouped cases are correctly classified.

Using the assessed discriminant model with the six predictors (Table 3) 78.5% of the cases were correctly classified according to their intention to change or not change mobile provider and the value of Wilks' Lamda is 0,808. These indexes present that the discriminant function can be accepted and use the assessed results for further analysis. The results shown indicate a unified relationship marketing strategy policy on behalf of mobile phone industries, which has as a target to manipulate the behaviour of consumers. The former leads to the inactivation of the consumers, letting them encaged to a specific initial selection. In order to change firms, the consumer has to recognize the benefits from the new firm both in the pricing policy and the innovation field. Consumer's perception of prices and innovation appear to be similar. This is a result of the intensity of the competition that exists between the industries of the sector. The intense competition concerns the similar offer packages that are promoted to the consumers through advertisement in the media. The policy of these mobile phone industries leads to inertia and lack of motive for the consumers, so as not to seek alternative solutions by changing service provider. As shown (Figure 3) the following model the present case of manipulation of the market.

Table 2. Descriptive statistics

Variables	Agree %	Neither Agree nor Disagree %	Disagree %
Customer Satisfaction			
- General customer satisfaction from the company	66.8	26.7	6.6
- Company comes up to customer's expectations	53.6	37.4	9.1
- Right choice of company from the customer	58.1	33.0	9.0
Price Perception			
- How fixed charges seem to the customer	21.1	52.1	26.8
- How SMS charges seem to the customer	27.8	36.3	35.8
- How charges seem to the customer	28.9	45.6	25.5
- How logical the charges seem to the customer	21.1	45.5	33.4
Switching barriers			
- Technical difficulties to change firm	70.8	12.2	16.9
- Difficulty in changing one's number while changing firms	28.3	32.8	38.8
- Costs a lot to change firm	31.7	28.5	39.8
- Needs effort to change firm	35.2	28.3	36.5
- Not able to start a procedure of changing easily	34.5	27.7	35.9
Service Quality Perception			
- Information for better use	61.7	25.5	12.7
- The personnel is helpful	64.5	28.3	7.2
- Better correspondence in the future	51.8	41.1	7.2
- Trust for the future existence of the firm	73.0	21.2	5.1
- Capable personnel	56.3	36.9	6.7
- Polite personnel	75.2	18.5	6.2
- Correction measures to a probable problem	43.5	36.4	20.1
- Easy access	57.7	14.0	18.3
- Understanding of needs	43.6	44.5	11.9
- Personal data security	52.0	36.1	11.8
- Coming up to one's expectations	51.6	34.3	14.1
- Economic offer packages	56.8	28.7	22.5
Trust			
- The firm is reliable	64.5	30.6	10.4
- The firm is a pioneer to the progresses	16.6	41.8	42.6
Indifference			
- There is no difference between firms	62.1	23.9	14.0
- There is little difference in the service between firms	45.7	23.2	31.1
Inertia			
- The don't in the procedure of changing firm	33	26.2	40.6

Table 3. Standardized canonical discriminant function coefficients

Factors		Function
Customer Satisfaction	Q15 Satisfaction from the selection of the given firm	.480
Customer Satisfaction	Q13 General satisfaction from the firm	.293
Prices Perceptions	Q22 The charges are reasonable (price perception)	.244
Prices Perceptions	Q20 SMS charges	.273
Inertia	Q25 Doesn't get in the procedure of changing (inertia)	.336
Indifference	Q23 There is no difference between them (indifference)	.244

Table 4. Classification results

		Predicted Group Membership		Total
	Intention	No Change	Change	
Count	No change	421	106	527
	Change	25	58	83
%	No change	79.9%	20.1%	100.0
	Change	30.1%	69.9%	100.0

Table 5. Function results

Test of Function(s)	Wilks' Lambda	Chi-Square	df	Sig.	
1	.808	129.300	6	.000	

Figure 3. Market shares and the communicating vessels phenomenon

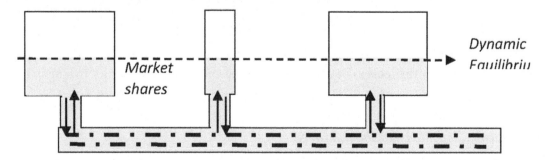

The market behaviour presents the phenomenon of the communicating vessels, where a dynamic equilibrium exists. The disappointed customers of a mobile provider (a small proportion of the market share) move to another while the same happens to the second mobile provider. The total balance of the market shares for every enterprise remains the same with minor positive or negative variation. This is more intense in this case where the majority of the market shares are split in only two mobile providers.

This conclusion comes as a result of the analysis of the customer with the intention to change enterprise for every operator. The findings (Table 6) emphasize that there were similar behaviours for customers' intentions for the two leader firms.

Solutions and Recommendations

Examining the first results of globalisation we notice the creation of oligopolies in the market conditions of various economic sectors. The E.U. and the USA government have developed mechanisms in order to watch the newly developed market forces and identify cases of market manipulation with a view to prevent such phenomena (i.e. Microsoft's case in the USA and Siemens in Europe). The existing mechanisms though are watching the market through its results rather than having a pro-active approach. This means that consumers have already suffered the consequences of political intervention or monopolistic and oligopolistic market forces that work together in the form of cartels in an effort to forward their policies. In this article we examine the development of political manipulation of consumer behaviour through marketing strategies applied by companies, aiming to achieve public inactivity that will limit reaction.

The intense competition of the mobile industry with similar tools can lead to a state of consumers' inertia. As a result of this, a state of communicating vessels is created between the specific economic units, meaning that the amount of customers, who change firm driven to the competitive one, equals the amount of customers, who come from the second firm to the first one.

The manipulation of the market can also be seen on the market shares that the great companies possess, which consist of the 82% of the total market, divided almost equally into the two greater companies. Firms have to operate in a competitive market following rules in favour of the consumers; they should differentiate their strategy with drastic interventions. This creates the need to further utilize all marketing tools in an appropriate mix in order to promote new technologies and services that increase revenue per customer, as well as create the need for customers to upgrade their mobile phones and subscriptions (Hackley & Kitchen, 1998). The drive for organizational integration contributes to greater influence over consumer perceptions.

Our research has shown that we can develop a model in order to present the situation of high competition among two firms. Through our findings elicited from the discriminant analysis, we saw that business firms using similar marketing tools, advertisement, package offers, pricing policy, try to manipulate the consumer's behaviour.

The main characteristic of the new economy is the great alterations in consumer purchase decisions; as a result it is increasingly difficult to develop long-term business programmes for two main reasons:

Table 6. Customers' intentions for the two firms

Intention	FIRM 1		FIRM 2	
	Count	Percentage	Count	Percentage
No Change	233	72,1%	212	65,4%
Doubt	59	18,3%	78	24,1%
Change	31	9,6%	34	10,5%
Total	323	100,0%	324	100,0%

1. These days, consumer awareness levels are significantly higher than in the past; and
2. There are a big number of new and departing companies in the industry as life cycles are continuously reducing due to the increased scientific innovations in all fields.

In order to face the above phenomenon, companies must develop relationship marketing strategies that will crystallise consumer loyalty through bettering their relationships' conditions with the public i.e. trust, switching cost, barriers etc. This way, companies can create the basis upon which they can build their development strategies.

REFERENCES

Anwar, S. T. (2003). CASES Vodafone and the wireless industry: A case in market expansion and global strategy. *Journal of Business and Industrial Marketing*, *18*(3), 270–288. doi:10.1108/08858620310471331

Athanasopoulou, P. (2009). Relationship quality: A critical literature review and research agenda. *European Journal of Marketing*, *43*(5/6), 583–610. doi:10.1108/03090560910946945

Bendall-Lyon, D., & Powers, T. L. (2003). The influence of mass communication and time on satisfaction and loyalty. *Journal of Services Marketing*, *17*(6), 589–608. doi:10.1108/08876040310495627

Bennett, R., & Barkensjo, A. (2005). Relationship quality, relationship marketing, and client perceptions of the levels of service quality of charitable organisations. *International Journal of Service Industry Management*, *16*(1), 81–106. doi:10.1108/09564230510587168

Chatura, R., & Jaideep, P. (2003). The influence of satisfaction, trust and switching barriers on customer retention in a continuous purchasing setting. *International Journal of Service Industry Management*, *14*(Iss: 4), 374–395. doi:10.1108/09564230310489231

Cronin, J. J. Jr, Brady, M. K., & Hult, G. T. M. (2000). Assessing the effects of quality, value, and customer satisfaction on consumer behavioural intentions in service environments. *Journal of Retailing*, *76*(2), 193–218. doi:10.1016/S0022-4359(00)00028-2

Dasgupta, K., Singh, R., Viswanathan, B., Chakraborty, D., Mukherjea, S., & Nanavati, A. A. (2008). Social ties and their relevance to churn in mobile telecom networks. *Proceedings of the 11th International Conference on Extending Database Technology: Advances in Database Technology*. doi:10.1145/1353343.1353424

Eagle, L., & Kitchen, P. J. (2000). IMC, brand communications, and corporate cultures. *European Journal of Marketing*, *34*(5/6), 667–686. doi:10.1108/03090560010321983

Everrit, B. S., & Dunn, G. (2001). *Multivariate data analysis*. London: Arnold Publishers. doi:10.1002/9781118887486

Fraunholz, B., & Unnithan, C. (2004). Critical success factors in mobile communications: A comparative roadmap for Germany and India. *International Journal of Mobile Communications*, *2*(1), 87–101. doi:10.1504/IJMC.2004.004489

Hennig-Thurau, T., & Klee, A. (1997). The impact of customer satisfaction and relationship quality on customer retention: A critical reassessment and model development. *Psychology and Marketing, 14*(8), 737–764. doi:10.1002/(SICI)1520-6793(199712)14:8<737::AID-MAR2>3.0.CO;2-F

Huang, H. H., & Chiu, C. K. (2006). Exploring customer satisfaction, trust and destination loyalty in tourism. *Journal of American Academy of Business, 10*(1), 156–159.

Jeng, J., & Bailey, T. (2012). Assessing customer retention strategies in mobile telecommunications: Hybrid MCDM approach. *Management Decision, 50*(9), 1570–1595. doi:10.1108/00251741211266697

Kim, K. Y., Yun, D. K., & Kim, D. Y. (2009). Expectations measurements in mobile data service: A case study. *International Journal of Mobile Communications, 7*(1), 91–116. doi:10.1504/IJMC.2009.021674

Kyriazopoulos, P. (2000). The modern firm at the beginning of the 21st Century (A. S. Ekdotiki, Ed.). Academic Press.

Kyriazopoulos, P. (2001). *Apply Marketing*. Athens Sychroni Ekdotiki.

Lam, S. Y., Shankar, V., Erramilli, M. K., & Murthy, B. (2004). Customer value, satisfaction, loyalty, and switching costs: An illustration from a business-to-business service context. *Journal of the Academy of Marketing Science, 32*(3), 293–311. doi:10.1177/0092070304263330

Light, C., Light, A., & Teulade, V. (2010). *A look at the future of mobile data*. Retrieved from www.pwc.com/en_GX/gx/communications/assets/Mobile_Content_final.pdf

Manoj, E., & Sunil, S. (2011). Role of switching costs in the service quality, perceived value, customer satisfaction and customer retention linkage. *Asia Pacific Journal of Marketing and Logistics, 23*(3), 327–345. doi:10.1108/13555851111143240

Papassapa, R., & Miller, K. E. (2007). Relationship quality as a predictor of B2B customer loyalty. *Journal of Business Research, 60*(1), 21–31. doi:10.1016/j.jbusres.2005.11.006

Ramaseshan, B., Yip, L. S., & Pae, J. H. (2006). Power, satisfaction and relationship commitment in Chinese store-tenant relationship and their impact on performance. *Journal of Retailing, 82*(1), 63–70. doi:10.1016/j.jretai.2005.11.004

Reinartz, W., & Kumar, V. (2000). The Impact of Customer Relationship Characteristics on Profitable Lifetime Duration. *Journal of Marketing, 67*.

Rust, R., Katherine, T., Lemon, N., & Zeithaml, A. (2003). *Return on Marketing: Using Customer Equity to Focus Marketing Strategy. Journal of Marketing*.

Seetharaman, P. B., & Chintagunta, P. (1998). A model of inertia and variety-seeking with marketing variables. *International Journal of Research in Marketing, 15*(1), 1–17. doi:10.1016/S0167-8116(97)00015-3

Sharma, N., Young, L., & Wilkinson, I. (2006). *The commitment mix: multi-aspect commitment in international trading relationships in India*. Unpublished Document.

Tabachmick & Fidell. (1989). *Using multivariate statistics*. New York: Harper Collins Publishers Inc.

Türkyilmaz, A., & Özkan, C. (2007). Development of a customer satisfaction index model: An application to the Turkish mobile phone sector. *Industrial Management & Data Systems*, *107*(5), 672–687. doi:10.1108/02635570710750426

White, L., & Yanamandram, V. (2004). Why customers stay: Reasons and consequences of inertia in financial services. *Managing Service Quality*, *14*(2/3), 183–194. doi:10.1108/09604520410528608

White, L., & Yanamandram, V. (2007). A model of customer retention of dissatisfied business services customers. *Managing Service Quality*, *17*(3), 298–316. doi:10.1108/09604520710744317

Wolfl, A. (2005). *The service economy in OECD countries*. STI working paper 2005/3. Statistical Analysis of Science, Technology and Industry, Paris Cedex.

Yanamandram, V. K., & White, L. (2006). Switching barriers in business-to-business services: A qualitative study. *International Journal of Service Industry Management*, *17*(2), 158–192. doi:10.1108/09564230610656980

Zeelenberg, M., & Pieters, R. (2004). Beyond valence in customer dissatisfaction: A review and new findings on behavioural responses to regret and disappointment in failed services. *Journal of Business Research*, *57*(4), 445–455. doi:10.1016/S0148-2963(02)00278-3

Zeithaml, V. A., Parasuraman, A., & Berry, L. L. (1990). *Delivering Quality Service: Balancing Customer Perceptions and Expectations*. New York, NY: The Free Press.

KEY TERMS AND DEFINITIONS

Customer Retention: The construct of customer retention focuses on repeat patronage, and it is different from, while closely related to, purchasing behavior and brand loyalty, in that in retention the marketer is seen as having the more active role in the customer-firm relationship.

Customer Satisfaction: Reflecting the degree in which the customer believes the service provider evokes positive feelings.

Indifference: Given a homogeneous supply and a heterogeneous demand, the satisfaction levels of the customer are reduced.

Inertia: Inertia is the re-buy of the same service provider passively without much thought.

Relationship Marketing: Emphasizes on a long-term interactive relationship between the provider and the customer, leading to long-term profitability.

Service Quality: Service quality of the product greatly affect consumer behavior.

Switching Barriers: Switching barriers are the factors which prevent a customer to change company.

Trust: Conceptualise trust based on interpretation of the construct of the commitment-trust theory of customer retention.

This research was previously published in Strategic Information Systems and Technologies in Modern Organizations edited by Caroline Howard and Kathleen Hargiss, pages 258-273, copyright year 2017 by Information Science Reference (an imprint of IGI Global).

Chapter 24

Brand Awareness Quotient:
A Metric for Effectiveness of Employer Branding Initiatives

Komal Ratra
Symbiosis Centre for Management and Human Resource Development, India

Netra Neelam
Symbiosis International University, India

ABSTRACT

There is a need to appropriately measure the effectiveness of Employer branding initiatives taken by an organization. There are a lot of questions to be addressed while measuring the effectiveness of the past or existing initiatives and formulating a new Employer branding strategy such as: Do the objectives of the Employer branding completely meet the initiative? What is the reach of the initiatives? Whether to continue with the same initiative or not in future? Hence while designing a new improved Employer branding strategy, there needs to be an appropriate initiative measurement methodology which can address the above questions quantitatively. This paper is an attempt to create A matrix "Brand Awareness Quotient" which will help in measuring the efficacy and support decision making for formulating the new strategy the same. This quantitative way of scoring and analyzing each and every initiative provides a 360-degree overview of the complete Employer branding strategy of the organization.

INTRODUCTION

In today's fluid employment environment, companies feel intense pressure to better define and promote their employment attributes, both internally to current employees and externally to prospective employees. This is known as "employment branding." The goal of employment branding is to create an effective "employment brand," a package of employment attributes that are readily identified with the company, and serves to attract and retain a desirable workforce. This package of attributes consists of "functional, economic and psychological benefits of working for a company." It is essentially the process of placing an image of being a great place to work in the minds of a targeted candidate pool.

DOI: 10.4018/978-1-5225-5187-4.ch024

A strong employer brand is related to:

- Pride of individuals expected from being organizational members
- Quality and Quantity of the Applicant pool.
- Stable and positive workforce attitudes and organizational performance as compared to broader market.
- Reduction in new hire premiums

According to a LinkedIn survey of more than 4,700 talent acquisition professionals, companies with a strong employer brand save up to 50% per hire[1]. That's more money you can save or put into strategic use for your business. Employer branding is how an organization markets what it has to offer to both potential and existing employees. A strong employer brand should connect an organization's values, people strategy and HR policies and be intrinsically linked to a company brand.

Every organization has internal and external Stakeholders. Employees, Managers, Executives, Board members, Union members and others who reside inside the company and benefit directly from their contribution to the growth of the company are the internal stakeholders. They commit to serve the organization. The concept of internal marketing specifies that employees of an organization are its first market. The most important of them are the Employees as they play a major role in the growth and sustainability of the organization. Organization culture reflects the brand promise made to its recruits and hence it becomes important to carry out effective internal marketing. Hence, internal branding becomes the major goal of internal marketing and aims to develop workforce committed to the set of values and organizational goals established by the firm. The bond and synergy between the brand value and the business model brings the feel good factor for the employee which in turn makes them to stay longer and be more engaged, leading to higher productivity. 'Employer branding' minimizes the loss of talented employees and enhances the level of staff engagement. It improves employee relations and helps in increasing the productivity thus yielding higher profitability to the organization. A good employer brand ensures that the brand is in the top choice list or is a 'brand of choice'. Employees who join the company and stay with it are better able to connect themselves with the brand and find it easier to align themselves as per the organization's visions and values. They commit to serve the company with high performance. In short, it helps in maintaining the organization's long term competitiveness and its core competencies.

Based on the information source that are not controlled by the employer, Job seekers or Prospective employees develop a strong employer brand association based. Hence a strong employer brand has the potential to attract and retain good and talented employees which in turn represents quality to its customers and helps in gaining global recognition in a sustainable manner. Hence every organization carries out some Employer branding initiatives to communicate the power of the brand amongst its employees who are its first market. On yearly basis, as a part of Human Resource Strategy, Employer Branding Strategy is formulated in lines to the Business goals and a separate budget is allocated to carry out these activities within the organization. The effective implementation of these initiatives determines the success of the Employer Branding Strategy. The challenge for most of the organizations here is to measure the effectiveness of these initiatives which is mostly subjective or opinion based. Some organizations calculate Return on Investment (ROI) for these initiatives based on the investment done and the benefits received by improving retention rates, reducing attrition and improving quality of new hire. But Return on Investment methodology has its own limitations as it does not takes into account the viewpoints of employees, manager or production workers who are the first market. These are the people who can actually tell that how connected they feel with the brand and how the Employer branding initiatives have helped in increasing the awareness about the brand they are working for. The problem arises when the feedback taken is mostly on the subjective side. An organization may use any one or a combination of the available data collection instruments like Questionnaire, Focus group interviews, Online surveys, One to One interviews or Feedback forms etc., but the primary objective is to get the data in a single format which can tell the efficacy of an initiative quantitatively considering the inputs of the different stakeholder.

This paper tries to comprehend the inputs from all these stakeholders (Employees, Managers and Production workers) and analyze their viewpoints through one single matrix named as "Brand Awareness Quotient" to compute a score which tells the efficacy of the branding initiative.

LITERATURE REVIEW

Managers argue that if an organization wants to establish a successful brand then it is essential to realize the internal implications and develop internal brand programs (Kotler & Pfoertsch, 2006). Hence the 'Holistic marketing' concept suggests that it is no longer to merely rely on external marketing efforts rather internal branding is also one of the essential pillars in achieving the organization goals (Kotler & Pfoertsch, 2006). Hence the process of internal branding should follow the same principles and procedures as an external branding exercise and it is very important to have sync between External and Internal marketing to avoid confusion among various stakeholders (A. Kumar, 2009). According to Ferrell and Hartline (2014) "Internal marketing refers to the use of marketing like approach to motivate, coordinate, and integrate employees towards the implementation of firm's marketing strategy" (p. 268). The term is defined as "the package of functional, economic and psychological benefits provided by employment, and identified with the employing company." (Ambler & Barrows, 1996, p. 187). Internal marketers need to understand that positioning is not what you to do to products; it is what you do to the minds of internal employees (Ahmed & Rafiq, 2002). In other words, employees are the first market or an internal market and employees being the first customers should always be attended first (Groonroos, 2007). This ensures that employees at all levels experience the business that supports customer consciousness. Hence, internal marketing aims in establishing a culture, developing human resource marketing approach, rewards and recognition systems and accurate flow of information to employees (Kotler, 2008). A strong employer brand can have a positive impact on the relations and pride that employees expect from the organization. Sparrow and Cooper (2003) states Employee Value Proposition as "a human resource management policy influenced very much by marketing thinking that cuts across the whole of the employment experience and applies to all individuals in the organization. It is the application of a customer value proposition – why should you buy my product or service –to the individual – why should a highly talented person work in my organization? It differs from one organization to another, has to be as distinctive as a fingerprint, and is tailored to the specific type of people the organization is trying to attract and retain" (p. 160). It's a direct application of internal branding concept to human resources by perceiving current and potential employees as customers and job as products of employer brand. (Berthon et al., 2005). Backhaus and Tikoo (2004) define employer branding as "the process of building an identifiable and unique employer identity" and the employer brand as "a concept of the firm that differentiates it from its competitors" (p. 502). This process begins with conducting marketing research to understand the need and wants of employees. The same concept of segmenting, targeting and positioning are used to set and match the requirements of different jobs (Verma, 2012). Accordingly, there is a need of internal branding initiatives, the depth of which should be in accordance with employee's relevance to communication of the brand promise and the breadth is represented by all the internal stakeholders as customers who are the target audience (Ravens, 2012). Giehl and LePla (2012) recommends that building a website, holding brand events, or employee marketing campaigns should not be seen as the only way to employer or internal branding rather it can be unrelated to the actual goal of internal branding rather branding is an evolving process which can be effectively managed through cross functional brand teams.

Different experts have different arguments to measure the efficacy of the employer branding initiatives. Despite its popularity, organizations are still unclear how to measure and evaluate the added value of employer branding initiatives (Dell et al., 2001). The first step is to measure the current stature of the employer branding initiatives which involves a market analysis of their current actual position as an employer and identification of positives and negatives as an employment organization. (Lukasczyk et al., 2014). Love and Singh (2011) have stated eight factors as inspired leadership, strategic plan, communication, performance management, training and development, employee benefits, ergonomics of work place and focus on corporate citizenship which contribute to make an organization as an 'employer of choice'. Nazemetz and Ruch (2013) suggests pulling power, recruitment cost, retention, employee engagement and employee satisfaction as some of the measures to evaluate the success of employer branding initiatives. The economist Bryan Finn (2007) suggests through his econometrics models that employer branding efforts can be well tracked from the advertising expenditure to stock market valuation. McLeod and Waldman (2011) presented a 20 questions self-assessment gauge to measure the effectiveness of employer branding initiatives. Rosethorn (2009) recommends that it depends on the organization which method they want to choose. It depends on a lot of factors and varies from organization to organization to decide on the standard of measures (Finney, 2008). Sartain and Deb (2006) presents a skeptical picture arguing that there is no clear best instrument method and organization use both qualitative and quantitative techniques like Hiring hit rate, retention rate, awareness of brand etc. Surveys reveal that most of the quantitative indicators used to measure the efficacy of employer branding initiatives are narrow, abstract and have a limited view (Yapp, 2009).Most of the companies measure the efficacy through conventional metrics such as quality of time, number of applicants or time of hiring etc. (Minchington, 2011). It's difficult to have a strong counter argument against these methods as they do measure the partial efficacy of the initiatives but lack in carrying out a holistic evaluation of the employer brand (Dell et al., 2001). Schumann (2006) opined that to accurately measure the impact of employer branding, an organization need to implement a 360 degree monitoring effort which can be similar to a 'full circle feedback' for an employer.

There are monetary metrics available to measure the Return on Investment (ROI), still there is a need of a measurement tool to assess the effectiveness of employer branding initiatives. Hence with respect to all the theoretical conceptualization, a measure of employer brand should cover all the relevant aspects associated and result into a holistic key figure which can summarize the employer brand as a whole.

OBJECTIVES OF THE STUDY

1. To develop a model of Brand Awareness Quotient for measuring the efficacy of employer brand development initiatives
2. To define a methodology to compute an overall key figure or score that can represent the Employer brand quotient for the organization as a whole.
3. To understand- Qualitative and Quantitative factors and capture the holistic view of the impact of current employer branding stature which can lead to the ideal set of recommendations in the particular HR Intervention.

METHODOLOGY

Data Collection was done using a 360 Degree Survey Model which included internal and external stakeholders. Details of the model are as follows:

Stakeholders

Different stakeholders were identified and suitable instruments were used for data collection. Different factors were identified though literature review and exploratory study. A 360 Degree Survey Model (Figure 1) had been used to carry out the data collection activity and analysis. The model includes both Internal and External stakeholders to understand the ground facts about the Employer Branding Initiatives. But as far as the applicability of Brand awareness Quotient is concerned, the study has been kept limited to Internal Employees as they are the first market.

Figure 1. 360 Degree Survey Model

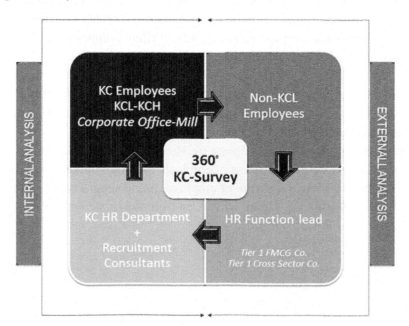

In Internal Analysis, the target audience were Employees of Corporate Office-Mill who were approached through Online Survey channel and Focus group interviews. Other segment of internal analysis were Employees of HR Department and Recruitment Consultants who were approached through Online Survey and survey through Social Media Channel (Facebook).

The instrument used for the above different stakeholders:

- Employees from Corporate Office-Mill
  ◦ Online Survey
  ◦ Focus Group Interviews
- HR Department + Recruitment Consultants
  ◦ Online Survey
  ◦ Survey through Social Media Channel-Facebook

Brand Awareness Matrix

New metric to measure "Internal Employer Branding" has been developed in this study.

Definition

Brand Awareness Matrix (Figures 2 and 3) defines the strength of awareness (strong or weak brand awareness) amongst the employees. It is designed to analyze the existing status of Internal Employer Branding and identify out the areas where Intensive Branding needs to be done.

Quotient

The magazine 'People in Business - Pioneer and Thought leader in Employer Brand Management' had identified the following two areas which employees of an organization should be aware of viz. 'Know the Business of the Company' and 'Know what's there for you in the company'. These areas have been further broken down into four sub areas in this study. This has helped in understanding the broader perspective of Employer Branding.

Figure 2. Conceptual Brand Awareness Matrix

These 2 major areas ("Know the Business of the Company" and "Know What's there for you in the company") have been then analyzed w.r.t 'Current System for Employees' and then 4 subareas have been identified – A,B and C,D (two subareas under each major area).

- Each of these sub areas are further categorized into 4 parameters (A.1 A.2 A.3 A.4 – B.1 B.2 B.3 B.4 – C.1 C.2 C.3 C.4- D.1 D.2 D.3 D.4) to carry out an in-depth analysis and understand the internal employer branding status.
- Each parameter (A.1 A.2 A.3 A.4 – B.1 B.2 B.3 B.4 – C.1 C.2 C.3 C.4- D.1 D.2 D.3 D.4) has a response as either YES (1 point) or NO 2(0 point). This cumulatively gives a score out of 4 to each subarea A-B-C-D.
- A B C D cumulatively gives a "BRAND AWARENESS SCORE" out of 16 which is scaled down to 4 to get the overall "BRAND AWARENESS QUOTIENT."

SAMPLING AND DATA COLLECTION

The study was conducted in Pune region. The subjects of the study were selected by using convenience sampling. 120 questionnaires were administered to the employees of the company, out of which 90 complete responses were returned. The responses were collected through a structured data collection process which was different for different stakeholders as mentioned above. The effective sample size of the employees turned out to be 90.

Figure 3. Brand Awareness Matrix

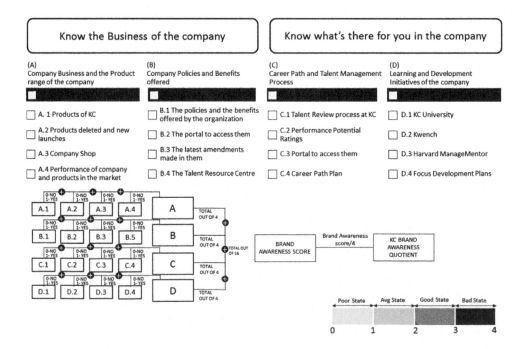

RESULTS

Demographic Profile

Diversity has been maintained across the pool of 90 respondents. 20% respondents were having an experience of more than 6 years, 10% were in the bracket of 4 to 6 years of experience, 35% belonged to 1 to 3 years of experience and rest 25% were having experience in the of less than 12 months. 60% of the employees were male and 40% were females. 26% of the employees were from Finance department, 26% from Marketing, 22% from Supply chain and the rest 22% from Human Resource department.

Company Business and the Product Range of the Company (A)

Under the section "Know about the company", the initiatives taken by the company to increase awareness about the "*Company Business and the Product range*" were evaluated. The responses (out of 90) were recorded in terms of "Yes" or "No", awarding 1 score for a "Yes" answer and 0 for a "No" answer. "Yes" means the respondent was aware about the initiative/product and "No" means, the respondent was not aware. Below is the Table 1 which sums up the responses and Table 2 shows an overall score was calculated for A part (Company Business and the Product range of the company).

Company Policies and Benefits Offered (B)

Under the section "Know about the company", the initiatives taken by the company to increase awareness about the "*Company Policies and Benefits offered*" were evaluated. The responses (out of 90) were recorded in terms of "Yes" or "No", awarding 1 score for a "Yes" answer and 0 for a "No" answer.

Table 1. Survey Responses of Stakeholders on "Company Business and Product Range"

SA	Initiative	No. of Respondents	Response (Yes)	Response (No)	Awareness Quotient (%)
A.1	Products of Company	90	65	25	72.50%
A.2	Products deleted and new launches	90	56	34	62.50%
A.3	Company Shop	90	38	52	42.50%
A.4	Performance of company and products in the market	90	50	40	55.00%
A	*Company Business and the Product range of the company (A)*	90	52	38	58.00%

Table 2. Brand Awareness Score of the organization for "Company Business and Product Range"

Brand Awareness Quotient for	Total Respondents	Total Responses (Yes) A.1+A.2+A.3+A.4	Brand Awareness score (out of 4) = Total Responses (Yes)/ Total Respondents
"Company Business and the Product range of the company"	90	209	2.322

"Yes" means the respondent was aware about the initiative/product and "No" means, the respondent was not aware. Below is the Table 3 which sums up the responses and Table 4 shows an overall score was calculated for A part (Company Policies and Benefits offered).

Career Path and Talent Management Process (C)

Under the section "Know what's there for you in the company", the initiatives taken by the company to increase awareness about the *"Career Path and Talent Management Process"* were evaluated. The responses (out of 90) were recorded in terms of "Yes" or "No", awarding 1 score for a "Yes" answer and 0 for a "No" answer. "Yes" means the respondent was aware about the initiative/product and "No" means, the respondent was not aware. Below is the Table 5 which sums up the responses and Table 6 shows an overall score was calculated for A part (Career Path and Talent Management Process).

Learning and Development Initiatives of the Company (D)

Under the section "Know what's there for you in the company", the initiatives taken by the company to increase awareness about the *"Learning and Development Initiatives of the company"* were evaluated. The responses (out of 90) were recorded in terms of "Yes" or "No", awarding 1 score for a "Yes" answer and 0 for a "No" answer. "Yes" means the respondent was aware about the initiative/product and "No" means, the respondent was not aware. Table 7 sums up the responses and Table 8 gives an overall score which was calculated for A part (Learning and Development Initiatives of the company).

Table 3. Survey Responses of Stakeholders on "Company Policies and Benefits offered"

SA	Initiative	No. of Respondents	Response (Yes)	Response (No)	Awareness Quotient (%)
B.1	The policies and the benefits offered by the organization	90	63	27	70.00%
B.2	The portal to access them	90	23	67	25.00%
B.3	The latest amendments made in them	90	34	56	37.50%
B.4	The Talent Resource Centre	90	36	54	40.00%
B	*Company Policies and Benefits offered*	90	39	51	43.33%

Table 4. Brand Awareness Score of the organization for "Company Policies and Benefits offered"

Brand Awareness Quotient for *"Company Policies and Benefits offered"*	Total Respondents	Total Responses (Yes) B.1+B.2+B.3+B.4	Brand Awareness score (out of 4) = Total Responses (Yes)/ Total Respondents
	90	156	1.733

Table 5. Survey Responses of Stakeholders on "Career Path and Talent Management Process"

SA	Initiative	No. of Respondents	Response (Yes)	Response (No)	Awareness Quotient (%)
C.1	Talent Review process	90	61	29	67.50%
C.2	Performance Potential Ratings	90	61	29	67.50%
C.3	Portal to access them	90	36	54	40.00%
C.4	Career Path Plan	90	47	43	52.50%
C	*Career Path and Talent Management Process*	90	51	39	56.94%

Table 6. Brand Awareness Score of the organization for "Career Path and Talent Management Process"

Brand Awareness Quotient for "Career Path and Talent Management Process"	Total Respondents	Total Responses (Yes) C.1+C.2+C.3+C.4	Brand Awareness score (out of 4) = Total Responses (Yes)/ Total Respondents
	90	205	2.277

Table 7. Survey Responses of Stakeholders on "Learning and Development Initiatives of the company"

SA	Initiative	No. of Respondents	Response (Yes)	Response (No)	Awareness Quotient (%)
D.1	Company University	90	34	56	37.50%
D.2	Kwench	90	56	34	62.50%
D.3	Harvard ManageMentor	90	23	67	25.00%
D.4	Focus Development Plans	90	38	52	42.50%
D	*Learning and Development Initiatives of the company*	90	52	38	41.94%

Table 8. Brand Awareness Score of the organization for "Learning and Development Initiatives of the company"

Brand Awareness Quotient for "Learning and Development Initiatives of the company"	Total Respondents	Total Responses (Yes) C.1+C.2+C.3+C.4	Brand Awareness score (out of 4) = Total Responses (Yes)/ Total Respondents
	90	151	1.677

Brand Awareness Quotient Score

Based on the Brand Awareness Scores of above individual sub areas (A, B, C, D), the overall Brand Awareness score of the organization is computed. Table 9 gives the current stature of the Employer Branding initiatives in terms of a consolidated score and represents the effectiveness of the Employer Branding strategy of the organization.

Table 9. Overall Brand Awareness Score of the organization

Overall Score	A	B	C	D	Average of A, B, C, D
Brand Awareness Score of the company as a whole	2.322	1.733	2.277	1.677	**2.002**

DISCUSSION

As per the score computations above, Table 9 shows an Overall Brand awareness score of the organization which is 2.002 out of 4 and represents that only 50% of the employees are aware about the branding initiatives taken by company. In absolute numbers, it can be stated that out of 90 employees only 45 are aware about the branding initiatives but at the same time it's not necessary that they know about all the initiatives. It may be the case that some of them know about only one initiative, others are aware about two or three initiatives and a few of them know about all of the initiatives being taken by the organization. An in-depth analysis of individual areas is required to know the exact bifurcation of who knows how much and to identify the focus areas of improvement.

In the case mentioned above, there are two major areas: "Know the business of the company" and "Know what's there for you in the company". Under first area, there are two sub areas viz. "Company Business and the Product Range of the Company (A)" and "Company Policies and Benefits Offered (B)". As per the Table 2. Brand Awareness Score of the organization for "Company Business and Product Range (A)" and Table 4. Brand Awareness Score of the organization for "Company Policies and Benefits offered (B)", the Brand Awareness scores for sub areas "A" and "B" are 2.322 and from 1.733 respectively. This means that for sub area "A", 58% (2.322 out of 4) employees are aware about the Initiatives and for sub area "B", only 43% (1.722 out of 4) employees are aware about the initiatives. Hence the company needs to focus on the initiatives under the sub area "B" as it has limited reach to the employees and either they are less effective or not well promoted in comparison to the initiatives under sub area "A". For instance, Table 3 shows Survey Responses of Stakeholders on "Company Policies and Benefits offered" and as mentioned, only 25% employees know about the initiative "B.2- The portal to access them" and similarly only 40% employees know about "B.3- The latest amendments made in them". This indicates the inefficiency in promoting the portal and to update the employees regarding the latest amendment and changes about the policies. Accordingly, on identification of the problem areas which are "B.2" and "B.3", the company needs to find out the root cause and take appropriate actions to increase the efficacy through improvements or scrap the initiative or design and develop more effective initiatives. Any initiative demands a lot of time and money and continuing with low efficacy initiatives in not healthy for an organization in longer run. So the Brand Awareness metric helps in identifying the low efficacy areas quantitatively and to know about the current health of the individual initiatives and the overall Employer Branding Quotient of an organization.

CONCLUSION

Employer branding is an emerging topic, and organizations are trying to formulate practices to implement the same in organizations. Employer branding involves promotion both within and outside the firm, a clear view of what makes a firm different and desirable as an employer. In order to develop a strong employer brand, it is necessary to demonstrate what is specific about an organization and its culture. The above analysis indicates the efficacy of the initiatives and addresses the questions (Reach of the initiative, efficacy of the same) which form the basis of brand awareness quotient.

Today, Organizations are facing the challenge of retaining their best employees. In order to retain the talented workforce they need to adopt practices like effective leadership, teamwork, training and development, challenging work environment, rewards and recognition, balance between personal life and career and flexible work schedule. These practices or initiatives needs a lot of time and monetary investment and the applicability of these initiatives varies from company to company as per the management goals. Hence, it is very much required to measure the efficacy of these initiatives at a regular frequency and keep revising the Employer Branding Strategy. As we have seen above Brand awareness quotient is one such metric which measures the effectiveness of the initiatives and helps in identifying the gaps which can be related to the implementation, reach or mismatch of the desired results with the actual results. Effective employer branding takes a proactive approach by identifying desired brand associations and then striving to develop these associations. It is through proactive efforts that the organizations can reduce the likelihood of losing the critical employees and surge ahead successfully, thereby creating a distinct edge in the marketplace.

REFERENCES

Ahmed, P., & Rafiq, M. (2002). *Internal marketing tools and concepts for customer-focused management* (pp. 158–164). Oxford: Butterworth-Heinemann.

Ambler, T., & Barrow, S. (1996). The employer brand. *Journal of Brand Management*, 1996, 185-206.

Backhaus, K., & Tikoo, S. (2004). *Conceptualizing and researching employer branding.* Career Dev Int Career Development International, 501-517.

Berthon, P., Ewing, M., & Hah, L. (2005). Captivating Company: Dimensions of Attractiveness in employer branding. *International Journal of Advertising*, 2005, 151–172.

Cable, D., & Turban, D. (2003). The Value of Organizational Reputation in the Recruitment Context: A Brand-Equity Perspective. *J. Appl. Social Pyschol. Journal of Applied Social Psychology*, 33(11), 2244-2266.

Deb, T. (2006). *Strategic approach to human resource management: Concept, tools and application* (pp. 273–280). New Delhi: Atlantic.

Dell, D. (2001). *Engaging employees through your brand.* New York, NY: Conference Board.

Ferrell, O., & Hartline, M. (2014). *Marketing strategy.* Mason, Ohio: Thomson/South-Western.

Finney, M. (2008). *Building high-performance people and organizations.* Westport, Conn.: Praeger.

Giehl, W., & LePla, F. (2012). *Create a brand that inspires: How to sell, organize and sustain internal branding* (pp. 11–26). Bloomington, IN: AuthorHouse.

Gronroos, C. (2007). *Service management and marketing: Managing customer relationships for service and manufacturing firms.* Chichester: Wiley.

Güntürkün, P., Haumann, T., & Lukasczyk, A. (2014). How to Evaluate Employer Brands: A Monetary Approach. In *Management for Professionals Human Resource Management Practices* (pp. 53-67).

Kotler, P., & Bowen, J. (2006). *Marketing for hospitality and tourism* (4th ed.). Upper Saddle River, NJ: Pearson Prentice Hall.

Kotler, P., & Pfoertsch, W. (2006). *B2B brand management.* Berlin: Springer.

Kumar, A., & Meenakshi, N. (2009). *Marketing Management.* Vikas House Pvt.

Love, L. F., & Singh, P. (2011). Workplace branding: Leveraging human resource management practices for competitive advantage through best employer surveys. *Journal of Business and Psychology, 26*(2), 175–181. doi:10.1007/s10869-011-9226-5

McLeod, C., & Waldman, J. (2011). The HR Trailblazer: Unlock the Potential of Your Employer Brand (pp. 1-10).

Minchington, B. (2011). Employer brand leadership: A global perspective (pp. 121-186). Torrensville: Collective Learning Australia.

Nazemetz, P., & Ruch, W. (2013). *HR and marketing: Power partners: The competitive advantage that will transform your business and establish a culture of performance.* Milwaukee: Versant.

Pride, W., & Ferrell, O. (2008). *Marketing* (14th ed., pp. 47–48). Boston: Houghton Mifflin.

Ravens, C. (2012). *Internal brand management in an international context.*

Rosethorn, H., & Group, M. (2009). *The Employer Brand Keeping Faith with the Deal.* Farnham: Ashgate Pub.

Sartain, L., & Schumann, M. (2006). *Brand from the inside: Eight essentials to emotionally connect your employees to your business.* San Francisco, CA: Jossey-Bass.

Sparrow, P., & Cooper, C. (2003). *The employment relationship key challenges for HR.* Amsterdam: Butterworth-Heinemann.

Verma, H. (2012). *Services marketing text and cases* (2nd ed.). New Delhi, India: Pearson Education/ Dorling Kindersley.

Yapp, M. (2009). Measuring the ROI of talent management. *Strategic HR Review*, 8(4), 5-10.

ENDNOTE

[1]   https://business.linkedin.com/content/dam/business/talent-solutions/global/en_US/c/pdfs/india-recruiting-trends-final1.pdf

This research was previously published in the International Journal of Applied Management Sciences and Engineering (IJAMSE), 3(2); edited by Carolina Machado and J. Paulo Davim, pages 62-74, copyright year 2016 by IGI Publishing (an imprint of IGI Global).

Chapter 25

Network–Based Targeting:
Big Data Application in Mobile Industry

Chu (Ivy) Dang
The Chinese University of Hong Kong, China

ABSTRACT

This chapter focuses on two kinds of targeting in mobile industry: to target churning customers and to target potential customers. These two targeting strategies are very important goals in Customer Relationship Management (CRM). In the first part of the chapter, the author reviews churn prediction models and its applications. In the second part of the chapter, traditional innovation diffusion models are reviewed and agent-based models are explained in detail. Customers in telecom industry are usually connected by large and complex networks. To understand how network effects and consumer behaviors – such as churning and adopting – interplays with each other is of great significance. Therefore, detailed examples are given to network-based targeting analysis.

INTRODUCTION

According to statistics from International Telecommunication Union (ITU), there will be more than 7 billion mobile cellular subscriptions by end 2015, corresponding to a penetration rate of 97%. In developed regions, penetration rates are much higher. For example, mobile subscriber penetration rate in Hong Kong reached 232.2% in April 2015 (Office of the Communications Authority, 2015). Mobile Internet connection are getting cheaper and easier thanks to technological progress, infrastructure deployment, and dropping prices. Globally, mobile broadband penetration reaches 47% in 2015, a value that increased 12 times since 2007 (ITU, 2015). All these figures give evidence to one bold prediction "Mobile to overtake fixed Internet access by 2014" made by Mary Meeker, an analyst at Kleiner Perkins Caufield Byers (KPCB) who reviews technology trends annually. With such an increasing customer base and huge potential market, companies are facing great opportunities to enlarge their existing market and gain more profit. Yet, their competitors are also preparing themselves to share this big market. Fierce competition makes customer retention and customer acquisition more difficult than ever before.

DOI: 10.4018/978-1-5225-5187-4.ch025

Consumers have many choices over mobile service providers and mobile devices providers. For mobile service provider, to keep the existing customer from churning is the main focus of their CRM as customer churn often entails great loss to mobile service providers. Whereas, for mobile device providers, they often launch new handsets every year to attract new customers or allure existing customers to upgrade their devices. Therefore, mobile device providers focus more on customer acquisition. According to Recon Analytics (Entner, 2011), American people replace mobile phones every two years.

This chapter will focus on the first step in customer retention strategy and customer acquisition strategy: *targeting*. Targeting is of great importance in CRM. If targeting goes wrong, companies will waste resources and efforts in marketing practice, leading to great financial loss. With such large and diverse customer base, customer related data in mobile industry is often very big. In order to properly process and analyze these data, big data applications are necessary. One important big data application in mobile industry is targeting. This chapter will focus on such models and applications. Especially, network-based targeting analysis will be emphasized. The whole chapter will be arranged as follows. The next section will introduce the background of this chapter. Then the author reviews models and applications in two kinds of targeting: targeting churning customers and targeting potential customers. Lastly, the conclusion of this chapter is given.

BACKGROUND

For any company, customer loyalty is an essential part for profit maximization. To obtain customer loyalty involves two steps: obtaining new costumers and then keep them from churning. The first step is called customer acquisition and the second is customer retention. Actually customer acquisition and customer retention is also the ultimate goal of most marketing strategies. For example, "free trial before buy" is a frequently used marketing strategy to attract new customers. "Membership" is also a common marketing strategy to keep existing customers. To obtain new customers and keep them loyal to the company is especially important for mobile industry in many countries since there are typically many wireless service providers as well as many mobile device providers within a region and customers can easily switch between them.

In Hong Kong, which has one of the highest mobile density in the world, for example, competition in public mobile services is vibrant. There are four main mobile network operators, namely, China Mobile Hong Kong Company Limited (CMHK), Hong Kong Telecommunications Limited (HKT), Hutchison Telephone Company Limited and SmarTone Mobile Communications Limited, providing a wide range of public mobile services (Hong Kong Government, 2015). Figure 1 shows the market share spectrum of mobile operators in Hong Kong. Indeed the competition within the mobile service sector is fierce. Operators use a variety of marketing strategies to maintain customer loyalty, ensuring high retention rate. One of the most frequently used strategy is Family Plan Packages, which give discount for communication between family members. Such plans also have dramatic consequence if customer churns. This will potentially induce their family members to churn because communication fee within the same operator is usually cheaper. As a result, customer churn will cause dramatic financial consequences for mobile operators. To tackle such churning effect, mobile service providers are developing sophisticated churn management strategies. First, they rank customers based on their estimated propensity to churn. Second, they offer retention incentives to a subset of customers at the top of the churn ranking. The core of this strategy is to *target* customer who are likely to churn. To be specific, such targeting strategy is

Figure 1. Mobile spectrum market share in Hong Kong
Source: Office of the Communication Authority.

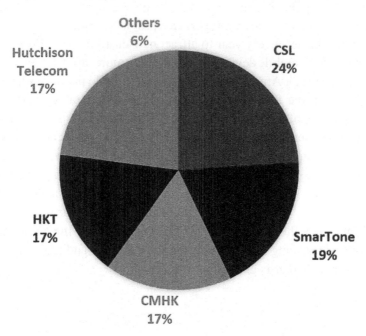

*For a more accurate representation see the electronic version.

usually called churn prediction. If churn prediction is inaccurate, companies will waste their money and effort on customers who would stay anyway. Therefore, companies want to predict churn as accurate as possible. The first part of this chapter will review the models and applications in targeting customers who are likely to churn. Specifically, the author will focus on models using big data technique and network analysis.

Besides mobile service provider, another important sector in mobile industry is mobile device provider. Figure 2 illustrates the market share of mobile phone of various brands in Hong Kong (by unit of shipment) in 2013. Although there are many mobile phone brands in the market, most of the market share is taken by two biggest players: Samsung and Apple. Each year, Samsung and Apple will announce its new mobile phone model and launch massive marketing campaign to allure customers buying new phones. According to Recon Analytics (Entner, 2011), on average American mobile phone user replace their mobile phones every 2 years. With such high replacement rate, customer retention is very hard to achieve. Therefore the marketing strategy of keeping customer loyalty for device providers is different from that of the mobile service providers. Mobile phone companies usually use new products to obtain new customers and allure existing customers to upgrade their handsets. That is to say, their marketing strategy focuses on customer acquisition instead of customer retention. From the companies' perspective, customer acquisition is equivalent to new product adoption. To understand how a new product diffuses in the market is essential for understanding the product adoption behavior of the customers. One of the most important steps in customer acquisition strategy is to *target* customers who are most likely to buy new products and then offer them incentives to induce buying behavior. The second part of this chapter will review the models and applications in targeting customers who are likely to adopt new products. The author will emphasis on models taking advantage of big data technique and network analysis.

Figure 2. Analysis of market share by brands of mobile phone
Source: Frost & Sullivan.

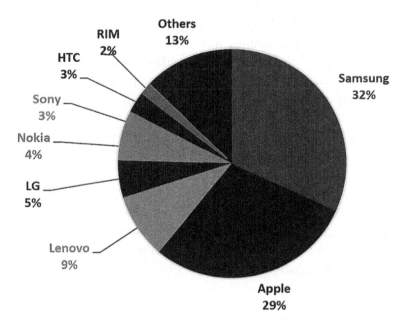

*For a more accurate representation see the electronic version.

TARGETING CHURNING CUSTOMERS

"Churn" is a word derived from change and turn. It means the discontinuation of a contract. Typically to gain new customers will cost much more than to retain the existing customers. Therefore, one of the most important goals in CRM is churn management. Churn management is about two things: predicting *who* is most likely to churn and analyzing *why* they churn. The "who" question helps mobile service providers target the right customers. The "why" question helps companies design proper customer retention strategies for these customers. If companies only predict churning without analyzing the underlying driving force of such behavior, retention effort will eventually be wasted. Churn prediction answers the "who" question and churn analysis answers the "why" question. In this section, the author will explain churn management from such two aspects: churn prediction and churn analysis.

In mobile industry, customer related data set are typically very big. Such data contains many information about customers, such as call details, 3G/4G data usage details, contractual information, demographics etc. With increasing popularity of mobile service and increasing frequency of use (ITU, 2015), such data set is becoming bigger and bigger. Therefore, CRM in mobile industry depends heavily on big data applications. Particularly, data mining technique is most frequently used (Wei & Chiu, 2002).

Data mining refers to techniques which analyze a very large data set from various dimensions and then "dig out" previously unknown, non-trivial, consistent patterns and/or systematic relationships between variables (Berry & Linoff, 2004; Chen, Han, & Yu, 1996). Such pattern and/or relationships can then be used to predict future events. The "mining" process typically includes a learning algorithm such that the model can be adaptive to different inputs. In CRM, the most commonly used data mining techniques include clustering (Ngai, Xiu, & Chau, 2009), classification (Neslin, Gupta, Kamakura, Lu,

&Mason, 2006; Lemmens & Croux, 2006), genetic models (Eiben, Koudijs, & Slisser, 1998), neural network (Tsai & Lu, 2009) etc. Since churn management simply cares whether customers will churn or not, such a binary behavior with known categories is best captured by classification models.

Classification, in simple words, is assigning data to one of some pre-defined categories. Usually, one classification model is composed of three steps. First, classify training data into some predefined categories, defined as label set. The features of the training data compose the feature set. Second, employ a learning algorithm to identify a model that best fit the relationship between the feature set and the label set. Informally, this classification model can be called a target function f. A target function maps each feature set x to one of the predefined labels y. Third, use classification model to classify test data with unknown class labels into different categories according to their feature set. After that, evaluate the model based on the accuracy of their prediction of the test data. Figure 3 illustrates how classification model works. A real life example would be an email system which can classify an email into either spam or not spam. In churn prediction model, such classification model would be the one which can classify a subscriber into churn or not churn according to their features such as demographics, contractual data, customer service logs, call details, complaint data, bill and payment information etc. Classification models applied in churn prediction include Naïve Bayes classifier, decision tree classifier, decision rule classifier, neural network etc.

General Customer Churn Management Methodology

1. **Obtain Data Set:** Mobile service provider needs to extract huge volume of customer related data. These data can be grouped into four categories (Van den Poel & Lariviere, 2004): customer behaviors (calling details, contractual information etc.), customer perceptions (can be measured via survey), customer demographics (age, gender, education etc.), and macro-environment variables (natural disaster, political revolution etc.).

2. **Data Reduction and Cleaning:** Typically the first-hand data set is very large with many noises. Data reduction will help to ignore unimportant variables and features such that the data can be reduced into manageable size. Data cleaning includes eliminating noisy data and estimating missing values. Interpolation is the most widely used method for missing value estimation.

3. **Build Model:** Randomly use a training set of data which contains both churners and non-churners to build churn prediction model. Typically this process is composed of a classification model with a learning algorithm. The churn prediction model will be reviewed in the following section.

4. **Evaluate Model:** After construction, test data with known category (churn or not churn) will be used in evaluation. Quality measures in churn prediction include *accuracy*, *sensitivity* and *specifity*.

Figure 3. How classification model works

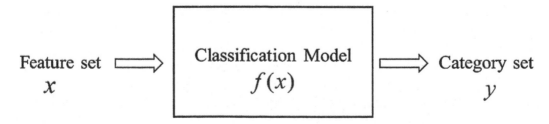

The most import quality measure in the evaluation process is *accuracy*. Accuracy is defined as the percentage of correct predictions. These measures can be obtained using a confusion matrix. Figure 4 is a confusion matrix in churn prediction models. According to Domingos (1999), an accuracy of about 90% is sufficient for a model to provide satisfactory churn prediction.

5. **Adjust Model:** If the model is not satisfactory after evaluation, it needs to be adjusted until it gets good quality measure results, such as a 90% accuracy score.

6. **Predict Churn:** Now the model is ready to predict customers who are likely to churn given a new data set with known features but unknown category.

7. **Analyze Reasons:** A huge drawback of churn prediction model is that it cannot answer the "why" question: why do those people want to churn? Effective customer retention strategies rely heavily on these reasons since the time and resources for retention is limited (Lazarov & Capota, 2007). Churn analysis models are used to analyze these reasons. Some of these reasons include social learning and network effect (Hu, Yang & Xu, 2015).

8. **Design Customer Retention Strategies:** After analyzing the reasons behind churn behavior, proper customer retention strategies can be designed. For example, if network effect dominates, strategies like family plan packages or developing exclusive network games would be effective. However, if social learning dominates, strategies like publicly recognizable handsets or accessories and positive word-of-mouth would be better (Hu et al., 2015).

Step 1 to 6 is churn prediction procedures and step 7 to 8 is churn analysis procedure. In the following section, the author will briefly review these models and their applications in mobile churn management.

Churn Prediction Models

Neslin et al. (2006) conducts a tournament in which both academics and practitioners use churn prediction models. In this practice, various churn prediction models are introduced. Among them, 45% are logistic regression, 23% are decision trees, and 11% are neutral networks. Other methods include discriminant analysis (9%), cluster analysis (7%), and Bayes method (5%). The author will review these models in this section.

Logit Model

Before big data age, the simplest and most traditional way of churn predicting is logit model (Hosmer & Lemeshow, 2004). Logit model, also called logistic regression, is frequently used to model binary outcome variables. It can be seen as a binary classification model. In the logit model the log odds of the outcome is modeled as a linear combination of the predictor variables. In churn prediction, the binary dependent variable is simply $y_i = churn$ or $y_i = not\ churn$. Vector $x = \left(x_{i1}, x_{i2}, ..., x_{in}\right)$ contains

Table 1. Confusion matrix

	Actual Churners	Actual Non-Churners
Predicted Churners	a_{11}	a_{12}
Predicted Non-Churners	a_{21}	a_{22}

features used for churn prediction which includes customer demographics, contractual data, customer service logs, call details, complaint data, bill and payment information etc. Regression coefficients $\beta = (\beta_0, \beta_1, \beta_2, \ldots)$ can be estimated by maximum likelihood estimation (MLE) using previous customer information (training data). After obtaining the coefficients, Equation 1 is used for calculating the probability of customer churn:

$$prob\left(y_i = churn\right) = \frac{Exp\left(\beta_0 + \sum_{k=1}^{n}\beta_k x_{ik}\right)}{1 + Exp\left(\beta_0 + \sum_{k=1}^{n}\beta_k x_{ik}\right)} \tag{1}$$

Logit model often serves as the benchmark model when comparing the performance of different churn prediction models (Neslin et al., 2006; Lemmenaswb s & Croux, 2006). Neslin et al. (2006) gives a comprehensive comparison of five most common churn prediction techniques to investigate their predictive accuracy. Lemmens and Croux (2006) apply bagging and boosting technique to churn prediction models. After comparing it with the standard logit model, they find significant improved prediction power in term of Gini coefficient top-decile lift. Logistic regression can also be used in feature selection (Masand, Datta, Mani, & Li, 1999). Usually, the data warehouse collects many features of each customer. To select the most predictive features as the input for churn prediction is of significant importance.

Decision Trees (DT)

As one of the most frequently used data mining methods (Berry & Linoff, 2004), DT is a powerful tool for classification and predition by finding out the patterns or relationships between data. DT is made up in the form of a tree built by making child-nodes until each branch reaches the terminal node. There are three kinds of nodes in a decision tree: root node, internal nodes, and leaf or terminal nodes. Root node and internal nodes contain feature test conditions to separate observations that have different characteristics. Each leaf node is assigned a class label. Figure 4 is a simple decision tree to judge whether a subscriber will churn or not. The classification starts from the root node with one feature test condition such as if the age of the subscriber is below sixty. If yes, the next internal node will judge whether the duration of his/her usual call is below 2 minutes. If yes, the subscriber will be classified as churner. If not, he/she will be classified as non-churner. Based on different split criterion, some of the algorithms for DT are CHAID (Kass, 1980), CART (Breiman, Friedman, Stone, & Olshen, 1984), and C4.5 (Quinlan, 2014).

Many researchers utilize decision tree classifier to model costumer churn behavior (Breiman et al., 1984; Wei & Chiu, 2002; Bin, Peiji, & Juan, 2007; Hung, Yen, & Wang, 2006). For example, based on customer demographics and contractual data, Breiman et al. (1984) use CART algorithm to predict customer churn. However, not all companies have customer demographic information. To tackle the problem of unavailability of customer demographics in the mobile service provider investigated, Wei and Chiu (2002) design a decision tree model to identify potential churners at contract levels. Their empirical evaluation results suggest that when more recent call details are employed for model construct, the prediction effectiveness will be more satisfactory. Also aiming at overcoming the limitations of lack of information of customers of Personal Handyphone System Service (PHSS), Bin et al. (2007) improve the existing decision tree model from three aspects: changing sub-periods for training data sets, changing

Figure 4. Decision tree for churn prediction

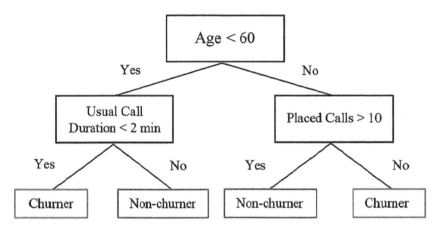

misclassification cost in churn model, and changing sample methods for training data sets. By carrying out three research experiments, some optimal parameters of models are found. Hung et al. (2006) empirically explore the effectiveness of data mining technique in churn prediction with a customer related data set provided by a wireless telecom company in Taiwan. Particularly, the data mining technique used by Hung et al. (2006) are decision tree model and neutral network. They show that both models can deliver accurate churn prediction by using customer demographics, billing information, contract/service status, call detail records, and service change log.

Neutral Network

The statistical technique neutral network is inspired by the way human brains process information. This information processing system is composed of a large number of highly interconnected "neurons" (processing elements) which send messages to each other. These elements work in unison to solve specific problems. By "learning" from previous experience, the weights put on these connections can be tuned, making this system adaptive to inputs. Such data mining technique is widely used in computer vision and voice recognition. Neutral network classifier is essentially a function $f : x \rightarrow y$ which maps feature set (inputs) to a label set (outputs). This function typically incorporates a learning rule such that it can be adaptive learning. In addition, this function allows complex nonlinear relationships between the feature set and label set. Figure 6 is one of the simplest neutral network which is equivalent to linear regression. There are four inputs or features in this model with attached "weights" for each of them. The prediction function is a linear combination of these four inputs. The weights are selected using a learning algorithm such that it can minimize a cost function, such as mean squared error (MSE).

Tsai and Lu (2009) evaluate the performance of two churn prediction models utilizing two hybrid neutral network techniques. Particularly, these two techniques are back-propagation artificial neural networks (ANN) and self-organizing maps (SOM). The hybrid models are ANN combined with ANN (ANN + ANN) and SOM combined with ANN (SOM + ANN). Their experiments show that the two hybrid models perform better than the benchmark neutral network model in terms of prediction accuracy and Types I and II errors. There are general two downsides of neural network analysis in churn

Figure 5. Neutral network which is equivalent to linear regression

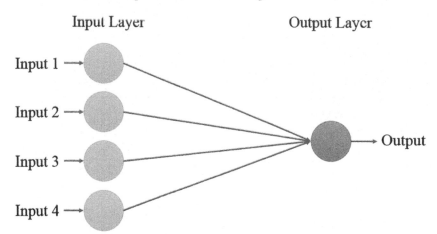

prediction. First, because neural network technique is a holistic approach to learning by encoding the classification model in the weights between nodes, its resulting knowledge often lacks interpretability. Second, due to the iterative nature of neural network analysis, it requires a long training time which will be a big problem for very large data set.

Naïve Bayes Classifier

Frequentist statistics defines an event's probability as the limit of its relative frequency in a large number of trials. However Bayesian probabilities is expressed in terms of level of certainty relating to a potential outcome. The simplest way to incorporate Bayesian statistics into churn prediction is Naïve Bayes classifier (Lazarov, Iba, & Thompson, 1992). Naïve Bayes is a type of supervised-learning module that contains examples of the input-target mapping which the model tries to learn. Such models make predictions about new data based on previous experience. The learning process is done by updating prior belief by posterior belief.

Given the same model, Naive Bayes calculates the probability that a given input data (e.g., the input feature vector $\boldsymbol{x}_i = (x_{i1}, x_{i2}, \ldots, x_{in})$) in churn prediction case) is generated by certain data generation process (DGP). Denote $\theta \in \Theta$ as the possible parameter vector in DGP. The posterior belief can be written as:

$$p\left(\theta \mid \boldsymbol{x}_i\right) = p\left(\boldsymbol{x}_i \mid \theta\right) p\left(\theta\right) = p\left(x_{i1}, x_{i2}, \ldots, x_{in} \mid \theta\right) p\left(\theta\right)$$

where $p\left(\theta\right)$ is the prior belief of θ. Naive Bayes assumes that the conditional probabilities of the independent variables are statistically independent. So the above equation can be re-written as:

$$p\left(\theta \mid \boldsymbol{x}_i\right) = p\left(\theta\right) \prod_{k=1}^{n} p\left(x_{ik} \mid \theta\right).$$

The estimation criteria of θ is given by:

$$\hat{\theta} = \arg\max_{\theta \in \Theta} p\left(\theta \mid \boldsymbol{x}_i\right).$$

Based on an Oracle database of fifty thousand real customers, Nath and Behara (2003) build a working database system for customer churn prediction using Naïve Bayes classifier. Their model obtained 68% predictive accuracy. Another application of Bayesian method is Kisioglu and Topcu (2011) who apply Bayesian belief network approach to identify potential churners and find out the most important features that influence customer churning behavior in mobile industry.

Churn Analysis Models

A huge drawback of churn prediction model is that the driving force behind such churning behavior is unknown. In order to understand such driving force, models which not only predict churning but also give insights on the reasons behind churning are constructed. Some of these techniques include evolutionary learning and self-organizing maps.

Evolutionary Learning

Au, Chan, & Yao (2003) propose a new data mining algorithm, called data mining by evolutionary learning (DMEL), to predict and analyze churn behavior. Unlike most classification models which fail to give likelihood for each prediction, DMEL can estimate the accuracy of each prediction. The model can be summarized as follows: 1. Using genetic algorithm to construct rules iteratively; 2. Identify interesting rules and measure them using objective interestingness measure; 3. Calculate the probability that the attribute values of an observation can be correctly determined using the encoded rules; 4. Estimate the likelihood of each prediction. Using the likelihood score and customer feature set, further analysis of customer churning is possible. For example, customers can be grouped into those with high likelihood and those with low likelihood. By identifying groups and features, companies will gain insight on real reasons for churning.

Self-Organizing Maps (SOM)

SOM is one of the clustering models in unsupervised learning. Clustering refers to a method which partitions a set of patterns into clusters without predefined classes. Cluster analysis refers to the grouping of a set of data object into clusters. In particular, no predefined classes are assigned (Jain, Murty, & Flyn, 1999). SOM was proposed by Kohonen (1987) and proved extremely useful when the input data are with high dimensionality and complexity. SOM is used to discover relationships in a dataset and then cluster data according to their similarity. Ultsch (2002) utilizes a combination of emergent self-organizing maps, U-matrix methods and knowledge conversion technique to predict potential mobile phone churners. The output rules produced by the model help mobile service providers get better understanding of who the clients are, how profitable they are and why churning is happening. With such information, better retention strategies, such as marketing campaign and service upgrading can be designed.

Network-Based Churn Analysis

As already been illustrated in the previous section, to understand what triggers consumers to switch wireless carriers is of great importance. Revealing the underlying mechanism behind this behavior will help telecommunication companies enhance product design and marketing strategy to avoid costumer churn, and ultimately optimize their customer retention efforts. For example, Dasgupta et al. (2008) examine the communication patterns of millions to address the role of social ties in the formation and growth of groups in a mobile network. They show that customers are more likely to switch wireless carriers if more of their contacts from the same operator switch. With the availability of data about individual interactions, there is a growing interest in understanding the mechanisms regarding this influence (Peres, Muller, & Mahajan, 2010).

Mantian Hu and her co-authors (Hu, Yang, & Xu, 2015) successfully identified the two underlying behavioral mechanisms, social learning and network effects, to explain such assimilation effect by proposing a two-step dynamic forward looking model. Figure 6 illustrates the modelling framework. According to their study, the individual costumer decides whether or not to switch carrier according to three sources of information:

1. Their own user experience of the current carrier and their idiosyncratic belief on the alternative carrier;
2. Feedbacks from their contacts who have switched to update their own quality expectations and learn about the alternative carriers;
3. Network effect induced by the switching decisions (for example, the more contacts a customer has, the more benefit she potentially receives).

(2) and (3) are two fundamentally different mechanisms why indiciduals imitates one another: the former is based on information exchange and it is called *social learning* (Moretti, 2011); the latter is based on direct benefit from aligning their behavior to others and it is called *network effect* (Katz & Shapiro, 1985). The network effect is a newly raised topic and it differs from social learning since others' behaviors are affecting someone's payoff directly, rather than indirectly by changing his information set. By proposing a dynamic structural model with strategic interpersonal interactions, Hu et al. (2015) find strong evidence for both social learning and network effect in mobile customer churn behavior. They show by simulation that 1% change in network size will lead to 11.5% change in customer retention rate in the same direction. And two-thirds of such impact can be attributed to network effects and one-third to social learning effects. Apart from simulation, they also apply this framework to data from a wireless carrier in a European country. Their empirical results indicate that, after controlling for mobile plan details and demographic information, learning from own usage experience, learning from contact neighbors' decisions, and network effects all have significant effects on customer mobile service switching decisions.

This is the first study to incorporate a learning framework within a social network context, where people's decisions affect one another endogenously. It disentangles two important mechanisms, social learning and network effects, by explicitly modeling the direct utility impact and the learning process. The disentanglement of the two behavioral mechanisms will provide great insight on how to avoid costumer churn or how to attract new customers for telecom companies. Given the fact that telecom industry experiences an average of 30-35 percent annual churn rate and it costs 5-10 times more to recruit a new customer than to retain an existing one, customer retention has now become even more important than

Figure 6. Modelling framework
Source: Hu et al. (2015).

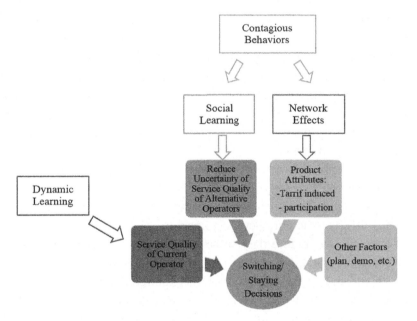

customer acquisition for mobile service providers. Hu et al. (2015) suggest that if network effect plays a dominant role, companies should focus on maintaining a large customer base to keep existing ones and at the same time attract new customers. However, if social learning prevails, information exchange is the key. So strategies like publicly recognizable handsets or accessories and positive word-of-mouth will be better. Moreover, this research also provides another angle to estimate wireless carrier's long-term customer retention rate and its profitability.

TARGETING POTENTIAL CUSTOMERS

Besides targeting customers who are most likely to churn, another important targeting goal is potential customers. In CRM, the ultimate goal of customer acquisition management is the acquisition of potential customers in an effective fashion (Saylor, 2004). "Effective" here means using the least effort and spending the least amount of money to acquire as many new customers as possible. Therefore, there are two main steps in customer acquisition management: first, target the right people; second, develop the right acquisition strategies. These strategies include customer loyalty programs, joining charitable events, launch mass marketing campaigns etc. In mobile industry, as already has been illustrated, the mobile device providers, such as mobile phone companies, new customer acquisition is more crucial than existing customer retention. Data shows (Entner, 2011) that typically one changes mobile phone every two years in countries like the United States. This is probably due to the low switching cost and fast technology innovation within the mobile device sector. According to Moore's Law, processor speeds, or overall processing power for computers will double every two years. Moreover, researchers showed that quality and inflation adjusted price of IT equipment declined 16% per year on average over five decades from 1959 to 2009 (Nambiar & Poess, 2011). More advanced technology with lower prices, this gives another reason for customers to adopt new handsets. In mobile device sector, the competition is even fiercer than the mobile service sector. To maintain or/and enlarge market share, mobile phone companies for example, develop many categories of phones to meet the needs of different customers. Particularly, big companies like Apple, Samsung, and Xiaomi launch their featured product every year to attract new customers and allure existing customers to upgrade their devices. In the meantime, they face extremely fierce competition with each other. A successful new product will diffuse very fast and take over competitor's market. For example, Samsung launched Galaxy S3 and Note II in 2012 which was a big success over Apple's iPhone 5. Apple's global smartphone market share dropped from 23% in the first quarter of 2012 to only about 12% in the third quarter of 2014 (International Data Corporation, 2015). However, after Apple launched its iPhone 6 model which was loved by the consumers in September 2014, its market share quickly climbed to the same level of Samsung by the end of 2014 (International Data Corporation, 2015). Customer loyalty in mobile phone sector is especially low, so companies devote many efforts to acquire new customers.

From companies' perspective, before they come up with any marketing strategies, they must first understand *who* adopt their product, *how* product diffuse in the marketplace and *what* drives diffusion process. The "who", "how" and "what" question can be captured in the new product diffusion process, which can be explained in innovation diffusion models or new product diffusion models. For traditional commercial products such as foods and durable goods, companies usually are incapable of obtaining customer related data and their social connections. However, one big advantage in mobile industry is the easy acquisition of consumer's behavioral data (e.g., detailed calling information), demographic data (age, sex etc.) and their mobile device information. With such rich data, companies can investigate the mobile device diffusion process conveniently. Diffusion denotes the spread of an innovation in the market (Peres et al., 2010). Rogers (2010) defines diffusion of innovation as "the process by which an innovation is communicated over time among the members of a social system. It is a special type of communication, in that the messages are concerned with new ideas". The diffusion process has many managerial implications. Some of those include how market mix (price, place, promotion, and product) affect the adoption process and brand image, how competitions influence the growth pattern of products etc.

Innovation Diffusion Theory

The innovation diffusion theory was first introduced by Rogers (1962). It seeks to understand how new ideas, products and practices spread throughout a society over time. In Rogers' model, the aggregate adopters follows an S-shaped curve. According to the different positions on the S-shaped curve, the adopters are grouped into five different categories: innovators, early adopters, early majority, late majority, and laggards. However Rogers' model is a conceptual framework rather than a quantitative model. Bass (1969) introduced a quantitative diffusion model which is the most frequently used model for diffusion research. Before Bass model, there are two other quantitative models proposed by Fourt and Woodlock (1960) and Mansfield (1961). Fourt and Woodlock (1960) is a pure innovative model where they assume new product adopters are influenced by external information such as advertising and mass marketing campaign, rather than internal influence such as word-of-mouth. On the contrary, Mansfield (1961) constructs a pure imitative model by assuming people adopt new things by internal influences such as word-of-mouth and interpersonal interactions. Bass model combines these two effects together. The Bass model assumes both external information (e.g., mass media) and internal information (e.g., word-of-mouth) influence potential adopters of innovation. Bass model has very good predictive power and it is the theoretical foundation for many diffusion models. These models are all traditional innovation diffusion models where they use aggregate level data. Therefore, they understand diffusion process from a macro-level.

In order to fully investigate the driving forces for each individual, micro-level diffusion theories are necessary. In the review of Mahajan, Muller, and Bass (1990), the authors also call for individual-level based diffusion models to explore the social communication pattern, and its impact on product perceptions, preferences and ultimate adoption decision. Such micro-level diffusion models will also reveal the relationships between individual adoptions and aggregate growth. These micro-level models include: microeconomic models, stochastic choice models and agent-based models (ABM). Microeconomic models and stochastic choice models typically rely on strong distributional assumptions about individual information and they also lack analysis of aggregated variables. Consumer-level data in mobile industry is very rich and thanks to the advanced information technology, especially to those related to big data application, researchers and companies are worrying less about long computation time and small computational power of computers. Therefore, in mobile industry, agent-based models are the most popular individual-level diffusion models. Many agent-based models are either extensions or variations of the Bass model with the same underlying logic. Cellular automata is one of these models. Agent-based models have many advantages, for example, they can incorporate heterogeneity and dynamics into individual behaviors, and they also link disaggregate individual-level choices to aggregate macro-level variables.

In the Bass model, the decision to adopt a new product at the population level is modeled as a hazard rate without considering the local network effects. However, in mobile industry, people are connected and communicated through their mobile devices. Ignoring the heterogeneity of consumers' local networks is one of the biggest drawbacks of the Bass model. To tackle this problem, agent-based models with network structure analysis are developed. For example, Hu, Hsieh and Jia (2014) investigated how dynamic network structure affects consumer's new smartphone adoption behavior. Their research showed that network structure is a good predictor of social influence. This study will be introduced by the author later in detail.

In the following section, the author will first briefly introduce the traditional Bass model and its agent-based extensions. Then a combination of agent-based model and network structure analysis will be introduced by a case study.

The Bass Models

The work done by Fourt and Woodlock (1960), Mansfield (1961) and Bass (1969) contribute to the foundation of traditional parsimonious empirical diffusion models, among which Bass (1969) is the most popular model. In the diffusion literature, there are many models which are based on refinement or extension of Bass model with the basic premise of the model (Mahajan et al., 1990). Therefore the author will briefly go through these three models.

Innovative Models

After examining the marketing penetration curves of many new products, Fourt and Woodlock (1960) proposed an innovation diffusion model which assumes adoption behavior is influenced by external sources such as advertising and marketing campaigns. In addition, the cumulative sales curve follows an exponential shape. The mathematic formula is:

$$f_t = \Delta Q_t / Q_p = rM\left(1 - r\right)^{t-1}$$

where ΔQ_t denotes the change in cumulative product sales at time t and Q_p denotes potential sales. r is the rate of penetration of potential sales and M is the ratio of total potential sales to all buyers. Parameters Q_p, r and M are constant across time.

Imitative Models

Imitative models (Mansfield, 1961; Fisher & Pry, 1972) assume adoptions are mainly influenced by internal sources such as word-of-mouth and interpersonal interactions. For example, Fisher and Pry (1972) assume that new product adoption rate is dependent on the fraction of the old product which are still in use. They regard advancing technology as a set of substitution processes. Therefore new products act as substitutions to old ones. The new product adoption rate in Fisher and Pry (1972) model is the classic logistic S-shaped curve:

$$f_t = \frac{1}{1 + e^{-2\alpha\left(t - t_0\right)}}$$

where α is half the annual fractional growth in the early years. α and t_0 is the time at which $f_t = 1/2$. The S-shaped curve is characterized by two constants: the early growth rate α and the time at which the substitution is half complete t_0.

Bass Model: A Combination

The Bass model assumes that new product adopters are influenced by two types of communication: mass media (external source) and interpersonal communication (internal source). Therefore external sources will have greater impact on innovative customers who is the main driving force for product takeoff. Whereas internal sources will impact more on imitative customers who are more likely to buy if more of their friends are buying. There imitative customer contribute more during the later periods of diffusion process (Rogers, 2010). One of the basic assumptions in Bass model is that the probability of adopting a new product at time t is a linear function of the number of previous adopters. In mathematic term, that is

$$f_t = \left(p + qF_t\right)\left(1 - F_t\right) \tag{2}$$

where f_t is the likelihood of purchase at time t and F_t is the cumulative fraction of adopters at time t. Parameter p captures the innovative influence and q captures the imitative influence. Aggregate models are primarily concerned with modeling ΔQ_t, the flow of consumers from potential market m to current market (Mahajan & Muller, 1979). Equation 3 is typically used to calculate ΔQ_t.

$$\Delta Q_t = \left(p + qQ_t / m\right)\left(m - Q_t\right) \tag{3}$$

Q_t is the cumulative adoption and m is the market size. ΔQ_t is a bell-shaped curve showing the speed of diffusion. Q_t is a S-shaped curve which shows diffusion in a cumulative way.

Some of the advantages of Bass model are: first, it gives an analytically tractable way to interpret the whole market diffusion process; second, Bass model use more readily available market-level data to forecast sales; lastly, the estimation methods for Bass model are well documented (Bass, 1969; Schmittlein & Mahajan, 1982; Srinivasan & Mason, 1986). Despite these advantages, Bass model unavoidably exhibits many drawbacks. For example, it doesn't incorporate population heterogeneity and dynamics into the model. In addition, it ignores the structure of social interactions. Moreover, the linkage between micro-level adoption behavior and macro-level growth is missed. In order to conquer these limitations, agent-based models are called in.

Agent-Based Bass Model

Bass model can be easily formalized using agent-based model. Therefore, Bass model is a special case that can also be captured by an analogous agent-based model (Kiesling, Günther, Stummer, & Wakolbinger, 2012). The author will explain this process to illustrate the differences in modeling. Assume there are M agents indexed by $i = 1, 2, ..., M$. Each of them is in one of the two states: potential adopter ($x_i = 0$) or adopter ($x_i = 1$). In the original Bass model, probability of adopting a new product at time t is a linear function of the number of previous adopters which is expressed using Equation 2. Equation 4 shows the agent-based analogy. Each agent's individual probability of adoption is influenced uniformly by the adoption state of all other agents. In addition, global connectedness and homogeneity are also implied in the equation.

$$f_i = \left(p + \frac{\sum_{i=1}^{M} x_i}{M} q\right)\left(1 - x_i\right) \tag{4}$$

Algorithms such as discrete time updating process are adopted to do the simulation. Since stochastic process is often included in the algorithm, ABM typically does not provide a single analytical solution, but involves uncertainty and variability. The relationship between ABMs and Bass model was studies by, for example, Fibich and Gibori (2010), and Rahmandad and Sterman (2008). Fibich and Gibori (2010) show that Bass model provide an upper bound for the aggregate diffusion dynamics in agent-based models with "any" spatial structure. Rahmandad and Sterman (2008) compare ABMs with differential equation (DE) models and examine the impact of individual heterogeneity and different network topologies.

Cellular Automata

The cellular automata model was originally introduced by Stan Ulam and John von Neumann in the 1940s to provide a formal framework for investigating the behavior of complex, extended systems (von Neumann & Burks, 1966). Agent-based cellular automata models differ from the traditional model in the following ways: 1. the state of an agent is more complex; 2. local interaction structures can be heterogeneous. Take a simple cellular automata model which fulfills the assumptions in basic Bass model for example (Goldenberg, Libai, & Muller, 2001). The cells in this model are all potential buyers and they all interact with each other, with binary state value "0" or "1". State "0" represents potential buyers who do not adopt innovation. State "1" represents potential buyers who adopt the innovation. Like Bass model, the mechanisms that govern the transitions of potential buyers are external influences such as mass media and internal influences such as word-of-mouth. The former is captured by parameter p_i and the latter is captured by parameter q_i. Equation 5 illustrates the mathematical formula. $f_i(t)$ is the probability of adoption at time t and $Q_i(t)$ the cumulative number of adopters at time t. In this model, p_i and q_i capture the heterogeneity of consumers in terms of external and internal influences, which differs from Bass model where the influences are homogeneous.

$$f_i(t) = 1 - (1 - p_i)(1 - q_i)^{Q_i(t)} \tag{5}$$

Network-Based Diffusion Analysis

Disaggregate models such as ABMs has many desirable properties. Some of them include: 1. It captures interpersonal interactions; 2. Heterogeneity can be incorporated into the model; 3. The model can include network dynamics and structures without knowing the exact global interdependencies (Borshchev & Fillipov, 2004); 4. Aggregate level variables can be obtained from the micro-level individual behaviors; 5. Linkage between micro-level adoption behavior and macro-level growth is recovered. Since agent-based models build on decisions of each individual, they are therefore more behaviorally based. In a word, agent-based models aim to capture macro-level phenomena such as diffusion process by simulating the decision process of each individual. Mobile industry therefore is a perfect place to apply these techniques.

Interpersonal communication is seen as a key influence on new product diffusion process (Rogers, 2010; Mahajan et al., 1990). In the agent-based model, interpersonal communication channels can be represented by networks. Usually, such network-level influence is called social influence. The notion of social influence in the diffusion of new products has been well accepted (Iyengar, Bulte, & Lee, 2015). In mobile industry, such influence is especially pronounced since people are connected by their wireless devices. For mobile device companies, in order to target the right potential buyers, they must first understand the relationship between social influence and new product diffusion process. While many studies have been focusing on identifying and quantifying the social influence effect (Van den Bulte & Lilien, 2001; Manchanda, Xie, & Youn, 2008; Iyengar, Van den Bulte & Valente, 2011), little has been done to predict its occurrence and even little has been done to reveal how network structures affect the adoption behavior.

By using a model which captures the co-evolution of both network structures and product diffusion process, Hu et al. (2014) reveals how dynamic network structures affect consumers' new smartphone adoption decisions. They get access to the complete information of the entire customer base of a major Chinese wireless carrier in two medium-sized cities in western China. Based on the calling records, they extract individual social network using snowball sampling. Since new cellphone diffusion process in each individual networks are different, they propose to examine how network topology interplays with the effect of social influence. Particularly, they examine this using the diffusion of Samsung smart phones. A difficult task of this study is how to distinguish social influence effect from homophily effect. Hu et al. (2014) solve this by using the stochastic agent-based dynamic network formation model. They use this model to identify and measure the sizes of homophily effect on network formation and social influence. The stochastic agent-based dynamic network formation model (Snijders, 1996, 2001; Snijders, Steglich, & Schweinberger, 2007) has been widely applied to model co-evolution of a dynamic social network and diffusion of behaviors. However, Hu et al. (2014) is the first study to apply this model in marketing context. After estimating social influence, they use meta-analysis to link it with network structure measures. For example, they find network size, density, clustering coefficients, diversity, assortativity, epidemic threshold and position of initial adopters are good predictors of social influence.

Besides the relationship between network structure and social influence, Hu et al. (2014)'s study also sheds light on many other aspect of mobile industry. For example, they apply the analysis to three choice levels for Samsung smartphones: mobile phone level (Samsung Note II), higher brand-tier level (Samsung high-end phones), and brand level (Samsung phones). They find that 6.0% networks exhibit social influence for Samsung Note II adoption, 12.3% for Samsung high-end phone adoption, and 10.2% for Samsung brand adoption. This result is quite counterintuitive given the fact that the adoption rate for Samsung branded phones is higher than that for the Samsung high-end phones. Hu and her co-authors find significant and positive social influence effects in all three behavioral cases. Their study also empirically demonstrates that if all the friends of an individual adopt a product, then social influence increases the chances of that individual adopting the same product by 7.38 times. Moreover, the pervasive homophily effect driven by product adoption has not been observed in their study; individuals do not connect with one another just because they have the same phone.

Hu et al. (2014)'s study gives many insights for mobile device providers. For example, before companies target the right individuals, they should first target the right networks. In addition, adoption rate and social influence are two separate concepts and they do not necessarily correlate with each other. Lastly, companies should develop some network-level customer acquisition strategies before targeting the individual customers.

CONCLUSION

In this chapter, the author gives a review of network-based targeting techniques for mobile industry. Emphasis is given to models which utilize big data applications. The author opens the chapter by explaining the concept of targeting and its importance. In mobile industry, there are two targeting goals: to target customers who are likely to churn and to target customers who are likely to adopt a new product. The main body of this chapter reviews churn prediction models and product diffusion models separately. Churn prediction models are used for targeting churning customers for mobile service providers. Product diffusion models are used to target potential buyers for mobile device providers. The network-based analysis of such targeting process is emphasized by the author. The author uses Hu et al. (2015) to explain network-based churn analysis. Network-based diffusion analysis is illustrated by introducing the work of Hu et al. (2014). Both of the two studies incorporate network-level analysis to investigate consumer behaviors.

The future research direction in mobile industry targeting is to refine the micro-level agent-based models and incorporate network-level analysis into them. Furthermore, big data techniques such as machine learning can be utilized to predict consumer behaviors. Lastly, developments in behavioral economics and psychology can be borrowed to analyze the decision making process of the consumers.

REFERENCES

Au, W. H., Chan, K. C., & Yao, X. (2003). A novel evolutionary data mining algorithm with applications to churn prediction. *IEEE Transactions on Evolutionary Computation*, 7(6), 532–545. doi:10.1109/TEVC.2003.819264

Bass, F. M. (1969). A new product growth model for consumer durables. *Management Science*, 15(1), 215–227. doi:10.1287/mnsc.15.5.215

Berry, M. J., & Linoff, G. S. (2004). *Data mining techniques: for marketing, sales, and customer relationship management*. John Wiley & Sons.

Bin, L., Peiji, S., & Juan, L. (2007, June). Customer churn prediction based on the decision tree in personal handyphone system service. In *Service Systems and Service Management, 2007 International Conference on* (pp. 1-5). IEEE. doi:10.1109/ICSSSM.2007.4280145

Borshchev, A., & Filippov, A. (2004, July). From system dynamics and discrete event to practical agent based modeling: reasons, techniques, tools. *Proceedings of the 22nd international conference of the system dynamics society*, 22.

Breiman, L., Friedman, J., Stone, C. J., & Olshen, R. A. (1984). *Classification and regression trees*. CRC Press.

Cantono, S., & Silverberg, G. (2009). A percolation model of eco-innovation diffusion: The relationship between diffusion, learning economies and subsidies. *Technological Forecasting and Social Change*, 76(4), 487–496. doi:10.1016/j.techfore.2008.04.010

Chen, M. S., Han, J., & Yu, P. S. (1996). Data mining: An overview from a database perspective. *Knowledge and data Engineering. IEEE Transactions on*, 8(6), 866–883.

Dasgupta, K., Singh, R., Viswanathan, B., Chakraborty, D., Mukherjea, S., Nanavati, A. A., & Joshi, A. (2008, March). Social ties and their relevance to churn in mobile telecom networks. In *Proceedings of the 11th international conference on Extending database technology: Advances in database technology* (pp. 668-677). ACM. doi:10.1145/1353343.1353424

Domingos, P. (1999). The role of Occams razor in knowledge discovery. *Data Mining and Knowledge Discovery*, *3*(4), 409–425. doi:10.1023/A:1009868929893

Eiben, A. E., Koudijs, A. E., & Slisser, F. (1998). Genetic modelling of customer retention. In *Genetic Programming* (pp. 178–186). Springer Berlin Heidelberg. doi:10.1007/BFb0055937

Entner, R. (2011, June 23). *International comparisons: the handset replacement cycle.* Retrieved from http://mobilefuture.org/wp-content/uploads/2013/02/mobile-future.publications.handset-replacement-cycle.pdf

Fibich, G., & Gibori, R. I. (2010). Aggregate diffusion dynamics in agent-based models with a spatial structure. *Operations Research*, *58*(5), 1450–1468. doi:10.1287/opre.1100.0818

Fisher, J. C., & Pry, R. H. (1972). A simple substitution model of technological change. *Technological Forecasting and Social Change*, *3*, 75–88. doi:10.1016/S0040-1625(71)80005-7

Fourt, L. A., & Woodlock, J. W. (1960). Early prediction of market success for new grocery products. *Journal of Marketing*, *25*(2), 31–38. doi:10.2307/1248608

Goldenberg, J., Libai, B., & Muller, E. (2001). Using complex systems analysis to advance marketing theory development: Modeling heterogeneity effects on new product growth through stochastic cellular automata. *Academy of Marketing Science Review*, *9*(3), 1–18.

Hohnisch, M., Pittnauer, S., & Stauffer, D. (2008). A percolation-based model explaining delayed takeoff in new-product diffusion. *Industrial and Corporate Change*, *17*(5), 1001–1017. doi:10.1093/icc/dtn031

Hong Kong Government. (2015). *Hong Kong: The Facts.* Retrieved from http://www.gov.hk/en/about/abouthk/factsheets/docs/telecommunications.pdf

Hosmer, D. W. Jr, & Lemeshow, S. (2004). *Applied logistic regression.* John Wiley & Sons.

Hu, M., Hsieh, C., & Jia, J. (2014). *The effectiveness of peer influence and network structure: an application using mobile data.* Working Paper.

Hu, M., Yang, S., & Xu, Y. (2015). *Social Learning and Network Effects in Contagious Switching Behavior.* Working Paper.

Hung, S. Y., Yen, D. C., & Wang, H. Y. (2006). Applying data mining to telecom churn management. *Expert Systems with Applications*, *31*(3), 515–524. doi:10.1016/j.eswa.2005.09.080

International Data Corporation. (2015). *Smartphone Vendor Market Share, Q1 2015.* Retrieved from http://www.idc.com/prodserv/smartphone-market-share.jsp

International Telecommunication Union. (2015). *World 2015.* Retrieved from http://www.itu.int/en/ITU-D/Statistics/Documents/facts/ICTFactsFigures2015.pdf

Iyengar, R., Van den Bulte, C., & Lee, J. Y. (2015). Social contagion in new product trial and repeat. *Marketing Science*, *34*(3), 408–429. doi:10.1287/mksc.2014.0888

Iyengar, R., Van den Bulte, C., & Valente, T. W. (2011). Opinion leadership and social contagion in new product diffusion. *Marketing Science*, *30*(2), 195–212. doi:10.1287/mksc.1100.0566

Jain, A. K., Murty, M. N., & Flynn, P. J. (1999). Data clustering: A review. *ACM Computing Surveys*, *31*(3), 264–323. doi:10.1145/331499.331504

Kass, G. V. (1980). An exploratory technique for investigating large quantities of categorical data. *Applied Statistics*, *29*(2), 119–127. doi:10.2307/2986296

Katz, M. L., & Shapiro, C. (1985). Network externalities, competition, and compatibility. *The American Economic Review*, 424–440.

Kiesling, E., Günther, M., Stummer, C., & Wakolbinger, L. M. (2012). Agent-based simulation of innovation diffusion: A review. *Central European Journal of Operations Research*, *20*(2), 183–230. doi:10.1007/s10100-011-0210-y

Kisioglu, P., & Topcu, Y. I. (2011). Applying Bayesian Belief Network approach to customer churn analysis: A case study on the telecom industry of Turkey. *Expert Systems with Applications*, *38*(6), 7151–7157. doi:10.1016/j.eswa.2010.12.045

Kocsis, G., & Kun, F. (2008). The effect of network topologies on the spreading of technological developments. *Journal of Statistical Mechanics*, *2008*(10), P10014. doi:10.1088/1742-5468/2008/10/P10014

Kohonen, T. (1987). Adaptive, associative, and self-organizing functions in neural computing. *Applied Optics*, *26*(23), 4910–4918. doi:10.1364/AO.26.004910 PMID:20523469

Langley, P., Iba, W., & Thompson, K. (1992, July). *An analysis of Bayesian classifiers* (Vol. 90). AAAI.

Lazarov, V., & Capota, M. (2007). *Churn prediction*. Bus. Anal. Course. TUM Comput. Sci.

Lemmens, A., & Croux, C. (2006). Bagging and boosting classification trees to predict churn. *JMR, Journal of Marketing Research*, *43*(2), 276–286. doi:10.1509/jmkr.43.2.276

Mahajan, V., & Muller, E. (1979). Innovation diffusion and new product growth models in marketing. *Journal of Marketing*, *43*(4), 55–68. doi:10.2307/1250271

Mahajan, V., Muller, E., & Bass, F. M. (1990). New product diffusion models in marketing: A review and directions for research. *Journal of Marketing*, *54*(1), 1–26. doi:10.2307/1252170

Manchanda, P., Xie, Y., & Youn, N. (2008). The role of targeted communication and contagion in product adoption. *Marketing Science*, *27*(6), 961–976. doi:10.1287/mksc.1070.0354

Mansfield, E. (1961). Technical change and the rate of imitation. *Econometrica*, *29*(4), 741–766. doi:10.2307/1911817

Masand, B., Datta, P., Mani, D. R., & Li, B. (1999). CHAMP: A prototype for automated cellular churn prediction. *Data Mining and Knowledge Discovery*, *3*(2), 219–225. doi:10.1023/A:1009873905876

Moretti, E. (2011). Social learning and peer effects in consumption: Evidence from movie sales. *The Review of Economic Studies*, *78*(1), 356–393. doi:10.1093/restud/rdq014

Nambiar, R., & Poess, M. (2011). Transaction performance vs. Moore's law: a trend analysis. In Performance Evaluation, Measurement and Characterization of Complex Systems (pp. 110-120). Springer Berlin Heidelberg.

Narayan, V., Rao, V. R., & Saunders, C. (2011). How peer influence affects attribute preferences: A Bayesian updating mechanism. *Marketing Science*, *30*(2), 368–384. doi:10.1287/mksc.1100.0618

Nath, S. V., & Behara, R. S. (2003, November). Customer churn analysis in the wireless industry: A data mining approach. *Proceedings-annual meeting of the decision sciences institute*, 505-510.

Neslin, S. A., Gupta, S., Kamakura, W., Lu, J., & Mason, C. H. (2006). Defection detection: Measuring and understanding the predictive accuracy of customer churn models. *JMR, Journal of Marketing Research*, *43*(2), 204–211. doi:10.1509/jmkr.43.2.204

Ngai, E. W., Xiu, L., & Chau, D. C. (2009). Application of data mining techniques in customer relationship management: A literature review and classification. *Expert Systems with Applications*, *36*(2), 2592–2602. doi:10.1016/j.eswa.2008.02.021

Office of the Communications Authority. (2015). Table 3: Telecommunications Services. In *Key Communications Statistics*. Retrieved from http://www.ofca.gov.hk/en/media_focus/data_statistics/key_stat/

Peres, R., Muller, E., & Mahajan, V. (2010). Innovation diffusion and new product growth models: A critical review and research directions. *International Journal of Research in Marketing*, *27*(2), 91–106. doi:10.1016/j.ijresmar.2009.12.012

Quinlan, J. R. (2014). *C4. 5: programs for machine learning*. Elsevier.

Rahmandad, H., & Sterman, J. (2008). Heterogeneity and network structure in the dynamics of diffusion: Comparing agent-based and differential equation models. *Management Science*, *54*(5), 998–1014. doi:10.1287/mnsc.1070.0787

Rogers, E. M. (1962). *The Diffusion of Innovations*. New York, NY: Free Press.

Rogers, E. M. (2010). *Diffusion of innovations*. Simon and Schuster.

Saylor, J. (2004, Oct 11). *The Missing Link in CRM: Customer Acquisition Management*. Retrieved from http://www.destinationcrm.com/Articles/Web-Exclusives/Viewpoints/The-Missing-Link-in-CRM-Customer-Acquisition-Management-44024.aspx

Schmittlein, D. C., & Mahajan, V. (1982). Maximum likelihood estimation for an innovation diffusion model of new product acceptance. *Marketing Science*, *1*(1), 57–78. doi:10.1287/mksc.1.1.57

Snijders, T., Steglich, C., & Schweinberger, M. (2007). Modeling the coevolution of networks and behavior. Academic Press.

Snijders, T. A. (1996). Stochastic actor - oriented models for network change. *The Journal of Mathematical Sociology*, *21*(1-2), 149–172. doi:10.1080/0022250X.1996.9990178

Snijders, T. A. (2001). The statistical evaluation of social network dynamics. *Sociological Methodology*, *31*(1), 361–395. doi:10.1111/0081-1750.00099

Srinivasan, V., & Mason, C. H. (1986). Technical note-nonlinear least squares estimation of new product diffusion models. *Marketing Science*, *5*(2), 169–178. doi:10.1287/mksc.5.2.169

Tsai, C. F., & Lu, Y. H. (2009). Customer churn prediction by hybrid neural networks. *Expert Systems with Applications*, *36*(10), 12547–12553. doi:10.1016/j.eswa.2009.05.032

Ultsch, A. (2002). Emergent self-organising feature maps used for prediction and prevention of churn in mobile phone markets. *Journal of Targeting, Measurement and Analysis for Marketing*, *10*(4), 314–324. doi:10.1057/palgrave.jt.5740056

Van den Bulte, C., & Lilien, G. L. (2001). Medical innovation revisited: Social contagion versus marketing effort. *American Journal of Sociology*, *106*(5), 1409–1435. doi:10.1086/320819

Van den Poel, D., & Lariviere, B. (2004). Customer attrition analysis for financial services using proportional hazard models. *European Journal of Operational Research*, *157*(1), 196–217. doi:10.1016/S0377-2217(03)00069-9

Von Neumann, J., & Burks, A. W. (1966). Theory of self-reproducing automata. *IEEE Transactions on Neural Networks*, *5*(1), 3–14.

Wei, C. P., & Chiu, I. T. (2002). Turning telecommunications call details to churn prediction: A data mining approach. *Expert Systems with Applications*, *23*(2), 103–112. doi:10.1016/S0957-4174(02)00030-1

KEY TERMS AND DEFINITIONS

Churn: In mobile industry, churn means to discontinue the contract with the current operator.

Customer Acquisition: To obtain new customers.

Customer Retention: To keep existing customers from switching to other companies.

Network Structure: Topological properties of the network.

Product Diffusion: The process of a new product accepted by the market.

Social Network: The social structure in which individuals are connected with each other according to their communication patterns or other social rules.

Targeting: In marketing context, targeting means to choose a particular group of customers based on their characteristics.

This research was previously published in Big Data Applications in the Telecommunications Industry edited by Ye Ouyang and Mantian Hu, pages 78-107, copyright year 2017 by Information Science Reference (an imprint of IGI Global).

Chapter 26
Financial Implications of Relationship Marketing in Airline Business

Hasan Dinçer
Istanbul Medipol University, Turkey

Ümit Hacıoğlu
Istanbul Medipol University, Turkey

Aydın Özdemir
Beykent University, Turkey

ABSTRACT

Relationship marketing promises a change from vendor, product and price centered marketing concept to a new people, long-term relationships and value centered marketing concept for airline companies in search of a messiah who will rescue them from bleeding to death because of monopolized supply market, duplicated services, financial crises, heavy pressure of competition and low profit margins. In this chapter, definitions and short background of relationship marketing are revised by focusing on components of the concept and relations with customer loyalty, customer value and basic notions. A glance at the airline industry takes place with a focus on relationship marketing and airline business on the basis of implication aspects such as frequent flyer programs, global distribution systems and internet. Specifically, domains of relationship marketing concept on the airline business are analyzed in detail specific to cost and profitability balance.

INTRODUCTION

Technological change brought by globalization, the pressure of population growth, inflation, and hard competition have forced companies to stand strong and sustain their activities in the middle of a high flow rate. In order to stand strong in the middle of this flow rate, companies have to strengthen their roots which are their customers.

DOI: 10.4018/978-1-5225-5187-4.ch026

While in the beginning of the century production was the center of industrialization in 1900's the center of companies turned into sales. In 1950s companies started to diversify their marketing applications and marketing centered companies started to appear. 1990s was the beginning of new experience in other words the beginning of customer era. (Palmatier, 2008, p.12). Nevertheless, increase in diversity of service and goods, distribution, dazzling increase in price and communication opportunities and hard competition conditions increased the amount of accessibility for service and goods for all income levels. Competition caused by goods and service inflation has increased the quality of goods and service relation in this area. It is very common to reach and experience desired goods easily both by virtual or real communication channels. In this marketing atmosphere formed by conditions that we stated above customers desire to buy the feeling of "satisfaction". Customers replaced the meaning of goods and service. Therefore marketing has to take customer relations into consideration instead of goods and service (Kotler& Keller, 2009, p.14).

It is very difficult for companies to find new customers in global arena, besides losing their customers is a matter of life and death for them. Looking from another aspect, it means that if companies want to have more advantages than the others it depends on their long life relationship with their customers. Today's business world is based on relationship with customers not the operations. All these marketing conditions have changed and evolved marketing literature, so relationship marketing has taken over. (Payne, Christopher, Clark, & Peck, 1999)

Marketing success of companies is related to their customer relations and their ability to be different from their competitors. Considered from this aspect the strategy of having long life relationship with customers and relationship marketing has become the center of marketing strategies. Relationship marketing which puts customers in the center of marketing takes customer loyalty as the most important factor for profitability. It is accepted that value given to customers and their loyalty will give competitive priority to companies in long term period. Gummesson describes this new process as "interaction and joint value creation" (Gummesson, 2002).

Relationship marketing is not a program to be implied in current marketing programs; on the other hand it means change in whole business strategies. Basically, trust and relations web which have been main principles of trade in eastern societies are applied to western trade principals which are based on distrust and solid engagement. (Gummesson, 2002) Product and seller based trade and marketing have lost power in nowadays world. Companies started to explore and institutionalize customer centered marketing which was taken from eastern societies.

The purpose of this article is to put the clock back the formula which has a potential of creating customer retention, customer loyalty and customer value and as result of this chain is to create profitability for airlines. As a result, according to Berry's expression "the spirit and heart of relations marketing is based on customers when they become customers" (Gruen, 1995, p.449).

1. BASIC PRINCIPALS OF RELATIONS MARKETING

1.1 Definitions of Relations Marketing

Relations marketing showed up in 1980s and still it doesn't have a generally accepted definition. There are several reasons of not having a proper definition of relations marketing. The reasons are not theoretical or practical inadequate but it is because of diversity and multifunctional structure of relations based marketing (Grönroos, 1994).

Direct marketing which was applied for centuries was replaced after industrial revolution with such a solid and mechanical marketing perception. After this change, human factor was redefined and imprisoned in specific roles. After industrial revolution, technology, individualization and internet revolution started to shape relations marketing by putting human factor into the center of focus (O'Malley &Tynan, 2000).

During this formalization period Bagozzi in 1975 open a discussion about relations marketing by putting "change (mutual communication)" into center of its definition (Man, 1998). Berry outlines service marketing and how to have long life customer relations and how to improve and develop them (Man, 1998, p.10).

- Finding a basic product or service to build customer relation,
- Adjusting the relation according to individual customers,
- Enriching the basic product or service,
- Pricing strategies to increase customer loyalty,
- Marketing for employees, employee satisfaction.

According to Grönroos who is taken as a reference nowadays business relation is mutual relation on both customer and company side and it is profitable for both sides. This mutual relation should be built and sustained with the intention of profit making for both sides. Grönroos, additionally to customers he puts B2B, distribution channels, employees, and competitors into relations perspective. In relations marketing, he also points that all departments of a company have to work in harmony. (Grönroos, 1994).

While Gummesson, who works on the subject, defines relations marketing as a long term relationship between seller and customer, he associates it with profitability. Another definition by Gummesson for relationship marketing is based on interactivity by relations and web network. He is the first person to state and offer that marketing relations should be put on an order according to their priorities (Gummesson, 2002).

According to Morgen and Hunt (1981) all activities in order to establish, maintain and develop successful business relations are relationship marketing. They put at the center trust which leads to cooperative and productive relations (Morris, Brunyee, & Page, 1998).

Among all mentioned definitions first time Manroe (1991) stated the "value of exchange" and formulated customer value by distributing value into cost per customer. Manroe interested in what customer gives to company and cost of it, simply (Dodds, Monroe, & Grewal, 1991).

Ravald and Grönroos mostly studied on time concept in relationship marketing and focused on effect of time on creating value. They argue repeated relations in time create customer value. With a wider scope, Evans and Laskin focuses on relationship marketing as creating service partnerships, supporting employees, total quality management and by using all these assets to create customer satisfaction, loyalty and profit increase (Ravald & Grönroos, 1996).

Despite all efforts and definitions are made in time are far from to create a common and de facto definition, yet. As in the given statistics in Figure 1, intangibility of the term is certified by the rareness of the words agreed on. However, most common explanation is focusing on retention of customers. ŞükranKaraca's extensive definition shines out because of facing implication of the concept. She builds its definition creating value by promise, trust, loyalty, and retaining this value for long run (Karaca, 2010).

Figure 1. Content analysis of definitions of relations
Source: Morris, Brunyee, & Page, 1998, p.361.

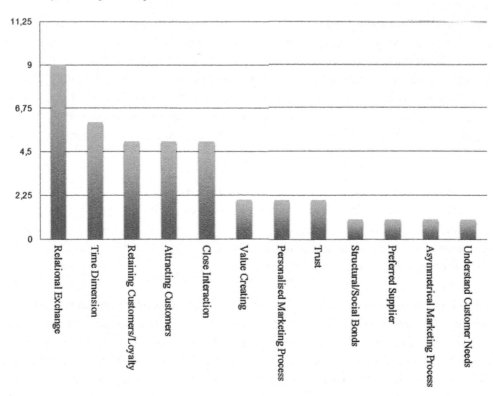

Consequently, relationship marketing is a concept aims to reduce costs and creating value, creating, maintaining long run relationships on a continuous win-win balance. In other words relationship marketing is a kind of consciousness that points how to gather all pieces currently on the stage but not used productively.

1.2 Relationship Marketing in Pieces

It is essential to understand components of relationship marketing content of the definition. Even in the definition of the term there is no consensus yet, however 6 elements which concept consists of had a general acceptance. Morgan and Hunt firstly stated these 6 elements but the last version which has a general acceptance was created by Sin and Tse. A company who accepts relationship marketing concept should invest on these areas shown in Figure 2 (Morgan & Hunt, 1994; Sin, Tse, Yau, Chow, Lee, &Lorett, 2005).

Between company and customer the first condition is trust. Not only in relationship marketing but also in all relational subjects of marketing trust has a big reputation. Although it has an abstract connotation, with very simple scales and surveys it can be measured and be converted into solid numbers (Sin, Tse, Yau, Chow, Lee, & Lorett, 2005).

Bonding or commitment rise upon trust and common aims and benefits between organization and customers. Communication both formal and informal with all possible channels is a company's weapon

Figure 2. Components of relationship marketing
Source: Sin, Tse, Yau, Chow, Lee, & Lorett, 2005, p.187.

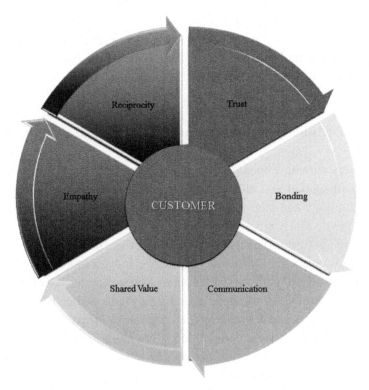

of attack and also defense, besides it's a pool where a company must pour its investments. Companies should invest this area in all possible ways. Shared values, are agreements between company and the customer on what is important to not, or what is true or not. Empathy is another concept that must be institutionalized and must accepted as the judge of relations or any problems that may rise among company and customer. Reciprocity is a value, must place instead of company centered marketing concept. Reciprocity must find its meaning in last few years and became a buzzword as "win-win" (Sin, Tse, Yau, Chow, Lee, & Lorett, 2005).

All six components, discussed above are also can be used as scales of relationship marketing application. Moreover it is a compass for companies how to distribute its marketing resources or they are elements a marketing campaign must include in order to be named as a relationship marketing campaign.

1.3 Relationship Marketing and Customer Loyalty

Creating and maintaining long and beneficial relations mostly thought with customer loyalty and customer satisfaction is also accepted as the first step of it. Because there is a general opinion that customer satisfaction triggers purchasing behavior and this opinion mostly true but a dozen of researched shows that customers can defect without a distinction weather satisfied or not. Variety of alternatives, price and some other must take into consideration (Payne, Christopher, Clark, & Peck, 1999).

It is very clear that customer loyalty increases customers' relation time with the company and lowers price sensibility and also feedback of these customers have positive effect on development of product or processes. This overlap with relationship marketing makes it more valuable. For instance, Sheraton hotels spend 50 million dollars for its loyalty program per year (Karaca, 2010).

A survey on customer loyalty made by Jones and Sasser shows that if defection cost for customer is low only loyal customers stays loyal. As a result of this research customers are classified according to their loyalty levels and purchasing behaviors. Metaphors that authors use really reflect the function of groups well (Jones & Sasser, 1995).

1. **Apostles:** Loyal customers, volunteered brand ambassadors, triggers of word-of-mouth.
2. **Mercenaries:** Price sensibility is high, loyal as long as satisfied, always in expectation from the company.
3. **Hostages:** Customers who have to stay loyal because defection cost is high. Satisfaction is low.
4. **Terrorists:** Aware of market and alternatives well. Seize every opportunity and in seek of new opportunities. Technology addicted and very high in using internet in daily life.

Relationship marketing also uses criteria of price sensibility and price incentives for customer loyalty. For instance, FFPs rewards customers with free flight tickets, extra luggage rights, lounge etc. but as long as customers buy from the company. Social relations are one another way to build customer loyalty (Leick, 2007). For example, banks or cell phone operators assign a dedicated staff for same customers. They address customer by name and celebrated special days and anniversaries. This method is effective mostly in market and some products were competition is not much dense.

Customer satisfaction, customer value, and customer loyalty terms have the biggest share in application of relationship marketing. These functions also have very simple measurements and can be tracked by surveys any time moreover these results will be a compass for relationship marketing. Rewarding mechanism inside organizations must be placed on results of these scales. For example Kentucky fried Chicken restaurants rewards branch managers who had high scores of customer satisfaction by 35% net salary increase each month (Karaca, 2010).

Airlines should lead all other sectors by designing measurements for each step of service. From reservation to airport check-in and to the end of flight every step must have own assessment channels. Today some airlines has such applications, while you buy a ticket at the end of reservation a small survey exists on the internet page or if the channel is call-center at the end of conversation they forward

Figure 3. Building value of customer
Source: Adapted from Kotler, Marketing Management, Millennium Edition, 2000, p.35.

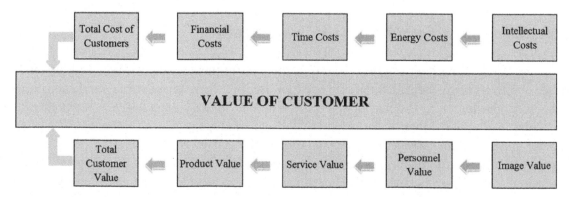

you for another survey (Belobaba, Odoni, & Barnhart, 2009). During the flight with a form on board or inside the airlines' magazine, or on entertainment system screen or within mobile applications customers forced to step up scale. Without omitting a step in all levels development and enhancements are done. Companies not only have to provide customer satisfaction and loyalty but also must reward customers for their complaints, and feedbacks (Taneja, 2010).

1.4 Stages of Development

For years, exchange is accepted as the core of marketing but it is clear that the relationship between seller and the consumer do not end with it. When global oil crisis rose in 1970s, energy cost of companies reflected to prices and companies could manage to survive with deep wounds. Customer retention notion was very popular in those years (Egan, 2011).

Term is used by Berry first in 1983 and focused on making customer relations attractive, developing and maintaining (Berry, 1983, 2000, 2002).

Grönroos and Gummeson defined the term "defining relations with customers, establishing, maintaining and increasing" (Grönroos, 1994).

Years after WWII market boom was only on manufacturing, selling and face to face or one toone marketing.1960s industrial markets, relations increased intellectual and practical experience of marketing. By 1970s' highly political atmosphere, focused came on non-governmental organizations but with 1980s markets meet the word globalism and global markets, management of diversities. Besides service sector became "in" but when in 1990s' marketing concept's mechanical and product centered structure disturbed "human" factor (Gummesson, 2002; Alabay, 2010; Selvi, 2007; Palmatier, 2008).

From 1950s to current day the center of marketing has changed from product to organization itself and finally back to people again. Just like the concept of market also customer concept is changed too much. Today's customers are well educated, demanding, suspicious, and have no mercy for waiting or time loss (Arslan, 2008).

Third and most determinant chance is on technology and namely internet. Internet is just like a new marketing karma which bring all classical and relational marketing elements together. Today people, product, promotion, price and more all in the internet and the internet himself.

Consequently, relationship marketing had six stages until today starting with Berry, Grönroos and Gummeson's approach mostly from service sector point of view and second stage where focused was on mostly inter organization relations mostly in 1980s. With the third stage effective and productive relations started to be discussed lately network of relations term added to the concept and with the fifth stage relations role started to be discussed in value chain (Berry, 1995; Grönroos, 1994).Sixth stage is going to be the merge of internet and all past experiences.

1.5 Purposes of Relationship Marketing

Relationship marketing aims to create values which make customers loyal and guarantee profit in long run. Relationship marketing concept accepts fixed production overhead as opportunities to build and maintain relationships. At the very beginning, relationship marketing should aim to define and group customers who produce net profit and who does not, which will point "right" customers for the airline. In other words, Relationship marketing orientation must have a well prepared scale to group customers according to why they should stay and go, who they are and what they produce and at the bottom line what is the lifetime value for the company (Gilbert, 1996; Selvi, 2007).

In today's market conditions, average customer defection rate is defined as 10%. Relationship marketing can help organization to find out which customers are inclined to leave and why. So, organization can decide how to keep and lock the customers in (Man, 1998).

Relationship marketing gives importance to customer share instead of market share and so gives companies a new type of measurement of success (Şendur, 2009). From this point of view objectives of relationship marketing are defined as (Selvi, 2007, pp.33-46).

- Customer retention, finding new markets and customers,
- Establishing cooperation's,
- Increase service quality,
- Ensure customer satisfaction,
- Increase net profit,
- Establish trust,
- Long term customer relations.

Copulsky and Wolf explains objectives of relationship marketing is a combination of direct marketing, CRM, sales promotions, advertisement in order reach high profit rates by gaining customer retention, satisfaction, loyalty (Copulsky & Wolf, 1990; Voss & Voss, 1997).

1.6 Types of Relationship Marketing

Types of Relationship Marketing vary according to point of view just as the definition of it. If it is considered as a strategy, the ideal approach will be to apply different marketing applications according to product and market segmentation. Rowe and Barnes popularize relationship marketing strategies into four main categories (Rowe & Barnes, 1998, p.288).

1. **Locking Customers In:** Organization must use all marketing resources and benefits in order to build strong relationships with customers but control of relationships are still in the hands of organization. Organization builds high walls to lock customer in by creating high costs for customer defection.
2. **Customer Retention:** Same focus with the previous item but this strategy indicates to place resources in order to keep profitable customers in.
3. **Database Marketing:** Indicates placing resources in order to a list which is formed by a database research. The main focus of this database work should be on characteristics and choices of customers.
4. **Strong, Close, and Positive Relations:** Apart from one-way and single channel communications this strategy indicates to build multi-channel and interactive relations.

Except from the last one, all strategies given above are organization centered or flow of the relations is one-way such as from organization to customer. Besides, in these first three strategies organization is the center and benefit of the company is underlined. Only the last strategy depends on win-win situation. The thing must be discussed is not the superiority of any one but advantages and special usage areas of each one has. It has to be considered which one is used at which level (Rowe & Barnes, 1998). For instance, customer retention is ideal for cost reduction.

Gummeson has a simpler and definition centered classification that he divides strategy into three (Gummesson, 1998, p.243):

1. **Market Relations:** Relations work in market, mostly likely relations with customer-seller, competitors etc. environments.
2. **Mega Market Relations:** Social relations' level which are built with authorities, media etc.
3. **Nano Marketing Relations:** Organization level relations which are conducted with employees.

Gummeson's classification approaches relationship marketing as the management of sales, society, market and organizational relations. Zineldin has created a more quality based strategy mostly depends on customer satisfaction, long term profitability and other environments such as banks, vendors to create "5Q" approach. (Zineldin, 2000, p. 24).

Q1 Product Quality: Quality of product or service with a technical point of view which is "what" a customer buys from the organization actually.

Q2 Process Quality: Functional quality of "how" a customer buys a product or service from the organization.

Q3 Infrastructure Quality: Exchange of information, experience, know-how, technology and motivation.

Q4 Interaction Quality: Interactional relations consists of information, financial assets etc.

Q5 Environment Quality: Environment which parties operate and in cooperation. The quality of this environment has a direct impact on quality of organization and customer relationships.

Concisely, Zineldin builds relationship marketing types on a set of inner organization relations, customer satisfaction, process improvements and employee satisfaction. Likewise, Zineldin gives responsibility in organization to every unit and individual for all these five strategies (Zineldin, 2000).

Gruen has drawn attention to a different spot and the distinction between B2B and B2C market environments. Gruen defines relationship marketing in B2B markets as "partnership" and in B2C markets as "membership" (Gruen, 1995).Considering airline business these definitions finds well its equivalent as FFP's.

1.7 From Kotlerism to Relationship Marketing

Traditional or classic marketing concept is designed mostly to achieve goals set by the seller side. This concept underestimates customer behaviors, away from interaction and puts customer in a position that needs to be managed or shepherd. On the other hand, relationship marketing estimates a transformation from so-called Kotlerist approach which is short-term, seller centered, to a new form of marketing which is long term relations (Zineldin & Philipson, 2007).

Kotlerist marketing concept can be described as hunter-gatherer era of marketing where movement and continuous search for new markets and customers is a matter of survival. So popular cliché of "swim or sink" fits here well (Kotler, 2000; Kotler & Keller, 2009; Kumar, Scheer, & Kotler, 2000). Simple measurement of this concept is sales increase rates besides except from sales, all other facilities and services of the organization are accepted as auxiliary and cost producers. Going through the same metaphor, relationship marketing can be described as settled land or early agricultural era of mankind. Relationship marketing is settled and trying to produce maximum benefit from a pre-defined land. In order to survive hunters are still active but some farmers also trying to domesticate captured preys. Performance measurement of this concept is rate of customer retention and return of investments. Main purpose of this era is to create customers who are always profitable, stable and loyal to the organization (Grönroos, 1994).

Classic concepts puts customer in a passive position where he has to accept offered 4P of marketing or deny. The entire role he has in this process is limited by choosing. Considering the post war era environment where this concept was born it can be accepted as reasonable but in today's internet shaped limitless market atmosphere it is now insufficient. In order to resolve this insufficiency, new elements were added by theoreticians such as "people", "physical environment" and "Process". Today it is almost accepted as classic concept with "8P" of marketing. Yet, new addings were not to cover today's needs "4C" (consumer, cost, communication, convenience) concept was born in the hands of Robert F. Lauterborn (Schultz, Tannenbaum, & Robert, 1993).

Focusing on each element of 4P concept it can be pictured the transformation (Figure 4). Product element can be match-up with customer value in relationship marketing where product or service has to create also a value for the customer. Customer Cost in classical 4P concept is accepted as the reciprocity of price which is providing the best priced service or product customer demands (Alabay, 2010).

Convenience for the customer stands for distribution element in 4C concept and can be formulated as getting the right product or service in right time to the right customers. Customer communication can be replaced with Promotion element in 4C concept. Customer communication means informing customers instead of convincing them, briefly (Schultz, Tannenbaum, & Robert, 1993).

One another concept is customer relations which relationship marketing put forward. It is commonly accepted that in today's market place it is not possible to create competitive advantages or differentiate by product or service itself (Hennig-Thurau, Gwinner, & Gremler, 2002). In todays' market conditions only way to differentiate is customer centered approaches. To be explained in detail, it can be possible by segmenting customers into micro sectors, than to create value by products or services according to their demands and creating interactive relations with customers that will build long and beneficial relationships for both sides. This formula can be offered as the new form of profit maximization. It should

Figure 4. Change of marketing concepts

Figure 5. Difference approaches to marketing concept
Source: Gummesson, Making Relationship Operational, 1994, p.9.

be kept in the mind always that relationship marketing based upon relations which will cover all life cycle of customer. Relationship marketing requires "special" relations instead of "good "relations like the one in 4P concept (Gruen, 1995).

While traditional marketing is focused on finding new customers and market share, relationship marketing is focused on customer retention and putting all organization resources to provide this. On the other hand, 4P concept is sharpened by competition while relationship marketing puts spot on co-operation and win-win situations. Traditional marketing gives particular importance on seller's needs and demands, but relationship marketing prioritise customers' needs and demands. It is the product or service in 4P concept which shapes marketing activities as in relationship marketing it is customer and customer value (Selvi, 2007).

As a result of comparing old and new concepts of marketing, it can be sum up relationship marketing seeks for creating new values for customers, who are not the people who buys but also who defines the value. Relationship marketing points all life time trade of customers not the short time purchases. Relationship marketing changed the center of gravity of marketing from seller to the customer, in other words from product to relations, from competition to cooperation (Table 1).

1.8 Relationship Marketing as a Competitive Advantage?

In new economic environment, customer who had freedom and power is now more demanding and asking relations from organizations. This also means that Kotlerist concept of marketing is not valid anymore (Sindell, 2000).

Competitive advantage mostly comes in sight when an organization finds out a creative strategy and application which opponents do not apply. In other words competitive advantage strategies Works until opponents imitate them. What make a strategy valuable are its effects on profitability, utilizing opportunities within or out of organization environment and cost cutting effects. Remembering "locking in

Table 1. From 4P to relationship marketing

Marketing Mix (4P)	Relationship Marketing
One-way	Interactive
On-and-off Communication	Continuous Communication
Product Centered	Customer Centered
Quality is for Quality Department	Quality is for All
Competition	Cooperation
Price	Value

Source: Adapted from Selvi, 2007, p.23.

strategy" previously stated where customers stays in and avoid of defection not to pay for finding new sources and new relationships (Rowe & Barnes, 1998).

If marketing here underlines "defection obstacles" and increases cost of defection. FFP which airlines are using for years can be the best example. In order to gain points and free flight tickets customers stays in the system but this application lost its top place on the list as a competitive advantage for year ago. It is not only imitated but also became a "standard" for all airlines even for a small carrier who has few aircrafts also has its own FFP program. So, imitation has a very destructive power. IBM applied locking customers in strategy for years. Customers could not break out even if they are not happy with product or services and stayed loyal involuntarily. However, this relationship has destroyed by entrance of new competitors into the market with similar product and services, as result of this IBM in 1993 had a dive from peak to the bottom and company market value fall from 106 million dollar to 30 Million dollar (Rowe & Barnes, 1998).

Customer retention strategy underlines the cost of retention of current customers instead of cost of finding new customers. Organizations especially who has direct access to retail market keep records of their customers in detail such as communication information, some personnel information etc. in order to create tools in marketing activities (Rowe & Barnes, 1998).

Even if it seems as a very strong competitive advantage for organizations to use these databases and create customized products and services for their customers due to its R&D and application costs it can be used by very few companies. Producing a product or service in small amounts means high cost rate per unit. According to airlines who serve millions of customers each year this is also another challenge to apply strategy (Kanagal, 2005).

All strategies stated has both advantages and disadvantages but is there a strategy which will be close, stable and creating benefit for both sides, moreover could this strategy can be a competitive advantage?

Consequently, creating a customized strategy which will be a response to this question shall have high and costly barriers of customer defection, second has a wide and detailed database of customers where keeps all necessary to support marketing efforts. Third, top management of organization must build strong and close relations with the units and individuals who have direct contact with customers. Considering airline business, check-in staff, cabin attendants, and call centers can best examples. As the last, organization must develop benefits and positive surprises for customers randomly. It is for sure that such a marketing strategy is going to lock in and retain customers also creates financial performance with reduce costs and keeps away from price competition.

1.9 Relationship Marketing Karma

Relationship marketing considered in Ceterus Paribus condition, where cultural and industrial variables are reset, rise upon six pedestals. Hansen (2000) as a reference to classical marketing karma named it as "6I" Marketing Concept. Intention, Interaction, Integration, Information, Investment, Individuality are proposed as new marketing paradigm (Karaca, 2010, p.445).

- **Information:** This element is known as also "database marketing". Today's technological potential and software availabilities with a limited afford, millions of can be processed within minutes. This opportunity gives airlines to create and customize, segmented all information it has and create micro markets as target.
- **Investment:** So called revolution in marketing actually happened in perception of customer but as the market is customer itself, it should be divided into pieces must be segmented and classified so placing an organization's resources and efforts must be conducted according to this classification. From this point of view, placing resources equally among customers will be wasting and so will cause customer defection in the end.
- **Individuality:** Relationship marketing requires having an aspect of seeing each customer as a niche market. Aside from product customizations, only applications which succeeds to make customers feel special or the product is customized for the customer.
- It is a very interesting point that airlines that serves millions of customers each year has a wide and detailed database collected from reservation systems and FFPs however very few of them have staff employed and systems to study this data and harvest useful marketing clues to feed marketing units. Airlines yet did not degrade marketing efforts from mass marketing size to individualism but in an effort to survive has to come this point soon.
- **Interaction:** Interaction also claimed as a most distinctive element between classic marketing concept and relationship marketing. Internet, mobile applications and social media tools creates a platform where multichannel, interactive, social and multi-layer communication and sharing is possible with a cheap and simple way. So this platform is no more a billboard or an option but an obligation.
- Interaction has also a meaning of communication between all layers of organization and society. This creates an opportunity gap for relationship marketing. For instance, a random Office staff's or front desk secretary's attitude can be affective more than a company worth of millions. Remembering the core of relationship marketing strategy, which was human, without limitations and prejudices enables this marketing concept work. According to latest researches of purchasing decision makers in airline business, it is surprisingly stated that even front desk personnel has an effect on to share travel budget among airlines. Because of this in previous years airlines started to offer incentives not only the travel agents but also their staff (Doganis, 2006).
- **Integration:** Communication platforms where all parties are met also provide a place to meet on a common point which is "product". Especially in B2B markets integration take place as a result of long relationship where information, experience and resources shared.
- **Intention:** Common ground of relationship marketing is named as "trust". In sales and distribution channels the message of the company and one-way dictation of messages irritate customers anymore and has a negative effect on purchasing attitude. Also, today organizations are not only

the constitutions that sell products but also have social responsibilities and environmental awareness. So, organizations have to state their intentions clear and briefly if they want to have a long time relationship.

1.10 Problems of Implication

The first and most obvious problem occurs in the process of relationship marketing concept is the wide gap between theory and practice. This gap occurred because lack of well-prepared application process and strategies and also dedicated and trained staff. Second common problem is trying to apply relationship marketing strategies for all customer groups. Every method could not be the best one for all customer segments. Companies should keep always in their minds that investing on low-profit customers is simply wasting. Besides, sometimes companies give importance and locate company resources excessively on the customer side and destroy financial balance (Selvi, 2007).

Third, return of investment in relationship marketing occurs in long-run so financial assets and resources must be placed on the ruler of time and campaigns according to these criteria (Hennig-Thurau, Gwinner, & Gremler, 2002).

Relationship marketing has a direct correlation with level of development. In Palmer's study on application of relationship marketing practices intercultural base, it is stated that, when level of development increases, customers' interest on companies' or products' functional or emotional importance also increase. Markets' culture, economic, political and technological infrastructures have a determining role on marketing practices (Palmer, 1995).

Finally, organizations should consider relationship marketing concept as a change of perception and strategy so it needs radical organizational changes. Airlines' organizations and formation are qualified by international organizations and rule makers (Alliances, IATA, EASA, and FAA etc.) This left very small room for airlines to create their own unique organizational structure.

2. CAN RELATIONSHIP MARKETING PUSH BACKAIRLINES FOR TAKE OFF? RELATIONSHIP MARKETING IN AIRLINE BUSINESS

2.1 Overall Picture of the Industry

Looking for the close traces of this ambiguous product, it can be seen a struggle against economic crises, epidemics, accidents but still attractive and still brilliant. Airline product concept is accepted among service sectors but considering specifications of the product, it is not very easy to classify it. This product first of all is not solid and customer does not have chance to see or experience it before consuming. Neither it can be packed nor shipped to the consumer. This is a special product where producing and consuming occurs in the same time lap (Shaw, 2007).

In the near history of the industry, sector faced its biggest financial crisis. Just a year before the 9/11 sector has a volume of 1, 82 billion passengers but just after the event it dropped to 1.79 billion passengers. Net profit of the sector dropped from 3, 7 billion dollars to -11, 3 billion dollars. Before 9/11 sector was growing with a rate of 8, 6% but after it fell down to a rate of -2,7%. But real shock wave came later with bankruptcies, decrease in traffic rates and a tragic decrease on barely surviving net profit rate with 1,1% fell to -4,2%(IATA, 2010).

Just after the 9/11, industry started to a session of recovery. Actually industry's playground has narrowed by new rules, increased security and safety precautions, new navigation applications. Airline industry with a dead cat bounce found a new way to survive and rose with mergers, partnerships and "low cost carriers". Solely, another beat was on the way. In 2008/9 global financial crisis, airlines were hit by another shock wave. This wave was lethal for some airlines and ended up with bankruptcy or turned them state-run companies. Following year European Volcano/ash cloud crisis did not even let industry trying to stand up. To sum up, previous 10 years in industry were shaped by all possible type crises (even with volcano eruptions) and made permanent changes in the structural and financial forms of airlines. New forms of airlines were born and some old big guys (Pan Am, Iberia, Swiss etc.) left the stage. Center of gravity of travel routes also moved from Atlantic to Europe and then now moving to Far East through Middle East (Shaw, 2007; Doganis, 2006; IATA, 2011).

Nowadays, apart from the low cost carriers airlines can be classified by their styles, products and way of doing business. American Carriers, which have large but relatively old fleet, multi hub, static and Atlantic based and generally do not have ambition to compete European Carriers. American Airlines, Delta and United are foremost representatives of this group. This group sells the image of "American" as American Airlines says (Doganis, 2005).

European Carriers have large fleets but flexible and renewing. Multi hubs and flying too many destinations enjoying having share from the traffic from west to east. They are still rule makers in Europe and mandating regions, they have a weakness of having very shallow local market and threat of Gulf Carriers. Still making money from far-old dominions. Lufthansa, British Airways, Air France are foremost carriers. This group sells the image of "European Quality" (Doganis, 2005).

Gulf Carriers, which are led by Emirates, Qatar and Etihad are relatively new in the market but had a good share. Well managed corporate structures by European CEO's, which powered by oil fields with large wide-body dominated fleets, shake the statue of European carriers. Currently picking fruits of geographical advantage and rising trend of Gulf countries but having no local market is their Achilles' heel. This group of carriers sells pure luxury (O'Connell, 2011).

Another group which can be named as new players rising from middle east, far east and mostly from Latin Americas. Most outstanding ones among them are Turkish Airlines, TAM, and Asiana. Speaking on Turkish Airlines, which has a new dynamic and flexible fleet where can make operations with narrow body aircrafts to all Europe, Russia and many countries of middle east, CIS and Africa (Doganis, Flying off Course, The Economics of International Airlines, 2005). This airline has the true geopolitical advantage comparing to all other carriers also has a very strong local market. Mostly managed by young managers Turkish Airlines, is the real threat for both European and Gulf carriers. This airline has a very unique service and business concept fed by a strong culture so other carriers are not accustomed to deal with. Turkish Airlines serves western quality with oriental luxury (Uslu, Durmuş, & Kolivar, 2013).

Another major change in the industry is on customer purchasing habits which are shaped by internet and mostly technology. Travel agents and airline offices are leaving their places to mobile applications, virtual agents, and internet sites (Doganis, 2005).

David Wessels from Pennsylvania University conducted a very remarking study on 1.406 random participants. Regarding to results of the study it is stated that 30% of today's customers certainly visit web sites like Expedia, Orbitz, Kayak, etc. where all possible airline choices are offered and ranked by price. On purchasing stage, 41% of subjects use these web sites. However, crucial point in this part is 80% of subjects always put the airline which they have FFP membership. From this point of view relationship marketing implications' center is to be FFPs (Wessels, 2006).

Another significant point in Pennsylvania University's study that major criteria in purchasing process of airline customers are schedule, price and FFPs. As a matter of fact results from a narrowed down study group of leisure travelers shown that FFPs are more important than safety. Also another result derived from the study is corporate travelers' have more loyalty and less price sensitivity which explains airlines' special interest in this group of customer (Wessels, 2006, p.9).

Airlines growth rate has a parallel progress with GDPs. Thus, airline industry have had four recessions, two global financial crisis, two gulf wars, one oil crisis and a few epidemics (SARS, Bird Flu etc.) and such an impact of 9/11 miraculously could manage to grow with a rate of 5%. However this rate is raised by developing Middle East and Far East markets. In financial portrait of industry starting from last ten years it can be seen a loss of 50 Billion Dollars. Loss in the 2008/9 crisis only is 11 Billion Dollars that Passenger capacity fell 7% and Cargo capacity 10% (IATA, 2010).

Considering the general portrait of the industry which is full of crises and problems, airlines are heading for stabile and steady sources of income. Just for this reason airlines re-focusing on productivity of customer incomes. It can be said that even if relationship market has a background of 30 years, airlines are discovering this concept nowadays.

2.2 Airline Economy 101

Airline product has high price sensitivity and under direct effect of travel time, schedule, and of course demographic variables. (Holloway, 2008).

Focusing on other financial area, costs and specifically capital costs which are 15% of total costs just after the leading cost factor which is fuel have a percentage of 30%. Labor costs, marketing and distribution, navigation, airline taxes are following these major costs. Under such a pressure of cost, airlines make yield management and flexible pricing strategies. Revenue management departments' main philosophy is to sell as much as possible in high fare classes and later on filling the rest by selling low fares (Belobaba, Odoni, & Barnhart, 2009).With this approach, in high fare class capacity is high and low fare class's capacity is designed low and also has time restrictions(IATA, 2012).

Other elements are sales channels and currency problems. As a result of operating in many countries and selling in many different currencies creates a loss in total. Airlines have to deal with this problem. Competition deeply affected by economic crisis or natural disasters, epidemics and has a very distributed organization structure make airline business very fragile. Even under these circumstances airline industry created a volume of 367 Billion Dollars in 2012 (IATA, 2013).

Main financial pans of airline business are divided into operational and financial revenues or costs. Financial revenues and costs are same as any corporate at any industry. Operational revenues can be summed up as, Scheduled flight revenues, charter revenues, cargo revenues, mail, excess luggage and additional revenues. Operational costs are fuel, maintenance, airport and slot costs, handling and catering, cabin and cockpit staff costs, fleet costs, staff costs and insurance costs (Shaw, 2007).

Financial performance of the network can be evaluated and routes can be classified according to the yield and Revenue per Available Seat Kilometer (RASK) achieved on routes (Figure 6).

Figure 6. Network structure and performance
Source: Serpen, 2013, p.15.

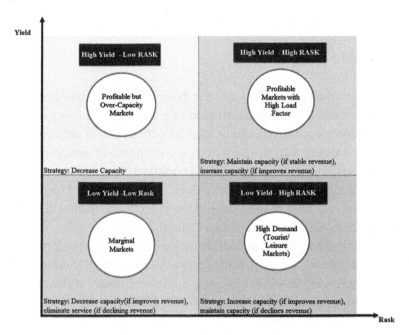

2.3 Relationship Marketing and Airlines

Airlines managed to reach today by assistance of genuine marketing inventions such as FFPs, capacity control, flexible fare systems, product (Cabin) segmentation, and reservation and distribution systems. All these inventions inspired other industries and applied in many different forms in daily life.

Today, airlines standing on cross-roads again because the sector is shared and dominated between two main aircraft manufacturers (Boeing, Airbus) airlines serves almost with same design aircrafts, same services, same seats, same foods, even the hairstyle of cabin attendants are the same. Under a massive competition pressure, they have to survive with a very slight margin of profit but increasing costs day by day. So, airlines will decide whether they will try to survive in this market with the same concept or they will re-design and allocate old marketing weapons with the touch of relationship marketing (Pilarski, 2007).

According to Hennig and Hansen, availability of capacity, punctuality, safety, security, on board service are today minimum requirements or musts which airlines have to provide for sure. Not fulfilling any of them will cause drastic loss of customers for airlines but fulfilling all of them will not create a competitive advantage. Because of this reason, airlines re-considering relationship marketing merged with new technological opportunities. In 1990s American Airlines and British Airways started to shape marketing strategies with relationship marketing concept and segmented their customers. İn 1996 Lufthansa established "Target Customer Unit" and institutionalized micro segmentation, one to one marketing and customer value processes (Hennig-Thurau, Gwinner, & Gremler, 2002).

Lufthansa use a scale for long, to group its customers in FFP according to value and purchasing attitudes (Figures 7 and 8). Such an organization and dense effort requires dedicated time and staff but it is also valuable because it allocates marketing resources to right customer (Thorsten & Hansen, 2000).

2.4 Southwest Example

Success of an organization is always depends on inner dynamics of relations. Southwest Airlines is one of the airlines that applied formally relationship marketing concept as a company strategy. Today this most profitable airline's name is mentioned almost in every publication in industry. Jody H. Gittell in his book explains Southwest's success with its mastering on creating and maintaining relations and claims four factors which are leadership, culture, strategy and coordination.

Under leadership title it should not be forgotten Southwest's ex CEO H.Kelleher's creation of an atmosphere of information, common respect and sharing. Kelleher formulated organization culture focusing on relations and commitment to each other (Gittell, 2003).

Strategy is defined as long run tactics to maintain relations in Southwest culture (Figure 9). Coordination in Southwest defined relations not only inside company but especially other circle of the company such as unions, airport employees, and other airlines. Southwest takes on the principle of relations in every direction and level but not a hierarchical one (Gittell, 2003).

Figure 7. Airline value pyramid
Source: Adapted from Hennig-Thurau, Gwinner, &Gremler, 2002, p.323.

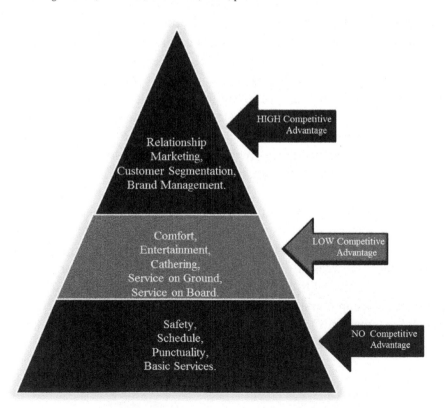

Figure 8. Customer segmentation and loyalty in airline business
Source: Hennig-Thurau, Gwinner, &Gremler, 2002, p.327.

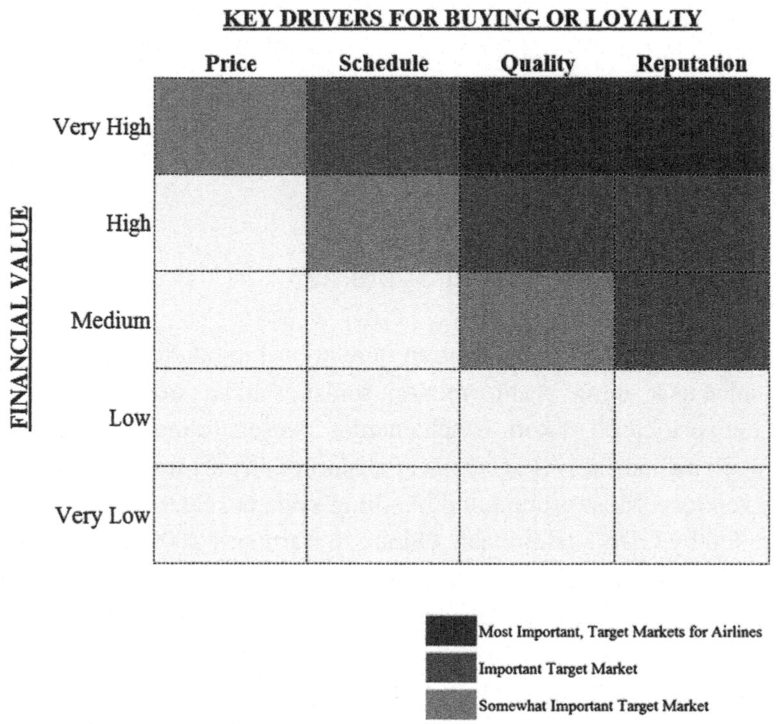

KEY DRIVERS FOR BUYING OR LOYALTY

	Price	Schedule	Quality	Reputation
Very High				
High				
Medium				
Low				
Very Low				

FINANCIAL VALUE

■ Most Important, Target Markets for Airlines

■ Important Target Market

■ Somewhat Important Target Market

Figure 9. Relationship marketing strategy
Source: Adapted from Gittell, 2003, p.55.

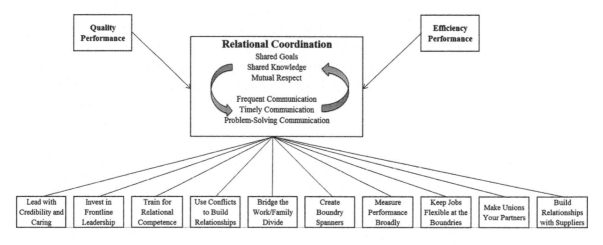

What Southwest earns with such a concept is efficiency, dedication, short ground times, more cycles in a day. It is well known by airport personnel that different from other airline staff, Southwest's' staff meets, jokes and "listens" them. Such courtesies worth millions in airport atmosphere where minutes means millions of dollars.

To sum up, what Southwest did is to put human and relations at the center and created such an organization culture, not works and procedures. However, as a result of this relationship approach relations make works and procedures easier and faster (Gittell, 2003). Southwest knows well "know-how" but also they developed a "know-who" perception.

2.5 General (Or Global?) Distributing Systems

General Distributing Systems are worth to mention in relationship marketing efforts in airline business because of its importance as a source of information, statistics and as market itself.

Simply a GDS is network based system which enables its users to make online transactions. Mostly the network is in between airlines, travel agents, and all sort of airport services. A GDS offers an online and real time link to vendors. Most ground and handling systems, catering, operational, financial and statistical systems are fed by GDS's (Belobaba, Odoni, & Barnhart, 2009).

First GDS was developed by American Airlines in 1960s with "Sabre" and today it is airlines' number one distribution, communication channel. Besides, because of the domination of a few GDS's in the market, it is a huge cost pan competing with fuel cost. Sabre was followed by Apollo which established by United Airlines, later on, Delta, Northwest and TWA created their own system named as "Worldspan". In Europe in 1987 nine airlines led by British Airlines and KLM created "Galileo" and four other airlines led by Lufthansa answered by "Amadeus" (Buhalis, 2003).

That is to say, in the research made by McKensey for IATA, it is stated as the most valuable item in value chain of airline industry. Airlines or carriers are coming far behind in this value chain after GDS's, travel agents, Cargo companies, finance, aircraft manufacturers, and airports.

In early stages GDS's were small software systems under airlines but because of the conflict on "to be seen on the first place" judicial process started and lasted for years but at the end it was claimed against competition law in USA. As a result of this they split up from airlines. (McKensey and Company, 2011).

In order to picture size of GDS's this "old" example can give idea about today's GDS's. In 1995 Sabre that was created and developed by American Airlines had reached the size which it serves in 54 countries on 130.000 terminals which contains 20.000 travel agents with all details, 57 rent a car companies, 50 touring organizations, 22.000 hotels all around the World, 641 airlines with all schedules, flight, pricing etc. Sabre in those years was a system which makes 2.700 transactions per second and files 750.000 passengers all reservation and personal data. Today GDS's are such huge systems (Gummesson, 1994, p.36).

For airlines using a global GDS also means buying a cost per reservation (weather it is ticketed or not), sharing its own customers data and could not find priority or ranking problems nevertheless if airlines use their own "in-house" reservation system they can keep all these advantages on their own side but this means also cannot reach such a big pool of travel agents, sales channels etc. or never be able to reach such terminal numbers.

Today, especially some low cost carriers leading by Easy Jet refuse to be in GDS's and insisting on their own sales channels. It is for sure that they are followed by legacy carriers enviously.

2.6 Frequent Flyer Programs (FFP)

2.6.1 Evolution of FFPs

First FFPs start in 1970s with Southwest's "Sweetheart stamps". Logically this application led to today's FFPs. The system used to work as collecting a defined number of stamps by each flight was converted to a free ticket.

Of course just like all successful invention it was imitated. American Airlines started in the same year "discount coupons" and followed by Western Airlines who gifts a 50 Dollar discount check after a passenger flied 5 times. Within all these primitive applications the idea was same and clear as much as today. The idea of FFPs is "rewarding repeated purchase behavior". On the other hand, due to technological insufficiency and lack of regulations it was hard to keep a campaign in tune with FFPs. FFPs were open defenseless to fraud and forgery of documents which used to cost airlines millions in those years. However, the real threat was usage of these programs without financial assessment namely, there was simply enough miles/credits cumulated in PanAm's FFP, "World Pass" to make all fleet operate a full month for free (Gilbert, 1996).

Maturity era started with American Airline's "AA Advantage Club" in 1981. Just five years later 24 national carriers of 27 in USA had FFPs just like this program and reached 22 million members. Growing each year it became such a complex structures. They made marriages with banks and payment cards and every card producing miles by every cent spent by the user. Besides, these credits or miles can be spent as a currency out of airlines for shopping, accommodation, rent a cars (Gilbert, 1996).

Inside airline alliances these FFPs became a covetable value or alliances integrated all members FFPs which each other. Shaw states this best as "FFPs are the glue of airline alliances." (Shaw, 2007, p.128).

Taking into account all of these today FFPs are the new currencies and have very complicated relations within financial systems and they became independent structures in airline industry but still needs the re-consideration with the touch of relationship marketing.

2.6.2 FFPs: Burden or Weapon?

FFPs are seen as the way of locking customers in or loyalty programs for airlines there are many ambiguous points in it. First of all unredeemed miles of airlines are growing with a snowball effect every day and became a heavy financial burden. Gillberts (1996) determination on the subject with an example is very interesting that if it is asked from airlines to redeem or melt all cumulated miles in a day they would need 600.000 Boeing 747s which will fly all day around the World. In other words today airlines can manage to melt only 25% of cumulated miles (Gilbert, 1996).

Another problem is corporates that finances business travels complaints about not having control on spending of miles. Companies paying for travels but benefit of these travels are spent by individuals because of FFP systems. This need forced many airlines to create special FFPs or memberships for companies (Holloway, 2008).

Governments are another party who puts a in a claim for benefits of FFPs. Governments see FFP miles as financial assets and want to excise them. Countries like UK which establishes its tax system on term of "benefit" and excises even mobile phone lines given by companies, vehicles for managers, bonus payments. So it is expected in such countries in short term that to excise benefits rise from use of FFP membership (Liston-Heyes, 2002).

On the side of airlines, miles causing another financial pressure. Unredeemed miles are converted as a currency and stays as "debt" on airlines balance-sheets which has a negative pressure on financial statement. After 2008/9 global financial crisis these huge amounts drew attention on board rooms and had the priority (Doganis, 2006).

International organizations and governments make new regulations in order to justify competition conditions for airlines. Nowadays, FFPs especially running by airlines under the roof of IATA, it is loudly discussed on charges of being against competition law and equality. Actually all FFPs are strong in their homeland or hub and do not provide living space for other airlines (Gilbert, 1996; Liston-Heyes, 2002).

In economic cycle of airlines, obviously, all FFPs work almost in same style, offer similar rewards and this raise competition threshold and increase customer retention cost.

As a result, FFPs shall be seen separate products of airlines which have financial roots and application availability in relationship marketing. FFPs will be successful if they can provide customer loyally, retention and reorder. In other words, FFPs have promising opportunities for airlines if they can be used as marketing tool.

2.6.3 Discussing FFPs in Relationship Marketing

Definition of FFPs and relationship marketing is overlapping on customer loyalty, customer retention and long run relationships. In order to renovate FFPs today there must be some certain steps to take from relationship point of view.

First of all, airlines while rewarding by FFPs must be generous to its customers. Putting strict and narrow time limitations for spending miles is not a good way of rewarding. Besides, the biggest problem from customer's side seems like finding available seat to spend miles as free tickets in certain seasons and destinations. Yield management departments are involuntary to give seats for FFP mile redemption in a top destination or high season but it must be remembered by these units that these customers must be seen as passengers already paid their seats in time (Shaw, 2007).

The most common reward in FFPs is free tickets but relationship marketing concept requires individualism and differentiation. So, airlines have to have a range of rewards from customized gifts or rewards to free tickets and actually must reward them by offering freedom of choice. As Shaw examples it will not be attractive for a passenger who flies 30 times in a year rewarding with a 31st flight (Shaw, 2007)

Additionally, today lots of airlines let their customers to change, share or sell their accumulated miles with other members. Airlines also can create some customized solutions for these demands. For example, airlines can promote members to spend their miles in low seasons when they have more empty seats. Airlines can make a setting if the member wants to fly in high season or fully booked top destinations have to spend more miles. In order to support weak or new destinations for airline members can be promoted to fly these destinations with spending very few miles. There can be created campaigns for specific destinations on mile spending (Holloway, 2008).

Mostly accumulated miles expire in three years which is an application that members do not like. This can be solved as miles can be kept unless member makes one flight per year. This would be just for both sides.

On balance-sheet of airlines balance of unredeemed miles can be converted also to relationship marketing tools. In order to melt this iceberg airlines have to inform their customers regularly and in different communication channels. There should open spending channels out of free flights and these channels must be less costly comparing to free flight tickets. There are some examples which bring relationship marketing, advertising, social responsibility and of course melting heavy burden of miles. When a customer starts reservation on the internet site of the airline, on routing step, an automatic system calculates total carbon emission of this possible flight per passenger and offers planting tree or trees on behalf of passenger in exchange for an amount of miles of course. This example application creates a feeling of doing something good for him and the environment and increase credibility of airlines ad also creates a win-win situation for all (Shaw, 2007).

Airlines can offer customers to join campaigns of charity or let them make donations to some charity or NGOs by spending from accumulated miles with a rate of exchange that company will decide. At the airport step of travel passengers should have availability to spend miles by limousine services, car parks or to get access to lounges. Besides a source of complaint, excess baggage fees can be made by miles and this can create another win-win situation.

On the stage of purchasing tickets there shall apply different rates, such if the customers choose to buy from airlines own channels such as internet site, sales Office, call center more miles would be earned and if other channels preferred less miles would be earned. This application will create a visible impact on cost area.

Another suggestion is enabling customers to be able make their shopping's with miles in certain internet sites. There is a common interest for airline promotional materials in public and this can be converted to an advantage by selling them and make it can be paid by miles. Airlines usually organize trips for corporates or staff of travel agents, airports etc. to their home based city and airline facilities such as operation, hangars, flight training centers, catering units and giving them chance to touch airline "product". These organizations are named as "fam trips" and mostly applied for B2B level. In order to make it a more profitable tool of marketing it must be adapted to B2C level. Melting miles by using this can be an option too. Today some airlines selling simulator flight hours in their flight training centers. Considering the crowded community of virtual airlines and pilots this would have an advertisement impact also.

All cases given above are examples for airlines to melt their mile icebergs without stepping out their main activities. Each example if considered with the impact of social media and advertisement support are nominees of being great campaigns or social media phenomenon's.

Consequently, FFPs are not only databases for airlines but has a potential of being source of information, analyses, segmentation and application instruments for relationship marketing. FFP members shall also be used as a pool for application of campaigns, surveys, new product launches.

2.7 Internet and Social Media

Internet is vital for relationship marketing just like it is a de facto of success for all industries today, not because it is a sales channel but also it is a multichannel, interactive and totally free place of share. From company perspective, customers today can access within minutes to cheapest product, can compare with related ones, can read and join user comments about the product even can order from all over the World and this makes traditional marketing karma dysfunctional. Especially the generation born in between 1997 to 1994 that also named as "Generation Y" use internet with all aspects in daily life to talk, meet, work, pleasure, shopping etc. purchasing power of this Generation Y is predicted 200 Billion dollars (İlban & Kaşlı, 2013).

So called word of mouth marketing has a more intense meaning with internet because in a latest survey related to the subject today's consumers consulting with a rate of 92% to their friends, colleagues or families moreover 73% admits that reading user comments in internet affects their choices and purchase behavior. Internet as a sales channel has reached 15% in total personal spending (İlban & Kaşlı, 2013).

A new updated survey on the subject made by Bright Local in USA, 83% of consumers read user comments about local companies and regarding to same survey 73% of total admits reading positive comments about the company increases trust to the company. Nielsen focuses on advertisement with its survey of "Trust on Advertisement" that studied with 28.000 internet users in 56 different countries. After family and friends who has an influence power with 92%, internet comes with 70% (Gazete Vatan, 2014).

Coming back to airlines, they will not reach their targets or will not turn into profit until they change their perception of internet and social media and abandon to try internet as a one-way channel to carry their messages from company to customers. Airlines should consider internet as a multi-channel real time communication channel, of course an advertisement area, a discussion forum, a CRM center, a sales channel, a distribution channel, a newspaper, TV channel, radio dedicated to airline, a place where you can meet and spend time with people(Chaffey, Ellis-Chadwick, Johnston, & Mayer, 2006).

For instance, Etihad Airlines makes announcement about itself and customers from twitter, for instance flight delays, cancellations. Airline replies all tweets and comments on Facebook one by through the channel "Etihad Help. Last year Turkish Airlines put its name on the top by a customer complaint made airborne during a flight from Istanbul on a social media channel. Just a few minutes after related department get in contact with the aircraft and inform cabin crew about the situation of passengers. Passenger's complaint had solved and informed also from same media channel within minutes during a flight. When passenger shared his complaint about something on Twitter it was a CRM issue but the way Turkish Airlines solved it is a good example of relationship marketing concept (kokpit.aero, 2013).

In 2008, Dave Carroll took a flight from Chicago to Halifax with United Airlines and gave its guitar to baggage because it was not allowed to the cabin because of its size, naturally. After the flight airline delivered the guitar broken. Related department in the airport offered to Carroll 250 dollars but actual price of it was more than 3.000 dollars. Passenger could not convince the airport about the real value of his instrument and backs to home with anger and disappointment. He wrote a song named "United breaks guitars" and after recording it uploaded to YouTube. In the first few days 150.000 people watched the video, later on news, and shows followed. United tried to cover but it was late. Just four days after the flight airlines value drop 10% of its value and lost 180 million dollars. This is a very solid example of how a CRM without awareness of relationship marketing (kokpit.aero, 2013).

Today American Airlines everyday replies 30.000 tweets one by one; KLM employs 60 experts in social media department. In addition to previous sections where from traditional marketing mix to relationship marketing is given, in this section with contemporary examples how CRM applications and relationship marketing should integrate is given (SocialBakers, 2014).

Consequently, today in such internet pages like Expedia, Orbitz all airlines are given according to best connection, schedule and price options from city A to city B. Airline logos are put side by side on a two dimension plane with prices and schedules under them. This is the simplest version of airline product. Because of the current market conditions and some sectorial peculiarities there is not much difference between airlines. In this case the most reasonable advice for airlines is to accept and immediately take necessary steps through relationship marketing concept.

3. FINANCIAL EFFECTS OF RELATIONSHIP MARKETING: IMPLEMENTATION MODEL FOR AVIATION INDUSTRY

3.1 Domains of Relationship Marketing

Adapting a cliché to the industry, A. M. Pilarski says in his book "Why Can't We Make Money in Aviation?" (Pilarski, 2007, p.9).

If you want to make millions in aviation, you must risk investing billions.

This is, in fact, a to-the-point statement underlining how bad the situation is considering the cost category of the industry, but still just points to the tip of the iceberg.

On the basis of three assertions, that even the small revisions to be made by the firm at the relations level could create great effects (Reinchheld, Markey, &Hopton, 2000, p.135).

1. It is less costly to serve long-term customers,
2. Loyal customers are less sensitive to price changes,
3. Loyal customers are voluntary marketing advocates.

In a 5-year study on loyal customers, Reinartz and Kumar have examined the customers with minimum 2-year commercial relation, accepting them as loyal customer, and observed that they have had positive effects on all cost items of the firm in different ratios (Sorce, 2002).

The domains of the relationship marketing, or in other words, expectations with regard to which domains will undergo changes in consequence of application of the relationship marketing are greatly important for effectiveness.

Among the studies conducted on this issue, especially Erdal Arlı's study conducted in Turkey is remarkable. The companies where the relationship marketing study would be conducted were given the simplest values, and the results of application were categorized by domains. As the relationship marketing practices, simple tactics such as customer retention, asking their wishes and needs, easy terms of payment, regarding the customers as members or stakeholders, remembering their special days, esteeming, offering special services, complaint handling, and one-to-one contact have been applied by the participant firms (Arlı, 2012). The results have had significant effects firstly on the repurchase criterion: an increase by 52.2%. The percentage in the categories such as satisfaction with management, intention to recommend, etc. has reached 80%. Briefly, it has been understood that even the basic practices that are in fact the simplest requirements of enterprise marketing but also cross-pathing with the relationship marketing have rather significant effects on the customers (Arlı, 2012).

The studies conducted indicate that the longer the relation lasts, the bigger is the gain. The possible reasons behind that are the decreases in the marketing costs, the decrease in the rate of leaving customers, and the increase in the SOW rate (Gummesson, 2002).

Figure 10. The chain of productivity
Source: Hanssens & Dekimpe, Models for the Financial-Performance Effects, 2008, p.502.

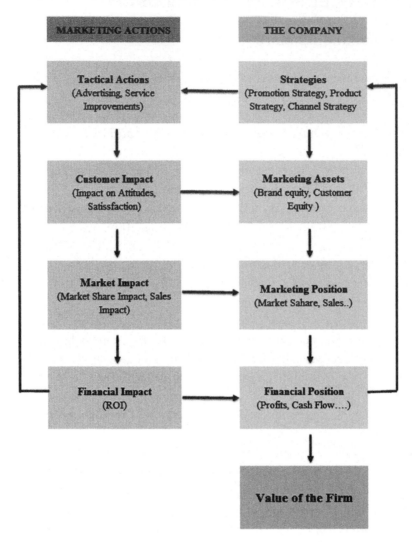

3.1.1 Effects of Relationship Marketing on Cost

Considering the abovementioned profile, for the present-day enterprises like the aviation industry trying to cope with heavy and multi-volume cost items, the most important cost item, among the visible ones, is in fact the customer defection.

For instance, an airline company's average annual customer defection rate is estimated to be 5%. Considering a medium-sized airline company carrying 32,000,000 passengers a year on average, this 5% defection corresponds to 1,600,000 passengers. Likewise, if we take the gross value as 1,000 dollars, the loss of the enterprise seems to be 1.6 billion dollars. Supposing, rather optimistically, that the profit margin of the company is 10%, the net loss of the company seems to be 160 million dollars. Although the ratios in this example are a little higher than the average, it will not be difficult to say that a company that might come to such ratios rather easily will go bankruptcy or at least be in a financially bad situation (Gupta, et al., 2006).

For another example, 15,30Billion TL out of Turkish Airlines' 18,77 Billion TL revenue for the year 2013 is the cost of the sales. And 1,94 Billion TL out of TL 3.47 billion gross profit seems to be the marketing expenditures (Turkish Airlines, 2014, March.).A relation with an enterprise, continued on the basis of long-term and mutual gains, will mean, first of all, a decline in the time cost. The customer will save the operating costs of finding new seller, such as time, labor, technology, transportation, etc.

Additionally, it must be remembered that the risk to be created by new customers also has its own cost. Although it has worn down today due to trust factor, the "open account" system applied in business life in Middle East societies deserves a review from the point of view of cost.

As per the principle that says the relationship marketing is to do marketing after the customer has become customer', the cost of the marketing efforts made to retain the customers in hand will be one-seventh of the cost of acquiring new customers (Grönroos, 1994).

Since the way of value creation passes through benefit creation, it is natural to regard it as a cost as well. However, the point to be reached is to create a value that can be the long-term value boosting the company's performance and providing the customer with benefit. Grönroos defines relationship costs as follows (Ravald & Grönroos, 1996, p.29).

- **Direct Relationship Costs:** The costs such as office, personnel, and system investments emerging with the supply of an idea, product or service.
- **Indirect Relationship Costs:** The costs such as incorrect billing, delayed deliveries, etc. caused by wrong execution of the supply function.
- **Psychological Costs:** The costs of safety precautions caused by the worries about whether the supplier can fulfill its promise, or whether it can solve the problems.

Decreasing the abovementioned cost types means creating a customer value without offering any additional benefit. This can be made possible through several changes to be made in the internal and external service quality and processes in the simplest and leanest manner. Activation of the strategies such as effectiveness, flexibility and zero customer loss in the areas of production, distribution and after-sales services will have reflections on the company's overall profitability. Grönroos mentions safety, security and credibility as the common costs that enable to establish long-term relationships and must be shared by the seller and the customer (Ravald & Grönroos, 1996; Grönroos, 2004).

3.1.2 Effects of Relationship Marketing on Profitability

The fundamental mission of marketing is to create or stimulate demand; thus, measuring the resulting sales and revenues under the marketing heading will not give the correct results. The effects of the marketing efforts must be searched in the sales and earnings of the company. In the US, the total value of the yearlong advertising and promotional activities is 10 trillion dollars, which corresponds to 10% of the Gross National Product. These figures and activities are regarded as the investments that must increase the profitability (Hanssens & Dekimpe, 2008).

The conventional profitability flow diagram starts with innovation, and this is the stage where the customers' demands and needs are also identified (Figure 11). Better products and services are offered to the customer at better rates and quality, and this creates a good experience for the customers. The satisfied customers are more loyal, and this returns to the company as the high repetition order rates and positive word-of-mouth marketing. Thus, the company that has up-sell and cross-sell items increases its profitability. And the increased profit finances the innovation to develop better products and services for the customer (Kumar, Pozza, Peterson, & Shah, 2009).

The Sprint Nextel example is included herein particularly for the questions it has caused. This company serves 53 million customers, and decided to cut off 1000 of them. Typical Nextel customer pays the company 55 dollars a month, 24 dollars of which seems to be profit. The company found out that this 1000-person group has called the customer services department several times a month, talked for 8 to 12 minutes on average, and complained about various services continuously. Since each minute in the customer services costs 2 dollars to the company, considering the fact that the said customer group does not yield any profit to the company, Sprint Nextel fired them following a radical decision strongly criticized in the industry. This example is important as it questions the relations in the classical, conventional profitability diagram. In his study of 1996, Reicheld observed a 60% defection among the satisfied customers as well. The author who gave examples from the automobile industry observed that only 40% of the customers who are 85% to 95% satisfied with the car they bought the same brand vehicle again (Kumar, Pozza, Peterson, & Shah, 2009).

A high amount of resources is used to create loyalty, or investments are made to increase the customer satisfaction in the aviation industry as well, but the profitability keeps being low. The factors such as time, connection type and quality, aircraft type, hub, etc. that affect the customer preferences despite the factors such as loyalty and satisfaction should also be regarded as standby diverters (Shaw, 2007).

In fact, such diversions occur as the customer satisfaction and loyalty are not connected to profitability in the first place. Therefore, discrimination between less and more profitable customers in the airline companies must be perceived as a compulsion. According to the classical FFP understanding, each customer gains as many miles as he flies, and this is generally the same for everyone (Gilbert, 1996). However, the purchasing processes are ignored at this stage. In such a situation, the relationship marketing prescribes analyzing the passenger firstly, drawing a conclusion by analyzing his flight segment,

Figure 11. Conventional path to profitability
Source: Kumar, Pozza, Peterson, & Shah, 2009, p.148.

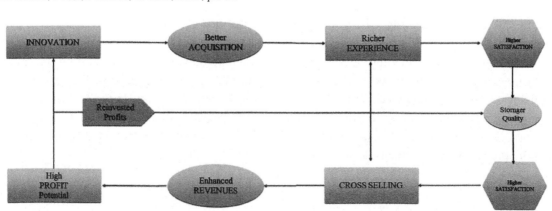

price class and amount of his ticket, and his previous buying behaviors. Likewise, numerous airlines have started to apply this. In previous years, the Continental Airlines has stated that it would reward the mile system on the basis of three statuses it has determined; likewise, Turkish Airlines changed its mile system by shifting to the price class, i.e. a rewarding system based on the amount paid by the customer, at the beginning of the year 2014(www.new-milesandsmiles.com, 2014). Thus, the mile accumulation will be diminished at the mile winning stage, and the frequent flyer loyal passenger will have a bigger share of the mile pie. And since the segment enjoying the bigger share of the mile pie is also the frequent flyer loyal segment, such miles will also be spent at a higher rate. What the airlines should do at this final point is to channel such accumulated miles to non-flying alternatives or idle routes.

According to the Pareto Principle, 20% of the customers generate 80% of the revenue. This 20% slice can be considered as the first, business or Premium class passengers or the passenger groups with high price class value such as the corporate, seamen, etc. Kumar's study measures the customer value in CLV, i.e. Customer Lifetime Value, from the relationship marketing perspective. In consequence of his study, Kumar has found out that, in parallel to the Pareto Principle, the 20% customer segment, i.e. the first two decile groups generate 95% of the company's revenue (Kumar, 2009).

In that case, companies who want to increase such type of customers of theirs must focus on and analyze their existing customers first, and then chase the customers that match the profile of such type of customers. The customers in this category will pioneer the companies about for which types of products and services they must apply innovations. For instance, as the first airline company offering the first lie-flat seats, British Airways owes this innovation to its first and business class passengers. Innovations made and the goods and services supplied considering the profitable customers will make contributions to both the total CLV and the company's overall profitability (Kumar, Pozza, Peterson, & Shah, 2009). The customer segmentation and tactics prepared from this viewpoint are shown in Figure 12.

Obviously, the success of the abovementioned scheme and segmentation depends on the organizational changes and qualified labor force to apply such patterns. Having applied the relationship marketing principles in compliance with the abovementioned tactics, IBM achieved a 20-million-dollar revenue growth in the year 2008 (Kumar, Pozza, Peterson, & Shah, 2009).

Figure 12. The new path to profitability
Source: Kumar, Pozza, Peterson, & Shah, 2009, p.151.

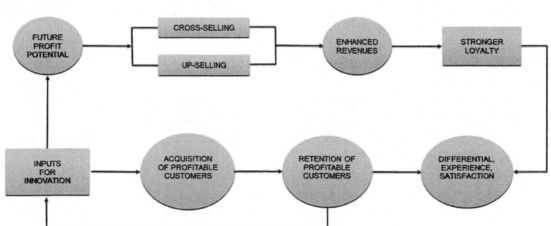

It is Monroe who has mentioned the exchange value in these exchanging processes for the first time and formulated the customers' customer value acquired in the simplest form. Having tried to attribute a numerical value by dividing the acquired values by the paid cost, Monroe has summarized the value as an evaluation of the customer's perception of what he has given and what he has received. (Man, 1998) On the other hand, a strong relationship set will facilitate the lives of the retail or corporate customers as it decreases the time to make a decision, because it creates a positive expectation for an award or feedback like the airline FFPs in consequence of an action or purchasing.

Considering from the perspective of the seller or the service provider, on the other hand, it is important as it reminds that the real motivation is "profit", though it seems rather difficult and costly to go beyond the motto of "Market share is everything" continuing for years (Bareika, 2010).

In consequence of this study conducted on over 100 companies from 20 different industries, it has been discovered that if the companies can decrease their customer defection rates by 5%, they can achieve a revenue growth by 25 to 85%. This study, which is capable alone to emphasize the importance of the relationship marketing, has revealed that not only the loyal customers yield more revenue in time, but also the cost of customer retention is much lower than the cost of gaining new ones. During another study conducted on a bank, it has been observed that if the customer defection rate is decreased from 20% to 10%, the average relationship period of a customer is extended from 5 years to 10 years, and that the average total profit per customer rises from 135 dollars to 300 dollars. If the defection rate can be decreased by 5% more, the profit rises from 300 dollars to 525 dollars by 75% increase (Reichheld & Sasser, 1990).

On the basis of the abovementioned two studies, it is possible to conclude that:

- The long-term customers are less sensitive to price changes,
- The long-term customers can perform free word-of-mouth marketing,
- The long-term customers tend to place more frequent, more steady, and less costly orders.

The long-term customers tend to buy additional products or services more rapidly and easily, and, as a general conclusion, their Life Time Values are higher.

As confirmed by Grönroos, after the first few successful communications, if the customer is satisfied, he starts to trust the supplier, becomes more tolerant towards the supplier, and refrains from complaining, or in other words, he may give the supplier a chance to solve the potential problems. The customer also keeps buying from the same supplier and provides the supplier with other job opportunities through the word-of-mouth marketing (Karaca, 2010).

3.2 Financial Scales of Relationship Marketing

"You cannot manage something you cannot measure", says an old management adage. Even an in-house scale to be developed by the company itself, without the requirement of universal consent, will assist the company in positioning its resources more effectively. Besides, this scale will also be a motivation and rewarding tool for the company.

Since the marketing measures are generally abstract and their effects or returns are mostly protracted, a tendency of measuring them as based on financial data has emerged. The most commonly used measurement units are market share, cost reduction, sales growth rates, and return on investment (ROI). Life Time

Value (LTV), which is mentioned frequently with the relationship marketing today, can also be included in this group (Sin, Tse, Yau, Chow, Lee, & Lorett, 2005; Hallowell, 1996; Lindgreen & Crawford, 1999).

As particular to airlines, the following scales can be concretized through the information sources like booking systems and FFPs:

1. **Customer Loyalty:** Whether the customer maintains his existence and the relationship within the unit of time.
2. **Customer Share:** The customer share is calculated by proportioning the gain brought to the company by a customer within the unit of time to the total.

The performance measurement is based on each customer's value and share according to the relationship marketing understanding, though it is based on the market share in the conventional marketing understanding.

3.2.1 Return on Relationship (ROR)

One of the leading theoreticians of the relationship marketing, Gummesson has adapted the Return on Investment (ROI) concept to the relationship marketing as shown in Figure 13.

The long-term net financial return on the network of relationships established and maintained by an enterprise is called the Return on Relationship Investment (ROR). Gummesson's description corresponds to satisfaction, loyalty and profitability in practice. ROI is a cost-based evaluation grounded in the return on the marketing campaign. What is important here is to calculate the cost items correctly and in detail whenever possible (Gummesson, 2002).

Figure 13. Return on relationship model
Source: Kanagal, 2005, p.9.

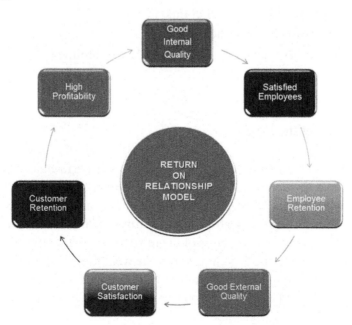

Four basic criterions must always be considered:

1.   **Costs of Customer Acquisition and Break-Even:** The point of maximum cost to bear to acquire a customer.
2.   **Depreciation Curves:** The indicator analyzing the customers' tendencies to depreciate in time, because the customers may lose their profitability in time. In the case of airlines, it is necessary to keep an eye on the passive members considering FFPs in particular, because the marketing strategy is based on the reason of this passivity: either the member has other memberships or he is really passive (Belobaba, Odoni, & Barnhart, 2009).
3.   **Life Time Value:** Life time values of customers must be calculated to be able to calculate the costs and gains of the acquisition and retention activities. Customer lifetime value (CLV) is generally defined as the present value of all future profits obtained from a customer over his life of relationship with the firm (Gupta, et al., 2006).It is possible to make a comparison among the airlines in particular today, thanks to the joint mile programs applied in codeshare flights and carrier alliances. The mile values that have become a currency so can be calculated in CPM (Cents per mile) and RPM (Revenue per mile). In the simplest way, the average LTV is calculated by multiplying the number of the customer's purchases within a certain period of time by the profit per unit. For example, the LTV value of a customer who has made 15 purchases in 2 years:
4.   LTV=15 x 1.45 (Profit Per Unit) =21.75 dollars. It is normal that some customer groups give negative values in consequence of this calculation. This indicator indicates the need to increase the number of customers as a unit. In detail, the formula is (Gupta, et al., 2006; 141):

$$CLV = \sum_{t=0}^{T} \frac{\left(p_{t-c_t}\right)r_t}{\left(1+i\right)} - AC$$

- c_t = direct cost of servicing the customer at time t,
- i = discount rate or cost of capital for the firm,
- r_t = probability of customer repeat buying or being "alive" at time t,
- AC =customer acquisition cost,
- T =time horizon for estimating CLV.

3.2.2 Relationship Marketing Scale

The effects of the relationship marketing practices on the company performance and the environmental factors in the process, the study conducted by Akyol and Ataman (2007) (Küçükkancabaş, Akyol, & Ataman, 2007) in Turkish beverage industry is a guiding one. The questionnaire used in 130 interviews made in various geographical regions basically deals with trust, loyalty, communication, shared values, empathy and reciprocity that are the basic factors of the relationship marketing. The financial indicators used in the survey completed using the 5-point Likert scale were the sales growth rates and the market share. This study is about the relationship marketing where the subjective inputs generate objective values, and the results of such marketing. The strong results acquired have failed to decrease the effects of the market fluctuations and the other environmental effects. However, the common values, empathy and loyalty have appeared to be the strongest factors while reciprocity, communication and trust have fallen rather behind.

3.2.3 Loyalty Scale

Although loyalty, as evoked by its name, is an abstract notion, it is a measurable and concrete notion in the relationship marketing as it has concrete indicators such as the Share of Wallet (SOW), payments to Premium services, and repetition orders. This scale, generally accepted for its behavioral aspects and repurchasing indicator, can be measured through simple survey methods and repetition orders accessible through databanks and accounting records (Gupta, et al., 2006). For the aviation industry, the survey must include such headings as the service quality, preference, Premium classes and products, trust, difference and convenience (Network, timetables, vacant seats, hub or airports flied, etc.).

3.3 Relationship Strategies for Airlines

Today, the airlines pursue different strategies to come out of the turbulence in the industry. The relationship marketing as a focusing strategy has recently found a place in the market in corporate sense, while the cost leadership or differentiation is the most preferred strategies.

The primary method used by the airlines to differentiate in terms of cost is to ensure lowering fleet costs. This method applied successfully by the low cost airlines particularly provides a considerable cost advantage by singularizing all cost items such as spare parts, maintenance, training, etc. through a single type of aircraft. Since there is no producer in the industry at the same scale with Airbus and Boeing, this method is restricted (Doganis, 2006).

Considering the differentiation strategy, the innovation expenditures and risk await the carriers. This differentiation may sometimes gain favor in the type of aircraft. The favorite airplane of the recent years Airbus A380 has brought a breath of fresh air to the market. The comfort and luxury brought into the forefront by the Gulf carriers today constitute a conscious differentiation strategy.

A shift from the classical marketing concept and the operational structure organized as per this understanding to the relationship marketing strategy means a rearrangement of the entire organization. The first thing coming to mind when it is the reorganization within the frame of relationship marketing is the fallacy of a customer relations department becoming the center of gravity of the company. It is necessary to make clear that the relationship marketing refers to the relations of all units with all business circles. The results of the relationship marketing provide the aviation industry with returns in very short times (Grönroos, 1999).

According to Rapp, an airline company that will apply the relationship marketing concept has to understand the headings presented herein, and ensure that the same are accepted throughout the corporate (Rapp, 2000, pp.328-330):

1. It is necessary to establish customer relations rather than customer databanks, The customer information collected through the airline company's booking systems, call centers, FFPs are nothing but burden for the company, unless it is used as marketing tool.

2. The information must be used to improve the service quality, the airline companies must gather information on their customers, especially the valuable customers from whom they earn considerable revenue, but such information must be used to improve its relations and service quality, otherwise the regularly sent template mails are worthless. When the companies have an opportunity to receive data on the market or themselves from the customers via complaints, mails, etc., they must make sure to use it. The present-day mobile applications and social media channels are appropriate channels for this purpose.

3. It is necessary to find out and focus on the roots of the customer's certain attitudes,

4. The relationship-based measurement units must be used, In case of the airlines, the relationship marketing must measure the segment-based, long-term values, and LTV must also be added to indicators such as occupancy, supplied seats, mileage, etc.

5. The long-term relationship marketing programs instead of the one-time ones must be developed and it must be remembered that the relations can be developed in time, step by step, strategically and within the scope of a program, as is the case with the personal relations.

It is necessary to ensure differentiation in relationships and services by utilizing the FFP systems detailed above. It is mandatory to base diversification of the products and services on the current and prospective customers' demands. Likewise, it is necessary to find out and utilize the life time value of each customer in the system. It is known that several airline companies sort the customers in their registered customer pools by different criteria through the computer systems running on the FFP system, and generate a life time value to be used by the analysts by giving point to every piece of information they have. This system, the customer's frequency of travelling, the price class used for ticketing during his travels, his destinations and flying periods are scored separately, and other than the same, his personal information is also utilized, and his residential location and the real estate values at this location, the agency card, if any, otherwise the credit card, he has used while buying a ticket are also scored. Obviously, what lies beneath all this scoring is the customer's earning value in the eyes of the company. The biggest obstacle to make the most of the FFPs by the airlines is the worry about taking the FFPs out of their principal activity area, i.e. the airport.

Consequently, the application areas of the Relationship Marketing can be reduced to the following three categories according to Palmatier and Houston (2006, p.479).

3.3.1 Financial Relationship Marketing Programs

Such a program rewards the customer loyalty with financial benefits. It has a Taylorian approach, which regards money as the most important motivator. The airline companies have been applying this through discounts, award tickets, incentives, etc. Aside from being easy to copycat by the rivals, it can be seen as a point of loss as it stimulates the price sensitivity, because the customer may shift easily to another carrier offering more affordable prices or better financial benefits.

3.3.2 Social Relationship Marketing Programs

They can be considered as activities ensuring that the customers can have social connections with the airline company or disregard the competitors' offers. In the aviation industry, there are applications that cannot be copycatted with the same effect, such as agency dinners, familiarization trips, sponsorships, golf tournaments, etc. Especially the activities in this group will create the difference when they are coordinated with a relationship marketing awareness.

3.3.3 Structural Relationship Marketing Programs

The activities during which the customer is supported with the systems, devices, or products assisting him in improving his own efficiency or effectiveness. The advertising materials, office products or designs, booking system installations provided by the airline companies to their agencies free of charge can be evaluated within this category. (Palmatier, Gopalakrishna, & Houston, 2006).

The study conducted by Palmatier, Gopalakrishna and Houston (2006) has revealed that the social relationship marketing practices are more effective on the profitability especially within the B2B environment. At the same time, it has been observed that its effects appear in the short run, though it promotes the long-lasting customer loyalty (Palmatier, Gopalakrishna, & Houston, 2006).

3.4 A Relationship Implication Model for Airlines

The company must aspire to accessing a segment that is low in quantity but high in value, and brings revenue to the company, in addition to its on-going efforts for new customer acquisition and market expansion. The marketing resources must be positioned relative to this new segmentation. Within the frame of the Pareto Principle, the easiest way to do this is to use the large databases of the airline companies.

- Airlines' Website Records,
- GDS, Booking System Records,
- CRM Records,
- Call Centre Records,
- Social Media Records.

The list in hand will transform from the alphabetical form to a list of values as per the scoring system created by the company in consequence of the assessments and analyses to be made on the databases. The company must establish the scoring system in line with its own purposes and interests, but it must basically include the following breakdown for sure:

3.4.1 Database Search

- **Passenger Information:** Number of Passengers, Residence City, Residence Neighbourhood, Occupation, Age, Marital Status, Extra Services (Golf Clubs, Wheelchair, etc.)
- **Flight Information:** Long Haul/Short Haul/Domestic/Beyond, Destination City, Destination KM, Cabin Class, (First, Business, Comfort, Economy), Fare Class
- **Sales Information:** POS (Point of Sale), Which flight within the current year, which flight in total, Sales Channel (Airline company Website, Agency, Virtual Agency, Call Centre, etc.)
- **Payment Information:** Payment Source (Individual, Corporate), Payment Method (Cash, Credit Card, Debit Card, FFP Miles, Paypal, etc.)
- **FFP Information:** FFP Type (Carrier's or Alliance's Card), FFP Status (Gold, Silver, Classic, Corporate Club), Total Active Miles.

Surely, when each piece of information obtained from the data repositories in hand is given a point, the travelling frequency, cabin and price classes, and active miles of the customer will receive the highest point values. Therefore, they will be the determinant values. The scoring of the other information can be changed in line with the importance of such information for different domains. In consequence of this scoring, the material value of each passenger for the company in question will have appeared to a great extent. This can be achieved rather rapidly and effectively through new software and applications to be articulated to or fed by the current systems thanks to the present-day software opportunities. When millions of passengers carried for one year are sorted in descending order according to the abovementioned criteria, the target customers who yield the real gain to the company will have been identified (McKensey and Company, 2011).

3.4.2 Re-Segmentation

In consequence of the customer value research, the value sorting can be realized and divided into percentiles. However, the right thing to do is a re-segmentation over this sorting so that it can constitute a target for the marketing units. The first segmentation value of an airline organization dispersed through various countries will be the geographical location. Then, sub-sections can be created on the basis of the criteria such as the travel purpose, business or personal travels, etc. Since the developing airline companies that have sufficient area to grow are always focused on growth, they do not give due importance to this application. The companies that have left this work to FFPs and CRM units believe that the FFPs cage the customers naturally and thus ensure the continuity. However, their current structures wait in the wings to generate more income with the touch of relationship marketing than what they can earn through growth (Teichert, Shehu, & von Wartburg, 2008).

The re-segmentation is quite valuable as it will have identified the target customers for each unit of the organization in the form of concrete name lists.

3.4.3 Analysis of the Valuable Customer Behaviors

Following the scoring, sorting and valuing processes, the customers have been divided into certain micro-segments. There are two probabilities relating to the customers ranking low within the percentiles, i.e. the sorting. The first one is that the customer has already reached the peak of his current potential, that is, maximum revenue is derived from the unit, but its potential is low. The second probability is the fact that the airline company itself is not much preferred by the customer, that is, its Share of Wallet is low (Gruen, 1995). The real target for the company is the customers in this group. At this point the airline company must find out why the groups prefer or do not prefer the airline company, what they are satisfied with, what they are complaining about through different surveys it will carry out through different communication channels (internet, social media, personal interviews, etc.), and it must set its strategy separately for each micro-segment on the basis of the results of such surveys (Leick, 2007).

The motives to prefer that are still effective though not determinant any more in case of the airline companies are tariffs, price, flexibility, FFP, the rate of timely departures, the cabin services and catering, and finally the ground handling services. Differentiation in these services provided by each airline company in standard is now possible only in the manner of offering such services and the communication with the customer while offering them.

A sort of SWOT analysis to be acquired this way will have a say in setting of the short and long-term targets of the company as well as repositioning of its resources.

3.4.4 Re-Organization and Implementation

The customer valuation, micro-segmentation, survey and repositioning works performed will bring along organizational changes as well. Accordingly, the red-tape in the FFP units must be decreased, and such units must be converted into units analyzing the customers and generating marketing materials, thus yielding gain to the company, instead of performing works that are used very limitedly by the card-issuing banks, rent-a-car companies, and the customers. At the moment, the FFPs have turned into compulsory but non-yielding units for the companies because of their current cumbersome structures and the financial burden caused by the accumulated miles. Even the mile depleting efforts can turn into high-yield values for the company just with the touch of Relationship Marketing (Gilbert, 1996). From this point of view such applications can be conducted:

When the customer's destination is determined at the ticketing phase, the system calculates the amount of carbon to be released at that travel automatically through the data such as flight distance, aircraft type, and average load factor. Then, the airline company suggests you to make a donation to an environmentalist organization or plant one or more than one sapling on your behalf against some of your miles. As per the mutual gain principle of the relationship marketing, both the passenger and the airline company generate joint gain over the environmentalist message on the one hand, and a great contribution is made to the customer loyalty on the other hand.

As is the case in this example, the customer can be guided to use the option of donating to the international aid organizations such as UNICEF, Red Cross, or the institutions like the local zoo, schools, etc. at the cost of some of his miles. Alternatively, certain airline promotional products that are in great demand may be sold, or a Fam trip covering the hangar, training, technical, kitchen, etc. departments of the airline company may be suggested. A full flight simulator (FFS) flight to be offered against a high amount of miles at the training facilities will receive great attention. As can be seen in all the above mentioned examples, the value the airline has or can access easily at present have been approached again with the relationship marketing perspective, and turned into values to generate mutual benefits and customer loyalty.

Likewise, the CRM units must have a structure enabling them to acquire customers and guide the other units and marketing units generating values for the acquired customers to make improvements, instead of being units trying the solve the customer complaints through formal and predetermined communication channels. At present, the CRM units respond every customer and every incident in the same way due to their mandatory procedures, and use the same compensation rates for all customers. With the customer value motivation and increased initiatives and authorities, they will cease to be a back office only and turn into an active marketing unit for the company.

In addition to the abovementioned existing units, a "Social Media Management" must be established (if not established already), thus ensuring 24-hour, uninterrupted and centralized management of the social media channels. American Airlines spends 20 minutes on average to answer the customer questions on Twitter, and is closely followed by KLM with 66 minutes (Social Bakers, 2013).Both airlines have established in-house departments in charge of this operation, and made a great progress on this issue.

Within the scope of re-organization, in case of a customer previously recorded and valued in the general distribution systems, the relevant units must be granted the initiative to offer this customer various extras such as awards, discounts, etc. If it is possible to annotate the passenger's PNR, which is not a difficult and costly change in systematic terms, he can be hosted in line with his customer position from ticketing to check-in, or even when he is aboard. For example, the call center, check-in officers or the pursers must definitely be authorized to do aboard last minute upgrade. In relation to this application, the airline companies must develop sub-programs or applications requiring membership. Such actions that can be described as efforts to raise the previously mentioned defection barrier will increase the passenger loyalty (Shaw, 2007).

Secondly, high-rate and frequent channels of communication with the customers must be sought. As a great channel that can meet this need fully, the social media are available to airline companies. For example, it is necessary to organize "Fam Trips", which are made in-house rather frequently, for the passengers as well, and to develop methods to give the passengers a chance to see the inside of the company or touch the product.

Services offered in standard by the airlines such as catering, onboard entertainment, etc. must be turned into an experience, thus achieving the differentiation. At present, the airline companies look alike from foods to aircraft types, from seats to advertisements, from uniforms to even smiles. In such an environment, differentiation can be achieved through understanding the precious value of "localness" and the high quantity-quality of the relations established with the customers. This is the factor behind the success and unique cabin experience of Turkish Airlines that have made a big break in recent years. From the catering concept to crew uniforms, airplane appearance to interior cabin designs, the company gives its passenger the message of difference under the motto of "Oriental Luxury with Western Quality".

In consequence, all of the abovementioned application models describe for the airline companies how to access the new source of income, which they have but cannot utilize. A long-term relationship built on mutual gain, which is the essence of the relationship marketing, can be transformed into revenue and profit that are the purpose of foundation of the company only through these stages. Otherwise, it will be nothing more than an abstract understanding and theory.

REFERENCES

Alabay, M. N. (2010). The process of transition from traditional marketing to a new one. *Suleyman Demirel University Journal of Faculty of Economics and Administrative Sciences*, *15*(2), 213–235.

Arlı, E. (2012). Effect of relationship marketing applications on re-purchasing intention, advising intention and satisfaction in marina management. *Anadolu University Journal of Social Sciences*, *13*(1), 61–76.

Arslan, A. (2008, July 25). Boosting relationship marketing. *Electronic Journal of Social Sciences*, *7*(25), 139–156.

Bareika, G. (2010). Customer Equity in Airline Industry. Master's Thesis, Universiteit van Amsterdam.

Belobaba, P., Odoni, A., & Barnhart, C. (2009). *The Global Airline Industry*. West Sussex: John Wiley & Sons. doi:10.1002/9780470744734

Berry, L. L. (1995). Relationship marketing of services: Growing interest, emerging perspectives. *Journal of the Academy of Marketing Science*, *23*(4), 236–245. doi:10.1177/009207039502300402

Berry, L. L. (2002). Relationship marketing of services: Perspectives from 1983 and 2000. *Journal of Relationship Marketing*, *1*(1), 59–77. doi:10.1300/J366v01n01_05

Berry, L. L., Parasuraman, A., & Zeithaml, V. A. (1983). Service firms need marketing skills. *Business Horizons*, 28–31.

Buhalis, D. (2003, November 13). *eAirlines: Strategic and tactical use of ICTs in the airline industry*. Guildford, England, UK.

Chaffey, D., Ellis-Chadwick, F., Johnston, K., & Mayer, R. (2006). *Internet Marketing: Strategy, Implementation and Practice* (3rd ed.). Essex: Prentice Hall.

Copulsky, J. R., & Wolf, M. J. (1990). Relationship marketing: Positioning for the future. *The Journal of Business Strategy*, *11*(4), 16–20. doi:10.1108/eb060069 PMID:10106864

Dodds, W. B., Monroe, K. B., & Grewal, D. (1991, August). Effects of price, brand, and store information on buyers' product evaluations. *JMR, Journal of Marketing Research*, *28*(3), 307–319. doi:10.2307/3172866

Doganis, R. (2005). *Flying off Course, The Economics of International Airlines*. New York: Routledge.

Doganis, R. (2006). *The Airline Business*. New York: Routledge.

Egan, J. (2011). *Relationship Markering: Exploring relational strategies in marketing*. Essex: Pearson.

Freiberg, K., & Freiberg, J. (1996). *Nuts! Southwest Airlines' Crazy Recipe for Business and Personal Success*. Austin, Texas: Bard Press.

Gazete Vatan. (2014, Ocak 13). *Türkiye'nin alışveriş istatistiği*. Retrieved Mayıs 17, 2014, from http://haber.gazetevatan.com/turkiyenin-alisveris-istatistigi/600264/184/haber

Gilbert, D. C. (1996). Relationship marketing and airline loyalty schemes. *Tourism Management*, *17*(8), 575–582. doi:10.1016/S0261-5177(96)00078-7

Gittell, J. H. (2003). *The Southwest Airlines Way*. New York: McGraw-Hill.

Grönroos, C. (1994). From marketing mix to relationship marketing: Towards a paradigm shift in marketing. *Management Decision*, *32*(2), 4–20. doi:10.1108/00251749410054774

Grönroos, C. (1999). Relationship marketing: Challenges for the organization. *Journal of Business Research*, *46*(3), 327–335. doi:10.1016/S0148-2963(98)00030-7

Grönroos, C. (2004). The relationship marketing process: Communication, interaction, dialogue, value. *Journal of Business and Industrial Marketing*, *19*(2), 99–113. doi:10.1108/08858620410523981

Gruen, T. W. (1995). The outcome set of relationship marketing in consumer markets. *International Business Review*, *4*(4), 447–469. doi:10.1016/0969-5931(95)00026-7

Gummesson, E. (1994). Making relationship operational. *International Journal of Service Industry Management*, *5*(5), 5–20. doi:10.1108/09564239410074349

Gummesson, E. (1997). Relationship marketing as a paradigm shift: Some conclusions from the 30R approach. *Management Decision, 35*(4), 267–272. doi:10.1108/00251749710169648

Gummesson, E. (1998). Implementation requires a relationship marketing paradigm. *Journal of the Academy of Marketing Science, 26*(3), 242–249. doi:10.1177/0092070398263006

Gummesson, E. (2002). Relationship marketing in the new economy. *Journal of Relationship Marketing, 1*(1), 37–57. doi:10.1300/J366v01n01_04

Gummesson, E. (2002). *Total Relationship Marketing*. Oxford: Butterworth-Heinemann.

Gupta, S., Hanssens, D., Hardie, B., Kahn, W., Kumar, V., Lin, N., & Sriram, S. (2006, November). Modeling customer lifetime value. *Journal of Service Research, 9*(2), 139–155. doi:10.1177/1094670506293810

Hallowell, R. (1996). The relationships of customer satisfaction, customer loyalty, and profitability:an empirical study. *International Journal of Service Industry Management, 7*(4), 27–42. doi:10.1108/09564239610129931

Hanssens, D. M., & Dekimpe, M. G. (2008). Models for the Financial-Performance Effects. In B. Wieranga (Ed.), *Handbook of Marketing Decision Models* (pp. 501–523). Los Angeles: Springer ScienceþBusiness Media. doi:10.1007/978-0-387-78213-3_15

Hennig-Thurau, T., Gwinner, K. P., & Gremler, D. D. (2002). Understanding relationship marketing outcomes. *Journal of Service Research, 4*(3), 230–247. doi:10.1177/1094670502004003006

Hollensen, S. (2010). *Marketing Management, A Relationship Approach* (2nd ed.). Essex: Prentice Hall.

Holloway, S. (2008). *Straight and Level: Practical Airline Economics* (3rd ed.). Aldershot, Hampshire: Ashgate.

Hooley, G., Piercy, N. F., & Nicoulaud, B. (2008). *Marketing Strategy and Competetive Positioning* (4th ed.). Essex: Prentice Hall.

Hougaard, S., & Bjerre, M. (2002). *Strategic Relationship Marketing*. Heidelberg: Springer. doi:10.1007/978-3-540-24813-2

IATA. (2010). *Annual Report 2010*. Berlin: June.

IATA. (2011). *The Impact of September 11 2001 on Aviation*. IATA.

İlban, M. O., & Kaşlı, M. (2013). A model of commitment for Generation Y: A survey on airline companies. *Istanbul University Journal of the School of Business, 42*(1), 133–152.

Jones, T. O., & Sasser, W. E. (1995, November-December). Why Satisfied Customers Defect. *Harvard Business Review*, 88-99.

Kanagal, N. (2005). Role of Relationship Marketing in Competitive Marketing Strategy. *Journal of Management and Marketing Research*, 1-17.

Karaca, Ş. (2010). Hizmet Sektöründe İlişki Pazarlaması. *Selçuk ÜNiversitesi İİBF Sosyal ve Ekonomik Araştırmalar Dergisi, 13*(9), 440–455.

kokpit.aero. (2013, Ağustos 21). *Kokpit.aero*. Retrieved Haziran 21, 2014, from http://kokpit.aero/index. php?route=content/flight_fear&flight_fear_id=55

Kotler, P. (2000). *Marketing Management, Milennium Edition*. Upper Saddle River, New Jersey: Prentice-Hall, Inc.

Kotler, P., & Keller, K. L. (2009). *Marketing Management*. New Jersey: Prentice Hall.

Küçükkancabaş, S., Akyol, A., & Ataman, B. M. (2007, August 15). *Examination of the effects of the relationship marketing orientation on the company performance*. Springer Science+Business Media.

Kumar, N., Scheer, L., & Kotler, P. (2000). From Market Driven to Market Driving. *European Management Journal*, *18*(22), 129–142.

Kumar, V., Pozza, I. D., Peterson, J. A., & Shah, D. (2009). Reversing the Logic: The Path to Profitability through Relationship Marketing. *Journal of Interactive Marketing*, 147–156.

Lee, D. (2007). *The Economics of Airline Institutions, Operations and Marketing*. Cambridge, USA: Elsevier.

Leick, R. (2007, October). *Building Airline Passenger Loyalty through an Understanding of Customer Value: A Relationship Segmentation of Airline Passengers*. PhD Thesis, Cranfield University.

Lindgreen, A., & Crawford, I. (1999). Implementing, Monitoring and Measuring Programme of Relationship Marketing. *Marketing Intelligence & Planning*, 231–239.

Liston-Heyes, C. (2002). Pie in the sky? Real versus perceived values of air miles. *Journal of Consumer Policy*, *25*(1), 1–26. doi:10.1023/A:1014594718701

Man, L. W. (1998). *Relationship marketing: the case of Cathay Pacific*. Hong Kong: The University of Hong Kong.

Maxim, A. (2009). Relationship Marketing: A New Paradigm in Marketing Theory and Practice. University of Iasi, 287-300.

McKensey and Company. (2011, October). Sales 2.0 For Airlines. *Cost Analyse*. McKensey and Company.

Michael, H., & Morris, J. B. (1998). Relationship marketing in practice. *Industrial Marketing Management*, *27*, 360–361.

Morgan, R. M., & Hunt, S. D. (1994). The commitment-trust theory of relationship marketing. *Journal of Marketing*, *58*(3), 20–38.

Morris, M. H., Brunyee, J., & Page, M. (1998). Relationship marketing in practice: Myths and realities. *Industrial Marketing Management*, *27*, 359–371.

O'Connell, J. F. (2011). The rise of the Arabian Gulf carriers: An insight into the business model of Emirates Airline. *Journal of Air Transport Management*, 339–346.

O'Malley, L., & Tynan, C. (2000). Relationship marketing in consumer markets: Rhetoric or reality? *European Journal of Marketing*, *34*(7), 797–815.

Palmatier, R. W. (2008). *Relationship Marketing*. Cambridge, MA: Marketing Science Institute.

Palmatier, R. W., Gopalakrishna, S., & Houston, M. B. (2006). Returns on business-to-business relationship marketing investments strategies for leveraging profits. *Marketing Science*, 25(5), 477–493.

Palmatier, R. W., Scheer, L. K., Houston, M. B., Kenneth, R. E., & Gopalakrishna, S. (2007). Use of relationship marketing programs in building customer-salesperson and customer-firm relationships: Differential influences on financial outcomes. *International Journal of Research in Marketing*, 210–223.

Palmer, A. J. (1995). Relationship Marketing:Local Implementation of a Universal Concept. *International Business Review*, 4(4), 471–481.

Payne, A., Christopher, M., Clark, M., & Peck, H. (1999). *Relationship marketing for competetive advantage*. Oxford: Butterworth-Heinemann.

Peter, M. S. (2007). *Airline Finance*. Hampshire: Ashgate.

Pilarski, A. M. (2007). *Why Can't We Make Money in Aviation?* New York: Ashgate.

Rapp, R. (2000). Customer Relationship Marketing in the Airline Industry. In U. Hansen & T. Hennig-Thurau (Eds.), *Relationship Marketing* (pp. 317–330). Berlin, Heidelberg: Springer-Verlag.

Ravald, A., & Grönroos, C. (1996). The value concept and relationship marketing. *European Journal of Marketing*, 30(2), 19–30.

Reichheld, F. F., & Sasser, W. E. (1990). Zero Defections: Quality Comes to Services. *Harvard Business Review*, 3-8.

Reinchheld, F. F., Markey, R. G., & Hopton, C. (2000). The Loyalty Effect: The Relationship Between Loyalty and Profits. *European Business Journal*, 134-139.

Rowe, W. G., & Barnes, J. J. (1998). Relationship Marketing and Sustained Competitive Advantage. *Journal of Market Focused Management*, 2, 281–297.

Schultz, D. E., Tannenbaum, S. I., & Robert, F. L. (1993). *Integrated Marketing Communications*. Lincolnwood: NTC Business Books.

Selvi, M. S. (2007). *İlişkisel Pazarlama*. Ankara: Detay Yayıncılık.

Şendur, F. (2009). The Importance of Creating customer Value in Relational context of Marketing: A Research on Bank Sector. *Master Thesis*, 25-29. Balıkesir, turkey: Balıkesir University.

Serpen, E. (2013, November 21). Airline Business and Financial Planning. *Aviation Economics and Financial Analysis*. Istanbul: Istanbul Technical University.

Sharma, A., Tzokas, N., Saren, M., & Kyziridis, P. (1999). Antecedents and Consequences of Relationship Marketing. *Industrial Marketing Management*, 601–611.

Shaw, S. (2007). *Airline Marketing and Management*. Hampshire, England: Ashgate Publishing Company.

Sin, L. Y., Tse, A. C., Yau, O. H., Chow, R. P., Lee, J. S., & Lorett, L. B. (2005). Relationship marketing orientation: Scale development. *Journal of Business Research*, (58): 185–194.

Sindell, K. (2000). *Loyalty Marketing for the Internet Age: How to Identify, Attract, Serve, and Retain Customers in an E-Commerce Environment: Search Results*. Chicago: Dearborn Trade Pub.

Social Bakers. (2013, April 01). *Havadaki Rekabet Sosyal Medya'da Nasıl?* Retrieved June 18, 2014, from http://www.pazarlamasyon.com/2013/02/havadaki-rekabet-sosyal-medyada-nasil/

SocialBakers. (2014). *Statistics*. Retrieved April 27, 2014, from Social Bakers: http://www.socialbakers.com/twitter/group/brands/tag/airlines/

Sorce, P. (2002). *Marketing Strategies that Build Customer Commitment and Loyalty*. Rochester, New York: Printing Industry Center.

Taneja, N. K. (2010). *Looking Beyond the Runway*. Farnham: Ashgate.

Teichert, T., Shehu, E., & von Wartburg, I. (2008). Customer segmentation revisited: The case of the airline industry. *Transportation Research*, 227–242.

Thorsten, H.-T., & Hansen, U. (2000). *Relationship Marketing*. Berlin, Heidelberg: Springer.

Turkish Airlines. (2014, March.). *Turkish Airlines 2013 Annual Financial Statement*. Istanbul: Turkish Airlines.

Uslu, A., Durmuş, B., & Kolivar, B. K. (2013). Analyzing the Brand Equity of Turkish Airlines Services: Comparing the Japanese and Turkish Perspectives. *9th International Strategic Management Conference* (pp. 446-454). Istanbul: Procedia - Social and Behavioral Sciences.

Verhoef, P. C. (2003). Understanding the effect of customer relationship management efforts on customer retention and customer share development. *Journal of Marketing*, *67*, 30–45.

Voss, G. B., & Voss, Z. G. (1997). Implementing a relationship marketing program: A case study and managerial implications. *Journal of Services Marketing*, *11*(4), 278–298.

www.new-milesandsmiles.com. (2014, april 28). *Miles and Smiles*. Retrieved May 21, 2014, from Turkish Airlines: http://www.turkishairlines.com/tr-tr/kurumsal/haberler/miles-smiles/pek-yakinda-miles-smilesta-yeni-bir-donem-yeniliklerle-basliyor

Wessels, D. (2006). *Consumer Loyalty in the Airline Industry*. Philadelphia: University of Pennsylvania.

Zineldin, M. (2000). Total relationship management (TRM) and total quality management (TQM). *Managerial Auditing Journal*, *2*, 20–28.

Zineldin, M., & Philipson, S. (2007). Kotler and Borden are not dead: Myth of relationship marketing and truth of the 4Ps. *Journal of Consumer Marketing*, 229–241.

KEY TERMS AND DEFINITIONS

Deregulation: Airline deregulation is the process of removing government-imposed rules and restrictions mostly on financial structure of airlines and slot rights, pricing and operational regulations of airlines. The term was born with "1978 Airline Deregulation Act" when control over air travel industry passed from the political to the real market and today it is identified with liberalization acts in sector. Deregulation process in USA also triggered the deregulation acts all over the World and helped to shape of free market conditions.

European Volcano/Ash Cloud Crisis: In 5th of April 2010, the volcano Eyjafjallajökull in Island started eruption and massive and dense volcanic ash clouds caused to stop air traffic in busiest air space of the world. All flights from or to major European airports have stopped and millions of passengers to be stranded in airports. This was the largest air traffic shut-down since World War II in Europe. IATA estimated that during this closure (5th to 21st of April, 2010) 100,000 flights were cancelled in total, and 10 million people stranded or unable to board their flights. According to IATA data Airlines lost 1.7 Billion Dollars, and Airports lost 250 million Euros. Specifically, low cost carriers which have inter Europe flights had the worse hit comparing to legacy carriers. Low cost carriers cancelled %61 of their flights. Besides, 75% of European and 30% of total worldwide airline capacity was cut during this period.

Kotlerist Marketing Concept: The concept named as also the marketing mix or 4P Concept. According to Philip Kotler, Marketing is defined as a social and managerial process by which individuals and groups obtain what they need and want through creating, offering and exchanging products of value with others is known as Marketing. The base of marketing is defined as exchange in this concept. Price, product, promotion, and place are major components. The four Ps can be expanded to the seven P's or eight P's according to different nature of services. Kotler also explains marketing as a social process.

Life Time Value: LTV is a way of measurement that can be defined as the net profit attributed to the entire future relationship with a customer. In other words, LTV is the financial value of a customer relationship, based on the present value of the future cash. This measurement focuses on long-term value of their customer relationships and defines the upper limit of spending to acquire new customers.

Low Cost Carriers: Low-cost carriers or low-cost airlines are airlines offer comparatively low prices but offer fewer comforts such low leg rooms, no on board meals. LCCs charge for all extra services such as meal, baggage. LCCs mostly has dense schedules for specific destinations with high turn around rates or prefer not to fly major airports. Especially after 9/11, LCCs had their golden age. In order to keep fleet costs low they use single type of aircraft. Southwest, Ryanair, and Easyjet are leading LCCs.

Pareto Principle: At the beginning of the century, first, it is mentioned by an Italian economist Vilfredo Pareto in order to formulate unequal distribution of wealth and resources in Italy. He finds out that twenty percent of the people owned eighty percent of the wealth. So, this was the base of so called 80/20 principle. Lately in 1940s, Joseph Juran, working on the theory of "vital few and trivial many" studied Pareto's work and named it as Pareto Principle. He applied Pareto's observations about economics to a broader body of work.Juran's observation of the "vital few and trivial many" states the principle that %20 of something always are responsible for %80 of the results.

Relational Coordination: Relational coordination is a research model which is developed and proposed by Gittell in 2002. The model is used to assess organizational coordination in four airlines in the United States. The idea of relational coordination is based on the interactive nature between both relationships and communication in business environment. A higher level of relational coordination will then affect organizational outputs as in efficiency and quality in operations. Relational coordination can be used for measuring and analyzing the communication and relationships networks through which work is coordinated across functional and organizational boundaries.

Share of Wallet: SOW is a term which refers to customers' total spending that a business captures in the products or services that it offers. As a performance scale it shows the amount of business in percentage that a company gets from a specific customer. This scale can be used to increase repurchase, customer loyalty, and find marketing opportunities. Moreover, SOW indicates unmet needs that the product is not satisfying.

Word of Mouth: WOM is an expected marketing outcome which becomes a marketing technique also by oral or written recommendations made by a satisfied customer to the prospective customers of a product or service. It is accepted as the most effective form of promotion. As a marketing tool WOM is an interactive process such that customers are collaborating with the business, product or service for which they have derived enough satisfaction that they are willing to speak out about it and even recommend it to others.

This research was previously published in the Handbook of Research on Behavioral Finance and Investment Strategies edited by Zeynep Copur, pages 405-447, copyright year 2015 by Business Science Reference (an imprint of IGI Global).

Chapter 27
Digital Marketing Analytics:
The Web Dynamics of Inside Blackberry Blog

Shirin Alavi
Jaypee Institute of Information Technology, India

Vandana Ahuja
Jaypee Business School, India

ABSTRACT

Technological advances and the speed with which new technologies are being embraced by organizations, along with the rising power of the consumers and their ability to get what they want, when they want it, from whomever they want, have opened up new challenges for customer relationship management and marketing. Thus the need for understanding the digital world and its application becomes one of the greatest competitive aspects for a business's survival. The exhortation of globalization holds no meaning without the concept of what is being termed as 'Digitization'. Blackberry has started a long and hard climb to regain its lost glory. Supporting its product improvement and repositioning strategies are a set of well-defined digital marketing strategies. This manuscript explores the dynamics of Inside Blackberry-an online endeavour of Blackberry to trace the E-Marketing objectives of the Blog and its ability to leverage the behavioral internet theory for online branding, building usability and reciprocity, strengthening credibility and consumer persuasion.

1. INTRODUCTION

Research In Motion (RIM), a global leader in wireless innovation, revolutionized the mobile industry with the introduction of the BlackBerry® solution in 1999. After several years of staying in business, Blackberry, armed with the tagline "Keep Moving", has mounted a make or break campaign to last all through 2013. BlackBerry products and services are used by millions of customers around the world to stay connected to the people and content that matter most throughout their day. The BlackBerry product line includes the BlackBerry® PlayBook™ tablet, the award-winning BlackBerry Smartphone, software for businesses and accessories.

DOI: 10.4018/978-1-5225-5187-4.ch027

As technology emerged as an enabler for a new generation of strivers, Blackberry has launched an aggressive relationship marketing campaign, to fight competition and to resonate with its consumers. This manuscript analyses in detail, one of the components of Blackberry's digital marketing strategy-*The Inside Blackberry Blog.*

2. LITERATURE REVIEW

2.1. Blogs

Blogs are customizable online web spaces that allow users to post content, which is displayed in reverse chronological order. Depending on the blogging software or service used, entries may include video and other rich media. Visitors to an individual's personal blog can typically post comments to specific entries and can also elect to be automatically notified whenever a new entry has been posted by subscribing to a blog's feed. Blogs are personal journals or reversed chronological commentaries written by individuals and made publicly accessible on the web. To many people, blogs are not much different from regular websites; however, they have distinctive technological features that differentiate them from other forms of computer mediated communication. These features include: (i) easy-to-use content management system; (ii) archive-oriented structure; (iii) latest-information-first order; (iv) links to other blogs; and (v) ease of responding to previous blog postings (Huffaker, D. A., & Calvert, S. L, 2005). However, with the evolution of blogging technology, and the fast expansion of the blogosphere, the form, content and functions of blogs have expanded tremendously. These weblogs are often perceived as low threshold tools to publish online, empowering individual expression in public. Although a weblog is a personal writing space, its public nature suggests a need to communicate, (Efimova, L., & Hendrick, S. 2005) and invites feedback. Weblogs can be positioned as their own genre, situated on an intermediate point between standard web pages and asynchronous computer mediated communication along dimensions of frequency of update, symmetry of communicative exchange and multimodality (Herring, S. C. 2007). Because of the flexible and interconnected nature of blogs, people can use blogs for various purposes including: keeping personal diary (Bortree, D. S. 2005), interacting with other bloggers building a virtual community; and disseminating messages to a mass audience (Lawson-Borders, G., & Kirk, R. 2005).

Even though the majority of blogs contain personal thoughts or feelings of authors that are not intended for mass dissemination, blogs exist in a public arena, the Internet, and messages posted in blogs are open to anyone with an Internet connection (Gurak, L. J., Antonijevic, S., Johnson, L., Ratliff, C., & Reyman, J. 2004). More and more bloggers are recognizing this mass communication potential of blogs and use blogs to publish their opinions on public issues and to disseminate them to a mass audience (Trammell, K. D., & Keshelashvili, A. 2005). Bloggers desire connection with their audience, want to insert themselves into known, sometimes unknown social spaces, to update, inform or advise, to greet or grumble, to pontificate, confess, create and to think (Nardi, B. A., Schiano, D. J., Gumbrecht, M., & Swartz, L. 2004). Blogs are a global phenomenon that has hit the mainstream. Discussions in the Blogosphere have been used by the media as a gauge of public opinion on various issues. The active Blogosphere can be defined as - The ecosystem of interconnected communities of bloggers and readers at the convergence of journalism and conversation (Barsky, E. 2006). Bloggers are not a homogeneous group. There are personal, professional and corporate bloggers, all having differing goals and covering a myriad range of topics, using different techniques to drive traffic to their blogs, different publishing tools on their blog and distinct metrics for measuring success. Social exchange via Blog fosters enterprise reputation (Wu, C. H., Kao, S. C., & Lin, H. H. 2013).

2.2. Corporate Blogs

This concept has found widespread acceptance in the corporate world with the emergence of 'corporate' or 'organizational' blogs. These are people who blog in an official or semi-official capacity at a company, or are so affiliated with the company where they work that even though they are not officially spokespeople for the company, they are clearly affiliated and endorsed explicitly or implicitly by the company. Also termed as a hybrid of the personal blog (Smudde, P. M., & Courtright, J. L. 2011), they are increasingly being explored by public relations practitioners and feature the insights, assessments, commentary, and other discourse devoted to a single company.

Organizational blogs seem to appear at the intersection of personal reflection and professional communication. They have evolved from both online and offline modes of communication and have characteristics of both personal and professional communication (Kelleher, T., & Miller, B.M, 2006). Posts in blogs are tagged with keywords, allowing for content categorization and also for gaining access to the content through tagging as a theme based classification system. Blogging is shaping into a useful organizational tool for brand propagation and interaction with consumers with several corporates having effectively launched Corporate Blogs. Perceived usefulness of bloggers' recommendations and trust had significant influential effect on blog users' attitude towards and intention to shop online (Hsu, C. L., Lin, J. C. C., & Chiang, H. S. 2013).

An effective blog fosters community and conversation (Kathy, 2004), drives traffic to the product website, and serves as a medium for interaction with consumers thereby shaping consumer perception, eliciting responses, and through a two way thought exchange process, aids in fostering a connection with the consumers. Further, consumer feedback can be leveraged for organizational consumption with respect to new product development, product features and consumer expectations. The elements of storytelling blogs, "perceived aesthetics", "narrative structure", and "self-reference", can indirectly influence readers' intention through empathy and attitude. Blog design needs to consider aesthetics, narrative structure, and relevance to readers (Hsiao, K. L., Lu, H. P., & Lan, W. C. 2013).

2.3. Digital Marketing

The entire value chain in a typical marketing organization starts at the supplier and ends at the consumer. Digital technology is playing significant roles in enriching the sales and marketing strategies of an organization. It has forced companies to find new ways to expand the markets in which they compete, to attract and retain customers by tailoring products and services to their needs, and to restructure their business processes to deliver products and services more efficiently and effectively (Shin, N. 2001).

Digital marketing has equipped the erstwhile consumer with greater access to information, more opportunities to compare products and services, greater convenience, thereby making him the dominating partner in the consumer-buyer relationship. This has pushed brands towards greater customer-centricity, emphasizing greater focus on the relationship between the organization and the consumer. The success factor for firms has been heavily dependent on the extent to which the Internet can be harnessed as a marketing tool and better service can enhance consumer relationships (Rust, R. T., & Kannan, P. K. 2003). Due to its potential for interactive communication, the Internet has been considered a promising tool for digital marketing (Thorbjørnsen, H., Supphellen, M., Nysveen, H., & Pedersen, P. E. 2002). The term digital marketing encompasses many activities carried out through computer networks and the Internet, including inter-organizational commerce, intra-organizational transactions, and transactions involving the individual consumer (Adelaar, 2000). The impact of the Internet has made a substantial difference in business-to-business (B2B) transactions. (Teo, H. H., Wei, K. K., & Benbasat, I. 2003; Venkatraman, N., 2000).

2.4. Influence of Internet on Digital Marketing

Internet is nowadays one of the key determinants of changes occurring in marketing. Digital marketing brings us closer to accomplish the mission of maximizing the satisfaction of buyers by simultaneous maintenance of profitability and considerable improvement of intra organizational processes of organizations.

The Internet has been highly influential in removing separations between IT and "the business" (Earl, M. and Khan, B., 2001).The Internet is a nearly perfect market because information is instantaneous and buyers can compare the offerings of sellers worldwide. The result is fierce price competition and vanishing brand loyalty (Srinivasan, S. S., Anderson, R., & Ponnavolu, K. 2002).Many applications of Internet such as online communities and blogs can help to provide interactivity to consumers (Holland, J., & Baker, S. M. 2001).Organisations will benefit from understanding the gains that can be acquired by utilising this medium for growth and enhanced profitability by leveraging the cost benefits offered by this medium coupled with ease of access and enhanced collaborative opportunities.

2.5. Building Consumer Engagement

Information overload in the internet age can force people to become passive receptors of information. It is hence important for an organization to make sure that the right information reaches the right people at the right time. A higher perceived value by the consumer in the organizational information will stimulate consumer interest leading to a desire to interact, achieving '*engagement*' from the organizational perspective. Each customer touch point has a significant role to play in the consumer life cycle by influencing the customer experience. The customer experience does not begin and end at a transaction, website visit, or conversation with an agent. The customer experience process encompasses the moment the customer becomes aware of the organization, product or service comprises multiple independent interactions, transactions, and contacts along the way. A customer's perception of an organization is built as a result of the interaction across multiple-channels, not through one channel, and that a positive customer experience can result in increased share of business (Pan, S. L., & Lee, J. N. 2003).

Consumer engagement can be defined as "Repeated interactions that strengthen the emotional, psychological or physical investment a customer has in a brand". These levels of engagement can be measured by the complexity and ultimate depth of user actions and the related amount of attention associated with each. This measurement also allows for the understanding of the time spent with the message or the causal action stemming from the attention. For example, a user might be engaged enough to read an article as well as related user comments following the text. But how is this situation different from a user that does the same, but also leaves a new comment of their own. The action of regarding content, followed by an action of engagement is the causal agent that defines this principal. Also worth noting is that each user action can provide different levels of attention as well as influence further interactions. While the viewing of a video online is considered an impression, there are different and unique tiers of attention and engagement in each play such as the length of active viewing as well as subsequent sharing, rating, favoriting, forwarding, and adding which are all secondary interactions that form the engagement.

The ability of marketing to engage and endear consumers will ultimately determine whether a user eventually enters into a greater relationship with a brand or organization. It is important to measure the engagement of customers, prospective customers and detractors with an organizational brand, in every area of engagement. Engagement needs to be understood by type, the factors leading to engagement and the value associated with each in terms of ultimate adoption, sales and brand loyalty. The engagement theory comprises the dimensions of Involvement, Interaction, Intimacy and Influence (Singh, A., Kumar, B., & Singh, V. K. 2010). The level of user engagement achieved by interaction between organization and consumer is an important factor contributing to product adoption, thereby driving sales and brand loyalty, as demonstrated in the case of a Corporate Blog, which allows consumers to interact with products, brands and organizations. In the Web 2.0 context, consumer engagement is visible through the means of publishing, posting comments, subscribing, bookmarking, emailing, distributing and networking. When measuring engagement, the level of user interaction is an obvious and important component, and each of the above stated user actions indicate a different level of engagement (Ghuneim, M., Salomon, S., & Katsunuma, M. 2008).

2.6. Brand Communication

Regular communication between organization and consumer reinforces organizational image and product messages, builds brand awareness and strengthens brand recall. By creating meaningful brand encounters, the consumer brand relationship can be strengthened. When consumers are regularly in contact with a brand, they may begin to perceive it as a person, a trusted friend who is part of their everyday life, thereby strengthening their loyalty towards the brand. Customer brand loyalty in cyberspace demonstrates an evolution from the traditional product driven, marketer controlled concept towards a distribution driven, consumer controlled and technology facilitated concept (Schultz, D. 2000). When consumers engage in a brand relationship, (Sheth, J. N., & Parvatiyar, A. 1995) they begin to perceive the value related to the brand. Brand knowledge affects future purchases via a brand relationship path that includes brand satisfaction, brand trust and attachment to the brand (Esch, F. R., Langner, T., Schmitt, B. H., & Geus, P. 2006).

2.7. Content Organization

In this dynamic blog landscape, the typology of content which attracts greater consumer interest and generates subsequent engagement by soliciting participation and involvement through comments needs to be identified to enable corporates to post in accordance with consumer receptivity. Customers will devour the content only when they perceive value in the same. The following outcomes of the previous research study (Ahuja, V., & Medury, Y. 2010) have been used in this research manuscript.

The content created by an organization can be classified on the basis of the objective of communication under 'Organizational', 'Relational' and 'Promotional' categories.

2.7.1. Organizational Content

Organizational posts can be directed specifically towards sharing news on organizational growth, new projects and endeavors, organizational activities directed towards Corporate Social Responsibility, employee experiences, to those talking about cultural events, awards and other organizational achievements etc. The aim is to use the blog as an outreach mechanism to enhance organizational brand image and build greater respect and value for the organization.

2.7.2. Promotional Content

They include posts sharing factual data with respect to product features, prices, new products, product comparisons, promotional campaigns and response to any product related grievances. Also included are posts passively persuading consumers to embrace the product and those addressing technological issues.

2.7.3. Relational Content

This category includes posts soliciting feedback, those addressing controversies or rumors about the organization, brand, product or service. Also included are posts addressing dealer issues, bloggers meets, consumer worries and those directed towards consumer redressal. All other posts are classified under the general category.

An increased organizational effort in terms of repeated contacts with the consumer through increased number of posts in a virtual environment can create an e-relationship between organization and consumer by stimulating consumer interest and achieving consumer participation by commenting on the posts hosted by the organization. Number of comments a blog entry attracts and the number of individuals that write the comments are indicators of participation that significantly load onto involvement (Dwyer, Paul, 2007).

2.8. The Inside Blackberry Blog

A careful exploration of the online domain, and analysis of online conversations have created for Blackberry, a customer relationship marketing opportunity, by listening to what the consumers are saying and leveraging the same by participating in the consumer discussions. *The Inside BlackBerry* blog is divided into three sub blogs - The *Developer* Blog, about the organization and its employees, The *Business* Blog, which deals with promotion and business related activities and the *Help* blog, which gives technical support as well as general service to those who are in need. Currently the archives span 1015 posts and over 12,609 comments, contained within the meager confines of 15 categories (Figure 1). They have gathered experts in social application, desktop software pro, software specialist and hardware experts as well in this community blog. It wants to take every opportunity to connect customers to the great conversations and expertise already being shared online. The global rank of the blog is 840 while the rank in India is 434.

This shows high involvement of visitors as average number of page views is more than the standard number of pages for returning back from the website (Figure 2). This shows that the blog is able to involve its visitors very well. Also the bounce back rate for the website is decreasing (Figure 3).

Figure 1. Quantitative analysis of blog

Figure 2. Daily pageviews per user

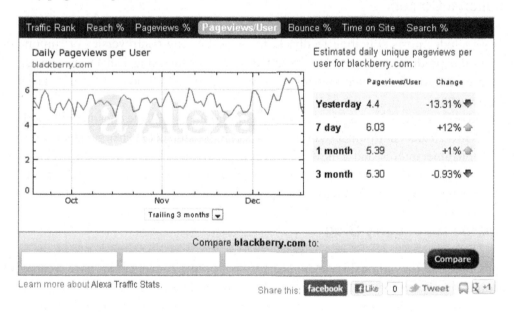

2.9. Behavioral Internet Theory

The behavioral internet theory states that users relate to virtual information with many of the same human traits and tendencies as they do in the physical world. This is extremely useful, as it indicates that the experience and guidelines of business will retain their validity in the online world also. There are striking differences between offline and online communication. Print messages are just not the same as a phone call or face to face meeting. This leads to important differences in the types of communication and interaction that occur with this limited communication method. The result can be inappropriate behavior. Thus a right online balance is instrumental in consumer's enjoyment of the medium.

Figure 3. Bounce rate (percent)

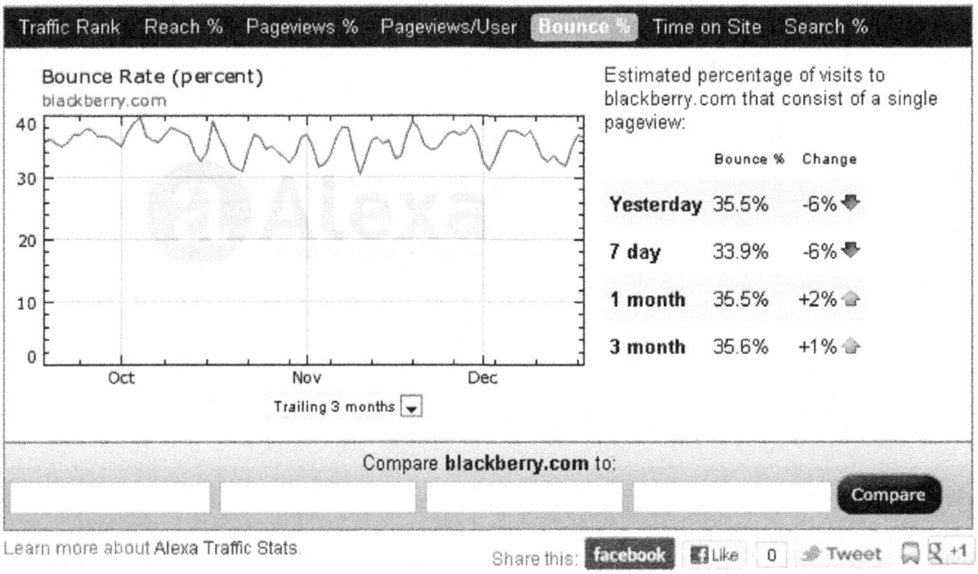

3. RESEARCH METHODOLOGY

3.1. Pilot Study

A pilot study was carried out as part of the research. This was conducted with a focus group *of experts in the field of Digital Marketing*. This focus group comprised a set of practitioners from the industry, who were already using the online web spaces for consumer engagement and participation. The experts were asked to *classify the 15 content categories under the content typologies viz* 'Organizational', 'Relational', 'Promotional' and 'General' categories (as presented in Table 1).

A Blog Analysis helps us identify the number of posts in each content typology, as presented in Table 2.

3.2. Content Categorization: Inside Blackberry Blog Analysis

The content has been organised on the blog under 15 categories viz. *CES, CES Event, Enterprise, Event, Feature, Global, How-to, Inside BlackBerry, News, Personalization, Product, Security, Top 5, Uncategorized and WES*. The total post in all categories is 1015 and these have garnered more than 12,609 comments.

It is clearly evident that *Inside BlackBerry Blog* focuses more on the promotional and relational categories. *This clearly implies how much of customer relationship effort they put in this blog.*

3.2.1. Promotional

Like any other company it gives updates on the different features and new product lines that have been introduced. Main features discussed are about camera and some game applications. Features are introduced by blogging of free demos and offers on particular features.

Table 1. Content categories under content typologies

Organizational	Promotional	Relational	General
About the Authors	Product Features	Top 5	Global
Enterprise	Products	Inside BlackBerry	Security
	CES Events	How-to	News
	Enterprise	Personalization	WES

Table 2. Percentage of posts under each content typology

ITEM	Organizational	Promotional	Relational	General
Percentage of posts in content typology	4.8%	32.5%	30.1%	37.3%

The Consumer Electronics Association (CEA) is a standards and trade organization for the consumer electronics industry in the United States. CEA works to influence public policy holds events such as the International Consumer Electronic Show (CES) and SINOCES, conducts market research, and helps its members and regulators implement technical standards. The CEA-sponsored show typically hosts previews of products and new product announcements. Inside Blackberry have categories for CES reviews, CES events and this very well shows the platform or the standard Blackberry is following. It keeps the viewer updates with their CES events.

3.2.2. Relational

Almost every week they have a system of blogging of Friday Top Five tips or techniques to make the use of blackberry more efficient by the user. Example: five ways to save battery life, five ways to setup and even top five applications needed for Blackberry product. The blog even provides a help section called How-to, in this category its main interest is solving customer's problem by acting as a help desk. Now Blackberry is thinking more about how friendly their product can be for the customer so they have started a conversation on personalization. It talks about Blackberry ID account, organizing message/inbox list, how to set up personal social networks etc. Blackberry blog also introduced fan of the month, as presented in Figure 4. They choose a lucky BlackBerry user and ask them series of question to know more about that winner and how he or she came across BlackBerry and how it's been useful to them so far.

3.2.3. Organizational

In this blog we don't find much description about the corporate itself except for mentioning some accomplishment they made. But it does have a tab called Authors where all the information right from name, designation to individual hobbies of each member who has posted on the blog is available. It is there to build connections between the one who post on the blog and those who comments.

Figure 4. BlackBerry fan of the month

3.2.4. General

Current and global news are discussed time to time about Blackberry as a whole and how its products are performing in the market. It gives awareness and sometimes brand recalls to the blog members.

3.3. Formulation of Research Instrument

A research instrument was formulated. 500 consumers were asked to rate their responses on a Likert Scale (1 to 5).

Q.1: The following statements (presented in Box 1) relate to the adherence *of Blackberry Blog to the Behavioral Internet theory*. As a consumer please indicate your choice by encircling one option out of 1, 2, 3, 4 and 5. (1-Highest, 5-Lowest).

3.4. Sampling Technique, Sample Size and Data Collection

The data was collected across 500 consumers who have been patronizing the Blackberry Blog and its products as well as services using *internet sampling technique*. Under internet sampling technique the *recruited panel* method was used. In order to maintain the integrity and reliability in the sample the password protection was done wherein a respondent is required to enter the password at the beginning of the survey to gain access into the survey. Password protection ensures that a respondent completes the survey only one time.

Box 1. Research instrument

S.No	Parameter		Choice			
1	I agree that Blackberry blog is motivating people to share their personal experience	1	2	3	4	5
2	I agree that Blackberry Blog also ask about members topic of interest and quality of service expected.	1	2	3	4	5
3	I agree that my personality traits and behavior is same online as it is in real life.	1	2	3	4	5
4	I agree that on the Blackberry blog the blog manager and other authors are posting interesting articles.	1	2	3	4	5
5	I agree that most of the articles also include supporting videos to involve people in the blog.	1	2	3	4	5
6	I agree that blog links its articles and conversations to popular social networking sites such as twitter, facebook etc.	1	2	3	4	5
7.	I agree that content on the blog is easily perceivable and accessible.	1	2	3	4	5
8.	I agree that content on the blog is written in simple language and is highly understandable.	1	2	3	4	5
9.	I agree that navigation through the blog is easy.	1	2	3	4	5
10.	I agree that articles on the blog have relevant data according to the topic as well as the blog.	1	2	3	4	5
11.	I agree that dynamics and personal communication systematically differ online.	1	2	3	4	5
12.	I agree that the tools of communication lack the richness and subtlety of face to face messages.	1	2	3	4	5
13..	I agree that the blog managers constantly ask the members for feedback and suggestions.	1	2	3	4	5
14.	I agree that with the help of this blog Blackberry is able to segment its customers and build quality for them.	1	2	3	4	5
15.	1) I agree that articles are being posted for complaints and problems and how they are being solved.	1	2	3	4	5
16.	2) I agree that blog has very simple graphic design.	1	2	3	4	5
17.	3) I agree that blog is compatible with all versions of web browsers.	1	2	3	4	5

The online questionnaire was drafted using Qualtrics (www.qualtrics.com). The appropriate link was hosted on the respective blog. The pre-requisite for a consumer to fill the questionnaire was that the consumer should have a minimum frequency of visiting the blog at least more than once a month.

3.5. Tools of Data Analysis

3.5.1. Factor Analysis

Factor analysis, also called exploratory factor analysis (EFA), is a class of procedures used for reducing and summarizing data. Each variable is expressed as a linear combination of the underlying factors. Likewise, the factors themselves can be expressed as linear combinations of the observed variables. The factors are extracted in such a way that the first factor accounts for the highest variance in the data, the second the next highest, and so on. In formulating the factor analysis problem, the variables to be included in the analysis should be specified based on past research, theory, and the judgement of the researcher.

These variables should be measured on an interval or ratio scale Factor analysis is based on a matrix of correlation between the variables. The appropriateness of the correlation matrix for factor analysis can be statistically tested. The two basic approaches to factor analysis are principal components analysis and common factor analysis. I have used the principal component analysis method. Here the total variance in the data is considered. The diagonal of the correlation matrix consists of unities, and full variance is brought into the factor matrix. Principal component analysis is recommended when the primary concern is to determine the minimum number of factors that will account for maximum variance in the data for use in subsequent multivariate analysis. The factors are called principal components. In principal component analysis the initial or unrotated factor matrix indicates the relationship between the factors and individual variables, it seldom results in factors that can be interpreted, because the factors are correlated with many variables. Therefore rotation is used to transform the factor matrix into a simpler one that is easier to interpret. The most commonly used method of rotation is the varimax procedure, which results in orthogonal factors. The rotated factor matrix forms the basis for interpreting the factors. Factor scores can be computed for each respondent. Alternatively, surrogate variables may be selected by examining the factor matrix and selecting for each factor a variable with the highest or near highest loading. The differences between the observed correlations and the reproduced correlations, as estimated from the factor matrix, can be examined to determine model fit. The principal components method of extraction was used for data reduction. Components with Eigen values greater than 1 were extracted. As the communalities were all high, the extracted components represented the variables well.

3.6. Data Analysis and Results

The research instrument drafted for assessing the adherence *of Blackberry Blog to the Behavioral Internet theory* was evaluated using Factor analysis. The data collected from the 500 consumers was subjected to a Factor analysis. The principal components method of extraction was used for data reduction. Components with Eigen values greater than 1 were extracted. As the communalities were all high, the extracted components represented the variables well. The rotated component matrix helped determine what the components represented, as demonstrated in Table 3. This was done by using the highest loading as a determinant of the factor an attribute belonged to. This procedure helped load the various attributes pertaining to Adherence of *Blackberry Blog to the Behavioral Internet theory* onto the factors of The Media Equation, Flow, Content Accessibility, Social Cues, Quality Cues and Friendly Technology (Table 4).

3.4.1. The Behavioral Internet Theory and the Blackberry Blog

1. **The Media Equation:** It says that people in the virtual world behave in similar way as they behave in real life. This blog is motivating people to share their personal experience with the Blackberry products, their views, or post complaints. The Blog also caters to the topics that members want to discuss, or the services they expect from the company.
2. **Flow:** It is about how much a visitor gets lost in the site and doesn't realize the time spent there. For this purpose the blog manager and other authors are posting interesting articles. Most of the articles also include supporting videos to encourage member engagement in the blog. It also links its articles and conversations to popular social networking sites such as twitter, Facebook etc. where people can join the conversation by merely login in from their respective accounts.

Table 3. Blackberry Blog and the Behavioral Internet theory

Rotated Component Matrixª						
	Component					
	1	**2**	**3**	**4**	**5**	**6**
BBM _MOT	.781	.242	.152	.133	.253	.187
TOPIC INT_SER_EXPECT	.681	.352	.021	.162	-.062	.049
ONLINE BEH SAME_OFFLINE	.489	.473	.268	.179	.351	.207
AUTH_POST ART	.011	.629	.499	.016	.209	.164
PRESC_SUPPORT VIDEO	.191	.670	.147	.192	.240	.277
ABILITY _SOCIAL NETWORK	.154	.847	.139	-.036	.251	-.018
CONTENT_PERCEIV_ACESS	.001	.403	.788	.199	. -.058	.505
CONTENT_UNDERSTANDABLE	.247	-.226	.769	-.026	.253	.302
EASY_NAVIGATE	.120	-.104	.633	.568	.354	.088
ARTICLE_RELEVANT	.523	.172	.857	.019	.630	-.125
DYNAMICS_DIFFER ONLINE	.333	.514	-.067	.738	.315	.067
TOOLS_LACK FACE TO FACE	.147	.461	.615	.742	-.290	-.051
BLOG MGRS_MEM FEEDBACK	.184	-.068	.333	-.067	.738	.315
BB_SEGMENT	.042	.044	.469	.569	.820	.311
ART_PROB_RESOLVED	.311	.071	.401	.247	.633	.072
SIMPLE _GRAPHIC	.434	.110	.251	.528	-.062	.687
COMP_WEB BROWERS	.104	.568	.485	.283	.240	.788
a. Rotation converged in 7 iterations. Extraction Method: Principal Component Analysis. Rotation Method: Varimax with Kaiser Normalization. Parameters of Blackberry Blog loaded onto media equation, flow, content accessibility, social cues, quality cues, friendly technology.						

3. **Content Accessibility:** The content on the blog is easily perceivable. It is written in simple language and is highly understandable. The articles have relevant data according to the topics as well as the blog. Also navigation through the blog is easy. The content can also be accessed month wise and category wise.

4. **Social Cues:** Although media equation is valid for this blog but in discussion group dynamics and personal communication systematically differ online as the tools of communication lack the richness and subtlety of face to face messages.

5. **Quality Cues:** On the blog, the blog manager consistently keeps the members in a loop for feedback and suggestions. He asks for feedback on products, suggests new ideas and modifications, as presented in Figure 5. Articles are being posted for complaints and problems and how they are being resolved. So, with the help of this blog the company is able to segment its customers and build quality for them.

Table 4. Parameters of Blackberry Blog loaded onto: The Media Equation, Flow, Content Accessibility Social Cues, Quality Cues, Friendly Technology

Factor	Attribute
The Media Equation	• Motivates people to share experience • Topics of Interest and Quality of service expected • Online behavior same as offline
Flow	• Presence of Interesting Articles • Presence of supporting videos • Ability to 'like' an article/post on a Social Networking Site
Content Accessibility	• Content perceivable and accessible • Content Understandable • Ease of Navigation • Relevant Data
Social Cues	• Dynamics differ online • Tools lack subtlety of face to face messages
Quality Cues	• Blog managers ask for feedback • Segment customers and build quality • Articles are posted for complaints and problems resolved
Friendly Technology	• Blog has simple graphic design • Compatible with all web browsers

6.   **Friendly Technology:** The blog has very simple graphic design as well as it is compatible with all versions of web browsers thereby enhancing the accessibility of the blog and providing its visitors a pleasant experience.

5. CONCLUSION

5.1. Unique Contribution of the Paper and Managerial Implications

According to the above study conducted the Blackberry Blog caters very well to the *Behavioral Internet theory* and its all factors. Organizations should identify the appropriateness of content to the target population of onsite visitors and host content that is attractive to them. By adopting adequate content management strategies, tools offered by the collaborative web, for instance, corporate blogs can be mobilized as channels for building relationships between organizations and consumers. As the organization increases contact with the consumer, by increasing its own efforts, the chances of forming a relationship with the consumer also increase proportionally. The website can generate more traffic from various ways:

• Keep track of blogs and leave comments on them. A good way to keep the conversation going is to install a MyBlogLog widget and visit the blog of people visiting the site. The blog is not generating revenue benefits through advertisements so it is highly recommended that the organization brings some advertisers on blog's website to generate some revenues.

• The advantages of advertisements on the blog are:

Figure 5. Feedback on BlackBerry blog topics

- ○ **More Money:** The first advantage of selling your own ads is the fact that you will cut the middlemen out, increasing your revenue potential.
- ○ **Flexibility:** The advantage of selling direct advertising is that you will have much more control over where and how the advertisements will be displayed.
- ○ **Credibility:** Finally, having sponsors and direct advertisers on the blog might help credibility.

5.2. Limitations and Future Research Directions

The entire study has been designed in respect of corporate blog as a medium for impacting effective digital marketing. Distinct studies can be designed for analyzing the usage of other Web 2.0 tools viz. online communities and other professional and social networks. There also exists scope of further research in replicating this study across diverse industry verticals.

REFERENCES

Adelaar, T. (2000). Electronic commerce and the implications for market structure. *Journal of Computer-Mediated Communication, 5*(3), 0-0.

Ahuja, V., & Medury, Y. (2010). Corporate blogs as e-CRM tools–Building consumer engagement through content management. *Journal of Database Marketing & Customer Strategy Management, 17*(2), 91–105. doi:10.1057/dbm.2010.8

Barsky, E. (2006). Introducing Web 2.0: Weblogs and Podcasting for health librarians. *Journal of the Canadian Health Libraries Association, 27*(2), 33–34. doi:10.5596/c06-013

Bortree, D. S. (2005). Presentation of self on the web: An ethnographic study of teenage girls' weblogs. *Education Communication and Information, 5*(1), 25–39. doi:10.1080/14636310500061102

Dwyer, P. (2007). Measuring the value of electronic word of mouth and its impact in consumer communities. *Journal of Interactive Marketing, 21*(2), 63–79. doi:10.1002/dir.20078

Earl, M., & Khan, B. (2001). E-commerce is changing the face of IT. *Sloan Management Review, 43*(1), 64–72.

Efimova, L., & Hendrick, S. (2005). *In search for a virtual settlement: An exploration of weblog community boundaries* (Vol. 5). Communities & Technologies.

Esch, F. R., Langner, T., Schmitt, B. H., & Geus, P. (2006). Are brands forever? How brand knowledge and relationships affect current and future purchases. *Journal of Product and Brand Management, 15*(2), 98–105. doi:10.1108/10610420610658938

Ghuneim, M., Salomon, S., & Katsunuma, M. (2008). Terms of engagement-Measuring the active consumer. Wiredset, http://wiredset.com/root/archives/008589.html, accessed 26 March.

Gurak, L. J., Antonijevic, S., Johnson, L., Ratliff, C., & Reyman, J. (2004). Into the blogosphere: Rhetoric, community, and culture of weblogs. *Online edited collection of scholarly articles.*

Herring, S. C. (2007). A faceted classification scheme for computer-mediated discourse. *Language@ internet, 4*(1), 1-37.

Holland, J., & Baker, S. M. (2001). Customer participation in creating site brand loyalty. *Journal of Interactive Marketing, 15*(4), 34–45. doi:10.1002/dir.1021

Hsiao, K. L., Lu, H. P., & Lan, W. C. (2013). The influence of the components of storytelling blogs on readers' travel intentions. *Internet Research, 23*(2), 160–182. doi:10.1108/10662241311313303

Hsu, C. L., Lin, J. C. C., & Chiang, H. S. (2013). The effects of blogger recommendations on customers' online shopping intentions. *Internet Research, 23*(1), 69–88. doi:10.1108/10662241311295782

Huffaker, D. A., & Calvert, S. L. (2005). Gender, identity, and language use in teenage blogs. *Journal of Computer-Mediated Communication, 10*(2), 00-00.

Kathy. (2004). *How can we measure the influence of the blogosphere.* Department of Communication, University of Washington, 2004, Retrieved June 2, 2008 from faculty.washington.edu/kegill/pub/www2004_keg_ppt.pdf

Kelleher, T., & Miller, B. M. (2006). Organizational blogs and the human voice: Relational strategies and relational outcomes. *Journal of Computer-Mediated Communication, 11*(2), 395–414. doi:10.1111/j.1083-6101.2006.00019.x

Lawson-Borders, G., & Kirk, R. (2005). Blogs in campaign communication. *The American Behavioral Scientist, 49*(4), 548–559. doi:10.1177/0002764205279425

Nardi, B. A., Schiano, D. J., Gumbrecht, M., & Swartz, L. (2004). Why we blog. *Communications of the ACM, 47*(12), 41–46. doi:10.1145/1035134.1035163

Pan, S. L., & Lee, J. N. (2003). Using e-CRM for a unified view of the customer. *Communications of the ACM, 46*(4), 95–99. doi:10.1145/641205.641212

Rust, R. T., & Kannan, P. K. (2003). E-service: A new paradigm for business in the electronic environment. *Communications of the ACM, 46*(6), 36–42. doi:10.1145/777313.777336

Schultz, D. (2000). Customer/Brand Loyalty in an Interactive Marketplace. *Journal of Advertising Research, 40*(3), 41–53.

Sheth, J. N., & Parvatiyar, A. (1995). The evolution of relationship marketing. *International Business Review, 4*(4), 397–418. doi:10.1016/0969-5931(95)00018-6

Shin, N. (2001). Strategies for Competitive Advantage in Electronic Commerce. *Journal of Electronic Commerce Research, 2*(4), 164–171.

Singh, A., Kumar, B., & Singh, V. K. (2010). Customer Engagement: New Key Metric of Marketing. *International Journal of Art and Sciences, 3*(13), 347–356.

Smudde, P. M., & Courtright, J. L. (2011). A holistic approach to stakeholder management: A rhetorical foundation. *Public Relations Review, 37*(2), 137–144. doi:10.1016/j.pubrev.2011.01.008

Srinivasan, S. S., Anderson, R., & Ponnavolu, K. (2002). Customer loyalty in e-commerce: An exploration of its antecedents and consequences. *Journal of Retailing, 78*(1), 41–50. doi:10.1016/S0022-4359(01)00065-3

Teo, H. H., Wei, K. K., & Benbasat, I. (2003). Predicting intention to adopt interorganizational linkages: An institutional perspective. *Management Information Systems Quarterly*, 19–49.

Thorbjørnsen, H., Supphellen, M., Nysveen, H., & Pedersen, P. E. (2002). Building brand relationships online: A comparison of two interactive applications. *Journal of Interactive Marketing, 16*(3), 17–34. doi:10.1002/dir.10034

Trammell, K. D., & Keshelashvili, A. (2005). Examining the new influencers: A self- presentation study of A-list blogs. *Journalism & Mass Communication Quarterly, 82*(4), 968–982. doi:10.1177/107769900508200413

Wu, C. H., Kao, S. C., & Lin, H. H. (2013). Acceptance of enterprise blog for service industry. *Internet Research, 23*(3), 260–297. doi:10.1108/10662241311331736

This research was previously published in the International Journal of Innovation in the Digital Economy (IJIDE), 5(4); edited by Ionica Oncioiu, pages 50-65, copyright year 2014 by IGI Publishing (an imprint of IGI Global).

Chapter 28
Digital Marketing Optimization

Neha Jain
Jaypee Business School, India

Vandana Ahuja
Jaypee Business School, India

Yajulu Medury
Jaypee Group, India

ABSTRACT

Digital marketing is a proliferating field that has opened new challenges for marketers. These challenges address concepts of website navigation, searchability, and garnering online traffic –issues that are critical to any organization's online presence. This chapter identifies website characteristics, studies the role they perform in the context of an organization's virtual presence, and proposes the creation of a framework that aids organizations in optimizing their digital marketing strategies for better return on investment.

INTRODUCTION

The web has become a place where many live, play and work. It is the ultimate customer empowering environment and in the emerging world of ecommerce where customers are surrounded with myriad choices, organizations are faced with a challenge of meeting consumer expectations in a highly competitive world. In the new digital marketplace, consumers are using mobile, interactive tools to become instant experts on product and service offerings and their relative merits as they decide who to trust, where to make their purchases and what to buy (Berman, 2012).

Consumers can access a virtually unlimited selection of products, brands, and sellers. They can switch brands or try different products in a single click. However, consumers have limited time and unlimited choice. They would naturally stick to the Internet merchants who meet their needs and provide quality services (Cheung et al., 2005). Recent statistics showed that 80 percent of the highly satisfied online consumers would shop again within two months, and 90 percent would recommend the Internet retailer to others. On the other hand, 87 percent of dissatisfied customer would permanently leave their Internet merchants without any complaints.

DOI: 10.4018/978-1-5225-5187-4.ch028

The Internet and web technologies created a new and unprecedented environment to governments, businesses, educational institutions, and individuals enabling them to webcast any information using multimedia tools. We are seeing a proliferation of websites with enormous amount of information (Hassan & Abuelrub, 2008).

LITERATURE REVIEW

The foundation of every online business is the e-commerce website that it creates. Once the website captures the attention of the visitors, they should feel the need to explore further. This feeling comes with good design, speedy navigation on the site and easy to understand instructions. The e-commerce specialists know these facts and therefore, they have the right kind of tools with them to "read" the mind of the users and to set up a site that would be beneficial to the client. In such scenarios, the experts look at the already running website and try to determine the reason for the lack of traffic (Ezinemark.com, 2013).

The Digital World

The internet has been identified as the world's fastest growing market place with an enormous increase in the globalization environment for marketing products and services (Domains, 1999). Projected estimates indicate that the worldwide internet population may reach 1.35 billion by the end of current year (Internet World Stats, 2010; eTForecasts, 2004; Gong et al., 2007). The internet today has been hailed as the single most important invention of the 20th century and digital marketing is transforming companies, customization and advertising (Majumdar, 2010). There seems to be rapid adoption of the internet by consumers for various purposes, including information search and online shopping (Ranganathan & Ganapathy, 2002).

Consumer behavior has changed dramatically in the past decade. The present day, consumers can order many customized products online, ranging from sneakers to computers. Many have replaced their daily newspapers with customized, online editions of these media and are increasingly receiving information from online sources (Schiffman & Kanuk, 2009). If nowadays, experts want to identify the most profound influences on consumer behavior in recent times, the answer would be the internet. One reason the internet is dramatically changing consumer behavior is that it helps us to search more easily and efficiently than ever before (*Roger et al., 2006*).

According to one report, internet household penetration in India reached 42 million households in 2007 (Internet Usage, January 2009), and there will be about 10.5 million broadband households in India by 2011 (e-Marketer.com, January 2008). Worldwide, more than 540 million people now have Internet access.

Websites

The very first website was posted in August 1991 by Sir Tim Berners-Lee (Lawson, 2009). There were 130 websites on the Internet in 1993 and 47 million websites were added to the Internet in 2009 bringing the total number of websites on the Internet to 234 million (Pingdom, 2010). This shows how fast the Web is spreading worldwide. The number of people using the Internet is growing exponentially world over. There were 1.8 billion Internet users by the end of 2009 representing 26.6% global penetration (Internet World Stats, 2010). The Internet is a virtual library containing an unlimited amount of information. Anyone is allowed to publish and access this information. The websites are not monitored, edited, regulated, or approved (Brown, Hickey, & Pozen, 2002).

A consumer's intention to purchase specific products may vary greatly, and hence predicting general intentions to adopt the internet for purchasing may be of limited use if customer's motives to purchase specific products are likely to differ (Coker, Ashill, & Hope, 2011). Website visitors may use both distant and nearby cues: consumers may click on a link because they seek that specific link. At other times, consumers click because they believe the link will bring them closer to what they seek. In summary, the motivations for search vary, but regardless of the motivation, the online searcher continually judges whether to continue to read, scroll, analyze or click (Hofacker & Murphy, 2009).

Website Characteristics

1. **Website Domain:** The domain name strategy of a company connects closely to an organization's branding and positioning strategy. It serves as a foundation for web and promotional activity. The ideal domain strategy lets a prospective visitor guess the website without any help (Hanson & Kalyanam., 2007).

2. **Longevity of Website Existence (Domain Age):** Domain Age (i.e. the date at which each domain was registered) has been posited as an important factor in the ranking of a site, as older domain names are said to be inferred by Google's ranking algorithm as conveying more trust, and therefore should rank higher than newer domains (Michael, 2007). It represents the age of a website's domain name. The SEO community currently speculates that older domain names will rank more highly than newer domain names for the same content (Web Confs, 2006).

3. **Specificity of Search Engine:** Search engine optimization (SEO) is a set of techniques used by websites in order to be better indexed by search engines and SEO tool tries to capture users who are actively looking for information about a product related to the firm, which converts them into potential clients openly expressing their needs (Gandour et al., 2001 ; Hernandez et al., 2009).

4. **Volume of Traffic on the Website:** Without visitors the best website is a wasted resource. Generating traffic, which can be expensive and difficult, is an essential web marketing skill (Hanson & Kalyanam., 2007). The important task of a company is to generate the traffic on the website. The higher the traffic, the topmost will be the website when someone triggers a search (Ezinmark. com, 2013).

5. **Ease of Navigation:** Navigability evaluates how easily users may move around the website and find the information that they require (Smith et al., 2001). Users should never feel lost and therefore, each webpage should be self-sufficient and provide links to the main contents (Mateos et al., 2001). Madu and Madu (2002) urged that consumers can be easily turned off when the website is not easy to navigate. Kateranttanakul (2002) therefore suggested several design guidelines for navigation efficiency. First, the website should facilitate users/consumers to obtain information in the fewest possible steps. Second, hyperlinks should be consistently provided on every web page. Third, the relevancy of hyperlink description and the expected destination should be described. Finally, there should be no broken hyperlink.

6. **Website Reputation and Reach:** Consumers worldwide can shop online 24 hours a day, 7 days a week & 365 days a year. Some market sectors including insurance, financial services, computer hardware & software, travel, books, music, videos, flowers and automobiles are experiencing rapid growth in online sales (Meeker et al., 1997).

7. **Faster Response Time/ Website Load Time:** According to a survey conducted by (Hamilton, 1997), speed (i.e., slow speed) was the number one complaint of web users (77%). Most potential e-commerce customers don't want to wait for a seemingly endless page to load. Instead, they hit the browser "stop" button and go elsewhere. Therefore, large, pretty graphic files and cool animation may come at a price to the web business owner in terms of lost business (Busc, 1997).

8. **Presence of Adequate Searching Capabilities:** Accuracy is the degree to which the information and materials available on the websites are correct and trustworthy (Eschenfelder et al., 1997; Tran, 2009).

9. **Clarity of Information on a Website:** It is nicely explained by Chuck Letoumeau (W3C, 2002) who defines Web accessibility to mean "anyone using any kind of web browsing technology must be able to visit any site and get a full and complete understanding of the information as well as have the full and complete ability to interact with the site if that is necessary.

10. **Volume of Detailed Information Available on a Website:** Coverage is the degree to which information and contents are presented according to various topics through the site. Good contents and coverage should be engaging, relevant, concise, clear, and appropriate for the audience (Sinha et al., 2001).

11. **Content Diversity of a Website:** The website of a company is such a powerful tool that it conveys huge amount of information cost-effectively, creates attitudes and action, triggers brand and product awareness and communicates company and brand image all at the same time (Leong et al., 1998), which is a portfolio of benefits that cannot be expected easily from any offline advertising or promotion tool. The visual appeal, creativity and attractiveness of websites are very important characteristics that influence product choices and purchases for both novice and expert users (Mandel & Johnson, 2002).

12. **Website Readability:** Websites are designed keeping in mind the concepts of interactivity, feasibility, convenience and user requirements. Information with regard to products and services must be easily accessible and of high quality in terms of customer satisfaction.

13. **Keywords Used for the Search:** One of the useful ways of elevating the search engine ranking is using targeted keywords. A targeted keyword is a word or a group of words that brings links back to the website for the terms that the customer is trying to find (Ezinemark.com, 2012). Consumers are not likely to buy anything online unless complete product information is available.

14. **Highest Level of Interactivity of a Website:** Interactivity refers to the interaction between users and computers that occurs at the interface of websites. Specifically, interactivity allows users to control what elements are to be delivered and when they are to be delivered through the interface (Tran, 2009).

15. **User Friendliness of Interface:** If a website meets a customer's expectations, then the customer is likely to reuse the website in the future, recommend it to his peers and become loyal. On the other hand, if the website does not meet the customer's expectations, then the customer is likely to switch to another website and perhaps never go back to the initial one (Dadzie et al., 2005). So the information provided by the website is an important factor that affects a customer's purchasing behavior and helps to make a website user friendly.

Research Methodology

An evaluation grid (Table I) was created, which listed the above website characteristics. A set of 500 online consumers were asked to help classify the above website characteristics in the context of the role they serve. The users were contacted using Intercept Sampling Technique. The results were subjected to a Factor Analysis.

Evaluation Grid (Table 1)

How do the following factors pertaining to an online site impact your information search? Rate your pre purchase information search decision on the 7 point scale (7 being the highest score and 1 being the lowest) (Jain et al., 2014).

Results

The 15 website characteristics loaded onto the following 3 parameters- Website Dynamics, Navigability, Content Findability, as depicted in Figure 1.

- **Website Dynamics:** The attributes of the website which differentiate it from the competing websites like the domain age (which shows the existence of website in the digital domain), traffic on website and the specificity of the search engine.

Table 1. Evaluation grid

Particulars	1	2	3	4	5	6	7
Ease of navigation							
Faster response time							
Level of interactivity of a website							
User friendliness of interface							
Presence of adequate searching capabilities							
Volume of detailed information available on a website							
Website readability							
Website reputation & reach							
Website domain							
Keywords used for the search							
Content diversity of a website							
Clarity of information on a website							
Website load time							
Longevity of website existence (domain age)							
Volume of traffic on the website							
Specificity of search engine							

Figure 1. Essential website characteristics

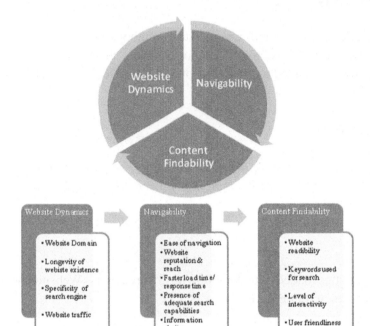

- **Navigability:** Website navigation is important to the success of any organizational website to streamline a visitor's online experience. The website's navigation system is like a road map to all the different areas and information contained within the website which includes the characteristics like website navigation, reputation & reach, load time, browsing capacity, clarity & detailed information available on the website.
- **Content Findability:** Site search is about more than a generic search box that helps point website visitors in the right general direction. Optimizing site search for efficient item or content discovery and findability is a business-critical function like readability, keyword search, interactivity and how friendly is the website.

FUTURE RESEARCH DIRECTIONS

The above parameters can be used to calculate a Digital Marketing Optimization Score (DMOS) in the context of respective websites. Future research can be conducted to calculate the DMOS across

1. Different websites in one industry vertical. This will help companies identify areas of improvement with respect to their website characteristics, in comparison to their competitors.

2. Comparative analysis of website DMO Scores across different industry verticals. This can help companies understand what types of products/industries benefit more by using the web as a media vehicle.

IMPLICATIONS AND CONCLUSION

Digital marketing is a fast evolving field which has immense potential. Companies will benefit from timely action with respect to how well and how fast they adapt to and adopt appropriate strategies to embed this marketing platform into their organizational fabric for marketing communication, both with the organizational employees, as well as the end customers.

REFERENCES

Berman, Saul. J. (2012). Digital transformation: Opportunities to create new business models. *Strategy & Leadership*, *40*(2), 16–24.

Brown, J., Hickey, K., & Pozen, V. (2002). *An educators' guide to credibility and web evaluation*. Retrieved from http://www.ed.uiuc.edu/wp/credibility-2002/methods.htm

Busch, D. (1997). Avoid the five cardinal graphical sins. *Internet World*, 98-99.

Cheung, C. M. K., Zhu, L., Kwong, T., Chan, G. W. W., & Limayem, M. (2003). Online consumer behavior: A review and agenda for future research. In *Proceedings of the 16th Bled eCommerce Conference eTransaction*. Academic Press.

Coker, B. L. S., Ashill, N. J., & Hope, B. (2011). Measuring internet product purchase risk. *European Journal of Marketing*, *45*(7), 1130–1151. doi:10.1108/03090561111137642

Dadzie, K. Q., Chelariu, C., & Winston, E. (2005). Customer service in the internet-enabled logistics supply chain: Website design antecedents and loyalty effects. *Journal of Business Logistics*, *26*(1), 53–78. doi:10.1002/j.2158-1592.2005.tb00194.x

Domains, C. (1999). *Business on the internet*. Retrieved from http://www.cleverdomains.com/business.htm/

E-Commerce Website Development. (2013). [Web Blog]. Retrieved from http://www.spyghana.com/e-commerce-website-development, Ezinemark.com

Eschenfelder, K. R., Beachboard, J. C., McClure, C. R., & Wyman, S. K. (1997). Assessing U.S. federal government websites. *Government Information Quarterly*, *14*(2), 173–189. doi:10.1016/S0740-624X(97)90018-6

eTForecasts. (2004). *World usage patterns & demographics*. Retrieved from http://www.etcnewmedia.com/review/default.asp?

Gong, W., Li, Z. G., & Stump, R. L. (2007). Global internet use and access: Cultural considerations. *Asia Pacific Journal of Marketing and Logistics*, *19*(1), 57–74. doi:10.1108/13555850710720902

Hamilton, A. (1997). *Avoid the website sin: Slow loading pages.* Retrieved from http://www4.zdnet. com/anchordesk/story/story_1244.html

Hanson, W. A., & Kalyanam, K. (2007). *Internet marketing & e-commerce.* Thomson South-Western.

Hassan, L., & Abuelrub, E. (2008). Assessing the quality of web sites. *Information and Computation, 7*(4), 11–20.

Hernández, B., Jiménez, J., & Martín, M. J. (2009). *Key website factors in e-business strategy.* Academic Press.

Hofacker, F. C., & Murphy, J. (2009). Consumer web page search, clicking behavior and reaction time. *Direct Marketing: An International Journal, 3*(2), 88-96.

Information on Internet Usage in India. (2009). [Data file]. Retrieved from www.internetworldstats.com

Internet World Stats. (2010). *Internet usage statistics.* Retrieved from http://www.internetworldstats. com/stats.htm#links

Jain, N., Ahuja, V., & Medury, Y. (2014). *E-marketing and the consumer decision making process* (Doctoral dissertation). Available from http://www.jiit.ac.in/uploads/SynopsisNehaJain.pdf

Katerattanakul, P. (2002). Framework of effective web site design for business-to-consumer internet commerce. *INFOR, 40*(1), 57–69.

Leong, E., Xueli, H., & Paul, J. S. (1998). Comparing the effectiveness of the web site with traditional media. *Journal of Advertising Research, 38*(5), 44.

Madu, C. N., & Madu, A. A. (2002). Dimensions of e-quality. *International Journal of Quality & Reliability Management, 19*(3), 246–258. doi:10.1108/02656710210415668

Majumdar, R. (2010). *Consumer behavior: Insights from Indian market.* New Delhi: PHI Learning Private Limited.

Mandel, N., & Johnson, E. J. (2002). When web pages influence choice: Effects of visual primes on experts and novices. *The Journal of Consumer Research, 29*(2), 235–245. doi:10.1086/341573

Mateos, M. B., Mera, A. C., Miranda Gonzalez, F. J., & Lopez, O. (2001). A new web assessment index: Spanish universities analysis. *Internet Research, 11*(3), 226–234. doi:10.1108/10662240110396469

Meeker, M., & Pearson, S. (1997). *The internet retailing report.* Morgan Stanley, Dean Witter, Discover & Co. Retrieved from http www.ms.com/insight/misc/inetretail.html

Michael, P. E. (2007). Analyzing Google rankings through search engine optimization data. *Internet Research, 17*(1), 21–37. doi:10.1108/10662240710730470

Pingdom, R. (2010). *Internet 2009 in numbers.* Retrieved from http://royal.pingdom. com/2010/01/22/ internet-2009-in-numbers

Ranganathan, C., & Ganapathy, S. (2002). Key dimensions of business-to-consumer websites. *Information & Management, 39*(6), 457–465. doi:10.1016/S0378-7206(01)00112-4

Roger, D. B., Paul, W. M., & James, F. E. (2006). *Consumer behavior.* Thomson South-Western.

Schiffman, G. L., & Kanuk, L. L. (2009). Consumer behavior. Prentice-Hall of India Private Limited.

Sinha, R., Hearst, M., & Ivory, M. (2001). *Content or graphica? An empirical analysis of criteria for award winning websites.* Paper presented at the Seventh Conference on Human factors and the Web, Madison, WI.

Smith, A. G. (2001). Applying evaluation criteria to New Zealand government websites. *International Journal of Information Management, 21*(2), 137–149. doi:10.1016/S0268-4012(01)00006-8

Tran, L. A. (2009). Evaluation of community web sites: A case study of the community social planning council of Toronto web site. *Online Information Review, 33*(1), 96–116. doi:10.1108/14684520910944418

Web Conference. (2006). *The age of a domain.* Retrieved from http://www.webconfs.com/age-of-domain-and-serps-article-6.php

Website Promotion for a Successful Online Business. (2012). Retrieved from http://www.spyghana.com/website-promotion-for-a-successful-online-business/ezinemark.com

KEY TERMS AND DEFINITIONS

Digital: Today's era which makes everything possible to purchase, consumer entertainment, profit making for marketers, great business.

Online User: Person who buys goods/ services by using online medium to satisfy his/her need.

Website Characteristics: Attractive keywords which used to influence consumers and create awareness to purchase.

Websites: Most emergent place where people come and fulfill their desires according to their need.

This research was previously published in Strategic E-Commerce Systems and Tools for Competing in the Digital Marketplace edited by Mehdi Khosrow-Pour, pages 162-170, copyright year 2015 by Business Science Reference (an imprint of IGI Global).

Index

A

Active Engagement 1456

Advertisement 1, 41, 73-74, 108, 110, 157, 222, 409-410, 415-419, 423, 449, 453, 456, 504, 519-520, 622-623, 658, 844, 848-850, 897, 1046, 1131, 1175, 1376, 1502, 1555, 1557, 1601, 1711

Affiliate 2, 73-81, 85, 759, 1130-1135

Affiliate Marketing 73-81, 85, 759, 1130-1135

Affinity Relationship 96, 99, 105

Affinity Scheme 97-102, 105

Analytics 2, 65, 101-102, 240, 475-476, 542, 627, 638-639, 657-658, 704-706, 936, 1141, 1173, 1189, 1220, 1230, 1237, 1297, 1387, 1498, 1635, 1641

Anti-Brand Community Behaviours 1354, 1369

Anti-Branding 1354, 1369

Attitudinal Loyalty 197, 1154, 1354, 1474, 1554-1555, 1561-1562

Audience Fragmentation 965, 1556, 1565, 1570

Augmented Reality 215-216, 218, 221, 224-225, 232, 425-427, 429-432, 434-437, 443, 1222

Authenticity 355, 928, 1037, 1046-1047, 1119, 1196, 1227, 1229, 1353-1364, 1369, 1668

Auto 695, 704, 707-710, 712-714, 716-719, 723, 806-807, 815, 898, 1253

Auto-Component 803-804, 806-807, 809-811, 813, 815

Aviation industry 521-522, 524, 529-530

B

Benchmarking 1016, 1018, 1022-1024, 1029-1030, 1033

Big Data 474-477, 479, 487, 491-492, 1647, 1710, 1713, 1718

Bipolar Analysis 588-589, 593

Bizarre Tourism Campaign 1354, 1356, 1369

Blog 130, 225, 240-241, 542-544, 546-553, 555-556, 640, 673, 735, 739, 771, 849, 851, 866, 874, 1131, 1143, 1172-1174, 1176, 1178, 1181, 1183, 1185, 1189, 1338, 1340, 1650

Blogging 433, 543-544, 549-550, 671, 850, 910, 1116, 1142, 1144, 1172-1173, 1177, 1185, 1189, 1338, 1713

BMW 717-719

Brand Affect 1154, 1555, 1558-1560, 1564-1565, 1570

brand alliances 383-386, 388-389, 395, 397-398

Brand Association 194, 214, 305, 333, 461, 1245

Brand Awareness 78, 147, 191-192, 195, 197-199, 206-207, 214, 239-240, 242, 256, 305, 460, 462, 464-466, 469-471, 546, 699, 733, 738, 747, 749-750, 788, 790, 792, 872, 899, 971, 983, 1120, 1255, 1300, 1314-1315, 1317, 1362, 1381, 1450, 1460, 1499, 1638, 1647, 1687, 1699

Brand Commitment 911, 1094, 1154, 1453-1454, 1559-1560

Brand Community 360, 610, 617, 619, 783, 910, 914, 918, 920, 963-964, 977-978, 1091, 1094-1095, 1266, 1283-1300, 1309, 1454, 1459, 1613-1615

Brand Engagement 398, 699, 701, 705, 789-790, 910, 1064, 1083, 1103, 1148-1155, 1158-1162, 1265-1267, 1272-1275, 1277, 1314-1315, 1398-1402, 1406, 1459, 1471, 1613

Brand Equity 113-114, 146-148, 150-151, 191-192, 196-199, 202-204, 206, 208, 214, 297, 304-305, 335, 385, 789, 808, 814, 898, 907, 944, 998, 1149, 1161, 1314, 1407-1412, 1415, 1420, 1422, 1426, 1429, 1460, 1557-1558, 1564, 1571, 1718

Brand Extensions 147, 305, 383-386, 388, 392, 396-398, 966, 1412

Brand Hate 1354, 1369

Brand Identity 108, 112, 114, 123, 129, 141, 147, 300, 305, 333, 339, 370, 384, 617, 804-805, 965, 987, 1363, 1684, 1707

Brand Image 108, 111-112, 114, 144, 191-192, 196-197, 206, 299-300, 303, 305-306, 326-329, 333-341, 348, 383-399, 445, 486, 547, 805, 872-875, 892-893, 898, 944, 979-990, 998, 1018, 1092-1093, 1142, 1151, 1180-1182, 1184-1186, 1353-1364, 1408, 1434-1435, 1441, 1447, 1449-1450, 1558, 1678, 1684

M

N

O

T

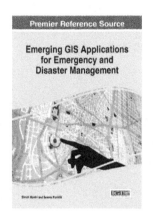
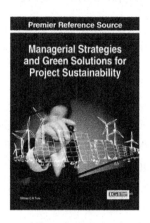

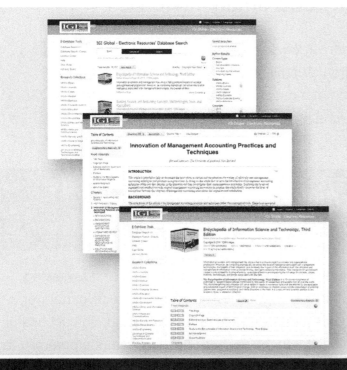

CPSIA information can be obtained
at www.ICGtesting.com
Printed in the USA
BVOW09*0318091217
502265BV00004B/11/P